Financial reporting, information and capital markets

Michael Bromwich

The London School of Economics and Political Science

Pitman

To Christine

Pitman Publishing
128 Long Acre, London WC2E 9AN

A Division of Longman Group UK Limited

© Michael Bromwich 1992
First published in Great Britain 1992

British Library Cataloguing in Publication Data

Bromwich, Michael
    Financial reporting, information and capital markets.
    I. Title
    657

ISBN 0 273 03464 2

Printed and bound in Great Britain

Contents

Preface   *iv*

Some useful symbols   *vi*

Abbreviations   *viii*

1 Introduction and overview   1

Part I Economic income and wealth measures

2 The market provision of accounting information   15
3 Wealth and income measurement: an economic perspective   31
4 *Ex post* economic wealth and income; problems with the economic
   approach to income and wealth measurement   52

Part II Accounting information under uncertainty

5 Accounting and decision making under uncertainty   81
6 Accounting and information economics   117
7 The value of information for private use and the utility of public
   information   145
8 Economic income and wealth under uncertainty   173
9 The informativeness of acounting reports: an empirical perspective   201

Part III The regulation of accounting

10 Some economic problems in the provision of accounting information   233
11 The regulation of accounting   250
12 The conceptual framework approach   278

Part IV Accountability, positive accounting theory and agency

13 Accountability, agency and positive accounting theory   307
14 Agent and principal models   331

References and further reading   *357*

Author index   *369*

Subject index   *372*

Preface

This book reviews the theory of the economic measurement of income and wealth in financial accounting and presents an informational perspective on accounting information. A major objective is to integrate the relevant aspects of current finance theory and information economics into accounting theory at a fairly general level.

This study is aimed at second and third year accounting undergraduates and first year postgraduates. It is seen as being used as a text for either a financial theory course or for the financial theory component of a more general financial accounting course. Used in these ways, it would need to be supplemented by material on the price change accounting debate and on current accounting problems. The considerable emphasis placed on the treatment of uncertainty and information is necessary to understand recent major contributions to accounting theory. It also allows students to obtain some access to much of the current research literature. Earlier drafts have been used for such courses with undergraduates at the (now) University College, Cardiff and at the University at Reading and with MSc students at the London School of Economics and Political Science for some five years. Parts of the book have also been used at a number of universities outside the United Kingdom.

Those who do not wish to get too involved in uncertainty and information economics should use in these courses Part I of the book, which deals with the economist's income and wealth concepts, and Part III, which deals with the regulation of accounting. These two parts also provide a course on accounting policy making when supplemented with some institutional material. Many teachers may however wish to incorporate references to uncertainty and information economics into such a policy course. Part II considers the impact of elements of uncertainty and some of the findings of information economics for accounting theory. This part could be used independently as an important element of finance courses and of courses on financial statement analysis. Part IV alters the focus and looks at accounting for accountability and monitoring purposes. It discusses both agency models and positive accounting theory.

Because of the somewhat unusual coverage of this book, fairly extensive details concerning its objectives and contents are given in Chapter 1. The material covered is treated as far as possible in a self-contained way and therefore the only essential prerequisites are an elementary accounting course and some exposure to economic reasoning (Chapter 1 gives more details concerning other useful backgrounds). It is also hoped this book will appeal to those in the profession who wish to understand the theoretical foundations of accounting seen from an economic perspective and to use this approach to solve current accounting problems.

A synthesis is provided of the work of a large number of scholars over a wide range of subject matter. The references give some indication of my indebtedness. Even a cursory study of the text will indicate my scholarly debt to the work of William Beaver,

Joel Demski, James Ohlson and the late Sir John Hicks, none of whom bears any responsibility for the use which is made of their work. I apologise to any authors not referred to in the text, and to all the authors cited, both for imperfectly capturing their ideas and for any errors in conveying them to the reader.

I have a strong personal intellectual debt to Will Baxter and Martin Walker, who also put up with many silly questions. I am similarly grateful to my colleagues at LSE, especially Christopher Napier and Christopher Noke. A number of people commented on parts of this book and I would especially like to thank John Board, Christopher Napier and Michael Power. A very special debt is owed to Ken Peasnall, Geoff Whittington and Martin Walker, who commented on much or all of this book and on material for a companion book on asset valuation and income measurement. The final outcome does not do justice to their comments.

I am also very grateful to the Chartered Institute of Management Accountants, who funded much of my later work on this book.

This book has been a long time in the making and I must thank a number of my secretaries, especially Katerina Pasternak and Dorothy Richards. A special acknowledgement is due to Meg Wells, who coped with the early versions of this and the companion book without the help of a computer.

Some useful symbols

a_j action $j; j = 1, \ldots A$

c_m quantity of commodity $m; m = 1, \ldots M$

C_i cash flows in period $i; i = 1, \ldots T$

$C_{i,i-1}$ cash flows in period i estimated in period $i - 1; i = 1, \ldots T$

$C(a_j, s_i)$ payoff function of state–action pair, $(a_j, s_i); j = 1, \ldots A, i = 1, \ldots S$

$\mathrm{Cov}(\tilde{R}_i, \tilde{R}_M)$
$= r_{im}\sigma_i\sigma_{M'}$ covariance between assets or securities i and M = where r_{im} is the correlation coefficient

D_i economic depreciation in period $i; i = 1, \ldots T$

$e_{i,t}$ abnormal return of security i in period $t; i = 1, \ldots Z; t = 1, \ldots T$

E_{pt} endowment of individual p in period $t; p = 1, \ldots P; t = 1, \ldots T$

$E(U)$ expected utility from a prospect

$E(U_a)$ utility function of an agent

$E(U_p)$ utility function of a principal

$E(\cdot)$ expected return operator

$f(a, x)$ joint probability of an action and an outcome in an agency context

F_i retained funds in period $i; i = 1, \ldots T$

N_z total number of securities issued by enterprise $z; z = 1, \ldots Z$

P_i price of an item in general, $i = 1, \ldots M$

$P_{i,t}$ uncertain price of security i in period $t; i = 1, \ldots Z; t = 1, \ldots T$

P_j price of a unit of state-contingent income in state $j, j = 1, \ldots S$

P_{jy} signal-contingent price of a unit of security j at the time of decision conditional on the receipt of signal y, where y is indexed to a time period, $j = 1, \ldots Z, y = 1, \ldots Y$

P_{st} price now for delivery of one unit of state-contingent income in a given state and time period, $s = 1, \ldots S, t = 1, \ldots T$

P^*_{st} spot price of a unit of state contingent income at time $t; s = 1, \ldots S; t = 1, \ldots T$

Q_{st} conditional price of a unit of income in state s in period t where the price is agreed prior to the period but paid on realisation; $s = 1, \ldots S; t = 1, \ldots T$

r_i	rate of interest in general in period t; $i = 1, \ldots T$
r_f or R_f	risk-free rate of interest
r_s	risk-adjusted interest rate
$\tilde{R}_{i,t}$	uncertain or random return from security i in period t; $i = 1, \ldots Z$; $t = 1, \ldots T$
$\bar{R}_{i,t}$ or $E(R_{i,t})$	expected or mean return from security i in period t; $i = 1, \ldots S$; $t = 1, \ldots T$
S_{it}	time–state contingent claim
$U(\cdot)$	general utility function
$V(a)$	disutility of effort
V_i	present value of a prospect at time i; $i = 1, \ldots T$
V_{ii-1}	present value of a prospect at time i estimated at time $i - 1$;
$V_{i,i-1}$	$i = 1, \ldots T$
$V_{p,i-1}$	wealth of individual p at time $i - 1$
W_i	wealth of individual i in a perfect market
y_i	signal i from an information system (η); $i = 1, \ldots Y$
Y_i	income for period i, $i = 1, \ldots T$
$Y_{i,\mathrm{I}}$	*ex post* economic income concept I for period i; $i = 1, \ldots T$
$Y_{i,\mathrm{II}}$	*ex post* economic income concept II for period i; $i = 1, \ldots T$
x_i	outcome in period i (especially in an agency context); $i = 1, \ldots T$
$(1 + r)$	the discount rate
$\mid$	'such that' or 'conditional upon', as in $\phi(s_i\mid y_i)$ = the probability of state i given the receipt of the signal i, $i = 1, \ldots S$, $i = 1, \ldots Y$; : is often used in the literature as a synonym for the symbol:
$\{\ \}$	a set of elements, as in $\{x_i, \ldots x_n\}$
$\tilde{\ }$ (tilde)	signifies a random variable
$\hat{\ }$ (caret)	signifies a realised or empirically estimated outcome
$\bar{\ }$ (bar)	signifies an expected value
$\in$	is an element of
$\cup$	union of
$\cap$	intersection of
$\emptyset$	empty set
β_i (beta)	beta factor for enterprise i; $i = 1, \ldots Z$
η_i (eta)	information system i; $i = 1, \ldots H$
η_0	null information system
λ (lambda)	opportunity cost of an agent's reserve price
μ (mu)	opportunity cost of effort in an agency context

π_i (pi)   profit for period i; $i = 1, \ldots T$; see also Y_i

Π product operator as in $\Pi(x_i) = (x_1x_2x_3)$

σ(sigma)   standard deviation of a probability distribution

σ^2 variance of a probability distribution

Σ summation operator

ϕ (phi)   probability of an event

Abbreviations

AICPA	American Institute of Certified Public Accountants
APB	Accounting Principles Board (USA)
API	abnormal perfomance index
AR	abnormal return
ARA	absolute risk aversion
ASB	Accounting Standards Board (UK and Ireland)
ASC	Accounting Standards Committee (UK and Ireland, predecessor to ASB)
ASSC	Accounting Standards Steering Committee (predecessor to ASC)
CAPM	capital asset pricing model
CAR	cumulative abnormal return
EMV	expected monetary value
FASB	Financial Accounting Standards Board (USA)
FIFO	first in first out
FRC	Financial Reporting Council (UK)
GAAP	generally accepted accounting principles
LIFO	last in first out
MRS	marginal rate of substitution
MRT	marginal rate of transformation
RT	risk tolerance
SEC	Securities and Exchange Commission (USA)
SIB	Securities and Investment Board (UK)
SAFC	Statement of Financial Accounting Concepts (issued by FASB)
SFAS	Statement of Financial Accounting Standards (issued by FASB)
SSAP	Statement of Standard Accounting Practice (issued by ASB)

1

Introduction and overview

This book reviews aspects of the theory of financial accounting from an economic perspective. Financial reporting is seen as the measurement and communication of financial and economic information to decision makers. We therefore investigate how far existing accounting theory integrates with modern finance theory and incorporates the current findings of information economics. Although these themes constitute the predominant approach in the current economically orientated research literature, with few exceptions they have not been comprehensively addressed in accounting textbooks. This is the task of this book. The presentation of these themes is not meant to be rigorous. It is sought to give only an intuitive understanding sufficient to appreciate some of the results of explicitly incorporating these themes into accounting.

Financial accounting or external accounting for profit making enterprises refers to formal corporate financial statements publicly issued to security holders and others external to the enterprise, either annually or more frequently (usually semi-annually or quarterly). These reports have to comply with the law and usually respect the requirements promulgated by accounting policy makers. The information contained in these reports becomes available to all in the community in a variety of ways. In most countries, financial statements have to be filed with the appropriate registration authority where they are usually available for perusal by all. Those who do not receive accounting reports through their connections with companies can request these reports and can read about financial statements in newspapers, financial journals and in analysts' reports.

The body of knowledge representing financial accounting has recently grown very greatly. Perhaps even more recently, the theories that seek to explain the information disclosed in such reports and the valuation bases used therein have similarly expanded.

It is unusual in an accounting book to consider the characteristics of capital markets. However, accounting theory seeks to aid, among others, participants in security markets. Moreover, recent research in information economics emphasises that the impact of publicly available information, which includes accounting information, can only be understood in the context of the capital markets in which the information will be used.

This book adopts an informational perspective on accounting theory. With this view, accounting reports are perceived as only one means of publishing information. Viewing information, including accounting information, as an economic commodity is the central strand of adopting an informational approach to accounting. Beaver has claimed that employing this perspective has resulted in a revolution in financial accounting theory. It certainly can be argued that its adoption has changed our view of accounting in terms of both its societal role and the difficulties associated with this role. This perspective has illuminated many issues which until recently had generally gone unconsidered, such as the regulation of accounting. From a more micro-economics stance, utilising an informational perspective has extended our understanding of the decision utility of information—a concept which forms the motivation for most accounting theories. This approach has also indicated the many difficulties faced by those who seek to provide more informative accounting reports. It has also contributed to the body of knowledge which has allowed the testing of some accounting theories against empirical evidence.

What this book is about

This study focuses in considerable detail on some of those general theories of accounting that utilise an economic perspective. These theories see accounting information as being used for decision making either for physical investment or for investment in the securities market and for the monitoring of the outcomes of such decisions. This perspective seems to be the predominant view of contemporary accounting policy makers in the United States of America and the United Kingdom. The aim here is to determine the fundamental elements of accounting theories which seek to provide accounting information consistent with our understanding of how well organised capital markets operate in an uncertain setting. This requires that we consider the role of accounting information in this setting in capital markets which reach equilibrium. An important objective of this book is to provide sufficient understanding of all these matters to appreciate how they impinge on accounting. This requires that the accounting models we consider are consistent with accepted models of financial decision making in well organised capital markets. We therefore present in more detail than is usual in accounting books uncertainty and the fundamental elements of capital markets.

This decision orientated approach to accounting has a distinguished history in accounting theory. Here, economic income and economic wealth measurement which base these measures on the present values of future cash flows have been advocated for many years as providing the accounting system most consistent with economic theory and as yielding a benchmark which other suggested accounting systems should satisfy.

Over the last three decades, major revolutions have occurred in the theories of finance and of capital markets. Of especial relevance to accounting theory has been the incorporation of information directly into these theories. The literature in these areas is now vast, often technical and inaccessible to accountants. An objective of this book is to make comprehensible to accountants the relevant parts of this literature. Here we express the necessary understanding of these elements in as non-technical way as possible to allow an assessment of their impact upon accounting theory and an appreciation of their likely contribution to future developments in accounting. Indeed, a knowledge in this area should help in providing sensible accounting procedures for dealing with the new complex financial instruments being issued in the securities market and for many of the complicated accounting problems presently being dealt with by accounting policy makers, such as accounting for goodwill and for acquisitions.

One major development incorporated in this book is the new appreciation that the role of accounting cannot be fully comprehended by considering only its contribution to measuring the economic performance of a specific enterprise but rather requires consideration of how accounting information facilitates the working of capital markets and integrates with these markets. One objective of our review is to show that the expected contribution of accounting information in a market context depends on how well organised these markets are, and the degree to which accounting information provides incremental information relative to other information sources available in such markets.

Throughout our study, we consider how far the provision of accounting information can be left to the market. The usual view in the literature is that the intrinsic character of information generally and that of accounting information specifically militates against such a market provision of accounting information. This book sets out the arguments for the extra-market regulation of accounting and reviews some of the available methods for prosecuting this regulation, including the use of a generally accepted conceptual framework for accounting. The regulation of accounting by accounting standard setters and others is seen here not as a technical accounting exercise but rather as involving social choice decisions for society. This view that accounting regulators make social choices reflects how different forms of accounting affect the wealth and income of those in the community in different ways. Accounting policy makers therefore have to decide which section or sections of the financial community they wish to favour in their deliberations. An objective of this book is therefore to indicate how social choice theory can illuminate such accounting issues.

The final objective of the book is to review the implications of agency theory, widely defined, for financial accounting. Here we deal with the situation where, in a setting of uncertainty, managers will seek to make accounting choices that maximise their personal welfare and will use their skills and any private information possessed for their own benefit.

Much of the material in this book is controversial and unsettled. As far as possible, all sides of the relevant arguments are discussed. The presentation does not examine the practical details of all accounting models embodying an economic perspective: thus, we will not look at price change accounting in any detail.

As the portfolio of subjects covered in this book may seem somewhat unusual relative to other financial accounting books, the next section of this chapter reviews briefly the detailed contents of the remaining chapters and further indicates the reason why these are being studied.

The contents of this book: a detailed review

This book is divided into four parts. Part I comprises Chapters 2 to 4 and presents a comprehensive review of what have come to be called the economist's income and wealth concepts, or economic income and wealth. Chapter 2 looks at the role of accounting information in perfect markets (where identical items command the same price) and complete markets (where all desired trade can be consummated) in both single and multi periods under certainty and uncertainty. This chapter commences our study of the economics of accounting information by considering the results which might be generated if the supply of accounting information were left to a perfectly functioning market, free of any regulation. The results obtained can be used to provide a standard of comparison for more realistic accounting regimes.

The first section of Chapter 2 looks at the type of accounting information which could be expected with ideally functioning markets in conditions of certainty in single and multi-period settings. Here, all necessary information is already available to all market participants. This part of the chapter shows that in some circumstances, rearrangements of already available information provide income and wealth measures which possess a number of characteristics which accounting policy makers and accounting theorists have deemed desirable. The results obtained here enable us to see later what factors of more realistic environments militate against the discovery of accounting measures possessing these characteristics in more complex settings.

Such measures can be shown to represent a unanimous ranking or measure of the opportunities available to market participants irrespective of preferences. The importance of this unanimity characteristic of accounting information is that it frees accounting theory and accounting policy determination from many difficult problems. It allows us to proceed in accounting choice without considering the heterogeneous tastes of individuals. It is important to consider the characteristics which allow 'value-free' accounting systems to be promulgated so as to ascertain whether such systems can be provided in the more practical world. Similarly, the chapter indicates that accounting information satisfies the stringent requirements for information to provide a measurement of income and wealth with the same properties as the usual measures associated with measuring weight or height. This suggests that the search for an accounting measurement system which serves all parties in their decision making, irrespective of their preferences, is not impossible in our ideal setting. Although accounting information can be shown to have these desirable characteristics in this setting, no one will pay for the provision of this information because it merely restates existing information.

The next section of Chapter 2 presents our initial attempt to incorporate uncertainty into our models. It shows that dealing with uncertainty *per se* causes no changes to our earlier conclusions. In this setting, accounting information may have no value.

Chapter 3 commences our study of the economist's wealth and income concepts. These concepts also form the subject of the following chapter. Although labelled economic, these measures are now the property of academic accountants and accounting policy makers and have been substantially developed by the accounting community. There is now considerable agreement amongst economists, academic accountants and some accounting policy makers that these measures do represent an important framework for measuring income and wealth.

As an introduction, the decision models usually favoured for multi-period decision making are reviewed. This section reminds us that the use of these models ensures that individual utility is maximised under specific assumptions and demonstrates that the economist's wealth concept generates identical results to these investment decision models.

The following section of Chapter 3 investigates the use of economic income in a 'planning' context. The definition of this income measure is discussed both in an intuitive way and, more formally, using symbols. The most important characteristics and virtues of the economic approach to wealth and income measurement are introduced. We conclude by looking at some of the criticisms of a more theoretical nature which have been made of some of the variants of income explored in this chapter.

The first major part of Chapter 4 introduces the after-event (*ex post*) income and wealth concepts advocated by economists which are consistent with the planning concepts considered in the previous chapter. These *ex post* concepts help to monitor forecasting ability, aid in the evaluation of managerial efficiency and of continuing project viability, and help in the *ex post* validation of contracts. Two generally accepted alternative definitions of *ex post* income are introduced. The choice between these two measures, which is a major subject of this chapter, is taken up in the next section. This part of the chapter is completed by a summary of the advantages of economic income *ex post*.

The second major part of Chapter 3 further considers some of the criticisms which have been levelled at the economist's approach to income and wealth measurement, both *ex ante* and *ex post*. The criticisms addressed in this chapter are those mainly concerned with the difficulties of making economic income and wealth concepts operational in the practical world. These criticisms include the very important view that the decision models which provide the foundations for economic income and wealth measurement may not yield optimal decisions for all individuals where markets are poorly organised. These market problems may mean that economic wealth and income measures will fail to work well, but that accounting information more generally may have value in aiding decision making in this environment. It should, however, be borne in mind that other accounting systems also face these problems in such environments.

Part II comprises Chapters 5 to 9. This part first develops the implications for accounting of the theories of decision making under uncertainty. Accounting information is considered in the context of information economics and the possible roles of this information in both well functioning and imperfect capital markets is presented. Considerable emphasis is placed on understanding the nature of information and outlining its characteristics.

Effort is devoted to explaining the difference between private and public information. It is indicated that public information, which includes published accounting information, is more difficult to handle analytically and has to be approached within the context of the complex financial markets in which this information is utilised. This provides one reason why accounting policy makers find it so troublesome to derive accounting methods applicable in ever more complex financial markets.

Chapter 5 first introduces some of the basic tools and decision making models for dealing with uncertainty. An acquaintanceship with these tools and models is necessary for understanding the problems of measuring income and wealth under uncertainty. This section assumes no previous knowledge of the subject. The material provided is also necessary to appreciate the contribution of information economics to accounting which forms the subject matter of Chapters 6 and 7.

The second part of Chapter 5 deals with optimal decision making in idealised securities under uncertainty. This is a difficult subject and may seem rather removed from financial accounting, but it is required in order to comprehend the literature that seeks to apply information economics to accounting. It also provides a perspective of great promise for analysing accounting.

The subject of uncertainty and accounting is taken up initially in the third part of Chapter 5. This part of the chapter suggests that market incompleteness and market failures are likely to appear in an uncertain setting thereby again inhibiting our ability to derive neutral accounting income and wealth measures, but rendering other items of accounting of value.

Chapter 6 is the first of three which use the tools provided earlier for understanding decision making and accounting under uncertainty. Most of the concepts introduced in this chapter are used in the same way in a multi-person setting.

The first part of Chapter 6 considers the meaning of the term 'private information' as it is used in information economics. Here, the term 'information' is restricted to new information, the possession of which leads to new decisions. It is shown that, in general, decision relevant information can be characterised as new knowledge concerning the likelihood of the occurrence of states of the environment.

The chapter then goes on to consider some of the characteristics of information systems. The informativeness of perfect and imperfect information systems is considered. Noisy information systems are those which yield signals that relate probabilistically to the occurrence of more than one state. The conditions under which information systems can be ranked in terms of their utility, without considering the preferences or probability beliefs of the individual, are then presented. Such comparisons are said to be possible only under restrictive conditions. The implications for accounting of information systems being comparable in terms of their usefulness are considered.

This chapter adopts an informational perspective to accounting, allowing us to define in a precise and rigorous way what we might mean by the decision utility of accounting information. This theory yields a precise definition of decision-useful accounting in contrast to other previous accounting theories and approaches in accounting.

Private information for optimal decision making having been reviewed in the previous chapter, Chapter 7 considers first how such information can be valued. This value is defined as the change in expected utility generated by utilising an information system relative to using the null information system, which provides no relevant information. The chapter then goes on to discuss a number of problems of information valuation, mainly flowing from the presence of risk averse (those who dislike risk) decision-makers.

The second major issue addressed by Chapter 7 concerns the economic characteristics of publicly available information. This type of information is defined as information which is simultaneously made available to all. It is suggested that a number of factors make public information more difficult to handle than private information, if only because this type of information must be analysed in the context of the equilibrium market setting in which it is to be utilised. A number of market regimes incorporating public information are considered. It is shown that they may possess different equilibrium characteristics.

It is indicated that some market participants may be made worse off by the introduction of public information because of the possibility of such information causing adverse revaluations of some individual endowments via changing market prices. However, several of the market regimes considered contain mechanisms which allow this problem to be either ameliorated or entirely avoided.

Chapter 8 represents a slight deviation from the themes of Part II. It extends our earlier treatment of economic wealth and income under uncertainty in Chapter 3. It is argued that if we are to understand the role of this type of accounting information, a multi-period model has to be entertained. In order to consider economic income over time in an uncertain setting, the concepts of spot, contingent and conditional prices for time-state claims are then introduced and the equilibrium conditions between these prices are presented. The satisfaction of these conditions is important in income measurement because such measures need to be grounded in a full equilibrium setting in capital markets.

These prices are then used to show that the economic income concepts introduced in Chapters 3 and 4 apply under uncertainty, though their calculation is more complex and their meaning is, perhaps, a little more difficult to comprehend. A new role for economic income over time is then suggested. In order to deduce income for a period with an information system that yields more detailed information over time about the likely occurrence of uncertain states, it may be necessary to know the history of the previous signals provided by the information system. It is indicated that *ex post* economic income could serve this role.

In the final section of Chapter 8, it is argued that models taken from economics and information economics do not fully allow information systems generally, including accounting information systems, to yield new or unexpected information, thereby ruling out the possibility of windfall (unexpected) gains and losses, which were demonstrated to be important in accounting in earlier chapters. In appraising our findings in this chapter, it must be remembered that we are assuming the existence of sufficiently well organised markets for the economic definitions of wealth and income to apply.

Chapter 9 reverts to the main themes of Part II. It reviews some of the approaches used in empirical work seeking to evaluate the informativeness of accounting reports in the practical world and to test the implications of some accounting theories for this world. This work also introduces two new theories about the working of the capital market which have important implications for accounting theory. Basically the questions to be answered in this type of empirical work are concerned with whether accounting information has any impact on the characteristics of securities (their returns and traded volumes) and whether the effect of accounting information on the market provides a means of testing theories about accounting. Affirmative answers to these and related questions would suggest that it may be possible in some settings to test whether different types of accounting information have differential impacts. Findings of this sort yield additional theoretical insights which may be helpful in selecting accounting systems and practices. The emphasis in this chapter is on the theoretical foundation and logic of the methods used in this work and the implications of this work for accounting theory. No attempt is made to provide any more than a flavour of the empirical evidence obtained using these methods.

Part III of this book considers the economics of accounting regulation. It moves our focus to considering the effects of poorly organised markets on accounting. Chapter 10 introduces our detailed discussion of these matters.

The important view that real world mechanisms for meeting demands for accounting information possess many of the characteristics of the ideal markets, is considered in the first sections of Chapter 10. The remainder of the chapter concentrates on analysing in an informal way some of the major problems which have been argued to inhibit the efficiency of contemporary regimes for the provision of accounting information. These problems are viewed as generated by market difficulties. It is further argued that such market problems often lead to some type of extra-market regulation, usually by the Government. This part of the chapter also examines the view that the lack of a well functioning market for accounting information means that accounting policy making cannot generally proceed by seeking neutral or value-free accounting measures of use to all. Rather, the choice between accounting systems may require value judgements as to which elements of society should gain and which should suffer losses.

The final major part of Chapter 10 reviews suggestions that characteristics of extant regimes for providing accounting information are likely to cause this information to have some of the properties of what are usually termed 'public goods', i.e. commodities and services which are, perforce, supplied simultaneously to the whole community or to complete sectors of the community. It is often argued that the case for regulating accounting information is strengthened if it exhibits some of the characteristics of a public good. It is generally argued in economics that goods of this type cannot always be handled well by the market mechanism. The problems raised in this chapter are important in appraising accounting theories intended for the practical world. They also lie at the heart of the arguments for the non-market regulation of accounting information which are surveyed in the following chapter.

Some of the various regimes used or suggested for the regulation of financial reporting from an economic perspective are reviewed in Chapter 11. Arrangements for accounting regulation differ between countries. The possibilities cover a wide spectrum. These range from a system that depends almost entirely on statute, for example in France and Germany, through a balanced mixture of statutory and private sector self regulatory systems (Australia and Canada provide contrasting illustrations), to regulation that relies mainly on private sector self-regulation or regulation by the accounting profession. The United Kingdom especially prior to the Companies Act 1981 (consolidated in the 1985 Act), which enacted the Fourth Directive of the European Community into British Law, and the United States provide examples of these types of system. The objective of this chapter is to appraise the strengths and weaknesses of some extant approaches to accounting regulation.

The first substantive part of Chapter 11 looks at the various institutional frameworks for accounting regulation and the political consequences of such choices. The second main segment of this chapter adopts a comparative approach to the strengths and weaknesses of public sector regulation relative to theories of private sector standard setting. It also considers problems common to both approaches.

A general problem common to public and private sector regulation is that of finding a system for making social choice decisions which satisfies some assumptions which seem reasonable for a liberal society. It is explained that all known public choice systems infringe at least one of these assumptions. While Government may be able to ignore these criticisms, standard setters unsupported by Government cannot so easily ignore or refute criticisms concerning alleged defects of their constitution. A second major problem faced by any accounting policy makers is that of determining individual preferences in the absence of a market which can be relied upon to deal with this automatically.

The third and penultimate part of Chapter 11 looks at two problems which seem unique to private sector standard setting. The first is to show from where standard setters obtain their authority to issue what some commentators regard as 'quasi laws' affecting many people, often external to the profession. The second difficulty unique to standard setters relates to the problem of having to rely on consensus seeking to enhance the acceptability of their conclusions.

Chapter 12 provides an economic analysis of the efforts of the Financial Accounting Standards Board (FASB; the United States accounting standard setting body) to determine a generally accepted conceptual framework for accounting in the United States of America, all the basic elements of which are now in place. The FASB's Conceptual Framework Project is probably the most comprehensive modern attempt to build a theoretical framework for financial reporting using an economic perspective and represents, perhaps, the major professional attempt so far to utilise some of the elements of the information economics framework of earlier chapters. It is thus is a case study in seeking to make operational some of the theory discussed in this book.

The early sections of the chapter introduce some of the advantages claimed for the conceptual framework approach by the FASB. Among these advantages, the conceptual framework provides a constitution guiding FASB's endeavours, clarifies the objectives of financial accounting and aids the FASB in selecting solutions to accounting problems. It is suggested that the possession of such a generally accepted framework could provide a defence for controversial standards because they could be shown to flow from a logically consistent structure. This conceptual framework should therefore provide additional authority for accounting standards and provide some defence from possible public sector involvement in standard setting.

Following these introductory sections, we review the Conceptual Framework Project in some detail from an economic and informational perspective and include a critical evaluation of the project.

The final part of the book (Part IV) comprises Chapters 13 and 14. This part complements our decision making approach by looking at accounting for accountability and monitoring purposes, commencing in Chapter 13 with the desired characteristics of accounting for such purposes. It then sets out the characteristics of the agency model which are used in the final part of the chapter to explain positive accounting theory. The final chapter of the book considers some of the implications for financial accounting theory of what is called the 'agent and principal model'. We now examine the contents of these two chapters in a little more detail.

So far, the contents of this book have generally concentrated on accounting information for decision making. One role of Chapter 13 is to consider some aspects of the use of accounting information *ex post* for the purposes of performance evaluation, for contracting and for monitoring contracts. In the practical accounting world, the use of accounting for monitoring the results of past periods is of great importance. Accounting information is used in practice for checking whether accountability responsibilities have been satisfactorily discharged, for ensuring that the enterprise is accountable to those with interests in the organisation, for monitoring performance and for ensuring that any prudential responsibilities have been fulfilled. In addition, accounting figures often serve as a basis for distribution of the benefits generated by the enterprise.

Chapter 13 demonstrates that accountability information is required to discharge organisational obligations to parties with interests in the enterprise. Such parties may include not only shareholders, creditors and labour, but also the Government and society more generally. Their requirements of the enterprise span a wide variety of types and may be very stringent. It is argued that such regulations may therefore substantially influence enterprise conduct and accounting choices.

This chapter indicates that the above subjects are very important, but they are only briefly examined. In order to continue to employ our decision-oriented approach, we will examine these issues from a decision making perspective.

In Chapters 13 and 14 we will also relax the assumptions generally maintained throughout this text that managers automatically work in the best interests of the security holders. With the uncertainty and imperfect information, we would expect managers to seek to maximise their own utility. Managers with superior skills and superior personal information will wish to utilise these advantages in their own best interests.

These problems are said not to be limited to relationships between managers and shareholders but may occur wherever one party employs others to carry out delegated functions. Such a contractual arrangement is described as an agency relationship where one person, usually called the principal, employs one or more other people to undertake tasks on his or her behalf. Agency relations pervade the real world. Agency theory seeks to deal with these problems in general. This part to the chapter explores, in a general way, the effects on decision making and resource allocation of entertaining various features of the agency model. Chapter 14 focuses upon a narrower approach which employs much of the theory presented in Part II of this book and is called the *theory of agent and principal*. Both approaches are sometimes labelled 'agency approaches'. The second part of Chapter 13 looks at some of the general ideas of agency theory.

The third and final part of the chapter briefly discusses what is now called 'positive accounting theory', which seeks to incorporate into accounting our understanding of agency and of contracting in markets in order to explain better why enterprise management makes accounting choices in the context of well organised markets. It also tests the hypotheses thus generated utilising the methods explored in Chapter 9. The theory is said to be positive in that it seeks to explain existing accounting phenomena rather than to provide a theory of accounting. Our review of positive accounting theory is fairly brief because this is a relatively new area and is subject to some controversy. It is also well explained by its proponents. The approach is said to represent a very important and rich research area with probably the fastest growing literature in financial accounting research.

Our discussion of agent and principal models in Chapter 14 will cover a number of subjects. First we shall discuss the general structure of the model and present an initial selection of the usual assumptions used with these models. The general form of these models will then be introduced in a non-technical way. Following this, we shall discuss in separate sections the two major elements of the agent and principal model—risk sharing and effort motivation—and then examine the effect of information on agency models. The following section of the chapter is more technical and introduces the general method of obtaining solutions utilised in the literature. We will then look briefly at extensions of the agency model. The final section of the chapter considers the uses that have been made of the agency model in financial accounting.

Using this book

Prerequisites

As far as possible the presentation in this book is meant to be self-contained, reflecting the wide span of knowledge addressed, some which most accounting students may not have otherwise encountered. There are a number of sections in the book which are clearly identified as capable of being left out by those with prior knowledge (for example, the section of Chapter 5 which introduces the rudiments of decision making under uncertainty). The only real prerequisites are good elementary financial accounting and economics courses. The presentation will be much easier to follow with an elementary background in corporate finance and some knowledge of statistics. Some ability to be comfortable with symbols will ease the reading of this book. No mathematical knowledge is required to understand the presentation, though a little mathematics will be found here and there, almost always in footnotes. Notation is used sparingly and is chosen for ease of understanding. The list of useful symbols (pp. vi-viii) might at first sight seem intimidating: however, very few symbols are used in any one chapter.

Aids to learning

A great deal of effort has been aimed at making this book as easy to read as possible; even so, many of the concepts used require much thought before they can be mastered.

For this reason, more difficult items are considered iteratively at different levels of sophistication as the book proceeds. There is a certain amount of repetition of difficult concepts and techniques. The leisurely development of ideas in this book is deliberately employed. Initial difficulty with any idea or concept should be overcome by encountering later application of the same idea or concept. There are plenty of references to other books where it is thought a more detailed presentation might help some readers. Advice about alternative presentations is often given in bracketed references in the text. Especially difficult technical matter is put in chapter endnotes, and those parts of the book which can be skipped without losing the flow of the argument are clearly indicated. As far as possible each argument is expressed separately in words and symbols and often a substantial example is also given. Each chapter commences with a plan which sets out its contents and the reasons why these matters are being studied. Chapter conclusions and summaries outline what has been covered in each chapter and indicate the most important points that readers should absorb.

Areas of this book, especially Part II (dealing with accounting information under uncertainty), may seem somewhat removed from the day-to-day practice of accounting. The recent development of finance suggests that well directed theory can improve the understanding of practice even though such theory may initially seem distant from practice.

This book focuses on the fundamental aspects of accounting. Such an understanding is necessary to appreciate how existing practices are consistent with these fundamentals, to develop solutions to new and urgent accounting problems and to contribute to the future development of accounting. Many of the perspectives considered here have in the past been absent from practical accounting debates which have tended to produce defective solutions subject to commercial pressures for further change. Many of the topics discussed have now begun to be embraced by accounting policy makers. The solutions to many accounting problems are coming to be understood to require a consideration of their market context, though the problems associated with accounting information being publicly available are not yet fully appreciated. Accounting has been loath to treat uncertainty explicitly and current practice is weak when seen from an uncertainty and information economics perspective. However, many of the problems now faced by accounting policy makers are forcing them to employ these approaches.

Our review suggests that we do not yet have a full analytical understanding of many of the subjects considered. Without further research in these areas practical accounting will never be more than a bundle of *ad hoc* technical methods. A major task facing practitioners and theorists is to provide workable theories which can be incorporated into practice. It is difficult to believe that this can be fully achieved without some relaxation and supplementation of the historical cost accounting system and its associated assumptions, at least for some purposes. For example, many of the benefits of the approaches considered here could be obtained if enterprise forecasts, which are in any case provided to many market participants in a variety of degrees of detail, were made publicly available in some form.

Economic income and wealth measures

2

The market provision of accounting information

Plan of the chapter

This chapter commences our study of the economics of accounting information by considering the accounting reports which might be generated if the supply of accounting information were left to a perfectly functioning market, free of any regulation. The results we obtain will be used later to provide a standard of comparison for more realistic accounting regimes. Wealth and income measures in this setting can be shown to possess a number of characteristics which accounting policy makers and accounting theorists have deemed desirable. The results obtained enable us to see what factors of more realistic environments militate against the discovery of similar accounting measures in more complex settings.

This market orientation is continued in later chapters where some of the characteristics of the actual systems used in providing accounting information in the presence of market difficulties are considered. The consequences of leaving the supply of accounting information to existing mechanisms free of additional regulation are initially investigated in Chapter 10, and further considered in later chapters.

The first section of this chapter looks at the type of provision of accounting information which could be expected with ideally functioning markets in conditions of certainty. To talk about the provision of information in such a setting may seem paradoxical. Here, all necessary information is already available to all market participants; thus accounting information represents merely a rearrangement of known information. Alternatively, and anticipating the approach of later chapters, we can say that we are considering a setting where everyone has costless access to perfect information. The aim of this part of the chapter is to show that, in some circumstances, rearrangements of already available information provide income and wealth measures which represent a unanimous ranking or measure of the opportunities available to market participants irrespective of preferences (see Beaver and Demski, 1979). The importance of this unanimity characteristic of accounting information is that it frees accounting theory and accounting policy determination from many difficult problems. Much of the debate between different schools of accounting thought arises because, when selecting accounting practices, heterogeneous tastes require a choice to be made as to the welfare of which individuals or entities is to be pursued. Various theories favour different market participants. It is important to consider the characteristics which allow 'value-free' accounting systems to be promulgated so as to ascertain whether such systems can be discovered for a more practical world.

The next major section of this chapter indicates that the stringent requirements of measurement theory can be satisfied by certain types of income and wealth measures in this 'ideal' setting. This suggests that the search for an accounting measurement system which serves all parties in their decision making, irrespective of their preferences, is not impossible in our ideal setting. Again, the importance of this finding is determined by whether any of the characteristics required of such systems apply in the world of practical accounting.

The characteristics of the income and wealth measures discovered in this simple setting suggest that many of the usual tricks used in income and wealth measurement in more realistic contexts, such as cost allocations, may be unnecessary and confusing in the simple setting employed here.

The third section of the chapter demonstrates that the above conclusions can be maintained in a setting of perfect markets and certainty even in a multi-period context.

The next section incorporates uncertainty into our models. It shows that dealing with uncertainty *per se* causes no changes to our earlier conclusions. Income and wealth measures can still be derived that are useful to all in a decision making context, irrespective of their preferences. These measures can be shown to be consistent with entertaining a measurement perspective using the same arguments as for the certainty case.

A fairly simple summary of the most elementary setting to be examined in this chapter commences our analysis. This section also introduces the set of assumptions usually employed by economists to describe an environment of perfectly functioning markets under certainty. The following sections deal with these matters a little more rigorously.

The provision of accounting information in well organised markets

In order to simplify the presentation, we will concentrate on accounting for decision making purposes. More specifically, we will restrict our concern to accounting for investors in physical projects and to reporting to investors in the securities markets. Enterprises are seen as planning and producing goods which they sell to consumers. Consumers are seen as only being able to trade—they buy enterprise output, and supply factors and finance to enterprises. The presence of perfectly competitive markets under certainty for all goods and factors will be assumed initially. The assumptions required for perfectly competitive markets are quite extensive, but in essence they ensure that the market will clear and that no market participants can by their actions affect market prices; that is, all actors in the market are price takers.[1]

No pretence is made that this assumed environment resembles the real world. However, the practical world of accounting is so complex that it is difficult, or impossible, to analyse without simplification. Simple models of the type used here should lead to a better understanding of the real world by indicating what factors make practical accounting problems so intractable. These simple models also help to identify those components of real world accounting systems which are likely to give rise to the need for complex accounting theories and to cause the advocacy of the non-market regulation of accounting.

The next two sections seek to show in some detail that in a perfect market with certainty the only information necessary to appraise an entity is its expected future cash flows, and that wealth and income concepts need to be based on these cash flows if they are to serve market participants as well as possible. This introductory section anticipates these more rigorous arguments by introducing them in an informal way in a multi-period setting.

We assume that all enterprises seek to maximise the present value of the cash flows from projects, net of outflows. With the assumptions of perfect markets and certainty, all enterprises face the same rate of interest for all purposes. Thus, only those opportunities that have a positive net present value (strictly, a non-negative net present value) when this interest rate is used in discounting should be accepted. The total present value of an entity's net cash flows can be determined by adding together the present values of all the enterprise's projects. The present worth of the enterprise will, therefore, equal the enterprise's value on the securities market.

No one will pay more than this for an enterprise because such an investment will generate less income than lending the equivalent sum on the market at the going interest rate. Whoever owns the enterprise will not be willing to sell it for less than this because the market will price the enterprise on the basis that its annual return will equal the going interest rate.

This means that the only information necessary, when appraising the enterprise in a perfect market with certainty, is its future cash flows. Present value information, once announced, will be immediately impounded in the market prices of enterprises. As these market prices are based on enterprise cash flows, announcing these flows themselves provides an alternative means to inspecting market prices of obtaining the only information necessary for optimal decisions.

In this setting all investors, irrespective of their specific preferences concerning the timing of cash flows, will unanimously agree that the market values of enterprises provide unambiguous measures of the contribution that investments in these enterprises make to their welfare. All will, therefore, be interested only in their wealth evaluated using the market prices of securities. Those whose preferences for cash flows are not met by their existing portfolios can use the perfect and complete market to rearrange the cash flow pattern of their net worth (by borrowing or lending) so as to suit best their preferences. In an ideally functioning market, any pattern of cash flows having the same present value as an existing portfolio can be achieved by trading on the market.

In such a market, as in many real world markets, there is no need for any regulator to ensure that preferences are satisfied and that resources are allocated efficiently. These matters can be left safely to the working of the familiar 'invisible hand' mechanism. Nor is there any need for accounting reports reporting wealth measures because these reports would merely duplicate market prices. No one would, therefore, pay for such reports. With certainty, income for a period can be computed by simply deducting closing wealth measured using market prices from opening wealth computed in the same way (see Hicks, 1946, pp. 171–181). This income measure will be equal in the assumed environment to receiving the going rate of interest on the opening value of wealth. No one will, however, pay for the provision of income information because this can be derived costlessly from market prices.

The existence of accounting measures of income and wealth that are entirely consistent with efficient resource allocation is important to accounting theorists and to accounting policy makers, even though these measures merely mirror stock market prices. This is because they clearly belong to a class of accounting measures that theorists and accounting policy makers seem to wish to promulgate. They provide general all-purpose statements of equal use in decision making to all users of accounts and financial reports, irrespective of any differing preferences and decision problems. More formally, they are neutral or value-free accounting measures that are optimal in terms of resource allocation irrespective of preferences and decision problems of individuals. Such measures do exist in the environment assumed here. They also satisfy the usual criteria used to determine whether quantities can be legitimately labelled 'measures'. An understanding of the characteristics necessary for the existence of such accounting measures allows us to consider whether such measures may exist in a practical world.

Income and wealth measurement under certainty with perfect markets

This and the next section present the above argument in a more formal way, starting here with a setting where the fruits of any decision become available immediately. Such a setting is usually referred to, perhaps confusingly, as a one-period analysis. A multi-period context is dealt with in the next section. The focus in this section is on the instantaneous transformation of factor quantities into saleable products. First, optimal decision making models for both producers and consumers will be considered. Second, income and wealth concepts which are congruent with these decision models will be derived.

Here we assume certainty with perfect and complete markets. A prefect market is one where all participants in the market face the same price for the same transactions; that is, only one price is associated with each commodity at the time of any transaction. In a complete market any desired trade is feasible. In such a market, the producer's decision problem is what level of production to adopt. This can be illustrated graphically (Hirshleifer, 1970, chapters 1 and 3).

A simple version of a representative firm's production decision is portrayed in Figure 2.1. The productive opportunities are shown by the locus QQ. The slope of QQ indicates the return in terms of commodity, c_1, obtained from the use of a given amount of the commodity or factor, c_0, which is also assumed to be the numeraire (the monetary unit). The productive opportunity locus (QQ) is drawn for an enterprise with a null endowment—resources must be obtained from investors, that is, consumers acting as finance suppliers. The slope of the line QQ reflects diminishing returns throughout its length. Any net return is assumed to be paid out to consumers in terms of additional amounts of the factor c_0 or commodity c_1. Optimal conduct for a profit-maximising firm is to produce at Q^*, where the return from additional production in terms of c_1 equals the market rate of exchange between c_0 and c_1. This rate of exchange is shown by the slope of the market line MW_0 which reflects opportunities to trade commodities on the market, $-P_0c_0/P_1c_1$, where $P_0 = 1$ and P_1 is the unit price of commodity 1. The firm's net 'profit' (π) is given by deducting the factor cost (P_0c_0) from the return in terms of commodity c_1 (P_1c_1). Thus profit (π) can be written as

$$\pi = P_1c_1 - P_0c_0 \qquad [2.I]$$

This equals OW_0 in Figure 2.1 when expressed in terms of c_0 or OW_1 in terms of c_1. The enterprise's objective is to maximise either version of this sum.

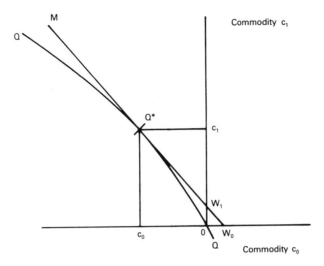

Figure 2.1 Optimal production activities

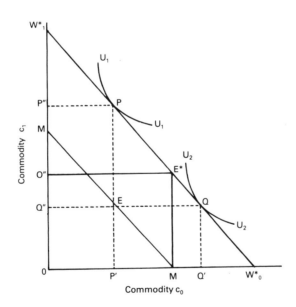

Figure 2.2 The consumer's optimal decision

Figure 2.2 illustrates the consumer's problem. For simplicity, it will be assumed initially that all the securities of a given firm are held by one consumer, who receives all the firm's income as defined in 2.I above. The consumer's original endowment is given by, say, E on the market line MM, which reflects the individual's opportunities to trade on the market. Its slope represents the market's rate of exchange between

c_0 and c_1, that is $(-P_0/P_1)$. The profit from the consumer's securities augments this original endowment. The augmented endowment in the figure (E^*) is assumed to equal OW^*_0 if the profits from the enterprise portrayed in Figure 2.1 were received in c_0 units (MW^*_0 in Figure 2.2 is assumed to equal OW_0 in Figure 2.1). It would be shown by OW^*_1 if the profits were paid out in c_1 units (MW^*_1 (Figure 2.2) = OW_1 (Figure 2.1)).

The consumer's decision problem is to maximise the utility obtained from c_0 and c_1 by trading, subject to a wealth constraint. This wealth measure represents the augmented endowment because, with certainty and perfect markets, enterprise profits are available to the consumer immediately the enterprise's plans are known.

The decision problem can, therefore, be written as

$$\text{MAX} = U(c_0, c_1) \tag{2.II}$$

subject to

$$P_0 c_0 + P_1 c_1 \leq W_i \equiv P_0 E_0 + P_1 E_1, \text{ where } P_0 \equiv 1$$

The first element of the expression says that the individual's objective in decision making is to maximise a utility function $U(\cdot)$, the elements of which are quantities of c_0 and c_1.

W_i in the wealth constraint stands for the wealth of the individual (i) and E_0 and E_1 represent his or her endowment of resources c_0 and c_1, respectively. The constraint says that the market value of the consumer's planned consumption shown on the left of the expression cannot exceed the market value of the individual's endowment shown on the right of the expression. The element on the right of the constraint ($W_i = P_0 E_0 + P_1 E_1$) will be referred to here as a wealth measure.

The individual's endowment, augmented by any realisations accruing from the plans of those firms he or she owns, is illustrated in Figure 2.2 by the market line $W^*_0 W^*_1$. This line indicates all the combinations of c_0 and c_1 the consumer can obtain by trading on the basis of any augmented endowment (E^*). The actual make-up of the consumer's endowment is irrelevant to optimal behaviour because trading in the market can convert any given endowment (E^*) into any preferred bundle lying on the same market line. An individual with preferences represented by indifferent curves like $U_1 U_1$ will maximise by trading to reach position P where the preferred rate of exchange between commodities c_1 and c_0, which is reflected by the slope of the indifference curve $U_1 U_1$, is equated to the market rate of exchange $(-P_0/P_1)$ between these commodities at the margin. This position will be obtained by selling MP' units of c_0 at the going market price and buying O"P" units of c_1.

By contrast, an individual with preferences like those represented by the curve $U_2 U_2$ will prefer position Q on the market line obtaining this by exchanging O"Q" units of c_1 at the going market rate of exchange for MQ' units of c_0. With perfect and complete markets, any other set of preferences can be optimised by trading on the market within the constraint imposed by the market value of the consumer's augmented endowment. It is well-known that this analysis can be extended to incorporate m commodities and p individuals (see Debreu, 1959).

Endowments constrain both individual and market trading. The individual cannot trade beyond his or her endowment and market prices are set to clear all desired trades which are feasible within the total of individual endowments of each commodity. Although the market clears without explicit knowledge of the economy-wide endowments of each commodity, it continually tests demand against supply in the process of obtaining these prices and in this sense knowledge of endowments is necessary for the economy to function as well as possible. The importance of a knowledge of these endowments is made clearer if we imagine that a central planner is charged with solving the allocation problem. Such a planner could not proceed efficiently without this knowledge. For optimal conduct, the individual needs to know his or her endowment or wealth. With complete and perfect markets, W_i in Expression 2.II measures the value of the ith consumer's wealth. The freedom to trade to achieve the most preferred bundle of goods means that W_i can be valued unambiguously using market prices, irrespective of individual preferences. This measure of the consumer's wealth can be expressed generally and unambiguously in a setting of certainty as

$$W_1 = \sum_M P_m c_m + \sum_Z P_z N_z \qquad\qquad [2.III]$$

where $P_m c_m$ is the value of the consumer's endowment of the $m=1$ to M commodities, N_z represents the total number of securities of enterprise z, $z=1$ to Z, all of which are assumed to be owned by the ith consumer, and P_z is the market price of a unit of the zth security.

All that is required for optimal individual conduct is to maximise the wealth obtained at the end of an instantaneous production and trading cycle, as measured by Expression 2.III. This is equivalent to seeking to achieve the highest market line in Figure 2.2. The end of period endowment provides a measure of the wealth available from all possible trading opportunities including those productive opportunities represented by the securities held. With well organised markets, following the above individual decision rules automatically ensures a market equilibrium of the type called *fully Pareto efficient* (see, for example, Hirshleifer, 1970). In such an equilibrium, markets clear at the equilibrium prices and the allocation of the commodities in the economy is such that all goods are exhaustively allocated to individuals in a way which ensures that the welfare of no one can be improved without harming someone else. The term 'fully' means that the market structure is such that all desired plans are feasible. Later in this book we will have occasion to consider market structures that do not possess this property.

The type of allocation in mind is efficient in the sense that all efficient production and trading decisions which market participants wish to action at the equilibrium prices with the given original distribution of resources are achieved. The equilibrium achieved ensures the efficiency of these decisions taking the opening endowments of resources as given. It says nothing about the reasonableness or otherwise of the final distribution of resources. For any given production and trading setting, there will be many Pareto efficient allocations, each reflecting different allocations of opening endowments (or more generally, opening welfare or utility levels).

As in this chapter, much of this book will seek to analyse the role of accounting using the above decision model. Adopting this approach means that accounting information and information more generally are studied when they are fully embedded and integrated into the usual model employed in economics to address economic efficiency. With this perspective, any conclusions concerning the roles of information and of accounting information will be deduced from their uses in this model and these roles will be consistent with helping to maximise economic efficiency. This is in contrast to many arguments for accounting reform which are generally based on the 'common sense' appeal of the reforms, leaving the relation of the reforms to economic models and to economic welfare generally somewhat unclear. This model will also help us to explore the problems that arise for accounting information and information generally when markets are not perfectly organised.

We will now briefly examine the underlying economic model in a little more detail and extend the findings of our earlier analysis in this chapter to multiple commodities. Above, it was shown that each consumer would seek to maximise by setting the rate of exchange between the two commodities in terms of preferences equal to the ratio of the prices of the two commodities. More generally, this will be true in equilibrium for every possible pair of goods. This rate of exchange between preferences is called the marginal rate of substitution in consumption. The equality of this rate with the ratio of the prices for every pair of goods means that no further trade will be beneficial once this equilibrium condition is achieved because further trade would involve paying a higher relative price for a good than is justified by the preferences accorded to the commodity relative to the other commodity in the calculations.

Similarly, it was shown above that production decisions were optimised by equating the rate of exchange of the two commodities in production to the ratio of their market prices. This rate of exchange was measured in Figure 2.1 by the slope of the product transformation curve and is usually labelled the marginal rate of transformation in production. Producing at any other level would mean that opportunities to transform any two goods which would be worthwhile at their market prices would be foregone. This finding also applies in economies with multiple goods and implies that the marginal cost of producing a specific good must be the same for all suppliers.

In perfectly organised markets, the equilibrium prices in our two-commodity example will be the same for all market participants and therefore the two rates of exchange will be equal for all in the market.[2] They will be equal to the ratio of the prices of the two commodities and therefore no further trade or change in production will be beneficial. These findings apply for every pair of commodities with multiple goods. The marginal rate of substitution in consumption between any pair of goods will therefore equal the marginal rate of transformation in production for the same pair of goods. Prices will be set so that demand equals supply in such markets and commodities will be fully allocated to those in the economy so that the welfare of no one individual can be improved without harming some other individual. Such an allocation is thus Pareto efficient.

Income measures

Income for the pth individual, $Y_{p,i}$, where Y_i represents the income for the instantaneous trading period i, could be measured by comparing the market value of wealth before and after the planned trading and production activities. This can be written as

$$Y_{p,i} = \sum_M (P_m c_m - P_m E_m) + \sum_Z \pi_z \qquad \text{[2.IV]}$$

where $P_m E_m$ stands for the consumer's opening endowment of the mth commodity. The profit realisation from the zth firm after repaying all commodities obtained in the market to allow production is represented by π_z, where this profit is arrived at using Expression 2.I (see Beaver and Demski, 1979, for an alternative approach). An income measure such as $Y_{p,i}$ is strictly unnecessary in choosing optimal conduct because knowledge of the planned end of period wealth (as expressed by Expression 2.III) is all that is required in the setting being considered. Wealth and income measures in this setting really represent different ways of looking at the wealth of actors in the market. Although both the measures are future-orientated, they are of the type conventional in accounting and can be expressed *ex post* using market prices. In the setting being considered, there is no role for accountants in providing these measures. Both quantities either will already be known to all or can be costlessly calculated. This assumes that there are no computational limitations upon any individual. The existence of such limitations may provide a role for accounting information, in certain circumstances, even in a setting of certainty and perfect markets (Radner, 1968). Such a role for accounting information could be incorporated in the above models.

Income and wealth concepts as measures

This section shows that these income and wealth measures have another desirable characteristic. They are given added strength because they possess the usual attributes required of measurements. Here we are concerned with whether the underlying objects in mind, bundles of consumption opportunities in our case, can be measured in a meaningful way and whether the income and wealth concepts discussed above correctly quantify the relationship between these bundles[3] (see Demski, 1980, chapter 2; Sterling, 1979, pp.168–169.) For a more general introduction to measurement questions, see Coombes *et al.*, 1970.

The essence of measurement is that we have in mind a set of items which we can distinguish empirically (say by their height) and for which we seek a measurement scale, usually of a numerical character (feet or metres), which when utilised preserves our underlying ordering of those items. For a measurement process to be applied, the primitive objects of concern must first exist and then be distinguishable using their empirical characteristics. Attempts to measure the weights and heights of a group of people satisfy these conditions. In our case the primitive objects in mind are bundles of consumption. These clearly exist and can be distinguished empirically. Some measurement attempts will fail because the underlying items do not possess the necessary characteristics.

The second step in measurement is to seek a set (or sets) of numbers, in our case income and wealth quantities, that captures the relationship between the items to be measured. This set must be chosen so that each underlying item is represented by one, and only one, number. The weight of a given person is, for example, a unique quantity of pounds or kilograms depending on the scale being used.

Such a measure can be found if, first, the criterion chosen for distinguishing the underlying items can be used to compare each and every pair of objects. More formally, such a relationship between objects is described as complete if it satisfies this test.

Secondly, the application of the criterion must not produce intransitive results. For all objects we must be able to say that if A is ranked higher than B and B to C then A must be ranked superior to C. These two conditions allow a set of numbers to be assigned to the underlying objects which preserve their fundamental ordering.

For our purposes, we can assume that the ordering between consumption bundles is complete and transitive. In the assumed setting, these bundles can thus be *measured* using their market prices. This exercise produces our wealth measure. The income from alternative plans can be expressed and ranked using these prices. The rankings obtained using these wealth and income measures are the same as would have been produced had the underlying objects and the fundamental distinguishing criterion, that of consumption, been used directly. The wealth and income quantities introduced here can thus be regarded as being measures in the formal sense (though they may not be the only ones based on market prices that could be used). Accounting measures using these quantities can, therefore, be defended on the same basis as can measures of, say, height and weight. Though arguments similar to whether height is 'better' measured in feet or metres can still be mounted, it cannot be argued that these accounting quantities do not represent legitimate ways of measuring the phenomena in mind.

As measures must reflect an underlying empirical relationship between objects, these accounting items have to represent items that exist in the real world if they are to be regarded as measures in this sense. They therefore cease to be measures if they are contaminated by conventional accounting artifacts such as depreciation and cost allocations, which have yet to be shown to be empirical phenomena (see Beaver and Demski, 1979, p. 40; Demski, 1980, chapter 2).

For this and other reasons, none of the above measurement characteristics necessarily apply to conventional accounting systems. Historical cost accounting would seem unable to provide measures consistent with the fundamental ranking of the underlying objects (bundles of consumption) which contribute to individual welfare. In the setting considered here accounting measures based on market prices do provide such measures. Similar reasoning shows that these findings concerning measurement can also be sustained for a multi-period context with certainty and well functioning markets, and with uncertainty under the same conditions. To avoid repetition, these points will not be specifically established when dealing with multi-period and uncertain settings which form the subjects of the next two sections (and, when discussing uncertainty in greater detail, in Chapters 5 to 9).

Reverting to the assumed environment of this section, it can be said that accounting measures of wealth and income, based on market prices, are consistent with individual optimal decision making. This is true for all individuals because these measures have been shown to be preference-free. We would seem to have found the universal income and wealth measures sought by many accounting theorists and accounting policy makers. The next sections show that allowing for time and uncertainty makes no difference to this conclusion. Later chapters indicate the factors in more realistic environments which render this achievement illusory. In poorly organised markets these characteristics may not apply in just those situations where accounting information can be shown to have value (Beaver and Demski, 1979).

Present value income and wealth measurement

In a setting of perfect markets and certainty, none of the above conclusions are altered by allowing for multi-period production and consumption. Decisions will now include investing between one period and another. The earlier diagrams can easily be adapted to illustrate this using the two-period analysis made familiar by Hirshleifer (1970, chapter 3).

Figure 2.1 above can be interpreted to incorporate investment by allowing c_0 now to represent current resources and c_1 to stand for resources at the end of the period. The slope of the market line (MW_0) now reflects the rate of interest relating to lending and borrowing. The slope of the productive opportunity curve (QQ) can now be interpreted as the return in terms of end of period resources (c_1) from investing c_0 beginning of the period resources. At Q* the market rate of interest is equated to the return from the marginal investment (that is, the slope of the market line equals that of the productive opportunity curve at Q*). The optimal conduct for the enterprise is, therefore, to plan to borrow c_0 from the market and undertake all investments up to Q*, yielding a gross return of Oc_1, in terms of c_1 resources. The profit of the zth firm can, therefore, be calculated in terms of c_0 resources as

$$\pi_{z1} = (P_1 c_1 \,|\, (1 + r)) - P_0 c_0 \qquad\qquad [2.\text{V}]$$

which equals OW_0 in Figure 2.1. Here π_{z1} indicates the profits of period 1 for firm z discounted back to the beginning of the period. The subscripts z and 1 represent the firm and the period in mind, respectively, r represents the interest rate, and the prices P_1 and P_0 are those obtaining at the end of period 1 and period 0, respectively (that is, at times t_1 and t_0 respectively). This expression can be generalised to n periods and is easily recognised as a variant of the well known economist's income concept (see Chapter 3).

Similarly, the consumer's problem over time can be illustrated by adapting Figure 2.2 so that the c_0 now represents present resources and c_1 represents resources at the end of the period. The investor's problem requires the choice of how much of any endowment, augmented by any planned profits from the enterprises, it is wished to receive in the form of present resources (c_0) and future resources (c_1). An individual with an augmented endowment represented by E* in Figure 2.2 and indifference curves of the type illustrated by $U_1 U_1$ will lend P′M on the market and so obtain position P where the rate of exchange between c_1 and c_0 in terms of preferences (the slope of indifference curve) equals the market rate of interest (shown by the slope of the market line $W_0 W*_1$). Consumers with the same endowment E* but who prefer present to future resources, as represented by indifference curves like $U_2 U_2$, would obtain their preferred position (Q) by borrowing MQ′ on the market and repaying this loan, plus interest, (a total of $O''Q''$) from their endowment of c_1 resources (represented by ME*).

In this setting, the wealth of the pth individual can be written, in general, over n time periods using the present value of his or her wealth constraint at the beginning of period i, or equivalently at the end of the previous period $i - 1$. This wealth can be represented in symbols as $V_{p,i-1}$, where V stands for wealth and the first subscript represents the individual in whom we are interested, and the second indicates the time to which this wealth appertains. With this nomenclature, time i refers to the end of period i and the beginning of period i is, therefore, represented by t_{i-1}, the end of the previous period. This approach assumes that no changes are made between the end of the previous period and the beginning of the next. (For more details see Chapters 3 and 4). Assuming that the individual has invested all wealth in securities, using this nomenclature, wealth at the beginning of period i can be characterised as:

$$V_{p,i-1} = \sum_Z \sum_{i-1} (\pi_{zi}) \,|\, (1 + r)^{i-1} \qquad\qquad [2.\text{VIa}]$$

where π_{zi}, represents the planned periodic profit from the zth enterprise, the period of receipt being indexed by subscript i (i equals $i - 1$ to n). $(1 + r)$ is the discount factor, where r is the rate of interest. This discount factor reduces the value of future receipts at the time of receipt to their present value at an earlier time, at time t_{i-1} *in our case.* *The second summation sign on the right (*Σ*)* is required because the present value of the discounted periodic profits from each firm must be aggregated over all periods to time $i - 1$. The first Σ sums these present values for all enterprise securities ($z=1$ to n), to obtain the total present value of the individual's endowment. This endowment constrains his or her actions and is, therefore, necessary for optimal decision making. The wealth constraint also serves to summarise all the market opportunities available to the consumer. Although strictly unnecessary for optimal decision making, the pth consumer's income for period i (Y_{pi}) can be written in the same way and using the same notation as above, as:

$$Y_{pi} = (\sum_{Z} \sum_{i} \pi_{zi} | (1 + r)^i) - (\sum_{Z} \sum_{i-1} \pi_{zi} | (1 + r)^{i-1}) \qquad [2.\text{VIb}]$$

The first element in brackets on the right of Expression 2.VIb represents the present value of the individual's securities at the end of period 1. To obtain this value the profits from enterprises in each period are discounted by one less period because we are valuing these at the end of period $i - 1$ or the beginning of the next period. This is signified by the second summation sign on the right summing the present value of profits over one less period, that is from i to n, and by the discount factor spanning one less period. The second bracketed element stands for the present value of the endowment of the individual's securities at the beginning of the period i, that is at time t_{i-1}, as given in Expression 2.VIa.

Again, both the wealth measure and the income measure are different ways of looking at consumer wealth. Further, no one will pay for either item of information. Both are either already available or can be costlessly calculated from other available items of information. This abstracts from computational limitations and the possible role of accounting in overcoming these difficulties as was explained above. The remainder of this chapter provides an initial consideration of whether the above rationale for our wealth and income measures can be sustained in an uncertain world. It also shows that neither extra market regulations nor accounting theories concerned with individual preferences are required only because of the presence of uncertainty.

Accounting information in perfectly functioning markets with uncertainty

It will now be shown that the introduction of uncertainty *per se* does not change the view that in perfectly functioning markets accounting reports merely reiterate information costlessly available from inspecting market prices. Nor does it alter the view that enterprise market values provide a unanimous ranking for all investors of the contribution that investments make to investor welfare only irrespective of differing preferences amongst investors. Again, no one would be willing to pay for external accounting reports.

These and other topics in a setting of uncertainty are addressed further in later chapters which deal with income and wealth measurement in uncertain settings and with accounting seen from an information economics perspective (Chapters 5–8).

To address this topic as simply as possible, we will revert to the instantaneous (one period) setting originally used above. All decision makers in perfectly functioning markets are seen as choosing their actions at the beginning of the instantaneous trading cycle. The results of these actions are then announced and they receive the fruits of their decisions. Uncertainty will be assumed to be associated only with the state of the environment which will reign. The returns from enterprise decisions will differ in different states of the environment. A given productive opportunity will yield different returns depending on the state of the environment which reigns. For example, a state equivalent to a depressed economy will cause a project to yield lower returns than a state associated with high economic activity. The amount of the end-of-cycle wealth will depend on the state of the environment which occurs. The type of uncertainty being studied concerns only the state of the environment which will be realised, and has, because of this, been labelled technological uncertainty. The returns to be yielded by all projects in each state of the environment are assumed to be completely known. The actual return from each project will depend only on the state of the environment which occurs.

To simplify this initial presentation, the familiar example of the consumer choosing a security portfolio will be used to illustrate the problems of income and wealth measurement in an uncertain environment (Sharpe, 1985). As is usual in this setting, we will also assume that all individuals have the same beliefs and differ only in their wealth and in their preferences between risk and return.

In our example (see Sharpe, 1985), the consumer is seen as deciding upon a portfolio of investments on the basis of only their forecast average, or mean, returns and their risk. This risk reflects the sensitivity of their returns to the possible states of the environment which may occur. The possible deviation of the actual return obtained from holding a security from its mean return will depend on how the security's returns are expected to vary under different states of the environment. The difference between the returns promised from a security under different states will be reflected in the spread of possible returns from the security around its mean return. (A measure of risk defined in this way is the standard deviation of a security's or portfolio's possible returns around its forecast mean return.)

It is well known that, in this setting, holding more than one risky security allows risk to be reduced. Investing a given sum of money in, say, the pharmaceutical industry and the bicycle manufacturing industry should reduce the risk associated with investment relative to that experienced by confining the same total amount of investment to just one of these industries. This possibility of risk reduction arises if the two industries are affected differently by the possible states of the environment. Indeed, a certain return in all states could be obtained by investing in these two industries if their returns were perfectly negatively correlated in all states—a high (above average) return from one investment would be associated with an exactly equivalent lower than average return from the other in each state.

In the above case, the specific risk attached to each industry individually is entirely diversified away by investing wealth equally in the two industries. More generally it cannot be expected that all risk can be eliminated in this way. All industries are affected to a degree by economy-wide influences. It can be shown that the maximum reduction of industry-specific risk can be achieved by investing in a portfolio consisting of all securities available in the market (such a portfolio is usually labelled the market portfolio). Those who wish to avoid all economy-wide risk should invest in a riskless investment, say a fully indexed government bond which gives the same real return in all states of the market. In the setting assumed here, the expected return from risky securities will incorporate premiums over that yielded by the risk-free bond, reflecting how each security's return is affected by economy-wide factors.

The investor's wealth invested in securities is measured by ascertaining the terminal value of these security holdings valued at their market prices. Investor income can be measured by comparing opening and closing wealth.

In the setting assumed here, the information required to determine security prices is automatically provided by wealth-maximising enterprises when seeking finance. The decision rule for physical investments is to accept all projects which offer the return required by the market for a security possessing the same degree of non-diversifiable risk as the project. Offering projects that satisfy this criterion to investors at their market prices is equivalent to announcing the return and non-diversifiable risk associated with each of an enterprise's planned projects. Such an announcement will automatically attract the resources required to fund such projects. Again, income and wealth measures incorporating market values provide unambiguous utility-free rankings of the contribution that investments make to individual welfare. Individuals who do not like the risk complex of their existing portfolio can use the perfect and complete market to trade this portfolio (their wealth endowment) so as to achieve their desired level of risk.

Thus, in this setting, those who see accounting policy making as seeking to provide general-purpose accounting statements useful to all in society, at least for decision making purposes, can achieve their objectives by basing income and wealth measures on market prices. Such measures are already available and no one will pay accountants for providing them.

Again, in a more realistic context, there may still be a role for accounting information in perfectly functioning markets in overcoming computational limitations in an economic way. Such limitations seem more likely to occur in an uncertain setting (Radner, 1968, pp. 31–36).

Regulation in an ideal world

There may be some grounds for expecting intervention even in the 'ideal' settings assumed here. The government may not like the distribution of wealth and income generated by 'ideally' functioning markets. Economists argue that any attempts to alter the functioning of 'ideal' markets would distort the price signals generated by such markets and reduce overall economic efficiency (Atkinson and Stiglitz, 1980, pp. 5–10). They would prefer any income and wealth transfers to be achieved via lump sum taxes on those who are perceived by the government to be over-provided by the market and lump sum subsidies to those who the government wish to aid. Lump sum transfers are generally held not to hinder the attainment of economic efficiency, though they may motivate individuals to behave in a way which is believed to attract subsidies and avoid taxes. It is unlikely that there is, or should be, any role here for private sector accounting policy makers in remedying any perceived defects in income and wealth distribution flowing from the market provision of accounting information. In democracies the transfer of income and wealth is usually held to be a matter for representative bodies. Private sector bodies which regulate accounting matters are unlikely to be perceived as representative of society.

The next two chapters continue our study of income and wealth in ideal markets by discussing what are generally called economic income and wealth concepts.

Chapter summary

This chapter examined some settings where the provision of accounting information can be left to the market free of regulation. It began with a brief description of the environment assumed here. An introductory description of the findings of the chapter was also given. It was then shown that, in the assumed setting, income and wealth quantities based on market prices provide unambiguous measures of the contributions that resource endowments and investments make to the welfare of each and every individual market participant. A diagrammatic treatment suggested by Hirshleifer was used to demonstrate these conclusions in some detail, first for a single-period setting (strictly, for an instantaneous setting) and then for a multi-period environment.

Prior to addressing this latter setting, a brief excursion dealt with some measurement issues. Here, it was shown that the income and wealth measures considered in this chapter could in the assumed environment (and, indeed, under uncertainty with well functioning markets) be legitimately regarded as measures. It was argued that this freed these accounting quantities from some of the controversy that usually surrounds them in a practical environment.

Earlier in the chapter the point was made that no one would pay for the provision of these measures. In perfect and complete markets this information is either freely available or can be costlessly deduced from information already held. The analysis of these simple settings does, however, provide a standard of comparison for more realistic regimes.

Some of the characteristics of accounting information in a setting of uncertainty were introduced in the final sections. It was shown, using a simple example of portfolio analysis, that all of the chapter's earlier conclusions survived the introduction of uncertainty, at least of the type being considered. Accounting systems can still be shown to be value-free and of equal use to all. Finally a brief note suggested government regulation of even ideal markets may be expected if the government dislikes the income and wealth distributions produced by the working of the market.

Notes

1. These assumptions usually include the following:

   (1) Each individual's and each enterprise's market activities are of a size insufficient to affect market prices, i.e. all actors are price takers.
   (2) There is freedom of entry and exit into all industries for all individuals and for all enterprises with resources which are assumed to be instantaneously mobile and perfectly adaptable.
   (3) There exists no artificial constraint on prices, demand or supply, and there are no taxes or transaction costs.
   (4) Certainty. This assumption does not usually mean that everyone knows everything. One alternative assumption often employed is that all individuals and enterprises are equally aware of all opportunities which are currently available and hold identical expectations concerning these opportunities (which later may be proved to be incorrect).
   (See Cohen and Cyert, 1975, pp. 49–51 for a discussion of the need for these assumptions.)

2. These three conditions are usually called the marginal conditions for Pareto efficiency. Generalising over m commodities, they can be written as:

$$\text{MRS}^r k, m = P_k/P_m = \text{MRS}^i k, m$$

The MRS represents the marginal rates of substitution between any two commodities k and m for any two individuals p and j. The market prices for the two goods are represented by P_k and P_m. The superscript $p = 1$ to P indexes individuals and p and j represent different individuals; the subscript $k = 1$ to M indexes commodities and k and m represent different commodities.

$$MRT^z k,m = P_k/P_m = MRT^b k,m$$

The MRT symbol represents the marginal rate of transformation in production between goods k and m for different enterprises z and b, where $z = 1$ to Z. The other symbols have the same meaning as above.

The above two expressions can be equated in an overall expression because the MSRs AND MRTs between k and m for all individuals and productive enterprises are equated to the same ratio of prices. This gives:

$$MRS^p k,m = MRT^z k,m$$

for all consumers and productive enterprises.

How exactly these conditions are derived is beyond the scope of this book (see, for example, Hirshleifer, 1970, chapter 1 or any intermediate microeconomics text book). The general idea is easily understood. The market can be envisaged as automatically behaving like an all-knowing central planner whose function is to maximise utility in a Pareto sense subject to market clearing constraints. These latter constraints require first that the plans of all market participants for each and every commodity cannot exceed the total endowment of that commodity plus planned production, and secondly that the total of each of the inputs used to produce goods cannot exceed the supply of each of these inputs. It is required that each producer works efficiently, thereby producing on the product transformation curve. Finally, certain conditions are required that allow a solution to emerge, such as that no firm encounters universal increasing returns to scale.

Allocation models of this type can be solved by what is called the Lagrangean method; this generates prices for each of the above constraints, many of which are market prices, which measure the benefit in welfare terms of relaxing each of the constraints. These prices measure the marginal cost of relaxing the relevant constraint or constraints in order to allow increased activity. Optimality ensues by ensuring that each activity is continued until the additional welfare generated equals the price of the relevant constraint or constraints encountered in changing the activity. The marginal conditions above follow by rearrangement and generally involve equating the marginal utility from switching from one commodity to another to the relative price of the two goods involved.

3. Such enquiries fall within the province of what is called 'measure theory'. This addresses the logical consequences of assuming that the underlying items in mind have certain properties, such as whether there exist ordering relationships that can be applied to the underlying items. More importantly, for our purposes, the theory provides tests that can be used to see whether measures exist for the objects in mind and whether any measure that exists is unique. In contrast, measurement theory seeks to test whether measurement systems have certain empirical characteristics.

3

Wealth and income measurement: an economic perspective

Introduction

This chapter commences our study of what have come to be called 'the economist's wealth and income concepts' or, more simply, 'economic wealth' and 'economic income'. These concepts also form the subject of the next chapter.

These views of wealth and income really refer to families of similar ideas. The usual description of these concepts as economic may be somewhat misleading. Although they are now identified in the accounting literature mainly with a specific economist (Hicks), they do not represent a major element of received mainstream economic theory. Moreover, there was little agreement even between those few economists who played a part in their formulation. In any case, they are now the property of academic accountants and accounting policy makers and have been further substantially developed by the accounting community. There is now considerable agreement amongst economists, academic accountants and some accounting policy makers that these measures do represent an important framework for measuring income and wealth. (To avoid the otherwise intolerable repetition of the qualification 'economist's' or 'economic', these adjectives will be used only where confusion might otherwise result.)

Plan of the chapter

This chapter starts with an introductory section which first considers the wealth concept and its usefulness in accounting. It then considers the income concept from a planning perspective and discusses its promise for improving accounting. The economic income concept, utilised as a monitoring device for periodic enterprise performance, is considered in the next chapter. Our main analysis of the criticisms of these income and wealth concepts is also deferred to Chapter 4.

The decision models usually favoured for multi-period decision making are reviewed in the first substantive section, which reminds us that the use of these models ensures that individual utility is maximised under certain assumptions. It also introduces the example we shall use throughout this chapter and the next and finally it demonstrates that the economist's wealth concept generates identical results to those of the investment decision models considered earlier in the same section.

The following section investigates the use of economic income in a 'planning' context. The definition of income is discussed both in an intuitive way and more formally, using symbols. The importance of distinguishing between income based only on the cash flows of the mainstream project and income encompassing any cash flows obtained on funds retained during the project's life is then explained. A definition of economic depreciation is first introduced, then incorporated into our expression for income. The most important characteristics and virtues of the economic approach to wealth and income measurement are then introduced. In the course of this discussion another useful way of defining economic income is suggested.

After this, the amendments necessary to our income model where alterations in interest rates and price changes are expected, are considered briefly. The chapter concludes by looking at some of the criticisms of a more theoretical nature which have been made of some of the variants of income explored in this chapter. Further criticisms concerning mainly the difficulties with making these principles operational are considered in the next chapter.

Introduction to economic income and wealth

Chapter 2 showed that in a well organised market (more precisely, in a perfect and complete market) there exist income and wealth measures which unambiguously reflect individual preferences for future prospects in a multi-period setting. Recall that, in this setting, the value of an accepted project or prospect is based on the consumption it is expected to make available. The value of multi-period projects can, therefore, be measured unambiguously by calculating the project's present value. In the assumed setting, this amount represents both the price at which the project can be sold on the market and the cost of buying identical prospects on the market. Individual wealth can, therefore, be determined by summing all the individual's resources and projects valued using their market prices. Changes in wealth defined in this way over a period were also shown in Chapter 2 to provide, in well behaved markets, an income measure of use to all individuals, irrespective of their preferences. Such an income measure is generally described as the economist's income concept because it was suggested by a few prestigious economists, especially Fisher (see Fisher, 1930a,b, for example), and Hicks, 1946. Here we similarly categorise measures based on present values of future cash flows as examples of the economist's wealth measure.

Wealth and income measures of this type really make operational those unambiguous and universally useful income and wealth concepts discussed in Chapter 2, at least in some settings, including that of perfect and complete markets which will be generally maintained throughout this chapter. Models of this type have been argued by economists, accounting theoreticians, accounting policy makers and some practitioners to provide 'ideal' measures of wealth and income. Hansen, writing about economic income, says it may be characterised as a theoretically complete concept which is superior to other concepts of profit as a definition or a guidepoint for practical procedures. In a similar vein Solomons (1961) says that as growth in present value 'seems to carry out the function generally attributed to income, growth in present value must be what we had better understand income to mean'. Much of the theoretical literature supporting these income and wealth measures really sees them as guidelines for thinking about difficult issues rather than as yielding completely practical measures. The choice amongst practical methods is seen as being made according to how far these procedures reflect the essentials of these more abstract measures. Many of the theories of accounting reviewed in this book can be appraised in terms of their ability to preserve as many as possible of the beneficial characteristics of these economic concepts.

A number of committees of practitioners have also advocated that income and wealth measures based on present values should be seen as 'ideal' measures towards which more practical endeavours should be directed. The Inflation Accounting Committee (1975) appointed by the British Government, explicitly advocated this role for such measures, saying that income based on present value was the 'ideal' income measure in certain settings. The Financial Accounting Standards Board (the United States standard setting body) believe that financial reports may aid decision makers if they convey information concerning the amounts, timing and risk of the future cash flows of enterprises (FASB, 1978). This objective for financial reports may be seen as an attempt to render income based on present values of utility in a practical environment. Economic income and wealth measures have thus achieved considerable and influential theoretical and practical support.

Income and wealth concepts for decision making

The motivation for utilising these concepts is that if income and wealth concepts are to be useful for decision making they must be consistent with the models generally held to be of utility for such purposes. Measures which lack consistency with decision making models may generate signals which cause behaviour to deviate from that which maximises welfare in a multi-period context. It is generally agreed in the economics and finance literature that decision models for this environment ideally should be based on discounted cash flow techniques, the present value technique being preferred for technical reasons (see, for example, Hirshleifer, 1970, chapters 2 and 3, and Copeland and Weston, 1988, chapter 2). To prepare the way for considering income and wealth measurement the characteristics of these decision models will now be presented briefly.[1]

As stated above, capital markets will generally be assumed to be complete and perfect throughout this and the next chapter. Chapters 4 and 10 will focus on the effects on accounting of imperfectly organised markets. In well organised markets, everyone can trade all rights to projects on the market and can borrow and lend as much as they wish at the same interest rate for the same purposes. It will also be assumed that any adjustment to projects to allow for risk has been carried out in a way which can be deemed appropriate. (A large number of such methods are reviewed in finance texts such as Brealey and Myers (1988, chapter 7), or Copeland and Weston (1988, chapters 4, 5, 6 and 7).

These assumptions restrict our study initially to the essentials of these decision models —the timing and the futurity of cash flows. Uncertainty will have to be considered directly when we turn in Chapter 4 to the use of income and wealth concepts to measure past performance.

Much of this and the next chapter use discounting procedures but in a fairly simple way. Any difficulty with the presentation should be resolved by referring to the investment appraisal section of a good finance text, for example Brealey and Myers (1988, chapter 3), and Copeland and Weston (1988, appendix A).

It will now be demonstrated in exactly what sense the net present value decision model produces optimal results. We will then demonstrate that the economist's wealth concept possesses these same optimality characteristics.

The NPV decision-rule

Throughout this and the next chapter we will use an example to give structure to what otherwise might seem a rather abstract discussion. This example involves Mr Flower, who has the opportunity to invest 100 monetary units at time t_0, the beginning of the first year of a project's life, in return for cash flows (net of variable costs) of 25 monetary units at the end of the first year (time t_1), 45 units at the end of the second year (t_2) and 74.88 units at the end of the project's third and final year (t_3). The project has no scrap value. The discount rate is assumed to be 10 per cent. The project can be regarded as completely separable from all other projects in the economy —that is, there is no advantage or disadvantage in carrying it out in conjunction with other prospects. It represents Flower's only possibility of earning more than the market rate of interest on his wealth of 100 monetary units.

Flower is, therefore, facing a straightforward accept/reject decision. The net present value decision criterion in this case is: accept if the discounted value of the net cash flows of all years is at least equal to the present value of the investment outlay. This can be written in symbols as:

$$\text{NPV}_0 = \sum_n C_i/(1+r)^i - I_0 \geq 0 \qquad [3.1]$$

where NPV equals the project's net present value at time t_0, C_i represents the net cash flows in period i, which are assumed to arise at the end of the period (at time t_i); $(1+r)^i$ is the discount factor for period i; and r is the rate of interest. The sigma sign (Σ), the addition operator, indicates that the discounted cash flows from period 1 to period n have to be added together. I_0 represents the investment outlay required at the beginning of period 1.

Table 3.1 shows that the project should be accepted. It has a net present value of 16.17 monetary units.

Table 3.1 The net present value of Flower's project

Net present value of the project at time t_0

NPV $= -100 + 25/(1.10) + 45/(1.10)^2 + 74.88/(1.10)^3$
$\qquad = 16.17$ monetary units

Calculations

The V_{10}^n column of a set of compound interest tables gives the present value of 1 unit to be received at the end of n years in the future with a 10 per cent discount rate. This allows us to calculate the net present value of the project by simple multiplication. This gives:

NPV $= 16.17$
$\qquad = -100 + 22.73 \,(= 25 \times 0.9091) + 37.19 \,(= 45 \times 0.8264) + 56.25 \,(= 74.88 \times 0.7513)$

In a perfect capital market, this positive net present value allows Flower, if he so desires, to spend this amount immediately by borrowing 16.17 monetary units. (Recall that Flower has to invest all his wealth of 100 to fund the project.) This positive net present value means that he can spend the loan in the knowledge that he can recover his investment, plus interest, and repay the loan, plus interest, out of the project's cash flows as they fall due. The project's net present value thus measures by how much his consumption opportunities, and therefore his wealth, have increased due to the project. The project proceeds are sufficient to repay the loan and Flower's investment. They also cover the loan interest and allow Flower to pay himself 10 per cent interest on his investment. This interest represents the opportunity cost of his investment. If Flower did not undertake the project he could have otherwise obtained 10 per cent by investing his original wealth (100 units) on the market.

These conclusions are unaffected by individual preferences. The net present value of a project and the present value of wealth holdings provide precise and unambiguous measures of the contribution made to welfare by projects and wealth irrespective of individual preferences. A perfect market allows any preferred pattern of cash flows over time which can be generated from a given set of future cash flows to be achieved. Any set of cash flows can be converted to any other having the same present value in the market. Table 3.2 shows how Flower could convert the stream of cash flows from his project to a lump sum at its end if this suited his preferences. Reinvesting all the project's cash flows as they appear would yield him a lump sum of 154.63 at the end of the third year. This has the same present value as the original project (116.17 at time t_0) with a 10 per cent discount rate.

Table 3.2 Flower consumes all cash flows at the end of the project

	Total accumulated cash from project at beginning of the year	Interest at 10 per cent	Proceeds at end of year	Total accumulated cash from project at end of year
	(1)	(2)	(3)	(4 = 1 + 2 + 3)
Year 1	0	0	25	25
Year 2	25	2.5	45	72.5
Year 3	72.5	7.25	74.88	154.63

The present value at time t_0 of the accumulated cash at the end of year 3 = 154.63 × 0.7513 = 116.17 monetary units

Table 3.2 provides an illustration of the finding in Chapter 2 that trading in a perfect market allows the present value decision rule to maximise investor welfare irrespective of preferences.

Economic wealth

Economists have argued that an *ex ante* measure of wealth consistent with the net present value decision rule is provided by measuring the *ex ante* wealth to be generated by any accepted project utilising the project's present value, where 'ex ante' signifies that we are concerned with measuring wealth at the planning stage prior to the commencement of the project. More generally, '*ex ante*' means before the event. Potential wealth arises in our assumed environment when an opportunity is perceived and quantified. This potential wealth is translated into wealth that can be traded on the market by the announcement of the project's acceptance to the market. With this view, once Flower's project is accepted, Flower has a total wealth (V_0) of 116.17 monetary units (as he has no other *ex ante* wealth) at time t_0, where V_0 represents wealth at time 0 (t_0).

This definition of wealth has intuitive appeal. It is the amount that the decision maker could obtain by selling a project on the market. Disposing of the prospect for less than this would amount to throwing money away. Such an action would value the project using a higher interest rate than the going interest rate. Similarly, no one will buy a project for more than its present value because this would imply accepting less than the going rate of interest.

Using this analysis, the economist's definition of the wealth obtained from an investment project, of either a physical or a financial nature (examples are building a factory or investing in securities, respectively), can now be stated:

An individual's total wealth from a multi-period project is equal to   [Definition 3.A]
and measured by the present value of the net cash flows expected
to be generated

More formally, the wealth at the beginning of a period generated by a prospect or project is represented by the present value of that project's expected net cash flows. Using symbols, this can be written for an individual project as:

$$V_{i-1} = \Sigma \, C_i/(1 + r)^i \qquad\qquad \text{[3.IIa]}$$

where V_{i-1} is the present value of the project at the end of period $i-1$ (at time t_{i-1}) or equivalently, at the beginning of period i. (This assumes no withdrawals or increases of capital between the end of the previous period and the beginning of the next.) The symbol i indexes the period and can take the values $i-1$ to $i+T$. The other symbols are as previously defined (see Expression 3.I).

To determine the total amount of the individual's wealth, the present values of all projects owned are simply added together. Total wealth can, therefore, be written as:

$$V_{i-1} = \Sigma_k \, \Sigma_i \, C_{ik}/(1+r)^i \qquad\qquad \text{[3.IIb]}$$

where the new subscript k indexes the projects and takes the value k to K (where these subscripts each represent a project owned by the individual). The second summation sign (Σ) says that the present values of the projects are added together. This operation implies that there are no interrelationships between projects such that two projects in combination will yield more net cash flows than the two projects undertaken separately (See Brealey and Myers, 1988, pp. 94–110; Copeland and Weston, 1988, chapter 2).

A more general version of the economist's wealth concept would incorporate those monetary resources (those which are denominated in money terms) and those non-monetary resources which are not presently being utilised on investment projects. This can be stated as:

Wealth at t_i is the sum of the non-utilised net monetary and non-   [Definition 3.Aa]
monetary resources at time t_i valued at their market prices[2] **plus the**

aggregate present value of all investment projects (calculated using Expression 3.IIb, or its equivalent using market prices).

(For more detailed and alternative presentations see Beaver (1981); Beaver and Demski (1979), Bromwich and Wells (1983).)

In the setting being considered, this wider definition, and its associated income definition, present few additional theoretical difficulties. We will therefore continue to consider only multi-period projects and ignore non-utilised resources in order to concentrate on the fundamentals of the economist's income and wealth measures. The essence of this approach is a concern with the proper evaluation of future cash flows with due allowance being made for their futurity.

According to our definition of wealth (Definition 3.A), Flower's wealth is 116.17 monetary units once the decision to accept the project has been made, given that he has no other resources. This sum will continue to represent his wealth if, at the end of each period, he consumes only interest based on the project's original capital value of 116.17 units.

This wealth concept, based on future cash flows, is different from those generally used in conventional accounting or suggested for such use. These other wealth concepts may well be useful for a variety of purposes, but they do not in general have the property of being completely consistent with a decision making model which is widely regarded as optimal, at least for the setting being considered here. Our wealth concept, in contrast, is built upon the same theoretical foundations as the decision model and incorporates the same constituents. This ensures that, if used in decision making, this wealth concept will lead to the same results as would be obtained using the more familiar net present value approach. It can be shown that this wealth concept can also be made consistent with other discounted cash flow models of investment appraisal.

Income concepts in decision making: income *ex ante*

Income can be defined in a great number of different ways. Different income concepts are likely to be useful to different people and in different environments.

The simplest version of income, which underlies most accounting systems, assumes that all changes in wealth, computed according to the accounting system being used, are incorporated in the income for a period. This is called the clean surplus method of income measurement in the United States of America. In practice, many accounting systems do not follow this approach: they use reserve accounting, thereby not allowing all changes in wealth to flow through to the income statement. However, where income incorporates all changes in wealth, income (Y) can be calculated by deducting the wealth (calculated according to the accounting system being used) at the beginning of the period (V_{i-1}) from the period's cash flows (C_i) plus the wealth at the end of the period (V_i) similarly defined, assuming that there have been no additions or withdrawals of capital (or that appropriate adjustments have been made). This general expression for income can be written as:

$$Y_i = V_i + C_i - V_{i-1} \qquad \text{[3.III]}$$

where V_i and V_{i-1} represent the 'value' of resources at the end of each period determined according to the accounting convention being used.

Expression 3.III declares an income only when the opening value of the project in mind has been maintained under the accounting convention being used. It is, therefore, consistent with one of the best known views of the role and significance of income suggested by Hicks (1946, p. 172) provided that we assume that the above value amounts can be costlessly converted into consumption, as it is consumption which we assume is ultimately desired. Hicks said that that the 'central' role of income *is to serve as a guide to prudent conduct and should give people an idea of what they can consume without impoverishing themselves.* Impoverishment here means reducing capital (strictly, reducing future consumption). The role seen for income is, therefore, to show how much can be consumed without withdrawing capital (see also Kaldor, 1955; Lindahl, 1935).

This view of income suggests that the rearrangement of known market data, which was the role suggested for accounting figures with well organised markets in Chapter 2, may serve a useful purpose in allowing the planning of consumption in this setting. As we will see shortly, sometimes complex calculations are required to generate income numbers. Thus, income figures may not be immediately apparent from already known information and may therefore not be costlessly derivable from such information. This supports the view expressed in Chapter 2 that there may be a role for accountants in generating income numbers, even in well organised markets.

Given this central meaning for income, Hicks defines income in the following way:

'A man's income is the maximum value he can consume during the   Definition [3.B]
week and still expect to be as well off at the end of the week as
he was at the beginning.'
Hicks (1946, p. 172).

This definition suggests that the necessary elements of income are:

1 the maintenance of an opening capital amount (V_{i-1} in Expression 3.III) out of the sum of
2 the expectations at the end of a period (V_i in Expression 3.III), plus
3 the proceeds during the period (C_i).

Apart from a clear concern with expectations, this definition does not imply use of the economist's definition of wealth. With suitable adjustments, the values in Expression 3.III could be based on historical cost, replacement cost and net realisable values. If historical cost were used, Expression 3.III would represent a budgeted income statement presented in historical cost terms.

Hicks converts his definition of income into the most familiar and most widely utilised version of the economist's income concept and renders it consistent with investment decision models, by defining 'well-offness' using the economist's wealth concept. This he does when he coins his first approximation to what he sees as the central meaning of income (as given by Definition 3.B). Hicks defines this concept which he labelled 'income concept Number 1' as:

'Income is ... the maximum amount which can be spent during a   Definition [3.C]
period if there is to be an expectation of maintaining intact the capital
value of prospective receipts (in money terms).'
Hicks (1946, p. 173).

This comes down to quantifying the V_i values in Expression 3.III using the economist's wealth concept[3]. This requires that we insert the appropriate present values for periods i and $i-1$ into Expression 3.III.

Income Number 1 is, therefore, given by:

$$Y_i = V_i + C_i - V_{i-1} \qquad\qquad [3.\text{IIIa}]$$

where V_i and V_{i-1} are now to be understood to be the present values of all future cash flows at the end of period i and period $i-1$ respectively, C_i represents the cash flows of the period, and Y_i now represents the economic income of the period. This is the usual formulation of the economist's income concept (using the Number 1 concept).

As a concrete illustration, Flower's *ex ante* planned income for the first year of his prospect can be computed using Expression 3.IIIa. This requires that we compute the present value of the project's expected cash flows at time t_0 (V_0) and its present value at the end of the first year (V_i). Table 3.3 shows the necessary calculations.

Section 1 of the table shows the present value of the project at the beginning of the project. Section 2 indicates the present value of the project at the end of the first year, including the cash flows retained in the first year shown by F_1. The amount of these retentions for the first year of the project are calculated on the third line of Section 2 of the table. This equals the amount required to maintain the original present value of the project, that is the difference between the original value (V_0) and that of the present value of the remaining future cash flows at the end of the year (V_i) Alternatively, the retained funds for a period are equal to the cash flows for the period minus the economic income for the period.

Section 3 similarly calculates the present value of the project at the end of year 2. The third line of this section (3.2) indicates the funds retained in this second year. The same calculations are given in Sections 4 and 5 of the table for years 3 and 4 respectively. Section 5 indicates that, at the end of year 4, the retentions in the previous years guarantee a continuing present value equal to that of the project's initial present value. The interest on the retained funds of previous years is given in symbols as rF_i, where r is the rate of interest. The necessary calculations for years 2, 3 and 4 are shown in the last lines of Sections 3, 4 and 5 respectively. Interest on the retentions of previous years is just sufficient to ensure that the total cash flows in each year are exactly the amount necessary to pay out an income equal to that of the project's first year, and allow retentions sufficient to maintain the project's original present value.

Thus, for example, the cash flows for the second year from the project are 45 monetary units (line 3.2). The necessary retentions in this year are 34.72 units (see line 3.2). The income in this year must be 11.62 units if income for this year is to be the same as for the first year (Y_1). Retentions and the income for the year sum to 46.34, which equals the cash flows of the year, 45 units plus interest on the funds retained in the previous year (13.38, see line 2.1). This interest equals 1.34 (10 per cent on 13.38, see line 3.2).

As we already know, V_0 is equal to 116.17 monetary units, and V_1 equals 102.79 units. Inserting the expected cash flows to be received at the end of the first year ($C_1 = 25$ units) into Expression 3.IIIa gives Flower's economic income (*ex ante*) for the first year of the project as

$$Y_1 = 11.62 = 25 + 102.79 - 116.17 \qquad\qquad [3.\text{IIIa(i)}]$$
$$ (C_1) \quad (V_1) \qquad (V_0)$$

Table 3.3 Present values of Flower's project including retained funds (Flower's wealth) at times t_0, t_1, t_2, t_3, t_4, and all future years

Section 1

1.1 At the beginning of year 1 (t_0)

1.2 $V_0 = \dfrac{25}{(1.10)} + \dfrac{45}{(1.10)^2} + \dfrac{74.88}{(1.10)^3}$

= 116.17

Section 2

2.1 At the end of year 1 (t_1)

2.2 $F_1 + V_1 = 116.17$
= 13.38 + 102.79

where $V_1 = \dfrac{45}{(1.10)} + \dfrac{74.88}{(1.10)^2}$

2.3 and where retained funds in the first year,
$F_1 = 13.38 = 116.17 - 102.79$ or $25 - 11.62$
$\quad\quad\quad\quad\quad (V_0) \quad\quad (V_1) \quad\quad (C_1) \quad (Y_1)$

Section 3

3.1 At the end of year 2 (t_2)
$F_1 + F_2 + V_2 = 116.17$
= 13.38 + 34.72 + 68.07

where $V_2 = \dfrac{74.88}{(1.10)}$

3.2 and where retained funds, in the second year,
$F_2 = 34.72$
= 102.79 - 68.07 or 45 + 1.34 - 11.62
$\quad (V_1) \quad\quad (V_2) \quad\quad (C_2) \quad (rF_1) \quad\quad (Y_2)$

3.3 and interest on $F_1 = rF_1 = 1.34$

Section 4

4.1 At the end of year 3 (t_3)

4.2 $F_1 + F_2 + F_3 + V_3 = 116.17$
= 13.38 + 34.72 + 68.07 + 0

4.3 where $F_3 = 74.88 + 1.34 + 3.47 - 11.62$

4.4 and interest on retained funds = $rF_1 + rF_2$
= 1.34 + 3.47

Section 5

5.1 At the end of year 4 (t_4) and all future years

5.2 $F_1 + F_2 + F_3 = 116.17 = 13.38 + 34.72 + 68.07$

5.3 and $\Sigma rF_i = 11.62$ = income for year 4 and all future years

where the symbols in brackets identify each numerical element in terms of the elements of Expression 3.IIIa.

As indicated in Table 3.3, any cash flows in the period in excess of this economic income for the period are retained and reinvested. These cash flows are equal to the difference between V_i and V_0 and generally designated in symbols as F_i. It will be assumed that these are planned to be reinvested to yield interest in the next period. Again, following Table 3.3, the consequent cash flows can be expressed in symbols as rF_{i-1}, where r is the rate of interest. This interest must be allowed for in computing the expected income of the second year and of succeeding years. Using the figures calculated in Table 3.3 gives the second year income as

$$Y_2 = 11.62 = \underset{(rF_1)}{1.34} + \underset{(C_2)}{45} + \underset{(V_2)}{68.07} - \underset{(V_1)}{102.79} \qquad \text{[3.IIIa(ii)]}$$

where the last three items appertain to the original project. Finally, Flower's third year income can be calculated in the same way. This gives:

$$Y_3 = 11.62 = \underset{(rF_1)}{1.34} + \underset{(rF_2)}{3.47} + \underset{(C_3)}{74.88} + \underset{(V_3)}{0} - \underset{(V_2)}{68.07} \qquad \text{[3.IIIa(iii)]}$$

where the last three elements flow from original project, 1.34 is interest on the cash flows retained in the first period and 3.47 is similarly the interest obtained on the cash flows retained in the second year (3.47 equals 10 per cent on the cash flows retained in the previous period, 34.72).

The above calculations illustrate the general finding that utilising income concept Number 1, the economist's income in each year can be expressed as interest at the relevant rate on the project's original or opening present value (or wealth). This finding follows directly from the economist's wealth concept which incorporates the present value of all opportunities once they are perceived or, perhaps more realistically, once they are accepted. Thus, the only difference there can be between the same prospect viewed from the perspective of, say, time 0 and time 1 is that we have passed through one period. At time t_1, each of the individual cash flow components becomes more valuable than at time t_0 because they are each weighed by one less application of the discount factor.

This can easily be seen by looking at any period. The value of the project at the beginning of the period (V_{i-1}) can be made equal to the total value at the end by multiplying it by the interest rate. This gives

$$C_i + V_i = V_{i-1} + rV_{i-1} \qquad \text{[3.IIIa(iv)]}$$

Switching V_{i-1} to the left-hand side of this expression converts it into our familiar expression for economic income, thus:

$$rV_{i-1} = C_i + V_i - V_{i-1} = Y_i \qquad \text{[3.IIIa(v)]}$$

This demonstrates that economic income from the mainstream project for the period (that is, ignoring interest on retained funds) is just equal to interest on the value of the project at the beginning of the period.[4] The economic income for a period from the project, plus interest on funds retained in earlier periods, can similarly be shown to be equal to interest on the opening present value of the project. That is, if the cash flows obtained in the period on funds reinvested in earlier periods are taken into account, $Y_i = rV_0$. This can be written as

$$C_i + \Sigma rF_{i-n} + V_i = V_0 + rV_0 \qquad \text{[3.IIIa(vi)]}$$

where $n = 1$ to $i - 1$. After rearrangement, this becomes

$$rV_0 = C_i + \Sigma rF_{i-n} + V_i - V_0 = Y_i \qquad \text{[3.IIIa(vii)]}$$

Income as a 'standard stream'

If we take a strict Hicksian perspective (Hicks, 1946, p. 184), income is not merely interest on the capitalised value of a prospect including the value of any retained funds at a given time. Rather, it is defined as the interest on the capitalised value of the prospect at the time of decision. With this view, income can be represented as the constant stream which can be obtained into perpetuity from the prospect while keeping the present value of the prospect intact as, for example, illustrated in Table 3.3 for year 4 (shown in Section 5 of the table).

The actual profile of annual cash flowing from any project can thus be represented, if so desired, by a standard and constant stream of annual cash flows which may be consumed without endangering the original capital value of the prospect. The mechanics of the determination of such a stream were portrayed in Table 3.3 and are implicit in Expressions 3.IIIa(i, ii and iii). Expression 3.III(a) shows how the income from the mainstream project was calculated. Expressions 3.IIIa(i to iii) show how the cash flows from the original project are augmented by interest on retained funds to yield a constant annual income in the face of the declining cash flows received from the mainstream project as it proceeds.

The irregular net cash flows from Flower's three-year project can thus be expressed equivalently as a constant stream of 11.62 monetary units per year into perpetuity. This annuity of 11.62 can be called the standard stream income of the prospect. It has a present value equivalent to the original capital value (116.17) of Flower's prospect. Table 3.3 shows that when the main project ends in year 3, the continuing interest on retained funds will be just sufficient to allow Flower to continue to consume 11.62 monetary units per year and thus still keep the original capital value of his prospect intact (see Section 5 of the table). The present value of this annuity, or standard stream of a constant amount in each year, is identical to the original present value of the prospect.

From an *ex ante* perspective, income can be represented as the constant amount in each year which is implied by the future plans made at the time of decision. This amount can be regarded as the permanent income of the business year by year and was the income concept preferred by Hicks. (See Hicks, 1979, for a similar explanation in an *ex post* context.) More generally, and allowing for random changes from one year to another, this standard stream might be called a business's 'normal' income (Hicks, 1979, p. 12).

Income seen in this light is remarkably similar to what investment analysts often say they are trying to discover when stripping the profits of a business in any one year of all exceptional and unusual items in order to assess whether the underlying capacity of the corporation to earn income has changed during the year (see Graham *et al.*, 1962).

This standard stream concept also may be of some aid to those who seek income concepts to help determine dividend decisions. Standard stream income is sometimes urged as a measure of the distributable or sustainable income of the enterprise (Revsine, 1973; Davidson *et al.*, 1979); but for the view that such income figures should, perhaps, have little bearing on dividend decisions, see Forker, 1980, and Eggington, 1980.

Economic depreciation

The funds planned to be retained in any year with economic income are budgeted provisions for maintaining intact the original present value of the project. In the assumed environment these provisions are necessary because the present values of a mainstream project calculated at the end of each year in the future will fall. This diminution in value results because some of the cash flows embedded in the project's original present value are expected to be realised as the project proceeds through time. Thus, in our example, the present value of the mainstream project is expected to have fallen by 13.38 units by the end of the first year (that is, $V_0 - V_1 = 116.17 - 102.79$). This results because the cash flows expected to be received after the end of this year are 25 units less than the cash flows embedded in the present value at the beginning of the first year. This decline in present value of the mainstream project over time represents economic depreciation. Our expression for the income of any period can be rewritten to incorporate this. This gives income as

$$Y_i = C_i - D_i \hspace{3cm} \text{[3.IIIb]}$$

where $D_i = V_{i-1} - V_i$ and C_i is now defined to include any interest accruing from the retention of cash flows in earlier years.

The retained funds generated by allowing for depreciation in any year can be seen to be just sufficient to recoup the fall in present value in the year concerned. Thus, in Flower's first year, depreciation is expected to be 13.38 and the funds retained are just equal to this. The income generated by these funds in future years will be just sufficient to remedy the otherwise expected fall in the annual cash flows of the mainstream project. This can be seen using the figures in Table 3.3. The income from the mainstream project in year 2 can be calculated by excluding the interest, shown in Table 3.3 (Section 3.2), on retained earnings. This gives the income for the year from the project itself as

$$Y_2 = 10.28 = 45 - 34.72$$

where 34.72 is depreciation in year 2. The interest obtained in year 2 from the funds retained in year 1 equals 1.34 which, when added to the income of the project itself, is just sufficient to allow Flower to consume income of 11.62 monetary units and maintain the original present value of his project. This income is made up of 10.28 units from the project plus 1.34 representing interest on retained funds in year 2.

In our assumed setting of perfect and complete markets, the value of a project is equal to the price the market places on prospects offering identical cash flows to the project in mind. Economic depreciation is based on a comparison of the market values of the cash flows offered by a prospect at the beginning and end of a period. This depreciation is, therefore, based on the prices the market is willing to offer for future cash flows at the beginning and end of a period.

These prospects could be traded at these market prices if so desired in the assumed market setting. Depreciation provisions of this type do not, therefore, fall foul of

Thomas's criticisms that depreciation provisions in general are arbitrary and have no empirical meaning in the real world (see Thomas, 1969, 1974, for a detailed discussion of these views). Thomas has, however, argued that the discount rates used in present value calculations are also generally arbitrary (Thomas, 1969, and 1974, pp. 12–13). This is because these rates are seen as being the creations of whoever imposes the discount rates to be used in present value calculations. This may be true of imperfect markets, but is not the case in the setting considered here. In perfect and complete markets, interest rates are market prices like any others.

With the above technical knowledge we can now proceed to consider some of the characteristics and virtues of the economist's income and wealth concepts. Some of the problems with these concepts will be considered later in this chapter, and others in Chapter 4.

Important characteristics and virtues of the economist's wealth and income concepts

Consistency with decision models

Earlier it was stressed that these concepts are entirely consistent with usual investment decision models. This has already been demonstrated for the wealth concept (see pp. 34–7). It is also easily shown for the income concept using the net present value method as an example. The usual accept/reject criterion used with the net present value model was set out in Expression 3.I. The net cash flows for any year in this model can be partitioned into economic income and economic depreciation. These two items can, therefore, be substituted for the cash flows in Expression 3.I. This yields an alternative expression for project NPV. This can be written as

$$\text{NPV}_0 = \Sigma(Y_i/(1 + r)^i + D_i/(1+r)^i) - I_0 \geq 0 \qquad \text{[3.IV]}$$

This shows that economic income is another, perhaps more complicated, way of writing the usual net present value criterion. This revised expression yields the same information as net present value models but in a way that may be more useful for budgeting. This is because Expression 3.IV shows the decision's potential cash flow consequences in each period partitioned between how much can be consumed in each period (Y_i) and how much is required to be reinvested (D_i) to maintain the originally expected present value of the project.

The wealth and income models used here are thus firmly grounded on well known and generally accepted decision models. Minimally, these concepts of income and wealth should be useful to guide our thinking when we are considering accounting models for decision orientated purposes. Some other wealth and income models which purport to be 'decision-useful' are generally less well grounded on these decision-theory foundations.

The economist's approach suggests that a full-blooded approach to decision usefulness clearly requires us to deal with expectations. Although, as will be seen shortly, the economist's approach to these matters is somewhat unsatisfactory, few, if any, other accounting systems incorporate forecasts in any reasonable way. Perhaps, the greatest strength of the economist's wealth and income measures is that they are fully in accord with the decision usefulness approach which presently pervades both accounting theory and accounting policy making.

The universality of these measures

The search for a general 'all purpose' set of accounting statements, which is the avowed objective of many accounting policy makers, has been interpreted as seeking to find that set of statements which are useful to all, irrespective of their preferences. The economic income and wealth concepts fulfil this role in the setting being considered here (and indeed with uncertainty in similar settings). If the cash flow proceeds from a project do not satisfy individual preferences, the rights to these cash flows can be traded on the market for any other set of cash flows having the same present value and which is optimal relative to the individual's preferences. This shows that the search in mind is not a completely impossible task.

Income as interest

One obvious characteristic of the economist's income concept has been made explicit in our presentation. This income represents, with the Hicksian Number 1 approach, interest on opening wealth. For Flower, for example, the expected total income from his project in any year was shown to be always equal to the interest on the present value of the project at the start of the project (see Expressions 3.IIIa(i), (ii) and (iii)).

To consider income as only interest on the opening capital value of a prospect is more prudent than the assumption usually made with the net present value decision model. This decision model sees an individual with a project as being able to spend the entire net present value of the prospect immediately if it is so desired, without reducing the opening value of the investment in the prospect (see Table 3.2). Economic income *ex ante* says alternatively that the individual should expect to consume only the interest on the original investment necessary for the project, plus the interest on the prospect's net present value (rather than the whole of this net present value).

This difference in the prescription concerning how much of the prospect's fruits can be consumed is a value judgement (or normative question) which cannot be resolved in an objective fashion. These divergences in view may arise from the different uses contemplated for the two models. The net present value model measures the amount by which wealth will be augmented if a given prospect is accepted. The *ex ante* income measure provides a periodical budget for projects and for consumption arising therefrom on the assumption that opening economic wealth, including the net present value of a project, is to be maintained intact.

In well organised markets, these differing viewpoints can be left to individuals to resolve by trading to achieve their preferences. Individuals whose income from a project was restricted to its economic income can realise some, or all, of a project's net present value, if so desired, by selling some or all of their rights to the project, by borrowing on these rights and by carrying out other similar market transactions. One or other of these two definitions of permissible consumption may be preferred by the individual if markets are less well conducted so that the conversion of wealth and income to obtain a more preferred alternative cannot be achieved by market transactions. The fact remains that an individual who seeks to consume more than the interest on the opening value of a prospect is not maintaining capital intact using the definition of economic wealth presented in this chapter.

Not all economists see income as being only interest. In 1906 Fisher (revised in Fisher, 1930(a)) regarded income as being based on actual consumption, thereby linking income more directly to the fundamental utility which is generated by projects and which it is assumed is to be maximised. See Kaldor (1955) for a critique of these and other income concepts. Lindahl (1935), although strongly in favour of income as interest, entertained three other meanings of income. Kaldor (1955) and others have suggested other income measures as useful for taxation purposes.

Uncertainty

One of the defects of the above treatment of wealth and income is that it does not treat uncertainty in any detailed way. This reflects the literature being considered. Hicks does not deal at any length with uncertainty when considering income for planning purposes (*ex ante* income). He and other authors prefer to deal with uncertainty explicitly only when dealing with after-the-event income (see Hicks, 1946; Lindahl, 1935). Alexander does seek to deal with uncertainty in a general way (Alexander, 1950, as revised by Solomons, 1962). This article represents a good comprehensive treatment of the economist's income concept. In a planning context, when dealing explicitly with uncertain prospects, the original proponents of economic income seemed to see the capital values utilised for income measurement as being certainty equivalents of the underlying uncertain prospects (see Chapter 5). A standard stream can, therefore, also be seen as a certain amount equivalent in value to the underlying uncertain prospect from which it has been derived (Kaldor, 1955, pp. 171–172). Chapter 2 implies that with perfect and complete markets this may be a legitimate way of proceeding (Hirshleifer, 1970, chapter 9). In such a setting, rights to income in different states of the environment in each time period have definite and certain market prices at any time which can be used to evaluate individual wealth at different times. Chapter 8 gives a more detailed explanation without getting involved in the details of a multi-period setting.

Our understanding of uncertainty, especially in a multi-period setting, is by no means complete (see Hirshleifer and Riley, 1979). Findings so far indicate that the introduction of multi-periods substantially increases the complexity of the models involved.

Results obtained for an uncertain environment, without considering time, do not always carry over in a straightforward fashion to multi-period settings. This is not surprising as the settings that have to be considered are likely to be more complex. For example, the set of trading instruments and the opportunities for trade may become much richer when the number of periods is increased. More germane to our concerns here is the fact that the utility function used to derive preferences for consumption in any given period (which forms the essence of the discounting treatment used above) may be very complicated. This may mean that preferences are not easily portrayed by simply using a discount rate in the conventional way. With this view, the preferences attached to the *ex ante* outcome in any state are determined by scarcity of benefits in that state, relative to those offered by other states. This suggests that, in a multi-period context, the prices attached to the state outcomes in different time periods may not conform with the underlying concept of discounting[5] (there are more technical reasons for expecting this difficulty, see Beaver, 1981(a), pp. 90–95).

In the present state of knowledge it is difficult to do anything other than assume that the discount rates used by individuals, and the appropriate market interest rates, do correctly reflect the market's valuation of uncertain prospects to be received at different times in the future. With these qualifications, there would seem no reason to assume that the Hicksian treatment of uncertainty, by using 'certainty equivalents' in planning, is incorrect in perfect and complete markets. With this view the certain standard stream equivalent of a prospect can be argued to summarise all expectations concerning uncertain states and to express these using 'certainty equivalents' utilising the known and certain prices which would have to be paid at the time of valuation to obtain rights to outcomes in each uncertain future state. Although not really dealing with uncertainty in any formal way, Hicks does find it necessary to introduce two additional income concepts to allow for expectations that the interest rate and general level of prices may change over the planning period. These are dealt with briefly in the next section.

Hicksian income concepts Number 2 and Number 3

Hicks suggests income concept Number 2 for use where the interest rate is predicted to change during a prospect's lifetime. Income concept Number 3 is similarly designed to cope with a situation of expected general price changes.

A complete analysis of income concept Number 2 is rather complex (see Hicks, 1946, pp. 184–188) and may be thought to represent a diversion from central ideas. This concept will, therefore, be dealt with only briefly here. Interest rate changes which are forecast at the time of decision making for future years may cause an income computed according to income concept Number 1, encompassing the mainstream project and funds retained as required by this income concept to become a variable stream. Amended calculations show that Flower's income in the first year of his project becomes 12.34 and 6.17 monetary units thereafter when the discount rate is expected to be 10 per cent in the first year and then 5 per cent in following years. Section 1 of Table 3.4 calculates the present value of the project under the assumption that the discount rate is 10 per cent in the first year and 5 per cent thereafter. The project is shown to have a present value of 123.43 monetary units under these assumptions. Recall that *ex ante* income for a period can be calculated as interest on the opening value of the project. Income in year 1 is therefore 12.43 (10 per cent on the revised present value of the project and 6.17 for all future years (5 per cent of 123.43 monetary units). The expectation of interest changes, therefore, means that the standard stream computed as interest on the opening present value may no longer have a present value equal to the original proposal's present value.

The question therefore arises of whether there is a correct income measure to use in these circumstances. Hicks seeks to answer this question by urging a variant (income Number 2) of his standard stream method. This approach comes into its own with expected interest rate changes because it allows a variable stream under income Number 1 to be converted into an equivalent constant periodical stream. Income Number 2 is defined as:

'The maximum amount the individual can spend in this week, and   Definition [3.D]
still   expect to be able to spend the same amount in each ensuing
week'
Hicks (1946, p. 174)

This definition yields the same results as income Number 1 when interest rates are not expected to change.

Table 3.4 Economic income Number 2 for Flower's project

1 Present value of Flower's project under the assumption that the interest rate is expected to be 10 per cent in year 1 and 5 per cent thereafter

$$V_0 = (25/(1.10)) + (45/(1.10)(1.05)) + (74.88/(1.10)(1.05)^2)$$
$$= 123.43$$

2 Annuity having the same present value under these assumptions

To find this annuity we have to solve the following expression for x:

$$V_0 = 123.43 = x/(1.10) + 1/(1.10)(x/0.05)$$

where the first term on the right yields the present value of the first instalment of the annuity. The final term in brackets yields the present value of an annuity of x received into infinity commencing at the end of the first year of the project. The penultimate figure in brackets discounts this amount to the beginning of the first year of the project. Solving for x yields 6.46 monetary units as the amount which must be received per year if an annuity of this amount received to infinity is to have approximately the same present value as the project under our assumptions.

Interest rate alterations cause the two concepts to differ. Hicks claims income Number 2 then provides a closer approximation to his central concept of income than does income Number 1. The second section of Table 3.4 calculates the approximate annual sum which if received for all years to infinity, will have the same present value. The table shows that an annuity of 6.46 monetary units per year is required under our assumptions. Thus, income Number 2 is equal, approximately, to a standard stream of 6.46 units in perpetuity.

One reason why we might wish to resort to a standard stream concept when interest rates are expected to change is that income concept Number 1 exhibits a discontinuity when interest rates are expected to change. Thus if we wish to see income as an approximation to the permanent income of the individual, we have to resort to income concept Number 2.

Income concept Number 1 also differs from income concept Number 2 in the amounts recommended as income for periods both before and after any expected interest rate alteration. This is because income concept Number 1, by the nature of its calculation, looks backwards to the present value of the project's cash flows at the beginning of the project and seeks to maintain this intact. With this perspective, any changes in interest rates which increase present values require more of the project's cash flows to be devoted to maintaining the increased present value of the project after the interest rate fall. Conversely, where the present value of a project falls because of expected increases in interest rates, income concept Number 1 would indicate that more of the project's original cash flows could be released as income without damaging the new lower present value of the project.

In contrast to the above perspective, income concept Number 2 looks forward to future cash flows and income is increased only if the new interest rate yields a greater income in future than does the standard stream income calculated prior to any interest rate changes. Whether this is a better measure of income than is obtained using income Number 1 can only be resolved by the decision maker in mind by reference to the central meaning of income. Income Number 2, Hicks's preferred alternative, may seem rather removed from the original prospect's cash flows and difficult to make operational in realistic circumstances.

Expected inflation

Similar problems arise where inflation is expected. Hicks coined his income concept Number 3 to aid in this situation. He says that:

'Income No. 3 must be defined as the maximum amount of money   Definition [3.E]
which the individual can spend this week and still expect to be able
to spend the same amount in real terms in each ensuing week.'
Hicks (1946, p. 175).

It is not intended to deal with this concept in detail here because general price level adjustment seems to produce no problems for the economic income concept additional to those which attend all attempts at adjusting accounting numbers for inflation in some way. Indeed, the economist's approach as characterised by income Number 3 probably faces less problems than other methods of price level adjustment suggested in accounting. The Number 3 income concept also uses a 'standard stream' approach and runs into similar problems to those which we found plagued attempts to use this approach to deal with expected interest rate changes.

Hicks recognises that a solution as to which is the 'best' measure of income in these difficult areas can only be resolved by the individual concerned by reference to the 'central meaning of income'. He also recognises that with poorly organised markets and a dynamic economic environment, income, along with saving, investment and depreciation, is not a suitable tool for any analysis that aims at logical precision. This is because there is far too much equivocation in its meaning (Hicks, 1946, p. 171). He, therefore, counsels that 'we shall be well advised to eschew income and saving in economic dynamics. They are bad tools which break in our hands' (Hicks, 1946, p. 177). But as a way of providing guidelines and ways of thinking about income and wealth, the framework provided by Hicks and other economists is as yet unchallenged.

Kaldor (1955) criticised the standard stream approach because, as we have seen, in some circumstances it separates income somewhat from the capital value of the prospect in mind. Most economists see income flowing from a source and being the yield offered on this source. Standard stream income measures are seen by Kaldor not as income calculations, but rather as restatements of original wealth. Such restatements may be a long way removed from project cash flows if, for example, we are dealing with standard stream income determined in terms of certainty equivalents. The need for fairly sophisticated calculations also renders the standard stream approach difficult to make operational.

Kaldor (1955) further argues that the change in capital values following expected interest rate changes, and the alterations in capital values resulting from expected general price changes, may be spurious and not represent real resource changes. He argues, for example, that any market-wide expectation of interest rate changes will be reflected in an alteration in the yield expected from assets. The change in capital values caused by an alteration in the expected interest rate will be just sufficient to offset the change in project cash flows consequent on any change in the generally anticipated yield from assets.

This argument means that in Flower's case a fall, say, in the interest rate, would be matched by a fall in the cash flows expected from his project, reflecting that the expected yield from capital assets has fallen. With this view, there may be no capital gain accruing from a fall in interest rates. Kaldor's argument concerning expected inflation is similar. With this view, the Hicksian Number 3 concept does not, therefore, necessarily capture the change in the real value of resources due to inflation.

This completes our review of the economist's *ex ante* income and wealth concepts.

Chapter summary

The contents of Chapters 3 and 4 will be summarised at a number of places in the following chapter, where an overview of the economic concepts of income and wealth will be given. Some of the advantages of economic income and wealth, concentrating on economic income, were summarised earlier in this chapter in the section entitled 'Important characteristics and virtues of the economist's wealth and income concepts (pp. 44–46).

Notes

1. This section can therefore be skipped by those with a good background in capital budgeting theory.

2. Market prices cannot generally be used to value individual wealth because with incomplete markets such prices may not exist. Alternatively, more than one price may exist for a given item.

3. Alternatively, Y can be defined as consumption during the period plus any savings during the same period, which may be negative if the individual concerned is consuming more than his or her income (dissaving), plus capital appreciation over the period. This can be written as

$$Y_i = (CO_i + (V_i + S_i) - V_{i-1}) \qquad \text{[3.III(1)]}$$

where CO_i and S_i represent, respectively, consumption and saving over the period. This second expression of income is introduced because some of the literature in this area is phrased in these terms (see Kaldor, 1955). Income expressed in this way may also be more easily measurable in the real world. Our two expressions for economic income are generally equivalent. As we are allowing for no withdrawal or increase in capital, consumption plus saving must equal the period's cash flows. Thus Expression 3.III(1) can be rewritten to give Expression 3.IIIa by substituting the period's cash flows for consumption plus saving. This transforms expression 3.III(1) into Expression 3.IIIa.

4. Alternatively, we can use our income expression more explicitly by dichotomising V_{i-1} into its component elements, $C_i/(1+r) + V_i/(1+r)$.
   Thus our income expression 3.IIIa can be written as

$$C_i + V_i - (C_i/(1 + r) + V_i/(1 + r)) = Y_i$$

Multiplying throughout by $(1+r)$ gives

$$C_i(1+r) + V_i(1+r) - C_i - V_i = Y_i(1+r)$$

which after deducting common elements leaves

$$C_i r + V_i r = Y_i(1+r),$$

which by rearrangement give

$$rC_i/(1+r) + rV_i/(1+r) = Y_i$$

The two terms on the left which are multiplied by r sum to V_{i-1}. Therefore, we can write Y_i as $Y_i = rV_{i-1}$.

5. Beaver (1981(a)), p. 5 and pp. 90–95) argues that the possible difficulties of deriving a discount rate to use with the economist's approach, under uncertainty, have contributed to the revolution which he argues has overthrown this approach in favour of adopting an information perspective (see Chapters 5 to 9).

4

Ex post economic wealth and income and problems with the economic approach to income and wealth measurement

Plan of the chapter

The first major part of this chapter introduces after-event (*ex post*) income and wealth concepts advocated by economists which are consistent with the planning concepts considered in chapter 3. These *ex post* concepts may help to monitor forecasting ability and aid in the evaluation of managerial efficiency and of continuing project viability. Any differences between the planned and actual income for a period, and opening wealth and end of period wealth, should aid the replanning of existing projects.

The first substantive section of the chapter explains the conceptual differences between *ex ante* and *ex post* figures used in planning. The following two sections consider some definitions of wealth and income *ex post*. It is shown that these definitions use the same conceptual framework as that which provided the theoretical foundations for our *ex ante* measures in Chapter 3. Two generally accepted alternative definitions of *ex post* income are introduced.

The choice between these two measures, which is a major subject of this chapter, is then taken up in the next section. This part of the chapter is completed by a summary of the advantages of economic income *ex post*.

The second major part of this chapter considers some of the criticisms which have been levelled at the economist's approach to income and wealth measurement, both *ex ante* and *ex post*. Some concerns of a more abstract kind were discussed in chapter 3 in the context of *ex ante* income and wealth measurement. The criticisms addressed in this chapter are those concerned mainly with the difficulties of making economic income and wealth concepts operational in the practical world.

These criticisms include the view that the decision models which provide the foundations for economic income and wealth measurement may not yield optimal decisions for all individuals where markets are poorly organised. These market problems may also mean that economic wealth and income measures will fail to work well. It should, however, be borne in mind that other accounting systems also face these problems in such environments.

Some difficulties which apply especially to the economic approach, including the subjectivity of the economist's figures and the rather unconventional depreciation calculations used,are then reviewed. Further difficulties of this type include the general impossibility of deriving economic income and wealth by following the conventional accounting practice of aggregating individual accounting items to obtain totals for corporate income and wealth.

The final section of this chapter looks at criticisms specific to the practical use of economic income and wealth *ex post*, concentrating on the subjectivity of the figures produced. A brief summary of Chapters 3 and 4 and our conclusions on the economist's wealth and income concepts, conclude this chapter.

Income and wealth *ex post*

We may learn additional information about an accepted project as it runs its course. The realised cash flows of a period may differ from those expected earlier. The pattern of realised cash flows over time may suggest that earlier estimates of yet-to-be- obtained cash flows, and of their timing, should be revised. Other items of information obtained as the project proceeds may also suggest that forecasts of future cash flows should be revised. Each time we pass through a period we may, therefore, wish to revise our plans, not only to incorporate the realised cash flows of the period, which may themselves differ from those which were expected, but also to incorporate in our forecasts of future cash flows any additional knowledge or information obtained during the period.

Measures or estimates encompassing any information available after a given event or period has occurred are labelled generally as *ex post*, relative to that period. This indicates that they reflect the information available after the passing of a given event, usually a period of time. In our case, *ex post* measures are those constructed conditional on the information set available at the end of a period in a project's life that has occurred. Wealth and income calculations concerning a given period, made prior to that period, provide those *ex ante* measures familiar from Chapter 3. The same calculations made after the completion of a period, and with access to the knowledge available at that time, provide *ex post* measures of income and wealth. Calculations and estimates obtain their *ex post* character because they are made after the passing of part of a project's span and with access to the knowledge available at that time. It is with respect to this period and this information set that the calculations or estimates can be characterised as *ex post*. Such calculations and estimates will generally include views as to cash flows expected in future periods. *Ex ante* estimates concerning wealth at a future time or income in a given future period can be made at any time earlier than the time period under consideration. In order to simplify our introduction to these difficult concepts, we will adopt the assumption made in the previous chapter concerning the time at which *ex ante* calculations are made. We will assume that *ex ante* figures refer to plans made at decision time prior to project commencement, that is at time 0 (t_0) in the terms of Chapter 3.

Comparisons between *ex post* and *ex ante* income for a project for a given period, and *ex post* and *ex ante* wealth measures at a specific time, aid in evaluating the project's progress and in monitoring the ability of those who manage the project. These comparisons and the *ex post* measures themselves may aid in assessing forecasting ability and may lead to new forecasts for both this and other projects. These comparisons may also facilitate the replanning of a project for the remainder of its life, or even the cancellation of the project.

Ex post versions of economic income and wealth employ the same conceptual framework as was used to calculate these items when planning. Thus, *ex post* results are obtained using variants of the models used to obtain *ex ante* wealth and income measures. *Ex post* figures are obtained by plugging into our models both the cash flows realised in a period and any revisions to future cash flows considered necessary in the light of knowledge available at the end of the period when these estimates are made. These changes will generally mean that the *ex ante* and *ex post* figures for a period of time will differ. All changes from what was planned must be unexpected at the time of planning, because all known expectations (including the characteristics of the information system being used and all possible signals from this information system; see Chapters 7 and 8) are incorporated into economic wealth the moment they become known. Such unexpected changes are often called windfall gains or losses.

In order to simplify our presentation of *ex post* income and wealth concepts, we will assume an environment of no price changes and of no interest changes. We are thus going to assume those conditions which allow us to use Hicksian income concept Number 1. (If neither unchanged interest rates nor a constant general price level could be assumed, we would have to use income concept Number 2 or Number 3, respectively (see Chapter 3, p. 47). We shall start our study of these matters by considering economic wealth from an *ex post* perspective.

Wealth ex post

The value of a project, or its contribution to wealth at the end of a completed period, is easily defined.

Ex post wealth is the value of the net cash flows of the period as reckoned at the end of the period, plus the present value at that time of the cash flows to be received in the remaining periods of the project's life.   Definition [4.A]

As in Chapter 3, we will assure that all cash flows are received at the end of a period. The definition set out above incorporates another assumption which we will use throughout this chapter, namely that we are determining *ex post* magnitudes prior to any distribution having been made to security holders. Our calculation of wealth *ex post* is undertaken with access to the information available at the end of the period when the calculations are being made. Our definition of wealth *ex post* will be applied only to what we called the 'mainstream' project in the previous chapter. The determination of the total wealth due to the project would require us to add to this sum the value of any funds retained in earlier years, including any interest accruing thereon. In order to concentrate on the essence of *ex post* measurement we will generally work only with a mainstream project in this chapter. References to the project, including retained funds and any interest thereon, will be confined to endnotes.

We will use the general notation of the previous chapter to express this informal definition in symbols. In order to differentiate between *ex ante* and *ex post* versions of the same items, some additional notation is helpful. This new notation has to be fairly complex because of the variety of similar items we wish to portray. Recall that in Chapter 3, cash flows were indexed by the subscript i to identify the period of their receipt. Thus C_i and C_n referred to cash flows expected to be received in periods i and n respectively. Such subscripts were also used to identify the end of the period to which each present value calculation related. Thus V_0 referred to the present value of future cash flows reckoned at the end of period 0 (or the beginning of period 1). *Ex ante* calculations referring to any given future period can be made at a great variety of times. Such estimates will be conditional on the information available at the time of the forecast. In order to avoid any confusion that the existence of a number of possible forecasts for the same item made at different times may cause, it is generally necessary to add an additional subscript which indicates both the time of the calculation and the time of the information on which the estimate is based. We will generally be assuming that the information set used at a given time is that which is available at that time and not one which was available earlier. This second subscript was unnecessary in the previous chapter because it was assumed that all *ex ante* calculations were made at time 0 (t_0) and no confusion resulted from omitting this second subscript. Although we will be making the same assumption in this chapter we will find it useful, especially when we come to deal with *ex post* income figures, to use a second subscript indexing when an estimate was made. This allows us to differentiate clearly between estimates of the same item, made at different times.

Using this more general notation, cash flows expected in, say, period 1 as estimated at, say, time 0 (time t_0) can be written as $C_{1,0}$, where the first subscript refers to the period in which the cash flows are to accrue and the second indicates when the estimates of these cash flows were made, time t_0 in the above case. Similarly, the present value of cash flows at the end of, say, period 3 as estimated at, say, time 3 (t_3) would be written $V_{3,3}$. The second subscript identifies the date of the information used or, more strictly, available for use in making the estimate. It also indicates that the project has proceeded at least up to the end of the period indexed by this second subscript. Wealth is *ex post*, in our sense, if the estimate of this wealth is made at the same time as that to which this estimate refers. Periodic cash flows are *ex post* if they are calculated at the time when these cash flows accrue. More strictly, we should also describe as *ex post* any later recalculations of earlier *ex post* figures. The two subscripts indexing *ex post* items are, thus, either identical or the second subscript is the larger. A larger second subscript indicates that later knowledge is being used to recalculate the estimates or calculations of earlier periods. The present value referred to above ($V_{3,3}$) is thus *ex post*, whereas the expected cash flows also referred to above ($C_{1,0}$) are *ex ante*.

With this background, we are now in a position to define, in a formal way, wealth *ex post* at the end of a period that has just been completed. The first element of this wealth is the realised cash flows of the period. This quantity can be written as:

$$\text{Realised cash flows of the period} = C_{i,i} \tag{4.I}$$

where the first subscript i indexes the period of receipt of the cash flow, period i in our case. The second subscript, also i in this case, indicates when the calculation was made. That the two subscripts are identical signals that the cash flows in mind are *ex post* magnitudes, and that they represent essentially a calculation rather than an estimate—though, of course, such calculations may still involve estimates.

The second element of wealth *ex post* at the end of a past period is the present value of the future cash flows still expected to be received from the prospect. This present value is estimated at the end of the period just passed using the information available at that time. It is the use of information from a past period, usually the period in which the present value is being estimated, which gives this present value its *ex post* character. *Ex post* does not signify that all the cash flows in mind have appeared. It merely means that our estimates are based on information from periods that have passed. The use of our second subscript now becomes crucial because in a prospect's life we may make a number of estimates of a present value at a given time, using information available at a variety of different times. The present value of the future cash flows expected at the *end* of a past period, period *i* in our case, can be written as:

$$V_{i,i} = \Sigma \ C_{j,i}/(1 + r)^j \qquad \qquad \text{[4.II]}$$

The first subscript following the present value symbol (V) indexes the present value to the end of a specific period, period *i* in our case. The second subscript represents the time at which this estimate was made, again, period *i* in our case. It also indicates the information set available for use in determining this estimate. The right-hand expression rewrites our expression for wealth using the underlying cash flows. The first subscript on the cash flows *j*, where *j* can take the values $j = i + 1$ to T, indicates that these cash flows are to be received in the *j* periods beyond *i*. The second subscript indicates the time when these cash flows were estimated, time *i* in our case.

The rest of the symbols on the right-hand side of our expression say that to obtain the present value of the cash flows at the end of period *i*, they must be discounted and summed in the usual way. A formal expression for wealth *ex post* is obtained by combining our two expressions (4.I and 4.II). This is portrayed in the expression below:

$$Ex \ post \ \text{wealth} = C_{i,i} + V_{i,i} \qquad \qquad \text{[4.III]}$$

This says that *ex post* wealth at the end of a period comprises the cash flows for the period plus the present value at the end of the period of all expected future cash flows.

This is the definition of *ex post* wealth which is now usual in the literature. Hicks, whose writings show him to be very sensitive to possible criticisms of economic income, does not advocate this definition, possibly because of its obvious subjectivity. Hicks believes that *ex post* wealth should refer to market values rather than estimates of present values. However, such market prices do not exist for many prospects. Hicks (1979), indicates the difficulties of constraining *ex post* calculations to depend only on market values.

Expression 4.III demonstrates that the same conceptual framework is being used *ex post* as was used in Chapter 3 to obtain wealth *ex ante*. This expression is clearly equivalent to that used in Chapter 3 to obtain the *ex ante* wealth generated by a project, ignoring any reinvested funds, i.e. by what we have called the mainstream project (Expression 3.III.a(v)). The only real difference between the two expressions is that the information set available is different. In *ex post* calculations the knowledge available at the end of a just completed period is available for use.

We can illustrate the *ex post* wealth concept in numerical terms using the Flower project of Chapter 3. Recall that at the beginning of the project Flower thought the opportunity would yield cash flows of 25, 45 and 74.88 monetary units at the end of the first, second and third years, respectively of its three-year life. Utilising a 10 per cent discount rate, the mainstream project had *ex ante* present values of 116.17, 102.79 and 68.07 at the beginning of the first year, the end of the first year and the end of the second year, respectively.

We will now derive the *ex post* value of the project, using its present worth at the end of its second period, as an example. It will be assumed that the results of the first period were as planned (25 monetary units were received at the end of this period), but that the cash flows realised at the end of the second period turned out to be 40 rather than 45 monetary units. We will also assume that knowledge available at the end of period 2 leads us to the view that the cash flows to be received in period 3 will be 67 monetary units rather than the planned 74.88 units. These quantities can be written, using the notation of this chapter, as:

1 the realised cash flows at the end of period 2 = $C_{2,2}$ = 40, and
2 the estimated cash flows at the end of period 3 as forecast at the end of period 2 = $C_{3,2}$ = 67.

The *ex post* value of the project at the end of period 2, prior to any income being withdrawn, can be found by plugging these amounts into Expression 4.III. This gives:[1]

Ex post value of the project at end of period 2 = $C_{2,2} + V_{2,2}$ = 40 + 67/(1.10) = 100.91

The *ex ante* counterpart of this amount as estimated at time t_0 is:

$C_{2,0} + V_{2,0}$ = 45 + 68.07 = 113.07

Strictly, the *ex post* wealth yielded by a project is the only information that the individual needs about the project for decision making purposes at the end of the period for which the wealth is calculated. It provides a measure of the contribution the project makes to the decision maker's endowment. Chapter 2 indicated that endowments determine the set of future actions which the decision maker can feasibly undertake. This is clearest in perfect markets where *ex post* wealth measures the sum of the values which the market assigns to the projects owned at the time of the calculation. It thus defines the amount the decision maker can realise to invest in other decision options. In disequilibrium or with poorly organised markets, the difference between the value of projects as estimated by the decision maker and their market values indicates what is called the subjective goodwill of the prospects at the time of calculation. This measures the amount which the decision maker hopes to tranform into market values as the project proceeds by the market coming to share the same views about the project.

Comparisons between *ex post* and *ex ante* project values, such as those shown above, may be useful in replanning. Differences generated by these comparisons may aid in measuring the enterprise's forecasting ability and be of help in later decision making. They may also facilitate the appraisal of project management if any deviations between *ex ante* and *ex post* magnitudes are due to managerial actions. Such appraisals may also lead to new decisions being taken. The next section seeks to show that income *ex post* is derived using the same conceptual framework as was utilised in obtaining *ex post* wealth.

Income ex post

In the last chapter, the *ex ante* economic income of a period was defined as the amount that could be consumed at the end of a period while leaving the capital value at the beginning of the period intact. In order to determine *ex ante* income for a period we compared the opening capital value V_{i-1} with the end of period capital value V_i *plus* the expected cash flows of the period (C_i). Recall that the only thing that can change in such *ex ante* income calculations as we move from period to period, is that time passes and therefore interest is expected to be obtained on the *ex ante* opening value at the beginning of a period. Thus, the *ex ante* income for period i, Y_i is equal to rV_{i-1}, where the opening capital value (V_{i-1}) is expressed in present value terms.

To be consistent with this conceptual framework, *ex post* income must be defined in the same way. To calculate *ex post* income we have to deduct from the closing wealth for the period a figure for the opening capital of the period. Before we can proceed, we therefore need to decide upon a definition of the amount of capital we wish to maintain intact at the beginning of the period. Two obvious candidates for this role will now be considered.

Ex post *income I*

The first method of defining the economic wealth we wish to maintain intact is to utilise the familiar *ex ante* value of the project at the beginning of the period (see Chapter 3). As we shall see, this approach is believed to pose a number of problems which make it less attractive than the second variant of *ex post* income. It is dealt with first because it involves no new concepts. Wealth defined in this way is measured by the opening value of the project used in planning or in *ex ante* calculations for the period in mind. This definition of wealth for period i can be expressed in our nomenclature for a mainstream project (i.e. ignoring reinvestment funds) as:

$$V_{i-1,0} = C_{i,0} + V_{i,0} \qquad [4.\text{IV}]$$

where the symbols being used have all been defined above.

Ex post income, using this definition of opening capital, will be called *ex post* income concept I. It can be represented in symbols for period i as $Y_{i\text{I}}$. Here, our second i subscript is omitted as no confusion should result, and the subscript I signifies that we are using *ex post* income concept I. This variant of *ex post* income for period i can, therefore, be written in full as:

$$Y_{i,\text{I}} = C_{i,i} + V_{i,i} - V_{i-1,0} \qquad [4.\text{V}]$$

The first two elements on the right are our familiar expression for *ex post* wealth calculated with the information available at the end of period i. The final element on the right represents the *ex ante* value of the project at the beginning of the period estimated using the information available at the beginning of the project (t_0).

The *ex post* income for period 2 of Flower's project, using this variant of income (*ex post*, concept I), can be calculated by plugging in the relevant figures. This gives:

$$Y_{2,\text{I}} = 40 + 60.91 - 102.79 = -1.88 \qquad [4.\text{Va}]$$

The first two figures on the right of the expression give the *ex post* value of the project at the end of period 2, calculated using the knowledge available at the end of this period. The final element on the right is the *ex ante* value of the prospect at the beginning of period 2 or the end of period 1, estimated using the information available at decision making time.

The income for the period, as calculated, tells us that no income can be distributed if we wish to maintain the economic worth of the project at the beginning of the period at the level which was expected at planning time. Indeed, the declared loss indicates that we must pay 1.88 monetary units into the project if we wish to maintain capital defined in this way. *Ex post* income concept I thus gives guidance about the actions required to maintain the original capital of the mainstream prospect as seen at planning time.[2]

Ex post *income II*

The second candidate for an *ex post* measure of income involves the deduction from *ex post* wealth, not of the original present value expected to reign at the beginning of the period, but rather this value recalculated to include relevant knowledge in the information set available at the end of the period. The capital value to be maintained intact is now defined as what we would have expected this to have been if we had access to the knowledge available at the end of the completed period in mind, when we were originally planning the prospect. This *ex post* income concept will be labelled *ex post* income II. The use of this concept requires us to recalculate the opening value of a project at the beginning of a period (V_{i-1}) incorporating the realised cash flows of the period ($C_{i,i}$) and the revised expectations of future cash flows ($C_{j,i}$, where j represents periods later than i) computed using the information available at the end of the period just completed. Thus we are estimating V_{i-1} incorporating the information available at the end of period i. This modified present value, V_{i-1}, can be written in the notation of this chapter as:

$$V_{i-1,i} = C_{i,i}/(1 + r) + V_{i,i}/(1+r) \qquad [4.VI]$$

The left hand part of this expression says that the present value at the beginning of the period (V_{i-1}) is estimated at time i using the information available at this time. Here, the second subscript i indexes the time of calculation and the information set available for such calculations. The first element on the right of the expression says that this present value includes the realised cash flows of the period discounted back to the beginning of the period. The second element on the right similarly says that this value also includes the present value of the remaining cash flows of the project estimated with the knowledge available at the end of the completed period discounted to the beginning of the period.

With this understanding, we can now formally express *ex post* income concept II as:

$$Y_{i,II} = C_{i,i} + V_{i,i} - V_{i-1,i} \qquad [4.VII]$$

The first two elements on the right of this expression are the same as those used in the expression for *ex post* income using concept I. They represent the *ex post* wealth of the project. The other element on the right represents the opening value at the beginning of the period estimated at the end of the just-completed period using any relevant knowledge available at this time.

Calculating *ex post* income defined in this way for period 2 of Flower's project indicates that our second *ex post* income concept is not really as difficult as our rather formal exposition may have made it seem. We will again use the same assumed realised figures as were used to obtain *ex post* income I for the project. Still working with the mainstream project, we deduct from the *ex post* value of the project at the end of period 2 the value of the prospect at the beginning of period 2, as estimated using the new knowledge available at the end of period 2. This revised value can be determined by expressing the present value of the received cash flows at the end of period 2 plus the present value of the new or revised third period cash flows as a present value at the end of period 1 (or beginning of period 2). Thus, the revised cash flows at the end of period 2 and the present value of the revised cash flows in period 3 at the end of period 2 have to be discounted back to the beginning of period 2. This gives, using our notation,

$$V_{1,2} = 40/(1.10) + 67/(1.10)^2 = 91.74$$

Plugging this new present value at the beginning of the period into Expression 4.VII gives the *ex post* income using concept II for period 2 as:

$$Y_{2,II} = 40 + 60.91 - 91.74 = 9.17 \qquad \text{[4.VIIa]}$$

This result is well behaved in that economic income *ex post* is found to represent the interest on the revised present value of the project at the beginning of the period just as it did *ex ante* (Chapter 3, pp. 41–2).[3] Income *ex post* measured using *ex post* income concept II says that 9.17 monetary units can be paid out while maintaining intact the *revised* capital value of the project at the beginning of the period.

There are, thus, at least two *ex post* income concepts which can be associated with each of Hicks' three approximations to his main criterion for income (see Chapter 3). This makes six income definitions in all. Above, it was shown in the context of Hicks' Number 1 income concept that income *ex post* as measured using *ex post* concept II was different from that obtained using concept I.

Ex post income and accounting

The complexity of the above calculations may provide a role for accounting even in well organised markets. It may be easier to allow an 'expert' to compute elements of income concept II, even though they can be derived from market prices (the revised value of the enterprise at the beginning of the period can be calculated as the amount on which the declared income would represent the appropriate rate of return for the enterprise). Similarly, it may be worthwhile allowing the accountant to maintain the data bank of past prices required to compute *ex post* income I and therefore to calculate this income. Such experts would have similiar roles within the enterprise and would have an even stronger claim to the above roles where we are dealing with *ex post* calculations based on managerial forecasts rather than market prices.

The choice between income concepts

Our first *ex post* income concept (concept I) (portrayed in Expression 4.V) compares the *ex post* value of the project at the end of a period with the original expected present value at the beginning of the period. Any positive *ex post* income can be taken out of the project without reducing the present value of the prospect as expected originally at the beginning of the period. A negative result can be interpreted as saying that the originally planned income must be foregone and that this amount must be paid into the project if it is wished to maintain the originally expected present value. Thus, with this *ex post* income concept all unexpected gains (windfall gains) are deemed to be available for consumption and all unpredicted (windfall) losses must be made up, first by foregoing equivalent income where this is available, perhaps from other projects, and then by the injection of new funds. The difference between the *ex ante* and *ex post* incomes, determined in this way, indicates how far the project's fortunes have been affected by unexpected developments. Such a comparison provides some crude indication of forecasting ability (sophisticated monitoring of forecasts might require a comparison not with the original present value, but rather with the *ex post* figures obtained by other managers in similar circumstances).

Most economic commentators prefer to employ the second model of *ex post* income (Expression 4.VII), in which the end-of-period value of the prospect, using the most up-to-date knowledge and perceptions, is compared with the opening value for the period, based on the same knowledge. Windfall gains are here treated as increments to capital and they therefore do not enter income. Unexpected losses are treated symmetrically. They reduce the prospect's capital value. Any difference between income *ex ante* and *ex post* for a period arises from the recalculated opening value of the project. In Flower's case, his windfall loss reducing the opening capital of the period from 102.79 to 91.74 decreased his income from the mainstream prospect from 10.28 (which was the expected *ex ante* income for the second period) to 9.17, a fall of 1.11 monetary units. This fall in income, therefore, reflects the fall in the interest obtained on the new opening present value of 91.74 monetary units relative to the original opening capital of 102.79.

Our second *ex post* income concept suggests we can spend only the interest on windfall gains without impoverishing ourselves and symmetrically reduces the original *ex ante* income by the interest on any unexpected losses. Thus, in Flower's case income falls from 10.28 to 9.17 monetary units. This decline is equal to interest on the decline in the capital value at the beginning of the period. This difference in capital values is 11.05. The reduction in income required to adjust for this change is 1.11. This is just the amount we calculated as the difference between *ex ante* and *ex post* income for the period.

The difference between the two *ex post* income concepts can perhaps be most vividly illustrated by assuming we have unexpectedly won a very large prize in some competition of, say, 1 million monetary units. Our first *ex post* income concept (I) advises that it may all be spent. After doing this, we will be no worse off in present value terms than before we won the prize.

Our alternative concept (II) says we should only spend the interest on the prize in each future year if we do not wish to reduce our capital. The two concepts, therefore, represent fairly extreme points on the spectrum of possible behaviour (see Figure 4.1 below). The most extreme conservative behaviour would be to say that you must spend nothing of the prize on consumption and should not recognise even the interest on the prize as part of income. Some variants of replacement cost accounting systems which seek to maintain the existing physical capital of the enterprise, rigorously defined, seem to come close to using this view of capital maintenance. We might suppose that actual behaviour may plot anywhere along this spectrum. However, it may be expected that people will spend some proportion of the prize and reinvest the remainder. Thus, neither of our *ex post* income concepts model likely actual behaviour.

Perhaps the treatment of losses by the two *ex post* income systems can, be best appreciated by considering ourselves faced by a large fine or financial penalty. Here the first *ex post* concept would suggest you pay the fine and somehow reconstitute your financial resources to the level at which they were before calamity struck. This would seem to be the most conservative treatment of losses which can be envisaged (see Figure 4.1 below). Our second concept does not expose you to the seemingly double jeopardy of having to pay the fine and of having to replace the capital thus lost. It suggests only that we recognise the loss by reducing capital and lowering income by an amount equal to the difference between the interest on the pre-loss and the post-loss capital.

The characteristics of our two *ex post* income concepts are summarised in an informal way in Figure 4.1.

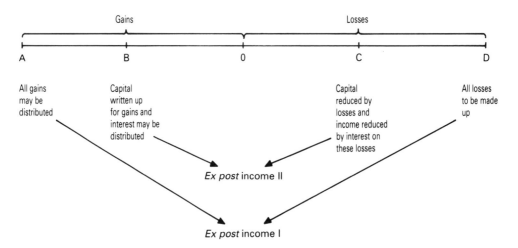

Figure 4.1 Treatment of gains and losses by the two *ex post* concepts

Line AD in the figure shows all possible treatments of unexpected gains and losses. Point A represents the distribution of all gains and point D signifies the making up of all losses. The two treatments represented by points A and D are those utilised by *ex post* income I.

Point B represents the writing up of capital for any gain and allowing only the interest on such gains to be distributed. Point C signifies reducing capital by any losses and reducing income by the interest on this adjusted capital. Points B and C in the figure illustrate the treatments used by *ex post* concept II.

It is generally impossible to say which of our two *ex post* income concepts is the best. This depends on the purpose of the income measurement. For example, many commentators would argue that all capital gains should be included in income if the wish is to tax those who can best bear the tax. Here, it is argued that windfall gains do make the recipients better able to bear taxation (see Alexander, revised by Solomons,

1962, p. 67 and pp. 82–83 and Kaldor, 1955, especially p. 174). In contrast, if the object in mind is to aid stewardship accounting by declaring a 'prudent' profit it will, perhaps, make some sense to disallow capital gains (at least until realised by being declared as part of conventional accounting income).

This chapter is, however, founded on the idea that income should be at least consistent with decision making models. Here the consensus amongst economists is that the *ex post* income model should exclude windfalls (i.e. unexpected changes between *ex ante* and *ex post* calculations for the same items in a given period). Alexander (revised by Solomons, 1962), Lindahl (1935) and Hicks (1979), provide some strong arguments for using our second *ex post* concept (concept II). Incorporating windfalls into capital is consistent with the discounted cash flow appraisal models which provide the foundations being used here for income and wealth measurement. If at decision time we had known about a gain or loss, it would have comprised part of the prospect's present value. The economist's *ex ante* definition of income would therefore allow only the interest generated on such gains to be spent. It would similarly reduce income by the interest lost because of windfall losses. It would, therefore seem consistent to incorporate any *ex post* windfall gains into capital as they become known, which is exactly how concept II treats windfall gains.

Income concept II also corrects any errors that we made at decision time in a way which is consistent with the model used at that time. It restates the original planning expectations using views formed as the project proceeds, and uses these changed expectations to calculate revised project values and incomes. It can be argued that unless this is done we are seeking to compare unlike items in income measurement. We would be attempting to monitor projects using out-of-date information (Hicks, 1979, pp. 8–l9). Avoiding this difficulty allows reassessment of a prospect's permanent income or standard stream income using the latest available information.

By contrast with the assumptions underlying *ex post* concept II, the logic of *ex post* concept I, which says that all windfall gains can be spent, is inconsistent with the decision making framework used at planning time.

The requirement under income concept I that a loss should be made up is also inconsistent with our underlying decision making model. Modern finance theory suggests that, in a perfect capital market in equilibrium, wherever we invest our money it will earn the appropriate interest rate for its risk. This is all any prospect can offer. Chapter 9 discusses this topic in a more technical way. Making up any *ex post* loss is therefore redundant because the valuation of each prospect already allows for the possibility of any such loss. This assumes the interest rate is correctly set to cover these possible losses on prospects of the same risk quality. Assuming investors hold diversified portfolios, the interest received on other similar projects which do not make such a loss will compensate for the failure of the project which has experienced losses. With this view, many incurred losses are not really unexpected relative to the portfolio of projects of a similar risk. Such losses were expected to be experienced somewhere in the portfolio and taken into account when arriving at the individual's optimal investment strategy, which Chapter 6 indicates may include stategies which allow insurance against such risks. The only uncertainty is which project will suffer these expected losses. The actual incidence of these losses is irrelevant to the future conduct of those holding investment portfolios which fully diversify the risk of individual projects. The future earnings from prospects will continue to be valued as if they will earn the going average return for their risk class. Thus, from the perspective of finance theory, any losses will apply only to the current period's cash flows because the expected returns from prospects are unchanged in the face of an expected deviation from their average returns in any given period. Such losses should, however, be recorded in *ex post* accounts. This is what *ex post* income concept I does with regard to realised cash flows. However, there seems no justification, at least from the finance view, for the suggestion of *ex post* income concept I that such losses should be made up. In contrast, Concept II reflects only the change in interest on the new capital value in income rather than the complete loss, thereby understating the accounting loss.

Using the usual finance framework, truly unexpected losses and gains would represent a change in the distribution of the expected returns from a given security or securities. Once this information becomes known, the security, or securities, affected would be revalued and this process may cause market-wide revaluations. The new capital values would again ensure that the securities offered the same average return as other securities of the same risk class. Such changes in capital values should be reflected in economic calculations of *ex post* wealth and income. *Ex post* income concept II seems to do this in a way consistent with the finance literature by altering capital values to reflect these changes.

Windfall changes and accounting

That windfall gains may be truly unexpected may yield an additional role other than those mentioned above for accounting reports embodying economic *ex post* wealth and income if these reports are based on management views rather than market prices. In this case, management may choose to announce these windfalls in the accounting reports. Such information, providing that it reflects the underlying productive activities of the enterprise, at least will have value in that it should improve society's decisions (See Chapter 7 which addresses the question of when public information can be said to possess value. It therefore expands and qualifies the above statement.) It is, of course, the information, and not its method of telling, which has value; but releasing information through accounting reports may be thought to allow a wide distribution of information and, perhaps, even increase the likelihood that the announced information will be accepted relative to other methods of announcement. This does give a possible further role for accounting information, even in well organised markets. This discussion of windfalls thus suggests a role for accounting income and accountants other than facilitating the complicated calculations referred to above (see p. 60).

The importance of perfect markets

We have now reviewed the conventional arguments for our two *ex post* economic concepts. Although this debate is generally conducted in the context of perfect capital markets, it seems to have overlooked a characteristic of such markets which may reduce this controversy substantially, at least when viewed from a decision making perspective. Whichever of our two *ex post* income concepts we use, this will not change the value the market assigns to a project. This value, prior to any distribution of income for the period, is that given within perfect capital markets by Expressions 4.II and 3.IIa.

Determining *ex post* income involves calculating the amount of net worth which can be distributed without reducing economic capital. Income can thus be represented as a deduction from the *ex post* net worth of a project.

It has already been said that generally our two *ex post* concepts may well involve deducting different amounts of income from this net worth. These deductions from *ex post* wealth under the two *ex post* income concepts are both taken from the same amount—*ex post* wealth. Thus, the different income concepts allow different amounts of this net worth to be regarded as available for distribution. Therefore, the two income concepts really advise partitioning *ex post* wealth between retention and distribution in different ways.

A perfect market allows prospects with the same present value but packaged in a different way to be converted into any other prospects having the same present value by borrowing or lending on the market. Thus, in perfect markets *ex post* period income for a prospect under concept I can be converted into that which would be declared under concept II, without reducing the *ex post* value of the prospect at the end of the period. With windfall gains in a period, income concept II will yield a lower *ex post* income than would concept I. An investor who prefers the distribution implied by concept I could convert his or her income under concept II into that of concept I by borrowing on the market. This expectation can be maintained because the cash flows not distributed early in a prospect's life under concept II plus the interest on them when paid out later, or when realised by selling the prospect, will just equal the value of the loan necessary to ensure that the individual receives income as determined under concept I, plus the interest on the loan.

As an example of the ability provided by a perfect market to switch between the two income concepts, recall that Flower had *ex post* wealth from his mainstream project of 100.91 monetary units at the end of period 2, prior to any income distribution or capital injection (see Expression 4.Va). His income under *ex post* income concept I was a loss of 1.88 monetary units, and investing this additional amount in the project gave an end-of-period wealth of 102.79 monetary units, thereby restoring the *ex ante* present worth of the project to that at the beginning of period 1. Income for the period computed, using *ex post* income concept II, was 9.17 monetary units and the end of period wealth after this distribution was 91.74 monetary units (see Expression 4.VIIa).

Assume that Flower delegates the managing of his project to the managers of the enterprise which operates his project and that enterprise management decides to determine *ex post* income using concept I, but that Flower would prefer income concept II to be used. By using the market he can convert the loss of 1.88 monetary units into an income of 9.17 units. To achieve this he borrows on the market 11.05 monetary units equal to the loss of 1.88 units plus 9.17 units income declared under concept II. He can thus spend an amount equal to income under concept II (9.17 units) and pay in 1.88 units to the firm in accordance to the dictates of *ex post* income concept I. Repaying this loan requires that at the end of the third year he can repay 12.16 monetary units, comprising the 11.05 units plus one year's interest at 10 per cent, the assumed cost of capital.

At the end of the third year, the *ex post* wealth of his investment in the company, assuming that the company distributes income according to the advice of *ex post* income concept I, will be given by the cash flows of the year, plus any funds generated by the project and reinvested, and any interest thereof. In Flower's case, the value of these reinvested funds equals 41.88 units (the opening value of the project at the beginning of the third period (102.79) less the present value at this time of the future cash flows from the project (60.91)). Thus, the total *ex post* wealth of the project at the end of the third period, using income concept I, is 113.07 monetary units, including reinvestment and interest thereon and assuming no further changes in the prospect's planned cash flows and no changes in the interest rate in the third period. This comprises the cash flows of this period equal to 67 monetary units, plus reinvested funds of 41.88 monetary units, plus interest thereon of 4.19 monetary units.

Deducting the terminal repayment of Flower's loan of 12.16 units from the *ex post* wealth derived under concept I of the project at the end of the third year yields his end-of-project wealth as 100.91. Deducting income under concept II for the third year, 9.17 monetary units, from this amount shows that he has maintained capital at 91.74 monetary units. He has thus been able to convert income, determined according to concept I in the second period, into that promised by concept II in this period. He will still have enough money to pay himself the income for the third period as determined by concept II of 9.17 units after having maintained his capital. (This capital, as we would expect, equals interest on the opening value of the project at the beginning of the third period calculated using the knowledge available at the end of period 3.)

This example, plus the early reasoning, suggests that a choice between the two *ex post* income concepts may be less important than the literature suggests, at least where there are perfect markets. In this case the individual can choose to receive income according to either concept, or indeed any combination of them. However, the choice remains crucial where markets are imperfect. Here, if an enterprise opts for one of our *ex post* income concepts, the individual may not be able to use the market to 'undo' the enterprise's policy by actions within the individual's control so as to adjust the enterprise's distribution policy to accord with the individual's own preferences. In imperfect and incomplete markets, a decision concerning which *ex post* income to follow may require a consideration of investors' preferences, existing endowments and decision problems. An investor who does not like the policy chosen will have no choice but to sell his or her shares (stock). Market difficulties may mean that the price obtained in such sales does not reflect only the present value of the cash flows promised by the investments being sold, where this value is obtained using the appropriate interest rate for the risk class of the cash flows. This is because share or stock prices, at least in disequilibrium, may incorporate a premium for desirable characteristics, including the adoption of a preferred *ex post* income concept and a discount for less desired income where rearrangements of the policies is not within an individual's power in the presence of market imperfections and incompleteness. Over time, one might expect market responses which cause these discounts and premiums to disappear. (For a similar argument with respect to financial gearing or leverage, see Modigliani and Miller, 1958.)

This highlights the point made in Chapter 2 which will be repeated in Chapter 10, that it is market imperfections which seem to require the existence of those accounting theories which help in explaining the distribution of income and wealth between various sectors of the business community.

The advantages of the economist's ex post *income concepts—summary*

All the advantages of the economist's *ex ante* concepts such as consistency with decision making models and a concern with the future, are shared by both the above *ex post* income concepts (and their associated wealth concepts). Both *ex post* concepts provide income treatments consistent with the models used for the original decisions, and those which would be used for making future decisions as projects progress. If used only in decision making, both *ex post* income models will yield the same decisions as would be generated if the projects in mind were being appraised for the first time, using our usual decision techniques utilising any information incorporated into these *ex post* income concepts. Additionally, it can be argued that *ex post* income concept II, which treats unexpected outcomes as part of capital, provides an *ex post* income concept which is exactly consistent with *ex ante* income.

The presentation in this and the preceding chapter has sought to provide as clear a view as possible of the merits of the economist's approach to income and wealth measurement. This 'ideal' system has not, however, swept all before it when considered as a practical system for the real world. The remainder of this chapter surveys the problems and disadvantages which it has been claimed surround the economist's approach to wealth and income measurement. These may account for the reluctance of the practising world to accept this system as an operational method of accounting.

Criticisms of the economist's wealth and income

The first criticism to be considered suggests that however useful economic wealth and income measures are found to be in the abstract environment of ideal markets, they function less perfectly in the less well organised markets of the practical world. It has recently become clearer that the optimality characteristics of the decision models underlying the economist's income and wealth measures may not apply where the market is poorly organised (that is, where the market is imperfect or incomplete), see Chapters 2 and 10 of this book, Beaver and Demski (1979); Bromwich (1977). The results of allowing for these difficulties, both for the underlying decision models and for the wealth and income models reviewed above, are still by no means fully understood. Their presence does mean that in at least some (perhaps most) circumstances the economist's income and wealth measures can no longer be utilised without considering individual preferences. Market problems may mean that it will be impossible for investors to rearrange investment portfolios in order to reflect their preferences better by trading in poorly organised markets. This may mean that all prospects having the same present value in the market are not regarded as equivalent by all individuals. With this view the emphasis moves from seeking income and wealth measures to searching for individual items of information, including accounting information, which are useful in poorly organised markets. This approach will be employed in the next three chapters.

Income for the individual

The accounting system discussed in this and the preceding chapter works for the individual, even in poorly functioning markets. With such markets, it still produces accounting results which reflect the individual's preferences because it is the individual who assigns those present values to the prospects which form the essence of the economic approach to income and wealth measurement. It is for this reason that the whole of this chapter has been set in the context of the individual. However, we have already seen in Chapter 2 that market difficulties may mean that a given proposal or set of proposals will be ranked differently by different individuals (for example, because of different preferences concerning the timing of cash flows). Similarly, in such a setting, the economist's accounting measures, while still consistent with the outcomes of the individual's decision, may now produce different results for two individuals faced with the same set of prospects because of differences in preferences, beliefs and endowments (see Chapter 10).

Hicks, and others among those who laid the foundations of economic income and wealth measures, clearly recognised the problems flowing from poorly organised markets because their careful arguments supporting these accounting methods were all phrased in terms of the individual. Indeed, Hicks made his view clear when talking of the possibility of aggregating individual incomes to obtain an income measure for the whole of society. He said that 'If A's income is based on A's expectations and B's income on B's expectations, and these expectations are inconsistent, then an aggregate of their incomes has little meaning', (Hicks, 1946, p. 80). Implicitly, he saw these differing expectations arising because of poorly organised markets.

It is later authors, and especially practitioners (see Alexander as revised by Solomons, 1962, and Inflation Accounting Committee; 1975) who have sought to apply our definitions of economic wealth and income for the individual without change to the enterprise as a whole. For example, Alexander said that 'We may define the income of a corporation in a given year as the amount the corporation can distribute to the owners of equity in the corporation and be as well off at the end of the year as at the beginning' (Alexander, as revised by Solomons, 1962, p. 44). His later comments make it clear that he saw well-offness as being measured using the present values of equity at the beginning and end of the year. Although Alexander qualifies this view in a number of ways, most accounting policy makers have accepted this switch of emphasis from the individual to the enterprise in wealth and income measurement without question.

The existence of poorly organised markets of the types discussed above may render illegitimate this change of perspective. Different individuals may now value an enterprise's portfolio of prospects variously because of, for example, differences in time preference or because of different attitudes to risk which cannot be traded away using the market. Market problems may inhibit any trading that seeks to obtain an alternative set of cash flows or a level of risk which better suits preferences. Wealth and income measures published by the enterprise of the type reviewed in this chapter (and generated, one assumes, by enterprise management) will presumably reflect the set of preferences used in decision making which may not match those of any given market participant (see Bromwich, 1977, and Beaver and Demski, 1979).

No longer, therefore, can the economist's wealth and income measures be generally defended on the basis that they provide unambiguous measures of the contribution that investment in an enterprise makes to each investor's welfare. Economic income may become a poor instrument for measuring individual welfare, unless carefully fashioned for the individual in mind and the market characteristics faced. Much contemporary research is geared towards isolating those characteristics of individuals and markets which would allow enterprise statements of wealth and income, drawn up according to the suggestions in this chapter and in Chapter 3, to continue to serve all or a subset of market participants in the face of market difficulties. For example, it can be shown that providing information on an enterprise's endowment of those resources which do have market prices in an incomplete market is, at least, unlikely to harm market participants, even where differing preferences exist (Bromwich and Wells, 1983).

Income for a project

For similar reasons the discussion of this chapter, and of Chapter 3, has all been placed in the context of only a single project. With perfect markets, dealing with a number of projects causes no difficulty. All projects will be priced in the market at the appropriate rates of interest. The present value of a given enterprise will be simply the sum of the present values of its prospects. This is the usual working assumption made in finance theory; see Copeland and Weston (1988) and Hirshleifer (1970). Similarly, where a project involves the use of a number of assets, a perfect market allows the aggregation of their market prices to obtain the value of the project, providing that there are no economies or diseconomies of scale and no other interrelationships between assets. This operation is rendered feasible by the ability in perfect markets to trade separately all the property rights contributing to a project's present value, including those special factors which enable the overall project to earn benefits above the going rate of interest. It is these special factors which give the project a positive net present value after paying the going price for all assets and other inputs used in the project. The value of these special factors has been labelled 'subjective goodwill' because it is based on the subjectively estimated net cash flows remaining after the present values of the costs of all other inputs have been deducted from the project's cash flows. In a perfect market in equilibrium, with certainty, all assets, including those representing these special factors, will be valued using the going rate of interest. Valuing project assets on this basis will just exhaust the present value of the cash flows from a project after meeting variable costs. There is thus, in perfectly functioning markets, no aggregation or allocation problem of the type familiar with conventional accounting. Similar conclusions can be demonstrated under uncertainty in perfect and complete markets which have reached equilibrium (see Chapters 5 and 6).

Market inhibitions on trading may introduce aggregation and allocation problems. The market prices of assets used by a project may not sum to the present value of the project's cash flows, net of variable costs. Any attempt to spread this present value amongst contributing assets may now involve allocation with all the difficulties which should be familiar (Thomas, 1969 and 1974).

Thus, one criticism of the economist's approach to income and wealth measurement concerns its weaknesses in less well functioning markets. We will return to this criticism regularly throughout our study. However, similar problems plague other accounting approaches in settings of market imperfections and market incompleteness. Indeed, many of the usual criticisms of historical cost accounting arise from these sources. There is, however, little evidence bearing on whether economic accounting concepts are more severely affected by market difficulties than those of other accounting systems. We can say that the decision models from which they obtain much of their strength are used in the real world with all its market problems. Similarly, the widespread advocacy of portfolio theory for making practical investment decisions about securities (see Sharpe, 1985), supports the economic approach to income and wealth measurement. Such recommendations carry with them an implication that the securities market is believed to be approximately perfect because this is one of the necessary assumptions of the theory. If this were the case, the claims for the economist's income and wealth concepts would be greatly strengthened.

It is fair to say that more research has been undertaken seeking to adapt the underlying decision models for some of the more crucial market difficulties, than has so far been devoted to similarly altering the economist's income and wealth concepts to cope better with poorly organised markets.

The remaining criticisms of the economist's system, discussed below, are those which are either unique to this system or which are believed to affect this system more severely than other accounting approaches. As we have already seen, some of the advocates of the economist's income and wealth concepts anticipated a number of the difficulties with this approach. Indeed, Hicks (1946) cautioned economists about utilising these concepts, especially in their empirical work. He felt that his suggested approximations to the central criterion of income became indeterminate in some settings. He sought to remedy some of the difficulties associated with income concept Number 1 by coining income concepts Number 2 and Number 3. Employing these additional concepts still left a variety of major indeterminacies outstanding. Hicks was especially concerned with those associated with income concept Number 3, which is designed to cope with general price changes. (These include the well known difficulty of defining the meaning of 'real terms' in an inflationary environment. This problem thus strikes at the essence of concept Number 3, which is meant to deal with items expressed in this way.)

Subjectivity

The overwhelming criticism of the use of economist's concepts are that they may be subjective and may yield figures which exist only in a decision maker's mind. There is no obvious way in which such figures can be audited in any objective fashion. There is, therefore, a clear danger that decision makers may seek to inflate their estimates of cash flows in the expectation that such forecasts will be accepted by other market participants, at least for a time. If share values may be 'talked up' in this way, any gullibility shown by the market can be exploited by the decision maker by selling any shares owned at the consequent higher prices. Similarly, enterprise managers who often are not long in a specific job may be able to inflate their forecasts with some impunity. The potential for these problems, even with more conventional accounting systems, has been offered as one reason for having auditors and employing other devices to monitor decision makers' conduct. Many commentators have argued that there are few obvious tools which can be used to check the subjective forecasts which lie at the heart of the economist's income and wealth figures.

These subjective figures may also provide a poor basis for those functions of accounting less directly concerned with decision making but which form a substantial element of the continued advocacy of historical cost accounting. Many commentators do not see how accounts based on the economist's concepts of wealth and income can, for example, either fulfil the function of stewardship accounting or provide a simple basis for levying tax on corporations. It is usually argued that such activities require figures that are as objective figures as possible. A similar view has been put concerning accounting figures which are meant to help in determining the distribution of the benefits from the enterprise amongst the various enterprise partners (Ijiri, 1975). It is argued that such benefits should be quantified on as deterministic a basis as possible, in order to minimise any debate about these calculations. Similar arguments are raised with regard to any accounting figures required for legally orientated purposes, such as determining whether contractual obligations have been fulfilled. Cost-plus contracts provide an example. Here, contractual payments depend on costs incurred determined according to rules laid down in the original contract between the parties. These payments equal costs plus an agreed profit margin. There is likely to be less debate concerning prices justified in this way, the greater the objectivity of the figures agreed on as the basis for payment.

Another related weakness of the economist's approach is that its results may be very sensitive to changes in those variables which may affect future enterprise cash flows. Such changes will alter the value of the enterprise and the amount of enterprise income. Thus, it can be argued that the operating performance of the enterprise in a period may be dominated by alterations in the predicted values of the cash flows expected to be received fairly far into the future. It may therefore be difficult for outside analysts to disentangle those profits arising from production and sales during a period in order to determine the 'permanent' income that may be expected from the enterprise for the period. Existing practices within the enterprise for appraising managers and those used by external analysts to monitor the enterprise seem to give little support for believing that any great weight is given to management's future expectations. Similarly, few executives are rewarded in a clear way for their forecasting performance, and even fewer management accounting systems within enterprises evaluate forecasting performance.

A strict interpretation of the economist's accounting model would seem to require decision makers to announce only the present value and income of the enterprise. This would deny much information of probable utility to those external to the firm. The FASB (the standard setting body in the United States of America) has recognised this by stressing the need for information concerning the timing, amount and riskiness of future cash flows. Further, it has been argued that the economist's concepts do not provide a comprehensive picture of the enterprise. For example, these concepts may say little about the enterprise's liquidity. This may reflect the perfect market foundation of the economist's concepts. Here liquidity is not a problem, because if a project has a present value it will be financed at the going rate of interest.

Profits and depreciation

To a conventional accountant, the definitions of capital gains, of profits and of depreciation used with the economist's income concept are unusual (Schwayder, 1967). From an economic perspective, capital gains should be taken into wealth and reflected in income immediately they become known. The net present value of a project is, therefore, regarded as available for consumption or reinvestment immediately the decision makers learn of the possibility, though such possibilities do not really become fully operational, even in a perfect market, until the project is announced to the market. In a realistic environment a project becomes valuable outside the enterprise when the market has become aware of that project.

Economic depreciation represents the difference between the project's economic value at the beginning and at the end of a period. Economic income is defined as interest on the present value of the enterprise's portfolio of prospects. These profit and depreciation concepts seem to have little to do with the conventional procedures used by accountants in the practical world. Profit under these conventional procedures is usually seen as determined by the excess of period revenues over costs. The economist's income does not represent profit as the gains of a period. All such gains have already been incorporated in economic wealth at the time they became known. Economic income merely represents the return required by the providers of equity capital on this wealth. The economist sees this return not as a profit but as interest reflecting the opportunity cost of those who finance the enterprise. Defining income as interest, when the Hicksian standard stream approach is being used, has been attacked by Kaldor because it separates income from its source—enterprise wealth. Standard stream income is only indirectly based on the cash flows of a project when changes are expected in interest rates (see pp. 42–4).

Economic income can be said to be determined not by production or by buying and selling, but rather by the accrual of information. According to the economist, the value of a set of physical activities can change not because of an alteration in activity, but simply because of a change in perception of the worthwhileness of that set of activities. From a decision making point of view this would seem reasonable. In the view of conventional accountants, this realisation criterion is very liberal and amounts to counting your chickens well before they have hatched. Cash flows expected in, say, 75 years' time which have present value now would be incorporated into the economist's wealth and profit concepts (Barton, 1974). The accountant generally expects to see an exchange of property rights before recognising profits.

There is no obvious objective way of deciding which realisation concept is correct. The choice depends on individual preferences, the decisions facing individuals and the use to which any envisaged realisation concept is to be put. In the same way as different income and wealth measures may be useful for different purposes, so may a variety of realisation concepts be of utility for different purposes. The economist's concept of realisation is consistent with the models recommended for decision making and, therefore, may well be of use for this purpose (if not for others). Doubt has been cast even on this role because the use of discounting (at least when not using market interest rates) has been said to represent yet another example of an arbitrary allocation (Thomas, 1969; 1974). This view has been insufficient to cause the use of discounted cash flow models in decision making to cease.

Aggregation difficulties

The economist's wealth and income concepts do not seem to lend themselves to the conventional accountant's wish to build up income and wealth figures by aggregating individual costs and revenues to arrive at income and aggregating individual assets and liabilities to obtain net worth, at least in poorly organised markets. The present value of an asset represents the increment to the wealth of the total enterprise, consequent upon the acquisition of the asset and given the enterprise's existing configuration of other assets. Present value calculations are, thus, marginal and ascribe to the item under consideration any interactions between an asset or prospect being considered and the portfolio of existing assets or prospects (Barton, 1974). Aggregating the present values of the individual assets or prospects of an enterprise obtained in this way may yield a sum greater than the total enterprise's present value, because the calculations of asset present values may ascribe some of the benefits of the same interaction to a number of assets or prospects. This problem does not arise in perfect and complete markets because, in this rather special setting, the rights to the benefits from these interactions could be traded on the market separately from other assets. For similar reasons, it can be argued more generally that attempting to spread the present value of an enterprise amongst its constituent parts represents a further exercise in arbitrary allocation (see Thomas, 1969, especially chapter 2).

Thus the economist's concepts of wealth and income, in contrast to those of conventional accounting, generally apply only at the enterprise level, or to easily separable portfolios of prospects. It can be argued that this perspective is the correct one. Enterprises exist because they yield a greater value than their individual components. Value flows not only from individual assets, but also from how they are combined together.

Most of the above criticisms can be answered by saying that they are necessary accompaniments to seeking to reduce the dissonance introduced when we use one set of models for decisions, and account for the results of these decisions in a different way. If we wish to reflect decision making in accounting, we have to recognise that the future is the essence of decision making. Advocates of the concepts reviewed in the previous two chapters may be said to have been forced to introduce subjectivity into accounting in pursuit of their wish to render decision models and accounting results consistent.

This suggests not that these ideas should be abandoned, but rather that different types of accounting should be used for different purposes and that efforts should be made to overcome the acknowledged difficulties we have considered. We should again recall the successful use in practice of the decision models which form the foundation for the economist's views of income and wealth.

Criticisms of *ex post* income

Some commentators would say that one major role of accounting is to monitor in the present what has occurred in the past (Barton, 1974; Chambers, 1966). For such critics, economic income *ex post*, in whatever form it is calculated, is irredeemably contaminated by the future. From this perspective, our *ex post* measures fail to distinguish between the past and the future and cannot, therefore, provide a reasonable *ex post* measure of income. This perceived weakness of economic income as an *ex post* measure is one of degree. All more conventional accounting systems encounter this difficulty and seek to solve it by intertemporal allocations. Accounting systems based on net realisable values do not experience this difficulty because they use market prices to value those asset services carried over to future periods. However, it can be argued that this problem is 'solved' only by replacing enterprise estimates of the worth of future services by the predictions of the market, which too are estimates.

In contrast to these approaches, economic income recognises the problem of interactions between the just-completed period and those yet to come, and seeks to tackle this head-on rather than by using arbitrary accounting procedures which may disguise the problem but do not cause it to disappear.

The other major problem with the economist's income concept, viewed as a monitoring device, is again its subjectivity.

The subjectivity of ex post *economic income*

Comparisons of the value of a prospect at the beginning of a period and at its end can be made non-subjective where we are able to compare the market price of the prospect at the two times. This calculation, which Hicks (1946) advocated as an *ex post* income measure, does not, however, provide a completely useful monitoring device because the two values being compared include all changes in market expectations. Therefore this comparison does not allow us to distinguish between the income flowing from operational performance and that accruing because of changes in market expectations. The variances which emerge from such a comparison may tell us very little. Monitoring exercises usually involve comparing some target expectations with the actual results. Without such a target, variances between enterprise values over a period cannot be easily interpreted. An obvious candidate for this target is the originally expected present value of the prospect at the beginning of the period adjusted for all the additional information appearing in the period, $V_{i-1,i}$ in our earlier notation, assuming that we are seeking an income figure for the *i*th period. This target, as portrayed by Expression 4.VI, is used in determining *ex post* income II. This involves comparing this target with the realised cash flows for the period ($C_{i,i}$ for the *i*th period), plus the present value at the end of the period of the remaining future cash flows to be generated by the project, determined in the light of knowledge available at the end of the period ($V_{i,i}$ for the *i*th period) (See Expression 4.VII).

Economic income *ex post* is, therefore, very subjective. Where the market value of the prospect at the end of the period is not used, economic income involves a comparison between an estimate made at the end of the period with earlier predictions adjusted for information obtained during the period. This comparison is rendered subjective because it utilises no objective figures other than the cash flows of the period. This subjectivity can be argued to be doubled because usually we would expect that the two estimates involved will, perforce, have to be made by the same person or group of people. Only project managers are likely to have the knowledge necessary to make these calculations.

Many critics would argue that this doubly subjective comparison is the one usually encountered in *ex post* income measurement using the economist's approach. This is because market prices for most prospects, as distinct from companies, do not exist in the practical world and, therefore, cannot be used in the calculation of economic income as Hicks suggested. Therefore *ex post* economic income calculations, may involve at least comparing a forecast made by a decision maker or group of decision makers ($V_{i-1,0}$) with a new forecast made by the same person or set of people ($C_{i,i} + V_{i,i}$). Indeed, if we use our second *ex post* concept, we are comparing a new forecast ($C_{i,i} + V_{i,i}$) with a revision of the original forecast ($V_{i-1,i}$), again made by the same person or set of people.

The only 'objective' item in any of this is the actual cash flows for the period. Any adverse variances arising from such comparisons can, therefore, be easily explained away, probably for a number of periods, by saying that the original present value estimate is maintainable because any variances reflect merely timing differences. Where unforeseen environmental changes do cause variances, the involved decision maker may say similarly, with impunity for a substantial period of time that action which will recoup the effects of these changes in the future has already been taken. The 'true' pattern of events may take a considerable time to appear. Edwards and Bell (1961, p. 44) summarise these arguments by saying that 'Expectations can be verified or disproved by the hard facts. Once the period has passed, one need not probe into the nebulous question 'Do you now feel as you thought you would feel . . . ?'

The problem is in fact worse than this because *ex post* calculations cannot of themselves aid in future decision making. Reforecasting is not sufficient for a new value for the prospect at the end of the period ($V_{i,i}$) to emerge. The present value of a project's future cash flows at the end of a period is indeterminate until after all the decisions which affect future cash flows have been made. The *ex post* present value of future cash flows at the end of a period thus only records any new decisions concerning the future. *Ex post* economic income serves only to quantify the results of decision making and replanning. Economic income *ex post* is formally redundant in actual decision making, though it may still be worthwhile in providing a useful summary of the rather more complicated calculations which it reports. Of course, it still has utility in providing income figures for the purposes surveyed in this and the preceding chapter.

Proponents of the economist's *ex post* income concept, in all its varieties, have to accept the burden of the above criticisms. It is recognised that the suggested monitoring techniques are unusual in their lack of use of 'objective' data and that they generally involve subjective comparisons. This is the cost we pay for using accounting systems consistent with the models used in decision making. Again, these problems really plague most other income concepts but remain somewhat hidden because most other accounting models do not seek to attain consistency with decision making models. These problems remain to be solved. At least, economic income *ex post* does make explicit the problems caused by seeking a decision orientated income figure.

In any case, perhaps too much may be made of the subjectivity of economic income when viewed from an *ex post* perspective. All managerial control techniques used in enterprises have subjective elements. Long-term planning on a rolling basis, for example, involves extending the plan to encompass another period as one period passes and is dropped from the plan. This process shares many of the elements of *ex post* income, as do other planning methods such as programme budgets. Standard costing and budgetary control processes often involve comparisons between actual results and targets revised for the conditions faced in the period under review. Post mortem meetings to review variances from plans often involve managers revising their original estimates in an effort to state that many of these variances were outside their control (see any management accounting text, for example Kaplin and Atkinson, 1989, chapter 9).

It can, of course, be argued that there is less opportunity for individuals to exploit the subjectivity of these control devices within the enterprise, than there is where subjective figures form part of the enterprise's external reports. Within the organisation there will be a number of ways of at least approximately checking what is claimed and forecast, and of rewarding honesty and penalising and discouraging any errant behaviour based on the subjectivity of the control devices used. It is usually argued that most of these methods are not available to the user of published accounts who is external to the enterprise. This, perhaps, has to be true in the present litigious climate that seems to surround auditing, but auditors could do much with appropriate safeguards to ascertain and to check the logic, consistency and reasonableness of the assumptions used in the forecasting which lies at the heart of the economist's approach to income and wealth measurement. Moreover, there are certainly investors and financial analysts who claim to have access to some internal corporate information and who can therefore monitor, at least to a degree, the reasonableness of any subjective information released by enterprises. The judgements of those with additional knowledge may well be communicated to other less informed investors by the effects which market actions based on these judgements may have on enterprise security prices.

Agency theory (see Chapter 13, and Jensen and Meckling, 1976) provides some possible reasons for believing that it may not be in the best interests of managements to seek to exploit the subjectivity of the economist's income and wealth figures. Security prices will be adjusted insofar as these activities are suspected. Managers who have shares in a company, therefore, have an incentive to behave honestly and to limit any excessive reductions in security values because of believed exploitation of the 'softness' of economic accounting figures by issuing information which allows the actual level of this exploitation, if any, to be ascertained.

Conclusions

It is not intended to reiterate here the rather long exegesis of the advantages and disadvantages of these measures. Full blooded practical acceptance of these measures is unlikely in the foreseeable future. Any practical acceptance has so far been piecemeal and seems to require, first, overwhelming evidence that the conventional accounting system cannot cope with specific accounting crises. Secondly, it has to be seen that conventional accounting provides an illogical way of handling a specific accounting problem and that the economist's approach seems to represent the only way out of whatever severe problems these defects are perceived to be causing. Bonds and annuities with definite incomes have for many years been valued using variants of the economist's method. Actuarial valuations of pension funds also rely heavily on the valuation methods described in this and the preceding chapter. Leases in a number of countries are now accounted for using the concepts being considered here. Each of the above cases seems to represent a situation where the economist's treatment has become difficult to deny. Many other practical accounting problems exist: concern over their treatment in conventional accounting may also be overcome by using the economist's wealth and income concepts.

It also seems reasonable to argue that the emphasis the economist places on the future has had effects on practical accounting. The FASB's concern with the timing, amount and risk of future cash flows may provide some evidence of this. Any increasing concern over the future of enterprises will, perhaps, lead to increased demands for forecasts from enterprises, so that individuals can attempt to construct their own estimates of enterprise value and income based on the economist's principles. This is probably the best way to implement the essence of the economist's approach in imperfectly functioning markets.

Any substantial adoption of the income and wealth measures reviewed here probably requires a general acceptance of the view that different accounting income and wealth measures are required for different purposes. A generally accepted pluralistic view of accounting would mean that adoption of the economist's measures was less likely to be hindered by the present-day concern that it fails to fulfil a number of criteria such as prudence and conservatism, which may be necessary for some accounting purposes but which have no obvious place in accounting systems geared towards aiding decision making.

The economist's model of income and wealth provides a useful base for appraising other, more practically acceptable accounting systems which may be suggested, and which are aimed at improving the decision making abilities of the users of financial reports and providing congruence between reported accounting measures and decision making. These economic concepts will be used in this way throughout the remainder of this book. The contemporary importance attached to 'user' relevance does suggest that the economist's income and wealth concepts may play a major role of this type.

The primary contemporary roles of the economist's wealth and income concepts may be perceived as to provide a guide to thinking about difficult accounting problems, and to provide a well understood analytical framework which can be used as a 'laboratory' to explore the advantages and disadvantages of suggested improvements to accounting. Over a fairly short period, modern finance theory has advanced from being an abstract theoretical framework, relying heavily on perfect markets and certainty, to providing a number of theoretically sound models, strongly grounded on empirical evidence, for practical decision making in poorly organised markets with uncertainty (to see this contrast compare Fama and Miller, 1972, and Brealey and Myers, 1988). Even the earlier idealised framework of finance theory cast practical doubt on a number of well established views (by, for example, saying that dividend payments as such may have no effect on an enterprise value). It can be expected that the concepts reviewed in this chapter may develop in a similar way.

This ends our formal review of the economist's wealth and income concepts but these ideas will continue to be used throughout much of the remainder of this book. The next chapter reviews elements of uncertainty and some of the tools available for dealing with uncertainty. This will allow us to begin to discuss the impact of uncertainty on financial reporting.

Notes

1. The *ex post* value of the project at the end of period 2 would be higher if the results of earlier reinvestment were included. Similar calculations to those in the text yield the *ex post* wealth of the project including any reinvested funds and any interest on such investments. The only alterations required to the calculations in the text are to add the value of the retained funds carried over from the first period (to be represented by $D_{1,1}$, where D stands for economic depreciation as defined in Chapter 3 (see Expression 3.IIIb), and the cash flows in the period representing interest on the retentions (depreciation) of the previous period. These cash flows are represented as $rD_{1,2}$ where r is the rate of interest. The *ex post* wealth results obtained for Flower's project incorporating retained funds and interest thereon at the end of period 2 is:

   Ex post value of total project at the end of period 2
   $$= CF_{2,2} + V_{2,2} = + D_{1,1} + rD_{1,2}$$
   $$= 40 + 60.91 + 13.4 + 1.34$$
   $$= 115.65$$

   where $D_{1,1}$ represents the retained funds (economic depreciation) set aside at the end of period 1, as calculated at the end of period 1, and $rD_{1,2}$ stands for the interest on these funds obtained in period 2 as calculated at the end of this period. This expression is again entirely consistent with the similar expressions utilised with an *ex ante* perspective in Chapter 3 (see pp. 43–4).

2. The *ex post* income for the project, using concept I when retained funds are included, is in this case identical to that given by the calculations for the mainstream project in the text. This is because the realised cash flows in the first period were assumed to have turned out as planned. Thus, in adopting a total project perspective, we have to add the same amounts of retained funds to both the *ex ante* and *ex post* wealth figures. These amounts are the

funds reinvested in the first year (13.4 units) as calculated earlier (see Note 1), and the interest obtained thereon (1.34 units in the second period (see Note 1). With these adjustments, the *ex post* income for the total project is:

$Y_{2,\mathrm{I}}$ for the total project $= (40 + 60.91 + 13.4 + 1.34) - (102.79 + 13.4 + 1.34)$
$$= -1.88$$

where the last two elements in each of the bracketed expressions represent funds reinvested in the previous period and the interest obtained thereon, respectively. *Ex post* income using concept I for a total project, including reinvested funds, will not generally equal that obtained when considering only mainstream projects. Differences will occur where the reinvested cash flows of earlier periods differ from those expected at planning time, and where there have been unexpected changes in interest rates.

3. Similar calculations for Flower's total project indicate that this second income calculation also provides a well behaved income number from this perspective. For the total project, this second definition of *ex post* income can be written as:

$$Y_{2,\mathrm{II}} = 40 + 60.91 + 13.4 + 1.34 - 105.14 = 10.51$$

where 1.34 and 13.4 represent respectively funds reinvested in period 1 and the interest obtained on those funds in period 2. This income represents interest on the revised capital value of the project at the time when given the new knowledge. This value equals:

$$V_{1,2} = 91.74 + 13.4 = 105.14$$

where the subscript 2 indicates that the knowledge available at the end of period 2 is being used to recalculate the original present value.

II

Accounting information under uncertainty

5

Accounting and decision making under uncertainty

Plan of the chapter

This chapter seeks first to introduce some of the basic tools and decision making models for dealing with uncertainty. An acquaintanceship with these tools and models is believed to be necessary when we seek to understand the problems of measuring income and wealth under uncertainty. The term 'risk' is sometimes restricted to those settings where the probabilities of risky events can be based on the frequency of their appearance in the past. With this view, the label 'uncertainty' is reserved for situations where probabilities of occurrence are not based solely on empirical evidence concerning the frequency of the occurrence in the past of the events of interest, but rather on subjective beliefs concerning their likelihoods. In this book, risk and uncertainty will both be used to describe decision problems where the probabilities utilised reflect perceived beliefs as to likely occurrences, irrespective of how these beliefs are determined. We will not deal with settings where probabilities cannot be determined. Such situations fall within the province of the theory of games (see Luce and Raiffa, 1957).

This review of the basic ideas required to understand accounting theory in a setting of uncertainty comprises the first part of this chapter. No previous knowledge of the subject, is assumed and this part can therefore be skipped by those with a knowledge of the state preference approach to uncertainty, and also by those who wish to obtain only an overview of the impact of information economics and of the effects of uncertainty on accounting theory. Such readers should go directly to the section entitled 'Uncertainty and accounting' on p. 102.

The presentation of the tools and models is not meant to be rigorous. It is sought to give only an intuitive understanding sufficient to appreciate some of the results of explicitly incorporating uncertainty into accounting theories.[1]

An understanding of these basic tools and decision models is required to begin to understand the impact of uncertainty on accounting. The material provided is also necessary to understand the contribution of information economics to accounting, which forms the subject matter of Chapters 6, 7 and 8. Uncertainty and accounting is taken up initially in the final part of this chapter, where it is shown formally that uncertainty as such makes no difference to our ability to derive the preference-free accounting measures introduced in Chapter 2. This part of the chapter also shows that market incompleteness and market failures are likely to appear in an uncertain setting. As in Chapter 2, this inhibits our ability to derive neutral accounting measures and yields reasons to expect some type of regulation.

The technical material of this chapter is also required to understand Chapter 9, which considers how information economics and recent developments in finance have allowed theories of accounting under uncertainty to be refined and have enabled empirical evidence concerning accounting information to be obtained.

The middle sections of this chapter deal with optimal decision making in idealised securities under uncertainty. This is a difficult subject and may seem rather removed from financial accounting. It can be left out, but knowledge of the topics discussed in this section is assumed in the literature seeking to apply information economics to accounting. It provides a perspective of great promise for accounting. Some understanding of this material will, therefore, make the comprehension of the final sections and Chapters 6 to 9 much easier.

The assertion (presented briefly in Chapter 2) that market failures under uncertainty will mean that the market mechanism cannot be relied upon to provide optimal accounting information is then considered in some detail. The results here echo some of the findings in Chapter 2 and anticipate those of later chapters.

The elements of individual decision making under uncertainty

The approach to uncertainty adopted here is called state preference theory (see Hirshleifer, 1970, chapter 8). With this approach the individual is seen as choosing between outcomes, the realisation of which are dependent upon the state of the environment which prevails. Therefore the only uncertainty that needs to be considered is that associated with which state of environment will reign. With this view, a given prospect is perceived as yielding different returns depending on the state of the environment which actually occurs. A state equivalent to, say, a depressed economy will cause a prospect sensitive to the state of economy to produce a lower outcome than it would generate with a state of high economic activity. The amount of wealth at the end of a trading cycle is thus seen as uncertain because it depends on the state of the environment which will appear. The only uncertainty in our model is that concerned with which state will arise. The outcome given by each and every state is assumed to be known. It is also assumed that a known probability can be attached to the occurrence of each state. This may seem a somewhat restrictive approach, but it does allow the essence of uncertainty to be captured in a fairly simple manner and it has contributed greatly to our understanding of uncertainty. In fact, this characterisation of uncertainty can, at least ideally, be made as comprehensive as we wish. Additional uncertainties can be portrayed by refining the detail captured in our definition of each state. For example, say, a manufacturer is uncertain not only about the state of the economy, but also about whether the variable cost of production will be high or low. Such an additional uncertainty can be handled by simply defining states such that they include this uncertainty. Thus, if the economy could take only two states—depressed or growing—the manufacturer's additional problem could be portrayed by defining four sub-states as follows:

1 depressed economy with low variable costs,
2 depressed economy with high variable costs,

3 growth economy with low variable costs, and

4 growth economy with high variable costs.

The only uncertainty involved in our models is that of which state will appear. This means that our decision problem can fairly easily be fully and completely specified so that nothing in the decision maker's experience which might be expected to impinge on a decision is left out of the model.

The type of uncertainty entertained here has been called 'event' or 'technological uncertainty'. Here individual decision makers are uncertain about exogenous events which they cannot themselves control, such as whether there will be a good or bad harvest and whether government economic policy will be expansionary or restrictive. There is, thus, no uncertainty over the market prices which will reign if a state is realised, or about the prices which reign at each stage in the trading cycle for the rights to commodities in each state if that state prevails. This assumption is similar to the traditional one of costless market exchange at market clearing prices which is usually made in an environment of certainty.

Uncertainty about the terms of market exchanges has been called, in contrast, 'market uncertainty'. This type of uncertainty is intimately related to market imperfections of one type or another which, according to Chapter 2, were likely to render impossible the achievement of preference-free accounting systems. This type of uncertainty has so far proved somewhat unamenable to any sort of general analysis (see Hirshleifer and Riley, 1979, pp. 1376–1378). In this chapter we shall concentrate on event uncertainty; market uncertainty will be covered only at the end of the chapter when we discuss the effects of additional market difficulties which may be caused by uncertainty. We shall also deal with individual decision making under uncertainty abstracting from the impact of information. This facet of uncertainty will be discussed in Chapter 6.

In order to keep the analysis as simple as possible, we will finally assume that we are only dealing with trading possibilities in a timeless setting. In the environment we are considering, individuals are seen as trading rights to consumption, commodities or incomes in specific states of the world, where consumption opportunities are the ultimately desired objectives. The basket of goods or portfolio of incomes belonging to an individual can thus be seen as indexed by the states to which they apply. The individual will obtain all the goods in his or her basket indexed to state 1 if state 1 appears. All rights to goods or income in state 2 will accrue if state 2 occurs. The basic items of trade can therefore be called contingent consumption claims, contingent commodities or contingent incomes. Unlike goods and incomes indexed by time periods, the total set of state-contingent items represent options, only one of which will be realised when a state occurs.

With this background, we can present the basic elements of individual decision making under uncertainty. The essential elements of a general model for this purpose are listed below and shown as in Table 5.1. Each element of the decision model is represented by a symbol. This symbolic representation will ease the later presentation and allow issues introduced informally to be dealt with in a more rigorous way.

The first necessary element in the table is a set of states of the environment, which is shown at the top. Two states, represented by s_1 and s_2, are assumed. In a two-state world, all possible events relevant to a decision must be contained in one or other of these states (a setting of certainty requires that only one state can appear).

The second required element of the model is a set of probabilities or likelihoods,

Table 5.1 The general decision model with uncertainty

State:	State 1 (s_1)	State 2 (s_2)
Probability of state:	ϕ_1	ϕ_2
Action (a_j)		
Action 1 (a_1)	$(a_1, s_1) \Rightarrow U(C_{11})$	$(a_1, s_2) \Rightarrow U(C_{12})$
Action 2 (a_2)	$(a_2, s_1) \Rightarrow U(C_{21})$	$(a_2, s_2) \Rightarrow U(C_{22})$

Assumed objective: To maximise utility, subject to constraints

one of which is attached to each state. These probabilities are represented by the symbols ϕ_i at the top of the table; ϕ_1 is the probability of state 1 and ϕ_2 is that of state 2. The total of these probabilities (ϕ_1 and ϕ_2 in the table) must add to 1 to signify that one, and only one, state will appear.

The third requirement is a set of actions (a_1 and a_2 on the left of the table). No decision making is possible without a choice of actions. Each action, together with a state, implies a given consequence or payoff (C_i in the table). A given payoff may be obtained from a number of state–action combinations shown by (a_i, s_i) in the figure. A table like Table 5.1 is therefore called a state–action matrix and indicates the consequences of each state–action pair.

The outcomes (C_i) need to be ranked in some way. Here it is assumed that the individual can assign a measure of utility to each state–action combination. We will leave the precise definition of utility for the time being. That we are dealing with utilities is shown in the figure by the U placed in front of each state–action combination (C_i). This symbol signifies that each outcome or payoff is expressed in terms of some measure of utility.

The decision maker requires some criterion which allows the 'best' act in terms of its contribution to individual welfare to be selected. The action which maximises utility is assumed to be selected. Finally, in addition to these elements, we would normally expect the decision maker to face constraints upon the actions chosen. Any individual can only undertake those trades made available by his or her original endowment—a usual constraint in the models used in economics and financial management. The endowment is a very important constraint as it restricts absolutely the individual's activities by constraining the cost of planned consumption to the individual's endowed wealth. Additionally, some otherwise feasible actions may be illegal. We will assume that no constraints of this latter type exist.

Table 5.1 summarises the problem in terms of a payoff matrix which shows the states of the environment, the feasible actions and their consequences in each state. All individuals and entities in the economy are generally assumed to be unable to change either the states of the economy that can be expected or the consequences that flow from combining an action with a state. Productive entities may affect the actions available on the market when they bring new opportunities to the market. A payoff matrix may be said, in an informal way, to be complete if it contains at least one opportunity to obtain an outcome in each state, thereby allowing the decision maker the possibility of a payoff in each state.

It is important to realise that although we are presently looking at decision making by a specific individual, much of what we are assuming for our individual is also assumed to apply equally to all others. It is generally postulated that all individuals are agreed as to the possible states of the environment and their consequences in terms of payoffs when combined with actions. Generally, the portfolio of actions available to one person is assumed to be available to all at the same cost for each action, and individual decisions do not affect these costs; that is, we are assuming perfect markets. Thus, in a multi-person environment, the payoff matrix portrays the market structure of the problem by showing all feasible trades. The remaining aspects of the decision problem may differ between individuals. Thus, people may have different preferences for consumption in different states and varying beliefs about the likelihoods of the states. Generally, endowments will be assumed to vary across individuals.

Prior to providing a numerical example of decision making under uncertainty and considering the meaning attached to utility in this setting, it is helpful to examine in a little detail what is meant by states of the environment and the probabilities of these states.

States of the environment and their probabilities

As has been stated, the only uncertainty in our models is that of which state will appear. A state is merely a set of possible happenings or events. Each possible occurrence is contained in one, and only one, of the states which comprise the collection of states of the environment. The total possible states of the world will be represented in symbols, when convenient, as S. This total set of states will be assumed to be finite. Any given set of states merely partitions or classifies this overall set of states in some way.

Few restrictions are necessary with regard to the states which comprise the overall set of states. States can be defined to be as fine as is convenient for the decision in mind, but the decision maker is assumed to know the consequences of each state for the prospect in mind. Each state must be relevant to the decision in mind and must be an element of the overall set of states with which we are working. This requirement can be expressed in symbols as $s_i \in S$ where $\in$ means that s_i is contained in the overall set of states, S. The states chosen must partition the overall set of states S in a mutually exclusive and exhaustive way. These restrictions mean that if the overall set of states (S) in mind relates to, say, the state of the economy, a possible partition is into a depressed economy (s_1), an average economy (s_2) and a growth economy (s_3). Such a partition must yield the overall set of states (S), that is $s_1 + s_2 + s_3$ must sum to S.

This may be expressed more precisely as $s_i \cup s_j = S$, where $i \neq j$, i and $j \in S$ and $\cup$ represents the forming of a set of states made up by s_i and s_j. These states must not contain the same elements or sub-states (where sub-states are the items contained in the states). That is, no common elements must exist between s_1, s_2 and s_3. This can be written more formally as $s_i \cap s_j = \emptyset$ for all i and j, where $i \neq j$, where $\cap$ stands for the intersection between two states and $\emptyset$ here signifies the empty set, as is normal in the mathematical literature. The intersection of states, signified by the symbol $\cap$, delineates any common elements between each pair of states.

Thus, the top line of Table 5.2 shows in symbolic form the complete set of states for a decision problem. This complete set of states is assumed to comprise five states, s_1 to s_5 (that is, $S = \{s_1, s_2, s_3, s_4, s_5\}$, where the curly brackets indicate we are dealing with a set). The remaining two rows of the table show two less exhaustive classifications of the states of the environment for the problem. Partition A groups s_1 and s_2 together in one set and the remaining states together in another. Partition B similarly combines states s_1 and s_2, but partitions s_3 from s_4 and s_5. The less detailed partitions still divide the states in a mutually exclusive way. Each state is contained in one, and only one, element of each of the less detailed groupings.

Table 5.2 Possible classifications of states

Complete set of states:	s_1	s_2	s_3	s_4	s_5
Partition A	$\{s_1, s_2\}$		$\{s_3, s_4, s_5\}$		
Partition B	$\{s_1, s_2\}$		$\{s_3\}$	$\{s_4, s_5\}$	

Which classification of states the decision maker will use depends on the decision problem to be solved. The state partition to be used for any decision needs to separate out all those states which yield different payoffs to other states when combined with any and all actions available to the decision maker. Such a partition is called payoff-adequate for the decision problem involved. It classifies states into those groups which yield different payoffs. The least detailed payoff-adequate state classification is all that is needed for an optimal solution. Further refinements yield no additional decision-relevant knowledge as this classification shows separately all decision-relevant events. It is therefore referred to as the 'payoff-relevant partition' in the literature.

The states chosen should be selected so that a mutually exclusive probability can be assigned to the realisation of each state. The occurrence of a given state may yield a different outcome from other states (states giving the same outcomes can be combined if desired, as discussed above). The use of states allows us to index outcomes, generally taken to be consumption, commodities or incomes, to the states which produce these consequences. As has been said, the amount of consumption, commodity or income arising in any state is said to be contingent on the occurrence of that state. The prices of consumption, commodities or incomes in a given future state, prior to the realisation of that state, are therefore referred to as contingent prices indexed according to the state which is expected to generate these outcomes.

Probabilities

The concept of probability is very difficult and one about which there are a number of different schools of thought, often with opposing views (see Kyburg and Smokler, 1964, pp. 3–15). The best known views of probability is that it represents the empirical frequency of the event or phenomenon in mind. The universally accepted 50 per cent probability attached to the prospect of obtaining a particular side uppermost upon tossing an unbiased coin over a series of trials is based on a large number of trials in the past. With this view, probability statements are hypotheses which can and must be tested by looking at the empirical evidence gathered in the past.

This empirical approach to probability may inhibit decision making under uncertainty, which often involves decisions which are not going to be repeated and for which no frequency data can, therefore, have been accumulated. We therefore adopt the interpretation of probabilities as subjective beliefs. With this view, the probability attached to an event is subjective and reflects the individual's degree of belief as to the likelihood of that event occurring. A high probability attached to a state does not necessarily reflect the empirical frequency of the state, but rather the possession of a high degree or substantial strength of belief in the state's occurrence. Empirical evidence forms only one basis for the determination of such probabilities. Rather, these probabilities reflect beliefs, however they are generated. This means that the likelihood attached to a set of events may be unique to each individual and may thus differ between individuals. Our accounting models, therefore, now have to cope not only with differences in tastes but also with differences in beliefs about the perceived likelihood of events.

Savage (1954) and others have sought to show that such subjective probabilities can be manipulated for decision making in exactly the same way as frequency based probabilities. Critical views concerning subjective probabilities will not be considered here as they require an intensive examination of the philosophies underlying probability concepts (see Edwards and Tversky, 1967).

That probabilities are subjective does not mean that the likelihoods involved in a decision can take any form. Any degree of belief in a given outcome is permissible, but the probabilities attached to other outcomes must be consistent with this degree of belief. Thus a rational decision maker may, if desired, believe that a given side of a coin will appear in a coin tossing experiment, say, 75 per cent of the time, but the same likelihood cannot also apply to the appearance of the reverse side. This would infringe the condition that subjective probabilities should be consistent.

Another reasonable restriction placed on subjective probabilities is that they must be consistent with the available evidence. Outcome *x* should be given the highest degree of belief if the available evidence favours outcome *x* over other outcomes. Moreover, subjective probabilities should follow the usual calculus used with empirical probabilities. Probabilities which follow these rules are labelled coherent. Such probabilities must possess the usual characteristics of being transitive and of totalling 1. This restriction helps us to rule out pathological behaviour.

Finally, subjectivists believe that people may learn from experience. They would, therefore, expect that once a sufficient number of observations has been accumulated to yield a frequency-based probability for an event, adopting a subjective perspective would generate an identical probability to that yielded by the frequency approach. This assumes that subjective probabilities are determined in accordance with the above restrictions. Those who take a subjective view of probability do, however, believe that the order in which empirical experience is obtained does not matter. In the end, beliefs will be amended so that they are consistent with frequency probabilities based on empirical evidence.

An example of decision making under uncertainty

As an example of decision-making in a two state environment, we will consider Mr Risky. He has a number of securities (common stock) in which he can invest, the details of which are shown in Table 5.3. These securities are available prior to state realisation at prices equal to their average outcomes (shown on the far right of Table 5.3), described by the more technical term 'expected monetary values'. The numbers associated with each action and state combination (a_i, s_i) in the table, refer to the monetary payoffs from each state–action combination.

Risky's wealth is at present invested in prospect A. Thus, his endowment amounts to 75 monetary units, prior to the realisation of either state. Each prospect promises income in both states. Only one of these promised contingent incomes for each security will be actually realised. His existing endowment is thus uncertain. Risky's view is

Table 5.3 Risky's decision problem

Probabilities of state:	State 1 (s_1)	State 2 (s_2)	Expected monetary value (monetary units)
	0.75 (ϕ_1)	0.25 (ϕ_2)	
Action			
Hold prospect A (a_1)	95 (a_1, s_1)	15 (a_1, s_2)	75
Accept prospect B (a_2)	50 (a_2, s_1)	150 (a_2, s_2)	75
Accept prospect C (a_3)	75 (a_3, s_1)	75 (a_3, s_2)	75

The expected money value of a prospect (say A) is given by:

$$\text{EMV} = \phi (a_i, s_1) + \phi_2 (a_i, s_2)$$

where a_i is the action which results in obtaining the prospect in mind. This decision rule is explained in the following text.

that the likelihood of state 1 will appear is 75 per cent (ϕ_1). The probability of state 2 is, therefore, 25 per cent $(s_2 = 1 - \phi_1)$. These probabilities must add to 1 because we are assuming that one or the other of these two states must appear. The table shows that if he continues to hold security A he will obtain 95 monetary units if state 1 appears and 15 units if state 2 is realised. He has only two other opportunities, prospects B and C, the possible monetary returns from which are also shown in Table 5.3. Each of Mr Risky's opportunities really represents complex opportunities made up of a number of elementary or primitive prospects. Each of these elementary prospects offers one monetary unit in one state and nothing in the other state. Thus, prospect A yields 95 units of the elementary prospect relating to state 1 and 15 units of that relating to state 2.

Risky's choice cannot necessarily be made simply by inspection, because each of his prospects offers its own attractions. Prospect A offers a larger outcome in the more likely state than either of the other options, but yields much less than these other prospects in the other state. Prospect B gives a higher return in the less likely state, but at a cost of income foregone, relative to the other options in state 1. Prospect C yields equal incomes in both states. The choice will, therefore, depend on Risky's preferences.

One well known decision rule is to assume that utility can be measured in monetary units. This allows us to use the Expected Monetary Value decision rule. This says 'Choose the prospect with the highest average value where the outcomes being averaged are weighted by their probabilities.' Thus, the expected monetary value of option A is found by multiplying its payoffs in each state by their probabilities and adding the results of these calculations for both states. This gives:

$$\underset{(C(a_1, s_1))}{95} \times \underset{(\phi_1)}{0.75} + \underset{(C(a_1, s_2))}{15} \times \underset{(\phi_2)}{0.25} = 75 \qquad [5.I]$$

where the symbols in brackets underneath indicate the meaning of each figure in the expression: $C(a_i, s_i)$ represents the outcome of a given state–action combination and ϕ_i is the probability of state i.

The expected monetary values for each of the prospects, which happen to be identical, are shown in the last column of Table 5.3.[2] The calculation required to obtain the expected monetary value of an action, or—in our terms—a prospect, can be written more formally and more generally as:

$$E(MV_j) = \sum_{s_i} (\phi_i C(a_j, s_i)) \qquad\qquad [5.II]$$

where $E(MV_j)$ represents the expected value of action j. The term on the right in brackets shows the monetary outcome produced by taking the action in mind (a_j) and a given state (s_i) being realised $C(a_j, s_i)$, weighted by the probability of that state (ϕ_i). C represents the payoff function which expresses the consequences or outcome of each state–action pair in monetary terms. The summation sign (Σ) says that to obtain the expected monetary values of an action, shown by $E(MV_j)$ on the left-hand side of the expression, all the payoffs obtained from a combination of an action and a state weighted by their probabilities should be added together over all states; E stands for the expectation operator, indicating we are calculating an expectation or average. The set of states over which the outcomes must be accumulated is represented by the symbol s_i at the bottom of the sigma sign, where i takes the value 1 to S, where there are S elements in the set of states.

Using the expected monetary value criterion, all three prospects have the same utility to Risky. This decision rule may work well where a project or prospect is going to be held for a number of trials. Each of the prospects in our example will, on average, yield its expected value or average value. Prospect A, for example, will yield 95 monetary units in some trials and 25 monetary units in others, but the average outcome generated by this process will equal the prospect's expected monetary value of 75 monetary units over a run of trials.

The expected monetary value of a prospect may also be obtained in one trial where a large number of units of the prospect are held. This result is conditional on the probabilities attached to states which govern the possible outcomes for the prospect being the same for all units and the outcome for each prospect being independent of those obtained on other units. That is, each unit of the prospect must represent an independent trial with the same probabilities as other units. If, in a given trial, Mr Risky held a large portfolio of independent investments, each identical to prospect A, some units would yield outcomes of 15 monetary units and others would yield outcomes of 95 monetary units. The average return on all units would however, be 75 monetary units, providing that Mr Risky's portfolio was of a large size.

Similar conclusions may also hold for one trial if a decision maker invests in a number of opportunities which promise different payouts in different states. Here, by diversifying, the individual may be able to obtain a certain payoff in each state different from any of those offered by the original prospects. For example, Mr Risky could obtain a certain return of 75 monetary units in both states if it were possible to invest funds in approximately 55.5 per cent of prospect A and 44.5 per cent of prospect B.

Risk attitudes

The expected monetary value decision rule has been subject to criticism. Risk may become important where the decision maker does not have multiple chances of undertaking the same projects, or the ability to diversify. Those who are averse to risk may dislike prospect A in our example, because of the very low outcome it yields if state 2 is realised.

Individuals who follow our earlier decision rule, and base proposal acceptance on the expected monetary value of prospects, must be unaffected by risk. Risky's three projects are deemed equivalent under this decision rule, even though prospect C yields a certain income (even when undertaken only once) and the other projects generate uncertain returns (prospect A produces very low returns in state 2). If Mr Risky is averse to risk he may prefer prospect C to either of the other two options because this guarantees him a certain income.

Attitudes to risk can be captured by use of appropriate utility functions. Three general attitudes to risk have been identified in the literature. Some people may like gambling. These are aptly labelled risk seekers. Such a person, forced to choose between Risky's three projects, would opt for prospect B because of the high promised return in state 2.

Those who dislike risk are labelled 'risk averse'. Such people would not accept a fair gamble. Such a gamble yields uncertain returns that have an expected value equal to the certain sum required to undertake the gamble. Fair gambles provide no expectation of a gain on average. Prospects A and B open to Risky would illustrate fair gambles if the investment required to undertake each of them is equal to the expected monetary value of each prospect, as we are assuming. Risk averse decision makers would accept such projects only if they were sold at a discount on this price. For such people the level of wealth received with certainty, which is deemed to be equivalent to the expected value of a risky project, will be lower than the project's expected value. The difference between the expected value of a project and the certainty equivalent of this amount is called a risk premium. Such a premium is the maximum amount of certain wealth an individual would be willing to sacrifice to avoid a given risky prospect. If Mr Risky were risk averse, the amounts of certain wealth he would be willing to pay to engage in prospects A and B will be less than 75 monetary units, the expected value of these projects.

It is generally assumed in the literature being followed that decision makers are risk averse (see Copeland and Weston, 1988, chapter 4, and Hirshleifer, 1970, chapter 8). Casual observation supports this view. Market participants are seen to diversify their asset portfolios, accepting less than a maximum expected return in order to reduce risk. Much insurance is bought in the practical world, people hedge against foreign exchange risk and, in a different context, undertake preventative maintenance. All these activities will be engaged in only by risk averse individuals. As will be explained later, the theory of uncertainty we are using here, state preference theory, itself offers a further justification for the concept of risk aversion (Hirshleifer, 1970, p. 233). This theory tends to favour the idea of diversification. It emphasises that investing in one project only will generally be more risky than diversifying. Most people would tend to accept prospect C rather than Risky's other possibilities because these other prospects involve plunging all funds on just one prospect. Accepting only project A illustrates this. Its acceptance involves the possibility of receiving a very small payoff in state 2.

Utility functions

Risk attitudes can be characterised using utility functions. A utility function provides a cardinal index of preferences for choosing between risky projects. The term 'cardinal' is used to indicate that we seek scales which do not simply order uncertain prospects. Rather, we are looking for scales which allow the relative ranking between any pair of prospects to be maintained when we switch from one ranking scale to another. The characteristic we seek is possessed by temperature scales, for example. Different amounts of heat measured on a Fahrenheit scale will not only be ordered as they would be using a centigrade scale, but the relative position of different amounts of heat will be preserved if we switch from one scale to the other. The difference between two temperatures on one scale can be converted into the units of the other temperature scale by a simple mathematical operation (a linear transformation, where x on one scale is expressed on another scale by applying, for example, either $y = b(x)$ or $y = a + b(x)$).

All this is a rather arduous way of saying that we wish different utility scales or functions to give the same ranking to prospects. This requires that the ratios of differences between any two prospects or outcomes, expressed using two different utility functions, must be constant for all such differences. This requirement means that the utility functions which can be legitimately used to describe an individual's preferences must be linear transformations of each other ('linear transformations' means we can add, subtract and multiply or divide the function by factors which do not involve power terms). Functions of this type allow us, as with choosing temperature scales, arbitrarily to assign utility numbers to two monetary amounts. Zero and the maximum monetary amount likely to be obtained are usually chosen for this purpose for convenience.

Representative utility functions for the three classes of risk attitude are shown in the three diagrams of Figure 5.1: (a) represents a utility function for a gambler, (b) represents that of a risk neutral individual and (c) shows a representative utility function for a risk averse individual. The vertical axes of the diagrams measure utility (a scale which reflects preferences). The horizontal axes measure amounts of money. The utility of a certain amount of money is found by moving from this axis to the utility function (OP) and reading off the utility from the vertical axis. Thus the utility $U(x)$ of a certain amount of money x is found by locating the point (Y) on the curve OP above x in each diagram and then reading off the point on the utility axis where a horizontal line from point Y intersects this axis.

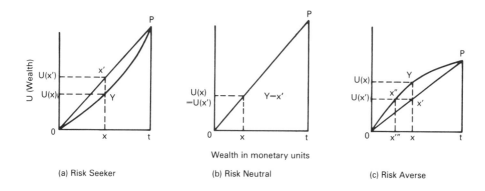

Figure 5.1 Representative utility functions

The utility of an uncertain prospect can be determined by ascertaining the utility of its expected monetary outcome. More generally, the expected value of a two-outcome gamble can be found diagrammatically by dividing that part of the horizontal axis connecting the two outcomes in a gamble at the point reflecting the probabilities of the two outcomes. Consider a prospect that gives an equal chance of receiving a sum t, where t equals twice x, as shown in Figure 5.1(a), or nothing. The expected value of this prospect is x', which is an uncertain amount equal in terms of monetary units to x. It thus plots on the line (OP) connecting the two outcomes 0 and t. This expected value can be calculated by multiplying the promised sums of t and zero by their probabilities. In our case the expected value is found halfway along the line, reflecting the equal probabilities of the two outcomes. This gives the expected value of the risky prospect as $0.5t = x'$.

Similarly, the expected utility of the outcome of a gamble is found by drawing a straight line connecting the two possible outcomes, shown by OP in each diagram, and dividing it at the point reflecting the probabilities of the two outcomes (shown by x' in the three diagrams). The expected utility of the outcome is then found by moving across to the utility axis. The utility of an expected monetary value x' equal in monetary units to x can be determined by moving up from x on the horizontal axis to OP. The utility of this amount is then found by moving vertically to the utility axis (the vertical axis). The utility of an amount having an expected value equal to x' is shown by $U(x')$ in the three diagrams of Figure 5.1.

Diagram (b) in Figure 5.1 shows that a risk neutral individual will value a certain amount equally to an expected monetary value of the same amount. In Figure 5.1(b), the utility scale of a risk neutral individual is identical to that obtained when measuring amounts in monetary units. The 45° line ensures that a given amount on the horizontal axis will plot in the same position on the vertical axis. It can be demonstrated that a risk neutral individual will value a certain sum of, say, x identically to a risky prospect yielding an expected value of x' equal in monetary units to x. Moving up from x on the horizontal axis of Figure 5.1(b) to the utility curve for a risk neutral individual and moving across to the utility axis shows that both amounts x and x' have the same utility $U(x) = U(x')$.

A risk seeking individual (a gambler) would give the uncertain prospect a utility substantially greater than 50 per cent of the utility of t. $U(x')$ is found to be greater than $U(x)$ in Figure 5.1(a). A risk averse individual accords the certain sum of x a greater utility value than the risky expectation of one-half the utility of the sum t. Figure 5.1(c) that $U(x)$ is greater than $U(x')$. This latter finding illustrates that for risk averse individuals the utility ascribed to monetary sums increases as the amounts involved increase ($U(t) > U(x)$ in Figure 5.1(c)), but at a decreasing rate.[3] This means that the marginal utility yielded by additional amounts of money decreases with wealth. Utility functions for risk averse individuals, therefore, slope upwards but are saucer-shaped from below (concave), reflecting the decreasing utility yielded by extra wealth. Similarly, the utility curves of a risk seeking individual slope upwards, but are convex (see Figure 5.1(a)) because each extra unit of wealth is regarded as more valuable than the previous units as extra units of wealth are accumulated.

To summarise, a risk averse individual will always prefer a certain amount equal to the expected monetary value of an uncertain prospect, rather than the expected monetary value of that prospect (that is, the utility of a certain sum equal to a prospect's expected monetary value will be greater than the utility ascribed to this expected monetary value). Similarly, a risk seeker will assign a higher utility to the expected value of an uncertain project than to the same amount received with certainty.

Above, a seemingly reasonable assumption was made that, for risk averse individuals, risk aversion decreased as an individual's wealth endowment increased. Such an attitude is called decreasing absolute risk aversion and can be informally associated with curvature of the utility function. Absolute risk aversion is what we have in mind when we talk of risk aversion without qualification. It can be shown that for small movements along a utility function, if these are generated by accepting prospects which involve fair gambles, absolute risk aversion is measured by minus the proportionate change in marginal utility with respect to wealth, with a definite amount of wealth in mind in order to give concrete dimensions to the measure that is, by $-U''(W)/U'(W)$, where U' represents the marginal utility of wealth and U'' is the second derivative of utility with respect to wealth; this second derivative indicates how the marginal utility of wealth changes with increased wealth).[4]

The expected utility of a decision

The certain amount of money or wealth having a utility equal to the expected utility of an uncertain amount is called the certainty equivalent wealth of the uncertain amount. This equivalent amount can be easily determined using graphs of the types shown in Figure 5.1 in the same way as they were used above. In this way, the equivalent certain amount can be found by going from the point on the straight line, OP, directly above the uncertain amount in mind to the utility curve and dropping a line down to the horizontal axis. The intercept of this line with the wealth axis yields the certain amount of money or the certain equivalent wealth having the same utility as the expected utility of the uncertain amount. This process is shown in Figure 5.1(c). Here x'' shows the expected utility accorded to the uncertain result of our gamble. The point on the horizontal axis directly below this point shows the amount of money received with certainty (x''') having the same utility as the uncertain amount x. It is less in monetary terms than the monetary value of the uncertain prospect because we are dealing with a risk averse decision maker. We can thus say that the difference between an uncertain monetary amount and the smaller certain amount of money or wealth which is its equivalent in money terms, measures the risk premium that a risk averse decision maker would be willing to pay to avoid the gamble. For the specific individual whose preferences are traced in Figure 5.1(c), this risk premium amounts to the difference between x and x'''.

To determine the utility of an uncertain prospect, we have to calculate the expected utility of that prospect. The ranking of the prospect, relative to other opportunities, depends on the utility function being used and on the probabilities associated with the outcomes. These probabilities even entered into our calculations when we determined the expected monetary value of a project. This means that if we are seeking to aid a decision maker we need to respect both individual tastes and probability beliefs. With certainty, the existence of a well functioning market allowed us to ignore individual tastes. The equivalent finding under uncertainty (to be presented later) allows us to ignore both tastes, including preferences concerning risk, and individual probability beliefs.

The expected utility decision rule provides a valuation (preference ranking) of uncertain events using a cardinal utility function and a set of probability beliefs. This decision rule says 'Choose that act which maximises expected utility', where the term 'expected' signifies that we determine the utility of a project by weighting the utility of each possible outcome by the probability of the state associated with this outcome and adding over all possible states. Using the state preference approach this decision rule can be written using the symbols already introduced in this chapter, as

$$E(U \mid a^* = \underset{a \in A}{\mathrm{Max}} \sum_{S_i} U(a_i, s_i)\phi_i \qquad \qquad [5.\mathrm{III}]$$

where A represents the set of mutually exclusive acts and $a \in A$ means that action a is contained in the total possible set of acts. The vertical line on the left indicates that expected utility is conditional on choosing the optimal act (a^*). This expression says that the expected utility ($E(U)$), conditional on choosing the optimal act (a^*), can be found by selecting that act (a_i) out of the set of mutually exclusive acts (A) available to the decision maker which maximises the expected utility yielded by the state–action combinations which involve this act. Here we suppress the payoff function by assuming that the payoffs in the state–action matrix are expressed directly in amounts or expected utility.

As is usual in economics, it is not being suggested that the decision makers explicitly make decisions in this way. Rather it is being asserted that we will obtain good predictions of the outcomes of decision making under uncertainty if we assume that decision makers act as if they used these procedures in decision making. Apart from the casual, but important, observations that the expected utility approach does allow us to explain many real world phenomena related to uncertainty and enables us to rationalise much of the behaviour aimed at coping with uncertainty observed in the practical world, empirical evidence bearing on this assertion is sparse (but see Grayson, 1960; Friend and Blume, 1975).

Before we can see what all this means for Mr Risky, we need to select a function to measure his utility. Ideally, the procedure for this is to invite the decision maker to quantify preferences by ascertaining choices between various gambles of the character of Mr Risky's prospects. This procedure is explained in detail in any of the references given earlier in this chapter (see Note 1), but we can start to measure preferences by asking the decision maker whether a gamble involving as one of two outcomes a monetary amount to which we have already arbitrarily assigned a utility, is preferred to a different certain amount to which we have also assigned an arbitrary utility (remember we are free to choose two points on a utility scale). Adjusting the gamble until the decision maker is indifferent between the hazard and the certain amount yields the utility of the gamble expressed on our chosen utility scale. We can deduce the utility of the other element involved in the gamble because we know the utility of two of the items involved in this calculation (that of the certain amount and of one item making up the gamble). We can then repeat the exercise by offering gambles and certain amounts which can now involve the monetary amount, the utility of which we have just determined. This process will yield the utility assigned to additional monetary items. Exhaustive use of this procedure will ideally allow us to determine the decision maker's entire utility function.

This procedure illustrates the principle that discovered utility functions are personal to the decision maker involved and are merely ways of representing the decision maker's observed preferences on one of a number of possible scales. Therefore, they cannot be aggregated across individuals. That moving from amount x to amount y moves two individuals up their respective utility functions merely means that both have experienced an increase in utility. We can say neither by how much either individual's satisfaction has increased nor which individual's utility has increased the most.

The above procedure for determining utility functions has both obvious and less obvious defects (see Simon, 1959). One clear worry is whether the individual will react as portrayed by a discovered utility function when confronted with actual risky choices. Utility functions could be derived by seeking to determine the utility function that seemed to be implied by past decisions (see Grayson, 1960), but preferences may have since changed.

Workers in the area of decision making under uncertainty, in the face of these and other difficulties, generally choose a seemingly realistic mathematical formulation of a utility function and use this in their studies. Two popular functions are the quadratic and the power functions. A quadratic function can be written as:

$$U = aW - bW^2$$

where W is wealth and the utility function $U(\cdot)$ is constrained to that segment of the function where $W \le a/2b$. Other segments of the function imply utility that decreases with wealth (Markowitz, 1952). An example of the power function can be written as $U = \sqrt{W}$, where W represents wealth; that is, utility is measured by the square root of wealth.

The utility functions generally used in the literature for portraying individual risk attitudes belong to that class which displays a characteristic which is called linear risk tolerance. Risk aversion relates to the individual's attitude to risk as wealth changes. Risk tolerance is the mirror image of this and measures the ability to tolerate risk as wealth changes. Not surprisingly, it is measured by the reciprocal of the risk aversion measure. (That is,

$$RT = \frac{1}{ARA}$$

$$= -\frac{U'(W)}{U''(W)}$$

where RT is a measure of risk tolerance and ARA is the usual measure of absolute risk aversion, which was defined earlier as $-U''(W)/U'(W)$.) Linear risk tolerance expresses a person's attitude to risk as a linear function of wealth, generally comprising a constant plus a stable proportionate factor of wealth. This stable factor measures the way the slope of the utility curve changes with wealth. Its stability ensures that these changes are smooth and the utility function does not change in abrupt ways as wealth alters. This factor is usually referred to as the individual's degree of cautiousness. An individual who is decreasingly risk averse with increased wealth will have a cautiousness greater than zero. Risk tolerance increases when the stable factor is greater than zero because a proportionate amount of increased wealth is added to the risk tolerance measure as wealth increases. Increasing risk tolerance (as with the power utility function with a positive stable factor) therefore implies decreasing risk aversion because this is defined as the reciprocal of risk tolerance. Cautiousness will equal zero for those who show constant risk aversion (RT will equal the constant in this case, which is portrayed by the negative exponential utility function) and be negative for persons displaying increasing risk aversion.

Mr Risky's decision employing expected utility

Table 5.4 below illustrates how Risky would rank his three prospects using utility functions drawn from each of the two classes of utility function introduced above, the quadratic and power utility functions. All we are doing is seeking to represent Mr Risky's preferences using mathematical functions which are assumed to mirror his preferences.

Table 5.4 The utility of Risky's projects

Action	State 1			State 2			Expected utility
		Utility function 1	Utility function 2		Utility function 1	Utility function 2	
	(1)	(2)	(3)	(4)	(5)	(6)	(7)	(8)
A (a_1)	$(a_1, s_1) = 95$	77	10.0	$(a_1, s_2) = 15$	15	4	62	8.5
B (a_2)	$(a_2, s_1) = 50$	45	7.0	$(a_2, s_2) = 150$	105	12	60	8.25
C (a_3)	$(a_3, s_1) = 75$	64	8.6	$(a_3, s_2) = 75$	64	8.6	64	8.6

The figures in the columns labelled utility functions 1 and 2 (columns 2, 3, 5 and 6) are obtained by plugging the monetary outcomes shown in columns 1 and 4 into the two utility functions. The columns labelled utility function 1 (columns 2 and 5) show the utility of each outcome evaluated using a utility function of the form $W - 0.002W^2$ (a quadratic function). The columns labelled utility function 2 (columns 3 and 6) show the same calculations employing a utility function of the form $\sqrt{W}$, a power function.

Each of the two columns labelled expected utility in the figure (columns 7 and 8) show the result of multiplying each outcome expressed using one of our two utility functions by the relevant probability and adding across states. Each row of column 7 shows the expected utility of taking one of the three actions computed using utility function 1. Similarly, each row of column 8 indicates the expected utility of each action evaluated using utility function 2.

Generally, different mathematical formulations of utility functions which are not linear transformations of each other may rank projects differently. However, with Mr Risky's problem, although the expected utilities assigned to the three prospects by the two utility functions are very different in numerical terms, they do rank the projects in the same way. Assuming they correctly reflect Mr Risky's preferences for this bundle of projects, we can see that Mr Risky's optimal conduct would be to invest only in project C if all three options were available in the market at prices equal to their expected monetary values. (This illustrates the general proposition for a risk averse individual, which will be discussed below, that if contingent incomes can be purchased at prices proportional to the probabilities which the decision maker assigns to state occurrences, the optimal decision will always involve buying a certain outcome (in our case project C; see Hirshleifer, 1970, pp. 232–235)).

Characteristics of the expected utility rule

The expected utility rule, used with utility functions of the type we have been describing, can be shown to reflect preferences for risky outcomes providing that certain postulates of rational choice apply. The utility of any outcome can be shown to be simply the probability that has to be attached to the best outcome in a lottery involving only the best and worst outcomes available to the decision maker to render the decision maker indifferent between this lottery and the outcome in mind received with certainty. The utilities attached to outcomes are nothing more than probabilities reflecting individual preferences. Utility functions are thus probability scalings reflecting preferences between outcomes.[5] It is, therefore, possible to manipulate these utilities as if they were probabilities without destroying the preference ranking attached to individual outcomes. The usual mathematical operations of addition, subtraction, multiplication and division can be applied to utilities.

This is all the expected utility rule does. (For an original presentation of this argument, see Schlaifer, 1959, chapter 2.) It weighs the utilities of outcomes (probabilities reflecting individual preferences) by the likelihood of the states of the environment under which these outcomes can occur. Finally, it aggregates these weighted preferences across all states (see Expression 5.III). The expected utility attached to complex proposals involving several possible outcomes is thus a weighted sum of those probabilities which reflect the preference rankings of each individual outcome. Thus, if the individual acts in accordance with this rule, individual preferences will be respected and individual welfare maximised.

The strength of the expected utility rule is that it reduces complex issues to their essential elements. With some simple, but compelling, assumptions, the utilities attached to outcomes and the probabilities of their occurrence capture all that needs to be known to ensure optimal decisions under risk. This is true even for one-off situations. The utility function encapsulates preferences in such situations and with the probabilities attached to states indicates all we believe about the events involved. By using the expected utility rule we are, therefore, doing the best we can unless we could obtain more information.

The expected utility rule is overwhelmingly accepted in the literature because the postulates necessary for its application are difficult not to accept (see Luce and Raiffa, 1957, chapter 2). The first postulate requires the usual behaviour for rational decision making, that is the individual in mind has complete and transitive preferences. Transitive merely means that if A is preferred to B and B to C then A must also be preferred to C in pairwise comparisons. The second postulate states that all uncertain outcomes can be ranked in a transitive way such that the larger of the two in any pairwise comparison is preferred, irrespective of the states of the environment which yield those outcomes (see Luce and Raiffa, 1957, chapter 2 for more detailed set of postulates). Thus, there are no preferences for the occurrence of specific states themselves as distinct from the outcomes they produce; results are desired only for themselves (Hirshleifer and Riley, 1979, pp. 1387–1389).

Decision making under uncertainty

One way of illustrating Mr Risky's decision problem diagrammatically is shown in Figure 5.2. This section uses our Risky example to illustrate optimal decision making under uncertainty. It is a little complex and may be left out by those who wish to

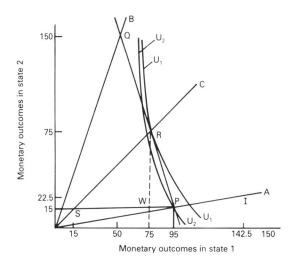

Figure 5.2 Optimal behaviour under uncertainty

obtain only an overview of the impact of uncertainty on accounting theory. Comprehension of this optimum and its consequences for decision making will help substantially in understanding some of the remaining chapters of this book. The literature of information economics and finance, the impacts of which on accounting theory are examined in the next few chapters, use this knowledge, at least implicitly.

Here the decision maker is seen as choosing between the only three equity securities (common-stock) available in a two-state world. Outcomes in state 1 (x_1) are plotted on the horizontal axis and those in state 2 (x_2) are shown on the vertical axis. The individual's original uncertain endowment is shown by point P, which represents Mr Risky's original holding of one unit of security A. This yields 95 monetary units in state 1 and 15 units in state 2. Holding additional units of this security would move the decision maker to the right and upward along the line OA (holding 1.5 units of the security would, for example, place the individual at point I with 142.5 monetary units in state 1 and 22.5 units in state 2). Initially the decision problem is assumed to be whether to change the security holding to one of the other two securities available.

The returns from holding increasing amounts of the second security (security B) are shown along the line OB. The line OC coincides with what is called the certainty line because security C offers equal returns in both states. A given holding of security C will yield a certain income, irrespective of the state of the environment which actually appears. The ray representing the certainty line has an angle of 45° from the origin, which ensures that it connects equal amounts of income in both states. Points S and R along this line represent a certain income of 15 and 75 monetary units, respectively.

Curves like U_1 are indifference curves, each of which connect bundles of the two state-contingent incomes or, more generally, commodities which yield an individual the same utility. There is an infinite number of curves like U_1 and U_2, each of which connect those combinations of outcomes in the two states which yield the same utility to the decision maker, given the probabilities of state occurrence. Each indifference curve represents a contour of the decision-maker's utility function, assuming fixed probabilities of occurrence for the two states. These curves are obtained by plotting all combinations of utilities of outcomes which satisfy the following equation.

$$\bar{U} = \phi_1 \, U(x_1) + (1 - \phi_1) \, U(x_2) \qquad\qquad [5.IV]$$

where $\bar{U}$ is a constant level of utility and ϕ_1 is fixed at some level. In our Mr Risky example, the probability of state 1 occurring is 0.75 and that of state two is, therefore, $0.25\,(= 1 - 0.75)$. The slope of an indifference curve will differ over its length, indicating that the utility lost by a given reduction in the outcome in a specific state will differ depending on how much of this state's income or wealth we already possess. The inverted saucer shape of such indifference curves follows from our assumptions about utility curves (see Hirshleifer, 1970, p. 233). Informally, this shape is necessary to ensure that we can model the desire to diversify which we observe in the world. The shape (convex) of the indifference curves means that, if possible, the individual will diversify so as to achieve outcomes in both states. This is shown in Figure 5.2. Holding either of the portfolios represented by points P and Q, which represent Mr Risky's opportunities if he held one unit of security A and B respectively, promises the same expected monetary value as the third security. However, they yield less utility than point R on the certainty line, which represents holding one unit of security C. Holding this security represents diversification between the two other securities and yields a certain income in both states.

Security C yields the income that would be obtained if Mr Risky was able to diversify his investments in the other two securities and hold approximately 55.5 per cent of his portfolio in prospect A and the remainder in prospect B.

The slope of an indifference curve at any point is given by calculating the loss of utility from reducing the outcome in state 1 weighted by its probability and dividing this amount by the contribution to expected utility of the extra amount of state 2 outcome needed to just compensate for the lost utility in state 2. This is the amount which just keeps the individual on the initial indifference curve. This clumsy verbal expression for the slope of an indifference curve can be written succinctly using symbols, as

$$\text{Slope} = - \phi_1 U'(x_i)/\phi_2 U'(x_2) \qquad\qquad [5.V]$$

where ϕ_1 represents the probability of state i and $U'(x_i)$ represents the marginal utility of the outcome in each state i. Where an indifference curve cuts the certainty line, the marginal utilities attached to the outcomes in the two states are equal. The marginal utilities at any point on the certainty line are the same. The slope of the curve at this point, therefore, reflects only the probabilities of the two states. (Here the slope of the indifference curve is given by $-\phi_1/\phi_2$.)

Optimality conditions for the individual

It is fairly clear from our diagram that the optimal security portfolio for our decision maker is to hold only security C, even if we relax the assumption that only one of the securities can be held. Dropping this assumption allows the decision maker to form portfolios comprising different proportions of the three securities. Such portfolios plot along the line PQ. Moving towards Q means that more of security B is added to the portfolio by purchase at its market price at the cost of less of security A, which is sold at its market price to fund the purchase of the other security. By moving to point R, which represents holding only security C, the individual will be exchanging state-contingent incomes at a rate determined by the slope of the line PQ. From the figure we can see that the decision maker is willing to sacrifice WP income in state 1 for extra income of WR in state 2. This indicates that our decision maker is risk averse and would be willing to pay a fair insurance premium of WP in order to avoid holding the outcomes promised by security A. Moving up the PQ line to the certainty line, therefore, increases his welfare. Mr Risky can act in this way because his opportunities represent fair gambles. We have assumed that these opportunities are priced at their expected values by the market. The slope of the PQ line is equal to minus the market price of a unit of income in state 1 over that of a unit in state 2, i.e. the slope of PQ equals $-P_1/P_2$.

With this view of prices, the line PQ can be thought of as a budget line showing feasible transactions at a rate of exchange represented by the market price of income in state 1 over that of a unit of state 2 income. This, in our case, equals the ratio of probabilities of the two states. This must be the case because this line is tangential to an indifference curve on the certainty line. The slope of this line is, therefore, the same as that of the indifference curve at this point (R). Here the marginal utility of an extra unit of money in state 1 must be the same as that for an extra unit of state 2 income and, therefore, the slope of the indifference curve must be ϕ_1/ϕ_2 (as the marginal utilities in Expression 5.V cancel out). We have now demonstrated that the optimal solution for our decision maker is to move to point R. This confirms our earlier advice to Mr Risky to invest in the certain security and indicates that any risk averse individual will, at fair prices, move to a certain position. This assumes that the market prices for the securities coincide with the probabilities attached to the two states by our decision maker.[6]

Our optimality condition requires that the decision maker will optimise by reallocating security holdings until the ratio of market prices for state income, P_1/P_2, is equal to the slope of the relevant indifference curve, which reflects the rate at which the individual would be willing to substitute one state income for the other. This ratio is formally called the marginal rate of substitution between state contingent incomes, which is a technical term for the slope of an indifference curve. It can, therefore, be represented by our earlier equation for this slope, Expression 5.V. The above optimality condition can, therefore, be written formally as:

$$-P_1/P_2 = -(\phi_1/\phi_2)(U'(x_1)/U'(x_2)) \tag{5.VI}$$

The first element indicates the rate of exchange between state incomes on the market as expressed by the ratio of their prices. The term on the right similarly represents the rate of exchange between state incomes as reflected by the decision maker's preferences. Gains in terms of extra utility can be made by revising security holdings if these two ratios are not equal. Expression 5.VI becomes equivalent to our verbal expression for an optimum on the certainty line if the market prices of state incomes are based on the same probabilities for the states as are entertained by our decision maker. This is because the marginal utilities of the state incomes must be the same on the certainty line and thus cancel out in Expression 5.VI. This yields an optimum on the certainty line of:

$$-P_1/P_2 = -\phi_1/\phi_2 \hspace{4cm} \text{[5.VII]}$$

This is equivalent to our earlier verbal statement of this condition.

In a perfectly competitive market where all individuals are price takers, the allocation of investment by each individual must satisfy our optimality condition. More generally, in equilibrium in such a market the marginal rates of substitution between every pair of state incomes must be equal for all individuals. All the benefits from trade must, therefore, be achieved in such a market when it has reached equilibrium. Further trade cannot improve the welfare of any one individual without making some other individual worse off. Any further change in portfolios undertaken at the going prices for any pair of state incomes will cause the marginal rates of substitution between these state incomes to be no longer equal to the ratio of prices between the two states. The additional utility obtained by an individual from further trade after equilibrium is reached will be lower than implied by the ratios of the market prices between any pair of securities. Additional trade would, therefore, mean that the individual was paying more for some state income than would be justified by his or her preferences. For an alternative treatment of these matters, see Hirshleifer (1970, chapter 9), and for a more succinct treatment see Copeland and Weston (1988, chapter 5).

The above analysis implies that, in a perfect and complete market, enterprises face no risk because they can issue securities which protect them from all eventualities. All risks will be accepted by security holders at the going market prices for the contingent incomes offered by securities. Enterprises can, therefore, treat projects as if they involve no risk for the enterprise. This means that enterprises need not concern themselves with the risk attitudes of security holders. All they need to do is announce the state-contingent income accruing from any new project and let security holders buy these incomes at the going market prices.

These prices are generated by the market and, by equating demand and supply for the contingent incomes in different states, will ensure that all securities or portfolios which yield the same payoff in terms of state-contingent incomes must be priced identically. All arbitrage possibilities concerning securities which offer the same payoffs will have been exploited prior to reaching this equilibrium. The prices of all complex securities can be deduced from the prices of the set of primitive securities, each of which yields one unit of income in only one state, that are required to give the same payoffs. No arbitrage opportunities can exist if this is the case.

The above conditions are those required for full Pareto efficiency as explained in Chapter 2. In the simple setting considered here, all that is required to reach a full Pareto solution in a one-period uncertain setting is that the marginal rate of substitution between every pair of state incomes must be the same for all individuals and must be equal to the ratio of the prices of the state incomes. More generally, in a two-period economy, the marginal rate of substitution between certain current consumption and uncertain consumption in each and every state must be equal for all individuals and must also be equal to the ratio of the prices of current consumption and of consumption in the uncertain state with which current consumption is being compared. This condition must apply relative to all states and current consumption. Similarly, production possibilities can be added to our problem. Such production adds additional conditions for full Pareto efficiency, which should be familiar from Chapter 2. The first of these additional conditions is that the marginal rate of transformation in production for output in each pair of states must be equal for all firms. It must also be equal to the marginal rate of substitution in consumption for each pair of states. Finally, the marginal cost of output in a state, which will be common to all firms (see Chapter 2), must be equal to the marginal rate of substitution in consumption between each state and current consumption. The reason we are concerned with Pareto efficiency is that any findings derived in such settings for accounting information will be fully consistent with maximising overall economic efficiency.

Uncertainty and accounting

The optimality conditions for individuals, demonstrated above, mean that in the setting considered here the market prices of state incomes will provide a unanimous ranking of prospects. Enterprises will be maximising the expected utilities of all their security holders if they accept all productive projects which have a positive value when the net state-contingent incomes they generate are evaluated using the market prices for such incomes. In order to finance such projects, the enterprise merely issues securities with the same state-contingent incomes as the projects in mind. That is, the enterprise announces its plans to the market.

Income and wealth under uncertainty

The state-contingent incomes promised by such plans and the associated securities will be valued using the going market prices for the incomes promised by enterprise management. Incomes evaluated in this way provide a unanimous ranking of prospects available on the market in exactly the same way as did using market prices in a setting of certainty (see Beaver and Demski, 1979, Bromwich and Wells, 1983). These findings allow us to define wealth, or endowments under uncertainty for a one-period setting.

In these conditions the wealth of any individual (j), who is assumed to hold only securities, is:

$$W_j = \sum_z J_z/N_z \sum_i (P_i q_{iz})$$
[5.VIII]

where W_j is the wealth of the individual in mind, q_{iz} is the net income promised in state i, net of any associated outgoings in this state, from all the securities of enterprise z, and p_i is the market price for a unit of income in state i. The quantity in brackets on the right-hand side of Expression 5.VIII is the income in state i promised by holding all the securities in enterprise z. Summing the bracketed expression over all states yields the total income offered by holding all the issued shares (stock) of enterprise z. N_z is the total number of securities issued by the enterprise z, and J_z represents the number of z's securities held by our individual. So far, we have determined the value of state-contingent incomes the individual derives from security z. The first summation sign indicates that total individual wealth is found by summing the individual's wealth derived from all securities held (some holdings may be negative where short selling is allowed).

In the setting here, *ex ante* income for the individual in mind is merely the difference between expected wealth at the beginning (W_0) and end of the trading cycle (W_k) (which is assumed here to be instantaneous in order to avoid the complications of discounting). Here the wealth amounts at the beginning and at the end of the trading cycle are defined according to Expression 5.VIII. *Ex ante* income for individual p for the ith trading cycle can, therefore, be written as.

$$Y_{pi} = W_k - W_0 \qquad\qquad\qquad [5.\text{IX}]$$

where the first term on the right is closing wealth and the second term on the right is opening wealth. *Ex ante* income is thus the expected increment in wealth from trading. Wealth at the end of the trading cycle therefore differs from opening wealth only by this increment.

Thus wealth and income measures are again found to be different ways of expressing the same basic information, as they were in a certain setting (see Chapter 2). These measures provide a unanimous ranking of prospects useful to all individuals irrespective of their preferences and probability assessments. Uncertainty of the type considered here does not inhibit the derivation of accounting measures which are universally useful to all market participants concerned with decision making. Individuals can again be left to deal with their own preferences, now including any differing probability assessments, by trading on the market. As explained above, those who do not like their existing security portfolio can trade on the market until their holding is optimised relative to their preferences and to their views as to the likelihood of the states. This was illustrated in Figure 5.2 where the individual facing the uncertain prospect represented by P trades in the market (moves up PQ) until a certain income is guaranteed. This illustrates that in a perfect and complete economy-wide market under uncertainty, the individual can, if so desired, obtain protection from any uncertainty that is not economy-wide and which, therefore, does not affect all prospects. Economy-wide uncertainty cannot be diversified away by trading, unless the individual has access to complete and perfect world markets). Even here world-wide risk cannot be diversified away (Copeland and Weston, 1988, chapter 6).

Accounting information with multi-periods

So far we have demonstrated our conclusions in a model with one trading cycle. These results easily extend to a multi-period model under uncertainty under the assumptions entertained. However, to do this it is necessary to make a little more explicit the role of information in decision making. In our single-period model we implicitly assumed that any common information system merely formed part of the experiential base of all decision makers. As we shall see shortly, introducing multi-periods allows us to make it explicit that information will constrain individual decision making and condition any market equilibrium attained.

In a multi-period economy, an information system, again assumed to be available to all in the market, will be expected to yield one of a set of known signals at, say, the end of each period. One reasonable assumption is that the signals expected be received as we pass from earlier to later periods will yield more details as to the outcomes of the prospects about which information accrues over time. This assumption formalises the idea that we may learn over time.

To illustrate the role of information in a multi-period model, first recall that the only uncertainty in our models is which state of nature will appear. Now let us assume that in a multi-period economy the same state of nature appears in all periods but exactly which state will be realised is unknown in intermediate periods. In this setting, an information system may yield more precise information over time as to state occurrence in a way such that we know at the beginning of the process which signals are possible in each intermediate period. Thus, with this approach, we know at the beginning of the process what signals will be available in each period and how much richer the information available will become over time, though in intermediate periods we have only limited knowledge as to which state has appeared, because the specific signal to be received in each period does not fully distinguish between states.

Table 5.5 An information system giving differential signals over time

Possible signals	Time		
	t_0	t_1	t_2
y_0	$y_0 = \{s_1 \text{ to } s_5\}$		
y_1		$y_{1a} = \{s_1, s_2, s_3\}$ or $y_{1b} = \{s_4, s_5\}$	
y_2			$y_{2a} = \{s_1\}$ or $y_{2a} = \{s_2\}$ or $y_{2a} = \{s_3\}$ $y_{2b} = \{s_4\}$ or $y_{2b} = \{s_5\}$

An example is shown in Table 5.5, where the possible information signals for a two-period economy are shown. The same state is realised in the two periods. The timing of the signals is shown at the top of the columns: t_0 is the initial date of the two-period economy and t_1 and t_2 represent the end of periods 1 and 2, respectively. We know what signals may appear at each time and these are shown in the figure. Signal y_0 in the first column says that at this time, we know only that there are five possible states represented by s_1 to s_5. The signal received at the end of the first period, y_{1a} or y_{1b}, indicates that the realised state will be found to be one of s_1, s_2, s_3 if signal y_{1a} appears or either s_4 or s_5 if signal y_{1b} appears. That is, at time 1 (t_1) we learn that the actual state is either one of three of the possible states (s_1, s_2, s_3), or that it will be either s_4 or s_5. Finally, at time 2 (t_2) the actual state that reigns out of the two sets of states that may be signalled at time 1 will be indicated. The final column of the table says that signal y_{2a} will indicate which of the three states signalled at time 1 is the realised state if signal y_{1a} was received at t_1. Similarly, the other signal y_{2b} or y_{2b} in the third column indicates which of the two states s_4 or s_5 signalled by receiving signal y_{1b} at time 1 is the realised state.

With information systems of this type in a perfect and complete market all desired trades can be made at the beginning of the period, provided that the information system being used is available to all. This is because in such markets the individual will be able to buy at time 0 (t_0) claims to consumption at time 0 and at each other time contingent upon what state will be realised at that time. The existence of such claims allows the individual to maximise utility because these claims permit trading across all combinations of time periods, states and commodities. By maximising subject to the prices of time–state-contingent claims at time 0, the individual maximises expected utility, given endowed wealth and the information system. As we would expect from our earlier analysis, in equilibrium the marginal rate of substitution between a given time–state claim and consumption at time 0 would equal the ratio of the prices of these claims for all individuals (That is, $\phi_{st} U'(x_{st})/U'(x_0) = P_{st}/P_0$, where s and t index the state and time, respectively and s and t take the values of, say, 1 to S and 1 to T, again respectively). It should be noted that time 0 consumption is not weighted by a probability as it is a certain sum and that the prices are those reigning at time 0).

In this setting, it makes no difference whether there are markets that open for trading at times 1 and 2. It can be shown that the original holdings at time 0 would be retained even in the face of markets that open in later periods. This is because the prices that would reign in these markets with a rational market would bear a specific relationship to their counterpart time 0 prices. Thus, the prices that would reign if markets were opened at times 1 and 2 could be fully anticipated at time 0. Thus, no new opportunities for the individual would be provided by opening new markets at times 1 and 2 (Krouse 1986, pp. 77–99). Later we will deal with the problems raised by new information becoming available over time and the absence of a full set of time–state-contingent claims.

The above analysis helps to clarify the role of information in our models. For the individual, information constrains what can be achieved by trading. In the market, a publicly available information system similarly conditions the equilibrium that can be obtained. Demand and supply are set equal using the available information system. Any equilibrium obtained is thus conditional on the information system being used. A different solution for a given economy may emerge when an alternative information system is used. This dependence of market equilibrium on the information system being used makes it difficult to analyse the effects of different information on decision makers without undertaking a full analysis of the market effects of the information.

Using the prices for time–state contingent claims derived above, we can construct wealth and income measures of the type that we obtained for the situation where trading was allowed in only one trading cycle. This is not really very surprising as, with our assumptions, the decision maker can maximise at the beginning of the exercise. Our assumptions of perfect and complete markets and full access to an information system at the beginning of the sequence of periods really mean that the multi-period problem being reviewed does not differ fundamentally from a single-period model. Thus, the income and wealth measures derived for a multi-period setting will have exactly the same characteristics in a full and complete multi-period market as they did under uncertainty in a single period. They are value-free, represent measurements and are either automatically available or can be costlessly constructed. Again, therefore, there is no role for accountants in providing these measures.

For the same reasons as in a certain setting, such accounting measures may no longer exist where there are market difficulties. Poorly organised markets inhibit the free trade which is necessary for the existence of such accounting measures. Incorporating uncertainty into our conclusions does not change this view. Items of accounting information, which do not possess these characteristics, may now be found useful for the information they convey. Thus Beaver and Demski (1979) suggest that where management have superior information in this setting, conveying this information to the market may improve welfare (see Chapter 2).

The next section considers in a little more detail the view expressed in Chapter 2 that the presence of uncertainty is likely to cause additional market difficulties which are not encountered in a certain world.

Uncertainty and market difficulties

The above analysis assumed that markets were complete and perfect. For markets to be complete under uncertainty, it can be shown that there must be as many separate securities as there are states of the environment. 'Separate' here has a special meaning. A security can be said to be separate in this special sense if the state-contingent incomes (the payoffs) it generates cannot be completely replicated by holding either some other security or some portfolio of other securities. A separate security, therefore, offers opportunities not available from other securities. (More formally, such a security is described as linearly independent.) This means its return in each state cannot be achieved by forming a portfolio comprising proportions of some other securities to give the same income as the original security in each state.

Our Mr Risky example can provide a crude illustration of this phenomenon under a number of assumptions, including that negative holdings are not allowed. With this assumption, securities A and B are separate. You cannot obtain exactly the state-contingent incomes offered by either of these securities by holding only either one of the other two securities or any mixture of these other two securities. Security C is not separate in this sense. The returns offered by point R in Figure 5.2 can be replicated by holding a portfolio of approximately 55 per cent of security A and 45 per cent of security B. The returns from security C are, therefore, said to be 'spanned' by the returns of these other two securities. Inspection of Figure 5.2 shows that all the returns contained between the rays OA and OB can be achieved by holding some combination of these two securities. It can be demonstrated that, with uncertainty, a market will be complete providing that the number of separate securities is equal to the number of possible states of the world (see Arrow, 1964; Debreu, 1959, chapter 7).

The meaning of 'spanning', in terms of the payoffs of a security spanning payoffs already offered in the market, is most easily seen by looking at two payoff matrices, one of which merely duplicates some of the consecutive columns of the other larger, payoff matrix. The smaller matrix comprises the possible payoffs of a number of consecutive states contained in the other matrix. The smaller matrix can be said to span, duplicate or contain the payoffs of part of the larger payoff matrix. The small matrix is thus of a lesser span than the large matrix. The larger matrix can be said to span a larger payoff space than the smaller one and can be said to contain the smaller matrix. Above, spanning was used in the sense of duplicating payoffs already offered by existing securities.

In our example, assuming that no one wishes to trade outside the area formed by the rays OA and OB, the two separate securities A and B in our two-state world allow all relevant feasible trades for optimal conduct to be consummated. Any point within the rays OA and OB can be achieved by holding a portfolio made up of some proportion of the two securities. The two securities span the relevant income state space. Markets which cannot be spanned using the available set of securities are not complete. Not all desired trades can be consummated. Figure 5.2 illustrates such a market if we consider all possible trades. The security portfolios in the area between the vertical axis and the ray OB and in the area between the horizontal axis and the ray OA are not available for trade by market participants. This inability to trade may, therefore, affect welfare if otherwise optimal conduct requires individuals to have security holdings in these areas. Issuing two primitive or basic securities, units of each of which offer a return of one monetary unit in each state, would allow all possible trades in our example to be completed. Such securities are called Arrow-Debreu securities. Relaxing constraints on trade in this way cannot, at least, make individuals worse off. This is because it expands the span or payoffs offered by the market (though this may require that some individuals are protected from the possible redistributive consequences of enriching the market by changing their original endowments).

In the real world it is clear that a set of separate securities, one for each of the total possible states of the world, will generally not exist, and the ability to maximise individual welfare will be inhibited. Thus, complete markets of this simple kind are unlikely to be encountered in the real world. More generally, market incompleteness is evidenced by the impossibility of insuring against all possible events, the lack of future markets which allow us to contract and obtain deliveries in future states for all states at an agreed price, and the inability to sell such assets as goodwill and R & D activities separately from other assets in real world markets.

The simple and abstract model we have been using in this chapter constrains trade to the area bounded by OA and OB. It therefore provides an example of an incomplete market; however, it does capture the essence of real world stock exchanges. It can be shown that such markets in securities are not complete but, with some special assumptions, do allow allocations of securities which maximise individual welfare, given the constraints on the trading opportunities available. In terms of our diagram, real world security markets allow optimal trades within the area bounded by the two rays OA and OB.

Such settings are said to obtain constrained Pareto efficiency. They do the best they can with respect to the incomplete market setting. With regard to security problems of the type encountered by Mr Risky, a constrained Pareto solution would ensure that all trades in securities which improved the lot of one person without harming anyone else would be achieved. It would ensure that the marginal conditions are satisfied across securities and are equal for all individuals, whereas full Pareto efficiency satisfies these conditions across consumption in all states. Generally, we would expect that a full Pareto-efficient solution would be economically preferable to the constrained Pareto solution that would emerge where the market setting entertained is constrained in some way. That a market is incomplete does not mean that a full Pareto solution cannot be achieved. Chapter 7 indicates that incomplete markets may be sometimes completed by providing additional information. Market completion may also be accomplished by allowing the issuance of special types of securities, such as options (Ohlson, 1987a, chapter 3; Strong and Walker, 1987, p. 55). Chapter 7 also indicates that we can sometimes overcome these problems by making assumptions about common beliefs and preferences. The well known capital asset pricing model (CAPM) used in finance achieves full Pareto efficiency in this way by assuming common beliefs for all investors and assuming either that individual utility functions are all of a specific type (the quadratic utility function) or that the probability of payoffs is of a certain type (normal). Even these conditions can be relaxed somewhat (Ohlson, 1987a, chapter

3). Thus, for many incomplete markets our existing findings for accounting may still apply.

More generally, incomplete markets mean, as they did under certainty, that not all desired welfare maximising trades may be achieved. More importantly for our purposes, the unanimity accorded to a preference ranking using market prices may disappear with poorly organised markets. Thus, we may lose our value-free accounting measures useful to all market participants.

With incomplete markets, the endowments of decision makers may include non-tradeable or only partially tradeable opportunities, the amounts of which are likely to differ among individuals. Whether they would wish to see the market value of their securities maximised may depend on these opportunities. Accounting systems based on market prices may, therefore, no longer satisfy all individuals. This does not mean that we should abandon the search for useful accounting information. We should rather seek to establish the conditions under which such accounting information may still be helpful to all market participants or a subset of those involved in the market in such settings.

A major reason why complete markets do not exist in the practical world is because of the transaction costs associated with the setting up and servicing of such markets. It would seem reasonable that such transaction costs are more likely to exist in risky rather than in certain settings and that their magnitudes are likely to be greater. These costs are, therefore, one example of the additional market imperfections which we are likely to encounter when we deal with uncertainty, rather than certainty. These market imperfections form the subject of the next section.

Market imperfections under uncertainty

The presence of large transaction costs is one reason why some markets do not exist. These costs may mean that any gains from trade are believed to be less than the costs of establishing and running a market in the commodity in mind. Insurance against the common cold may provide an example. Such insurance is not generally available even though the probabilities involved are well defined and colds impose costs on individuals. That insurance schemes do not exist suggests that the costs of running these schemes are large relative to the losses occasioned to individuals who suffer colds.

If insurance for colds were available, our example would provide an illustration of one of those market imperfections which are uniquely associated with uncertainty, but which are also intimately tied up with transaction costs. If insurance were obtainable against colds, those with complete insurance would have no incentive to take the actions which are usually recommended in order to avoid a cold. This is an example of what has been called a *moral hazard*, where the outcome of a given event may be affected by the conduct of the individual involved. Fire insurance is generally held to lead those in possession of such insurance to reduce the precautions they would otherwise take against the risk of fire. Such possibilities require expenditure by those offering the insurance on monitoring the behaviour of those with insurance policies. Insurance policies usually have conditions which render the policy invalid in the event of certain actions by those being insured. Monitoring whether these conditions have been fulfilled is expensive and may be impossible. Insurance contracts, and contracts in general, may therefore be restricted to only certain types of trade in an endeavour to minimise the likelihood of moral hazards. Insurance policies, for example, may be offered which only cover any determined loss less a fixed penalty (those claiming for vehicle damage under motor insurance often have to pay the first x amount of any damage, where x may be high). Alternatively, the insurance company may seek to motivate the individual to undertake loss prevention behaviour, and base the cost of insurance on the amount of this behaviour that can be easily detected. No-claims bonuses for drivers provide an example, as does the determination of burglary insurance based on the numbers of security devices installed. Such efforts can only be imperfect. A householder with the maximum number of security devices may still leave doors open because of the possession of anti-theft insurance.

A closely related phenomenon, which again arises only in an uncertain setting, is that of *adverse selection*. Here the problem is that high transaction costs or the difficulty of obtaining information may make it impossible to distinguish between different types of individuals who are each aware of their own type. Contracts, therefore, which allow for the different characteristics of individuals may not be able to be framed. This inability may have effects on the behaviour of the contracting individuals. The usual example is that of the same insurance terms being offered to high- and low-risk individuals because of either the cost or the impossibility of determining the class into which any specific individual may fall. The terms offered will reflect the average or past experiences of losses. High-risk individuals may, therefore, be offered a bargain whereas the low-risk class may feel the terms to be too expensive for their circumstances and may, therefore, take no insurance. Insurance companies may thus be left with only high risk individuals.

An accounting example of this phenomenon of adverse selection might arise where enterprises could not distinguish *ex ante* between high- and low-quality auditors and will, therefore, offer a fee appropriate to the average quality of audits to their auditors. High-quality auditors will not be rewarded for their special skills and will drop out of the market or adjust the quality of their performance to that usual for low-quality auditors. At the extreme, only low-quality auditors would be available in the market. Relatively skilled auditors may seek to publicise their special skills in order to overcome these problems.

Market uncertainty

The possibility of further market imperfections being introduced in a setting of uncertainty arises when we abandon the assumption of no uncertainty concerning items such as market prices, quantities and product qualities. Consideration of these types of uncertainties introduces the possibilities of substantial market imperfections which are likely to inhibit any attempt to leave the provision of accounting information to unregulated markets. For example, in these circumstances those providing accounting information may have to choose which of the differing prices that may exist for the same commodities should be reflected in accounting reports. Such choices seem to plague debates about price change accounting. Similarly, with uncertainty about market exchange possibilities, potential traders will incur transaction costs in the search for trading partners and in the search for possible prices and product qualities. They may also experience additional risks because of uncertainty about these items. This setting is one of market imperfections where there may be no unique prices known in advance attached to transactions.

In ideal conditions, any uncertainty associated with prices can be considered as similar to a public good where a commodity, which may have a negative value, is distributed simultaneously to all in the relevant community. Such a public good characteristic may arise because the probability distribution of commodity prices will depend on the joint actions of suppliers seeking to maximise their expected utility, given the knowledge available to them. The form and level of risk borne by individual suppliers will depend on the characteristics of this price distribution. This allocation of risk is unlikely to be ideal because markets will, in general, fail to distribute public goods in an optimal way. We will see later that the presence of public goods similarly gives rise to the view that market provision of commodities with these characteristics will be less efficient than can be achieved by some type of regulator, usually the Government (see Newberry and Stiglitz, 1981, chapter 15, especially pp. 210, 233–234). Regulating such markets and accounting information relating to these markets may not necessarily produce any improvement because the required interventions may demand information which is unavailable.

These and other additional imperfections generated by uncertainty, together with the incomplete markets introduced into the market by uncertainty, are likely to make impossible in some cases the search for value-free accounting systems, as they did under certainty, in just the setting where accounting information may have value. This is because market values may no longer capture the preferences of all individuals. Non-marketable characteristics may dominate any attributes of projects which are reflected in market prices. Wealth and income concepts are no longer well defined, nor is their significance clear. An optimal accounting system for any given individual can only be designed with a full knowledge of the individual's preferences, endowment opportunities and decision environment. Such systems may be expected to differ between individuals. In such a setting, accounting information may have value in overcoming market and information defects.

For these and other reasons, a number of commentators, including Beaver and Demski (1979), have suggested that the economist's approach to income and wealth already surveyed in Chapters 3 and 4) cannot be used generally. Incomplete markets and market imperfections mean that the values of enterprises at the beginning and end of periods may not serve all individuals as ranking devices for prospects.

Beaver and Demski have therefore suggested that accountants should pursue an alternative emphasis (see Beaver and Demski, 1979; Beaver, 1981(a), chapter 4). It is argued that accountants should adopt what has been called an *information perspective*. The objectives here are to discover the characteristics of what might be called useful information, and to determine whether accounting information possesses any of these characteristics, both from an individual and a multi-person perspective. The objective of this approach is to provide useful items of accounting information, both at the individual and social levels, using tools and concepts drawn from information economics. This concern with a multi-person setting in situations where individuals may have different preferences and beliefs requires explicit consideration of the welfare aspects of accounting which seem to underlie many of the controversies over accounting in the business community. A review of the information economic perspective of accounting forms the subject of the next chapter. However, in contrast to Beaver's (1981(a)) approach, this subject will not be characterised as a perspective to accounting distinct from that utilised with the economist's approach which was reviewed in Chapters 3 and 4. Rather, the attitude taken here will be that the utilisation of information economics allows some of the strengths of the economist's approach to income and wealth measurement to be preserved in more realistic settings than were considered in these earlier chapters.

However, there are grounds for believing that the above analysis and the similiar analyses in earlier chapters do not fully reflect the role of information, including accounting information, in financial markets. Our treatment of uncertainty allows us to begin tackling this problem in the next section.

Information in capital markets

Our analysis of accounting information up to this point has rather artificially constrained the role of information and especially accounting information. In Chapter 2 we considered information in a certain environment both for single periods and multi-periods with perfect and complete markets. In these settings, information has no real role. Here existing knowledge can be rearranged and expressed in a conventional accounting format. Accounting information of this kind can be shown to have many characteristics which would be desirable if possessed by accounting information in the practical world. Income and wealth measures were shown to be measures in the proper sense, to be completely consistent with optimal decision making and value-free in that they were unaffected by individual preferences. However, no one would pay for the provision of such measures as they could be obtained from existing knowledge in a costless way. These desirable characteristics of accounting information were shown not necessarily to be maintained in conditions of poorly organised markets.

These conclusions were shown to be unaltered with single- period uncertainty, both in Chapter 2 and more rigorously in this chapter. Accounting information is usually seen as appearing at the end of a period and obtaining any value it may have from the unanticipated messages it may yield. There is no way in which accounting information of this type can impact in a one-period analysis. Our one period analyses did suggest that not all market imperfections will cause accounting information to lose all the desirable characteristics it was shown to possess under perfectly organised markets. These were shown to be maintained, for example, under the assumptions of portfolio analysis in Chapter 2, and where spanning existed in this chapter. In both cases, accounting information was shown to be value-free and the underlying unanimity accorded to the ranking of prospects by accounting information was maintained in the face of certain types of incomplete markets. This suggests that an important research avenue for accounting is to seek to discover those poorly organised markets where accounting information can still be shown to possess at least some of those desirable characteristics it has in perfect and complete markets.

Indeed, Ohlson, (1987b) makes the point that unanimity can be obtained even with no market, where we are postulating identical individuals. More importantly, he suggests that there is a still more compelling reason to expect unanimity not to hold even in well organised markets. His argument, which is important but rather technical and is therefore put in Note 7, gives additional reasons to those provided by Beaver and Demski (1979) for expecting that unanimity will reign only in restrictive circumstances.

Ohlson suggests that one way to proceed in the face of these difficulties while still trying to integrate accounting information with capital markets, is to seek to determine income and wealth measures ignoring their wealth and income redistribution effects. He provides such a model (Ohlson, 1989). We will not go further down this route because it is very new and because so many of the problems of accounting seem to centre on its wealth and income effects.

Reverting to the role of information and especially accounting information in our models, as was suggested in Chapter 2, we would expect information to have substantial utility only in a multi-period uncertain setting. A possible criticism of Beaver and Demski (1979) is that it is not clear that they deal with such a setting, in which case accounting information has no value. All information is already known. We have not yet dealt with this more complex setting, preferring to wait until the basic tools for dealing with uncertainty have been provided. Even now, we can only treat this subject in a tentative way until we have studied the meaning and value of information in more detail in later chapters.

Our analysis of this multi-period setting under well organised markets suggests that even here the role of information and especially accounting information may be limited. The information system and its possible signals are known at the beginning of the multi-period sequence at the time of the only necessary decision. Information at the end of any period can therefore bring no new information, other than signalling a possibility which was fully anticipated and allowed for when the decision was made. Again, accounting information as such has no value. This is because it provides no new information as we proceed through time. All possible signals are known at the beginning of the time sequence and are fully allowed for in the allocation decision.

In some ways the approach used in this chapter, which is standard in economics, would not seem very helpful in analysing the role of accounting information where we see it as providing new information. It does, however, allow us to say that even in perfectly organised markets additional information may be valuable. This is because economics seeks an equilibrium conditional on the information system being used. Another information system which might be an accounting information system may allow a preferred equilibrium to be obtained. This suggests that we are more likely to find a role for accounting if we relax some of the assumptions we have so far made. For example, accounting information may be of value where its signals are received prior to decision making. We may also expect that accounting information is more likely to have value where it helps to overcome market difficulties. These and other ideas are investigated in the next three chapters.

Chapter summary

The first substantive section of this chapter presents the elements of the state preference model under uncertainty for the individual. It was indicated that we are dealing with event uncertainty in only a trading setting. This type of uncertainty considers risk arising from uncertainty about technological events, rather than market items. The basic elements of this model were shown to comprise, first, states of the environment and their probabilities, the only uncertainty being the likely occurrence of these states. The model, secondly, comprises actions and an objective to be achieved, subject to any constraints. We then discussed in more detail each of these items. States were suggested to be mutually exclusive and exhaustive partitions of the events which are relevant to the decision. The items of interest are the payoffs contingent on each state.

Such payoffs may be purchased in the market, prior to state realisation. Such prices are called 'contingent prices' and the purchased payoffs are conditional on the occurrence of the relevant state.

The probabilities being used were said to be of a special type. They reflected not the frequency of state occurrence, but rather the decision maker's belief in the likelihood of the occurrence of each state. Such probabilities, for the same set of occurrences, were said to be likely to differ between individuals. Adopting this view of probability allows decision making in one-off situations and permits the usual calculus used with frequency-based probabilities to be utilised with subjective probabilities, providing that these probabilities satisfy certain conditions.

A numerical example of this approach to decision making under uncertainty was then presented, and was used to illustrate the objective of maximising the expected monetary value flowing from decisions. It was then argued that the expected monetary value decision rule did not allow for risk attitudes, which were considered next: these could be conveniently divided into three types, those who ignore risk (who are called risk neutral), those who dislike risk (risk averse), and gamblers (risk seekers). It was suggested that such attitudes to risk need to be incorporated into decision models. The approach used in this chapter to achieve this objective was to introduce utility functions of a specific type. It was demonstrated that such utility functions could incorporate risk attitudes. It was shown how the utility attached to both certain and uncertain amounts of money could be read off a utility function.

We then introduced the expected utility decision rule, which says that we should approach decision making by seeking to maximise the expected utility we obtain from our decisions. The expected utility promised by a decision was shown to be found by multiplying the utility of each payoff by its probability and adding over all the states which may occur. How such utility functions may be obtained empirically was discussed briefly.

We then reconsidered our example using mathematical formulations for two popular forms of possible utility functions for a risk averse individual. The strength of this approach is that utility functions allow individual welfare to be maximised under uncertainty, providing that some simple and seemingly compelling assumptions are satisfied.

The next main section of the chapter utilised the state preference model to derive the conditions that need to be satisfied if the individual is to make optimal decisions. It was shown, using our simple example involving the trading of securities, that these conditions are those familiar in economics. The individual should seek to equate the rate of exchange between the market prices of pairs of state incomes to the ratio of the preferences for these incomes at the margin. This condition is simplified in settings where the market prices of prospects reflect the same probabilities of state outcomes as attached to these outcomes by the individual. Here the condition for an optimum was demonstrated to be that the ratio of market prices for each pair of state incomes is equal to the ratio of the probabilities assigned to the two states.

The part of the chapter modelling behaviour under uncertainty ended by indicating that, with the state preference approach, enterprises bore no risk. In this setting, the outcomes of prospects would be purchased on the market using the state-contingent prices for these outcomes. It was shown that in this case all individuals would subscribe to enterprises, accepting all projects or prospects which are worthwhile when the outcomes are evaluated at their state-contingent prices in the market.

The last main part of this chapter commenced our study of the impact of uncertainty on accounting theory. This subject is further considered in the following three chapters. Chapters 6 and 7 introduce the results for accounting theory of adopting an information economics perspective. Chapter 9 considers how developments in information economics and in finance theory have allowed theories of accounting under uncertainty to be further refined, and have enabled empirical evidence concerning accounting information to be obtained.

In the final section of this chapter, it was first shown that uncertainty, as such, makes no difference to our earlier conclusions in a certain setting that it was possible to derive measures of income and wealth which provided value-free accounting measures for all individuals concerned with decision making. Again, as with certainty, such measures are based on market prices and no one will pay accountants to provide this information in accounting statements. This information is already available, or can be calculated costlessly from information already available to the public.

It was then suggested that uncertainty is likely to cause additional market difficulties which, as under certainty, may inhibit the determination of value-free accounting information. Additional market difficulties which arise only under uncertainty were then introduced. Two of these phenomena were called 'moral hazard' and 'adverse selection'. The first of these arises where individuals have some ability to determine outcomes in uncertain situations. Fire insurance was given as an example. Adverse selection means that individuals are unable to determine the quality of the market actors they are dealing with and, therefore, cannot write contracts which reflect fully the characteristics of contracting parties. Uncertainty concerning market characteristics was suggested to be likely to generate further market imperfections and lead to demands for extra market regulation. Given these difficulties, it has been suggested that accountants should seek to provide useful information using the understanding given by information economics. Lastly, we looked in a little more detail at the role of information in models of decision making under uncertainty. It was suggested that accounting information could not have a role in one-period models. Even in multi-period models, no clear role was found for accounting information. However, evaluating whether one accounting system was better than another required deriving an equilibrium solution for both models and selecting that which gave the preferred optimum. It was stated that finding a role for accounting information required the consideration of more complex models; this is the task of the next few chapters, starting with a discussion of the meaning and utility of information, which are considered in the next chapter.

Notes

1. There are vast number of books and articles dealing with uncertainty, suitable for further reference. Among the books are Hirshleifer (1970), chapters 8 and 9, and Malinvaud (1972), chapter 11. Most modern finance books adopt a similar approach to that of this chapter; see for example, Copeland and Weston (1988), chapters 4 and 5. Newberry and Stiglitz (1981) approach many of the issues of this chapter from a different perspective. Beaver (1981b) provides a good alternative and extended coverage of the material in this and the next chapter. Hirshleifer and Riley (1979) present a very good review of the whole area of decision making under uncertainty, including its effect on markets. A more advanced treatment is provided by Dreze (1974). The latter part of this chapter draws heavily upon Ohlson (1987a), Krouse (1986) and Strong and Walker (1987).

2. The calculations for prospects B and C are:

$E(MV_B) = 37.5 \; (=50 \times 0.75) + 37.5 \; (=150 \times 0.25) = 75$
$E(MV_C) = 56.25 \, (=75 \times 0.75) + 18.75 \, (= \; 75 \times 0.25) = 75$

where $E(MW_B)$ and $E(MV_C)$ represent the expected monetary values of prospects B and C respectively. The symbol E on the left of the expressions signifies that we are taking a mathematical expectation (a probability-weighted average) of the outcomes of each state–action combination.

3. The marginal utility $U'(W)$ yielded by extra amounts of wealth decreases with wealth, that is $U''(W)/U'(W) < 0$, where $U'(W)$ and $U''(W)$ are respectively the first and second derivatives of utility with respect to wealth.

4. If we wish to consider how risk attitudes change as the relative proportion of our endowment at risk changes, we are concerned with relative risk aversion. This can be calculated by weighting the first of the components of the absolute risk aversion formula by the level of wealth. Relative risk aversion is therfore measured by $-WU''(W)/U'(W)$. There is no obvious *a priori* or empirical view as to how this measure might respond as wealth increases. A popular view with some empirical backing is that it will stay constant.

5. To understand this, consider a gamble involving only the best and worst outcomes on offer to Mr Risky. His best outcome is 150 and we will take the worst outcome to be zero. Assume that a gamble offers these outcomes with equal probability. The expected monetary value generated by this hazard would be 75 monetary units. The utility attached to this uncertain prospect is 52.5 utiles with a utility function of the form of $U = W - 0.002W^2$. The utility of 150 monetary units obtained using this utility function is 105 utiles (see Table 5.4, column 5, row 2) and multiplying by the probability of receiving this amount (0.5) yields a utility of 52.5 utiles for this uncertain sum, i.e.

$U(150) \times 0.5 = 105 \times 0.5 = 52.5$

Our assumed utility function can be used to determine the amount of money received with certainty which has the same utility as our uncertain prospect. This can be determined by solving the following expression:

$52.5U = x - 0.002x^2$

where x stands for the certain amount of wealth having a utility equal to 52.2 utiles. Solving this expression yields 59.6 monetary units as the certain sum having the same utility as our original uncertain prospect.

Thus, this sum of 59.6 monetary units has the same preference ranking as the original gamble. These items have the same utility and are, therefore, both on the same indifference curve. This allows us to write:

$U(\overline{59.6}) = U(\tilde{0}) \times 0.5 + U(\tilde{150}) \times 0.5 = U(\tilde{75})$ [5.X]

where the bar over the 59.6 monetary units signifies that this is a certain amount and the ($\tilde{}$) over the sums of 0, 150 and 75 monetary units indicates that these are uncertain amounts.

Expression 5.X says that 59.6 monetary units received with certainty have the same utility as a risky prospect involving the sums of 150 and zero, each having a likelihood of 50 per cent and thus yielding an expected monetary value of 75 monetary units.

The argument in the text is that the product of the best uncertain outcome and its probability should equal the the utility of the certain sum, which renders the decision maker indifferent between the uncertain prospect and this certain sum. This implicitly assumed that the utility scale being used ranged from 1 to zero. Our utility scale spans 105 to zero; to show that the assertion is correct we need to transform our figures into those of this alternative scale.

We therefore need to divide the right-hand side of Expression 5.X by 105 to give the utility of 59.6 monetary units received with certainty on the simpler scale of 1 to zero. This operation gives:

$U(59.6) = 52.5u/105 = 0.5u$

Thus, the utility assigned to 59.6 monetary units received with certainty is just the probability of best outcome in the basic lottery, as is claimed in the text.

6. Where this is not the case the optimal portfolio will contain more of the state-contingent income to which the individual gives a higher probability than is implied by its market price, and less of the other state income because the individual will back personal beliefs. The decision maker proceeding in this way will reach an optimal indifference curve. Differences of views with the market thus provide a reason why risk averse individuals may well hold risky portfolios in the real world. With such beliefs the individual will seek to optimise by reallocating investment until the ratio of the market prices between the states is equal to the rate at which the individual would be willing to substitute one state income for another so as just to keep utility constant.

7. In Chapter 2 we were able to show that every one would agree to an investment decision, because this decision maximised wealth irrespective of preferences which could be left to the individual to look after. Any other decision amounted to throwing away wealth.

This required well organised markets. Hidden in this assumption are a number of conditions, two of which are especially important to obtaining unanimity (see DeAngelo, 1986). The first is the spanning condition referred to in the body of this chapter. This condition is equivalent to assuming that the mix of opportunities available in the market is not altered by the decisions of firms. New prospects which offer opportunities which cannot be replicated by some combination of already available prospects cannot be brought to the market. This avoids the problem that such new prospects may change individual utility substantially and in a variety of ways, thereby possibly losing unanimity. The second condition for unanimity similarly holds the perceived prices of claims to uncertain wealth constant in the face of changed plans, because such changes may affect individuals differently, thereby again losing unanimity. Ohlson (1987a) says that the general view in the literature is that this second assumption is unlikely to be met except under very restrictive conditions. This is perhaps not surprising, as firms with monopoly power may have the power to affect the wealth of their owners who consume their products, via the prices they charge. With this view we still lose unanimity but for reasons additional to those given by Beaver and Demski (1979).

6

Accounting and information economics

Introduction

So far in this book we have often explicitly or implicitly employed an informational perspective on accounting theory (Beaver, 1981(a), chapter 1). With this view, accounting reports are perceived as only one means of publishing information. Viewing information, including accounting information, as an economic commodity is the central strand of adopting an informational perspective to accounting. A later chapter (Chapter 10) discusses many of the problems generated by current institutional arrangements for providing accounting information. These are said to be likely to inhibit any ability to trade information on markets easily as if it were a conventional economic commodity.

Chapter 11, on the regulation of accounting, emphasises the additional problems encountered when we are looking at the provision of accounting information explicitly in a multi-person context. Chapter 11 suggests that the need for the regulation of accounting reports might be generated by some of the rather unusual properties seen to be possessed by accounting information when such information is viewed as an economic commodity. Chapter 12 shows that this view has substantially influenced the Conceptual Framework Project of the Financial Accounting Standards Board, the standard setting body in the United States of America.

Our chapters on the economist's approach to income and wealth measurement, Chapters 3 and 4, have emphasised a different aspect of the informational approach to accounting by seeking to determine that decision-useful information which would allow a decision maker to make optimal investment decisions concerning both new physical projects and security investment under the assumed objective of seeking to maximise economic wealth. The aim was to determine information that was optimal by specifying in some detail the decision model used by investors. This allowed us to determine in an unambiguous way what accounting information would possess decision relevance and utility to a decision maker characterised by the assumptions employed in these chapters. Chapter 5 widened this analysis by presenting a variety of models of decision making under uncertainty. It sought to indicate the information requirements implied by such models.

In Chapters 3, 4 and 5 we sought to discover accounting information that would seem to have decision utility under various entertained assumptions. In this search the value of different information to different individuals in society was given less emphasis than in other parts of the book. This was because our primary objective in these chapters was to derive examples of accounting information which could be shown to have decision utility for, at least, the entertained decision models. We also generally assumed in these three chapters that accounting information and information generally could be traded in well functioning markets. In such markets, varying preferences for accounting information can be left to individuals to deal with in the market.

Beaver has claimed that utilising an information perspective to external accounting amounts to a revolution in financial accounting theory. It certainly can be argued that the recent adoption of this type of informational perspective to accounting has changed our view of accounting, in terms of both its societal role and the difficulties associated with this role. This perspective has illuminated many issues which until recently had generally gone unconsidered, such as the need for the regulation of accounting. From a more micro-economics stance, utilising an informational perspective has extended our understanding of decision utility—a concept which forms the motivation for most accounting theories. This perspective has also indicated the many difficulties faced by those who seek to provide more informative accounting reports. It has also contributed to the body of knowledge which has allowed the testing of some accounting theories against empirical evidence. This particular use of the informational approach to accounting is reviewed in a later chapter.

This chapter is the first of three which uses the tools provided in Chapter 5 for understanding decision making and accounting under uncertainty. Here we present a fairly detailed exploration of the meaning of information for private use and of the concept of user relevance or decision utility, mainly from the perspective of an individual decision maker using a specific but fairly general model in decision making. We will also consider in this context how far information systems (including accounting systems) can be ranked in terms of their utility for decision making purposes. In the next chapter, we will consider how information may be valued.

We generally adopt a single-person perspective in this chapter to ease the presentation of a difficult subject and because more clear-cut research results have been obtained for this setting than for the multi-person context. However, most of the concepts introduced in this chapter are used in the same way as suggested here when a multi-person view is taken.

This single-person approach does ignore many of the problems facing accounting. The second part of Chapter 7 discusses the multi-person setting with information being made generally available and considers the value of such information, which includes accounting information, to individuals and to society. Many other problems arise because accounting information is made generally available using a quite complex institutional framework and cannot be used privately by the individual. These matters will be addressed from a society-wide perspective in Chapters 10 and 11.

The informational approach to accounting utilises that area of economics which is called the economics of information, which itself is a product of economic and statistical decision theory. Information economics seeks to describe information in a rigorous way and to model the selection of optimal information systems for decision making in both a single-person and a multi-person context. Our presentation is therefore a little technical and uses elements of a mathematical language. However, those who have knowledge of decision making under uncertainty to the level of Chapter 5 should not find the material in this chapter too difficult.

Plan of the chapter

The first part of this chapter considers the meaning of the term 'information' as it is used in information economics. This part firstly reintroduces the concepts discussed in the previous chapter. It then defines the meaning of 'information' from an informational perspective. Here, the term 'information' is restricted to new information, the possession of which leads to new decisions. It is shown that, in general, decision-relevant information can be characterised as new knowledge concerning the likelihood of the occurrence of states of the environment. Although introduced in a single-person context, the ideas discussed in this chapter generally have equal relevance to the multi-person environment.

We then go on to consider some of the characteristics of information systems. The characteristics and informativeness of perfect and imperfect information systems are considered. A perfect information system yields a unique signal for each possible state of the environment. Incomplete information systems continue to associate a specific signal with each state but such a signal may be associated with a group of states rather than just one. Noisy information systems are those which yield signals that relate uncertainly to the occurrence of more than one state. The concepts of payoff-adequate and payoff-relevant information systems are reintroduced. The conditions under which information systems can be ranked in terms of their utility, without considering individual preferences or probability beliefs, are then presented. Such comparisons are said to be possible only under restrictive conditions. The implications for accounting of information systems being comparable in terms of their usefulness in some circumstances are then considered.

Finally, the concept of information is illustrated quantitatively using our Mr Risky example of the previous chapter. The approach is formalised by showing how prior probabilities concerning state occurrence may be revised in the light of new information utilising a theory of probability revision named Bayes' Theorem. Note 2 discusses this theorem informally and gives an intuitive explanation of the reasoning behind it. Our Mr Risky example is again utilised here to provide an illustration of this approach. Note 3 demonstrates how Mr Risky's expected utility can be calculated when information is available.

Adopting an informational perspective is shown to allow us to define in a precise and rigorous way what we might mean by the decision utility of accounting information. This yields precise definitions relative to other accounting theories and approaches to accounting which have tended to leave these ideas rather vague (for an example, see Chapter 12).

The chapter concludes with a summary of the usefulness of some of these ideas for accounting. The next chapter (Chapter 7) considers how information for both private and public use may be valued.

There is a large amount of literature dealing with information economics. Two important general sources are Marschak and Radner (1972), chapters 2 and 6, and McGuire and Radner (1972), especially chapters 5 and 6. A sample of the more technical approach to information economics is provided by Marschak (1974), Volume II, chapters 25, 29 and 31. A fairly non-technical approach to the implications of adopting an informational perspective to accounting is provided by Beaver (1981(a)). More technical expositions of some elements of this approach are given by Demski (1980) and Feltham (1972). Strong and Walker (1987) examine this approach in the context of capital market theory in a fairly non-technical way. Ohlson (1987a) provides a fully integrated treatment of information and capital markets at a more technical level.

Prior to considering the meaning of information in the context of this chapter, we shall review some of the ideas concerning decision making under uncertainty introduced in Chapter 5. Those who feel comfortable with these ideas can skip the next section.

Review of decision making under uncertainty

In a fully specified setting with uncertainty, decisions are hypothesised to depend on a number of items which are listed below (see also Marschak and Radner, 1972; Demski, 1980).

Elements of a decision model

The elements of a decision model can be seen as comprising:

1 A set of decision alternatives or actions (A) from which one and only one action, a_j, where $a_j \in A$, is to be selected.
2 A set of relevant states, S, only one of which, s_i, $s_i \in S$, will occur.
3 A set of outcomes (X), each of which, x_i, is the result of taking a given action (a_j) and specific state (s_i) occurring, that is $x_i = C(a_j, s_i)$. It is normally assumed that decision makers are concerned only with the wealth generated by action and state combinations.
4 The subjective probabilities attached to the occurrence of each relevant state which for improved clarity will now be written as $\phi(s_i)$ (instead of ϕ_i as usual in the previous chapter). These probabilities for a set of mutually exclusive states which comprise all states which are of concern, must be consistent in that they must add to one when summed over all states, where $\phi(s_i) > 0$.
5 A utility function representing the decision maker's own preferences for outcomes. Such a utility function can be written in a completely general way as $U(\cdot)$. This becomes a specific utility function when a mathematical relationship expressing the individual's preferences is chosen. The expected utility of specific action combined with a specific state (a_j, s_i) is given by applying a utility function to the uncertain wealth (x_i) promised by this action and state combination (a_j, s_i). The expected utility of an act can be represented as $E(U \mid a_j)$, where the vertical line indicates that expected utility $E(U)$ is conditional on a given act (a_j) being taken. This sum is obtained by weighting the utility of each action–state combination that may flow from taking a specific action by the probability of the relevant state and then summing over all states.

   This expected utility can be represented in symbols as

   $$E(U \mid a_j) = \Sigma U(a_j, s_i)\phi(s_i)$$

   where the probability of the state, s_i, is now represented by $\phi(s_i)$.
6 The person or persons whose welfare is to be maximised. In this chapter we shall usually assume that it is wished to maximise the decision maker's welfare.
7 Any constraints on the decision, including the decision maker's opening endowment.

A model in which each of the above elements is exhaustively specified for the decision in mind is described as complete. No further refinements of the model will improve the decision. Such a complete specification enables us to proceed on the assumption that all uncertainty concerning the decision is impounded in the probabilities associated with the states relevant to the decision. Thus, we are dealing with what was called technological uncertainty in Chapter 5 as distinct from market uncertainty.

Optimal decision making without information

As was explained in Chapter 5, modelling decisions in this way yields an abstract decision rule for expected utility maximisation for the decision maker. This can be written using Expression 5.III of the previous chapter as

$$E(U \mid a^*) = \underset{a \in A}{\text{Max}} \sum_S U(a, s)\phi(s) \tag{6.I}$$

where a^* is the optimal act. The decision maker is seen as first calculating the expected utility of each act. The first element on the right of Expression 6.I indicates that the individual then optimises by choosing that act which maximises the remainder of the right-hand part of the expression.

The specification of this model will reflect the individual's past knowledge and experience which will be influenced by any information gained over the decision maker's lifetime. Thus, the above decision model is strictly conditional on the decision maker's past experience.

Defining the meaning of information

Thus, when we talk about information we are talking about additional information over and above that contained in the decision maker's experiential base. In common parlance, information is often defined as anything that yields new knowledge to an individual. This definition is too imprecise for use in information economics. Here information is defined as information relevant to decisions and which will change decisions. Thus, additional knowledge which does not impact on a decision is not classified as information when an information economics perspective is adopted. Knowledge which confirms the decision maker's existing beliefs, or which although changing these views does not generate any change in decisions, is therefore not characterised as information in the strict sense used here.

This narrow definition of what is considered as information is adopted because a major thrust in information economics is to seek to value information by determining what an individual would pay for it for private use, where 'private use' implies that the information cannot be passed on to others once it has been used by the decision maker. In order to be able to view the decision maker's acts in isolation, we will assume in this chapter that any actions following from private use of information do not affect market prices or quantities. With the objective of valuing information for private use, knowledge which does not require decision alterations has no effect on behaviour and therefore does not change the expected utility which the decision maker expects to obtain from selecting the optimal solution to a decision problem.

Recall that, in the model being considered, the only uncertainty concerns the state of the environment. Knowledge which confirms or strengthens beliefs about the probabilities attached to the relevant states clearly does not change existing decisions. Even objective evidence concerning these probabilities which just confirms extant views does not alter the degrees of belief about the likelihood of the states. Therefore, it cannot change the optimal decision.

Issues of some subtlety are involved here. For example, knowledge which changes probabilities without changing the optimal decision may still alter the value the market places on a prospect (and may therefore impact on the decision maker's utility). Such knowledge is not regarded as information from the perspective of the economics of information. However, changes in the market value of the outcome of an already selected decision may be useful knowledge where outcomes can be traded on markets.

According to information economics, information can be defined in a non-formal way as follows.

Information is decision-relevant knowledge which alters existing optimal conduct or decisions.   Definition [6.A]

Accounting and information

Much of what we usually regard as accounting information may not be information under this definition. This is because many items in accounting reports do not obviously lead to changes in decisions. Moreover, those items which might have this characteristic may only yield knowledge which has already been made publicly available from other more timely sources of information.

That accounting reports may replicate information available in a more timely way from other sources is an important insight for accounting theory. There may be a large number of sources of a given item of knowledge, and therefore the information content of messages from any given source may be small or non-existent because of the redundancy of such messages. Empirical studies concerning the information content of accounting reports, which will be discussed in Chapter 9, suggest some of the information contained in accounting reports is new to stock markets and therefore does affect security prices but to only a modest degree. The next main section examines this definition of the meaning of information in more detail and introduces the characteristics of information systems assuming for the time being that information is available at no cost. The following section gives a quantitative example of the impact of information on decision making using the Mr Risky example introduced in Chapter 5.

Characteristics of optimal costless information systems

The usual notation used to represent an information system is η (eta) and the symbol for a message from an information system is y. More technically, an information system is referred to in the literature being followed as an information structure or information function (Marschak and Radner, 1972, chapter 2). The term 'information structure' is used because the available information system provides the structure of the events within which the decision maker seeks to optimise. The use of the term 'information function' is, perhaps, more obvious because it makes it explicit that an information system is a function of the states of the environment, which associates states with specific signals. Such an information function can be written as $\eta(s) = y$. That is, knowledge of a signal yields some view of the state that reigns, where the amount of state knowledge obtained from the signal depends on the character of the information system being used. Here we will continue to use the term 'information system' because of its familiarity.

Information here is defined without reference to its cost. Costly information raises a number of complexities with which we will deal later. We will assume at present that any information being considered is available at no extra cost.

Perfect information systems

A perfect information structure would associate a unique and precise signal on a 'one for one' basis with each and every state of the environment. Thus, in a three-state environment represented by states s_1, s_2, s_3, a perfect information structure or system would associate a specific and unique signal y_i with each state. One such information system is given below.

$$y_1 = s_1$$
$$y_2 = s_2$$
$$y_3 = s_3$$

An example of such an information system would be a set of traffic lights which correctly signal the underlying state of a crossroad as dangerous, in need of care, or safe. Here the usual signals might be associated with states in the following way:

Green signal, (say) $y_1 = $ (say) s_1, safe state

Yellow signal, (say) $y_2 = $ (say) s_2, proceed with care

Red signal, (say) $y_3 = $ (say) s_3, dangerous

A system that does not distinguish between states, which is called the null information system, would associate the same signal with all states. In our traffic light problem, an information system which always showed a green signal would provide an example of a null information system.

An information structure or system thus yields signals which partition the underlying states in some way but not necessarily in a perfect way. State partitionings induced by information systems have to follow two sensible rules. First, combining the subsets of states in the partition must yield the overall set of states. Thus combining the subsets of states that could be signalled by our information system above yields the full set of states. Secondly, the same sub-state cannot be in more than one element of the partition. Thus an information system can, perhaps, with some difficulty, be thought of as merely partitioning the underlying states following these rules, and associating signals with the subsets of states induced by the information system.

Information systems and outcomes

Another helpful way to look at information systems is to see how they restrict decision making by constraining the possible plans which can be made. This perspective requires that each individual signal from an information system is viewed as grouping together outcomes and that information system itself is the collection of the subsets of outcomes which are associated with its signals. A plan can be seen as being made for each signal from the information system. Each plan seeks to maximise utility from the opportunities available, given the signal. Plans can therefore be seen as commitments contingent on the signals provided by the information system. The achievement of any desired outcome is thus limited by the signals from the available information systems. Richer information systems enhance the opportunities available to decision makers.

As an example, consider the five-state–two-action problem set out below. Outcomes in each of the five states are shown vertically in the five columns of the example. The outcomes of the two actions are shown in the two rows of the example.

$$\text{States:} \begin{bmatrix} 1 & 2 & 3 & 4 & 5 \\ 3 & 4 & 5 & 1 & 2 \\ 1 & 2 & 3 & 4 & 5 \end{bmatrix}$$

States: / Action 1: / Action 2:

Now assume that an information system which yields two signals is available. Signal y_1 says that either state 1 or state 2 has occurred and signal y_2 signifies the appearance of one of the other three states but without distinguishing which state out of these three has actually appeared. Thus the two signals group the possible outcomes from the decision problem with the two signals in the following way:

$$y_1 = \begin{matrix} 3 & 4 \\ 1 & 2 \end{matrix} \qquad y_2 = \begin{matrix} 5 & 1 & 2 \\ 3 & 4 & 5 \end{matrix}$$

The plans the decision maker can make are contingent on the signals from the information system. Assuming the decision maker wishes to maximise the outcome in any state, there are only three plans which are maintainable with this particular information system. The first is to plan to obtain outcomes of 3 in state 1 and 4 in state 2 by taking action 1 when signal y_1 is observed (the other action contingent on signal 1 will not be taken as it is dominated by action 1). The other two plans are to take actions 1 or 2 when signal y_2 appears. Taking action 1 yields an outcome of 5 if state 3 appears and outcomes of 1 and 2 in states 4 and 5 respectively. If action 2 is taken in these circumstances, the decision maker can plan to obtain an outcome of 3 in state 3 and outcomes of 4 and 5 in states 4 and 5 respectively. Which action will be chosen will depend on the decision maker's preferences, but chosen plans are limited by the information system.

A richer information system would free the decision maker from some of the constraints imposed on his or her plans by the available information system by allowing more detailed plans to be made. Thus, in our example, an information system, say η_b, which yielded three signals would allow more detailed plans to be made and achieved. Assume, for example, that with this richer information system the signals are the same as before except that signal y_2 is now divided into two so that state 3 is now signalled separately from states 4 and 5. Thus the signals from information system b group outcomes together in the following way:

$$y_1 = \begin{matrix} 3 & 4 \\ 1 & 2 \end{matrix} \qquad y_2 = \begin{matrix} 5 \\ 3 \end{matrix} \qquad y_3 = \begin{matrix} 1 & 2 \\ 4 & 5 \end{matrix}$$

This allows the decision maker to make more detailed plans and, in this case, to determine an optimal action for each signal by taking action 1 if either y_1 or y_2 appears and action 2 if the other signal is obtained. We now take a first look at imperfect information systems.

Imperfect information systems

An imperfect information system may still yield signals which partition the underlying states into a set of mutually exclusive and exhaustive subsets; that is, the occurrence of each state will be associated with only one signal and all states will be associated with a signal. However, such signals may be associated with the occurrence of more than one state. Here, a signal, say y_1, may appear whenever, say, state 2 or state 3 has occurred. Using this signal, we are sure that state 2 or state 3 obtained but are unable to distinguish which of these two states has appeared. An information system with this characteristic is said to lack completeness, which requires that a unique and specific signal is associated with the occurrence of each and every state.

Noisy information systems

An imperfect information system may also yield signals which do not unambiguously signal the occurrence of a state or subset of states. With this type of information system, signals lack precision in that there is only a probability that a given state or set of states has occurred following the receipt of a specific signal. Such systems are therefore called noisy, because the signals contain an element of uncertainty. An example is given later.

Reverting to our three-state problem, two possible imperfect information but non-noisy systems for our traffic light problem would be:

Information system A (η_A)   Information system B (η_B)

$y_1 = \{s_1\}$ $y_1 = \{s_1, s_2\}$

$y_2 = \{s_2, s_3\}$ $y_2 = \{s_3\}$

Here the two information systems partition the underlying states in different ways. Information system A signals state 1 (the Safe state) separately from the other two states (Dangerous, and Proceed with care) whereas information system B partitions state 3 from states 1 and 2. The former system might be preferred by anyone who was especially safety conscious.

Decisions would be consistent with such an information system if they assumed that the results of any state conveyed by a specific signal produced the same decision outcome or payoff as did the other states contained in the same signal. Technically, this property of information systems is termed the 'measurability' of outcomes with respect to an information structure. Informally, this term reflects that where this condition is satisfied the information system involved measures outcomes using the same outcomes as are used in planning. Such plans would therefore be achievable with the information system in mind; they can be said to be *adapted* to the information system.

Reverting to our information systems above, plans that foresee one outcome in state 1 but the same outcome in states 2 and 3 are adapted to information system A and can be achieved with this system. Such plans are not compatible with information system B, which is built on different assumptions. Under this system, states 1 and 2 yield the same outcome but state 3 provides a different outcome. The earlier plans are therefore not compatible with this information system and cannot be achieved using it. Available information systems thus restrict what plans can be made. A perfect information system is compatible with all possible plans, whereas the null information system allows no additional decision making over that allowed by the information originally possessed by the decision maker. More detailed information thus allows a richer mix of state outcomes to be achieved.

An idea closely related to the compatibility between plans and information systems is the concept of an information system yielding a set of signals adequate to allow the decision maker to optimise with respect to a specific decision problem. This matter is discussed in the next section.

Payoff adequate information systems

Information systems which are not perfect in either of the senses used above, but function as if they were are characterised as payoff-adequate. There are several ways of defining this property. One is to say that information systems which allow the same decision as would a perfect and complete information system are payoff-adequate. Another criterion for payoff adequacy is to ask whether access to an imperfect information system would allow the decision maker to select an *ex post* optimal action.

Both of these conditions are satisfied if an imperfect information system classifies underlying states so that all states which give the same payoff for each action are combined together. A traffic light system which separated the dangerous state from the other two would be payoff-adequate if drivers were concerned with only whether they have to stop or to proceed. The state classification or partitioning provided by an information system which generates a payoff-adequate partition can additionally be characterised as payoff-relevant if there is not a coarser classification of the underlying states that is payoff-adequate. If an information system provides too coarse a classification, its signals will subsume underlying states which, when combined with an action, may yield outcomes which do not have the same utility. Traffic light signals which combine the states Proceed with care and Safety may be too coarse for adequate decision making by a risk averse driver. Too fine an information system divides states into sets of sub-states which are not different from a decision making point of view. Traffic lights which were able to signal each of the three states would be too fine for a driver concerned with only whether to stop or proceed. Using reasoning of this sort, it can be shown that only one information system (state partition) will be payoff-relevant for any decision problem and set of preferences and expectations (Marschak, 1974, pp. 131–132).

Accounting implications of payoff-adequate and payoff-relevant information systems

Payoff-relevant accounting information systems would thus seem to be what the designer of financial accounting systems should be seeking to achieve. However, as payoff relevance is generally individual and decision-specific, it does not offer much help to those who wish to design general all-purpose accounting statements. This again emphasises the fact that accounting policy makers would seem to have to choose that set or sets of accounting users they wish to favour. In the next main section, we will discuss one way of overcoming this rather disappointing finding in some restrictive circumstances.

Prior to this we will consider some characteristics of imperfect information systems in a little more detail.

Imperfect information systems

An example

Let us now consider all the distinct sets of traffic signals that can be constructed using a maximum of three conventional colours—red, yellow and green. Each set of signals maps the underlying states in a different way. Here we will be dealing with some information systems which do not distinguish between all states. The signals from the systems are, however, assumed to be related deterministically to the underlying states; that is, a given signal is assumed to be related in a specific way to a given state or set of states without any uncertainty about this relationship.

Table 6.1 shows the total set of unique information systems which are available for our problem. The first column of the table indicates the label attached to each information system. The second column indicates the possible signals which may be generated by each information system. The third and final column indicates the relationships between the underlying states and the signals from each information system. The states are signified in the same way as they were above: s_1 represents the underlying state Safe, s_2 stands for the state Proceed with care and s_3 represents the state Danger.

Table 6.1 Possible signals from information systems

Information system	Signals from the information system	Partition of the underlying states introduced by the information system
η_1	y_1 = green	States reported together: Safe, Proceed with care and Danger; $y_1 = \{s_1, s_2, s_3\}$
η_2	y_1 = green	States reported together: Safe; $y_1 = \{s_1\}$
	y_2 = red	Proceed with care and Danger; $y_2 = \{s_2, s_3\}$
η_3	y_1 = green	States reported together: Safe and Dangerous; $y_1 = \{s_1, s_3\}$
	y_2 = red	Proceed with care; $y_2 = (s_2)$
η_4	y_1 = green	States reported together: Safe and Proceed with care; $y_1 = (s_1, s_2)$
	y_2 = red	Dangerous; $y_2 = (s_3)$
η_5	y_1 = green	States reported together: Safe; $y_1 = (s_1)$
	y_2 = yellow	Proceed with care; $y_2 = (s_2)$
	y_3 = red	Danger; $y_3 = (s_3)$

Table 6.1 indicates the total number of distinct information systems that can be constructed using a maximum of three possible signals. Each of the information systems shown partitions the underlying states in different ways. There are a number of additional information systems which could be constructed but they are informationally equivalent to those in the table. A system of red, yellow and green signals can be constructed which reverses the usual mapping of the red and green signals in a three-light system with the underlying states. It would associate a green signal with danger, and a red signal with safety. This system is informationally equivalent to the conventional system, as shown by system 5 in Table 6.1.

Comparable information systems

Only information system 5 (η_5) of the above information systems provides all the information conveyed by any other system. These other systems can however be ranked to a degree. The first information system in Table 6.1 is not really an information system at all. It provides no information to the decision maker. The second, third and fourth information systems all provide differential information which may be viewed differently by those with various preferences and probability beliefs. For example, a risk averse driver may prefer information system η_2 because among these three systems only this one distinguishes clearly the Safe state. Information system 4 (η_4) may be preferred by those who value their waiting time very highly because here the green signal indicates that stopping is not essential.

It is difficult to see who might use our third information system other than, perhaps, someone who is truly risk seeking. This is because the green signal compounds together both the safe and the dangerous states. It is fairly obvious that information system 5 (η_5) contains all the information of each of the information systems. Each of these other systems can be constructed from information system η_5 by leaving out some of the information conveyed by this information system. For example, the results of information system 2 (η_2) could be constructed merely by treating all yellow signals from information system 5 as if they were red. This amounts to throwing away information in order to convert a more detailed information system into a coarser information system. Thus we can argue that the finer information system will be preferred by an individual in a costless setting because any details not required can be ignored. This conclusion applies irrespective of the individual's preferences and probability beliefs. This is because all rational decision makers will either prefer our more detailed information system (η_5) or be indifferent between it and our less detailed systems. Those who are indifferent can convert information system 5 at no cost into the less detailed system.

An information system which contains at least the same information as another system is said to be at least as fine as the other system. The test for whether two information systems are comparable in terms of fineness is whether the signals from one system can be converted into those of the other by the application of some mathematical rule. Thus, with our example, signals from information system 5, our more detailed information system, can be converted into those of any of our less detailed systems by adding one of the signals in the more informative system to one of the other two signals provided by the coarser systems.

This means that the signals from one information system which is comparable in terms of fineness with another system can be 'garbled' so as to mimic exactly the signals received from the other information system (see Maguire, 1972). As an example, consider the traffic light system which reverses the mapping of colours of the signals of our information system five (η_5). Here, red will now be associated with the Safe state and green with the Dangerous one. Such a system contains all the information contained in the conventional traffic light system. Signals from this system can be converted into the signals from the conventional system simply by reversing the red and green signals. Both systems are of the same degree of fineness.

The importance of this finding is that if one information system is as fine as another, then and only then is the first system at least as valuable as the second for all preferences and beliefs. Looking at Table 6.1, it is clear that information system η_5 not only yields the same information as do the other systems, it also generates additional information for at least some decision makers. Anyone who does not wish to use all the information conveyed by an information system may jettison any additional information at no cost. This result implies that perfect information costlessly provided can never damage anyone. Perfect information can be either used or ignored. It is, however, important to remember that here we are involved with information systems that are comparable in terms of fineness (perfect information is comparable in these terms with all information systems with respect to the same events). If one non-comparable information system yields more detail than another, this does not mean that the more detailed information system will be preferred. This will depend on preferences and beliefs concerning the states of the environment (see Marschak and Radner, 1972, pp. 53–59).

The above findings concerning comparable information systems are very powerful. They say that we can, in some circumstances, compare information systems for an individual by considering only the signals from these information systems. We must therefore expect that ordering information systems in terms of their fineness will only provide a partial ranking among information systems. Using our example again, information systems 2, 3 and 4 are not comparable in terms of fineness. There is no way of converting any of these information systems into one of the others without access to additional information. Table 6.2 shows the state partitions induced by the information systems in Table 6.1.

Table 6.2 State classifications induced by various information system

Information system	State classification		
η_1	$\{s_1, s_2, s_3\}$		
η_2	$\{s_1\}$	$\{s_2, s_3\}$	
η_3	$\{s_1, s_3\}$	$\{s_2\}$	
η_4	$\{s_1, s_2\}$	$\{s_3\}$	
η_5	$\{s_1\}$	$\{s_2\}$	$\{s_3\}$

In the table, the states signalled together by each information system are grouped together and surrounded by a set of curly brackets, { }. System 1 groups all the states together. Information system 2 segregates state 1 (s_1) from the other two states. Similarly, our third and fourth information systems each classify the underlying states in a different way. Only information system 5 is comparable in terms of fineness with the other systems. Choices between η_2, η_3 and η_4 would require a consideration of preferences and beliefs. Different preferences mean that the decision makers may attach importance to the occurrence of different states. Thus, we might be able to say that system 2 which segregates the state of Safety from the other two states will appeal to those who are risk averse and want to proceed only with the assurance of complete safety. Those who value highly any time lost in not proceeding may prefer information system 4 to information system 2. With information system 4, they will stop at the road junction only when it is absolutely essential in order to avoid danger.

This example illustrates that it is generally impossible to define a single measure of the 'quantity' of information (without considering preferences or costs) such that if one information system yields more information than the other, it is the more valuable for an individual, irrespective of preferences and beliefs. Value-free orderings of information systems are only possible within the context of fineness for information systems which are comparable in terms of fineness. Another way of expressing comparability of this type is to say that the actual physical signals used are unimportant in themselves. The significance of a signal comes from the set of states which give rise to the signal and not from the physical form of the signal.

In our example we have dealt with a noiseless system in which each signal is deterministically related to a state or a set of states. Similar findings apply to noisy systems where signals are only probabilistically related to states but under more restrictive conditions (see Marschak and Radner, 1972, pp. 64–67). This matter is discussed in Note 1 at the end of this chapter.

Even these limited findings concerning comparable information systems do not extend straightforwardly to a multi-person context unless all have the same probability beliefs. Although individual probability beliefs do not affect our conclusions concerning the comparability of information systems for the individual, they do have to be taken into account when modelling market equilibrium. It can be shown that findings similar to the conclusions of this section require that any differences in beliefs between individuals are of a limited character and that some minor restrictions are placed on preferences (see Ohlson, 1987a, pp. 143–146; Amershi, 1988).

To summarise our findings in this section, we have explored some conditions which allow some costless information systems to be compared, irrespective of preferences and beliefs. Ranking such systems by the fineness was indicated to produce only a partial ordering. Even where information systems are comparable in the terms of this section, they may not be regarded as equivalent when costs are taken into account.

Accounting applications of comparable information systems

The above analysis can easily be applied in an accounting context. Chapter 12 provides some examples of this. A set of accounting reports containing both current cost and historical cost information is more informative in the technical sense than accounts prepared on either of the two bases separately. One reason why many accounting debates go unresolved is provided by the realisation that these usually involve accounting systems which are technically incomparable. Debates concerning the virtues of such systems cannot therefore be settled at the technical level and their resolution requires value judgments.

This is one reason why the choice between accounting theories is so difficult. The selection of a given theory cannot be determined by considering only technical issues.

This provides a reason why we would expect to see some form of regulation of accounting information.

Some methods for the regulation of accounting information are reviewed in Chapters 11 and 12. The requirement that comparable information systems should be at least as fine as each other also suggests that accounting policy makers who seek a conceptual framework for accounting of equal use to all are likely to fail if they approach this as a technical task. Accounting policy makers are able to make value-free choices between accounting systems only where these are comparable in the sense used in the previous section. Our discussion suggests that accounting policy makers should seek to consider accounting problems which involve comparable information systems.

Cushing (1977) has suggested that some accounting problems may be of this character. Segmental reporting would seem to be such an issue, assuming that no additional cost is encountered in providing this information. Basically, the fineness argument of this chapter, ignoring costs, would suggest the provision of as much information as possible on any accounting item because any user of accounting reports may ignore any additional detail not required.

This suggestion suffers from problems because it essentially recommends looking at accounting issues in isolation from each other. The conditions for the use of this approach are known but they are rather restrictive (see Bromwich, 1980). More generally, our approach also suggests that accounting policy makers need to understand the stringent requirements before accounting problems can be approached as choices between comparable accounting systems, even if there are no cost consequences attached to such choices.

Demski (1973) has argued that the general inability to fulfil these conditions means that attempts to lay down desired qualitative characteristics for accounting information, such as decision usefulness and a desired level for the reliability of accounting information, which are implicitly of equal use to all or to a subset of accounting report users, are likely to fail (see Chapter 12). This is because such an exercise requires that the accounting systems being considered are comparable in terms of fineness. Ranking accounting systems in terms of their fineness is generally impossible because many accounting systems are incomparable.

Vickrey (1982), in answer to Demski (see also Cushing, 1977; Chambers, 1976), has sought to show that decision relevance is a characteristic which can be applied to all accounting systems, irrespective of their general comparability. However, in his analysis he assumes the existence of perfect markets. Chapter 2 suggests that accounting systems could be ranked in this situation in the sense that individuals can be assumed, by trading on the market, to be able to look after their own preferences. Therefore Vickrey's findings do not seem to refute Demski's suggestions, which are more general (see Bromwich and Wells, 1983).

The next section discusses the effects on our decision model of allowing for the impact of information using a quantitative example.

Information and decision making: an example

The meaning being propounded here for 'information' can be exemplified by considering again Mr Risky's decision problem which we considered in Chapter 5, namely to determine which of three security portfolios to hold in order to maximise his individual utility. The returns from these portfolios depend on which of two mutually exclusive states of the environment will appear. Table 6.3 gives relevant information, with an assumed utility function of the form $\sqrt{W}$ (see Table 5.4).

Table 6.3 The utility of Risky's possible decisions

Action	State s_1 (probability 0.75)	State s_2 (probability 0.25)	Expected utility of action a_j
Hold portfolio A	$U(a_1s_1 = 95) = 10.0$	$U(a_1s_2 = 15) = 4$	8.5
Hold portfolio B	$U(a_2s_1 = 50) = 7.0$	$U(a_3s_2 = 150) = 12$	8.25
Hold portfolio C	$U(a_3s_1 = 75) = 8.6$	$U(a_3s_2 = 75) = 8.6$	8.6

The outcomes of each state–action pair shown in brackets are expressed as monetary units.

Without additional information, Mr Risky's optimal decision was found in Chapter 5 using the same facts as in Table 6.3 to be to hold security portfolio C. This yields an expected utility of 8.6 units. We will now consider the consequences of his obtaining costless access to information, assuming that he has access to an information system which will give him a completely reliable message as to which state of the environment will appear and that he is restricted to investing only up to his endowment (the problems where individuals are free to exploit their information by undertaking more general market operations will be considered in the next chapter).

Perfect new knowledge allows Mr Risky to plan to hold the optimal portfolio for the state which will occur. If the message he obtains is that state 1 will occur, he will hold portfolio A because this yields him the largest return in state 1 (10 units of utility). If the signal is that state 2 will appear, he will move to portfolio B, which yields the largest return in state 2 (12 units of utility). He will no longer plan to hold portfolio C. This portfolio rearrangement is sensible because access to a perfect information system relieves much of the uncertainty which led him to the holding of portfolio C as a protection against risk.

Thus we can say, as we would expect, that perfect information can be regarded as information in the sense of information economics because it changes Mr Risky's optimal decision.

Some uncertainty still remains, even when a perfect information system is available. This is because Risky will not know which message will be revealed by the possessor of the perfect information. In order to assess the worth of this information prior to receiving a message, he will have to assign probabilities to receiving the two messages when he has access to this information system. It seems reasonable to assume that he will use his previously believed likelihoods of the two states occurring for this purpose. Thus, to determine the worth of an information system, we must first calculate the utility accruing from taking the optimal action, conditional on each signal. We must then determine the expected utility obtained with access to the perfect information system by weighting the utility expected on receipt of each message by the probability of the message and summing for all messages. For Mr Risky these calculations yield:

$$E(U \mid a^*, y_i, \eta_p) = 0.75 \times 10u + 0.25 \times 12u = 10.5u \qquad [6.\text{II}]$$

The element on the left of this expression says that Expression 6.II shows Mr Risky's expected utility *conditional* on taking the optimal act a^* on the signals provided, y_is, using the perfect information system (η_p, where the subscript p reminds us that this is the perfect information system). The second element of the expression indicates the quantitative value of this expected utility. The remainder of the expression indicates how this value is obtained.

The first element of the right-hand part of the expression shows the utility obtained by taking the optimal action for state 1 (10 units) weighted by the perceived probability (0.75) that the message to be received from the information system will say that state 1 will appear. The second element, similarly, weights the expected result expressed in utility terms of multiplying optimal action in state 2 by the probability of a message indicating that state 2 will occur. Summing these two elements yields the expected utility of the decision made with the assistance of a perfect information system.

The maximum expected utility that Mr Risky can expect from employing any information system is 10.5 units. This is because the value of the perfect information provides an upper bound on the value of information systems. By employing this system and taking the optimal action on the basis of its signals, Mr Risky gains the maximum utility relative to using no information. Prior to using the perfect information system, Risky's maximum expected utility from his decision problem without information was a utility of 8.6 units: thus he gains 1.9 units of expected utility from employing the perfect information system when this is available costlessly. We can see that, as we said earlier, the provision of free private information can never do him any harm. He can either use it or ignore it. This finding can be generalised to apply to all individuals. Anyone in receipt of costless information can always jettison it. They therefore cannot be put into a worse position than prior to the receipt of the information. Much of the remainder of this chapter and Chapter 7 explore the qualifications to this finding which become necessary as we introduce practical matters, such as the cost of information.

We will now express our findings for Mr Risky in a more general form using our usual notation.

To quantify the maximum expected utility obtainable from an information system η_j, $E(U \mid \eta_j)$ where η_j represents a given information system, we go through two steps. First, for each signal from the given information system, we determine the expected utility obtained by taking the optimal act (a^*), given that signal. This process can be expressed for signal i and information system j as:

$$E(U \mid a^*, y_i, \eta_j) = \underset{a \in A}{\text{Max}} \sum_{S} U(a, s)\phi(s \mid y_i) \qquad [6.\text{III}]$$

where a specific signal is in mind. The term on the left represents the expected utility conditional on taking the optimal act, given a specific signal from a given information system. The new term on the far right signifies the probability of a state conditional on a specific signal. For each possible signal from a given information system we use Expression 6.III to determine the expected utility of taking the optimal act on each signal. The second step is to sum each of these conditional expected utilities, weighted by the probabilities of the signals to which they relate. This operation can be written for information system j as:

$$E(U \mid \eta_j) = \sum_y (EU \mid a^*, y, \eta_j)\, \phi(y) \qquad\qquad\qquad [6.\text{IV}]$$

Here the term on the left of the expression is the expected utility conditional on optimally using a specific information system. On the right-hand side, $\phi(y)$ represents the probability of a given signal. The summation sign (Σ) and the following terms tell us that the expected utilities conditional on using each signal optimally, as shown by the first element on the right, are to be weighted by the probability of the signal to which they relate and added together over all possible signals (y) from the information system (η).

The impact of the signals from an information system on decisions

So far we have considered the worth of information systems in a very general way. We have said that the role of an information system and its signals is to change the prior probabilities attached to the states of the environment. We will now consider this process of revising probabilities in a little more detail. How the signals from information systems can lead to revised probabilities is a complex matter; see Demski (1980) and Marschak and Radner (1972), especially chapter 2. This section may be skipped by those who are not interested in the technical detail of probability revision. Here the aim will be only to give a flavour of the analysis. A slightly more detailed treatment is given in Note 2 at the end of this chapter. However, an understanding of the analysis is important for accounting theory because it provides what many commentators believe is a compelling and rigorous rationale for how information, including accounting information, might be used by decision makers. Basically, information is seen as leading in a consistent way to a revision of a decision maker's subjective beliefs concerning state occurrence. Although approached here in the context of information for private use, this role of information as leading to the revision of probabilities applies to all information, whether provided for general or for private use.

This perspective also provides a rigorous meaning for the term 'decision usefulness' (or 'utility') which is used throughout the accounting literature as a major criterion for judging the worthwhileness of the figures produced by implementing accounting theories. The discovery of a rigorous definition of 'decision usefulness' (which, recall, states that information has utility for a decision if it changes the outcome of that decision) is important because the term is generally used in the accounting literature in a rather vague and non-operational way. This has allowed the advocates of most, if not all, accounting theories to claim that their favoured theory has some type of decision utility.

We will, again, proceed using our Mr Risky example. We now assume that Mr Risky is given costless access to an information system which yields two signals. One, which we will label economy 'unfavourable', purports to indicate the presence of state 1 and the other, which we will label economy 'favourable', similarly signals the occurrence of state 2. These signals are assumed to be imprecise in that they do not exhibit a one-for-one relationship with the state to which they purport to be related.

Table 6.4 shows, in columns 1 and 2, all the possible combinations of states and signals. Column 3 presents the assumed likelihood of each message, given the occurrence of a state. Thus the first entry in this column indicates there is assumed to be a 75

Table 6.4 An information system for Mr Risky's decision

Possible message	Possible state	Assumed likelihood of a message, given the occurrence of a state	Prior probability of state occurrence
(1)	(2)	(3)	(4)
Economy unfavourable (y_1)	State 1 (s_1)	$(y_1 \mid s_1) = 0.75$	0.75
Economy unfavourable (y_1)	State 2 (s_2)	$(y_1 \mid s_2) = 0.50$	0.25
Economy favourable (y_2)	State 1 (s_1)	$(y_2 \mid s_1) = 0.25$	0.75
Economy favourable (y_2)	State 2 (s_2)	$(y_2 \mid s_2) = 0.50$	0.25

per cent chance of signal 1 being observed and state 1 actually occurring. Similarly, the second row of this column indicates that there is a 50 per cent chance of signal 1 appearing, given that the actual state is state 2. The actual probabilities assigned to the occurrence of states conditional on the signals may result from past experience with similar information systems and from any knowledge provided by information suppliers. The notation used in column 3 $(y \mid s_i)$ says that each of the probabilities represented in this column indicates the likelihood that a signal will appear, conditional upon the occurrence of a given state. Finally, column 4 shows the probabilities that Mr Risky originally assigned to the two states occurring.

This information system does fulfil some obviously sensible requirements. The probability of receiving one or other message, given that a state has occurred, is 100 per cent as we would expect. The probabilities of receiving one or other of the two signals in both states must sum to 2. This is because there is a probability of 1 of receiving one or other of the two signals in each state, and there are two states. This indicates that the information system we are considering yields signals which overlap the two states. The probabilities of obtaining the two signals in both states would sum to 1 if each signal were associated with only one state.

In order to determine the impact of the signals from an information system, we wish to calculate revised probabilities of state occurrence, given each signal. Ultimately, we want to use these revised state probabilities to make an optimal decision. The first step in this process is to calculate the probabilities of receiving a given signal if a specific state has occurred (the conditional probability of a message, given a state). These probabilities for all messages were given in column 3 of Table 6.4. The probability of a message being observed because the state we are considering has obtained can be determined by multiplying the probability of a message, given the occurrence of the state, by the likelihood of the state obtaining, as indicated by Risky's prior beliefs about the states. Thus we are calculating Mr Risky's expectation of receiving a given message and a specific state obtaining bearing in mind his prior views concerning state occurrence. These calculations for each message are shown in Table 6.5.

The table has two panels. Panel A refers to signal 1 and Panel B refers to signal 2. Panel A shows in column 1 the probability of the signal given a specific state. The original probabilities of the states are shown in column 2 and the joint probabilities of the signal and the states are indicated in column 3. Panel B gives the same information for signal 2.

The entries in column 1 come from Table 6.4. Those in column 2 are Mr Risky's

Table 6.5 Probabilities of receiving messages, given the occurrence of either state

Panel A

State	Signal 1		
	Probability of y_1, given state i $(y_1 \mid s_i)$	Original probability of s_i $\phi(s_i)$	Joint probability state and message $(y_1 \mid s_i)((\phi)(s_i))$
	(1)	(2)	$(1 \times 2 = 3)$
State 1 (s_1)	0.75	0.75	0.562
State 2 (s_2)	0.50	0.25	0.125
Probability of message 1 conditional on the believed occurrence of either state.			$\overline{0.687}$

Panel B

State	Signal 2		
	Probability of y_2, given state i $(y_2 \mid s_i)$	Original probability of s_i $\phi(s_i)$	Joint probability states and message $(y_2 \mid s_i)((\phi)(s_i))$
	(1)	(2)	(3)
State 1 (s_1)	0.25	0.75	0.188
State 2 (s_2)	0.50	0.25	0.125
Probability of message 2 conditional on the believed occurrence of either state.			$\overline{0.313}$

prior expectations of the two states occurring, which are also shown in Table 6.4 in column 4. Each entry in column 3 tells us the combined probability of obtaining a message and a given state occurring. The totals of columns 3 in the two panels, indicate the probability of a specific message conditional on either state appearing.

The final step in obtaining the probabilities of the states, given each message, is to work out the probability of each of the states conditional on the receipt of each of the messages.

It can be shown that the probability of obtaining a state given a specific message is found by dividing the joint likelihood of the relevant signal and the relevant state by the total probability of receiving this message in all states. Intuitively, what we are doing is assigning the total probability of obtaining a message in the two states to each of these two states. This assignment is based upon the known likelihood of observing the message and each state together relative to the total likelihood of obtaining the signal in both states. We know, for example, that the total probability of observing signal 1 is 68.7 per cent. We therefore assign this probability to the two possible states in the proportion that the joint likelihood of receiving the signal and observing a state bears to the total probability of receiving the signal (see Note 1). Thus the total probability of observing signal 1 is 68.7 per cent and the chances that state 1 will occur when this signal is observed contributes 56.2 percentage units to this sum. The probability of the other state appearing, given signal 1, contributes the other percentage units to this sum. Therefore, if signal 1 is observed, it seems reasonable to say that there is a likelihood of 56.2/68.7 that state 1 has occurred, given signal 1. This equals 0.818 when expressed as a probability.

This operation yields the probability of a given state occurring conditional on the appearance of a specific signal. The same operations for all signals therefore yield new probabilities for the two states, given the occurrence of each of the two messages. These probabilities are shown in Table 6.6. It is this ability to bring about revisions

Table 6.6 Revised or posterior probabilities of states, given signals

State	Probability of state, given signal 1	Probability of state, given signal 2	Probability of state, given either signal
	1	2	3
State 1	0.82	0.60	1.42
State 2	0.18	0.40	0.58
	1.00	1.00	2.00

of the prior probabilities which renders information systems valuable. These revised probabilities are called posterior probabilities, reflecting that they are determined after information is received and are conditional on that information. They are shown for our Mr Risky example in columns 1 and 2 of Table 6.6.

Column 1 shows the probability attached to each state conditional on signal 1 occurring and column 2 gives the same information, given that signal 2 has occurred. The final column shows the probability of each state when either signal is received. The new probabilities satisfy all the earlier conditions which we said would seem sensible to apply to the probabilities in our example.

Inspection of Table 6.6 reveals that the revised probabilities attached to state occurrence are proportional to the product of the prior probability of the occurrence of the state and the likelihood of observing the signal in mind, conditional on the occurrence of that state. Our method of calculation provides a means for determining the posterior probabilities of states and for the consistent revision of state probabilities as more evidence appears. It really formalises the learning process in the face of information. Indeed, in a stable environment we can expect such posterior probabilities to converge to the objective probabilities for the same event, as was suggested in Chapter 5.

A more formal explanation of the operations required to calculate these revised probabilities involves the use of what is called Bayes' Theorem. This provides a formula for calculating revised state probabilities in the face of new information (see Mood, Graybill and Boes, 1974, p. 36). This formula has been used implicitly in the above calculations. A short intuitive treatment of the theorem is given in Note 2 at the end of this chapter.

These probability results allow us to proceed to the final step in the process. This is to see whether our revised probabilities make any difference to Mr Risky's decision.

Only if this is the case will the information have value to Mr Risky. To determine this, we first work out the expected utility which will accrue to Risky if he takes the optimal action on each signal. Thus, we first calculate the optimal action for each signal and add together the outcomes accruing in each state conditional on the signal expressed in terms of expected utility weighted by the probability of the signal upon which they are conditional. This is shown in Table 6.7, where the optimal acts in face of each signal are starred.

Table 6.7 New optimal acts for Mr Risky

Possible action	Utility of an action, given signal 1	Utility of an action, given signal 2
Hold portfolio A	8.92*	7.60
Hold portfolio B	7.90	9.00*
Hold portfolio C	8.60	8.60

*Optimal act: hold portfolio B

These figures are calculated by determining the expected utility of each act for each signal. To do this, the utility generated by each state in combination with an act is weighted by the revised probability of the state conditional on a signal, and added across all states. The detailed calculations for our example are shown in Note 3. For example, if we hold portfolio A when in receipt of signal 1, we can determine the expected utility generated using a variant of Expression 6.III.

This general process is written out in Expression 6.V. The figures for Mr Risky's problem where he takes action 1 after receiving signal 1 are shown below this expression as an illustrative example.

$$E(U \mid a_i, y_l, \eta) \quad = \Sigma U(a_i, s_i)\phi(s_i \mid y_1) \qquad\qquad [6.V]$$
$$8.92u \qquad = 10u \times 0.82 + 4u \times 0.18$$
$$\qquad = 8.2u + 0.72u$$

The numerical utilities and the state outcomes for Mr Risky come from Table 6.3 and the revised state probabilities come from the first column in Table 6.6. The optimal action when a given signal has been received is determined by calculating in this way the expected utility obtained from each action, given the specific signal. The action which yields the highest expected utility is then selected. This operation is undertaken for all possible signals. The optimal action for Mr Risky, if he received signal 1, is to hold portfolio A obtaining an expected utility of 8.92 units, as shown in Table 6.7. If he receives signal 2, he should hold portfolio B because in this way he will obtain the highest expected utility of 9.00 units, again as shown in Table 6.7. The two optimal actions associated with the two signals are starred in Table 6.7.

The second and final step in the last stage of this rather long process is to determine the value of the information system using Expression 6.IV. For our Mr Risky problem, this simply requires the addition of the expected utilities from taking the optimal act for each of our two signals (taken from Table 6.7) weighted by the revised probability of receiving each signal. To show this we write out Expression 6.IV again and show below this expression the relevant figures for Mr Risky's problem.

$$E(U \mid \eta) = \sum_{y}(EU \mid a^*, y, \eta)\phi(y)$$ [6.IVa]

$8.95u = 8.92u \times 0.687 + 9.00u \times 0.313$

$\qquad = 6.13u + 2.82u$

The expected utility from taking the optimal act conditional on signal 1 (taken from Table 6.7) is shown by the first element on the right of our numerical expression. This is then multiplied by the probability of receiving signal 1 (taken from Table 6.6). This weighted figure is then added to similar calculations for signal 2. Our calculations show that the expected utility from using our information system is 8.95 units of utility. As we would expect this yields a higher expected utility than when the null information system is used (8.95u − 8.6u = 0.35u, where 8.6 is the expected utility obtained without access to an information system (see Table 6.3)). It also generates a substantially lower expected utility than would be obtained with access to the perfect information system. The optimal decision using this perfect information system yields 1.55 more utility units than are obtained when using our imperfect information system (10.5u − 8.95u = 1.55u). The perfect information system yields an expected utility equal to 10.5u, (see Expression 6.II). With this background we are ready to deal in the next chapter with the value of information for private use and to consider how far we can deal with the costs of information.

The next section briefly summarises the application of our findings, thus far, to accounting.

Accounting aspects of information systems

The approach discussed in this chapter provides a framework for thinking about informativeness and decision usefulness in an accounting context in a much more precise and careful way than is usual in accounting debates. It also yields a framework for the use of *ex post* information. This role of information will be briefly discussed in the next chapter and more fully in Chapter 13. The ideas reviewed here give a specific meaning to many of the terms which are generally used rather casually in accounting textbooks. Information economics provides us with a clear and precise definition of information which can be used to help determine the informational value of accounting reports. Similarly, decision relevance is given a clearer meaning using information economics. Information economics also indicates the many difficulties that have to be solved before we can value information.

The perspective employed in this chapter has really been that of an information system designer seeking to provide an optimal information system for decision makers in an assumed environment. From an accounting point of view, we have described how accounting policy makers might proceed at a technical level abstracting from problems caused by different preferences amongst users. Accounting systems, to have user utility, must affect user views, and strictly should change user decisions by causing alterations to the probabilities assigned to states. The decision models reviewed in this chapter suggest that external accounting reports are likely to be only one information source and probably a fairly minor one, because a large number of information sources, perhaps of a more timely character, exist.

Our approach in this chapter can serve only as a guideline for thinking about the informativeness aspects of accounting reforms. This is not so much because the models used in this chapter seem far removed from the outputs of accounting systems, although it may be difficult to see just how accounting information systems yield signals about states of the environment. This problem can be overcome, at least, in principle, by reformulating all our earlier models, definitions and theories which concentrated on probability revision using payoffs (action–state combinations), which represent a more familiar concept to accountants. Such a reformulation of our work would not alter our conclusions. This change of emphasis does, however, suggest that a clear aim for accounting information would be to report the payoffs from activities.

For example, with this view, the economist's approach to income and wealth measurement (see Chapter 3 and 4) adjusted specifically for uncertainty (as is done in Chapter 8) would seem entirely consistent with the models employed in this chapter.

Looking at conventional accounting models more generally, it has proved very difficult to determine how the outputs of conventional accounting are used in decision making generally, and more specifically how these outputs might be incorporated into the models of this chapter. Thus, the contribution of the informational perspective to much of accounting is generally limited to providing a clearer understanding of how accounting systems might obtain value, yielding a more rigorous definition of the decision relevance of accounting information and indicating some of the problems that this approach to accounting needs to solve.

The main obstacle to using any of the rigorous definitions of this chapter in accounting policy making is the lack in the real world of any generally accepted decision making models, even for investment decision making. Accounting policy makers may have reacted to this and other problems flowing from a thorough-going use of the models of information economics in accounting, by seeking only to define any terms borrowed from this approach in a rather general way; see, for example, the FASB's definitions of the value of information and of decision relevance (FASB, 1978, 1980a). However, the FASB's Conceptual Framework Project suggests that adopting an information perspective even at this level of generality does substantially change ways of thinking about accounting (see Chapter 12).

The work of researchers who have adopted an informational perspective suggests another problem with any direct application of information economics to accounting. Our emphasis in this chapter has been on the design of optimal information systems for decision making. However, those seeking to monitor such systems for policy making or research purposes have to work with their *ex post* results. Such workers therefore have to utilise the payoffs (outcomes from action–state combinations) reported on the basis of whichever accounting system is in use. When working with *ex post* payoffs, it is difficult to separate out the results of the accounting procedures being adopted from all the other items which may impact on reported payoffs. Accounting policy makers and others wishing to monitor the actual results of policy making in accounting may also find it difficult to generalise from outcomes for specific entities in a way which is likely to command any general acceptance.

This conclusion should now be familiar and is to be expected whenever markets are imperfect (see Chapters 10 and 11). Thus we cannot say that adopting an information perspective frees us from all of the major problems of accounting.

Chapter summary

In this chapter we introduced a large number of new concepts. The two main parts of this chapter have already been summarised in the 'Plan of the chapter'. We will therefore merely reiterate in summary form some of the most important findings for accounting of adopting an informational approach.

1 Information is new knowledge which leads to a change in the actions of a decision maker.
2 Perfect information is knowledge which gives a completely reliable message or signal as to each of the states which may occur, with each message relating uniquely to one and only one state. What is called the expected value obtained from using a perfect information system places an upper bound on the value of the other less perfect information systems which can be utilised for the same decision.
3 Perfect information can never place the decision maker in a worse position than if perfect information were not available, because any information not required can always be ignored.
4 Two types of information system from which imperfect information is obtained are:
   (i) Ones from which the signals do not relate uniquely to a specific state but rather relate to a number of such states. This type of imperfect information system still provides signals which partition the underlying states in a mutually exclusive and exhaustive manner, but not in a complete way (i.e. each signal does not signal the occurrence of one and only one specific state).
   (ii) Systems from which the signals partition the underlying states in an exhaustive manner, but more than one signal may be associated with a specific state (these are labelled noisy information systems).
5 Some costless information systems may be ranked in terms of the richness of the detail they convey about states of the environment.
6 An information system which can be changed to yield the same signals as some other information system without access to additional information is said to be at least as fine as this other system.
7 The optimal costless information system for a given decision is that which contains all information systems which are comparable with it. Such an information system yields at least all the information provided by these other information systems, and perhaps more.
8 A ranking of costless information systems in terms of their fineness or informativeness is generally impossible because costless information systems are generally not comparable in terms only of the information they yield.
9 A general accounting implication of (8) is that, in the present state of knowledge, it is not always possible to choose between accounting theories or accounting treatments on the basis of only their informativeness. The findings summarised above have, according to some commentators, revolutionised attitudes to accounting. Adopting an informational perspective to accounting has emphasised a number of facets of accounting that previously had gone unexplored. This approach provides the foundation stone for much of the theory reviewed in this book with its emphasis on viewing information generally, and accounting information, as economic goods or commodities subject to the usual economic influences.

Notes

1. Fineness with probabilistic information systems

Blackwell's Theorem provides similar conditions to fineness for probabilistic information systems (see McGuire, 1972; Marschak and Miyasawa, in McGuire and Radner, 1972). This theorem says that, given the existence of a payoff-adequate partition of the underlying states, one information system can be said to be as fine as another if the probability of a signal from the first information system can be converted into the probability of a signal from the other information system by using a garbling system (more precisely, a randomising device of a specific character).

In more detail, this garbling mechanism must be such that, given the appearance of a specific state from the payoff-adequate partition, the signals (y) received from one of the information systems which we wish to compare, η_i, can be converted into a signal from another information system, η_j, by using a random device which generates new signals from the first system, η_i, with a given probability. It can be shown that if the choice of a signal from η_j is determined only by the signal from the system i, perhaps, with noise, information system i is at least as valuable, as fine or as informative, as information system j.

This is only a sufficient condition for such information systems to be comparable. A necessary condition additionally requires that the probabilities used in converting a signal from one system to the other take a specific form. Very crudely put, this requirement is that the probability of any signals from one system, given a state occurrence in the payoff-adequate partition, can be converted into the probability of a specific signal from the other by applying a weighting factor to the signals from the first system, conditional on the given state. The weighting factors applied to the signals from the first information system to obtain the probabilities of the signals from the other system must sum to unity when added over all the signals from the second system. In essence, all this means is that one information system is as fine as another if and only if the signals from the first system can be transformed into those of the second by applying some specific probabilistic device to signals from the first system.

2. Bayes' theorem

Here we give a short intuitive explanation of the reasoning underlying Bayes' Theorem; for a more formal treatment see Demski, 1980; Mood, Graybill and Boes, 1974, p. 36; also Degroot, 1970. Consider a set of messages y and a subset of states, s, from the set S. Recall that an information system is itself a subset of the set of states, S. Information systems merely partition this set in some way. We first calculate the probability of the occurrence of a specific message (say, y_1) and a specific state (s_1) by multiplying the probability of the message conditional on the state by the probability of the state. That is we use the following expression:

Joint probability of $(s_1, y_1) = \phi(s)\phi(y) = [\phi(y \mid s)\phi(s)]$. 　　　　[6.VIa]

where the subscripts are suppressed on the right-hand side for ease of presentation. The likelihood of obtaining a given signal conditional on a specific state occurring for our Mr Risky problem is given in Table 6.4, expressed in the form of the bracketed element in Expression 6.VIa above. Columns 3 of Table 6.5 in the chapter give the joint probability of each state and signal calculated according to Expression 6.VIa.

This probability can also be obtained by calculating the probability of the state, given the message weighted by the probability of receiving the message. This can be written in the same way as above, i.e. as

Joint probability $(s_1, y_1) = \phi(y)\phi(s) = [\phi(s \mid y)]\phi(y)$ 　　　　[6.VIb]

The element in square brackets in this expression is what we are seeking, the probability of the state, given the message. This can be obtained by substituting Expression 6.VIa for the joint probability into the second expression for (s_1, y_1) and rearranging. This gives

$$[\phi(y \mid s)\phi(s) = \phi(s \mid y)\phi(y)]$$
$$= [\phi(s \mid y) = \phi(y \mid s)\phi(s)/\phi(y)] \qquad \text{[6.VIc]}$$

The right-hand side of this expression says that the probability of the state conditional on the signal is given by the known probability of the signal, given the state, divided by the probability of the signal. The probability of the signal is simply the probability of the signal conditional on the state occurring plus the probability of the signal occurring in all other states weighted by the respective state probabilities. The probability of the signal can therefore be expressed as:

Probability of the message $= \phi(y \mid s)\phi(s) + \phi(y \mid \text{not } s)\phi(\text{not } s)$ \qquad [6.VId]

Substituting this last expression into Expression [6.VIc] yields Bayes' Rule for probability revision, which can be written using our usual symbols as:

$$\phi(s \mid y) = \phi(y \mid s)\phi(s)/\phi(y \mid s)\phi(s) + \phi(y \mid \text{not } s)\phi(\text{not } s) \qquad \text{[6.VIe]}$$

This is Bayes' Theorem. Table 6.6, gives these revised state probabilities for signals 1 and 2 for Mr Risky's problem. These are calculated using the above formulae for each signal by dividing the joint probability of a state and a message by the overall probability of receiving the message (as shown in Table 6.5). To obtain the revised probability of each state, given a message (say, signal 1), the joint probability shown in Panel A, column 3 of Table 6.5 is divided by the overall probability of receiving the message. The overall probability of obtaining message 1 is obtained in Table 6.5 by summing the two joint probabilities in Panel A, column 3. Similar calculations using Panel B, column 3 of this table yield the revised state probabilities, given message 2.

3. *Calculations to obtain the expected utility of each of Mr Risky's actions, given the occurrences of either Signal 1 or Signal 2*

The top panel of Table 6.8 yields the expected utility of each of the three action options, given the revised state probabilities flowing from the occurrence of signal 1 (y_1 = economy favourable). The utility obtained from each action and state combination (column 1 for state 1 and column 3 for state 2) are taken from Table 6.3. The revised probabilities attached to the two states consequent on signal 1 (y_1) occurring are taken from column 1 of Table 6.6. The expected utility of each action (shown in column 5 of Table 6.8) is found in the now familiar way using Expression 6.V. (This expected utility is found by weighing the expected utility of each state combined with a given action by the now-revised probability of the occurrence of each state.) The top panel of Table 6.8 shows that the optimal act (a^*), given that signal 1 has been received, is to hold portfolio A, which yields an expected utility of 8.92 units. The bottom panel shows that if signal 2 appears, the optimal action is to hold portfolio B yielding an expected utility of 9.0 units.

Table 6.8 Expected utility from each action, given the occurrence of signal 1 and signal 2

Signal 1

Possible action	Utility of action (a_j) in combination with state 1	Revised probability of state 1 given signal 1 $(\phi(s_1\mid y_1))$	Utility of action (a_j) in combination with state 2	Revised probability of state 2 given signal 1 $(\phi(s_2\mid y_1))$	Expected utility of action
	(1)	(2)	(3)	(4)	(5 = 1 × 2 + 3 × 4)
Hold Portfolio A	10.0	0.82	4.0	0.18	8.92*
Hold Portfolio B	7.0	0.82	12.0	0.18	7.90
Hold Portfolio C	8.6	0.82	8.6	0.18	8.60

*Optimal act: hold portfolio A

Signal 2

Possible action	Utility of action (a_j) in combination with state 1	Revised probability of state 1 given signal 2 $(\phi(s_1\mid y_2))$	Utility of action (a_j) in combination with state 2	Revised probability of state 2 given signal 2 $(\phi(s_2\mid y_2))$	Expected utility of action
	(1)	(2)	(3)	(4)	(5 = 1 × 2 + 3 × 4)
Portfolio A	10.0	0.60	4.0	0.40	7.6
Portfolio B	7.0	0.60	12.0	0.40	9.0*
Portfolio C	8.6	0.60	8.6	0.40	8.6

*Optimal act: hold portfolio B

7

The value of information for private use and the utility of public information

Optimal decision making with private information has been discussed in Chapter 6; this chapter first considers how such information can be valued. The second main part of this chapter introduces the concept of publicly available information.

Plan of the chapter

The first major part of this chapter considers the value, if any, of information for private use. The definition of this value as the change in expected utility generated by utilising an information system relative to using the null information system, which provides no relevant information, is discussed first. An example is provided using the Mr Risky problem outlined in previous chapters. Here, using a perfect information system, the value of information is defined as the net expected utility obtained from using an information system for a decision relative to the expected utility of the decision employing the null information system. It is then shown that attaching a monetary value to this gain in expected utility is not without problems where individuals are risk averse. Such an expression of the benefits of private information is shown to be possible with risk neutrality. Here again, we use our Mr Risky example.

Two methods of valuing information for private use in the face of risk attitudes are then considered. The demand value of information is said to be given by the amount the individual would be willing to pay to obtain the information on the market. Alternatively, the supply value of information is defined as the amount for which the individual would be willing to sell the information and the prospect to which it applies on the market.

We then go on to discuss a number of problems with valuing information, mainly flowing from the presence of risk averse decision makers. It will be suggested that these problems make it very difficult for accounting regulators to use a cost/benefit test when deciding on changes in accounting regulations.

The second major part of the chapter considers the economic characteristics of publicly available information. This type of information is first defined as information which is simultaneously made available to all. It is suggested that a number of factors make public information even more difficult to analyse than private information. Public information will impact on security prices and affect equilibrium prices. This type of information must therefore be considered in an equilibrium market setting if it is to be analysed fully. A number of market regimes incorporating public information are then considered from this perspective and shown to possess different equilibrium characteristics.

It is indicated that market participants may be made worse off by the introduction of public information even though the market regime with this information can be shown to be able to obtain Pareto efficiency. This problem arises because of the possibility of such information causing revaluations of individual endowments via changing market prices. Such revaluations may mean that some individuals are worse off with the introduction of public information. However, several of the market regimes to be considered contain mechanisms which allow this problem to be either ameliorated or entirely avoided.

A central topic of this chapter is the value, if any, of privately available accounting information—a theme which has been discussed a number of times in this book. In this chapter, this subject is considered using the more rigorous and comprehensive framework provided by information economics.

The value of private information

We have implicitly calculated the value of information in the preceding sections. The usual definition of the so-called 'expected' value of information is the increase in expected utility resulting from use of an information system relative to use of the null information system. This comparison with the null system is made because it avoids technical difficulties involved with comparisons between information systems (see Demski, 1980, pp. 34–35).

Reverting to our Mr Risky example of the previous chapter, we can calculate the value of perfect information in utility units by recalling that taking the optimal action on the basis of this system yielded 10.5 units of utility. This can be written as:

$$E(U \mid \eta_p) = 10.5u$$

As a first step in dealing with this complex subject, we can say that the value of a perfect information system can be measured by the expected utility of this system (η_p) less the expected utility using the null system (η_0). Using our notation this can be expressed as:

Value of an information system = $E(U \mid \eta_p) - E(U \mid \eta_0)$ [7.I]

Applying this expression to our Risky problem yields $10.5u - 8.6u = 1.9u$ as we calculated earlier. This is the expected value of the perfect information system to Mr Risky, expressed in terms of expected utility. Expression 7.I measures the value of information systems in general. It thus provides a step towards defining the value of information in a precise way which can be substituted for the usual usage of this term in accounting. However, this expression can only be used to value information in utility terms. Expressing such values in monetary terms, which is what we can reasonably assume accountants wish to do, is only possible in special conditions. One example is where a decision maker is risk neutral, and where expected monetary values therefore provide an unambiguous description of the contribution to welfare made by a prospect.

With risk neutrality, the value of an information system can be determined straight-forwardly by deducting from the expected monetary value of the decision made with an information system, the expected monetary value that would have been generated for this decision problem without utilising an information system. In this case there is no difficulty in working with the net payoffs yielded by a costly information system. Assuming the cost of using an information system is a definite lump sum, all we need to do is to deduct this cost from the expected monetary value of the system (discounted if necessary). If this net expected monetary value is positive, the purchase of the information system is worthwhile.

The expected monetary value of information: an example

To illustrate the expected monetary value of an information system we will revert to our Mr Risky example, but will reinstate our original assumption that he is risk neutral. This means he will seek to maximise the expected monetary value of his decision. Recall that without information he is indifferent between our three prospects. The expected monetary value of each decision is 75 monetary units (see Chapter 5, Table 5.3).

Now assume that he is offered the use of the imperfect information system of Chapter 6. One possibility is to calculate the maximum amount he would be willing to pay for this system for his own private use. This sum is what we earlier called the expected value of information (see Expression 7.I) when we determined the expected utility provided by this information system. Here, however, all our calculations will be done in monetary amounts. The revised probabilities according to the states are, of course, the same as determined in the previous chapter (pp. 134–9). The requisite calculations are shown in Tables 7.1 and 7.2. Panel 1 of Table 7.1 determines the expected monetary values of Mr Risky's three options, given that signal 1 has been observed. It uses the monetary values of the outcomes in each state shown in Table 6.3 of the previous chapter. These monetary values (columns 1 and 4) are multiplied by the revised probabilities that we have already calculated in Chapter 6 for states 1 and 2 conditional on the receipt of signal 1 in Table 6.6. Summing the monetary values in each state weighted by its probability, as shown in columns 3 and 6, yields the expected monetary value of each strategy (column 7). The star attached to outcome A indicates this is the act which yields the highest expected monetary value, given signal 1. Panel 2 of the figure shows the same calculations for the three acts, given the receipt of signal 2. It indicates that holding portfolio B is optimal, conditional upon the occurrence of signal 2. Table 7.2 calculates the expected monetary value generated from taking these two optimal acts. This requires that the two optimal outcomes are weighted by the probabilities of receiving the two signals.

Column 8 of each of Panels 1 and 2 of Table 7.1 reminds us of the expected utilities we obtained earlier in Chapter 6 (p. 138) on the assumption that Mr Risky used our information system and was risk averse. Column 4 of Table 7.2 similarly shows the expected utility offered by the decision when our information system is used (see Expression 7.I). These results will be used in due course when we discuss the determination of the value of information when the individual is not risk neutral. A comparison of columns 7 and 8 of Panels 1 and 2 of Table 7.1 indicates that, in our case at least, the optimal actions on receipt of either signal are invariant with Mr Risky's assumed risk attitude. This is by no means a general finding (see Hilton, 1981).

Table 7.1 The expected monetary value of Mr Risky's optimal decision for each signal using an imperfect system

Panel 1: Expected monetary values of actions conditional upon receipt of signal 1

Action	(a, s_1)	$\phi(s_1\mid y_1)$	EMV	(a, s_2)	$\phi(s_2\mid y_1)$	EMV	Total EMV	Total expected utility†
	(1)	(2)	$(3 = 1 \times 2)$	(4)	(5)	$(6 = 4 \times 5)$	$(7 = 3 + 6)$	(8)
Hold Portfolio A	95	0.82	77.9	15	0.18	2.7	80.6*	8.92*
Hold Portfolio B	50	0.82	41.0	150	0.18	27.0	68.0	7.90
Hold Portfolio C	75	0.82	61.5	75	0.18	13.5	75.0	8.60

*Optimal act: hold portfolio A.
†(See Table 6.8).

Panel 2: Expected monetary values of actions conditional on receipt of signal 2

Action	(a, s_1)	$\phi(s_1\mid y_2)$	EMV	(a, s_2)	$\phi(s_2\mid y_2)$	EMV	Total EMV	Total expected utility†
	(1)	(2)	$(3 = 1 \times 2)$	(4)	(5)	$(6 = 4 \times 5)$	$(7 = 3 + 6)$	(8)
Hold Portfolio A	95	0.60	57	15	0.40	6.0	63.0	7.60
Hold Portfolio B	50	0.60	30	150	0.40	60.0	90.0*	9.00*
Hold Portfolio C	75	0.60	45	75	0.40	30.0	75.0	8.60

*Optimal act: hold portfolio B.
†(See Table 6.8).

Table 7.2 The expected monetary value of Mr Risky's optimal decision using an imperfect information system

Optimal action conditional on signal	Outcome EMV	$\phi(y_i)$	EMV	$E(U)$
	(1)	(2)	$(3 = 1 \times 2)*$	(4)
Hold A $\mid y_1$	80.6	0.687	55.37	6.13
Hold B $\mid y_2$	90	0.313	28.17	2.82
Total			83.54	8.95

*(See Expression 6.IVa)

The demand value of information

What is called the 'demand' value of our information system, assuming that Mr Risky is risk neutral, can now be calculated using the above results. To do this, we deduct the expected monetary value generated by taking the optimal action without any information, 75 monetary units, from the equivalent value obtained with our information system. Thus, the demand value of our information system is given by deducting from the expected monetary value of the decision with the information system the amount which would produce indifference between using this information system and using the null information system. These calculations for our example are shown below:

$$83.54 - 8.54 \, (= 83.54 - 75.00) = 75 \qquad\qquad [7.\text{II}]$$

The element on the right is the optimal expected value of our decision problem without access to any information system. The first element on the left of the expression is the expected monetary value of the decision using our information system. The second element on the left is the maximum amount a risk neutral individual would pay for the private use of our information system (8.54 monetary units). It is, of course, what we have called earlier the 'expected' value of an information system, when this is expressed in monetary terms.

The maximum demand value of information can be defined more generally allowing for attitudes to risk, assuming that the payoffs from actions and the value of information are expressed in cash flow terms. (For a rigorous treatment see Hilton, 1981, or Demski, 1980, pp. 34–35). This value can be expressed in a casual way, using Expressions 6.III and 6.IV, as:

$$E(U \mid \eta_\text{h}) = \sum_y \phi(y)[(\text{Max}_{a \in A} \sum_S U((a, s,) - h)\phi(s \mid y)] \qquad\qquad \text{Definition } [7.\text{A}]$$
$$= E(U \mid a^*, \eta_0)$$

The expression on the left indicates the expected utility obtained from taking the optimal actions on the signals from an information system costing h monetary units, where h represents the maximum demand value for information. The second element on the right of the first equality sign contained in large brackets rewrites this expected utility in more detail. It says to optimise expected utility, with the information system, we first maximise the expected utility of the net payoff from each action, given a specific signal (shown by the element $(\text{Max} \, \Sigma \, U(a, s, -h)\phi(s \mid y)$ in the expression). These utilities are then summed over all signals weighted by their probabilities, indicated by the $\Sigma \phi y$

element of the expression. The payoff in each state is written net of the maximum value of the information system (h) because this amount must be paid in each state. The left-hand side of Definition 7.A must have the same value as the final element of the definition ($EU \mid a^*, \eta_0$) which represents maximum expected utility that can be obtained using no information.

The maximum monetary value, h, assigned to the information system is thus the amount that renders the decision maker indifferent between using and not using the information. The maximum value of an information system is the value which implies that:

$$h = E(U \mid \eta_h) - E(U \mid a^*, \eta_0) \tag{7.III}$$

This value is the certain amount of money which renders the choice between utilising the information system and not using it a matter of indifference. This value can be shown to be approximately 5 monetary units for our example. This can be demonstrated by first deducting this amount from each of Mr Risky's monetary payoffs and then using Expression 7.III to convert these payoffs into utility amounts. The expected utility of the state outcomes with the information system, net of the cost of the information system in each state, is equal, as we would expect, to 8.6 units—the expected utility of the null system. Thus, the expected utility yielded by the information system can be expressed as equivalent to a certain sum of monetary units (5 monetary units in our case).

The supply value of information

An alternative to utilising the demand value of information is to compute its supply value (see Hilton, 1981). Here we calculate the amount of money which represents the minimum for which the individual would sell the choice problem together with the information system being considered.

The minimum selling price (G) for an information system can be written as G in:

$$E(U \mid \eta_0, G) = E(U \mid \eta) \tag{7.IV}$$

The element on the left of this expression is the expected utility obtained by selling the decision problem and the information system, where G is the minimum price at which the decision maker would sell the information system on the market. The element on the right-hand side of the expression is the expected utility of the outcomes using the information system. Expression 7.IV implies that G is the amount which makes the decision maker indifferent between using the information system and selling it and the decision problem as a package. The supply value of information to Mr Risky expressed in monetary amounts, assuming that he is risk neutral, is starred in the expression:

$$83.54 = 75 + 8.54^*$$

In other words, the expected monetary value obtained using the information system is the sum of the other two items in the expression, i.e. the expected monetary value obtained using the null information system and the selling price of the information system.

The supply value of information for our example where Mr Risky is risk averse and his preferences are described by our assumed utility function can be shown, using Expression 7.IV, to equal approximately 5 monetary units. This amount also equals the demand value of information in this case. Optimal action without access to our information system requires that we select option C, which yields the maximum utility of 8.6 units. This selection yields a constant payoff of 75 monetary units in each of our two states. Adding five certain monetary units to this monetary payoff yields an expected utility of approximately 8.95 units. This equals the expected utility obtained using our information system, as shown in Table 7.2.

Problems with valuing information

The above two definitions of the value of information, one adopting a demand perspective and the other using a supply orientated view, express this value in certain monetary units. We would have thus seemed to have obtained operational measures for the value of information which allow us to look only at the net payoffs yielded by information systems. These concepts would seem to allow us to put a value on the information generated by accounting systems and make our choices accordingly.

This section looks briefly at some of the major problems which militate against the easy practical use of the above measures of the value of the information in accounting (see Demski, 1980, pp. 34–35; Marschak & Radner, 1972, pp. 82–86).

We can only adopt these approaches easily where risk neutrality can be assumed. Here our measures of information do provide measures of the value of information expressed in certain monetary amounts. In these circumstances we can determine whether the value of information exceeds its cost and can place an unambiguous monetary value on information systems. This is what we did for Mr Risky when we calculated the maximum price he would pay for our information when he was assumed to be risk neutral. Using this approach, we found that the value placed on our information system was 8.54 monetary units (shown by Expression 7.II).

Thus, with risk neutrality we can proceed to determine whether the cost of information exceeds the benefits it produces. This is a variant of the much advocated cost/benefit test for accounting information (see Chapter 12). Benefits and costs are here, however, defined in a far more rigorous way than is usual with such calculations in accounting. With our approach, costs and benefits are also defined in a way consistent with the decision models which should be used if it is wished to maximise the expected monetary value of wealth. As explained below, this perspective does however also suggest that cost/benefit tests in general cannot be used widely without explicitly considering preferences and opting to favour one party in society over another.

The value of information and risk attitudes

The value of information we calculated above differed depending upon our assumptions concerning Mr Risky's preferences concerning risk. We calculated above that he would pay up to 8.54 monetary units for private use of our information system if he were risk neutral, whereas he would only pay approximately 5 monetary units for use of the information system when he was risk averse to the degree represented by the utility function we are assuming for Risky in our example. This suggests that the value of an information system for private use is sensitive to the decision maker's risk attitude. As our example suggests, the effect of different risk attitudes on the monetary value attached to a given information system may cause this value to change. Such alterations in value may not be easy to predict and their determination may be difficult (see Hilton, 1981).

It may seem surprising that Risky would pay more for the information system when he was risk neutral than when he was risk averse. The reason for this is that risk aversion affects not only the valuation placed on the uncertain fruits of the decision obtained using the information system, but also on the certain sum of money required to pay for the information. Risk aversion means that the enhanced but uncertain benefits from using the information will be valued relatively less highly by a risk averse person than by a risk neutral decision maker, thereby reducing the value of the information system to the risk averse person. Similarly, the certain money to be sacrificed to pay for the information system will be valued more highly by the risk averse decision maker relative to a risk neutral one. For both of these reasons, a risk averse person may be willing to pay less for an information system than someone neutral to risk. The valuation of an information system for an individual can only be done by consulting that person's preferences.

An important problem, once we allow risk attitudes into the analysis, is that our demand measure does not provide a ranking of information systems. It merely expresses the maximum amount an individual would pay relative to utilising the null information system. That the demand value of one information system is greater than the demand value of another information system does not imply that the expected utility obtained with the first information system is greater than the expected utility conditional on the use of the second information system. This is not a problem with our supply definition of the value of information. This is because the certain monetary value attached to the decision problem and to the information system is a measure of the total expected utility of these two items taken together. Expected utility is therefore a good ranking device. However, to obtain such monetary values we must know individual preferences. This means that we have not succeeded in obtaining any generally useful measure of the value of information. It also suggests that those accounting regulators who seek to choose between accounting systems on the basis of cost/benefit tests face many difficult problems, even in the context of a single individual, let alone in the multi-person and more realistic institutional environment to be discussed later in this chapter.

Indeed, the next section raises a second problem in generating such a measure, and shows that we cannot even use net payoffs to value information systems directly where individuals are risk averse.

Problems with using the net payoffs of information systems

Recall that, in the above calculations to ascertain the value of information, the basic elements were the net payoffs from each state–action combination after paying for the information system being used. The problem with using instead the utility assigned to the net payoff (after meeting the cost of the information system) is that the net utility of an outcome minus the cost of an information system will not in general be the same as the difference between the utility of the outcome and the utility of this cost. As will be explained below, this means that we cannot express the value of an information system in terms of the certain sum of money which renders a non-risk-neutral individual indifferent between using and not using an information system (the net payoff from using the information system).

This inability to value the net benefits of information systems arises because the usual conditions which allow utilities to be manipulated arithmetically are absent from this problem. Usually, in decision making, the utilities in mind are those for mutually exclusive events, only one of which will happen. In such problems, assigning utilities to events therefore does not require us to consider any possible complementarity between events because such an interrelationship cannot arise. However, such a relationship between events can appear where we are evaluating information systems.

Here we are considering two events, the gross payoff from using an information system, and its cost. Both of these events occur simultaneously. We therefore have to consider the utility generated by this combination of events considered as a whole.

Seeking to value an information system by valuing separately the net benefits over costs in order to determine the net payoff from the system may be likened to attempting to assess the benefits of having a cup and a saucer by considering the benefits accruing from the possession of each piece of crockery separately. Such an exercise ignores any benefits obtained from using the cup and saucer together. With this reasoning, the utility ascribed to the net payoff from an information system may well be different from that assigned to the net benefits obtained from the entire prospect represented by the decision problem, the information system and its cost. For a more technical presentation, see Hirshleifer (1970) pp. 251–255. The remainder of this section is a little technical and may be skipped by those willing to accept this conclusion.

The above conclusion can be illustrated by returning to our Mr Risky example. Above we determined that in utility terms our information system was worth some 0.35 units of utility to Mr Risky when compared with the null system (see page 139). This net payoff in utility terms cannot be expressed in monetary terms by simply converting it into a certain monetary amount by reference to Mr Risky's utility function.

Figure 7.1 shows that proceeding in this way generally may yield a certain monetary amount different from that which we obtain using either our demand or supply definition of the value of information.

The essence of the problem is illustrated in this figure, where a decision involves a gamble offering outcomes OX″ and OY″. The expected monetary value of the optimal decision without information is assumed to be OX, which lies halfway between OX″ and OY″ because the probability of obtaining either of the two outcomes is assumed to be 50 per cent. The expected monetary value of the decision made with an information system is assumed to be shown by OY on the horizontal axis, where the probability of the more favourable amount OY″ is now 75 per cent. This higher probability of the more favourable amount reflects the information conveyed by the information system. Moving up the monetary value line to points B and C and reading across to the vertical axis yields the utility of these two uncertain amounts as $U(y)$ and $U(x)$. The difference in utility accruing because of the information system is utilised is therefore given by $U(y)$ minus $U(x)$. These two basic utility amounts can be converted into the certain amounts of money which are equivalent to them, by first locating the positions on the utility curve horizontal to $U(y)$ and $U(x)$ shown by points B′ and C′ respectively, and reading down to the horizontal axis. This yields the certain amounts of money equivalent in utility to $U(y)$ and $U(x)$. The certainty equivalent of $U(y)$ is thus shown to be OY′, and that of $U(x)$ is OX′.

The value of the information system in certain money units is thus given by OY′ − OX′. It might seem that the difference between these two certain monetary amounts, shown in the figure by OP (OP = OY′ − OX′) gives the monetary value of the infor-

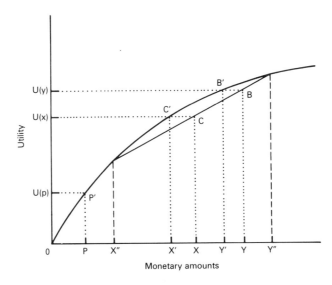

Figure 7.1 Monetary value of information

mation system. That this is not the case is easily seen. The utility of OP is found by moving to the point on the utility curve vertically above P (shown by point P′ in the figure) and reading across to the utility axis. These calculations show that the utility assigned in this way to the net benefits from using the information system $U(p)$ is substantially greater than was obtained when we looked at the benefits of the package as a whole.

This is because $U(p)$ does not capture the essence of the problem which requires determining the certain monetary amount equals to $U(y) - U(x)$. This involves determining the utility of benefits and costs, the size of which depends upon the segment of the utility curve being consulted in the calculations. Appraising only the net benefits means that the wrong segment of this curve may be being used.

Cost and benefits of information for the individual: conclusions and summary

The above analysis says that only if the decision maker is risk neutral can the net benefits of costly information systems be valued in monetary terms without consulting the individual's preferences. More generally, to value information we must consult the individual's preferences and we cannot proceed by evaluating just the net payoff from a costly information system. These difficulties mean that all we can say in general when seeking to compare two costly information systems is that one system will be at least as good as another for a given individual if the expected utility it yields is at least equal to that of the second system. In our usual notation, this can be written as:

$$E(U \mid \eta_i) \geq E(U \mid \eta_j) \qquad [7.V]$$

This may seem disappointing but, generally, we do not expect to find universal rankings which reflect preferences for commodities and services for all individuals, where endowments, preferences, beliefs and uses differ between individuals.

There are a number of ways forward. One is to see what progress can be made in characterising optimal information systems when we ignore the costs of information. This approach was fully discussed in Chapter 6 in the section entitled 'Characteristics of optimal costless information systems'. Another is to consider how the value of information might change for the individual with alterations in the variables that might reasonably be expected to change the value accorded to information.

A number of studies have considered how changes in some of the elements of the environment in which information systems are used may alter the value of the information systems (see Hilton, 1981, for a review of some of these studies). The determinants of the value of information systems which have been studied include changes in the degree of risk aversion, alterations in the amount of the decision maker's original endowment of wealth, and variations in views concerning state occurrence. These studies suggest that information value may change with alterations in these items but not in a way which is consistent between decision makers or decision problems. This is because changes in these items may affect both of the elements in our most general expression for the expected utility of an information system (Expression 7.I). This expression says that the expected utility of information equals $E(U \mid \eta_j) - E(U \mid \eta_0)$. Changes in any of those items which impinge on the value of information will affect the left-hand element of this expression. This element shows the expected utility obtained with an information system. Such alterations may, however, also affect the utility obtainable using the null system, the second element of the expression. The results obtained when both these effects are considered may mean that the results of consistent increases (or decreases) in those items expected to increase the value of information will not necessarily cause a consistent increase (or decrease) in the value of information.

It can be shown, for example, that the result of reducing the actions available to the decision maker may have a variety of effects, depending especially on whether the optimal actions with the information system and with the null system have been removed from the decision maker's range of actions. These investigations suggest that the number of general results in the area of information value are likely to be fairly sparse, with current knowledge. However, further developments in understanding the determinants of the value of information can be expected to have a substantial impact on accounting.

Public information*

So far in this chapter and in Chapter 6 we have discussed the meaning of private information and its value in private use. We have also discussed certain characteristics of information systems for individuals. We now consider publicly available information. The utility of information was said in the previous chapter to stem from the ability it provides for (Bayesian) revisions of state probabilities. This view of the utility of information carries over to publicly available information.

Public information defined

Public information systems may be defined as those which simultaneously make the same information available to all in the market at no cost—at least no direct cost.

---

* This section raises some relatively subtle and technical points.

This simultaneity of the provision of the information is important because otherwise those who received the information early may be able to make gains at the expense of those who receive the information with a timelag. Those obtaining early access to the information may be able to treat it as if it were private information. Similarly, it is important that public information is made widely available because otherwise those in possession of the information may make gains out of those who have not received it. The coverage or width of the distribution of the information is thus important in defining whether information can be said to be publicly available. However, it is not clear how the adequacy of such a distribution can be determined for this purpose. All that seems to be required is that whatever distribution mechanism is decided upon for public information does not allow its private use. However, such information may not be provided by markets where there is no possibility of private gain from the possession of information. As we have seen above, information will be paid for by individuals only if they expect to gain from its use. They will not expect benefits in trading from information where this is widely distributed, because all in the market will have the same information. In our example, Mr Risky gained from using private information for trading purposes because he knew something others did not know. There would be no possibility of such gains if this information were available to all. Thus, there has to be a possibility of private gain if we want public information to be provided by the market and financed by (at least) some users (see Grossman and Stiglitz, 1980). In the absence of the possibility of such private gains, some extra-market mechanism may have to be used to provide public information. Chapter 10 considers the various possibilities for the provision of public accounting information and the problems associated with these regimes for accounting policy making. The right of individuals to exclude themselves from being given public information should be recognised in defining the characteristics of public information.

The concept and definition of public information given above are of great importance in accounting theory because these characteristics of public information are just those which are meant to govern the distribution of external accounting reports. Thus external accounting information would seem to be part of the public information available in a commercially sophisticated economy. Unfortunately, the theory of public information is not yet as developed as that addressed to private information. This is because the analysis of public information is more complex than that required for private information. Discussing public information requires the specific consideration of a multi-person setting involving markets and of the ability of such markets to generate equilibrium prices in the face of interactions between market actors. Public information will have market-wide and social effects and these must be considered in any analysis. Chapter 10 is devoted to this task, employing a societal perspective. Here we confine ourselves to presenting the economic characteristics of public information and seeking to determine the value of such information to market participants.

One reason why public information is difficult to analyse is that its release may change market prices and consequently alter the ability of individuals to trade by changing their budget constraints. Public information may thus give rise to wealth effects for individuals. The resultant revaluations of individual wealth may affect individuals differently. Thus, it is possible that information which otherwise would produce an improvement in economic efficiency may not lead to an actual Pareto improvement because revaluation effects may leave some in the community worse off under the allocation reigning with information than under the original allocation. This is because receipt of public information may lead to a change in the price of state claims and securities. Thus, for example, those endowed with state claims for states which a received signal says will not now come to pass will suffer a loss of wealth, and those holding claims to states which the information suggests are now more likely will gain. Such revaluation effects may thus affect some individuals adversely even though the introduction of public information would otherwise lead to an allocation of securities which dominates that attainable without public information.

Before discussing situations when public information can be shown to have a positive value, we will consider a number of one-period regimes for the provision of public information and some of their economic characteristics. Generally, our findings will carry over to similar multi-period settings. Here, we will consider when it is possible to say that public information will potentially have value in the various regimes. We will do this by ascertaining whether each of the regimes can with public information attain the equivalent of full Pareto efficiency. (The conditions for this have to be amended to allow for the presence of information. This requires that markets are complete, given the information system employed; see Ohlson, 1987a, p. 110.)

The provision of public information

This section relies strongly on Ohlson and Buckman (1981) and on Ohlson (1987a), though the aim here is to give only a flavour of these more rigorous works (see also Strong and Walker, 1987, chapter 4).

To model the effects of public information we need to stipulate a number of items concerning the environment in which this information is to be utilised. These include:

1 the information system being used;
2 the character of the signals from the information system;
3 the knowledge possessed by decision makers of the character of the information system and its signals;
4 the time of receipt of the signals from the information system relative to the timing of the decision and the timing of trading;
5 the types of markets faced by investors, including their completeness and how often they allow trading in the period being considered;
6 the beliefs about the probabilities of states of the environment and about these likelihoods of signals from the information system, and how far these beliefs are common among individuals.

The results obtained concerning the utility of public information may be sensitive to changes in any of these items.

To model public information, we also have to make assumptions about the character of the claims that are available and the constraints faced by decision makers. A variety of assumptions can be made but we will generally assume that, for each prospect, it is possible to buy individually its return contingent on the receipt of a specific signal. These securities are purchased at the time of decision: P_{jy} is the price at the time of decision of the return from a unit of security j conditional on the receipt of signal y. We shall also sometimes use P_j as the price of a unit of security j. The results of the models may well depend on these assumptions. One important question to be answered is 'When will different models produce varying results?'

The multi-person aspect of public information also needs to be considered in our models. We may obtain different results depending on the degree of heterogeneity between the individuals we admit into these models. Generally, we can cope with allowing decision makers to differ to a degree in their risk attitudes, in their state beliefs, in their beliefs about the likelihoods of the signals from the information system (called signal beliefs) and in their endowments. We shall generally avoid this problem by assuming that complete markets allow us to leave it to individuals to trade to satisfy their individual characteristics.

The aim is to describe the impact of public information on decision models and to indicate when models encompassing public information can be expected to obtain Pareto efficiency. An important point to note is that, as stated above, if a market with public information does achieve this type of efficiency it does not guarantee that the introduction of such public information may not make some market participants worse off. This problem arises because information affects market prices and therefore the endowments of individuals. Such revaluation effects may affect some individuals adversely even though the introduction of public information would otherwise lead to an allocation of securities which dominates that attainable without public information.

One way round this problem is to reallocate the original endowments. It can be shown that any Pareto-efficient solution can be achieved as an equilibrium solution in a complete market under some specific original allocation of resources which may not be the one that originally reigned. In a later chapter it will be argued that, at least in the accounting area, it may not be possible to rely on such reallocations in order to introduce accounting systems which, except for their revaluation effects, improve society's welfare. This is because such reallocations require powers of subsidy and taxation which accounting policy makers generally do not possess.

Another more practical solution to this problem is to adopt trading processes which allow individuals to insure themselves against the revaluation effects of public and accounting information. This really means that the market must not only be complete in terms of allowing all state claims to be traded, but it must also be complete in terms of allowing all trades contingent on signals from the information system employed. This allows insurance from the revaluation effects that otherwise would be experienced. Thus it is important in our survey of trading models in the presence of public information to ascertain which ones possess those characteristics that allow insurance against signals and to consider whether such models or their variants are available in the practical world. The lack of such models in real world markets would mean that accounting policy makers would have to make value judgements as to the individuals they wish to favour (see Chapter 10).

Information for public use concerning state occurrence can be provided at a number of times in the decision process and under different trading assumptions. We will review a number of possibilities in sequence. These models are illustrated in Figures 7.2–7.5.

(a) Full details of the information system and the realised signal from this system are provided prior to the decision and individuals can trade in normal securities.

This trading process is shown in Figure 7.2, where timing runs from left to right. Thus, the information system and its signal are shown on the left. The operation of decision making is later in the time sequence and is therefore shown further along the line. Trading is the final event and is therefore shown on the right.

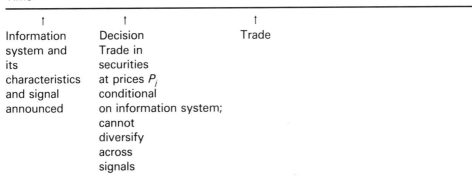

Figure 7.2 Characteristics of regime (a)

Even without information, this regime may not obtain Pareto efficiency without additional assumptions as it is not sufficiently rich in securities to allow all possible trades. The introduction of information may make this system more inefficient as it would expose individuals to revaluation effects on the announcement of the information system and its signal which they cannot escape by trading. This would further inhibit trading. The distribution of any gains and losses flowing from the information depends on the endowments possessed by the decision makers. Those relatively well endowed in the states favoured by the information system will gain and those possessing claims in other states will lose. Such markets with information may thus also fail to obtain Pareto efficiency because there is no way individuals can protect themselves from signal effects before receiving information.

Consider two risk averse individuals who each owned all the claims in one state in an equally endowed two-state problem of this type with each state having the same probability. Without access to an information system, they would trade so as to diversify. This trading ensures that they would each obtain half of the amount arising upon the realisation of either state with certainty. They would become worse off in the presence of a perfect information system which provided its signal prior to trading. Both would feel they would suffer the revaluation effects which would flow from the information system. With the information system, both would now feel that there is an equal chance of receiving their full endowment and obtaining nothing. The expected utility of this is less than the utility accorded to receiving half the endowment in each state with certainty.

(U(0.5 endowment) > 0.5U(endowment in, say, state 1)

$$+ 0.5U \text{ (zero endowment in state 2)}$$

In this setting public information introduces an additional uncertainty associated with its signals which cannot be insured against. A similar problem may arise with the next regime (b). However, the almost continual trade allowed in actual financial markets may substantially mitigate this effect.

Prior to considering this second regime, we will illustrate the inherent intricacies of public information by considering a situation where public information may help even in the above setting. It can be shown that public information received after the event may help to complete an otherwise incomplete market and facilitate trading.

Assume our investors were unable to distinguish the realised state just by considering the outcomes obtained by them at the end of a trading cycle. This may inhibit them from entering into risk sharing agreements of the type which were suggested above to be optimal. This is because contracts contingent on state realisation could not be enforced using information only available to each individual. The parties to the agreement might argue that the realised outcome they have received was due to a state other than the state which was actually realised. In this way they may make gains from others who could not with their own information ascertain which state had actually appeared. This possibility may mean that otherwise worthwhile risk sharing contracts will not be completed. Knowing that public information would allow the realised state to be deduced after the event would therefore allow such trading to take place and so improve economic welfare. The role of information here is not to reduce state uncertainty prior to the decision but rather to report objectively that a state has occurred. This is similar to one of the roles claimed for accounting reports, and research in this area may help us to understand the characteristics that accounting information must possess if it is to fulfil the role of *ex post* validation. We can go a little further in the area of validation by information and say that any information system useful for this purpose needs to distinguish all those states by which each individual party to a risk sharing agreement is affected differently.

(b) The decision is made prior to receiving the signal from the information system but with full knowledge of the characteristics of the information system and of its possible signals; individuals trade in claims contingent on each signal separately, i.e. for each possible signal they make a plan subject to a budgetary constraint for that signal only and the relevant plan is actioned on receipt of a specific signal.

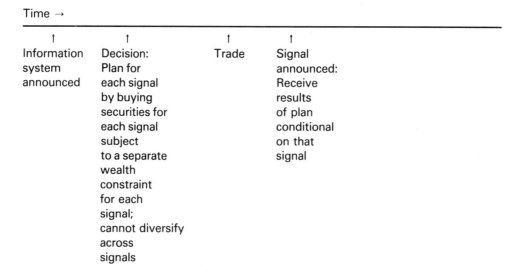

Time →

↑	↑	↑	↑
Information system announced	Decision: Plan for each signal by buying securities for each signal subject to a separate wealth constraint for each signal; cannot diversify across signals	Trade	Signal announced: Receive results of plan conditional on that signal

Figure 7.3 Characteristics of regime (b)

This process is illustrated in Figure 7.3 where, reading from left to right, the information system and its full possibilities are announced first, the decision is then made, following which the signal is received and receipts from the plan conditional on this signal are obtained.

The special characteristic of this model is that a plan is made for each possible signal in full knowledge of the characteristics of the information system by buying securities conditional on each signal. There is no possibility of coordinating plans across signals and there is therefore no way of insuring against the effects of signals. Thus this system of the provision of public information may also fail to achieve Pareto efficiency.

Again, the public information may make individuals worse off. Without information, individuals would trade on the basis of state outcomes and, assuming there were primitive securities each of which offered a return in only one state (these securities were called Arrow–Debreu securities in Chapter 5), would achieve a Pareto-efficient outcome. The introduction of information changes the probabilities of the states which now become conditional on the information signals, but does not provide any mechanism for protecting the individual from these effects, unless there is a basic security of the Arrow–Debreu type for each signal. Without this type of signal-based securities, a lack of insurance possibilities arises because the individual cannot trade across signal-contingent states. Mr Risky would experience this difficulty in his two-state problem if he were constrained to hold only security A which, it may be recalled, although yielding 90 monetary units in state 1 provides only 15 units in state 2. He would suffer major revaluation effects against which he could not protect himself if the public information system signalled that state 2 would appear. However, he could escape this problem if he were allowed to devote a proportion of his wealth to holding security A conditional on the signal for this state appearing and devote the rest of his endowment to holding security B conditional on the second signal appearing. Security B yields 150 monetary units in state 2 and 50 units in state 1. If he held approximately 55 per cent of his wealth in security A and the remainder in the other security, he would obtain 75 monetary units conditional on either signal and therefore would be protected from revaluation effects. Such protection cannot be achieved in our more general setting. It requires that the number of securities equals the number of possible signals. Attaining such protection may therefore require the use of more sophisticated market regimes. The next regime to be considered, which is a variant or a combination of regimes (a) and (b), allows the individual more freedom in planning.

(c) There is a multi-stage decision process and trade is first in securities in full knowledge of the information system and its possible signals (as in (a) above), the signal is then received, and further trade can then be undertaken in signal-contingent claims as in (b) above.

Figure 7.4(c) illustrates this. First the information system and its possible signals are announced, as shown on the left of the figure. Trade in normal securities then takes place with the individual seeking to optimise, subject only to not yet knowing the realised signal and being unable to trade in signal-contingent claims. This is shown in the middle of the figure. This trade generates a new portfolio. The signal is received and trade then takes place in signal-contingent claims as in (b) above, subject to the revised portfolio achieved in the first stage, as shown on the far right of the figure.

This model does have the advantage that it incorporates some of the characteristics of the sequential decision making observed in security markets. This regime does allow

Time →

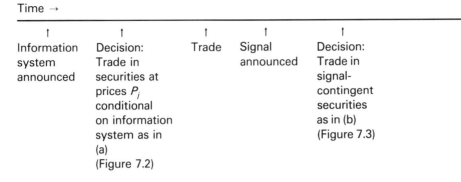

Figure 7.4 Characteristics of regime (c)

individuals in the market to insure across states. Indeed, if Mr Risky were free to diversify fully as suggested above, he would be able to obtain his optimum in the first round of this process. Both its non-information variant and the model with information achieve Pareto efficiency, assuming trade is in Arrow–Debreu securities. This means that we can say that public information has a potential value and, under specific assumptions, we can say that richer information has more potential value. There is a presumption in this model that public information will be socially useful and that enriching information should increase this utility but may not always do so. This adverse finding arises because the second round of this model has some of the same characteristics as regime (b) above and full coordination of plans over all signals may therefore become impossible in the face of fuller information. Insurance across signals is not fully possible with this two-state model because of the imperfect second stage and therefore the allocations that can be achieved with this regime may not be the best possible. The next model allows full coordination across signals and does not encounter this problem. However, to achieve this we have to forego the sequential character of the above model and move away from modelling actual financial markets. With regard to accounting information we also lose the attractive feature that having received information, decision makers were able to act upon this information in the market.

In fact, the realism of our third regime (c) is rather artificial. The second stage in regime (c) is not really necessary to take advantage of information but rather to allow the better coordination of plans across signals as this cannot be fully achieved in the first stage. The previous chapter presented the usual economic analysis applied to information. This suggested that to possess a full knowledge of the possible signals and to be able to trade on these signals on a complete market is all that is necessary to take full advantage of information, as Mr Risky could in the first stage of this process by diversifying between securities A and B as suggested above. Thus there is no role for an information system to give an unexpected signal. This possibility is brought out by the next regime to be reviewed.

(d) Information appears after the decision, which is made with full knowledge of the information system and its possible signals; trade is in signal-contingent securities and is possible across signals.

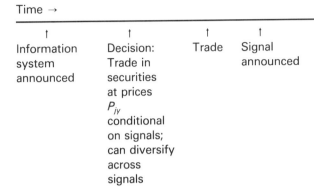

Figure 7.5 Characteristics of regime (d)

Here Figure 7.5 shows that we first have full knowledge of the information system and then make a decision involving constructing a portfolio diversified across signal-contingent securities.

As we would now expect, this model obtains full Pareto efficiency with information. All required information is known at the time of the decision and full protection from revaluation effects can be obtained by using the market. Again, public information has potential value and enrichment of the information system is likely to have social value.

Embedding accounting information into these types of model really requires that we consider different information systems. This is an under-researched area but some extant findings will be considered in the next section.

The value of public information

Before appraising these arguments for relying on the market system to provide accounting information without any extra-market intervention, it is necessary to consider whether the accounting information, however provided, has any value to society. First recall how the private value of information to an individual is determined (see Chapter 2 and Chapter 5). To simplify presentation, it is assumed that the information being considered is useful only for trading purposes and will become available to all in due course. Hirshleifer (1971) has argued that no resources ought to be devoted to supplying such information because acting on it does not alter any of the economy's productive activities. Information that alters available productive opportunities should obviously be produced, except where the cost of such information exceeds its benefits. In Chapter 5, it was argued that for information to be worthwhile for trading purposes to an individual investor it needs to permit either an expected gain or the avoidance of an expected loss.

Such gains arise from wealth transfers from other investors. Private information which suggests that security prices will rise allows an investor to gain by buying securities at the going market price, which does not yet reflect this private information. An equal amount is therefore lost by the holders of the shares who sell to the informed investor. The persons who supplied our investor would forgo a gain which would otherwise have been obtained in due course. Similarly, the people who are left holding securities which private information suggests should not be bought at present lose money once the private information becomes public. The gains to Mr Risky which we discussed earlier in this chapter and in Chapter 6 were of this character. Access to this information allowed him to gain because with this private knowledge he could purchase state claims from the market at prices that did not reflect this private knowledge. Information of this type is therefore seen as facilitating only wealth transfers. Any real resources devoted to information production are therefore wasted in the sense that they do not produce additional resources for the economy.

Another way of illustrating this lack of an economic case for public information for trading purposes is to ask whether a society made up of individuals identical in their endowments, preferences and beliefs as a whole would be willing to pay for this information to be made public. No such purchase will be made because no action follows from access to the information. All that happens is that an earlier announcement of the realised state is made. This announcement will cause the prices of state claims in other states to fall to zero at this time rather than when the state is actually realised. No one in society can anticipate what state will be announced and they will therefore continue to hold whatever was the optimal allocation of state claims for their beliefs, preferences and endowments without information. Indeed, we can go further and suggest as was said earlier that in certain circumstances public information may actually reduce welfare because of its possible redistributive consequences where individuals are not all identical. Here, some individuals may gain and others lose because of the existence of public information. If this information is announced before the trading cycle, those who are disproportionately endowed with claims in the state of which the realisation is announced by the system will gain, and others will lose. Similarly, those who believed that some other state was very likely to occur will also gain because they have avoided the loss they would otherwise have made.

We can use Mr Risky where he is risk averse to illustrate the effects of providing a public information system which yields perfect information as to state occurrence in the uncertain environment he faces. Recall that without information as to which state would occur, his welfare was maximised by holding security C, which yielded him the same certain income in both states. This conduct was optimal because it equated his marginal rate of substitution between consumption in the two states he faced to the ratio of the prices of these claims in the market. It is especially easy to see that this amounts to optimal behaviour in the face of risk in Mr Risky's case. For him the optimum involves equating the ratio of the probabilities of the two states to the ratio of prices of income in the two states, where these prices reflect the same probability of state occurrence as Mr Risky expects. He can therefore spread his existing wealth between the two states in a way that ensures that he holds no risk, which is the optimal amount of risk sharing for Mr Risky.

The probabilities he would assign to the signals to be received from a public information system concerning each of the states would be just those he has already used in his calculations and against which he has already optimised. Therefore he would not subscribe to any public information system because use of such a system cannot improve his risk sharing. In our example, as soon as the signal is announced market prices would adjust so that claims in the state that has occurred would be valued at one monetary unit and claims in the other state would have no value. This is just what Mr Risky expects and what he has already protected himself against. It is this change in market prices on the signals from a public information system that make impossible the gains he made when this information was privately available to him. He is thus fully protected from any changes flowing from a perfect information system and he is therefore also fully protected from the consequences of any imperfect information system.

This example suggests that public information will generally not affect the optimal allocation of prospects where the market is already perfect and complete and in other settings where full Pareto efficiency can be achieved (remember that for ease of understanding our simple example does not fully possess these characteristics). This finding is not inconsistent with the general view that more information cannot be less valuable than less information. All that we are saying is that public information will not change optimal decisions in markets that have already obtained full Pareto efficiency. More precisely, we can say that additional public information will not lead to a Pareto improvement where:

(i) individual utility functions are of the type that the benefits received in different periods can be added together as they are, for example, in discounting;
(ii) individuals have the same beliefs about the likelihood of signals from the public information system; and
(iii) the allocation of securities attains full Pareto efficiency for a given exogenously fixed production plan. (For a more rigorous and comprehensive discussion see Strong and Walker, 1987, chapter 4; Ohlson, 1987a, pp. 52–71 and chapter 5.)

The first condition above is a technical one, necessary because we may wish to be able to deal with multi-periods but, without this assumption, information may otherwise allow investors to coordinate better their plans across time. The second means that there will be no desire or ability to trade differing claims following the receipt of signals from the information system; otherwise people may wish to back their beliefs about signals in their investments. The attainment of full Pareto efficiency for a given production plan means that optimal risk sharing has been obtained prior to the information system being provided and information cannot yield information about productive opportunities. As suggested in Chapter 6, there is a variety of ways in which full Pareto efficiency can be assured, the most obvious one being to assume that markets are complete, but other less stringent market conditions may suffice providing that we impose additional conditions on the characteristics possessed by individuals in our models. Two possible settings that lead to full Pareto efficiency without complete markets are:

(a) the existence of a risk-free security, homogeneous beliefs and some restriction on attitudes to risk, and
(b) the more restrictive setting of homogeneous beliefs and identical, constant, relative risk aversion.

Thus we can reasonably say that public information may not be worthwhile in certain circumstances. This is a disturbing finding for accounting and again may stem from a different view as to the function of information. The models being reviewed here assume that the only unknown with respect to the information system is which signal, from those which are expected, will appear. In contrast, in the practical world accounting information may be thought to obtain its value from any unexpected signals it provides. Chapter 8 looks at this problem in more detail.

Even if it were found that public information did not generally improve economic welfare, this would not mean that there would be no pressures for the provision of accounting information for trading purposes. Wealth and income transfers, even though they may not interest economists concerned with the efficient allocation of resources, do interest politicians and investors.

Possible reasons for public information to have value

In any case, our earlier analysis of some models of public information provision suggested that there were good reasons to anticipate that public information was likely to have value. Recent research has supported this by suggesting a number of reasons for believing that, even in the trading settings being considered here, information may be useful. This section reviews this research in an introductory way. It is argued that information may not just facilitate wealth transfers but may have utility for resource allocation decisions, providing that perfect information is available costlessly in perfect markets (for a simple review, see Ohlson and Buckman, 1980). The studies involved are highly technical and their results are still tentative. First, it can be shown that, given a suitable set of individual endowments, which may not be the set which actually reigns, perfect information costlessly provided will allow at least a no-less-preferred allocation of resources to be achieved. This seems reasonable because those who wish for less detailed information may always jettison any excess detail provided by perfect information. Secondly, in such a setting, the utility attached to risky wealth transfers may differ, and therefore additional information concerning such matters may allow favourable trades among individual investors with different risk attitudes and/or beliefs. More information may allow the lot of someone in the economy to be improved without harming others. Additional information may also act as a substitute for some markets which are unavailable in the economy, thereby allowing trade which could not otherwise take place (model (a) above provided an example of this). Finally, public information may be less costly to provide than if the same information were generated for private use by some people in the community. Above, we saw that costly private information concerning which state would appear may be privately worthwhile, but not socially, where all had homogeneous beliefs in a trading setting. Making such information publicly available may be less costly to society than the total cost of the private endeavours to ascertain this information (Marshall, 1974).

However, the first reason given above for expecting publicly available information to bring benefits requires the rearrangement of the distribution of endowments in the economy by a 'benevolent dictator'. This would require Government intervention. This may not be a role to which the Government gives high priority. This would not seem a function that could be legitimately fulfilled by private sector accounting policy makers.

The other three roles for information listed above do seem to fall in to the purview of private sector accounting policy makers and accounting theorists. However, it is difficult to see how these roles for information can be made operational, other than by suggesting that accounting theorists and policy makers should seek to provide accounting theories and therefore accounting information which aids in remedying defects in the market system. Accountants are unlikely to have the skills necessary to determine whether any item of accounting information actually serves these purposes. Moreover, such attempts to improve markets may well have distributional consequences which may make any necessary accounting changes difficult to enforce. Such problems are also likely to attend attempts to resolve the cost dilemma stated above. Attempts to substitute less costly public information for more expensive private information may be resisted by those who stand to gain from such private information. The next section explores these points in a little more detail. It is a little technical.

When public information will have value

The obvious way forward is to seek to relax the assumptions listed above that cause public information to have no value. There have recently been a number of attempts to do this (see Ohlson and Buckman, 1981; Ohlson, 1987a, chapter 5; Strong and Walker, 1987, chapter 4 for reviews of this work). Here we will consider only a few of the above assumptions. The first assumption that may be relaxed is that the market is complete. Information may have a role in the completion of incomplete markets. The second is that requiring homogeneous beliefs or risk attitudes. Where people differ in their preferences or beliefs in incomplete markets, additional information may allow improved trading. We will explore both these avenues together, because they both require us to consider different regimes concerning when information is received. The role of information received prior to trading may be very different from that of information obtained after the event. Finally, as was said earlier, public information may be useful where we allow production into our models.

Information completes the market

One way of considering this problem is to recall that not all desired trades can be executed in an incomplete market. Information received prior to trading may therefore help to extend trade. In order for a market without information to be fully complete, at least for our purposes, there must exist the same number of securities as states. If we have, say, four states and only two securities, a possible way to complete this market would be to provide an information system which distinguishes between pairs of states, thereby allowing the number of securities to match the number of states, providing that trading is allowed both before and after signal receipt.

As was illustrated above, it can be also be shown that public information received after the event may also help to complete an otherwise incomplete market and to facilitate trading.

Information received prior to trading can also bring about a welfare improvement where we allow production to enter into our model. Information about which state is to be realised may allow production decisions to be reorientated to optimise for the declared state. Here it is assumed that production decisions are made by those active in the market. It can also be shown that, where beliefs differ amongst individuals, information may have value where production decisions are made outside the system. Where beliefs differ, the probabilities assigned to the various states will no longer be independent of the beliefs about signals as they were in the full Pareto-efficient setting with common beliefs discussed earlier; see Hakansson *et al.* (1982), which also shows that information may have value if we relax the assumption that utility functions are time-additive where production decisions are made outside the system.

As is usual in a fairly new field of research, this whole area of debate is subject to great controversy (see Verrecchia, 1982; Watts, 1982). When a multi-person environment is assumed, it is difficult to see how information can be valued without considering any consequent wealth transfers. Economics generally provides little guidance here. The only uncontroversial welfare criterion—the Pareto criterion—is not relevant for such choices. The application of this criterion is limited to choices where one or more individuals are made better off without harming others.

One reason for the variety of conclusions suggested by these studies is the application of different views on how the social value of information can be measured.

Admitting a multi-person setting also means that we have to allow for complex responses to any publicly available information. Attention has also to be paid to the information which actors find it worthwhile generating themselves. Verrecchia (1982) goes as far as to say that, for these reasons and because it is difficult if not impossible to structure research in this area, any future research efforts may not provide useful insights. Others argue that this sort of research has deepened our understanding of some very complex issues which are of fundamental importance to understanding accounting and which have not been considered sufficiently by accounting theorists (see Ohlson and Buckman, 1980, 1981). The meaning of the term 'information' and its value when provided both publicly and privately would seem to be central for understanding accounting in the practical world.

This ends our discussion of public information made generally available. This and the preceding chapter have analysed private and public information. The final part of this chapter looks briefly at the setting where individuals possess differential information. This topic is tackled only briefly because accounting information is meant to be publicly available.

Differential information

We can illustrate the problems that arise with differential information by reverting to our earlier example of Mr Risky in which he has access to a perfect information system not available to anyone else in a complete market (see Chapter 5). In this case, Mr Risky would seem able to make infinite sums of money as only he knows what state will appear. He could, for example, short sell claims at the going market price to the state which he knows will not appear. Short selling means to sell now claims to a future state which one does not currently possess. Those which do not have this information will be happy to buy these claims at the going market prices, which (as will be recalled) reflect their probability beliefs. The result of this process is suggested by Hirshleifer (1971) to be that Mr Risky will become infinitely rich.

This suggestion does not accord with reality and results in markets being unable to clear. In this regime the market cannot achieve a competitive equilibrium. The problem here is that all market participants assume that market prices will not change in the face of their actions. In fact, Mr Risky's activities will depress the price of the claim he is selling short. Those who do not know which state will appear can therefore learn from observing prices. That the price of the state that Mr Risky knows will not appear falls means the probability that others attach to the realisation of this state should be revised downwards. More generally with differential information, market participants learn both from their own information systems and from market prices. Market prices now serve two purposes. As before, they determine budget constraints. They now additionally provide information. A price system which plays these two roles in complete markets can be shown to obtain what is called a rational expectations equilibrium.

Consider a setting where five possible states can appear but the individuals in the economy have differential information as to which state will appear. One set of individuals know that only states 1 or 2 will appear. The other set know only that one of the first three states will appear. Learning from prices will mean that, in equilibrium, only states 1 and 2 will have positive prices. This is because someone in the economy knows that none of the other states will appear and the consequent trading on this information will drive the prices of the non-appearing states to zero. Equilibrium prices obtained in this way will fully reveal all the information in the economy. In our example all participants in the market will know that the state to be realised is either state 1 or state 2. The equilibrium obtained is a rational expectations equilibrium in that all individuals know the relationship between the equilibrium prices and the signals in the economy, and these prices are consistent with these signals and with the information contained in these reigning prices themselves (Grossman, 1976; Radner, 1979). This has to be the case, otherwise equilibrium would not reign at these prices. The trading activities of anyone who believed that all available information was not reflected in these prices would cause them to change.

This equilibrium result can also be shown to be true even with incomplete markets (see Strong and Walker, 1987, chapter 5). Another way of explaining this type of equilibrium is that the reigning prices are just those which would obtain if all individuals rationally predicted them on the basis of both their private information systems and the information contained in these prices.

Such an equilibrium has many desirable properties. It aggregates diverse private information so that it provides information that summarizes all the information in the economy. Moreover, a central planner with access to the same information could not provide a better allocation of securities than is provided by this equilibrium.

However, the equilibrium also provides a number of paradoxes. It conveys information that is superior to that of any individual; to optimise, all the individual needs is a knowledge of the equilibrium prices. Individuals will thus disregard their own information, for which they will therefore be unwilling to pay. This means that such equilibria may contain the seeds of their own destruction. Under these conditions, there will exist no differential information for markets to use to form a rational expectations equilibrium because it is not worthwhile to buy information. The obvious way out of these problems is somehow to inject into the system an uncertain (noisy) variable, information about which cannot be aggregated by the markets (Grossman, 1976, 1977; Grossman and Stiglitz, 1976, 1980). With such a variable, individuals will wish use their own information system in decision making and be willing to pay for such information for private use. Such partially revealing systems have been constructed but we do not know how they would function in securities markets. The assumption that two separate types of uncertainty exist does not sit well with the usual assumption that all uncertainty is embodied in uncertainty about the states of the environment which will reign.

This type of model has been used to provide a theory of why firms might voluntarily disclose information publicly, thereby replacing individual endeavours to obtain private information. Such studies combine a concern for a number of topics discussed in this chapter, including public information and differential information (Diamond, 1985; see also Dye, 1986). Here individuals are postulated to enter into costly transactions to obtain private information in the absence of enterprise-provided information. As was indicated above, there may be substantial resource savings where the enterprise provides the information; these savings flow from reducing the duplicated costs where a number of individuals are seeking to obtain the same private information. Just how great the saving may be is very difficult to ascertain: information is a very difficult item to market in the usual way because it is not exhausted by use and may be able to be sold-on. Such activities may substantially reduce the price of information to individuals. This may mean that the saving from public provision is not as great as might be thought because not all private consumers of the information will have to pay the full cost of providing it from scratch.

Additionally, public information provided by firms should improve risk sharing. The public provision of information should reduce the differences in beliefs in the market, thereby reducing the number of speculative transactions that privately informed individuals would otherwise wish to undertake. Such transactions produce very unequal risk sharing arrangements that would be inefficient where individuals are all assumed to have preferences which are, to some degree, common. This is clearly a very important area for further research which may have far-reaching results for accounting theory.

The next chapter uses the tools provided in Chapters 5–7 to consider again the economist's income and wealth measures discussed in Chapters 3 and 4.

Chapter summary and conclusions

This chapter continued our study of private information by considering how such information may be valued for the individual. It was first shown that the value of an information system to an individual in terms of expected utility was given by the expected utility of the decision with information, less the expected utility obtained from the decision using the null information system. The value in terms of the net expected utility generated by employing a perfect information system in our familiar Mr Risky example was then calculated. It was suggested that seeking to express these gains in monetary terms was not free of difficulties where individuals were not risk neutral. That there were no problems in doing this where risk neutrality could be assumed was illustrated, again using the Risky example.

In the next major section two different definitions of the value of information which could be used where the decision maker was not risk neutral were then considered. The demand value of information was defined as the price of information that rendered the decision maker indifferent between utilising or not using the information. The supply value of information was similarly defined as the amount of money which rendered the decision maker indifferent between selling the information and the related decision opportunity as a package on the market and using the information personally.

Although these definitions can be used where the individual is risk averse, it was then indicated that risk attitudes render their quantification difficult. This was said to be because both the benefits and costs of information systems impact on the individual. Care is therefore needed in ascertaining the net effect of these two items. This suggests that those cost/benefit tests which accounting regulators seem to favour are not easy to use, even at the level of the individual.

The next section looked in a little more detail at the problems introduced by the cost of information systems. It was shown that to avoid problems we have to work with the expected utilities of the gross benefits and of the costs of information systems, rather than the expected utilities of their net payoffs. Converting the utility of the net payoff from an information system into monetary units was suggested to mis-specify the monetary value of the information system because it obtained its figures from the wrong part of the utility function. This and other difficulties mentioned in the chapter mean that all we can say in general, in comparing two costly information systems for an individual, is that one system is at least as good as the other if and only if the expected utility (correctly determined) of the first system equals or exceeds that offered by the second system.

It was then indicated that there were at least two ways to expand our analysis of information systems in the face of these difficulties. The first was to ascertain how sensitive the value of an information system was to changes in the variables affecting the information system. Such studies were indicated to demonstrate that the impact of even simple changes of this type might have very complex results. This result appeared because alterations in some variables may impact on the results of the decision, both with and without information. The other approach, which was to assume that information systems were provided costlessly, was considered in Chapter 6.

The second major part of the chapter turned to discussing public information as distinct from private information, which had been the focus earlier in the chapter. Public information was stated to provide the same information to all market participants at the same time. This property of public information was said to result in no one being willing to pay for such information because its provision to all on a simultaneous basis meant that private gains could not be achieved. This theme will be taken up later (Chapters 10 and 11). It was suggested that the wide dispersal of public information made the analysis of such information even more difficult than when we focused on private information. Public information was shown to impact on market prices and therefore differentially on individuals in the market. This meant that a multi-person and market equilibrium perspective had to be employed when dealing with such information. This type of information was said to be likely to impact on market prices and therefore cause individual endowments to rise or fall in value in different ways. These effects were suggested to militate against what otherwise might be the economically efficient result of using a public information system. Thus, the introduction of public information might well make people worse off because of the consequent revaluation effects.

The next section introduced a number of models for the provision of public information in different market regimes. Especial attention was paid to which models would lead to an economically efficient outcome. It was argued that there was a presumption for most of the models surveyed that public information will at least do no harm and might do good, especially where the market regime adopted allowed market participants to protect themselves from any adverse revaluation effects following the introduction of public information. Indeed, it was argued that a strong case could be made that this type of information has potential value and that the use of richer information systems may lead to preferred economic equilibria.

In the next section we reversed the analysis and outlined the conditions under which public information would not have value. Such a situation was said to arise where access to information gave market participants no additional opportunities. Thus, trading information was said to be unlikely to have value in an already complete market. We then considered the view that trading information can never have economic value to society because any gains to some individuals would be exactly offset by losses experienced by others. The arguments behind this view were considered and a number of recent suggestions indicating that public information will have positive value in some settings were presented, including the views that public information might complete an otherwise imperfect market, might facilitate trading that otherwise would not take place, and might indicate new productive opportunities.

The final part of the chapter provided a brief survey of the problems and opportunities that arise when we allow market participants to possess different information. The view was considered that a so-called rational expectations equilibrium would ensure that all the information possessed by individuals would be impounded in market prices in such a way that all would learn this information. Indeed, it was argued that we could go further and say that the information contained in market prices in this setting would dominate that possessed by any individual. This introduced the paradox that individuals would not use their private information and would therefore not pay for such information, thereby destroying the possibility of achieving such an equilibrium. The way round this problem was said to be to add 'noise' to the system. The chapter concluded by presenting some findings in this area which indicated its potential for accounting research, and suggested that there were still problems to be solved in this type of research.

8

Economic income and wealth under uncertainty

Introduction

This chapter extends the brief survey of the economist's income and wealth concepts under uncertainty in Chapter 5 using the tools provided in Chapters 5–7. It therefore provides a review of the material in the preceding five chapters. It also gives some of the flavour of issues that are being addressed in contemporary research.

In Chapters 3 and 4 we said that the treatment of uncertainty in the classical approach to economic income and wealth was not very satisfactory, at least when seen from the perspective of modern treatments of uncertainty in decision making. This was because *ex ante* income and wealth were generally treated as if they were certain (however, see Alexander as revised by Solomons, 1962, where an approach utilising expected monetary values was suggested for both *ex ante* and *ex post* use). The classical approach generally takes uncertainty into account explicitly only when dealing with *ex post* calculations where the impact of 'windfall' or unexpected gains and losses is allowed for in measuring *ex post* income and wealth.

This does not mean that these authors were unaware of the importance of uncertainty in income and wealth measurement. Hicks, in the book *Value and Capital* (1946, originally published in 1939), discussed the approach to the economist's wealth and income used in this book and in most of the current writings adopting this perspective. In this book, he talked about uncertainty. He viewed expectations about the future as able to be seen as the expected values of probability distributions (Hicks, 1946, pp. 124–126), though he did not explicitly adopt this treatment in that part of the book dealing with wealth and income measurement. He also discussed what we now call risk aversion, and stated explicitly that he could not handle this topic with the methods available to him at that time. However, he made it clear that he intended to work generally with certain, rather than uncertain, numbers in planning but would occasionally 'interpret these certain expectations as being those particular figures which best represent the uncertain expectations of reality' (Hicks, 1946, p. 126, including footnote 1).

Neither did the classical treatments of economic income and wealth deal with information in any explicit way. The decision maker was generally assumed to be in a certain setting *ex ante* or to have a complete knowledge of the expected values of relevant cash flows. *Ex post*, the decision maker was assumed to have access to information which gave certain knowledge of the realised cash flows of the period and definite signals about any future cash flows. There was little concern to indicate which part of this information was private to the individual and which part was publicly available, nor was there any concern with the details of the market on which items were traded—which was suggested to be important earlier in Chapter 7 in determining the welfare predictions that could be made in different settings. Earlier work on economic wealth and income measurement simply assumed that the market was complete and perfect.

Plan of the chapter

This chapter restates the classical views of economic income and wealth using the concepts for dealing with uncertainty and information introduced in the last few chapters. This will enable us to see whether the findings of Chapters 3 and 4 carry through to a setting where uncertainty is treated explicitly. It will also help us to integrate our understanding of information economics with the concepts of economic wealth and income, thereby allowing us to suggest what utility these concepts may have in more complex but more practical settings. As has been made clear in previous chapters, there are many difficult and unsettled ideas in these areas. Our treatment will therefore be at a simplified level but even this should be helpful in understanding the strengths and weaknesses of the economic perspective on income and wealth under uncertainty. The presentation will however address most of those issues identified in this book and the literature more generally, as necessary for any adequate treatment of accounting in an uncertain market environment with information (see, for example, Ohlson and Buckman, 1980). Thus, we will deal with a multi-period model because it is difficult to see how any role can emerge for accounting information in a less complex model. We will place this model clearly in an equilibrium market setting and will seek to sketch the role of information in such a setting because, as was shown earlier, the impact of information may depend crucially on the assumed market setting (pp. 155–63). The traditional economic income concept assumes complete and perfect markets. We will follow this assumption. However, our findings also apply in those imperfect and incomplete market regimes which were shown in Chapter 7 to possess market characteristics which allowed them to obtain Pareto efficiency, and to other market structures which also possess properties which allowed them to achieve this type of efficiency. Regimes (c) and (d) in Chapter 7 (pp. 161–3), where trade was allowed in either signal-contingent claims or in securities, provide examples of such market structures. Chapter 7 also suggested that some incomplete markets may obtain full Pareto efficiency providing that we are willing to make assumptions about the common character of individuals in the market, such as homogeneous beliefs and restrictions on permissible risk attitudes (see p. 165).

Thus we are able to escape the problems raised in Chapter 5 that the economist's income and wealth concepts may not be well defined in poorly organised markets, at least for some market regimes of this type which are widely used in finance.

We shall follow Chapters 6 and 7 and consider accounting information, as but one source of information because the importance of accounting information may depend on the availability of other information sources. We shall, however, allow accounting information to provide incremental information, at least in some settings.

In the next section, before addressing our task of amending the economic approach to wealth and income measurement specifically, we shall briefly restate the basic findings of Chapters 3 and 4 where the classical treatment of economic income and wealth were reviewed. The following section lists the assumptions we shall make in our analysis; the numerical example we will use is introduced in the next section, which also discusses in a little more detail the various types of prices for securities and contingent claims which may be used in multi-period uncertain markets, together with the characteristics of these prices. This is followed by a discussion of the conditions that need to be satisfied if such markets are to obtain equilibrium.

We then derive *ex ante* and *ex post* measures of economic wealth and income under uncertainty. The chapter concludes with a brief summary of the role of accounting information in an uncertain environment.

The classical treatment of economic wealth and income

Ex ante economic wealth was defined in Chapter 3 as the present value of the cash flows from an opportunity in perfect and complete markets under certainty. *Ex ante* income for a period was defined in the same setting as the going rate of interest on the present value of the opportunity at the beginning of the period. Income was also defined as the amount the owner of an opportunity could plan to spend in the period and still expect to be as well off at the end of the period as at its beginning. *Ex ante* income and wealth could be used in decision making if so desired and would produce the same results as more conventional discounted cash flow techniques. The economic perspective on income and wealth was argued to be attractive because it adopted the same concepts as the appropriate decision model and, if used for further decision making as the project proceeds, would yield the same results as would be obtained using the relevant decision model directly.

More generally, it was indicated that the economic approach encompassed all the elements that should be incorporated in any accounting system aimed to aid investors in their valuation activities in the assumed setting. This is what has constituted its appeal as an 'ideal' system to be used to judge the decision utility of other accounting systems.

Chapter 4 focused on reviewing the two different *ex post* income concepts suggested for the setting where windfall gains and losses accrued (see pp. 57–66). What was called '*ex post* income concept I' in Chapter 4 declares as income for a project the difference between the *ex post* value at the end of the period plus the cash flows of the period and the originally expected value at the beginning of the period, thereby allowing windfall gains and losses to flow through to income. It was suggested in Chapter 4 that most commentators preferred *ex post* income concept II, which in computing income compares the present value at end of the period *plus* the cash flows of the period with an opening present value recalculated using any information obtained during the period.

This amounts to capitalising any windfall gains and losses and declaring as the *ex post* income for the period the appropriate rate of interest on the recalculated opening value of the business or project. Those writers who originated these concepts saw income *ex post* concept I as being useful where nothing unexpected happened during the period and income *ex post* concept II as useful when the unexpected materialised.

Whether published economic value and income numbers have decision utility depends on whether they convey new information to users.

There is little doubt that those who advocate using the economist's concepts, at least as guidelines for other accounting systems, do see them as yielding valuable information, in some contexts anyway. Edwards, in the course of an article advocating the economic approach, says, for example, that 'Published accounts should have as their object the provision of information for a judgement of net worth ...' (Edwards, 1938, p. 138; see also Whittington, 1983, pp. 30–31).

From an information perspective, reports based on economic concepts are not valuable for the usual decision making purposes where they contain no new information, as they merely record known decisions (Kaldon, 1955). They may, however, still be useful for the original purpose entertained by Hicks of guiding the individual in determining how much can be consumed out of periodic income without the expectation of being worse off than at the beginning of the period. Any need for skill in the computation of economic wealth and income may also serve to give value to reports of these items.

The remainder of this chapter will consider these points in an uncertain setting from an informational perspective. We commence the presentation using a simple example.

Economic income and wealth under certainty

In our example we shall use the state preference approach to uncertainty, making all the associated assumptions introduced in Chapter 5 and used in subsequent chapters; these include the assumptions that investors seek to maximise their utility over the period being considered and that they supply all resources to firms, the role of which is to make decisions and to produce outputs. Investors are assumed to own the net worth of all firms. We shall assume a perfect and complete market where any trade in time–state-contingent outcomes is possible, i.e. market participants can trade in claims indexed by period and by the possible states in each period. Initially we shall assume that markets are open for trade in all periods. For simplicity, we shall assume initially that all such trades are made at their expected values. That is, we are assuming that all participants in the market are risk neutral and that markets clear at prices reflecting the expected values of claims. We shall also assume that all participants in the market attach the same probabilities to state occurrences and have the same signal beliefs when using the same information system (see Chapter 7).

We shall assume the entertained information systems convey the only information concerning state outcomes and that no other relevant experience or item which might impact on the probabilities assigned to state outcomes is available. With regard to information systems, we shall assume that there is a public information system which is available to all and gives completely reliable information about economy-wide events. That is, this information system partitions in some way those states which affect all in the economy. Again for simplicity, we assume that this information system has already revealed a signal about the state of the economy at the beginning of the sequence of time periods we are considering, and that this signal will remain unchanged for the remainder of these time periods.

We shall secondly assume that an additional public information system is available for each firm in the economy. This second information system yields information about only the firm to which it relates, i.e. it conveys firm-specific information. This information says nothing additional about the state of the economy that reigns, nor does it say anything about firm-specific states for any other project or firm. The reason for adopting this approach is because we wish to avoid the possibility of the information affecting one firm providing information about economy-wide events. The effect of this information might otherwise dominate our analysis, which is meant only to examine our earlier findings concerning economic wealth and income in a setting which explicitly includes uncertainty and information.

An alternative way of looking at our assumption concerning firm-specific information systems is to say that their informational impact on the market is small in the same way as are the results of the activities of perfectly competitive firms in economic theory.[1]

Any combined signal from our two information systems will provide a signal as to the state of the environment and signals for firms conditional on that environmental signal. (For a more formal treatment, see Feltham and Christensen, 1988.)

As we shall be dealing with more than one time period, we have to indicate the detail provided by these information systems over time. Here we shall generally assume that, as we progress through time, an information system yields a finer partition of the states. We shall also assume that the complete set of possible signals and the sequence of these signals from an information system over time are known to each user at the beginning of the sequence of periods being considered; that is, users of an information system know, at the beginning of the time period under consideration, all possible signals from the entertained information system at all times within the overall time period being considered and the probability attached to each possible signal. The only thing users do not know is which signal will actually appear at any time.

Finally, we shall assume that management take the optimal action from the perspective of enterprise investors in each period. Thus we are abstracting from any problem of providing incentives to management to maximise on behalf of investors. (Problems of this type will be considered in Chapter 10 and 13.)

With this rather complicated background, which reflects the complexity of the situations we are going to consider, we can now introduce our example, which in due course we will use to restate economic income and wealth explicitly, taking into account uncertainty and information.

An example of economic wealth and income under uncertainty

We shall consider a firm which has just been set up to undertake one project over two periods. The general economy-wide state has already been revealed and will not change over the span of the project. Prior to any firm-specific information being revealed, it is believed that any one of four firm-specific states (s_1, s_2, s_3 and s_4) may occur in each of the two periods with equal probability. Prior to any information system being available, there is no belief (or evidence) that any state is more likely than any other. It is therefore believed that each state may appear with a 0.25 probability in each period. The enterprise management are assumed to make the optimal decision for investors, who are assumed to wish to maximise the expected monetary value of cash flows. For simplicity, it is assumed that planned production occurs instantaneously at the end of each period and any funds obtained from investors to finance this production are instantaneously raised and paid back at this time. Thus we will be dealing with net cash flows after this transaction with investors. All time–state-contingent claims are assumed to be traded on perfect and complete markets, which are open at the end of each period. These claims will be written in symbols as s_{it} where the first subscript (i) indexes the state and the second (t) the time period.

Table 8.1 Project details

| State | Time | | | $\phi(s)$ |
	t_0	t_1	t_2	
s_1		90	150	0.25
s_2		90	100	0.25
s_3		90	400	0.25
s_4		80	50	0.25
Total		$\overline{350}$	$\overline{700}$	
Expected value		$\overline{87.5}$	$\overline{175}$*	
Present value	224†			

*Expected values for the two periods = 350 (0.25) and 700 (0.25).
†Present value at time 0 using a 10 per cent discount rate = 79 (=87.5/(1 + r)) + 145 (=175/(1 + r)^2) = 224.

Table 8.1 shows the estimated cash flows for the project, their probabilities, their expected values in each period and the project's expected present value using a 10 per cent discount rate prior to any information system being available: t_0 represents the beginning of the first year of the project or the end of the previous year, t_1, the end of the first year of the project and t_2 the end of its second year; $\phi(s)$ indicates the probability of a state. The table shows that the project has a present value of 224 monetary units prior to any firm-specific information system becoming available.

We shall now assume that all market participants have knowledge at time 0 of the character of the enterprise's information system that will provide signals at the end of periods 1 and 2.

At the end of period 1 this information system will provide either signal y_{II} or signal y_{III}, where the first subscript in Roman numerals indexes the signal and the second indexes the time when the signal will be received. The notation used is somewhat cumbersome, reflecting the complexity of the situation being considered. Signal y_{II} indicates that either state 1 or state 2 has been realised at time 1 but not which of these two states obtained. Similarly, signal y_{III} signifies that either state 3 or state 4 has been realised at this time, again without distinguishing which of the two states has occurred. At time 2, the information system will indicate which of the possible two states declared at time 1 has actually appeared. Thus the receipt of signal y_{I2} will indicate that out of the two states declared by signal y_{II} (s_1 or s_2), state 1 (s_1) has appeared. Similarly, signal y_{II2} indicates that state 2 has occurred out of the two possible states signalled by y_{II}. Similarly, signals y_{III2} and y_{IV2} signify respectively that state 3 or state 4 have occurred out of the two states signalled by the second possible signal at time 1 (y_{III}). This information system is an example of one frequently used in the literature. It gives finer signals as to the realised state as we progress through time. The system used here is deliberately a simple one. This system is imperfect in that it does not associate a unique signal with each state. However, it does not contain noise nor are its signals inconsistent with the originally entertained probabilities (see Chapter 6).

The probabilities attached to the signals for period 1 are 0.5 for both signal y_{I1} which indicates the realisation of either state 1 or 2 and for the signal that indicates the occurrence of either state 3 or 4. These probabilities are consistent with the opening probabilities. Given that signal y_{I1} is associated with states 1 and 2 in period 1 and they both have an original probability of 0.25, the probability of receiving this signal is 0.5. Given that signal y_{I1} was received in period 1, the probability of state 1 being signalled in period 2 via the receipt of signal y_{I2} is similarly 0.5 and the probability of state 2 being signalled is therefore also 0.5 (signal y_{II2}).

Similarly, the probabilities attached to signals y_{III2} and y_{IV2} conditional on receiving signal y_{III} are both 0.5. Thus the revised probabilities of the states conditional on the receipt of a signal obtained using the Bayesian methods introduced in Chapter 6 are not surprisingly 0.5 in period 1 and 0.5 in period 2.

The details of this information system are set out in Table 8.2.

Table 8.2 Characteristics of the information system

Signal, period 1 (y_{i1})	States signalled (s_{i1})	Probability $(\phi(y_{i1}))$	Signal, period 2 (y_{i2})	States signalled (s_{i2})	Probability $(\phi(y_{i2}))$
y_{I1}	$\{s_1, s_2\}$	0.5	y_{I2}	s_1	0.5
			y_{II2}	s_2	0.5
y_{II1}	$\{s_3, s_4\}$	0.5	y_{III2}	s_3	0.5
			y_{IV2}	s_4	0.5

We can now work out a new present value for the project with this information system. One approach is to work out the expected present value of the stream of the cash flows predicated on each of the two signals in period 1 and then to add these present values together.

If signal y_{I1} is observed, the project is expected to yield 90 monetary units in period 1, but at time 0 there is believed only to be 0.5 probability of observing this signal. Thus the expected value of receiving 90 units at time 1 is 45 monetary units (90 × 0.5), which has a present value at time 0 of 41 monetary units with a 10 per cent discount rate (45/1.10).

With this signal in period 1, there is also a 50 per cent chance of obtaining 150 monetary units at the end of period 2 and a 50 per cent chance of obtaining 100 monetary units at this time. Weighting these sums by their probabilities yields the expected value of the cash flows expected to be received at the end of the project, i.e. 125 monetary units (75 (= 150 × 0.5) + 50 (100 × 0.5) = 125). This assumes that the signal in period 1 has actually occurred, whereas at time 0 there is only believed to be a 50 per cent chance of observing this signal. Therefore the expected cash flows at the end of period 2 only have 0.5 probability of appearing . Adjusting for this means that their expected value at the end of the second period is only 62.5 units (125 × 0.5). Discounting this amount back to time 0 yields 51 monetary units (62.5/1.21, where $1.21 = (1 + r)^2$ with a 10 per cent discount rate) as the expected present value of the possible period 2 outcomes conditional on the occurrence of signal y_{11} at time 1. Thus, the present value at time 0 of the cash flow stream conditional on signal y_{11} is 92 monetary units (41 + 51 monetary units). Expression 8.I below summarises the calculations by showing the present value of the expected cash flow stream contingent on the first signal in the first period.

$$V_0 \mid y_{11} = 0.5 \times 90/1.10 + [0.5 \times 0.5 \times 150/1.21 + 0.5 \times 0.5 \times 100/1.21]$$
$$= 45/1.10 + [37.5/1.21 + 25/1.21]$$
$$= 92 \qquad\qquad [8.I]$$

Here the decimal figures in the numerators of each element on the right of the expression represent the probabilities of signals, the non-decimal figures represent cash flows and the denominators represent the discount factors. The first element on the right is the expected present value of the cash flows in the first period. The other two elements are the same sums for the second period, one for each possible signal in this period.

To obtain the present value of the second cash flow stream, we first have to determine the expected present value of the cash flows in period 1 of 90 plus 80 units. This requires that these cash flows have to be multiplied by their probabilities, 0.5, and the probability of the associated signal as perceived at time 0 of 0.5, and the resultant sum discounted back to time 0. This yields $170 \times 0.5 \times 0.5$ which equals 42.5 units, which when discounted contributes 39 monetary units (42.5/1.10) to the overall cash flow stream contingent on the second signal in period 1.

Secondly, the expected present value of the state 3 and 4 cash flows conditional on the observation of the second signal can be similarly worked out: s_{3II} will yield 400 monetary units with a 0.5 probability, given that signal y_{III} has occurred, and s_{4II} will yield 50 units with a 0.5 probability in these circumstances. Weighing these sums by their probabilities gives 225 monetary units $[(0.5 \times 400 =) 200 + (0.5 \times 50 =) 25]$. Again, this assumes that signal y_{III} is certain whereas at time 0 it is believed to have only a 0.5 likelihood of appearing. Adjusting for this yields the expected value of 112.5 monetary units at the end of period 2 and discounting to time t_0 yields the expected present value of the cash flows at the end of period 2 as 93 units (112.5/1.21). Summing the expected present values of the cash flows in periods 1 and 2 gives 132 monetary units as the present value of the cash flow stream contingent on the second signal in period 1. Expression 8.II summarises these calculations by indicating the expected present value of the possible cash flow stream contingent on receiving the second signal in the first period, where the figures have the same meaning as in Expression 8.I

$$V_0 \mid y_{III} = 0.5 \times 0.5 \times (90 + 80)/1.10 + [0.5 \times 0.5 \times 400/1.21 + 0.5 \times 0.5 \times 50/1.21]$$
$$= 42.5/1.10 + 112.5/1.21$$
$$= 132 \qquad\qquad [8.II]$$

To determine the expected value of the total project, we have to add these two present values together. Thus the value of the project at time 0 (V_0) can be written as

$$V_0 = 92 + 132 = 224 \qquad\qquad [8.III]$$

As we would expect, the new information system has no effect on the present value of the prospect because no new information is revealed until time I and the original probabilities were used to evaluate this information.

As we are dealing with a public information system, we determined the above present values using the market prices for expected cash flows indexed by time and state. We obtained these expected present values by multiplying the expected price of a unit of cash flow at the time of realisation by the quantity of cash flow at that time weighted by the probability attached to the cash flow and discounting back to time 0. The price of a unit of cash flow at the time of its realisation is called the *spot price* of such a unit, which we write as P^*_{st}, where the subscript s refers to the realised state and t indicates the time period. In our case, the realised spot price will equal unity because the price of one unit of realised income in a given state and time period must equal 1 unless we are using a price in some other period as the numeraire. The prices of all other cash flows in this time period will, of course, fall to zero on the realisation of a specific state.

More generally, the realised spot price of one unit of a good which yields varying outcomes in terms of uncertain consumption units in different states will not equal unity because it will be expressed relative to the price of the good chosen as the numeraire good for that period, which will generally be taken as unity. Thus, generally the spot prices of goods are prices relative to buying one unit of the numeraire good in the same period (see Krouse, 1986, chapter 2; Ohlson, 1987a, Chapter 3).

We could alternatively use the time–state-*contingent* prices reigning at a time previous to that of realisation, say at time 0, to value our project. Time–state-contingent prices written as P_{st} are what one has to pay now to be sure of the delivery of one unit of a commodity or of cash flow in a given state in a given time period. Time–state-contingent income contracts yield one monetary unit if the state in mind is realised and nothing otherwise, though the price has to be paid at the time of contracting and before realisation.

To see what this means in terms of our example, we shall calculate the contingent price of a unit of state income if state 1 is realised in period 2. The realisation of state 1 at that time promises 150 monetary units as the outcome. We need to ask how much a rational expected value maximiser in our case would pay for such an outcome at time 0. In order to determine a value at time 0 for such an outcome, the decision maker would deflate the outcome to allow for its uncertainty and for its futurity; that is, the investor would multiply the outcome by its probability, which equals 0.25 (the probability of receiving signal y_{II2} (0.5) multiplied by the probability of receiving signal y_{II} (0.5)), and discounting by $(1 + r)^2$. This gives 31 monetary units ($= 150 \times 0.25/1.21$), where 31 units is the cost at time 0 of 150 units of state-contingent income in period 2. The (approximate) time–state-contingent price at time 0 of one unit of state 1 outcome in period 2 is thus 0.21 (31/150) monetary units. The full set of time–state-contingent prices calculated in the same way for our example are shown in Table 8.3 on the assumption that time–state claims sell in the market at their expected values. Using these prices to value the outcomes of our project at t_0 would yield the same valuation for V_0 as we obtained using spot prices.

More generally, these prices would differ between states in any time period, reflecting the economy-wide demand and supply for specific state claims.

Finally, we could also value our project utilising what are called *conditional* prices (Q_{st}) which are prices we agree to now but will pay at the time of state realisation.

Table 8.3 State-contingent prices

State	Monetary outcome	Probability	Present value	Contingent price at time t_0
	(1)	(2)	(3)	(4 = 3/1)
s_{11} or s_{21}	90	0.5	41	0.46
s_{31}	90	0.25	21	0.23
s_{41}	80	0.25	18	0.23
s_{12}	150	0.25 (0.5 × 0.5)	31	0.21
s_{22}	100	0.25 (0.5 × 0.5)	21	0.21
s_{32}	400	0.25 (0.5 × 0.5)	83	0.21
s_{42}	50	0.25 (0.5 × 0.5)	10	0.21

An example of the use of these prices is provided in futures contracts, where we contract now for certain future delivery of a good at a specific time in the future, at which time we pay the price agreed at the time of contracting.

Equilibrium conditions

As we wish to set our analysis firmly in markets in general equilibrium, we have to respect the general conditions presented in Chapter 5 which ensure that no profitable opportunities for arbitrage exist in markets generally. Here we will focus upon those additional conditions which are required to be met by multi-period prices to ensure that arbitrage is not possible using these various prices. This rather more technical section shows that the settings we are examining in discussing economic wealth and income do satisfy these conditions. Later we shall see that it is these conditions which determine the character of economic wealth and income under uncertainty. A first equilibrium condition can be specified as stating that the spot price for income in a given state at the end of a period must be equal to the contingent price of that income at the beginning of the period divided by the contingent price of the numeraire. This comes down to saying that, for example, $(P^*_{s2})/(P_{s1}) = P_{s2}$, where we are taking s_1 income as the numeraire. This says that in equilibrium, if we wish to be able to buy one unit of the state 2 income on the spot market at the end of the period, we must now buy enough units of money contingent on that state to be able to pay the expected spot price. The number of units of state-contingent money required is given by the spot-price, and the cost of a unit of state-contingent money is given by the state-contingent price of the numeraire. The above equation says that obtaining one unit of income in period 2 in this way must cost exactly the same as buying such a unit on the market for state- contingent incomes.

A final set of conditions is required for the non-existence of arbitrage between the various prices for goods with given state outcomes in the various markets. The first of these conditions requires that the cost of buying one unit of a good in a given period in the spot market divided by the cost of buying this good at its conditional (future) price which is agreed in the previous period must equal $(1 + r_f)$, where r_f equals the risk-free rate. Similarly, the rate of exchange between the future price of buying one unit of a specific good in a period and its price in the prior period, i.e. valuing the outcomes promised by the good at their state-contingent prices, will also equal $1 + r_f$.

We can use these conditions to gain insight into the relationship between contingent and spot prices which will be useful in our later analysis of economic income. The cost of one monetary unit of income in the next period in a given state is the expected spot price of this one monetary unit in the state multiplied by the probability of the state. In equilibrium, this cost should equal the state-contingent price of this income multiplied by $1 + r_f$, otherwise profitable arbitrage could take place.

Ex ante wealth and income in the example

In Expression 8.III, we have already calculated the *ex ante* wealth of the project conditional on the information system at time 0 using expected spot prices as:

$V_0 = 92 + 132 = 224$ monetary units

where the first numerical value represents the expected present value of the project conditional on the signal that s_1 or s_2 will be realised. The second value similarly represents the expected present value conditional on the second signal at time 1.

The present value of the cash flows at the end of period V_1 conditional on the information available at time 0 can be derived easily. The value of the expected cash flows to be obtained at the end of the second period conditional on signal y_{II} was calculated above as 62.5 monetary units (see page 179). This value was shown to be 112.5 units conditional on signal y_{III} (see page 180). V_1 is therefore found by discounting these amounts by $(1+r)$ rather than by $(1+r)^2$. This gives V_1 as:

$V_1 = 62.5/1.10 + 112.5/1.10 = 159$ monetary units

V_2 equals zero as no cash flows are expected to be obtained after period 2.

The cash flows at the end of the first period will be 90 units if signal y_{II} is received and either 90 or 80 units if signal y_{III} is realised. At the beginning of the project, it is not known which of these signals will be obtained. The two possible cash flows therefore have to be weighted by their probabilities to obtain the expected cash flow in period 1 as seen at time 0. This gives an expected cash flow of $90 \times 0.75 + 80 \times 0.25 = 87.5$ monetary units. Similarly, to obtain the expected cash flows at the end of the second period the various cash flows have to be weighted similarly by their probabilities in that period and also by the probability of receiving the signal in the first period on which they are contingent. The necessary calculations are set out in Table 8.4 for each state in period 2. Thus the cash flows expected in the second period as estimated with the information at time 0 are shown in the table to have a total expected value of 175 monetary units.

We can now calculate *ex ante* income using the expression introduced in Chapter 3 and reviewed above in a general way. We will continue to use the symbol Y for income as we did in Chapters 3 and 4. The context should make clear when we are talking about income and when we are talking about signals from an information system. The general expression for economic income *ex ante* was given in Chapter 3 (Expression 3.III) as:

$Y_i = V_i + C_i - V_{i-1}$ [8.IV]

Table 8.4 Expected cash flows in second period as perceived at time 0

Time–state	Monetary outcome	Probability	Expected cash flow
	(1)	(2)	$(3 = 1 \times 2)$
s_{12}	150	0.25	37.5
s_{22}	100	0.25	25
s_{32}	400	0.25	100
s_{42}	50	0.25	12.5
Total			175

where V_i and V_{i-1} represent economic wealth at the end and beginning of the period respectively, C_i represents the cash flows of the period and the i subscript indexes the period. Plugging the numbers from our example into this expression yields the *ex ante* income in the two periods of our example obtained using spot prices as:

$$Y_1 = 159 + 87.5 - 224 = 22.5$$
$$\quad (V_1) \quad (C_1) \quad (V_0)$$

and

$$Y_2 = 175 - 159 = 19$$
$$\quad (C_2) \quad (V_1)$$

where the symbols represent relevant items from our general formula for economic income.

The income figures of the type obtained above were characterised as 'well behaved' in Chapter 4 in that they merely represent interest on the opening value of the project at the beginning of each period. They also indicate that even though we are dealing with uncertain amounts, economic income only measures the interest expected to be obtained as we pass through a period. This is not surprising as all the uncertainty is known about at time 0 and the only change that occurs when we compute *ex ante* income is that we are assuming that we have passed through a period.

Thus all our findings in Chapter 3 still apply to *ex ante* income. Although consistent with the decision model, it does not provide valuable information because it merely recasts information in the public domain, though market participants may be willing to pay for its computation if it is difficult to calculate. Its only obvious role is to serve as a guide to sensible spending, as suggested by Hicks.

Risk aversion *ex ante*

Generally the above findings remain unchanged if we allow for risk aversion. Here we would expect the economic value ascribed to our project at the beginning of each period to be lower if market participants were all risk averse than if they were expected value maximisers. Risk averse investors would have to be offered a higher return to hold the project because they are now concerned with the variability of the cash flows in each period and not just their expected values. The value of the project would now also depend on the possibilities offered for insurance against possible adverse wealth effects which arise as the project proceeds. For these reasons we would expect the various time–state prices to be different from those reigning in an expected value-maximising environment.

The calculations of *ex ante* income with risk aversion are a little different from our earlier calculations because now income additionally has to take direct account of risk aversion. Using a two-period, four-state example, as in our illustration, the easiest way of proceeding is to work out V_0 using state-contingent prices for the relevant time period. This requires that we evaluate all time–state claims at their contingent prices at time 0, P_{si}, where $t = 1,2$ and $s = 1–4$. These prices reflect the scarcity and futurity of the claims and the effect of risk aversion. To obtain the income for the first period we have to calculate V_1 and the period's expected cash flows, C_1. The value of the cash flows at the end of the period can be calculated using their expected spot prices (P^*_{s1}) weighed by their probabilities (remember that we are calculating income before the event and do not know which state will actual reign). The valuation of cash flows using spot prices makes no allowance for time preference or risk aversion. Deducting the value of these cash flows evaluated using state-contingent prices at time 0 (P_{s1}) which do incorporate these factors therefore yields the income expected to be generated by the period 1 cash flows as compensation for bearing risk and as a return for time preference. Similarly, valuing the period 2 cash flows at their spot prices (P^*_{s2}) at this time and deducting their value using their state-contingent prices at time 0 (P_{s2}) indicates the expected contribution these cash flows offer towards rewarding risk bearing and foregoing earlier consumption.[2]

It is therefore possible to dichotomise this total income into that which is due to time preference calculated as the risk-free rate obtained on the opening value of the project ($r_f V_0$, where r_f is the risk-free interest rate). Secondly, the difference between income for a period and the risk-free rate on opening capital ($Y_i - r_f V_0$) equals the expected periodic return for risk bearing available in the market.

Thus, even with risk aversion, *ex ante* economic income merely reflects the passing of time and amounts only to obtaining interest at a rate reflecting risk on the opening value of the project at the beginning of the period.

The amount of the *ex ante* income described above will not be realised when the period concerned comes to pass because our income measure under uncertainty involves a weighted average value of cash flows, only one of which will be realised in each time period. Thus, it is possible to define an income measure that reflects attitudes to risk, but only by deviating from the essential characteristic of economic income of providing a measure of how much can be spent in the period with the expectation of being as well off at the end of the period as one was at the beginning.

We shall now consider *ex post* wealth and income under uncertainty using our example.

Ex post wealth and income

In Chapter 4 we discussed two alternative definitions of *ex post* income. One variant of this measure, labelled *ex post* income concept I (see Expression 4.V), compared wealth at the end of a period plus the cash flows of the period revised for any new information accruing during the period with the original value of the project at the opening of the period. We shall now derive this measure for the two periods of our project.

Ex post income under concept I for period 1

For period 1, there are two possibilities for the cash flows of the period. One possibility is that cash flows of 90 monetary units appear and the other is that cash flows of 80 units are realised. Thus, to determine economic income in period 1, we have to undertake two calculations.

Calculation A: value at end of period 1, given signal y_I

If signal y_I appears, this means that states 1 or 2 will appear in period 2. Wealth must therefore be revised to reflect this. Wealth at the end of period 1 will now comprise expected cash flows of 150 monetary units with a probability of 0.5 and expected cash flows of 100 with a probability of 0.5. These two sums have to be added together yielding 125 monetary units (0.5 × 150 + 0.5 × 100) and discounted back to the end of period 1 to obtain the revised wealth at the end of period 1. These operations yield cash flows with a present value of 114 units (125/1.10), yielding a total present value at the end of the period of 204 units (90 + 114).

Calculation B: value at end of period 1, given signal y_{II}

If this signal is received in period 1, the cash flows in period 2 will be either 400 units or 50 units. However, this uncertainty can be resolved by considering the cash flows that have been realised in period 1. If cash flows of 90 are obtained in combination with signal y_{II} we can be certain that the realised cash flows in the next period will be 400 units. Similarly, we will know at the end of period 1 that the cash flows in the next period will be only 50 if the cash flows in the first period amount to 80 units.

The value of the project at the end of the first period conditional on receiving the second signal will be either 363 monetary units (400/1.10) conditional on realised cash flows of 90 units in period 1, or 45 units (50/1.10) if the cash flows in the first period amount to 80 units.

The above finding that original knowledge about the project can help in interpreting the signals from a separate information system is important. In an accounting context this result means that the full informativeness of accounting items cannot be evaluated without considering any information they convey when taken together with other accounting signals and, indeed, with the signals from other information systems. Considering the signals from separate information systems together may yield more information than when they are used separately. This provides a logic for not just looking at profits, for example, but for also considering the information obtained when all the signals yielded by the items determining profits are evaluated as a whole.

We can utilise the above calculations to determine *ex post* income using concept I in period 1. We will first calculate this measure assuming that signal y_I is obtained in period 1. To do this we add together the revised wealth at the end of period 1 contingent on the occurrence of signal y_{II} and the period 1 cash flows contingent on this signal. Finally, from this sum we deduct the original opening value of the project.

This allows us to write *ex post* income for period 1 contingent on signal y_{II} as

$$Y_1 \mid y_{II} = \underset{(V_1 \mid y_{II})}{114} + \underset{(C_1 \mid y_{II})}{90} - \underset{(V_0)}{224} = 204 - 224 = -20 \qquad \text{[8.Va]}$$

where the symbol | indicates that the element on the left of this line is conditional on the element on its right. The other symbols represent income for the period (Y_1), the value of the project at time $1(V_1)$ and the cash flows in period 1 (C_1) contingent on signal 1 in that period and the original value of the project (V_0), respectively. The figures come from Calculation A above.

Ex post income in period 1 contingent on signal y_{III} and on the cash flows obtained in period 1 can similarly be written as

Either

$$Y_1 \mid y_{III}, 90 = \underset{(V_1 \mid y_{III}, 90)}{363 \,(400/1.10)} + \underset{(F_1 \mid y_{III})}{90} - \underset{(V_0)}{224} = 229 \qquad \text{[8.Vb(i)]}$$

where the symbols now represent end-of-period value and cash flows in the period contingent on signal 2 and on the cash flows in the first period, as shown by the 90 to the right of the conditional sign. The figures come from Calculation B above.

or

$$Y_1 \mid y_{III}, 80 = \underset{(V_1) \mid y_{III}, 80)}{45 \,(50/1.10)} + \underset{(F_1 \mid y_{III})}{80} - \underset{(V_0)}{224} = -99 \qquad \text{[8.Vb(ii)]}$$

We shall now calculate *ex post* income for period 2 using the same logic as above. In order to do this we need to know what happened in period 1 because the actual states to be realised in period 2 depend on the realised state in the previous period. Without a knowledge of what happened in the first period, it is impossible to compute income in the second. This operation highlights a new role for economic income. Earlier *ex post* income and wealth figures record the history of the enterprise. Thus one possible role for economic income is to provide a history of the enterprise's economic development. This history can be obtained by keeping other records, but accounting using economic concepts does provide an easily accessible and very low cost method of retrieving the enterprise's financial history. This general use of income is reflected in practice, where analysts often refer to a run of historical income andother figures to aid them in predicting current results.

Ex post income under concept I for period 2

Here there are four possible *ex post* income numbers, one for each state at the end of period 2. Two of these are contingent on signal y_{II} which indicates that the cash flows at the end of period 2 will be either 150 or 100 units. The other two arise following the receipt of signal y_{III} and the realisation of cash flows of either 90 or 80 units which indicate that the cash flows in the second period will be 400 or 50 monetary units respectively.

The calculation of the *ex post* income concept I requires that from the actual cashflows for the period is deducted the opening value of the project as seen at the beginning of the period. In our case, the latter values would be either $V_2 \mid y_{II}$, 90 which equals 114 monetary units and either $V_2 \mid y_{II}$, 90 which equals 363 units (400/1.10) or

$V_2|y_{III}$, 80 which equals 45 units (50/1.10); see Calculations A and B respectively. Thus our four possible *ex post* income numbers for period 2 indexed by the signals which apply to them are

$$Y_2 \,|\, y_{I2} = 150 - 114 = 36 \qquad\qquad\qquad\qquad\qquad\qquad\qquad\qquad\text{[8.VIa]}$$
$$Y_2 \,|\, y_{II2} = 100 - 114 = -14 \qquad\qquad\qquad\qquad\qquad\qquad\qquad\text{[8.VIb]}$$
$$Y_2 \,|\, y_{III2} = 400 - 363 = 37 \qquad\qquad\qquad\qquad\qquad\qquad\qquad\text{[8.VIc]}$$
$$Y_2 \,|\, y_{IV2} = 50 - 45 = 5 \qquad\qquad\qquad\qquad\qquad\qquad\qquad\qquad\text{[8.VId]}$$

The term on the left of each expression says that the income expressed on the right of the equation applies if a specific state has obtained in period 2. The two subscripts associated with each signal are first state occurrence in the period and the second the time period. Expression 8.VIa indicates *ex post* income in the second period, given that signal 1 (y_{I1}) was received in period 1 and signal 1 (y_{I2}) was also obtained in the second period. The second expression similarly presents income if signal 1 is received in the first period and signal 2 is obtained in the second period (y_{II2}). Expressions 8.VIc and 8.VId calculate income in the second period, given that the second signal is obtained in period 1 (y_{III}). The third expression assumes that realised cash flows are 90 monetary units and that signal y_{III2} will be obtained in period 2 and the final expression indicates that cash flows of 80 units appear and that signal y_{IV2} is then obtained in the second period. The first element on the right of each expression is the realised cash flows, given the indexed pattern of signals. The second element on the right is the expected value of the period 2 cash flows at the beginning of the period conditional on the signal received in period 1. *Ex post* income using concept I is shown in numerical terms on the far right of each expression for the signals assumed by each expression.

Adding each of these income figures for the second period to the appropriate income figure for the first period yields the four possible *ex post* income histories for our project.

These histories are:

History 1	$Y_{yI1} + Y_{yI2}$	$= -20 + 36 = 16$	
History 2	$Y_{yI1} + Y_{yII2}$	$= -20 - 14 = -34$	
History 3	$Y_{yIII,90} + Y_{yIII2}$	$= 229 + 37$	$= 266$
History 4	$Y_{yIII,80} + Y_{yIV2}$	$= -99 + 5$	$= -94$

Thus with *ex post* income concept I, in order to maintain the original wealth of the project as it actually unfolds, we have to pay in money whenever the first signal appears in period 1. Once we have received signal y_{I1} we are recommended to declare an income only if signal I is received in period 2. Following these recommendations for all our histories generates wealth of 224 monetary units at the end of the project for all histories.[3] Thus history 2 yields cash flows of 90 plus 100 monetary units. It requires a payment in period 1 of 20 monetary units and of 14 units in period 2 (90 + 20 + 100 + 14 = 224). History 3 allows us to declare an income in period 1 on receipt of signal II. The final history requires us to pay in 99 units and to declare an income of 5 units in the second period.

While the calculations for *ex post* income using concept I are still fresh in our minds, we will carry out the same calculations using *ex post* income concept II before considering the impact on our calculations of allowing for risk aversion and discussing the economic meaning of the income figures generated by the two *ex post* income concepts.

Ex post income under concept II for our example

The presentation of our second *ex post* income numbers is easier, given the calculations discussed above. For each period, this second concept of income compares the same end-of-period wealth and the cash flows for the period as above with a revised figure for opening period wealth. This revised figure incorporates the information that accrues at the end of a period. We are thus going to compare end-of-period wealth and period cash flows conditional on the information available at the end of the period with these values discounted to the beginning of the period. The justification for revising opening period wealth in this way is that this what a rational person would have expected end-of-period wealth to be with full access to the information available at the end of the period. It is opening period wealth with the mistaken views as seen at the end of the period stripped out.

The first column of Table 8.5 rewrites the end of period wealth and the cash flows for each period and for each signal within each period, indexing the figures by the signals to which they relate. The wealth at the end of the second period is represented by only the end-of-period cash flows, as the project terminates in this period. These figures are obtained from Expressions 8.Va, 8.Vb(i) and 8.Vb(ii) for period 1 and from Expressions 8.VIa–d for period 2. They are the first elements on the right of each of these expressions.

Table 8.5 *Ex post* income for project under income concept II

Ex post wealth (V_i) and cash flow in the period (C_i) conditional on signals		Wealth at beginning of period revised for information available at end of period $V_{i-1} \mid y_{ii}$	*Ex post* income using concept II
(1)		(2)	(3 = 1 − 2)
$(V_1 + C_1) \mid y_{I1}$	= 204	185	19
$(V_1 + C_1) \mid y_{II1}, 90$	= 453	412	41
$(V_1 + C_1) \mid y_{II1}, 80$	= 125	114	11
$C_2 \mid y_{I2}$	= 150	136	14
$C_2 \mid y_{II2}$	= 100	91	9
$C_2 \mid y_{III2}$	= 400	363	37
$C_2 \mid y_{IV2}$	= 50	45	5

The value of the project for each signal at the beginning of a period revised for the information available at the end of the period is found simply by discounting end-of-period wealth under that signal back to the beginning of the period. This provides the estimate of opening period wealth we would have made with access to the end-of-period information at its beginning. The discounting is required because we are making the estimate at the beginning rather than the end of the period. The results of these calculations are shown in column (2) of Table 8.5.

Ex post income under concept II is obtained for each signal in each period by deducting from closing period wealth, calculated using the signal at the end of the period, the opening value of the project conditional on the signal received at the end of the period. The results of this calculation are shown in the third column of the table.

Our second income concept yields a different set of income histories for our project than did the first concept. The income histories with income concept II are

History 1	$Y_{yI1} + Y_{yI2}$	$= 19 + 14 = 33$
History 2	$Y_{yI1} + Y_{yII2}$	$= 19 + 9 = 28$
History 3	$Y_{yIII} + Y_{yIII2}$	$= 41 + 37 = 78$
History 4	$Y_{yIII} + Y_{yIV2}$	$= 11 + 5 = 16$

Inspecting the *ex post* figures we have calculated using income concepts I and II indicates that here these accounting income numbers fully reveal the signals received from the underlying information system. The income figures for each period inform us of all that the underlying information system could tell us. Thus they tell us as much about the future as does the basic information system. This ability of the accounting system to indicate something of the future provides a logic for the practical belief that accounting information may provide information about the future. This perspective provides a foundation for the Conceptual Framework Project of the Financial Accounting Standards Board (the United States accounting standard setting body; see Chapter 12). Generally, accounting figures may not fully reveal the information provided by an information system without adjustment (see Demski and Sappington, 1990).

Risk aversion and income concepts I and II

Our two *ex post* income concepts can be used without change when risk aversion is brought into the analysis employing the approach utilised for determining *ex ante* income with risk aversion, but we have to be very clear as to the meaning of the elements used to deduce income in this setting. Consider first the *ex post* cash flows for the period under income concept I. These will be automatically stated in terms of actual spot prices as determined by the information at the end of the period. The contribution that the actual cash flows of the period make to income for the period is therefore found by netting off the actual cash flows and their value determined using state-contingent prices reigning at time 0. The end of-period-wealth can be stated in terms of its total value at the end of the period in a number of ways. It can be evaluated by pricing all the time–state contingent claims it encompasses, given the information received in the completed period at their anticipated spot prices in the period in which they are expected to be realised, and multiplying them by their probabilities. Their value at the opening of the period using their state-contingent prices is then deducted from this sum. Adding these two sums together yields the economic income for the period using concept I.[4]

Again, this concept tells us how much we can take out of the project or have to pay to maintain its opening value intact. It really reflects the actual variability of the project's cash flows and indicates the actual periodic return for risk bearing.

One of the weaknesses of this income concept is that it is difficult to analyse in further detail by dividing income into the actual return for risk bearing and the return for forgoing consumption in any meaningful way, though a variety of calculations are possible.

Using income concept II, the original opening value of the project at the beginning of the period is updated for the information received during the period. The detailed computations are given in Note 5 at the end of the chapter. These show that this second measure of income is well behaved with income being the risky rate of interest on the revised opening value of the project. The return for risk bearing can be quantified by deducting from this income the amount that would have been obtained if only the riskless rate had obtained on this revised opening value. Income representing the return for risk bearing will also be well behaved as it represents the going rate of return for this purpose on the value of the project at the beginning of the period.

As we have seen, the prices of time–state claims and income will be affected by the flow of information up to the period we are considering but in a perfectly organised market these revised prices will have already been fully anticipated at the start of the project. Thus the changes in these prices as a project unfolds come as no surprise and will have been allowed for in optimal decision making. They merely reflect necessary alterations, as the actual direction to be taken by an uncertain project is revealed as it passes through time and information is obtained. None of these changes will therefore reflect changes in demand or supply or in preferences over time.

We will now compare the two income concepts, concentrating on their special attributes under uncertainty and using our numerical example to help understanding. It is not intended to reiterate the long discussion of the two concepts in Chapter 4.

The two income concepts compared

Inspection of Table 8.5 suggests two things which are immediately noteworthy on comparing the two income concepts. First, the table shows that income numbers under concept II are well behaved in the sense that they yield the interest rate on the revised opening value of the project. Secondly, they differ substantially from both *ex ante* income numbers derived earlier and from the *ex post* figures we obtained using *ex post* income concept I. For example, they show none of the losses yielded by income derived using our other *ex post* concept. These losses still accrue but instead of passing through income they are immediately deducted from capital. Recall from Chapter 4 that use of concept II indicates the income that can be declared while maintaining our capital revised for information obtained in the period. As was said in that chapter, our second income concept really involves deducting a different sum from *ex post* wealth at the end of a period.

Consider the treatments of capital losses and gains in period 1 under income concept II in our example. If signal 1 is received in period 1, this income concept writes down capital as the difference between what we originally expected the value of the project to be at the beginning of the period, a sum of 224 monetary units, and what it was expected to be at the beginning of the period revised using the information available at the end of the period, 185 units. Thus, under concept II, capital values are reduced by a capital write-down of 39 units, but some of this write-down is compensated for by an income for the period of 19 units. The net loss to investors is therefore 20 units, which is just the amount required to be paid in using income concept I.

Similarly, if signal 2 and cash-flows of 90 units had been received in period 1, income concept II would have written up capital by the difference in the original value at the beginning the period, 224 monetary units, and its revised value obtained using the information at the end of the period, 412 units. This yields a revaluation of 188 units. The total wealth change to investors under concept II is this revaluation plus the declared income for the period of 41units, a total of 229 monetary units. This is the amount of income declared in this setting with the other *ex post* income concept.

Thus, as was said under certainty, it does not matter if one of the two income concepts is chosen by management for reporting purposes and for determining dividends. In a perfect market investors who prefer the income declared under the other concept can obtain this through personal operations on the market (see Chapter 4, p. 64).

Expected versus unexpected changes

Those who originated these concepts saw them as applying in different settings. *Ex post* income concept I was meant to applywhere there were no unexpected losses and gains. It was seen to be appropriate where the setting was one for which the assumptions of a project do not change as it proceeds. Thus, it would be suggested for our project if it were to proceed according to the original plan, because no unexpected changes will occur. This does not mean that violent changes in project value do not occur as the project unfolds. The value of our project alters substantially over time. Rather, it means that all possible changes and the probabilities of these changes are known at the start of the project. Each individual is therefore able to use the well organised market with full information to satisfy preferences at the beginning of the project. Income numbers are really irrelevant in so far that the decisions made at this time are Pareto efficient. This is because no later decisions can improve welfare. The attainment of a Pareto efficient allocation of all present and future claims at the time of the original decision means no further decisions can improve welfare. If this were not the case the marginal conditions for overall and individual optimality would not be satisfied at the time of the original decision. Possibilities for profitable arbitrage would therefore exist at the various prices for claims at that time, leading to a new allocation of claims amongst market participants. Our example with its assumptions represents an illustration of a decision model where no unexpected changes are possible. Knowing what actually happens as the project proceeds allows no possibility of gain or any further avoidance of loss.

What is being said applies where individuals are risk averse. The market settings discussed above and that applying to our project allow all desired adjustments for risk to be made at the time of decision. If we allow people to be risk averse when considering our project, such individuals could insure against the outcomes they do not like at the time of decision making. Chapter 7 demonstrated that with a full set of markets in Arrow–Debreu signal-contingent securities, each of which yields one unit of outcome in one and only one time–state/signal combination, all decisions would be made at the time of the original decision. The opening of markets in the future and information about state realisations would therefore be unnecessary to improve welfare. As an example of this, recall from Chapter 6 that an investor who was risk averse and who subscribed to the probabilities impounded in the market prices of state claims (see pp. 99–102) would trade to obtain a certain outcome in all states. With our example, such a result could be obtained by trading the original holdings of contingent claims at their contingent prices shown in Table 8.3 to obtain rights to approximately 128 units of contingent claims in each state. An investor who has carried out these operations would be uninterested in any information concerning state realisations.

The choice of income concept may be important if decisions based on *ex post* income have to be made during a project. This is because the prices used to calculate *ex post* income using concept I do not reflect the opportunities available at the end of the period. Indeed, some of the prices used to calculate the opening value of the project no longer exist. The prices used by income concept II are consistent with those used to determine the end-of-period wealth and the use of this concept in decision making will lead to decisions consistent with those obtained if this end-of-period wealth had be used in decision making.

The introduction of risk aversion into our analysis does suggest another use for *ex post* income I with perfect markets. The original value of a project in this setting measures the amount the owner of the project could invest on the market in a variety of less risky opportunities if so desired. If the owner invests in the project it must be expected to yield sufficient return for the additional risk taken on. *Ex ante* income using concept I measures this expected return and *ex post* income according to this concept measures the actual result of bearing this risk. Thus the traditional view that income concept I should be used in situations of no unexpected changes seems justified. This concept charts the progress of a project as it proceeds and compares this with the original value of the project, thereby allowing investors to compare what the project is yielding with what they could have obtained if they had allocated their funds differently.

Thus, with the usual models entertained in the literature of financial markets, optimal decisions are made at the beginning of a project and nothing changes as projects unfold. There is therefore little role for income measurement as decisions are not changed by the receipt of signals as the project proceeds.

The assumptions of the models of uncertainty and information economics reinforce this lack of a role for income measurement. Such models are assumed to be completely specified. Thus, no unenvisaged states can appear, no new actions can become available and all possible outcomes are known. The only changes in state probabilities and therefore in the various prices of time–state claims that can occur are determined in a known way depending on the known possible signals to be received from a known information system.

These assumptions concerning markets and information economics mean that windfall gains and losses cannot occur. In this setting, the originators of economic income would therefore recommend the use of income concept I.

A role which income measurement, and accounting more generally, is seen to play in the practical world is that of, at least, yielding some information with surprise value. Research is needed to make the above analysis richer in order to allow the possibility of unexpected gains and losses.

Windfall gains and losses

One way to bring windfall gains and losses into our analysis is by permitting the possibility of introducing richer information systems into the market over time. This was really how we evaluated the role of public information in the previous chapter. The results of such an introduction may cause major shifts in enterprise values (without changing the character or prices of securities offered in the market) and therefore generate windfall gains and losses. As an example of these effects, consider how our numerical example would change if an information system were suddenly made available at the end of period 1 which told us at the end of this period which of our four states reigned in that period and would continue to reign in the next.

We will now recalculate the possible end-of-period wealth at time 1 for each of the states, given this new information system. For each of the states, this gives wealth of:

$$V_1 \mid s_{11}, s_{12} = 90 + 150/1.10 = 90 + 136 = 226$$
$$V_1 \mid s_{21}, s_{22} = 90 + 100/1.10 = 90 + 92 = 182$$
$$V_1 \mid s_{31}, s_{32} = 90 + 400/1.10 = 90 + 363 = 453$$
$$V_1 \mid s_{41}, s_{42} = 80 + 50/1.10 = 80 + 45 = 125$$

The terms on the left are the values of the project conditional on a given state occurring in both periods 1 and 2. The first term on the right of each of these expressions is the project cash flow in period 1 and the second term is the value of the second period cash flows when discounted back to the end of period 1, both conditional on the occurrence of the same state.

One measure of the extent of windfall gains and losses is obtained by deducting from the above revised values the value for the project at the end of period 1 which we calculated earlier for the previous information system; see the first column of Table 8.5. Here, the value of the project at the end of period 1 was 204 monetary units if signal y_I was received and either 453 units or 125 units if signal y_{II} was received in conjunction with cash flows of 90 units or 80 units respectively. Thus the windfall gains and losses with the new information system for each new signal are:

Windfall gain $\mid s_1 = 22 \quad = 226 - 204$
Windfall loss $\mid s_2 = -22 = 182 - 204$
Windfall gain $\mid s_3 = 0 \quad\;\; = 453 - 453$
Windfall loss $\mid s_4 = 0 \quad\;\; = 125 - 125$

Here the final set of notation in each expression indicates the total value of wealth with the original information system conditional on the signals received in the two periods.

Table 8.6 shows the *ex post* income for period 1 with the new information system using our two *ex post* income concepts. *Ex post* income concept I deducts from the end-of-period value for each signal from the new information system the opening value of our project of 224 monetary units. A reconciliation between our original calculations for this number and our new income numbers for each signal shows that this method of calculating income passes all items through income and again allows all gains to be spent and requires all losses to be made up. Our second income concept deducts from the new value of the project for each signal its opening value revised for this signal. The table also indicates the gain or loss capitalised by income concept II. The total of *ex post* income II plus the capital changes for each signal is equal to the income announced under the other concept, as we indicated earlier.

Income according to concept II does seem to make good sense where unexpected

Table 8.6 *Ex post* **income calculation with new information system**

Ex Post **Income Concept I**

Income conditional on signal from the new information system	Capital change*	Original Y_1†
$Y_1 \mid s_1 = \quad 2 = 226 - 224$	$= +22$	$- 20$
$Y_1 \mid s_2 = -42 = 182 - 224$	$= -22$	$- 20$
$Y_1 \mid s_3 = \quad 229 = 453 - 224$	$= 0$	$+229$
$Y_1 \mid s_4 = -99 = 125 - 224$	$= 0$	$- 99$

*The capital change is calculated in the text.
†The original income figures come from Expression 8.Va and 8VIb.

Ex Post **Income Concept II and capitalised gains and losses**

Income	Changes capitalised $V_{1\text{revised}} - V_1$
$Y_1 \mid s_1 = 22 = 226 - 204 \ (= 226/1.10)$	$204 - 224 = - 20$
$Y_1 \mid s_2 = 17 = 182 - 165 \ (= 181/1.10)$	$165 - 224 = - 59$
$Y_1 \mid s_3 = 41 = 453 - 412 \ (= 453/1.10)$	$412 - 224 = +188$
$Y_1 \mid s_4 = 11 = 125 - 114 \ (= 125/1.10)$	$114 - 224 = -110$

changes in the time–state claims generated by the firm occur, especially where this causes major changes in enterprise values. It capitalises all past changes and declares an income based upon the economic value of the project at the end of the period; thus income is related to an economically meaningful figure, end-of-period wealth.

Income declared using this concept therefore automatically gives the same signals for future decision making as would use of the usual decision making models. This is not generally true of income concept I where changes have occurred from original expectations. This is because concept I compares the end-of-period value and period cash flows conditional on the latest available information system $(V_i + C_i) \mid \eta_i$, where η_i refers to the information system available at the end of the period) with the value of these quantities at the beginning of the period estimated using an earlier information system, usually that available at the time of the original decision, say, time t_0. That is, income for period i according to concept I is calculated as

$$Y_{i,1} = (V_i + C_i) \mid \eta_i - V_{i-1} \mid \eta_0$$

An opportunity is worth continuing in a perfect and complete market providing that its value at the end of the period, which is indicated by the first term on the right, is positive. Income concept I yields negative signals if the originally expected value of the project $(V_{i-1} \mid \eta_0)$ is greater than its revised value $(V_i \mid \eta_i)$ unless this difference is offset by larger cash flows for the period than originally expected being declared by the later information system.

With regard to our project, inspection of the first numerical columns of the income history yielded by income concept I on p. 188 indicates that this concept yields negative signals for two of the signals in the first period generated by our original information system, even though the end-of-period value of the project is positive in these cases. Of course, with sufficient information it is possible to recover the end-of-period values from these income numbers and make the correct decision. Thus again, we can confirm the traditional view and say that it is easier to use *ex post* income concept II, at least where unexpected changes have occurred.

Thus we can overcome the problem that the theories being used do not allow unexpected changes in the variables that determine income, by seeing such changes as flowing from the introduction of new or refined information systems. It is unlikely that the change in the quantity of time–state claims offered by the firm is likely to be sufficient to change extant market prices. Similarly, in many cases, if not in most, changes in time–state claims flowing from the firm are unlikely to change their market prices as few changes will produce outcomes which cannot be formed using time–state claims already available on the market. This means that any changes can be evaluated by using existing market prices.

Thus where we are talking about unexpected changes we are speaking of items not expected by the firm. If for example a new information system gave more information about the firm's productivity, this would change the outcomes the firm could place on the market, but the prices used to evaluate these outcomes could be taken from the market. However, in the course of a general review of this area, Feltham and Christensen (1988) have suggested that we have not entirely escaped the problem that no gains may flow from additional information for trading purposes where we are dealing with firm-specific events in a pure trading setting, as such events should be irrelevant to a well diversified individual. Our numerical examples did show that accounting information may have other purposes than just trading: managers could use the information to make production decisions and also finance could be refused for the project. However, there do seem to be problems here that require additional research.

Further research is also required into settings where enterprise information, contrary to what we have assumed in this chapter, does change the market prices of time–state claims. Here we would compute income after the market has regained equilibrium, utilising the revised prices generated by this process. However, enterprises having information of this type may be able to exploit any monopoly accruing because of its possession.

The role of accounting in information provision

So far in this chapter, we have been talking about information generally. The various models of economic wealth and income were based on an underlying information system rather than upon an accounting information system. The output of such underlying information systems may be available separately from the accounting reports at a time no later than when the accounting reports are issued. In this case, the accounting reports will have no public or private value (see Beaver and Demski, 1979). Thus the value of accounting information must stem either from the elements of the information system which it uniquely reports or from those unique elements which the accounting system itself generates. Demski and Sappington (1990) have recently shown that even traditional accounting systems can under certain conditions accurately portray any incremental information from the underlying enterprise information system reserved for publication in the accounting reports.

The above analysis also indicates that the accounting systems of firms cannot provide all the information required to value the enterprise. Our analysis allowed for this by concentrating on firm-specific events and assuming that an economy-wide information system also existed. The outputs of both systems impact on the value of the enterprise. Demski and Sappington (1990) have suggested that enterprise accounting reports need augmentation from an economy-wide information system if they are going to allow a valuation of the firm taking into account all information. They concentrate on the information value of the enterprise information system. There is another view; that is that management in decision making have to consider the outputs of both information systems and because of their special knowledge should be in a better position to evaluate how economy-wide information impinges on the firm. Thus, it can be argued that enterprise should seek to portray the economic value of the enterprise as seen by management. This at least would seem to be what was in the minds of those who originated the economic perspective on income and wealth concepts. Providing the outputs of all relevant information systems are utilised in arriving at these estimates, it would seem possible to maintain this view without abandoning the informational perspective.

Our analysis in Chapter 7 and in this chapter also suggested a reason why accounting information may be less valuable than we might expect. Well organised markets may require very little information from enterprises as projects proceed where all the possible signals about the project were known about at the beginning of the project. In such markets, earlier market transactions may substitute for later information. This is one reason why the unexpected changes we have focused on towards the end of this chapter are so important.

Overall the analysis in this chapter may not suggest a strong role for accounting information either from an information perspective or for aiding in enterprise valuation. It is the underlying information system that serves this role. Research is needed into how far the accounting system forms part of the enterprise information system and the degree to which the accounting information systems yields independent signals unavailable from other sources. With this perspective the accounting system itself is seen as generating incremental information. Unless this is the case, it is difficult to reconcile our views of accounting with the view that seems to be entertained in the practical world. As Ohlson said in commenting on views expressed by Beaver and Demski (1979), 'The argument in favour of income measurement simply rests on income as being a primary piece of information when investors value a firm.' (Ohlson, 1987b, p. 3). Ohlson's own research suggests one direction for discovering a role for accounting of the type he insists upon in the above quotation. He is trying to site accounting earnings and book values in a valuation model of the firm within a general equilibrium setting (see Ohlson, 1989).

The above analysis was undertaken in the context of markets that could obtain Pareto efficiency. As has been said a number of times, poorly organised markets may mean that economic income and wealth may no longer serve as value-free measures useful to all individuals. The problems that this brings are taken up in the following chapters. Chapter 9 first considers how the findings flowing from adopting an informational perspective on information and on accounting information allow the construction of empirical tests concerning the effects of additional information. Some of the findings concerning accounting information obtained using this approach are presented.

Chapter summary

This chapter extended our earlier treatment of economic wealth and income under uncertainty (see Chapter 5). It commenced by indicating that the originators of these concepts were aware of the importance of uncertainty in this area but generally ignored its effects in their presentations.

The first substantive section of the chapter revised the classical treatments of these subjects, first presented in Chapters 3 and 4. The following section introduced the uncertainty models we would use later in the chapter. In order to simplify the presentation we first assumed that participants were risk neutral, though the effects of risk aversion were treated in later parts of the chapter. It was argued that a multi-period model had to be utilised so that a role for accounting information could emerge. The firm-specific information system which was mainly to be used in the chapter was introduced; it was indicated to be of a character such that it yielded finer signals as we proceeded through time.

The example to be used was then presented. Periodic *ex ante* wealth for our example was shown to have the same characteristics as it did under certainty (see Chapter 3). In order to consider *ex post* income over time in an uncertain setting, the concepts of spot, contingent and conditional prices for time–state claims were reviewed and the conditions between these prices which must be satisfied in equilibrium were presented. These and our earlier equilibrium conditions were argued to be important in income measurement because we wished to ground such measures in a full equilibrium setting.

These prices were then used to derive *ex ante* income for our example. Again, it was indicated that uncertainty made no difference. The next section showed that introducing risk aversion made no difference to the results obtained thus far, except that with risk aversion income could be dichotomised into a return for risk bearing and a return to foregone consumption.

The two *ex post* income concepts introduced in Chapter 4 were then shown to apply under uncertainty, though their calculation was shown to be more complex and their meaning, perhaps, a little more difficult to understand. Again, introducing risk aversion was shown to make no difference of principle.

A new role for economic income over time was then suggested. In order to deduce income for a period with an information system that yields finer information over time, it may be necessary to know the previous signals provided by the information system. It was indicated that our two *ex post* information systems could serve this role. Although the two income models generally yielded different income histories for the enterprise, they can be reconciled as we would expect, recalling that in Chapter 4 it was shown that the results of using either income concept could be converted into the other in a well organised market.

An important new point was introduced in the next section, where it was said that the models we were using taken from economics and information economics did not really allow information systems generally, including accounting information systems, to produce new or unexpected information. This is because these models assume that the only unknowns at the time of decision making are which signals out of a known set will appear in each period. Those who dislike the risk this engenders can rearrange their affairs in the market to avoid this risk. Thus, this perspective really rules out the possibility of windfall gains and losses being shown in accounting reports. This is at variance with the practical world, where these reports are assumed often to provide information having surprise value. One approach to reconciling these perspectives was suggested to allow a richer information system to appear during the development of an opportunity over time. This approach equated obtaining information with a surprise value with unexpected access to a richer information system. Reviewing our two *ex post* income concepts suggested that income concept II was the more suitable in the setting where new information systems became available.

The chapter concluded by arguing more generally that, for accounting information to have a role in the context of our usual models, it must provide information not yielded by a more timely information source. It was then suggested that in a well organised market for any incremental information provided by an accounting system to have value, this information must be unexpected. Otherwise, the decision maker could at the time of decision making adjust for any possible signal using the market, and would not then be interested in the signals realised.

The major questions which remain are whether economic income and wealth, accounting systems built upon them, and accounting information more generally, may have a stronger role in imperfectly organised markets. These questions are taken up in later chapters.

Notes

1. The easiest way to visualise what is being assumed with regard to information systems is to say that usually the overall set of states S can be split into a number of subsets of states. Here the first of these is a set of economy-wide states, say, S_E, the representative member of which is s_e, where $e = 1$ to E (that is, $s_e \in S_E$ in terms of our earlier notation). The remaining subsets of states are sets of states, one for each firm, specific to that firm and conditional on each economy-wide state s_e. That is, there is a set of states for each firm conditional on each economy-wide state.

2. This approach to *ex ante* income determination can be written in symbols for the first period of a two-period problem as

$$Y_1 = \{\sum_S C_{s1}(P^*_{s1})\phi s - \sum_S C_{s1}(P_{s1})\} + \qquad \text{[8.VII]}$$

$$\{\sum_S C_{s2}(P^*_{s2})\phi s - \sum_S C_{s2}(P_{s2})\}$$

The first element on the right is the cash flows end of period 1 evaluated at their expected spot prices weighted by their probabilities. The second element represents the value of the same cash flows evaluated at their contingent prices at time 0. That is, it represents the present value of these cash flows at time 0 evaluated using time- and state-contingent market prices at that time. The third element is similarly the period 2 cash flows evaluated using spot prices at that time. The final element of this expression is the value of these cash flows evaluated using contingent prices at time 0. It is important to separate the two elements in this calculation as the first set of state-contingent prices relate to period 1 and the second set relate to period 2.

3. We are working with project cash flows rather than the total cash flows of the project (see Chapter 3). The income declared at the end of the second period is therefore understated. For example, our calculations of income under signal I, make no allowance for the interest that would be obtained on the retention of 90 monetary units in the first period and the

payment-in of 20 monetary units in the second period. This reinvestment would yield additional income of 11 units ($=110r$, where r equals 0.10). Thus, the income that could be declared in the second period while maintaining intact the original value of the project at that time is 47 units rather than 36 units.

The total cash flows at the end of period 2 taking interest into account can be written as $90 + 20 + 11 + 150 = 271$ monetary units. Deducting 224 units (the original value of the project) yields a sum of 47 monetary units. This sum can be declared as income without causing the terminal value of the project to fall below its original opening value.

4. These operations for the first period of a two-period, four-state problem are shown in symbols below:

$$Y_{1,\mathrm{I}} = \{\hat{C}_{s1}(P^*_{s1}) - \sum_{s} C_{s1}(P_{s1})\} + \{(\sum_{s} C_{s2} \mid y_1)(P^*_{s2})\phi(s \mid y_1) - \sum_{s} C_{s2}(P_{s2})\} \qquad [8.\mathrm{VIII}]$$

The second subscript on the income symbol indicates that we are using *ex post* income concept I. The first expression on the right indicates the realised cash flows for period 1 priced at their actual spot price, where the caret ($\hat{\ }$) over the cash flow symbol indicates that these cash flows have been realised in that they have been signalled as received by the information system being used. The second element of the expression is the cash flows for the period expected at the beginning of the period evaluated at the contingent prices reigning at that time (time 0). The third element represents the cash flows expected in the next period conditional on the signal received in period 1 (indicated by the $|y_1$ symbols) valued at their expected spot prices and weighted by their probabilities, which are also conditional on the signal. The final element of the expression represents the originally expected cash flows in the second period valued at the contingent prices that reigned at the beginning of period 1.

5. Income for the period using this concept is expressed in symbols for our usual two-period, four-state problem below.

$$Y_{1,\mathrm{II}} = \{\hat{C}_{s1}(P^*_{s1}) - \sum_{s} \hat{C}_{s1})(P^*_{s1})/(1 + r_s)\} + \{(\sum_{s} C_{s2} \mid y_1)(P^*_{s2})\phi(s \mid y_1) -$$
$$(\sum_{s} C_{s2} \mid y_1)(P^*_{s2})\phi(s \mid y_1)/(1 + r^2_s)\} \qquad [8.\mathrm{IX}]$$

The new second subscript on the income figure indicates that we are using *ex post* income concept II. The first element in each of the curly brackets ({ }) is the same as in our earlier expression for income using concept I. The first element of this type represents the sum of the realised cash flows in period 1 evaluated at the spot price for these claims, where the caret ($\hat{\ }$) symbol indicates that these cash flows are declared realised conditional on the signal received in that period. The first element in the second set of curly brackets is the sum of expected second-period cash flows conditional on the signal from the information system in period 1 evaluated at their expected spot prices multiplied by the probability of the relevant states conditional on this signal.

The final element in the first set of curly brackets represents the present value of the realised cash flows of the period at the beginning of the period. This present value is obtained by discounting these cash flows by the risky interest rate signified by $(1 + r_s)$. It represents the present value of these cash flows revised for the information obtained in period 1. The items in the first set of brackets thus indicate the contribution made to periodic income by the cash flows of the first period. The second element of the second set of curly brackets similarly is the present value at time 0 of the expected cash flows of period 2, revised to allow for the information obtained about these cash flows in period 1. The items in the second set of brackets thus generate the contribution of second-period cash flows to the income of period 1.

9

The informativeness of accounting reports: an empirical perspective

Introduction

The information economics perspective on accounting reports is a persuasive one and is a theme which runs throughout this book. Chapters 2 and 10, for example, treat information as if it were a commodity of the type usually traded on markets. Similarly, Chapter 11 considers accounting regulation from this perspective. This chapter concentrates on another thrust in accounting theory provided by adopting this approach.

Here we review some of the approaches used in empirical work seeking to evaluate the informativeness of accounting reports in the practical world and to test the implications of some accounting theories for this world. The methods used for this task rely heavily on information economics. Basically the question to be answered in this type of empirical work is limited to whether accounting information has an impact on security characteristics, including prices, returns and trading volumes. An affirmative answer would suggest that it may be possible in some settings to test whether different types of accounting information have differential informational impacts. Enquiries of this sort yield additional theoretical insights which may be helpful in selecting between accounting systems and practices. The testing of the informational characteristics of accounting systems also utilises models drawn from the theory of finance. This chapter therefore also indicates some of the additional insights finance models provide for accounting theory.

The subjects discussed in this chapter are intellectually demanding and technically complex. The aim here is only to give a flavour of the approach. Additional treatments are given in Foster (1980), Lev and Ohlson (1982), Watts and Zimmerman (1986) and Beaver (1989), but see also Dyckman and Morse (1986) and Fama (1976). For a less technical treatment, see Keane (1983). The relevant chapters of any good finance text books should also be consulted (see, for example, Copeland and Weston, 1988, chapters 7 and 10). The emphasis in this chapter will be on the theoretical foundations and logic of the methods used in this work and the implications of this work for accounting theory. No attempt is made to provide any more than an indication of the empirical evidence obtained using these methods. A comprehensive review of this evidence would require a book to itself (see Foster, 1980).

Plan of the chapter

The first section of this chapter reviews very briefly the theoretical concepts utilised to provide a methodology for testing the informativeness of accounting reports. This first substantive section deals with these matters in a general and informal way.

The next two major sections consider in more detail the two theories which have helped research workers to construct models useful for testing the informativeness of accounting information. The second section of this chapter reviews the security valuation model used in empirical testing. This valuation model indicates how securities may be valued in a multi-period and uncertain setting. Our review of this model is fairly brief; this exposition is further developed in any good finance book. This model and its more tractable substitutes have been used almost universally in advanced academic work to value securities under these conditions.

The third section of this chapter discusses the model of information processing by the capital market used in the empirical testing of the effects of accounting information on security prices. In this section the empirical evidence supporting this model is also examined. These two models of security valuation and of information processing are well known in finance theory. These two sections may be skipped by those with a good knowledge of the Capital Asset Pricing Model (CAPM) and associated models, and of what are labelled 'informationally efficient' markets.

The fourth section of this chapter looks at the implications for external accounting of the way in which the capital market processes information. Many of these implications run counter to conventional views in accounting. For example, the entertained theory of information processing suggests that the disclosure of an accounting item may be more important than where it is sited in accounting reports. In contrast, the conventional accounting view is that the most important items should be in the accounting reports proper and that less important items may be put in the notes to the accounts. The implications of this model are of especial importance in determining how accounting regulation might proceed. It suggests that the disclosure of new information is far more important than measurement issues.

The fifth section provides an introduction to how the informativeness of accounting information can be tested empirically.

The theory

The approach used in obtaining empirical evidence of the impact of accounting information on the security market is based only in a general way on the information economics approach reviewed in the previous chapters. The theoretical models used in gathering empirical evidence are specified in far less detail than were the more formal models of Chapters 6 and 7. In contrast to these chapters, we have no generally accepted theory which tells us which elements of investor decision models will be affected by any signals provided by accounting systems. Any messages obtained by investors from accounting information may be expected to lack precision. This is because the theoretical roles in investor decision models of many accounting concepts, such as the accrual concept and realisation principles, are still unknown. The complexity of these concepts may mean that any signals generated by accounting systems are indirect and imprecise. Such signals may therefore lead to revisions in investor understanding in ways which are far less formal than the Bayesian procedures introduced in previous chapters (see Demski, 1980, chapter 4).

Research workers seeking to test the informativeness of accounting information have therefore been forced to use much less formal and less precise models than those discussed in Chapters 6 and 7. Some of the hypotheses used are, however, very sophisticated in their specifications. They generally come down to a view that accounting information, if it has any information value, will affect prices and trading volumes on the securities market. The actual mechanism causing this effect is generally treated as some type of black box operation. The focus in the studies to be reviewed is on the inputs into the black box (accounting information) and on the consequent outputs (security characteristics), without concern for the internal workings of the box.

It is important to be clear that even if these exercises did find a high correlation between accounting information and changes in security characteristics, this would not allow us to ascribe a value to accounting information (see Lev and Ohlson, 1982, section 2.4). This is because the value placed on information by any individual depends on a wide range of factors, some of which were reviewed in earlier chapters. For example, although additional information affects security prices, it may still harm some individuals unless markets, including the market for accounting information, are well functioning. As will be indicated in Chapter 10, many commentators think that there are strong reasons for believing that the mechanisms for providing accounting information do not really resemble a perfect market. These mechanisms do not therefore allow individuals to use the market to adjust their position to suit best their preferences.

Thus, seeking to rank accounting information systems according to their impact on the security market in an imperfect market setting implies that we are willing to aid those who gain from such changes in security prices. As was indicated in Chapter 2, this means that the selection of accounting systems cannot be based on logic alone (see also Chapters 10 and 11). Empirical evidence can help in these choices but has to be augmented by a consideration of a wide range of other factors.

This general approach to evaluating the informativeness of accounting reports has been used to look at a number of major areas in accounting. The most important thrust is probably that which seeks to assess whether accounting information, generally concentrating upon earnings, has effects on the securities market. Here, the questions concern the impact of earnings and other financial data on security returns, including the risk attached to these returns, and trading volumes. A somewhat different question is to consider empirically the relationships between accounting risk measures, such as gearing (leverage) and market-based risk measures. Beaver *et al.* (1970) and later workers have found significant correlation between accounting and market risk measures. Measures of gearing and the change in enterprise earnings relative to market-wide changes seemed especially useful.

Studies have also been undertaken concerning whether accounting changes made at the discretion of management impact on the securities market. Earlier studies suggested that the market could 'see through' these accounting changes where these disguised the economic reality of the enterprise. As we shall see, later studies are much more equivocal. The other major research stream has been into the security market effects of accounting changes mandated by accounting policy makers. These studies have concentrated on a few important changes of this type. The results achieved so far seem generally consistent with economic reasoning (see Lev and Ohlson, 1982, section 2).

In the remainder of this chapter we shall focus on the information effects of routine accounting figures, though we shall briefly look at the evidence concerning some discretionary changes.

The underlying valuation philosophy used in accounting information studies is invariably the capital asset pricing model (CAPM), (see Foster, 1985; Beaver, 1981a; Keane, 1983). As a practical matter, what are called market models are used in empirical work. These models will be explained later.

In order to gauge the effects of accounting information on the security market, we also need a theory of how well the security market processes new information. To predict how information impinges on security prices we need to understand whether information will be impounded into security prices and if it is, whether this will happen quickly or will take several periods before any information is fully understood and completely impounded into stock market prices.

Theories concerning these matters are contained in a body of literature addressing what are called 'efficient' markets (see Foster, 1980; Beaver, 1981a, chapter 6). With this theory, a market is said, for example, to be 'efficient' with respect to a specific set of information, which may include accounting information, if all the available information from this information set is fully reflected in security prices. There is strong evidence that well established stock markets, such as those in the United States of America and the United Kingdom, do substantially reflect publically available information and impound such information into security prices very quickly. Such markets are therefore argued to be efficient with regard to such information. (This use of the term 'efficient' may be somewhat confusing. This usage *per se* has no implications that markets with this property will necessarily lead to the efficient allocation of resources within the economy.) However, recent evidence suggests that this process is by no means perfect. A number of exceptions to the theory, which are called anomalies in the literature, have been found (see Lev and Ohlson, 1982, section 2.4.1). For a more favourable view of the evidence, see Copeland and Weston (1988), Chapter 11.

These two theories of asset valuation and of market information processing provide the foundations for utilising the information economics approach in attempts to determine the impact of accounting information on the security market. That they command substantial operational acceptance in research is very important for the empirical studies to be considered later in this chapter because these take the correctness of the two theories for granted.

These theories have gone a considerable way towards giving accounting an empirical base and do aid in testing some views concerning accounting. Accounting theories would otherwise remain essentially assertions and continue to be the subject of relatively fruitless debate. The facility to test at least some aspects of hypotheses about accounting allows researchers to proceed in the same way as has proved so fruitful in science. The next section describes briefly the bare bones of the CAPM which provides the intellectual underpinning for this type of study. The model generally used in practice, the market model, will also be reviewed.

The capital asset pricing model

This model asserts that any security has only two characteristics of interest to investors—risk and return. Before defining these terms, we shall introduce the usual assumptions of the literature being followed. These include the assumptions that the relevant market is perfect and there are no transaction costs, taxes or any other impediments to trading. Generally this literature assumes a one-period setting. Investments are made at the beginning of period and the fruits of investment are obtained at the end of the period. Investors are assumed to have the same knowledge (the same information set) and beliefs, though they may have different preferences. All investors calculate the expected return from a security and its risk in the same way. Finally, a riskless asset is assumed to exist. Such an asset could be represented by an indexed government bond which yields a guaranteed real rate of return in the face of inflation. This last assumption is in fact unnecessary but eases the presentation substantially.

Portfolio return

The expected return from a security or portfolio is defined as the average expected return forecast from holding a security or portfolio over a period. This return for any period is given by deducting the opening value of the security or portfolio, P_0, from its expected (mean) market value at the end of period, $E(\tilde{P})_1$, where E represents the expectations operator, including any dividends expected to accrue over the period. This return, in terms of expected wealth, is then expressed as a percentage of the opening market value P_0. The expected return for any security, j, is thus calculated as

$$\bar{R}_j = E(\tilde{R}_j) = \frac{E(\tilde{P}_1) - P_0}{P_0}$$

where the bar over the return, $\bar{R}_j$, indicates that it is an expected return. This return is the weighted average of all possible returns from the security during the period, weighted by the probabilities of these returns.

The individual risk of a security is usually measured by the possible distribution of the returns from the security around this average or mean return, using the standard deviation σ or variance (σ^2) of the probability distribution of returns. Some of this risk will be specific to the investment in mind. Whether a new product introduced by a firm will be accepted by the market provides an example. Other elements of security risk will be the result of economy-wide factors (such as an economic depression) which will be experienced to varying degrees by all firms in the economy.

The essence of much of modern finance theory is that the risk of any given security cannot be determined in isolation. Holding a mixed portfolio of securities affected by different specific factors may reduce risk below that associated with holding only any one of the individual securities making up this portfolio.

Mr Risky's problem discussed in Chapters 5 and 6 illustrates this. Recall that Mr Risky could invest in any one of three portfolios. Portfolio A represents investing all his resources in security A, which yielded 95 monetary units if state 1 appeared and 15 if state 2 occurred (see Table 5.3). Portfolio B yielded a return of 150 monetary units in state 2 but only 50 if state 1 appears. Portfolio C yielded 75 monetary units irrespective of the state of the environment. Portfolio A provides its higher returns in what we have earlier labelled (see Chapter 6) the unfavourable state of the economy, yielding a payoff in money terms of 95 and a lower return in the other state, 15 (see Table 6.3). Portfolio B yields its higher return if the 'favourable' state occurs (150 monetary units). It generates only 50 monetary units if the other state is realised.

Holding combinations of securities A and B reduces the risk of investment. Indeed, holding a specific combination of the two portfolios allows risk to be entirely diversified away. Mr Risky's portfolio C provides such an opportunity. It is made up of a specific combination of security A and of security B. This complete reduction of risk is obtained at a cost. The return from portfolio C is less in each state than would have been obtained if the most favourable portfolio for that state had been held. (Portfolio A yields a payoff of 95 monetary units in state 1 against a return from C of 75 units. Similarly, portfolio B yields 150 in state 2 whereas portfolio C yields only 75 monetary units in this state.)

More generally we would expect to be able to diversify only that risk which is specific to a given security. This type of risk is called a security's unsystematic risk because it is special to that security and does not reflect the system-wide risk experienced by the economy as a whole. This second type of risk, which is called systematic or market risk, can be expected to affect all securities to a greater or lesser degree. Such risk cannot be reduced by diversification unless investment in international portfolios is allowed. It can be shown that by holding all securities on offer in a market, an investor can diversify away all the unsystematic risk associated with securities. This means that holding the market portfolio which is made up of all securities on issue, held in the proportion that their market prices bear to the value of the market portfolio, yields the highest return for a given level of risk. This is because the risk involved with the market portfolio is due only to economy-wide factors. All other risks have been diversified away.

Portfolios which by diversification minimise the risk attached to obtaining a given level of expected or average return are called efficient portfolios. They allow all the specific risk attaching to each security to be diversified away. Rational investors will only hold portfolios that belong to this efficient set. Such portfolios yield the highest return for a given level of risk and minimise the risk that must be borne to obtain a specific amount of return. The complete set of efficient portfolios is shown by the PN segment of the curve in Figure 9.1.

Combinations of securities lying along the segment PE of the line EN are clearly inefficient because investments on the PN part of the curve yield a greater return but involve either the same amount of risk or less risk than those lying on the remainder of the EN line. Other investment opportunities, including investment in individual securities, lie in the area to the right of the EN curve and are bounded by it. These opportunities are also inefficient.

An individual's choice among efficient portfolios will depend upon the amount of risk the individual is willing to bear. Moving down the segment PN from N reduces risk but also lowers expected return. The return from the risk-free security is shown by R_f on the return axis. The slope of the line drawn from the risk-free return (R_f) tangential to the efficient set indicates the extra return per unit of risk obtained from investing in the portfolio (portfolio M), which occurs at the point of tangency. Risk cannot be further reduced by diversification unless investment in international portfolios is allowed. Moving along this line (from the risk-free security to the market portfolio (R_fM)) towards point M substitutes portfolio M for the risk-free investment. Such conduct yields a higher return for a given level of risk than investing in a portfolio chosen from the efficient set. Proceeding beyond M on the R_fM line indicates the risk and return from borrowing and investing in the market portfolio.

In equilibrium, security prices must be such that there are no unfilled demands at

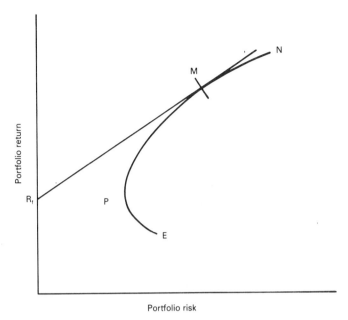

Figure 9.1 Efficient portfolios

the going prices for securities. All securities must therefore be held by someone. All securities on offer must therefore be incorporated into the market portfolio because rational investors who wish to bear risk will hold only this portfolio. This is why this portfolio is called the market portfolio. It thus consists of all securities available in the market held in the proportion which their aggregate market values bear to the aggregate value of all securities in the market.

Securities obtain their value from the contribution they make to the market portfolio's expected return and risk. The return on the market portfolio can be calculated as the weighted average returns on the securities comprising the market portfolio where the weights are the percentages invested in the securities.

A security's contribution to market risk must relate only to that part of its risk which is correlated with market-wide risk. This is because all the security's individual risk has already been diversified away by holding it as part of the market portfolio. In order to calculate the contribution of a security to the risk of the market portfolio, we need to measure how each security's return is affected by economy-wide influences relative to how the return from the market portfolio is affected by these factors. We therefore have to measure what is called the covariance of a security's returns with those of the market portfolio in order to quantify this correlation between the risk of an individual security and the risk of the market portfolio. For security i, this covariance can be written as $\text{Cov}(\tilde{R}_i, \tilde{R}_M)$, where M represents the market portfolio and i, the ith security.[1] Intuitively, the risk that security i contributes to the market portfolio can be thought of as the amount of commonality of risk between the security in mind and the market portfolio. One measure of the volatility of a security's return with respect to the returns from the market portfolio has been called the security's beta factor. This factor shows how the returns of a security vary with those of the market portfolio, expressed relative to a measure of the risk of the market portfolio. A security's beta factor is defined as

$$\beta_i = \frac{\text{Cov}(\tilde{R}, \tilde{R}_\text{M})}{\text{Var}(M)} \qquad\qquad [9.\text{I}]$$

where β_i is the beta factor of the ith security and $\text{Var}(M)$ is a measure of the dispersion of the returns of the market portfolio.[2] Multiplying a security's beta factor by its relative market value yields the proportionate contribution of the security to market risk.

The relationship between a security's return and its beta factor is called the capital asset pricing model and can be expressed by what is called the security market line. This is obtained by plotting return against the value of beta. All securities will plot somewhere on the security market line depending on their beta factor. The intercept of this line with the return axis will be the risk-free rate of return. The line will slope linearly upwards from this intercept. As we would expect the market portfolio will have a beta factor of 1.

In equilibrium, securities must be priced so that the rate of exchange between risk and return they offer is the same as the reward the market offers for bearing risk. In equilibrium, a security will not be held at a price which offers a lower return for bearing risk than the market price of risk. Any unsatisfied demands for a security which originally offers a higher return for bearing risk than does the market will increase the security's price until the reward the security offers for bearing risk is equal to the reward offered by the market.

The market price of risk can be expressed as the difference between the return on the risk-free security (R_f) and that on the market portfolio (R_M) divided by a measure of the risk of the market portfolio (the standard deviation σ_M). The equilibrium relationship between the market price of risk, or the reward offered by the market in terms of return for bearing an extra unit of risk, and the rate of exchange between risk and return offered by a security, expressed using the beta factor, can with a little mathematical manipulation yield the capital asset pricing model.[3] This can be written as:

$$\bar{R}_i = R_\text{f} + (\bar{R}_\text{M} - R_\text{f})\beta_i \qquad\qquad [9.\text{II}]$$

This says that the price of a security in equilibrium must guarantee that its return is equal to the risk-free return plus a premium for risk. This risk premium is determined by evaluating the risk of the security as expressed by its beta factor using what is called the market price of risk ($\bar{R}_\text{M} - R_\text{f}$) in CAPM terminology. (Here, the quantity of risk is measured by the beta factor ($\text{Cov}(\tilde{R}_i, \tilde{R}_\text{M})/\sigma_\text{M}^2$) rather than by $\text{Cov}(\tilde{R}_i, \tilde{R}_\text{M})/\sigma_\text{M}$ which is consistent with our earlier definition of the market price or risk.) Thus with the CAPM, all securities must be priced so that their risk-adjusted returns plot exactly on the security market line.

Expression 9.II represents a very generally accepted theoretical model or relationship for determining the equilibrium return from a security. This model and models based on its logic can be used to price security. In empirical studies of the impact of information, including accounting information, on security prices and returns, this model is used to price securities on the basis of what these prices would have been without the information in mind. A comparison between the returns predicted using these prices and those which actually reigned in market with access to the information being studied gives a measure of the impact of information, in our case accounting information.

Market models

There are problems with the CAPM model which we will not pursue here in any detail. Like many other powerful models used in empirical work, it runs into very difficult statistical problems and methodological difficulties. These are generally beyond the scope of this text (see Roll, 1977). For a discussion of these problems in the context of assessing the impact of accounting information see Lev and Ohlson, 1982, section 2.4.2; Ricks, 1982; Foster, 1985.

Similarly, many of the assumptions of the model deviate from our understanding of the practical world. For example, distributions of security returns do not seem to fit the normal bell shaped distribution assumed by the model (Fama, 1965). For a good review of some of these problems see Copeland and Weston, 1988, pp. 212–230.

Much theoretical work has been done in order to relax many of the assumptions of the theory. The non-existence of a riskless asset seems to cause no particular problem for the analysis (Black, 1972), nor does considering a multi-period model (Fama, 1970). Attempts are beginning to be made to tackle problems such as market failure (Mayers, 1972), thin trading (where securities are traded infrequently) Dimson, 1979), and difficulties associated with the non-normal distribution of security returns (Fama, 1965). There are still substantial econometric problems associated with testing the theory. Many of these pervade all empirical work in finance and economics. Many commentators therefore believe that there are numbers of unsettled issues associated with the theory. Few commentators, however, believe that these problems are sufficient to lead to the theory's rejection as a theoretical framework for our purposes. There is some evidence that CAPM is mis-specified in terms of firm size. The risk-adjusted returns of small firms have been found to differ from those of large firms in the same risk category, whereas there should be only one market return for a given level of risk. It has also been argued that the excess returns relative to those which would be expected using the CAPM, that have been associated with portfolios comprising securities which have low price/earnings ratios, also flow from a mis-specification of the CAPM. There is also considerable evidence that the one-factor approach used by the CAPM, where security prices depend only on the market risk shared by the firm, may not be rich enough to fully capture the effect of risk on returns (Roll and Ross, 1980).

Generally, the empirical evidence available strongly supports, at least, variants of the CAPM. The empirically determined slope of the security market line differs from the price of risk ($R_M - R_f$), and suggests that the return required for holding risk in the real world is less than the model would suggest. This slope does, however, reflect a positive linear relationship between beta factors (β) and expected security returns. However, these empirical security market lines do not, as we would expect, always show that the market portfolio yields a higher return than the risk-free security.

Adding other factors to the model does seem to help obtain a better fit with empirical data. This is consistent with the finding that the model does not completely explain security returns.

One major problem with attempting to use the CAPM in empirical work is that it is not easy to calculate or quantify the market portfolio. This would require us to calculate a vast number of covariances. Many workers in this area have therefore used surrogates or proxies for the returns on the market portfolio. These surrogates are those indices of stock market prices which are familiar from the newspapers such as Standards and Poor's composite index in the United States of America or the various

Financial Times indices in the United Kingdom. Such models assume that the returns from a security $(R_{i,t})$ exhibit a statistical linear relationship with the returns on the 'market' portfolio being used $(R_{M,t})$. This model can therefore be written in symbols as a relationship of the form:

$$R_{i,t} = a + \beta_i R_{Mt} - e_{i,t}$$

where a is the intercept term which equals the expected return on the security $E(\tilde{R}_{i,t})$ minus the expected return on the market portfolio $E(\tilde{R}_{M,t})$ weighted by the security's beta factor (β_i) and $e_{i,t}$ is the disturbance term or the abnormal return on the security. It is assumed that the joint probability distribution of the two returns is normal. This assumption introduces the linearity into the above expression because it implies that the mean return from the security conditional on the return from the market portfolio is a linear function of the intercept term and the beta factor (see Fama, 1965, chapter 3). It is this assumption which therefore gives the market model its character. No other theory supports the approach.

Additional assumptions are made with the market model. It is assumed that the return on the market portfolio captures the effects of factors which impinge on the returns of all securities and the disturbance term $(e_{i,t})$ is presumed to measure the results of variables impinging on the return of asset *i*.

Although the substitution of indices for the CAPM market portfolio is helpful in empirical work, it does rob empirical tests using these indices of the full theoretical support yielded by the CAPM. The theory behind the CAPM provides a strong foundation for predicting security returns based on their beta factors. Market models using indices are not based directly upon this theory but rather on the assertion that security returns and prices are determined by a consideration of market-wide risk and beta factors. Market models cannot claim the support of the CAPM because, for example, the securities portfolios which form the base of the indices will plot on the curve showing the efficient set of security's portfolios at different places than would the market portfolio. Indeed, even the efficiency of such portfolios may not be guaranteed. Such portfolios may therefore plot to the right of the efficient set curve.

The problem of determining the market portfolio before the CAPM can be used to support empirical findings lies at the heart of a very important critique of this model (Roll, 1977). Here it is argued that to test the theory, the market portfolio should include not only all securities but also all other assets. A portfolio which encompasses all assets, including, strictly, even those assets which are not traded, cannot be constructed. This requirement therefore renders the testing of CAPM impossible. However, work is proceeding on adapting approaches to testing for this problem and to adding assets to the portfolios being used in empirical work (see Shanken, 1985, 1987; Kandel and Stambaugh, 1987).

In much empirical work, the CAPM is used to determine what security returns would have been without the information in mind. Roll has under consideration a rather different use for the CAPM, that of measuring the past performance of securities. Here an *ex post* average return over and above what the CAPM would predict for a security might be thought to represent a 'good' performance by the security being examined. Roll's contribution is very technical but his major point can be understood by first assuming that we initially choose a securities index which lies on the efficient set boundary as our standard of security performance. This index is then used to calculate security beta factors. Such securities will all perform as the CAPM would lead us to expect after the event if the index used lies on the boundary of the efficient set of portfolios. If the index portfolio is found not to be efficient after the event, the ranking of portfolio performance will depend on the index used. With this view, tests of the CAPM using market indices are seen as not being tests of the CAPM. Rather they are tests only of whether the index portfolio was *ex post* efficient. Thus, evidence that security returns are well explained by betas based on a given market index cannot be said to be evidence supporting the CAPM. This does not mean that the CAPM is invalid as a theory but rather that conclusions based on its applicability should be treated with considerable care. One way of overcoming this problem is to use market models which do not rely upon the validity of the CAPM model to give them authority. This approach is theoretically acceptable for information content studies as the need is only for a statistical model of expected returns. However, tests of the efficiency of markets do require the use of an equilibrium pricing model. Models for pricing securities which are not vulnerable to Roll's criticism have also been developed. These have been used to explain security behaviour (see Ross, 1976; Roll and Ross, 1980).

This concludes our discussion of the security valuation models used in testing the impact of accounting information on security prices. These tests also depend on the degree to which details of accounting information are absorbed by the market and the speed with which this operation is accomplished. These characteristics of the market determine whether the market can be called 'efficient' in processing information. The next section discusses briefly what this means and how this theory impinges on the testing of the effects of accounting information on the security market.

Information efficiency

Markets which fully and quickly process information are called efficient. Efficiency when used to describe how well capital markets impound information does not guarantee a Pareto optimal allocation of resources, if only because of inefficiencies in other markets. However, informationally efficient markets for securities fully process available information and impound it into market prices in a way consistent with some equilibrium pricing model. These prices therefore yield accurate signals for resource allocation, conditional on the available information and the security price model being entertained. The contribution of informational efficiency to optimal resource allocation is thus dependent on the security price model being used.

It was argued in Chapter 6 that information has value only in so far that it tells us something we do not know and leads to a change in decisions. A utility-maximising individual will act on such information. Such transactions will in time affect market prices. This is likely to happen quickly, given the incentives for informed individuals to publicise any information in their possession once they have arranged their transactions so as to gain from any expected price changes.

This process leads us to expect that security returns and security prices will quickly reflect all available information. This implies that the expected prices of securities will impound the information in the available information set which is relevant to the security pricing model in use. Different amounts of information and various information sets may therefore yield different security prices. Expression 14.III below indicates formally, but in a general way, how information may affect security prices, assuming that the CAPM is a valid valuation model for securities.

$$\bar{R}_{i,t} \mid \hat{y}, \eta_{t-1} = R_f + ((\bar{R}_M \mid \hat{y}, \eta_{t-1} - R_f)(\beta_i \mid \hat{y}, \eta_{t-1})) \qquad [9.\text{III}]$$

This expression rewrites Expression [9.II] and incorporates the effects of information. The term on the left is the expected return of security i in period t as indexed by the second subscript. Here, the expected return is conditional on the information set η_{t-1} available at the end of the previous period, indicated by the subscript $(t-1)$ and on the actual signal received from this information system. That this signal has been realised is indicated by the symbol $\hat{y}$ where the caret ($\hat{\ }$) over the y indicates that these signals have been received. The risk-free rate (R_f) shown as the first element on the right is assumed to be known. The return from the market portfolio (the second element on the right) and the beta factor (β) of security i are shown to be conditional on the available information system in the previous period (η_{t-1}) and the actual signal received in the previous period ($\hat{y}$). Utility maximising individuals will act to ensure that any of the signals available from an information system relevant to security prices but not as yet impounded in security prices will be quickly incorporated in such prices. That there are incentives for individuals to act to ensure that all information relevant to security prices are impounded in these prices allows us to define an efficient capital market in a general way. This definition, which is a variant of what is called the efficient market hypothesis, is:

A securities market is efficient if the probability distribution of security   Definition [9.1A]
prices it generates for a period is the same as that which would exist
if all the relevant information available in the previous period had
been utilised.

This definition merely says that forecast security prices for the next period are fully explained by two items—the valuation model being used for securities and the information presently available (Beaver, 1981). It therefore emphasises that for the efficient market hypothesis to be meaningful it has to be entertained jointly with what is taken to be a valid security valuation model, such as the CAPM. It is the valuation model entertained which determines whether information is relevant to security valuation. Information must therefore affect some element or elements of the security valuation model being used. Tests of the impact of accounting information on security prices assume not only that a given valuation model is used by the market but also that the efficient market hypothesis is valid. Accounting information has also figured strongly in endeavours seeking to test the efficient market hypothesis. Here the view is taken that accounting information does have an impact on security market prices. The item now being tested is therefore the efficient market hypothesis.

   The above definition is too general to be tested. However, an implication of market efficiency does provide a testable form for the efficient market hypothesis. If a market is efficient this implies that no one can make any abnormal gains from using available information. All such information will have already been impounded into security prices in such a market. The possibility of any individual making further gains using this information is therefore ruled out. This variant of the efficient market hypothesis can be defined as saying that:

An efficient market is one in which it is impossible to make a gain   Definition [9.1B]
from using information already available to the market.

This inability to gain from using information already utilised by the market allows us to predict that security prices and security returns may follow any of a number of patterns over time which allow no gain to occur for an individual using the same information as the market. There are a number of behaviour patterns of prices and rates of returns over time which satisfy this condition. The pattern of security prices and returns of this type with the longest history is called the random walk model. This says that the security prices or returns will vary randomly over time. With this view, a time series of the changes in security prices will look as if the direction of alterations in prices were decided by independent drawings from some known set of possible prices. This means that knowledge of today's price or the change in prices experienced today gives no guide as to tomorrow's price change. The *ex post* distribution of price changes will, however, help in assessing the future distribution of price changes. It is the sequence or order of the price changes that is of no use in estimating the distribution of future price changes.

More generally, it can be said that an implication of market efficiency is that the returns from investing in securities using an information system, the signals from which are fully impounded in the market, will be such as to offer no possibility of gain or loss, on average. This finding can be written more formally as:

$$\bar{e}_{i,t} = E(\hat{R}_{i,t} - (\bar{R}_{i,t} \mid \eta_{i,t-1})) = 0 \qquad\qquad [9.\text{IV}]$$

where $\bar{e}_{i,t}$ is the expected abnormal return from investing in security i in period t. The bar over the $e_{i,t}$ indicates that this is an average or expected value. As usual, E is the expectations operator. $\hat{R}_{i,t}$ represents the actual return on security i in period t. This is an *ex post* magnitude as signified by the caret over the return variable. $\bar{R}_{i,t} \mid \eta_{i,t-1}$ is the expected return or mean return on security i based on an information system (η_{t-1}) available at the beginning of the period or the end of the previous period.

Expression 9.IV represents a fair gamble, or a fair game in the parlance of efficient markets. With respect to an information system, such games offer the expectation of neither a gain nor a loss, on average. Using Expression 9.IV, we can say that a security market is efficient and fully reflects an information set if the returns obtained using this information represent a fair game. Many other variants of the fair game model have been used in empirical work (see Fama, 1970).

The literature in the area has concentrated on testing three types of information efficiency. Markets which fully reflect all the information contained in historical security prices are called weak-form efficient. The empirical evidence supports the view that developed security markets are weak-form efficient (see Alexander, 1961; Fama, 1965, 1970; Foster, 1985).

Markets are said to be semi-strong efficient if all publicly available information, including published accounting information, is reflected in security prices. The testing of this hypothesis has concentrated on evaluating specific items of publicly available information, frequently accounting information. Especially attractive to those undertaking this type of work has been the information contained in income statements (Ball and Brown, 1968; Beaver, *et al.*, 1979). The value of any information conveyed by stock splits has also been intensively studied (see Fama *et al.*, 1969). Another rewarding study has been to determine whether those who manage mutual funds (unit trusts) can make profits using all publicly available information (see, for example, Jensen, 1968, but recall Roll's criticism of using the CAPM in measuring security performance). The available evidence supports the view that developed stock markets are semi-strong efficient, though substantial inefficiencies have been found.

Finally, markets which are efficient with respect to all information including 'inside' information are called strongly efficient. The difficulties of validly testing this hypothesis are severe. For example, it is difficult to define precisely what is privately available information and to identify those individuals with access to such information. For these and for other reasons only relatively few studies of strong-form efficiency have been undertaken. Even these studies have been forced to concentrate on indirect evidence of inside practices. For example, Lorie and Niederhoffer (1968) considered whether information can be obtained by studying the declared trading activities of corporate insiders. These activities should yield a profit if corporate insiders possess privileged information, not impounded in market prices. This was found to be the case. Findings of this sort support the general view that stock markets are inefficient with respect to private information.

Some studies have indicated the existence of a number of inefficiencies with regard to some items of information. A number of recent studies have suggested that price changes may continue well after the announcement being studied has occurred. This finding runs counter to the market impounding instantaneously all new information into prices, though whether profitable trading strategies exist which can take advantage of these inefficiencies is still unresolved. Other findings have suggested, for example, that it is possible to obtain gains from studying the published quarterly earnings announcements of United States companies and that the market is inefficient with respect to securities with low price/earnings ratios. More generally, it has been shown that abnormal returns may accrue from considering enterprise size. These results have been argued to be the result of using imperfect research methods, in which, for example, some variables are incorrectly defined (see Keene, 1983, chapter 5; Beaver, 1981a, pp. 157–158).

To evaluate these results, a much better understanding of the theoretical foundations of market efficiency is required. The general weight of the theory in the academic literature is founded mainly on the evidence supporting weak and semi-strong efficiency and on its utility in market-based accounting research. There is as yet no generally accepted theory explaining how market efficiency arises.

One possible theory suggests that there exists a small band of insiders who provide new information to the market which is then instaneously impounded into stock prices. Indeed, it has been argued that a fully efficient market could not function (Grossman and Stiglitz, 1980). Here, it is argued that new information will be sought and available information processed only if some reward can be expected after meeting costs. This implies that some inefficiency with regard to information must exist if private information is to be communicated to the market. No profits would otherwise be made from private information. This theory does seem consistent with findings that the market is not strongly efficient, at least for some inside information. However, this reasoning may be regarded as weak because it does not indicate in any precise way how privileged information reaches the market, nor does it enable us to predict in any definitive way the likely sources of such information.

Other work dispenses with the need for there to be an élite of informed individuals (see for example, Kihlstrom and Mirman, 1975; Grossman and Stiglitz, 1980). Here market prices are seen as instruments which aggregate the information held by all actors. Market prices therefore represent some type of weighted consensus of individual views (see Chapter 7, pp. 168–70). As a more specific example, Grossman and Stiglitz have used analytical models to study markets where some individuals choose to be informed and the rest opt to remain uninformed. Informed individuals will take trading positions on the basis of their information and expect to make profits after paying any costs of information. The aggregate of such activities will affect security prices. Uninformed investors can infer the information possessed by informed individuals by observing consequent changes in security prices. Thus, market prices may come to contain all available information so that all market actors are ultimately equally informed. All investors will be indifferent to acquiring information in equilibrium, because in equilibrium the marginal utility obtained from being informed, after deducting any costs, will equal the marginal utility obtained from remaining uninformed. This process will work only if markets were initially inefficient. Without this, those who choose to be informed would not be able to make sufficient gains to offset the cost of any information they acquire.

The theory of efficient markets and the theory of security valuation introduced in this chapter have substantial implications for accounting information. Some of these are considered in the next section, concentrating on the possible effects of market efficiency as a preliminary to reviewing some of the empirical work which uses these theories to improve our understanding of the possible effects of published accounting information.

Some implications of efficient markets for external accounting

The major effects on external accounting of accepting that security markets are informationally efficient impact especially upon accounting policy making. The implications of efficient markets form an implicit foundation for our later review of accounting policy making; see Chapter 11. This section therefore seeks only to make explicit some of the implications of market efficiency for accounting, concentrating on efficiency with regard to published accounting information; that is, we are concerned with semi-strong efficiency.

We can expect that many of the implications of efficient markets result from viewing such markets from an information economics perspective. This section discusses the implications for accounting of this perspective (see Beaver, 1974, for an early review of these matters). The objective is to give a flavour of the support the evidence provides for adopting an information economics perspective with regard to accounting information. Further discussions are contained in Dyckman and Morse, 1986, chapter 6; Fama, 1976; Foster, 1980; Ricks, 1982.

One implication of efficient markets for accounting is that it does not matter how information is disclosed. It is the information itself which matters. Thus accounting information is seen as merely one possible source of information which may often repeat items already available from other sources. With this view, disclosure via accounting reports of information not available from other sources would seem likely to improve decision making.[4] Thus, for example, it might be expected that the disclosure of the accounting earnings of segments of enterprises would be welcomed by the market. Studies of segmental disclosure as mandated by the Securities and Exchange Commission (SEC) in the United States of America have suggested that this disclosure does affect the market's views as to the overall risk of diversified enterprises.

If efficient markets are effective processors of information, one way to resolve accounting choices is to publish the results of a variety of treatments of an accounting item, subject to cost and let the market decide which accounting method is most informative. Some of these treatments may provide information not contained in the others. Thus the efficient market hypothesis may well favour reporting using a variety of accounting bases, as might the information economics approach discussed in the preceding chapter.

Efficient markets also imply that we should not be too concerned with whether lay users of accounting statements can interpret accounting reports. It will pay relatively skilled users of accounting information to exploit their special talents. All information contained in accounting reports which is detectable by experts will become impounded into security prices via this process. This view also provides a clear role for financial intermediaries which seems to be consistent with one of their functions in the practical world.

A combination of the above ideas has been used to suggest one reason why price change accounting has not been received very favourably by the financial community. The evidence is that external accounting statements adjusted for price changes do not seem to have affected security prices; see, for example, Beaver and Landsman, 1983. It has been argued that this unfavourable reception means that the financial community has already estimated any effects of price changes using other information available prior to the issuance of price-change-adjusted accounting reports. A number of studies have shown that a fairly good representation of inflation-adjusted accounting numbers can be derived from conventional published accounting reports. Similarly, evidence concerning the replacement cost of enterprise assets may be obtained from inspecting published price indices.

Another implication of efficient markets for accounting is that it is the information itself which is of concern, not how it is presented. Any new information contained in published accounting reports will be discovered quickly in efficient markets, irrespective of how or where the information is positioned in accounting statements. Thus debates concerning whether items should be in the main body of the accounts or in notes to the accounts are unnecessary in the context of efficient markets. Similarly, the European concern to promulgate very precise and rigid formats for accounting reports by law seems unnecessary in efficient markets. The information conveyed in such formats will be impounded into security prices if it is relevant to security prices, irrespective of its position in any prescribed format.

The required treatment in the United States of America of accounting for leasing activities provides insights on this point. Large companies were first required to provide supplementary disclosure of leases in 1973. In 1976, the Financial Accounting Standards Board required that this disclosure of leases should be incorporated into the body of the accounts. Ro (1987) studied the market's reaction to the introduction of footnote disclosure of leases in 1973 and found a negative reaction in security prices for those firms which were required to disclose their leasing activities. How one interprets this finding depends on your theoretical view of the effect of leasing on a company's net worth. A reduction in security prices after disclosure would be consistent with the view that this disclosure suggests to the market that the enterprise is more highly geared (levered) than previously expected and that gearing (leverage) is believed to affect shareholders adversely. This finding is also consistent with the recent view that an important effect of using non-equity finance is the constraints that the providers of such funds impose upon enterprise behaviour. Such inhibitions placed upon management can take a wide variety of forms, including restricting the ability to pay a dividend prior to meeting the interest payments on debt finance, and the acceptance of imposed liquidity targets. Such reasoning suggests that the disclosure of previously unknown substantial leasing commitments by an enterprise might depress the price of the enterprise's securities. This would occur if it were felt leasing activities meant that management were more restricted in their financial management activities than was previously expected.

Some studies of leasing failed to find any risk effects generated by requiring information about leasing to be shown in the accounting reports, whereas others using different methods and cross sectional data did find some effect of this type (Bowman, 1980). Later requirements concerning lease capitalisation seem not to induce a change in market prices (Abdel-Khalik *et al.*, 1981). The evidence from the markets suggests that the later more detailed requirements concerning the accounting for leases provided little, if any, information additional to that provided by the earlier footnote disclosure.

With efficient markets, it is the economic meaning of any information for security prices which is important, not the way in which it is portrayed in the accounts (see Ricks, 1982). Early studies which look at changes in accounting treatments which seem to have no economic effect (here interpreted as having no obvious effect on enterprise cash flows) have generally been unable to detect any effect of such changes on security prices. As an example, consider the work of Hong *et al.* (1978), who looked at the market reaction to the accounting treatment used for mergers and acquisitions in the United States of America. Mergers could be accounted for using what in the USA is called the 'pooling of interest' method and in the United Kingdom the 'merger' method. Here the conventional accounting results of the companies being merged are added together, and profits accumulated in the past can be distributed as dividends. In contrast, acquisitions are treated as if one company purchases another, thereby creating goodwill where the value of net assets of purchased company are less than the aggregate purchase price. For technical reasons any accumulated profits of the purchased firm are not available for distribution following an acquisition. Generally, the pooling of interests method of accounting allows higher profits to be declared than the acquisition method. The underlying cash flows of the combined enterprise are unchanged whichever method is used. Security prices should therefore be unaffected by the accounting treatment chosen providing that the market is not 'fooled' by the accounting technique selected. As we would therefore expect, Hong *et al.* (1978) found that when the pooling or merger method was used there was no market reaction near the time of the mergers or at later reporting dates, after adjusting for economy-wide influences. They therefore concluded that the market was not misled by the higher profits resulting from the pooling method. However, later authors have suggested that this result may be due to self-selection bias. Firms which, in any case, expected relatively high abnormal earnings may because of this favour the purchase method.

Some changes in accounting procedures have a direct economic effect via inducing a change in enterprise cash flows. Studies of some of these changes have generally indicated that the market can 'see through' the accounting techniques used to the underlying economic variables. Last In First Out (LIFO) inventory valuation methods are permissible in the United States of America for both accounting and tax purposes.

Valuing inventory (stock) using LIFO rather than First In First Out (FIFO) methods will result in tax savings when inventory prices are rising. The actual amount of such savings depends on a number of factors, including the degree of the price changes, whether inventory levels are stable and the stock turn-over rate. The switch to LIFO will, however, decrease enterprise accounting earnings. This decrease in earnings occurs because the switch to LIFO increases the cost of sales figure in the income statement relative to what the cost of sales would have been under FIFO.

Thus, studying the effects of switches from FIFO to LIFO allows us to see whether the market is fooled by the 'depressed' accounting earnings reported consequent on such changes and therefore adjusts security prices downwards. Such investigations may alternatively show that the market can 'see through' the accounting effects of such changes and therefore adjust security prices upwards, reflecting any expected enhanced cash flows occurring because of tax savings.

Such tests are not straightforward and a great deal of ingenuity is required to avoid obtaining conclusions because of the methods used. Sunder (1973) computed the monthly residual abnormal returns (that is, returns over and above those predicted allowing for market-wide influences) of some enterprises that made the switch during a long period, 1946–1966. He found that such switches were associated with increased residual returns for the 12 months prior to the annual report incorporating the switch. This finding suggested that the market anticipated the good news of tax savings. Unfortunately, in the study Sunder made no adjustment for the possibility that firms making the switch were having an unexpectedly 'good' year and in any case would therefore have exhibited positive abnormal returns. Other studies of these matters have not come up with an entirely clear finding that the market does see through to the underlying events.

A more recent study (Ricks, 1982) went to great lengths to avoid problems like that of switching forms having higher earnings than non-switching firms. It was found that switching enterprises had lower residual returns near the date of the announced change to LIFO than did non-switching, but otherwise similar, firms. This is consistent with the hypothesis that the market does not see through accounting numbers to the underlying economic effects. However, it was also found that the negative effect on security prices was reversed after three or four months, thereby correcting any naive market reaction to changes to LIFO. Another study (Biddle and Lindahl, 1982) suggests that Ricks (1982) did not succeed in avoiding all the possibilities that some other characteristics of firms in his samples generated his results; in this case, any differences in the results for the samples may not be due to the LIFO switch but to some other characteristics which differ between the samples.

Biddle and Lindahl (1982) suggest that the change and no-change firms may have been affected differently by an economic recession that occurred in 1973–1975. They argue that the results of the switching firms studied by Ricks were affected less by the depression than were those of the no-change firms he considered. The results obtained by Ricks may therefore be due to the omission of the differential effect of the economic environment on the two types of enterprise. Inspecting the beta factors of the two samples may provide evidence concerning the possibility of such a differential effect. This result could occur if the no-change firms had larger beta factors than the enterprises that switched. It could also arise if the difference in the beta factors of the two samples became relatively greater over the period. Ricks indicated that the beta factors of the no-change firms were less sensitive to the economic environment than those of switching enterprises. Ricks also tested for changes in the relative riskiness between the samples in order to show that his results were not consequential upon this. He found that the differential risk between the two samples had increased during the period studied. The relative riskiness of the LIFO firms had increased. This cannot explain his result because it would have reduced the difference in the cumulative abnormal returns for the two samples. In contrast to the findings reported by Ricks, elementary reasoning, which is unlikely to capture the richness of a very complex situation, might lead us to expect that the beta factors of the no-change enterprises would increase, reflecting their seemingly greater sensitivity to the economic environment if the Biddle and Lindahl results were to obtain.

Ignoring this problem, when Biddle and Lindahl adjusted for the differential effect of the economic environment their results again supported the view that accounting results did not 'fool' the market. Thus, data concerning the LIFO switch phenomenon are at present unable to yield unambiguous evidence as to whether the market can see through accounting reports to the underlying economic reality. This rather detailed discussion of the problems encountered in this debate illustrates some of the general difficulties of obtaining clear results for accounting from empirical studies, at least in this general area. It also illustrates the great sensitivity of the results obtained to the correct modelling of the setting being studied. Such studies also show a similar sensitivity to the econometric methods being used. As both modelling processes and econometric methods seem to be always capable of improvement, any results obtained must be regarded as tentative in the present state of the art.

The evidence concerning the ability of the market to penetrate accounting figures and discern underlying economic effects is thus not unequivocal. Recent theoretical advances also suggest that accounting changes may be taken at their face value for rational reasons (see Watts and Zimmerman, 1986, chapter 7). This does not imply that the market is fooled by accounting figures. Rather, it is suggested that the market perceives economic effects not captured in past empirical studies. With this view, reactions appear because the market perceives that the change in accounting earnings has effects on managerial perquisites which are often based in part on accounting figures. These reactions may also be based on inhibitions imposed on managerial conduct by fund providers in some areas, such as in determining the amounts of dividends they can pay out. In the context of the LIFO studies, any decrease in earnings following the adoption of LIFO might be seen by the market to cause enterprises to move nearer to restrictions on their conduct imposed by the providers of finance. Studies which seek to incorporate such possible effects should improve empirical research in the area of accounting and efficient markets.

The efficiency of markets has many other implications for accounting policy makers. It supports the view discussed in many parts of this book that information generally, including accounting information, should be regarded as a commodity. If publicly available information is plagued by the externalities to be discussed in Chapter 10, then market efficiency of the strong form suggests that requiring the disclosure of private information is important not only in terms of improved decision making but also because of income and wealth effects.

Entertaining an information economics perspective and a belief in efficient markets in the weak and semi-strong form really provides a further foundation to our later discussion of accounting regulation. Findings that the market is efficient in these forms would ease many of the difficulties which accounting policy makers experience when dealing with information which is already in the public domain (see Beaver, 1973). Proposals involving additional disclosure become more important with this perspective. Consider, for example, the question of whether research and development expenditure should be charged to the profit and loss account, or income statement, or whether it should be capitalised as an asset. This question, which has generated a considerable debate in a number of countries, becomes of secondary importance from an information economics perspective relative to the decision to report the relevant figures whichever option is chosen. These figures might well contain information not at present available to the community.

The enhanced understanding of security valuation and the meaning of efficient markets provided in this chapter makes it now possible for us to review briefly how research based on these foundations can be used to test the effects of accounting information on security prices and security returns. This subject is taken up in the next section of this chapter. Here we will focus on the effect of accounting information on security returns. Other accounting informational studies have sought to evaluate the impact of accounting information on security trading volumes and on the risk associated with security returns. With regard to trading volumes, Beaver (1968) found that increased trading volume relative to the average trading volume was observed around information announcement dates. Such effects may not necessarily be correlated with the security price effects flowing from the release of accounting information.

Testing the impact of accounting information on security prices

An introduction

These tests use findings from the efficient markets literature and usually utilise the market model. The detailed methodology is often very complex and, perforce, highly technical in order to overcome difficult econometric and statistical problems. Here, it is only intended to give an intuitive understanding of the procedures adopted. Further and more technical descriptions are given by Fama (1976) and Foster (1980). Some of the findings obtained are reviewed briefly in this and the next section. Some understanding of these matters is important because these studies have yielded very powerful results which some commentators believe have revolutionised our understanding of some of the effects of accounting information. As has already been suggested, these studies and their theoretical foundations have also contributed much to our understanding of external accounting, more generally.

Prior to these approaches becoming available, endeavours to obtain empirical evidence in accounting used a variety of approaches, deficient in their logical and theoretical foundations. The results produced in this way usually lacked in any clear meaning. These studies often turned out to support the accounting theory advocated by the researcher. Reasons for rejecting such findings were usually easily found by those who supported other theories of accounting. In contrast to these earlier approaches, the methodology to be reviewed here uses a clear and logical approach and often produces substantive results which are difficult to refute, other than by further and more sophisticated empirical work.

The approach

The methodology used is very simple in concept. It is assumed that some equilibrium pricing model, usually the CAPM, or alternatively the market models discussed earlier in this chapter, describe how the security market determines expected returns.

Generally, the security valuation model being entertained is not used directly. Rather, the model is utilised to predict the returns that can be expected from securities, assuming that it does explain the prices of securities observed in practice. It is also assumed that the security market being considered is efficient, usually in the semi-strong form.

The aim of these studies is to determine how accounting information impacts on security returns and volumes. It is generally assumed as a working hypothesis that accounting information contains new information and that the effect of this can be determined using a security pricing model which incorporates this information.

In evaluating these studies, it is of importance to understand the meaning of any findings which show an unequivocal relationship between accounting changes and security returns and volumes. The existence of such effects has nothing necessarily to say about the desirability of such accounting changes. Such insights are an important preliminary to considering the desirability of alterations in accounting systems. Extant results promise progress in accounting because they enhance our empirical understanding of the effects of accounting changes. They do not, however, necessarily have anything to say about the effects of accounting changes on economic welfare. The theme that information provision may take place in an economy characterised by market incompleteness and market failures runs throughout this book and recent literature (see, especially, Chapters 6, 10 and 11). Market difficulties of this type can be argued to mean that accounting policy choices cannot be made without an explicit consideration of, and a value judgement between, different preferences. Information about the effects of accounting changes on security returns and volumes may be an important input into this process (Marshall, 1974; Ohlson and Buckman, 1981). However, in conditions of market difficulty, an assessment of whether changes are desirable requires an assessment of preferences.

The presentation in this chapter has not yet fully indicated the role of information in the models being discussed here. The CAPM assumes that all investors have the same expectations about all the factors assumed to determine the price of securities. Each element in the model is therefore conditional on the information, which may include accounting information used in forming these expectations. It is this information to which we are referring when we assert that information is fully incorporated in security prices. Expression 9.III makes clear the importance of information in a security valuation model by indicating that some elements of this model could, at least in principle, be dependent on the information system used and its signals. This expression will now be used to discuss the effects, if any, of accounting information on security prices. *A priori*, the role of a piece of accounting information is to change the information on which security prices may depend. This role can be expressed in symbols using the left-hand side of Expression 9.III as:

$$\Delta \bar{R}_i = (\bar{R}_i \mid \eta_i) - (\bar{R}_i \mid \eta_j) \qquad \qquad [9.\text{V}]$$

Here η_j is the information set defined to exclude the accounting information in mind; η_i is this set including the item of accounting information which it is desired to study.

The term on the left of the expression, $\Delta\bar{R}_i$, is the expected change in the estimated average return from security i resulting from using an information system (η_i) incorporating the accounting item under study rather than an information system without this item of information (η_i). The above formulation implicitly assumes that any new signals from the augmented information set are immediately impounded into security prices. This expression therefore relies upon the hypothesis that the security market being studied is efficient in the semi-strong form in terms of information processing. Thus the two models reviewed in this chapter come together to give a theoretical model explaining the expected effect of accounting information on security prices and security returns.

This formulation provides a theoretical model for predicting the effects of providing published accounting information which contains new information utilising both the CAPM model and the efficient market hypothesis.

In order to test the impact of accounting items empirically, this theory has to be expressed in an *ex post* form. A possible first step in this process is to look at a long run of *ex post* returns for a security and for the market. This long run of returns could be used to estimate what we earlier called the CAPM relation for the security in mind. Generally, for practical reasons, we usually estimate this relation using a market model which relates the returns from a given security to an index portfolio.

Such a market model can be written in empirical form as

$$R_{i,t} = \hat{a}_i + \hat{\beta}_i R_{M,t} + e_{i,t} \qquad \text{[9.VI]}$$

where $t = 1$ to T. $R_{i,t}$ is the observed return from security i in period t, $\hat{a}_i$ is an empirically based estimate of the intercept of a line relating security risk to return (where the caret over the alpha symbol now indicates that this is an estimate based upon actual data). $\hat{\beta}_i$ is the estimated beta for security i, and $R_{M,t}$ is the return yielded by the market index at time t. The final term, $e_{i,t}$ is the return from the security which is not explained by market-wide influences. Earlier, in this chapter, we have called this the abnormal return of a security. More technically, this term is the unsystematic return generated by a security. Henceforth the terms 'abnormal return' and 'unsystematic return' will be used interchangeably. The mean value of this unsystematic return is assumed to be zero, i.e. $E(e_{i,t})$ or $(\bar{e}_{i,t}) = 0$, where the E stands for the expectation operator and the bar over the e_i indicates that we are dealing with an average. This average of unsystematic risk is assumed not to be correlated with the average market return over time. It is this assumption which allows us to say that this element measures unsystematic risk. It is also assumed that this mean unsystematic return is not correlated with itself over time. A final technical assumption is that the mean unsystematic return and its variance are constant over time.

The first step in deriving an empirical form of this relation is to run a time series regression between market returns and the returns from security i normally using monthly returns over some reasonably lengthy period, say five years, in order to derive estimates of a_i and β_i which are assumed to be constant over the test period. These estimates are obtained from a series of returns occurring prior to the test period. Estimates of the unsystematic returns of the security during the test period are obtained by employing the estimates to help in predicting the returns. The usual procedure is to compute the difference between the return estimated using a market model for each security and its actual returns in a period, typically a month. Averaging these differences across all enterprises will yield the average abnormal return for the month. This average of the abnormal returns (AR) for a sub-period of time is given by:

$$AR_t = \frac{1}{n} \sum_i e_{i,t}$$

where $e_{i,t}$ is the unsystematic proportion of the return from a security. The addition operator (Σ) says that these returns are summed over all n securities in the sample. Dividing this aggregate of returns by n yields the average abnormal return for all securities for the month. These average returns for each sub-period of the test period can be summed over all sub-periods to give a cumulative average of abnormal returns (CAR) which can be written as

$$CAR = \sum_T AR_t$$

where T signifies the number of sub-periods in the sample being aggregated ($t = 1$ to T).

Abnormal returns are often expressed in a slightly different way in the literature being followed. This entails calculating what is called an abnormal performance index (API), which indicates the value of one monetary unit invested in a security or portfolio for a period of time, often the period between annual reports. This index for a security can be expressed as

$$API = \frac{1}{n} \sum_n \prod_T (1 + \hat{e}_{it})$$

where $\hat{e}_{it}$ is the abnormal return for the sub-period and the $\prod$ symbol says that abnormal returns are to be compounded over time by multiplying together the terms in brackets for each sub-period, typically all months in the period. Summing over all securities and dividing by the number of securities yields the average cumulative abnormal return over the test period.

The length of the test period should be sufficient to cover the period of time over which the accounting information was believed to become known. Even with items announced in the annual report, it may be difficult to predict confidently when this item of information became known to the market. There is considerable evidence that the market may anticipate information. Announcements may be made by different firms at different times. Even with an item of information that is released by each firm unambiguously on a given day, the information may still be released by different firms at different times over the test period.

Having obtained estimates of the abnormal returns from a sample of securities over the test period, we need to consider whether these returns are explained by the item of accounting information we are studying. We must therefore measure the correlation between the accounting item of interest and the cumulative abnormal returns we have obtained. Such a correlation should emerge and should be statistically significant if the accounting item affects security prices. Normally, studies also seek to indicate what proportion of abnormal returns are explained by the accounting item in mind. For a more technical discussion see Ricks (1982) and Foster (1980). Much of the above discussion was modelled on that contained in Beaver *et al.* (1979).

The remainder of this section reviews briefly two studies which have sought to discover whether information from historical cost accounting reports have any effect on security prices. The objective is to give examples of the results of what has come to be called market-based research. It is also hoped to provide some feeling for the technical difficulties that are encountered in applying the approach, and for the ingenuity that is required in seeking to overcome these difficulties (see Beaver *et al.*, 1979). For other illustrations see Foster (1980). Beaver and Landsman (1983), chapters 3 and 4, provide an example applying this approach to a different topic—the information effects of price change accounting.

The seminal article concerning the informativeness of historical-cost- based accounting reports is by Ball and Brown (1968). They investigated whether the direction of unexpected changes in conventional accounting results were associated with unsystematic returns which moved in the same direction. They used monthly data for a sample of 261 firms over a period of 20 years terminating in 1965. They first calculated forecasts of changes in future earnings using conventional accounting numbers after allowing for market-wide influences. They then compared these predicted changes with what actually happened. Securities were partitioned into two sets. One set contained those enterprises where the earnings forecasts were in error in a negative direction. The other contained those exhibiting positive errors. Finally, the securities in the two sets were tested for any abnormal returns before and after the announcements of accounting earnings. Their results suggested that the price of shares tended progressively in the same direction as subsequent unexpected earnings during the 12 months leading up to the earnings announcement. This suggests that accounting earnings do have an effect on security prices and returns. This association becomes fairly minimal by the time of earnings announcement. The tendency for share prices to move progressively nearer the direction of the unexpected earnings changes as announcement approaches was taken to mean that the share prices anticipated any information content of the earnings announcement using other information sources. Security prices almost fully adjusted for the information in the earnings figures over the total period prior to the announcement. The annual report as such seems therefore to contain little new information.

Beaver *et al.* (1979) investigated whether, over the years 1964 to 1975, share prices were sensitive not only to the direction of any unexpected change in earnings but also to the amount of any change. They used methods aimed to overcome statistical and other difficulties not fully dealt with in the Ball and Brown study and other earlier studies: their four methods of defining forecast earnings errors turned out to be highly correlated and seemed to show similar results. They considered 25 portfolios ordered according to the relative size of the forecast error they exhibited. They found a highly significant statistical relationship between the average accounting forecast error and unsystematic return. Unsystematic return increased in a positive way with the magnitude of forecast error. They thus found some clear correlation between accounting numbers and changes in security prices and security returns. (Strictly, the relationship is between abnormal returns and errors in earnings forecasts.) As we might expect, this correlation is not complete. The percentage changes in security prices are generally less than the changes in earnings, often by substantial amounts. Beaver *et al.* (1979) suggest that the correlation between these items at the individual security level is around about 0.35, and substantially higher at a portfolio level. What this means in the case of securities can best be seen by assuming that securities are ranked according to the size of errors in their forecast earnings. On average, this ranking will explain some 35 per cent of the ranking obtained if these securities were ordered according to their abnormal returns.

The finding of this and similar studies suggests that a large number of items of information other than accounting earnings affect security prices. The results so far obtained by studies of accounting earnings have been summarised by Beaver (1981a, p. 85), who says that accounting earnings explain a modest proportion of the alterations in security prices, as do Lev and Ohlson (1982, p. 261). This proportion is, however, important because other items of information also explain only small amounts of the changes in security prices. Beaver additionally points out that these other sources of information may allow investors to anticipate earnings changes which will be announced later, though not to the degree suggested by Ball and Brown (1968) because of perceived technical defects in their study. Finally, Beaver states that these findings may in any case reflect the impact on security prices of other accounting items of information with which earnings and other items may exhibit an association.

It has to be said that the results of this approach, both for practice and for theory, have not been as fruitful as, perhaps, was once expected. This seems a general problem with empirical work in the social sciences. In the recent past, disciplines such as economics, sociology and organisational theory effusively embraced empirical studies in the belief that this would add a new dimension to these subjects. Generally, the view now is the results of this work have not yet produced the revolution in these disciplines which many had forecast. Any disillusion is, perhaps, much less with market-based research. This research is very impressive: it represents a very strong and coordinated programme. However, this approach is not universally accepted and there are still substantial problems associated with market-based research, which can be seen as of two types. There are problems of a theoretical nature and difficulties of a technical nature. These two categories of problems are dealt with below.

Some difficulties with market-based research

Justifying accounting policy choices on the basis of discovered security prices effects requires that expected utility for all actors will be optimised by maximising the market values of securities. Earlier chapters indicated that such an assumption cannot be made generally in the face of market difficulties. Studies of the sort reviewed here, for example, say nothing about any effects of accounting changes on those not active in the security market, such as those enterprise employees who do not own securities.

Market-based research is based on movements on the securities market induced by accounting changes. It therefore has nothing to offer in evaluating possible accounting changes until such alterations have been enacted and used for sufficient time to give a statistically valid series of data. Therefore, this method cannot be easily used for a wide class of important disclosure debates where some of the possible disclosures have not yet been used in practice.

Although the theoretical support for market-based accounting research is stronger than for many other accounting theories, its theoretical underpinning is still substantially lacking in theoretical rigour. Models of the way in which security prices are formed and of how the security markets process information provide the theoretical foundations for market-based research. The theoretical strength of this research is therefore dependent on that of these two models. The efficient market models of information processing still lack any compelling theoretical basis. As was indicated earlier, these models are essentially empirically based. CAPM does provide a very strong theoretical basis for understanding the determination of security prices, though its critics are becoming more vociferous. It does suffer from defects (see pp. 209–11). As indicated earlier,

Roll's findings (1977, 1978) suggest that it would seem to be untestable in many settings and is likely to introduce bias into empirical results (see Mayers and Rice, 1979, for one setting where testing is said to be possible). These and other uncertainties concerning the model do mean that the foundation it provides for capital market research is not yet entirely firm. The empirical work reviewed here would seem less subject to some of these difficulties than other applications of the CAPM, such as in performance measurement (see pp. 210–11 and Roll, 1978). Studies using market models are free of this difficulty but only at the cost of dispensing with any strong theoretical foundation for the approach.[5]

There is another emerging programme of research that some commentators, mainly from mainstream economics, regard as possibly casting doubt on the informational efficiency of markets. This work examines the variances of aggregate stock prices using a past series of such prices expressed in real terms. These studies suggest that the observed *ex post* variances are far too great to be explained by a valuation model based on the *ex post* present value of subsequent actual aggregate real dividends over the period being studied, of a type similar to those used in Chapters 3 and 8 (Shiller, 1981a; LeRoy and Porter, 1981). The differences between the time series of actual price changes and the prices given by the valuation model are argued to be too large to be explained by new information appearing in the market. One of the contributions made by Shiller is that he calculates upper bounds for the stock price variability that could be justified by the pattern of subsequent dividends, using logical relationships derived from his valuation model. The actual behaviour of stock prices far exceeds these bounds. This suggests that the market is under- or over-reacting to information and therefore cannot be efficient, at least in terms of the valuation model being used. This valuation model gains strength because it is widely used by economists and financial analysts seeking a plausible theoretical model to explain movements in aggregate share prices.

It is still too early to assess the importance of Shiller's results. A number of suggestions have been made that the results flow from a mis-specified model. His use of a constant real discount rate in his valuation model has been criticised, for example. Shiller (1981b) has, however, shown that the discount rate would have to vary to an impossible degree to explain his results. As would be expected with a new approach to a well researched subject, many other doubts about the model have been raised, but only to be rebutted in that they seem to be unable to explain the very great volatility of actual stock prices relative to using a seemingly sensible valuation model. Some commentators have argued that the valuation model is deficient because it does not take into account attitudes to risk. It has also been argued that the model does not allow for major changes in beliefs, such as that a major depression is round the corner, where the expected events do not subsequently actually appear.

More importantly in some ways, the connection between Shiller's results and market efficiency as discussed here is not yet clear. He is dealing with aggregate data that may smooth away much of interest at the individual security level. Nor is it clear how the risk dimension actually fits into the definitions of efficiency used here, all of which are concerned with average returns. Shiller's results suggest that there are vast amounts of noise contained in stock prices but he does not suggest any source capable of generating this phenomenon. There is a need for a pricing model for securities to be suggested and for strategies to obtain gains from the excess volatility of stock prices to be formulated. This is an important area of work. Future developments may substantially change views on market efficiency and on the role of accounting in informationally efficient markets.

Chapter summary

The first major section of this chapter reviewed the theories which form the foundation of empirically based research in accounting. It was first indicated that the theoretical models used in this work are less detailed than those discussed in the preceding chapter addressing information economics. This work was said to be based on a view that accounting information may affect security prices, returns and volumes. This requires the use of some model or models to determine the value of securities with and without the accounting information being studied. Some model of how information is processed by the market is also required to be entertained by workers in empirical research.

The next two sections of the chapter looked at two classes of models, starting with the valuation models entertained by those undertaking market-based research. The capital asset pricing model (CAPM) was first introduced. This model sees corporate value as depending on the expected return from an enterprise and its risk. This uncertainty concerning enterprise returns was said to be measured by how the enterprise's returns are correlated with those of a portfolio comprising all the securities on offer in the market. The proportion each security forms of this market portfolio is the proportion which each security's aggregate market value bears to the total value of the market portfolio. The relationship between the risk of each security and that of the market portfolio was said to be measured by its beta factor (β_i). This measures how the security's returns covary with the market's returns. With this model, the value of a security is given by the risk-free rate of return plus a premium based on the beta factor of the security. It was suggested that technical and computational problems with this approach mean that market-based accounting researchers substitute indices based on a sample of securities for the market portfolio. These index models allow empirical work to proceed but at the cost of weakening the theoretical foundation for the valuation model used.

The following section examined how information is processed by the security market. A market is defined as efficient if it quickly impounds information into security prices. Varieties of forms of efficiency were discussed. The empirical evidence suggests that security markets are efficient in their weak form (where all evidence contained in past security prices is impounded in current stock prices) and in their semi-strong form (where all public information is incorporated into security prices). The theoretical arguments for expecting security market efficiency in information processing were said to be rather weak.

The fifth substantive section discussed the implications of market efficiency for published accounting statements. One of these implications is that it does not matter where information is disclosed. The actual position of an item of accounting information in accounting statements does not matter if the security market is informationally efficient. In this setting, it has also been argued that the market can 'see through' accounting tricks to the underlying economic reality, though the evidence on this was indicated not to be unequivocal. Efficient markets also have major effects on the way accounting regulators should proceed.

The penultimate part of the chapter discussed how the effect of accounting information on security prices and on security returns is actually estimated using empirical methods. The approach introduced in this section was very simple in essence. Some security valuation model is assumed to explain security prices in informationally efficient markets. Accounting information, if it contains information, should change the return from a security from what would have been predicted using the entertained security valuation model, assuming the accounting information being studied was not being utilised. An explanation was then offered of that part of the actual returns over and above those predicted by the security valuation which are called abnormal returns. An accounting item should be correlated with abnormal returns if it does affect security prices or returns. We then indicated that this work allows us to determine statistically the proportion of the abnormal returns explained by an accounting item.

Two specific examples of this approach were discussed. The general finding from this type of work is that accounting information is one source of information which impacts on security prices. As with other information sources, this impact is modest. Finally, some of the difficulties with market-based research were examined. The major problem addressed was the lack of a compelling theoretical basis for market efficiency. Some important technical difficulties were also considered, as were extant methods of avoiding these difficulties. To summarise, it may be said any problems with the approach are not to be regarded as substantially weakening the contribution that the empirical testing of the information effects of accounting information has so far made to our understanding of accounting systems and their effects. This approach has made substantial contributions to accounting theory.

Notes

1. $\text{Cov}(\tilde{R}_i, \tilde{R}_M)$ represents $r_{iM}\sigma_i\sigma_M$ where r_{iM} is the correlation coefficient between the returns from security i and from the market portfolio (M) and σ_i and σ_M represent a measure of the dispersion of the returns of security i and of portfolio M, respectively (the standard deviations of the returns for security i and portfolio M). This covariance measure is used to express the correlation between the returns of the security and the market portfolio, rather than the usual correlation coefficient in order to express this measure in terms of rates of returns.

2. $\text{Var}(M)$ is given by squaring the standard deviation of the market portfolio (σ_M). This measure is used because it is expressed in the same units as $\text{Cov}(\tilde{R}_i, \tilde{R}_M)$ (that is, in rates of returns squared).

3. For strictly presentational purposes we have omitted some of the steps necessary to derive the CAPM relationship.

4. Accounting information which duplicates presently available information but is less costly to produce may also be thought to be beneficial. It represents a more cost-effective way of producing the information. The substitution of the accounting information for the more costly source cannot, however, be unequivocally regarded as an improvement because the income or wealth of those who previously provided the information may be reduced.

5. Roll argues that the zero beta or risk-free rate in empirical work is defined in a way that may make its value depend on the index chosen to approximate the market portfolio's performance. This association between the risk-free rate and the index used means that the proxy index chosen for measuring the performance of securities will generally turn out to be efficient. This is because no deviation is allowed in these studies from the empirically estimated beta factor and the risk-free rate. This problem is not shared by residual analysis unless the risk-free rate or zero beta rate is affected by the accounting event being studied, in which case there would be a deviation from either the estimated beta factor or the risk-free rate.

III

The regulation of accounting

10

Some economic problems in the provision of accounting information*

This chapter introduces a detailed discussion of the effects of poorly organised markets on accounting. Chapter 11 looks at modes of regulation of accounting and the following chapter (Chapter 12) considers the roles of a conceptual framework for accounting in private sector standard setting. We will see that uncertainty and information economics figure strongly in parts of these chapters.

Plan of the chapter

The view that real-world mechanisms for meeting demands for accounting information possess many of the characteristics of the ideal markets will be considered in the first sections of this chapter.

The reasons for believing that the provision of accounting information should be left to the imperfect market mechanisms of the practical world will be presented first.

If this view were correct, it would lighten substantially the need for accounting theorists to produce theories to deal with problems of differing preferences and decision environments between individuals. Accounting could seek to follow received microeconomic theory and leave these matters to be dealt with by the market. If real-world regimes for supplying accounting information possessed some of the characteristics of perfectly organised markets, this would reduce the need for accounting regulators to make decisions concerning the sectors of the community they wish to aid. Some criticisms of using the market to provide accounting information in the practical world will then be presented.

The remainder of the chapter concentrates on analysing in an informal way some of the major problems which have been argued to inhibit the efficiency of contemporary regimes for the provision of accounting information. These problems are viewed as generated by market failures. Much of what is said applies to other sources of information but we will concentrate on accounting information in all its forms. It is further argued that such market problems often lead to some type of extra-market regulation, usually by the Government. Three short sections introduce these difficulties and some of their effects. The first looks at the problems which might be caused by the lack of markets for some goods (incomplete markets). The second introduces the setting

---

* This chapter relies heavily upon and is a development of parts of Bromwich (1985), chapter 4.

where markets exist but do not function perfectly. The third considers whether the existence of these problems is rendered more likely under uncertainty.

This part of the chapter also examines the view that the lack of a well functioning market for accounting information means that accounting policy making cannot generally proceed by seeking neutral or value-free accounting measures of use to all, except where the information systems in mind provide similar information which varies only in detail. Market difficulties are argued to mean that policy makers cannot proceed by selecting the most informative accounting system or items of accounting information from those available. This is because existing accounting systems differ in character, not just in detail. Choices between such accounting systems and between accounting data more generally may require value judgements as to which elements of society should gain and which should suffer losses.

The final major part of this chapter considers in more detail the view that such choices are necessary with accounting systems and the information they provide because of the characteristics of existing accounting regimes. We review suggestions that characteristics of extant regimes for providing accounting information are likely to cause accounting information to have some of the properties of what are usually termed 'public goods'. These are commodities and services which are, perforce, supplied simultaneously to the whole community or to complete sectors of the community. It is often argued that the case for regulating accounting information is strengthened if it exhibits some of the characteristics of a public good. This is because it is generally agreed in economics that goods of this type cannot always be well handled by the market mechanism.

The final sections of this chapter are addressed to a consideration of the reasons usually given for expecting accounting information to possess some of these characteristics. The intrinsic character of accounting information and current legal requirements in most economically developed countries suggest that it is impossible to keep accounting information private. This is argued to render market solutions to the provision of accounting information difficult because in these conditions no one will be willing to pay for it.

The final reason that has been given for expecting the provision of accounting information to have non-market characteristics stems from the nature of the cost structure encountered in accounting reports. This cost structure is argued to be of the type where, when one consumer has been supplied, remaining consumers can be satisfied at a very low additional cost. Items of this type, including accounting information, are unlikely to be supplied by private enterprise unless a degree of monopoly power is allowed to be exercised.

The problems raised in this chapter are important in appraising accounting theories intended for the practical world. The chapter suggests that one important attribute of accounting theories is the degree to which they are able to address the difficulties introduced by the poorly organised markets or poorly functioning systems used for the provision of accounting information.

The problems surveyed in this chapter also lie at the heart of the arguments for the non-market regulation of accounting information which are surveyed in Chapter 11.

Relying on the market to supply accounting information in a realistic context

Many accounting theorists believe that any imperfections encountered in the real world, with its uncertainty and its lack of markets for accounting information are insufficient to stop existing regimes for providing accounting information from behaving as would a well functioning market as described in Chapter 2.

One attraction of discovering that a well functioning market for accounting information exists is that each individual can be generally assumed to look after his or her own preferences. There is no need for choices about whether accounting reports should aid this or that section of the community or for theories aimed at helping in this choice (see Benston, 1983). In a well functioning market where information was a private good, those who wished for additional information could pay the market price and obtain it. Those who required little or no additional information could desist from trading. Actors in the market would be willing to pay for information which could be kept private and which changed their decisions (see Chapters 2 and 6), provided that any benefits from this exceeded the cost of obtaining the accounting information.

Most of those who urge that the provision of accounting information should be left to the free market accept that the present institutional framework does not correspond to the 'ideal' market settings examined earlier in Chapter 2 (Benston, 1976), nor would they expect practical regimes for providing information, including accounting information, to fully resemble these market settings. They do believe, however, that enterprises which produce additional information will have their share prices bid up relative to otherwise identical enterprises that do not provide such information. They also argue that other information sources and the activities of information intermediaries such as bankers, stockbrokers and financial analysts serve to satisfy the demand for any additional information not provided by published accounting information. Advocates of this view argue that there is little evidence of pent-up demand for greater accounting information concerning enterprises. They would expect all demands for accounting information which covered the cost of providing this information to be met (see Watts and Zimmerman, 1986, chapter 7).

Advocates of letting the market work believe that this would place all individuals in approximately the same situation as those who today can, to varying degrees, acquire certain information when they want it. Banks negotiating loans with companies do not have to wait for the annual accounts before making a decision and can obtain information not in the accounts. Much of Government, in transactions with business, has the same ability to obtain tailor-made information. Trade unions, investment analysts and pension fund managers also may obtain additional information not available to the general public at a time convenient to them.

Those who favour leaving the provision of accounting information to the market are able to point to evidence that supports their theory. They cite, for example, the voluntary provision of accounting information by enterprises prior to any legal or societal requirements for such information (Benston, 1976, early part), the provision of information not required by statute or convention in present-day accounting reports, and the giving of information to financial intermediaries (Watts and Zimmerman, 1986, chapter 7).

Further, supporters of allowing a free market for accounting information would expect management to be willing to issue sufficient information to allow interested outsiders to monitor their behaviour (Jensen and Meckling, 1976, pp. 305–318). To establish this view, it is first argued that the business community perceives that the managers of enterprises have greater knowledge about their enterprises than the rest of the community and will seek to guide enterprises in a way that provides benefits to them. It is suggested that investors would, therefore, allow for this likelihood by adjusting share prices of enterprises to reflect the benefits it is thought that managers will procure from enterprise activities and for the cost of any monitoring of these activities which investors feel would be forced upon them. If managers are part owners of the business in which they are employed, it will be in their interest to publish information which allows any expropriation of benefits to be quantified, thereby limiting the discount that investors might otherwise apply to enterprise securities. Such actions will be in the interests of managers, as stockholders, because they will not wish share prices to be depressed below those necessary to reflect their actual expropriations. Similarly, the proceeds they would receive when they sold all or some of their shares would be net of any costs of monitoring management behaviour. They therefore have an incentive to issue any required information themselves so as to reduce monitoring costs to a minimum.

Chapters 2 and 5 suggested that using a market to allocate information, including accounting information, is feasible, at least in an 'ideal' world. The question, therefore, is why is this method not used in contemporary economies? One answer is that the above arguments for allowing the market to proceed unfettered are thought to be unconvincing. The remainder of this chapter considers the reasons for this in some detail and suggests that the existence of market failures may provide *a priori* reasons for expecting some non-market regulation of the contents of accounting reports, and for the provision of accounting theories seeking to guide any such intervention. However, this is a very controversial subject and a major school of thought, mainly in the United States of America, is convinced that market solutions generally are better than those entailing extra-market regulation because of the costs and distortions that may be introduced by such regulation; see Stigler (1971) and Peltzman (1976). For similar arguments in an accounting context, see, for example, Watts and Zimmerman (1986), later part, and Chapter 13.

The politics of accounting: an introductory look

Some commentators find unconvincing the above arguments in favour of allowing as free a market as possible in the provision of accounting information. The existence of market failures and imperfectly functioning markets may result in accounting information sharing some of the characteristics of public goods. It is argued that such goods are not dealt with efficiently by the market. The possible existence of these market problems and their consequences are empirical questions, as are concerns that existing levels of regulation cannot be justified by extant market difficulties. Laws and conventions against inside trading may provide necessary conditions for accounting information to share some of those characteristics which are believed to make goods difficult to trade on markets. Evidence of economies in the production of published accounting information gives additional support to this view. Whether trading accounting information as well as possible on an imperfectly organised market or utilising some non-market form of regulation is the best way to provide accounting information in the face of these problems is a matter for cost/benefit analysis once the empirical evidence concerning any market problems for accounting is in. Only one major empirical study seems to yield evidence on whether a market or a non-market solution is likely to work best in accounting. Benston (1976) studied early British and American systems of accounting regulation and felt the evidence supported the view that the less regulated British system was to be preferred. More research of this sort would seem to be urgently required.

The possibility that management acting in their own self-interest will be motivated to provide sufficient information to allow their performance to be monitored has also been questioned. It is not clear how security holders and others will be able to assess managerial efficiency from reports voluntarily provided by management. Consumers of managerially provided information may not be able to check its accuracy without considerable cost. Similarly, security holders using this information may be unable to distinguish between securities issued by managers who can be relied upon to act in the shareholders' interests and those who act to their own advantage. This difficulty is called the problem of adverse selection in the economics literature; Chapter 5. Those executives who wish to maximise share values will not be especially rewarded, if the market does not have the ability to distinguish between the different types of managers. Shareholder-orientated managers will, therefore, either join those who wish to pursue their own self-interest in decision making and in information provision, or not attempt to sell their securities on the market. It has been claimed that this phenomenon will lower the attractiveness of securities generally and reduce the size and efficiency of the market. Regulation of accounting reports may be required to offset these effects (Ronen, 1979).

Some economic problems for the provision of accounting information

Most of the remainder of this chapter concentrates on analysing, in a intuitive but fairly detailed way, some of the major problems in the real world which have been said to inhibit the efficiency of contemporary mechanisms for the provision of accounting information. With this view, the imperfect mechanisms at present utilised to allow the expression of demands for accounting information and for supplying accounting information are at the heart of the need for both the regulation of accounting information and accounting theories. These problems have been argued to require intervention by either public or private sector accounting policy makers in an attempt to overcome the consequent difficulties. Similarly, accounting theories are thought to be needed to aid policy makers in their difficult decisions. Regulators, users and preparers of accounts also need theories of accounting to help them choose the most efficient accounting systems for their purposes. In contrast it has also been argued that theories are needed to render respectable the desired accounting systems in the face of the different wishes of others (Watts and Zimmerman, 1979). Here the accounting theory to which an individual subscribes is seen as being determined not only by efficiency considerations, but rather by the degree of congruence between the individual's desire to use a certain type of accounting system and the support of theories for this view.

Generally, poorly functioning markets, such as those which are held to give rise to the need for accounting regulation, are argued to arise either because of market imperfections or because of a complete absence of markets for certain types of goods (the inability to obtain insurance for some types of risk is one example). The term 'market imperfections' covers a wide range of phenomena but basically the presence of such imperfections means that people face different prices for the same items. An obvious example is the different interest rates charged to borrowers, even where they are all borrowing for the same purpose. The presence of such market imperfections and a lack of markets is usually seen as requiring intervention to cure these problems. A wide range of tools is available for this purpose: the choice of which to use is usually a matter for the Government. Evidence of the regulation of markets is easily found. For example, the market mechanism is often completely superseded in the defence area. Public utilities are usually subject to considerable Government regulation. Legislation concerning monopolies and restrictive trade practices attempts to control monopoly suppliers.

Below it is argued that these problems of market imperfections and the lack of complete markets seem to plague the provision of external accounting information. Such problems may not require regulation, nor may they require the degree of regulation that at present exists. For this to be the case necessitates that the results of a such regulation are demonstrably 'better' than the results of a freely functioning but imperfect market mechanism. They do, however, require theories to explain these effects.

One problem in providing a demonstration of the relative superiority of intervention is that it generally involves political judgements. Even with regard to efficiency issues, efforts to judge superiority between an imperfect market mechanism and an alternative intervention system will generally require the use of value judgements. In accounting, this means that there may be disagreement as to the consequences of the implementation of any given reform. The relevant policy makers will have to choose between different views as to the outcome of any intervention. More important is a lack of an agreed view as to the objectives of intervention systems. In an accounting context, this amounts to there being no 'agreed' conceptual or theoretical framework.

Income and wealth measurement in poorly functioning markets

Not all resources and investment opportunities can be traded on perfect markets in a practical environment. Examples of the absence of complete markets are provided by the inability to market 'human' assets, the fruits of research and development expenditures and enterprise 'goodwill', other than jointly with other assets. The lack of a complete set of forward markets and complete insurance opportunities provides further examples of incomplete markets. The differences between an asset's realisable value, its replacement cost and its present value in use provide a familiar and important example in accounting of the results to be expected in an imperfect market. The presence of transaction costs, contractual difficulties and asset specificity are usually held to be important causes of market difficulties, including both incomplete and imperfect markets. These market difficulties may make accounting information a valuable commodity. They may also give a reason for seeking the regulation of accounting. This is because, as is shown in the next three sections, they render the provision by the market of utility-free measures of income and wealth difficult or impossible in some settings.

Incomplete markets

Robinson Crusoe on his desert island provides an 'extreme' example of the possible problems of accounting with incomplete markets. In order to allocate his efforts, over and above those necessary to ensure his subsistence, between investment activities (making fishing rods, for example) and activities leading to additional consumption (obtaining more bananas) he needs to estimate his labour endowment. Crusoe can value the optimal outcomes of these efforts by reference to his preferences. Such a valuation is personal to the valuer. Crusoe and any successor may thus value income and wealth differently but their non-overlapping stays on the island mean they cannot trade to take advantage of this.

Incomplete markets and, indeed, imperfect markets inhibit the individual's ability to use the market to transform a given bundle of goods into a preferred bundle. Such inhibitions mean that market activities cannot be relied upon to resolve differences in preferences between individuals via trade.

It is for this reason that Beaver and Demski (1979, p. 41) claim that 'without market-ability of *all* the factors and commodities, it is possible to lose the unanimous ranking of production plans'. Some shareholders may prefer one plan over another based on non-marketable opportunities. In poorly functioning markets, income measures may not provide correct measures of an enterprise's contribution to welfare for all individuals. Similarly, in these circumstances reporting the entity's present value as seen by the management cannot be defended on the basis that it serves as an index of individual welfare in all circumstances (Bromwich, 1977).

Imperfect markets

The introduction of market imperfections into the analysis may have a wide range of effects which may also cause difficulties for accounting measurement. For example, an enterprise subject to limitations on funds available for investment (capital rationing) may need to know the preferences of its shareholders prior to making investment decisions. Those shareholders with different views may not be able to satisfy their preferences by trading on the market. With such market imperfections, it may again be impossible to arrive at preference-free accounting measures.

Market failure with uncertainty

It may well be thought that the above difficulties caused by market imperfections and market incompletenesses are more likely to arise with uncertainty. Where some risky opportunities are unmarketable, there may be again no way of valuing these opportunities without considering individual preferences. Similarly, individuals may optimise either using different prices or using only their own preferences (Hirshleifer, 1970, chapter 7), where market imperfections yield different prices for a given risky opportunity.

The above arguments suggest that those accounting policy makers and theorists who address their task by seeking neutral or value-free accounting measures are generally likely to fail in practical markets. The determination of accounting standards and accounting regulations cannot generally proceed in such markets without considering individual preferences, the decision environment faced by each individual and the character of the decisions themselves. As we saw in Chapter 7, the conditions under which information systems can be ranked without considering these items are known but they are very restrictive (Demski, 1973; see also Chapter 6). Judgements abstaining from preferences and decision problems can generally be made only if the costless information systems being considered are comparable in terms of their information content. Such systems are those where an information process provides at least all the information available from competing systems, and may yield additional amounts. A more informative system must be preferred because it is always possible to revert to the less informative system by disregarding information. A balance sheet showing replacement and historical cost figures would thus be comparable with a conventional balance sheet.

Generally, accounting policy makers seem to have turned their backs on any extensive use of multi-columnar statements which might provide a solution to this problem. Conventional wisdom holds them to be confusing.

Many of the suggested reforms for accounting systems are not comparable in this way. For example, there is no obvious way of converting accounting statements prepared on a general price level or constant purchasing power basis into those embodying replacement cost figures, without additional information. A choice between such non-comparable information systems can generally be made only by considering the preferences and decision problems of those it is wished to aid. Thus progress in regulation can be made only by making extensive value judgements.

In this light, one important development is the finding that even in incomplete markets (where all desired trades cannot be consummated), investors with differing preferences may still be unanimous as to whether a given project is worthwhile to a specific enterprise (see Chapter 7). This occurs where, for example, the projects being considered offer or span the risks and returns having the same characteristics as are already available to investors, and where competitive markets prevail. Given such unanimity concerning project acceptability, it should be possible to derive accounting variables of use to all investors irrespective of their preferences, at least in some circumstances. Thus sometimes accounting policy makers may be able to abstain from considering individual preferences and from choosing which sector of the community they wish to aid. In general, this will not be the case.

Problems of the character indicated above are likely to be pervasive in a real world context. Thus, they provide a reason for expecting some element of intervention in the institutional framework which generates accounting reports. Policy makers of all types may need to make value judgements as to which sectors of the community they wish to aid where preferences differ. The next sections consider some major practical market failures which may affect current mechanisms for supplying accounting information. Even if these effects were felt to be of little importance, this would not necessarily provide support for the advocates of the free market treatment of accounting information. Poorly organised markets in other sectors of the economy may well have some effect on the type of accounting information that might be required by market participants. Indeed, supplying additional information may be one way of mitigating the effects of these difficulties which cannot, or will not, be removed by other means.

Accounting information: a public good

It has been suggested that some of the characteristics of the contemporary process for providing accounting information endow this information with some of the properties of what are called 'public goods' in the economics literature. The essence of a public good is that if one person is supplied with a commodity its benefits are conferred generally and indiscriminately on all, or some, others in the community. Some aspects of defence are said to provide examples. Nuclear deterrence, some other elements of national defence and public broadcasting programmes provide illustrations of what are generally regarded as public goods. A 'pure' public good probably does not exist. This would require that the good provides the same physical services to all in the community, that these services are consumed simultaneously by all and, strictly, that there could be no opting out of the level of service provided. This is perhaps the case with nuclear deterrence. It is the simultaneity of consumption which gives rise to the name 'public goods'.

The joint supply characteristic of public goods means that their supply is not, as with a normal good, reduced by the consumption of any individual (Samuelson, 1966). An individual's consumption of one unit of a typical good, say a chocolate bar, reduces the supply of this good by one unit, whereas the individual consumption of accounting information leaves such information intact for others to use. It is the amount of commodity, or of the services in mind, which is being left intact, not the benefits accruing from their use. For example, the benefits to the individual flowing from a unit of education, provided to all, may depend on the uses others make of that unit. Similarly, the pleasure experienced by watching a television programme may be affected by the number of people who also watched the programme. Matters such as these are reflected in the valuation the individual puts on public goods. They do not alter the quantity supplied to each individual.

The concern with whether accounting information has some of the characteristics of a public good arises from the view usually held in economics that such goods cannot be supplied by the market with complete efficiency (see Atkinson and Stiglitz, 1980, pp. 482–518). The usual view is that commodities with public good characteristics will be underprovided by the market. Some of the demands of those consumers who would be willing to pay the incremental cost of supplying them will not be met. A *prima facie* reason for some type of regulation of accounting information would be provided if it could be demonstrated that accounting data have major public goods characteristics.

The following two sections will be devoted to considering two major market imperfections that may generate such characteristics for accounting information. These two alleged market defects will be considered sequentially. The first problem is that arising from the present institutional arrangements for supplying public accounting information which, put crudely, requires that no one should be denied any accounting information that has been made available to others not involved in transactions with the company in mind. The second imperfection to be addressed is that of the joint supply of accounting information to all. Accounting reports may be of the type that, having been provided to one individual, their provision to others who demand them can be made at zero or a small cost.

Accounting and 'free riders'

The present mechanisms utilised for providing accounting information seem to resemble a market only imperfectly. However, recall that advocates of a free market in accounting information do not necessarily believe that this imperils the superiority of market provision relative to supply by regulated systems.

Generalising, perhaps too far, it can be said that the current institutional arrangements for the provision of accounting information do not usually provide any obvious system whereby bids for additional information can be expressed. Rather, enterprises are supposed to issue the same package of information at a minimal cost to users. It would seem to be regarded as sufficient by the business community that this information satisfies only conventional minimum standards and legal requirements. The enterprise does, however, have considerable discretion as to the accounting practices embodied in the accounting package. Choices are often permitted in the method of dealing with given accounting items. It is likely that those charged with these decisions within the enterprise will resolve the question by selecting those procedures which best achieve their own wishes (that is, which are thought most likely to maximise their welfare). Similarly, where information over and above that which should be contained in the minimum package is provided, it might be expected to support the picture of the financial position of the enterprise which those in power in the corporation wish to present to the outside world in order, for example, to repulse take-over bids.

The absence of the usual price system for accounting information means that, in general, there is no clear mechanism to be utilised by those with needs unsatisfied by conventional published statements in order to make known those desires which they are willing to back by money. They cannot, therefore, expect to cause resources to be directed towards the provision of their information requirements.

A number of people such as investment analysts, stockbrokers and financial journalists do, at least, claim to be able to obtain access to non-public information. They also claim that they derive additional insights from publicly available information because of the superior analytical techniques which they possess. Such individuals contribute to economic efficiency in so far as the claims to have superior ability to analyse public information are justified. However, where they do have access to non-public data, such a provision may reflect their superior bargaining power relative to the general user of accounting information. The explicit or implicit price for this type of accounting information which emerges from these activities may, therefore, reflect neither society's preferences for accounting information nor the opportunity cost of its provision. Only a relatively small number of individuals have access to such non-public information. It is likely that they will have some monopoly power, and therefore will not provide the information to all those willing to pay the incremental cost of their demands. Moreover, it is possible that any financial data given by enterprises to favoured individuals such as investment analysts and financial journalists will minimise that information which reflects badly on those in power in the enterprise. This suggests that 'city experts', even if they do have special information cannot be relied upon to satisfy all demands for information. The question remains, therefore, why a more comprehensive market for accounting information, and indeed other information, has not appeared.

One major reason for the absence of such a market for accounting information is the desire in many developed economies to avoid the problems arising from 'inside trading'. Anti-inside trading legislation usually requires that no one should be excluded from receiving any information the enterprise has issued to any one for purposes not expected to facilitate the enterprise's normal operations. Those who obtain privileged information through their commercial activities with the enterprise, such as supplying raw materials and components, are generally regarded as becoming 'insiders' and are restricted in their ability to trade on this information. Therefore, people may well be unwilling to pay for any additional information. Effective prohibitions on inside trading mean that any 'non-insider' information obtained by an individual will flow to all, irrespective of whether they have paid for it. No rational person will buy any information unless those who have not paid for it can be excluded from using it. Similarly, rational individuals will be unwilling to attempt to bid up the share prices of those enterprises which voluntarily provide supplemental information relative to otherwise identical but non-disclosing firms. Such additional information would provide no private advantage to any investor.

Those who share such benefits without paying for them are usually labelled 'free riders'. In the example in Chapter 7, an investor using our imperfect information and seeking to maximise expected monetary value would pay up to 8.54 monetary units for information concerning which state of the environment will prevail if, and only if, exclusive use of the information were obtained (see pp. 131–9). If this information had to be announced to all once it was purchased, security prices would immediately impound the new information. In this case, the purchaser of the information would not be able to exploit this information by trading. This inhibits the flow of information because otherwise possibly desirable information will not be demanded even though individuals would be willing to pay its incremental cost if it were made available for their private use.

This example also suggests that similar problems will be encountered in attempts to market accounting information, even without inside trading legislation. This is because the process of arriving at a price for accounting information to be used privately may leak some information to the market. The determination of these prices requires that the information supplier gives potential purchasers some indication of the contents of any information being offered. Such preliminary information releases may be impounded into security market prices. There is strong evidence that the contemporary stock market does quickly reflect all public information in security prices (see Beaver, 1981b). Private negotiations of this type may involve high transaction costs, which may also be generated by attempts to ensure that primary buyers do not resell to others the information they obtain. Without such a prohibition, secondary selling will quickly affect security prices.

Even if these problems could be resolved, there is reason to assume that non-purchasers can 'free ride' by observing security prices. The actions taken by traders informed by private information, in order to capitalise on their knowledge, may affect security prices. Those who have not paid for the information can, therefore, share some or all the knowledge possessed by informed traders by observing price behaviour. This will make private information bargains less valuable (Grossman, 1977).

All these reasons for expecting the existence of 'free riders' with the existing institutional mechanism for providing accounting information suggest that published accounting information possesses some of the characteristics of a public good. This is likely to cause accounting information to be underprovided relative to the amount of this commodity for which consumers would be willing to pay the costs of supply.

It would be possible to reduce substantially the problem of free riders in accounting, by allowing inside trading. This has not been seriously suggested in political circles. Indeed, on the contrary, definitions of what is inside trading have been widening in a number of countries and the penalties attached to such illegal activities have been strengthened in some countries. One assumes that this attitude reflects the view that the income and wealth redistributions consequent on any relaxation of the insider trading legislation would be too large to be politically acceptable. Rationally, recent strengthening of anti-insider trader legislation should be based on the view that the net benefits following any such legislation are greater than those which would accrue from the better functioning market which would result from a more relaxed attitude to inside trading.

The problem caused by the inability to exclude purchasers of accounting information may be somewhat reduced in severity by the existence of private sector regulation bodies such as the United Kingdom's Accounting Standards Board and the Financial Accounting Standards Board in the United States. These rule-making bodies have some, albeit weak, power to enforce their solutions. This may help to reduce any alleged underprovision of accounting information. This depends on how far their imposed requirements for additional information are congruent with the unfulfilled desires of any erstwhile users of additional accounting information. There may also be a related publicness on the supply side. For example, many of the benefits from accounting reports are held to stem from their comparability across firms. This necessitates a degree of uniformity between firms in order to obtain comparability.

Public goods and the supply of accounting information

Under the present system of providing accounting information, the costs of any additional requirements imposed by standard setters and other accounting policy makers are left to fall where they may. This introduces the second major problem which is argued to inhibit the provision of accounting information by the market. This problem is generated by the rather unusual characteristics of the contemporary mechanism for the production, distribution and financing of the provision of accounting reports.

With the current institutional arrangements for the supply of accounting statements, the costs of their provision amounts in the first instance to imposing a lump-sum tax on enterprises. These costs arise from meeting legal and other requirements, including those imposed by any standard setting process. They amount to a lump-sum tax if the view is taken, as it will be here, that the cost of fulfilling any requirement for accounting information by the enterprise is mainly composed of set-up costs, the variable costs of supplying information to users being sufficiently small to be ignored. Indeed, the total costs of providing external accounting information may be small, where such information is already supplied to enterprise management. With this view the set-up costs of external accounting systems, and any changes to such systems, should not alter the profit-maximising behaviour of enterprises. Any set-up costs associated with regulation will be absorbed by reducing profits in the short run, as would any other increase in fixed costs. Enterprise price or output levels may, however, be altered by the imposition of additional accounting requirements if cost-plus pricing is practised. Here additional overhead costs will be treated as if they were variable costs with such a pricing system. Additional costs of this type will increase the perceived cost of output and therefore cause output to decline below what would otherwise be the profit maximising level.

In the longer run, the cost of providing external accounting information will be borne by, among others, one or more of the following parties—the consumers of enterprise products, the holders of enterprise equity, enterprise management and the taxpayer—via the tax deductability of such costs. Within the present framework these costs are allowed to lie wherever they fall. The prediction of their actual disposition is difficult and will depend on factors like the characteristics of the demand curves for enterprise products, how efficient enterprise managers are and how much bargaining power managers have relative to others concerned in enterprise activities. With this view, the provision of accounting information can be seen to be imperfect because those who bear the costs of providing it have little incentive as the bearers of these costs *per se* to supply the amount of information desired by the community. Indeed, they have clear incentives to discourage such demands.

The present institutional arrangements for the supply of accounting reports suggest another reason for assuming that accounting information possesses some of the characteristics of public goods; this has been rather overlooked in the accounting literature. The usual view of the cost structure for the provision of accounting reports is that there are large economies of scale in the production of such reports and that the costs associated with supplying further copies of existing accounting reports are very small. The presence of these economies is one traditional cause of goods being in joint supply. Having incurred the costs necessary to supply one consumer, others may either be supplied automatically (defence and television programmes provide examples) or at low cost. Economic logic dictates that in such situations the demands of all potential consumers should be met, providing they are willing to pay the low or zero cost of their supply.

One example of this logic is given by the willingness to allow all costlessly to use a road bridge with spare capacity. Low fares to encourage the off-peak use of under-utilised rail services which it has already been decided to run provide another example. Additional use of a service of this type, say the under-utilised roadbridge, increases the welfare of the additional users without placing any incremental costs on either the community or on other individuals in that community. Potential passages across the bridge in a given time period disappear if not used. This argument applies only if capacity constraints do not bite.

The cost structure sketched above for the supply of accounting reports would seem to justify the free or very low-cost provision of existing accounting reports to all who require them. Refusing to supply accounting reports to all who are willing to pay the associated incremental costs amounts to not fully using society's resources.

However, in a market-based regime, enterprises would have little incentive to provide information on these terms because the average cost of provision would be greater than the incremental cost of supplying one extra user and each unit would, therefore, be supplied at a loss if priced at its marginal cost. It is therefore normally argued that the provision of goods with decreasing costs in well functioning markets requires either the use of monopoly power, thereby allowing firms to recoup average costs, or some type of intervention (normally by the Government). Arguing for regulation implies that the social benefits of such regulation relative to those which would accrue from accepting whatever would be supplied by an unregulated market are larger than the costs imposed by regulatory action. Allowing enterprises to exercise any monopoly power they may possess would also impose costs on the economy.

This latter alternative is not at present feasible for the provision of accounting information because of the difficulties of exclusion of non-purchasers. Legal requirements in most developed economies require that accounts must be lodged at a central location and be freely available for perusal by all. Also, supplying one user means that others automatically obtain use of the accounts, either indirectly via the reports of intermediaries such as financial journalists or directly by repeat use of the reports supplied to another individual.

This centralised access to accounting reports and the activities of financial intermediaries mean that it is unlikely that capacity limits will be encountered. The joint supply aspects of accounting reports therefore militate against the application of any straightforward market solution to the supply of accounting information.

These difficulties yield a further reason for expecting the underprovision of accounting information if this were left to the market.

Thus the two major reasons for suspecting that accounting information has some of the characteristics of public goods—exclusion difficulties and joint supply problems—here combine and act together.

There are, therefore, good *a priori* reasons for expecting some intervention by regulators in the provision of accounting information.

Criticisms of the public good case

Watts and Zimmerman (1986, chapter 7) illustrate some of the arguments of those who are not convinced that accounting information can be shown to be a public good. For instance, they argue that many examples of the non-provision of accounting information becomes rational once account is taken of the cost of setting up and monitoring the usual contractual arrangements necessary if the market were to provide this information. Provision by the market actors would be rational only if the users of accounting information were willing to cover these costs. The countervailing argument is that the paying of these costs and trading accounting information are rendered irrational by perceived market problems. In our case, major factors causing these perceptions are the outlawing of inside trading and the usual characteristics of information.

Leftwich (1980) and Watts and Zimmerman (1986, chapter 7) illustrate the views of those who argue that providing an *a priori* case (or even empirical evidence) for the existence of market difficulties is not sufficient to justify extra-market regulation. This is first because the arguments for expecting market difficulties in the provision of accounting have been deduced in settings far removed from the practical world. It is also asserted that intervention mechanisms which could simulate the results which would be yielded in an ideal market setting do not exist (Leftwich, 1980). This requirement that intervention mechanisms should reflect the results which would be obtained from an ideal market may be too strong. Intervention can be justified, providing that regulation offers greater net benefits, after allowing for its costs (both direct and, more important, indirect), than those flowing from using the market regime.

This is an empirical question which is probably insoluble with existing knowledge and with a lack of any clear uncontroversial method of valuing net benefits. The views of those, like Watts and Zimmerman (1986, chapter 7), who additionally believe that regulatory mechanisms are vulnerable to failures in their functions (so-called administrative failure; see their chapter 11) are also questions that can only be resolved empirically. How such studies should be structured so as to produce generally acceptable results is not yet clear.

Many of those who favour the use of the market for providing accounting information accept the possibility of the difficulties caused by any public goods characteristics of accounting information. They argue that because of the costs and other difficulties of regulation, including the temptation of over-regulation, markets will still function better than regulatory bodies. Others argue that public good problems are insignificant for accounting policy making because a variety of arrangements may spring up to overcome these difficulties. They have in mind, for example, the very considerable incentives to financial intermediaries, such as investment analysts, to seek to disseminate any private information in their possession. Such activities may ameliorate any market failures that would otherwise exist. Any improvement in the market process is, however, obtained at the cost of possibly allowing financial intermediaries to make monopoly profits from their customers, the size of which depends on how well the intermediaries can restrict access to their private information by those who have not paid for that information. It has already been suggested that the implicit or explicit prices for information which emerge from any special access to enterprise information may not reflect either society's preferences or the opportunity cost of information production. Those who seek a market solution cannot argue against this by suggesting that access to enterprise information is sufficiently free to avoid the generation of monopoly profits, because this reintroduces into accounting the public good problem arising from non-exclusion. Moreover, the fee structures of financial intermediaries are complicated and the provision of information is often tied to the joint provision of their other services. The inability to pay separately for accounting information may cause additional market failure difficulties.

Few studies have been undertaken to ascertain empirically the importance of public good characteristics generally in the economy. Such exercises are very difficult to structure in a way sufficient to satisfy all parties with an interest in the results. In any case, any evidence on its own of public good properties in the provision of accounting information says little about the importance of these characteristics. Such statements require a consideration of the market's response to these characteristics. Present empirical evidence in the area of public goods generally amounts to little more than saying that casual observation supports the view that it is not starkly obvious that commodities and services with public goods characteristics are underprovided in the economy as a naive application of the theory would suggest (Atkinson and Stiglitz, 1980, pp. 515–516).

A possible and rewarding study of public goods problems in the accounting area would be to attempt to compare economies with different degrees of regulation of accounting along the lines used by Benston (1976), paying special attention to the reasons for regulation. A cost/benefit study of the relaxation of insider trading regulations could throw some light on the importance of public goods problems in the accounting sphere. Similarly, an investigation of how far there are currently unfulfilled demands for accounting information might give some clues as to the significance of these problems for the economy.

This completes our review of the approach of allowing markets to provide accounting reports. The difficulties of this approach, identified especially in this chapter, represent major challenges to accounting theorists.

Whatever view we take of the above debates, the degree to which various accounting theories can be expected to cope with these difficulties, and therefore their appeal to regulators is important to an understanding of accounting theory.

Whatever view we take of the promise of accounting regulation, we have to recognise its ubiquity in practice in a large number of countries. Chapter 11 therefore reviews in some detail the regulation of accounting by a variety of means. It considers how well each type of regulation can be expected to answer the challenges raised in this chapter.

Chapter summary

The first section of this chapter considered the advantages for accounting if practical methods of providing accounting information were found to yield similar results to those of an 'ideal' market (see Chapter 2). A major advantage of such findings is that individuals can be left to optimise the amount of accounting information they trade according to their preferences without any need for accounting policy makers to make judgements between different preferences.

The arguments of those who believe that actual systems for providing information, including accounting information, share many of the characteristics of information when traded in ideal markets were then considered. Such advocates believe that an unregulated system of providing accounting information will yield greater benefits than any system of regulation.

The arguments that existing regimes for providing public accounting information are flawed in a number of ways when considered from a market perspective were presented. After an introduction to these problems and to the *a priori* case they provide for expecting extra-market regulation, some of the likely effects of both imperfect and incomplete markets were presented. The *a priori* reasons for expecting these market problems to cause public accounting information to share some of the characteristics of what are usually called public goods were also presented. This perspective on accounting information is important because one view is that public goods need to be provided by non-market mechanisms.

The next section explained in a little more detail the characteristics of public goods. The two following sections looked at major reasons for expecting public accounting information to have such properties. The first of these reasons was said to be the possible existence of 'free riders' arising from institutional arrangements, such as any inside trading legislation, and from the intrinsic nature of information generally and accounting information in particular. It was suggested that the presence of free riders may inhibit any willingness to pay for accounting information which would be otherwise demanded.

The second reason considered in this chapter for expecting public accounting information to have public good characteristics was the cost structure of the process used to generate external accounting reports. This cost structure was argued to comprise a high set-up cost and a very low cost of providing additional copies of reports. With this type of cost structure, economic logic suggests that all who are willing to pay the marginal costs of providing accounting reports should be supplied. Such goods may be only imperfectly provided by the market. This is because prices set in this way will not cover all costs. One possible solution to this problem is to allow suppliers to exercise enough of any monopoly power they may possess to ensure that all costs are covered.

The existence of free riders, however, reduces any monopoly power accounting information suppliers might otherwise possess. Thus, it was argued that our two reasons for suspecting that accounting information has some of the characteristics of public goods interact together seem to provide a strong *a priori* case for expecting market difficulties in providing accounting information. They therefore yield grounds for expecting the intervention of regulators in this area.

The final section of this chapter adopted a critical perspective on both the public goods characteristics of accounting information and the need for intervention of regulators seeking to remedy any consequent defects in the provision of accounting information. Sceptics see any seeming market problems as actually arising from contractual costs of supplying accounting information. Non-provision is rational in such a setting. The arguments of those who believe that regulation is a doubtful way of dealing with market difficulties were presented, emphasising the very high perceived cost of regulation.

Irrespective of whether these arguments are convincing, in studying accounting theory we have to recognise the pervasive presence of regulation in the accounting world. Similarly, we have to recognise that the ability of various theories concerning accounting information to deal with the difficulties raised in this chapter is an important area of study for accounting theorists.

11
The regulation of accounting

Introduction

Chapters 2 and 10 examined the argument that 'ideal' markets could produce value-free accounting systems. With our earlier definition, an accounting system is value-free where it does not favour any specific sector of the community and is useful to all, irrespective of their preferences, beliefs and endowments. Chapter 10 suggested that accounting choices in the environment of the practical world necessitated judgements as to which sectors of the community should be favoured in these decisions. It also suggested that market difficulties may give rise to calls for the regulation of accounting. This chapter examines some of the various regimes used or suggested for the regulation of financial reporting from an economic perspective.

Arrangements for accounting regulation differ between countries. The possibilities cover a wide spectrum. They range from a system that depends almost entirely on statute, for example in France and Germany, through a balanced mixture of statutory and self-regulatory systems (Australia and Canada provide contrasting illustrations), to regulation that relies mainly on self-regulation by the accounting profession. The United Kingdom, especially prior to the Companies Act 1981 (consolidated in the 1985 Act, which enacted the Fourth Directive of the European Community into British law), and the United States provide examples of this last type of system.

The objective of this chapter is to appraise the strengths and weaknesses of some extant approaches to accounting regulation. All the earlier chapters have suggested, in one way or another, that accounting theories cannot be appraised using only analytical methods to determine how well they achieve their objectives, such as aiding investors' decision making. The implementation of such theories may have substantial consequences for some sectors of society. An accounting reform can be expected to aid some sector, or sectors, of society and impose costs on other members of the community. For example, an accounting reform which aids investors may cause extra costs in the preparation of accounting reports. Alterations to accounting systems may also require the release of information helpful to competitors'.

Each suggested theory and theoretical approach to accounting should ideally be appraised in the context of the regulatory requirements being utilised, and with a consideration of the societal consequences of the accounting changes based upon each theory.

Plan of the chapter

In this chapter we shall deal in a general way with some of the problems that surround accounting regulation. The first substantive part looks at the various institutional frameworks utilised for accounting regulation and the political consequences of such choices. This section commences by suggesting that there are a large number of approaches to accounting regulation, though most rely upon a general framework, at least, provided by statute. The regulatory environments for accounting in a number of countries are reviewed.

The second major segment of this chapter adopts a comparative approach to the strengths and weaknesses of public sector regulation relative to theories of self-regulatory standard setting. It also considers problems common to both approaches.

This part commences by considering the strengths of accounting regulation by the legislature. Secondly it addresses the social choice aspects of accounting regulation. In the absence of well functioning markets, accounting choices are argued to yield benefits to some in the community and impose costs on others. For example, a requirement to publish segmental income information may aid investors but possibly at the cost of giving information to competitors. The costs and benefits adhering to accounting choices are argued here to render accounting 'political' and to give rise to political activities designed to influence accounting policy decisions. The view that accounting solutions should not be amended in the light of these pressures is also considered.

The general problem common to public and private sector regulation is that of finding a system for making social choice decisions which satisfies some assumptions which seem reasonable for a liberal society. It is explained that all known public choice systems infringe at least one of these assumptions. Appendix 11.1 considers this matter in more detail. We also review some objections to this finding. It is suggested that Government, with a strong majority, can ignore these criticisms, as can public sector regulators backed by such a Government. Standard setters unsupported by Government cannot so easily ignore or refute criticisms concerning alleged defects of their constitution. We then take up the problems faced by any accounting policy makers of determining individual preferences in the absence of a market which can be relied upon to deal with this problem automatically.

We next look at the difficulties associated with accounting policy making by the legislature as an introduction to policy making by governmental agencies. Here it is also suggested that some of the problems of legislative regulation can be overcome by the legislature delegating much of the responsibility for regulating accounting to an agency, such as the Securities and Exchange Commission (SEC) in the United States. The advantages and disadvantages of using an agency for this purpose are then considered. These possible disadvantages, which include inefficiency and capture by those who are meant to be regulated, may be shared by private sector bodies. Finally, with respect to public sector regulation, we consider the strengths and weaknesses of accounting regulation by bureaucracy.

The third and penultimate part of this chapter looks at two problems which seem unique to private sector standard setting. The first is to show from where standard setters obtain their authority to issue what some commentators regard as 'quasi laws' affecting many people often external to the profession. A number of ways in which private sector standard setters can enhance their authority are introduced. It has been argued that discovering a conceptual framework for accounting may help in this area, by giving a generally accepted theoretical foundation to the output of standard setting bodies.

Our review of this approach to generating accounting theory is delayed until Chapter 12. We do, however, deal with a second problem facing standard setters and accounting policy makers of seeking consensus for their solutions. Consensus seeking is another major strategy that might be used by standard setters to enhance the acceptability of their conclusions.

The framework of accounting regulation and its political nature[1]

For most countries the question is not whether governmental regulation of external accounting is better than private sector standard setting. Rather, it is whether the existing balance between the two is correct. In some countries, such as Germany and France, state regulation is predominant. In most others, the form of external accounting reports is determined using what might be called a 'mixed' system in the same sense as economies are often described as 'mixed' in terms of their balance between Government regulation and the use of the market system.

The institutional framework for accounting standard setting

A review of standard setting in a number of countries (see Bromwich and Hopwood, 1983) suggests that private sector accounting standard setting cannot be considered separately from the requirements imposed by law and by governmental regulation. In most countries the activities of the government and its agencies, the judiciary and standard setters, and any other accounting policy makers not mandated by the Government in the accounting sphere, must be viewed as a whole. In most commercially developed countries, accounting policy is not the sole preserve of a 'self-regulating profession'. Rather, standard setters and policy makers in the profession can be seen as building on the law and generally dealing only with items which have not been addressed by the legislature in any detail. The standard setting system (if any) used in different countries seems to reflect their differing social, political and economic environments.

Australian and Canadian standard setters seem to have the most explicit mandate for accounting reform because accounting standards correctly promulgated in the authorised way may become part of statute law. In a number of other countries, including New Zealand, the United States of America and the United Kingdom (prior to the Companies Act 1981), standard setters seem to have a good deal of freedom, though they are all restricted by Government in one way or another. For example, the Financial Accounting Standards Board (FASB) in the United States of America has indirect delegated authority from the legislature. The power to set accounting standards for companies quoted on stock exchanges has been given by the legislature to the SEC which, in practice, mainly delegates the task to the FASB. However, this power is weakened by the SEC issuing its own accounting requirements for quoted companies, and by the number of government bodies in the United States of America who may have a degree of power to determine their own requirements for accounting regulations which fall within their purview and seek to overthrow or amend accounting standards impinging on their area of authority. Congress itself has not entirely abstained from promulgating detailed changes to accounting reports. It is not so much the actual intervention of these powerful bodies which restricts the freedom of standard setters and non-legislatively backed accounting policy makers in the United States of America. It is rather the threat of such intervention following lobbying by those dissatisfied with suggested solutions to accounting problems.

Standard setters in the United Kingdom have, perhaps, at least until recently, been less constrained than their American counterparts. Previously, legislation in the United Kingdom relating to accounting had been of a fairly general character. The courts have tended to rely on the profession for evidence of 'good business practice'. Other bodies, such as Government departments, seem to have been generally uninterested in accounting matters. However, recent legislation, especially the Companies Acts 1980 and 1981, has changed the character of the environment faced by British standard setters (and other non-governmentally backed policy makers). This legislation has moved the legislative environment somewhat towards that experienced in parts of continental Europe. Both these Acts may be seen to have reinforced the concern with objectivity and prudence in accounting matters. The 1981 Act follows continental European practice by providing for a much more complete codification of accounts with fairly rigorous valuation rules. It also stated, perhaps more clearly than in the past, the need for accounting statements to give objective evidence of stewardship so that creditors and investors can ascertain whether their interests in the enterprise have been protected and whether any proposed profit distribution is reasonable.

This legislation must constrain British standard setters. The body charged with standard setting for the United Kingdom and Ireland, the Accounting Standards Committee (ASC), was renamed in 1990 the Accounting Standards Board (ASB). Its financing and the Board itself were substantially reorganised at that time. References in this book to standard setting in the United Kingdom will refer to the experience of the earlier body. As an example of the possible constraints imposed on standard setters by legislation, it has been argued that, given the fairly detailed disclosure requirements now enacted by the British legislature, any further disclosure suggested by standard setters might be resisted on the basis that the United Kingdom legislature, if it had wished, could have insisted on more detailed accounting disclosure. Similar arguments could also be put concerning extra-statutory valuation or measurement standards being used by British standard setters. Taken to extremes, these arguments, which apply to a degree to most national standard setters, would restrict the role of UK standard setters to that occupied by accounting reformers in some parts of continental Europe. These European accounting policy makers are mainly concerned with non-mandatory information that supplements statutory accounts, making recommendations to the legislature and to the Government and to acting generally as opinion formers concerning accounting reform.

A more optimistic view of the future role of accounting standards relies on the lack of definition in the Companies Act of the dominant statutory requirement in the United Kingdom, that the accounts must give a 'true and fair' view. This places an important duty on the profession and on the ASB in helping to determine the constituents of a true and fair view. Accounting standards may also be required where the 'substance' of the underlying economic reality is not fully conveyed by adhering to the statutorily determined accounting 'form'. The 1981 Act introduced a true and fair 'override' which individual companies can use where compliance with statutory requirements does not convey the substance of the believed economic reality. A more recent act (the Companies Act 1989) may have widened this provision so that it may be available to standard setters seeking to ensure via accounting standards that the substance, rather than form, of an accounting item is reported, by placing a gloss on the law. In the past, one or two standards, including that dealing with foreign exchange, have been issued relying in part on the earlier override provision. This ability to ensure that economic reality is reflected in accounting, irrespective of statutory requirements, is given to only a few standard setters internationally. Any such power is often implicit and can often be utilised only to a very minor degree.

The British standard setting scene has not yet moved as far as in some countries, including France and Germany, in giving pre-eminence to the government in accounting regulation. In Germany, for example, external accounting is generally said to be dominated by the commercial and the tax laws. Enterprises must follow exactly the form laid down by statute for the published accounts, including specified valuation rules, if they wish to gain the fruits of these laws.

The large amount of governmental and professional resources involved in standard setting and accounting regulation indicates the importance ascribed to published accounts in many political and economic regimes. These activities also support the views expressed in earlier chapters that the form and contents of accounting reports are seen as matters for social judgements of one form or another. The reasons why accounting regulation requires social choices to be made will be considered from a fairly pragmatic stance in the next section. This section indicates that accounting regulation requires decisions to be made as to whose welfare should be aided by choices concerning accounting reports.

Social choice and accounting

In Chapter 10, it was indicated that badly functioning markets such as those which are often said to be encountered in the accounting area mean that market actors cannot necessarily trade away differing preferences for accounting information using the market. Similarly, without well functioning markets, individuals may not be able to avoid entirely the effects of any regulations imposed by governmental or private sector accounting policy makers. The benefits and costs of such regulations will, therefore, remain where they fall. A reform of accounting statements which forced management to release publicly 'bad news' concerning an enterprise's fortunes may harm the existing holders of the enterprise's securities and may reduce the welfare of the firm's management and workers where their rewards are based on the enterprise's accounting profit. Such a reform will favour other investors, providing that accounting information does have an effect on share values. Other parties, such as consumers and creditors, may be able to make better decisions concerning their future involvement with the enterprise using this information. Additional information about, say, research and development or segmental profits may aid competitors and, therefore, aid investors in other enterprises, even though the cost of providing such information is borne by others. The debates over a wide range of accounting standards in many countries indicate that a large number of parties perceive themselves affected by proposed and actual accounting standards.[2] For example, in all cases where additional requirements are promulgated, those who finance the provision of accounting statements will suffer when considered only as providers of such funding, because of any additional requirement for accounting information. Even those who do not use accounting information may be put at a disadvantage relative to those who do utilise accounts if accounting regulations alter the information conveyed by accounting reports.

Such views may well be imperfectly perceived and the arguments for intervention may be imperfectly articulated. Those actively involved in the standard setting scene are beginning to see their activities not as purely technical matters as was perhaps the view in the early days of standard setting (see, for example, Leach, 1981; Slimmings, 1981). One view, perhaps only reluctantly and perhaps implicitly accepted, is that they are making social choices or value judgements for society. This view has been made explicit in the United States; see, for example, Gerboth (1973) and Horngren (1973), both of whom suggested that this view renders standard setting political in most meanings of the word. Gerboth (1973), for example, argues that 'The politicization of accounting rule making is not only inevitable, but just ... When a decision process depends on public evidence the critical issues are not technical, they are political'. For a more recent American statement of this view, see May and Sundem (1976), who say that the FASB 'must consider explicitly political aspects (i.e. social welfare) as well as accounting theory and research in its decisions'. The concern with political issues in the United States of America has taken a rather different direction from the United Kingdom in that whilst it is generally accepted that accounting standards have economic consequences, it has also been authoritatively argued that these effects are not matters for accounting standard setters. For an especially strong argument for adopting this approach, see Solomons (1986), chapters 11 and 12. Solomons quotes the then-Chairman of FASB who has said that 'the role of financial reporting is to provide information in assessing the relative returns and risks of various investments. Business managers, investors and creditors make those decisions: it is not a function of financial reporting to try to determine or influence their outcome' (Kirk, 1979). With this view, although accounting standard setters must be aware of the political pressures and the economic consequences associated with accounting standards and may have to bow to the pressures exerted by those who may be affected by accounting standards, they should not alter standards substantially for these reasons because this would be seen as injecting politics into accounting and as really destroying accounting self-regulation.

Solomons (1983, 1986) argues that accounting information should be neutral in the sense that it should not be biased towards a given outcome favouring any given section of society. He uses map making as an analogy and suggests there is little demand for non-neutral maps. With this view, accounting standards should be directed either at disclosing empirical items or at the provision of rules for measuring empirical phenomena. Any effects on society of reporting essentially empirical phenomena must not be allowed to militate against using the best measurement methods. Seeking to ameliorate such effects should not lie in the province of standard setters.

However, in contrast to maps, accounting statements comprise mainly non-empirical phenomena. Few accounting items can be observed in the real world. Many accounting theories are not hypotheses about empirical matters. Rather, they generally concern ideas originated by human beings. Debates about different measurement systems seem to concentrate not on their ability to measure items empirically but rather how useful they can be claimed to be to all of, or part of, society. It was argued earlier in this book that such arguments cannot be resolved by considering only empirical evidence, nor of course can they be advanced without reference to such evidence. Those who see accounting issues as political argue that such choices can be made only by considering which sectors of the community it is wished to favour. It is this need to make value judgements when making accounting choices which is argued to render accounting policy making political.

The history of United States and United Kingdom standards provides ample evidence of political activities of one type or another. The history of any recent controversial standards yields further evidence of this type of activity. These political activities in the United States of America seem, perhaps, more sophisticated and more comprehensive than most other countries—ranging from explicit lobbying, appeals to higher level authority, and the misrepresentation both of preferences and of the likely effects of accounting standards. Such activities can also be observed in other countries. If this view of accounting policy decisions as 'political' choices is accepted, the question arises as to whether public sector or private sector regulation of accounting reports is likely to deal best with these political issues, and with accounting reform generally. These matters are considered in the remainder of this chapter, commencing with public sector regulation.

The approach adopted will be comparative: we shall compare some of the strengths and weaknesses of public sector regulation with those of private sector regulation. Problems common to both regulatory systems will also be considered.

Government regulation: the advantages of public sector regulation of accounts

In democracies the usual view is that important social choices should be made by the appropriate legislative body. Such arrangements applied to accounting would reduce any questioning of the mandate of accounting policy makers to the level that is normally encountered by legislators. With this arrangement for making accounting choices, judgements concerning accounting matters would be made in the same way as society's other major value judgements. The problem of enforcing accounting reforms would also be minimised. Any difficulties experienced here would be similar to those encountered with any legislation. In promulgating accounting regulations the legislature would provide whatever penalties they felt necessary for non-compliance. Finally, any income distribution or wealth redistribution effects of accounting regulation would be considered by the highest representative bodies in the land.

Under present arrangements for non-legislative accounting regulation, standard setters and accounting policy makers generally have to allow these redistributive effects to fall where they may. Private sector organisations generally have no power or authority from society to ameliorate these effects. As unrepresentative bodies, they have no obvious right to seek to counter these effects. These weaknesses of non-public sector accounting regulation and the lack of authority of such policy making bodies may well cause major criticisms of standard setters. This may lead to non-compliance with the accounting recommendations and standards issued by private sector accounting policy makers.

The legislature is better equipped than existing standard setting bodies with tools to control these effects and attenuate their impact on any sector of society if this is desired. The legislature can counter any such effects using their powers of subsidy and taxation. Standard setting bodies have but minimal powers to alter or ameliorate the redistributive effects of their proposals. The only direct items of cost or benefit they can usually control is the cost imposed on the producers of accounts. The only other way such effects can be taken into account is by altering the substance of proposed standards so as to reduce or increase their effects on those parts of society it is wished to aid, or protect, from adverse effects. Such activities may have a cost in terms of distorting accounting standards away from what otherwise would be thought to improve the efficiency of resource allocation. Much of the debate about the 'economic consequences' or indirect effects of accounting standards concern where the benefits and costs of accounting standards should fall (See Zeff, 1978). The Government may be better able to meet legitimate arguments of this type without distorting the efficiency effects of accounting regulations by using its powers of taxation and subsidy. Further, these powers may enable the Government to deal better with any 'economic consequences' arguments concerning the effects of accounting regulations on the efficiency of resource allocation without altering what might otherwise be regarded as an accounting 'ideal'.

Taxation and subsidy powers can also be used to encourage the full-hearted acceptance of promulgated accounting requirements. This would seem to be in the minds of those who, for example, urged the acceptance of current cost accounting proposals for taxation purposes. In contrast, standard setters who wish to provide what many people see as an extra incentive for the acceptance of current cost accounting could only lobby Government. It would seem reasonable to assume that if accounting regulation was a matter for Government, packages of accounting reform and tax alterations would be easier both to evaluate and to introduce, if so desired. Accounting regulation by the legislature may also be less vulnerable to pressures from concerned parties. Government may not have to devote as many resources to obtaining consensus for proposed accounting reforms as do private sector standard setting bodies. Non-compliance and explicit criticisms by important organisations have often either put the survival of the various United States standard setting bodies in doubt, or helped to lead to their replacement by a reorganised body (Zeff, 1972). Legislative regulators seem less vulnerable to such pressure over accounting matters.

Similarly, Governments who command a reasonable majority in the legislature may promulgate accounting reforms which they desire without engaging in major and costly consensus seeking activity, though such reforms may be argued often to introduce party political influences into accounting. Governments may be able to forgo elements of those activities practised by private sector accounting bodies which may be ascribed to the wish to establish a mandate by explicitly showing that they consult extensively over all their proposals.

A final advantage of governmental accounting regulation is that the ultimate enforcement agency and appeal mechanism are those usual in democracies—the courts. This overcomes the criticisms levelled at private sector standard setting bodies either that they provide no ultimate appeal mechanism concerning extant accounting standards or that any appeals system which is available is not sufficiently independent.

Social choice difficulties

Critics of governmental activity have suggested that there are problems which even an ideally functioning legislative system cannot overcome. These difficulties spring from a wish to ascertain individual preferences and respect them in decision making. Such problems are also encountered by private sector decision making organisations which wish to aid society's welfare, and will be considered shortly from this perspective. Even if such preferences could be accurately determined, as indicated earlier in Chapter 10, there still exist major problems in choosing between alternatives. Arrow (1963) has shown that there exists no obvious social choice mechanism that fulfils simple requirements which are likely to be generally acceptable in a liberal society (see Mueller, 1989, chapter 20, for a fairly simple proof). This finding causes problems for both public sector accounting regulation and private sector standard setting and is one reason why it will be argued in Chapter 12 that those who seek a generally accepted conceptual framework for external accounting may have taken on an impossible task. The requirements on the mechanisms which might be used for making value judgements for society are fairly straightforward, though the proof that all existing social choice mechanisms cannot meet these requirements is subtle, as are those associated with efforts to relax these requirements (Sen, 1970; Mueller, 1989, chapter 20).

The proof of Arrow's theorem is well explained by Sen (1970) and Mueller (1989, chapter 20). Appendix 11.1 illustrates in an informal way how this proof proceeds. Knowledge of these matters is unnecessary for the purposes of this book. However, an understanding of the requirements which Arrow imposes on social choice systems is important. Failure of the choice mechanisms used for non-legislative accounting regulation to fulfil these conditions may lead to the criticism that such mechanisms are irredeemably flawed. The first requirement is that any entertained social choice mechanism should mean that no one, nor any group of people, can act dictatorially, or be able to force through wishes, irrespective of the preferences of the other members of society. Some writers have argued that the lack of general conduits to accounting standard setters and the ability of accounting policy makers to override the wishes of other members of the community to some degree mean that private sector standard setting procedures contain an element of dictatorship. Many of the endeavours of private sector policy makers to seek consensus can be seen as ways of attempting to assuage this criticism.

The second requirement is that decisions which represent a Pareto improvement (see Chapters 2 and 5) should be deemed acceptable by the choice mechanism. Such options improve the welfare of at least one member of society and harm no one else. There is little evidence that private sector standard setters consider themselves as involved in choices of this nature.

The third requirement is that any selection between alternatives should consider only the impact on social welfare of the acceptance of these alternatives. Thus, considerations irrelevant to the choice in mind should not affect the decision. This restricts the information which is to be considered by policy makers and probably requires superhuman restraint on the part of decision makers. Preferences expressed in making past decisions often impinge on current decisions. This is clearly the case in standard setting, where consistency between standards is often a declared aim. Arrow's requirement restricts decision makers to considering only preferences concerning the options upon which a decision is required. This excludes information that many would find useful in decision making. Consider the decision to continue to retain a service in the public sector or to privatise it. Attitudes to public sector services in general might well play an important part in such a decision in practice. Such a consideration would infringe the requirement that only preferences concerning the services under review should be considered.

Finally, Arrow suggests that the choice mechanism must allow all rational and logical preferences to be considered in the decision making process and it should allow them to be reflected as possible outcomes of the choice mechanism being utilised. He also requires that such choices must be transitive, both for individuals and society. This means that if policy Choice A is preferred to policy Choice B and Choice B is preferred to Choice C, then logically policy Choice A must be preferred to policy Choice C.

All known existing legislative systems infringe one or more of these requirements, at least for some decisions. For example, the usual majority voting system may infringe the requirement that all possible individual preferences can enter as inputs into the decision making system and can figure as the outcome of the decision process. Consider an adaptation of the above example, which involves a choice between a privately provided service and two types of public systems. One of these systems gives a high quality of service but entails high expenditure and the other requires only a low expenditure but yields a low quality service. Assume society consists of only three people, one rich, one poor and one of average wealth and income. Assume that the rich man always prefers the private service and that public provision only increases his taxes. The poor person is assumed always to opt for public provision but prefers low expenditure to high expenditure because of the impact of high taxes. The average person prefers the private service when the government provision of resources produces low quality services, but public sector provision if the resources devoted to it generate a high quality service. There is no determinate outcome to majority voting on such pairwise choices between options. Not all individual preferences can therefore emerge as an outcome to the decision process.[3] Resort to other voting systems seems to offer no solution to this problem (see Mueller, 1989, chapter 20).

The importance of Arrow's theorem for accounting and ways of overcoming the problems

That majority voting is generally accepted as a choice device by many societies suggests that Government does not need to be too concerned with its inability to fulfil all Arrow's requirements for social choice mechanisms. A similar failure by private sector policy makers may cause their mandate to be questioned. Such a criticism would seem difficult to refute or override by private sector policy makers. The effect of this criticism on private sector standard setting bodies will be considered again when the search for a generally accepted conceptual framework for accounting is considered in Chapter 12.

It has been argued that some choice problems may avoid the problem raised by Arrow for majority voting. Cushing (1977) has suggested this applies to some accounting problems. Such choices are those which involve issues where all prefer at least some of the commodity being offered. For example, all may prefer the disclosure of depreciation provisions but may differ concerning the amount of detail to be provided. Majority voting, and some other voting systems, do not infringe Arrow's requirements in these and some similar circumstances (all of which involve the existence of what are called single peaked preferences) (Sen, 1977). With such views, the level of disclosure chosen would be that preferred by the median voter.[4] This characterisation of choices concerning accounting items would not seem to apply to those choices which need to be considered by those who wish to solve more wide-ranging accounting problems, such as seeking a generally accepted conceptual framework (see Chapter 12).

There are a number of other ways of overcoming the problems caused by the Arrow theorem. These difficulties have been investigated in the social choice literature; see Sen (1970, pp. 47–55) and Mueller (1989, pp. 88–201). For example, the transitivity condition may be relaxed for societal choices by requiring transitivity only where options can be clearly ranked but not requiring this where indifference is exhibited. Transitivity can also be relaxed by requiring that preference rankings be of the nature that option X can be ranked only in terms of it being at least as good as option Y, even though a finer ranking is available. Both of these approaches may still encounter the problem of allowing dictatorial power to be manifested, though this power will now be spread more widely throughout the community. This approach may also mean that we are no longer able to select the best alternative in any decision because not all options are now completely ranked.

It has also been argued that the decision model in mind could be made more realistic if we dropped the requirement calling for the independence of irrelevant alternatives. Consider the problem of choosing which one item of accounting information to provide to two users of accounts. Strictly, we should continue to consider only preferences for each possible pair of items until the preferred item is selected. However, a more informed judgement may be made if we are aware of all the preferences of the two individuals. Assume that the accounting report users, A and B, have the preferences set out in Table 11.1, where the item on the left of the inequality sign is preferred. In an isolated pairwise comparison between only profits and debt information (possibility 1, Table 11.1), we might give equal weight to the two items. From inspecting the

Table 11.1 Preference of accounting report users

	A	B
Possibility 1	Debt > profits	Profits > debt
Possibility 2	Assets > debt	Assets > debt
Possibility 3	Debt > liquidity	Liquidity > debt

list of preferences we might feel that this is not the fairest arrangement. B quite clearly values debt information far less than any of the other options. Thus, we may feel that because of B's preferences we can rule out providing debt information. However, this conclusion involves interpersonal comparisons. Great discretion would be given to those making social choice decisions if they were allowed to make such comparisons.

Difficulties with the revelation of preferences

Policy makers, if they are to serve society, should seek ideally to ascertain individual preferences in some way in the absence of a well functioning market for a commodity. A major problem here is that there is no automatic incentive for individuals to reveal their true preferences for commodities not provided by the market. When normal goods are traded on an ideally functioning market, it is in your best interests to reveal your true demand if you wish to buy a good. Understating your demand at any price will mean that some of this demand will go unfulfilled. Excess demands will merely yield more goods than required without any obvious advantages and may increase future prices if others also adopt this strategy.

There may be incentives not to reveal your true preferences where goods are not supplied by a market. The funding of a publicly provided good will be spread amongst all consumers or all taxpayers. The level of the good provided will, therefore, depend overwhelmingly on other people's contributions to its financing. The amount of the good decided upon will, however, generally be available to all and be seen by an individual as not dependent on the finance provided personally. An individual can therefore expect to free ride on the provision that is eventually decided upon by society's policy makers. The individual therefore has every incentive to mis-state any willingness to pay for the good. Thus, it is usually argued that public goods will be underprovided by the Government if it relies on expression of individual preferences. This is because individuals will understate their preferences in case they have to pay for them, in the hope that others will not take this attitude. It is possible, however, that incorrectly revealed preferences could lead to overprovision.

Private sector accounting standards bodies can also be expected to run into the problem of incorrectly stated preferences. The existing system of paying for accounting information means that any number of those parties involved with the enterprise may expect to pay for the provision of accounting information. These groups of people could include consumers of enterprise products, managers, shareholders and the community (via any tax deductibility of enterprise expenses). The great majority of users of accounting statements can therefore expect to escape paying the cost of any additional information for which they reveal a preference. However, casual observation does not suggest the existence of a flood of unfulfilled demands for additional accounting information. This does not necessarily refute the above suggestions. The mechanism for making such demands is not clear with existing systems for the provision of accounting information. Uncoordinated individual demands are unlikely to be given much weight by accounting policy makers. In this setting, the few who can make effective demands will not be willing to bear the cost of making these demands where others may free ride on any information obtained.

Both the Government and private sector policy makers will have to solve the problems of misrepresentation of preferences if they wish to gauge preferences for accounting information. The technology for overcoming these problems is imperfect but the literature suggests that the Government is more likely to be able to extract true preferences than a private sector body, though Governments generally, perhaps, show little wish to get involved with such systems. The Government is likely to be able to ascertain preferences better because most systems for overcoming these problems rely on the provision of incentives to reveal true preferences via subsidies, or the imposition of penalties for misrepresentation by taxation (see Mueller, 1989, chapter 8).[5] Schemes not involving taxation and subsidy would seem to be no less complex and yield little more promise for aiding private sector accounting policy makers. One such scheme involves voting procedures. This scheme, which has been called 'voting by veto' allows the individual to veto that one scheme suggested by others which the individual regards as most objectionable. It can be shown that this procedure selects as the winning choice the proposal which yields the highest total benefits when the proposal's benefits are shared equally amongst all.

The mechanisms available for obtaining the true revelation of preferences seem rather complex. This problem renders it difficult to believe that such schemes lie within the capacity of, at least, non-governmental bodies. Equally, it is difficult to believe that the above schemes are really practical. Thus the correct revelation of preferences remains a major problem for both Government regulators and for private sector accounting policy makers. One strength that legislative regulation has over private sector accounting standard setting is that a Government with a reasonable majority can, at least to some degree, dispense with such detailed and complex procedures to ascertain 'true' preferences, at least where detailed accounting reform is not regarded as a major political issue. It is not clear that private sector accounting policy bodies have sufficient authority to dispense with consultation, imperfect as it is. Indeed, detailed consultation procedures are one element which some see as a way of strengthening the mandate of standard setting bodies.

Some problems of the legislative regulation of accounting

There are clear potential difficulties with legislative control of accounting reform. Technical accounting issues may be decided on the basis of the political views of the party in power at any time. It has also been argued that the low perceived political importance which would be accorded to accounting matters would not allow accounting to obtain scarce legislative time. Thus the legislature may be generally expected to rubber stamp the ideas of interested civil servants and those who have influence on them and on politicians. That this type of civil-servant-dominated regulation of accounting is better for society than private sector regulation is doubted by many commentators in the accounting profession.

Even advocates of legislative accounting regulation admit that this process is lengthy and lacking in flexibility, even where an item is judged of sufficient importance to obtain legislative time. Difficulties in getting items on to the legislative timetable and through the legislature may discourage efforts to change established accounting regulations and may lead to rigidity. However, Von Wysocki (1983) argues that the German experience of dealing with accounting problems in this way produces very similar outcomes to those achieved by other systems. In his opinion, therefore, the results of the process are certainly no worse than those of other systems.

Some of the above problems with legislative regulation of accounting can be overcome by the legislature delegating most, if not all, accounting decisions to some agency with more or less government backing. This is similar to the position in the United States, where Congress delegates the power to set accounting requirements in certain areas to a number of agencies, notably the SEC. Similarly, in Australia, standard setting is delegated to a review board. Standards which this board issue are given legislative backing.

These agencies may be of various types and their direct relation with Government may also be of a wide variety. Generally, with this system of accounting regulation, agencies are given some delegated responsibility by the legislature for laying down the accounting requirements for major companies. Some possible strengths and weaknesses of such agencies relative to private sector regulation form the subject of the next section.

The case for a Securities and Exchange Commission

In some ways it is surprising that more countries have not taken to using Government agencies for accounting regulation. Those agencies that do exist generally arise from a wish not to rely generally on self-regulation by the securities industries. Any interest in accounting statements by such agencies is but one of their concerns. United States and Australia provide examples, though other countries also have some degree of governmental agency regulation of accounting reports.

Regulation of the securities industry is the major task of the SEC. It regulates the format of accounting statements filed by companies registered with it for the purposes of being listed on stock exchanges. It also issues its own accounting requirements in the form of so-called Accounting Series Releases (Benston, 1976, pp. 238–242). The SEC has, however, generally chosen to accept for their purposes those accounting principles generally accepted by the American accounting profession and it accepts accounting standards promulgated by the FASB (see Sprouse, 1983). The division of responsibility between the FASB and the SEC can be summarised as that the FASB is concerned with measurement standards and the SEC generally restricts itself to disclosure matters. However, this division may be difficult to maintain in practice because measurement issues often require additional disclosures. Similarly, new disclosures may also require measurement problems to be solved.

At first sight the advantages of using an agency would seem considerable. There should be no doubt about such an agency's mandate, which can always be confirmed in the courts. Ideally, the agency has the clear and explicit backing of the legislature from which its power clearly springs. It might, therefore, be argued that many of the advantages claimed above for legislative regulation of accounting should also accrue to public regulation by agencies controlled by the legislature.

A governmental agency of the character of the SEC should be able to approach accounting regulation not as an end in itself, but as part of its overall responsibilities. It may, therefore, be able to take a wider view than bodies concentrating solely on accounting standard setting. There would be little reason to expect its technical expertise to be less strong than that of alternative private sector accounting standard setting bodies. The employment of qualified professional staff would help overcome the problems which a lack of expertise is said to cause the legislature when dealing with technical legislation. Agencies of this type should be able to promulgate accounting regulations in a more speedy and efficient way than legislative bodies.

Agency regulation may indeed seem to have some advantage over legislative regulation. Agency regulation may offer reasonable methods of regulation without the large cost and severe disruption associated with the imposition of taxes and subsidies which would be necessary for a full-blown attempt to regulate accounting reports using the legislature. Giving power to prescribe the contents of published accounting statements and the necessary disciplinary powers to ensure compliance to an agency might be thought to provide as feasible an alternative to legislative regulation as can be reasonably afforded.

An agency may be more easily seen as independent than any self-regulating body drawing the majority of its members from the profession. It may also be seen as more explicitly accountable to society than private sector bodies of this type.

Some disadvantages of agency regulation

An SEC approach has not commanded substantial approval in all counties, not least in the United Kingdom. In the view of some commentators this is because of a desire to defend entrenched interests. However, the experience in some countries and *a priori* speculation suggests that the system may suffer from a number of defects. Some of these possible problems will be reviewed here. The likelihood that these defects may also be manifested by private sector standard setting bodies will also be investigated. The first potential disadvantage of agency regulation is that much of the agency's activity may be seen as arbitrary. Although such agencies would normally be set up by statute, this legislation may not be sufficiently detailed to constrain completely the staff of the agency in their actions. Nor can the legislature be expected to delineate completely the underlying principles and philosophy that the agency should utilise in its tasks. Benston (1976, pp. 241–253) has argued that the SEC in America has been a conservative force in the accounting area and that it has in its judgements often acted in its own best interests. It is certainly difficult to believe that the rulings of such agencies based on extant accounting theory can be any less arbitrary than those of private sector bodies. Moreover, the agency rulings may have more authority than their private sector counterparts and such agencies may, therefore, be more able to enforce arbitrary rulings.

There is a good deal of evidence that such agencies are susceptible to political pressure. In the United States of America, for example, both Congress and the SEC have been unwilling to abstain from threats and sometimes actions to override the pronouncements of private sector regulators, including the FASB, concerning accounting standards which the SEC are pledged to accept as definitive elements of generally accepted accounting principles (GAAP) in the United States. The FASB's concern with 'due process' and its attempt to seek a generally agreed conceptual framework might be seen as examples of the actions which public sector agencies could take to attempt to reduce political pressure and strengthen their authority in the face of challenges from sister regulatory organisations and superior bodies.

There will usually exist a large number of governmental agencies who may be lobbied to overturn proposed actions by any other agency when these can be argued to impinge on their own domains. Further restrictions in the accounting sphere in the United States of America on the SEC arise from the ever-present possibility, which has been an actuality more than once, of intervention by the legislature. It is a matter of judgement whether such agencies are more susceptible to lobbying than the legislature itself. In the United Kingdom, lobbying and other challenges would seem directed more heavily towards agency subordinates than to the legislature.

It is not so much actual intervention by superior bodies that restricts the freedom of subordinate agencies; it is rather the knowledge that those discontented with or jealous of an agency's activities may seek to challenge them, using more authoritative bodies. The concern by the FASB to be seen to use procedures which are neutral between individuals and its search for a strong conceptual framework can be seen as defensive actions to protect it from potential and actual challenges. All responses of this type take considerable time and resources and are likely to retard the agency's progress.

Most of these problems would seem likely to be encountered by private sector standard setting systems. Indeed, it can be argued that attacks are more easily mounted against bodies with no authoritative mandate and are less easy to repulse. Actual attacks on private sector standard setting bodies such as the ASC would, however, suggest that some importance is given to their outputs. It is also argued in the literature that both public and private sector agencies are susceptible to charges of inefficiency and to 'capture' by those who are supposed to be under the control of the agencies. There is a large body of literature which speculates that the phenomenon of 'Government or administrative failure' is as likely as market failure.

Judgements between the benefits of using the market or the administrative system thus require complex cost/benefit analysis. It may be suspected that these are at present beyond our capacity. Many case studies of administrative action suggest that all the results of these activities cannot be said to aid the achievement of social welfare obviously (for a general summary see Jordan, 1972; Posner, 1974).

There is little reason to believe that this finding is unlikely to apply to accounting regulators. It has been argued that failures to improve social welfare by agencies are due only to agency inefficiency. Others seeking to explain the conduct of agencies suggest first that the legislature is not necessarily very rational in the charges it places on administrative agencies. Secondly, they argue that the legislature may require the agency to attempt the impossible. An agency response in the face of imposed tasks of these types is to do the 'best' it can. The incentive to achieve even this may be weak, because it may be difficult to gauge the achievement of success where results depend on bargaining with interested parties, and because the interest of the legislature in the agency's results may wane over time. The usual reasons put forward for expecting the agency to be as efficient as it can may seem to be weak. The first view is usually that the staff of the agency want increased salaries and promotion, and therefore will be no less diligent than private sector employees. Secondly, it is argued that an agency accountable to the legislature will need to get its budget renewed regularly. It will thus have an incentive to show its masters that it is proceeding efficiently.

These views for expecting efficiency by public sector agencies would seem to apply equally to many private sector bodies charged with regulating accounting. However, the relatively small size of private sector bodies means that the staff of such bodies have easier access to the chief policy makers and may therefore work harder to give a good impression. Further, the ultimate superiors of such bodies are more diffuse than the legislature; therefore, irrational and impossible demands can be more easily ignored than, perhaps, they can by public sector regulators.

The capture of agencies

It is doubtful whether private regulators are any less susceptible to 'capture' by those who are supposed to be regulated than are public sector agencies. The first element in the general argument for expecting this capture by the regulatees is that the regulation is an economic good like any other and will, therefore, be supplied to those who value it most. It is argued that those who place a high value on regulation are those who cannot ensure in other ways, such as via cartels, that their industry will do what they think is in their own best interests. Those who wish to obtain a regulatory regime which performs in their perceived best interests need to be able either to cause difficulties to those with the power to regulate and to determine the type of regulation to be imposed, or to have something the regulators want (votes, for example).

This theory as it stands would seem to have some relevance to the accounting area. There may be reasons why a number of parties in accounting might expect to achieve benefits from regulation which cannot be obtained in other ways, such as by forming cartels. Firms of auditors cannot enter explicitly into plans which operate in their industry's best interests without putting their independence in question. Those who prepare accounting reports would have difficulties in forming a cartel of their own because of the cost of doing this and the difficulty of policing any cartel. The demands of such a cartel of preparers of accounts may also be inimical to business success in other areas of enterprise activities. Similarly, some groups of users such as investment analysts may share similar desires concerning accounting but not with regard to other matters. However, the price these groups can extract from the regulators may be high. They can make creditable threats to cause substantial difficulties to the regulators. Their favourable opinions of what the regulating body desires to achieve may be important in successfully obtaining these aims.

The general empirical evidence for the capture of regulators by those who are being regulated is by no means conclusive. The theory is held to explain why regulation, at least in the United States, covers all types of industries and not just those where there is danger of the exercise of monopoly power or where it is thought *a priori* that there is the possibility of heavy external costs being imposed on the community. It also explains why regulation often seems to take the form which the industry concerned would favour.

If this theory is accepted, one might expect accounting regulatory agencies to be 'captured', at least to a degree. Many commentators would argue that auditors may have a preference for a clear ruling as to the best accounting practice for each controversial accounting problem. The theory suggests that private sector standard setting bodies might, if anything, be more susceptible to 'capture' than a public sector agency charged with accounting regulation. Indeed, this criticism was levelled directly at the American Accounting Principles Board (APB), an earlier standard setting body; the majority of its membership comprised the senior partners of the 'Big Eight' accounting firms. This criticism has been argued to have contributed to the demise of the APB. Sprouse (1983), the then-Vice-Chairman of the FASB, places considerable emphasis for the survival of the FASB on its more explicit independence from auditors and the preparers of accounts, and on the perception of this by the business community (see, however, the Metcalf Report 1977).

Some empirical studies have sought to discover characteristics of the voting behaviour of standard setters. They concentrate on the frequently expressed concern, especially in the United States of America, which was introduced above, that those standard setters with existing, or previous, affiliations with large auditing firms have dominated voting on various United States standard setting bodies (see Newman, 1981a, b; Selto and Grove, 1982). A concern to test empirically hypotheses about how individuals and entities will react to proposed and actual accounting standards is part of that school of accounting research called positive accounting theory, which is reviewed in Chapter 13.

With regard to voting studies, the approach used concentrates on predicting, at a fairly abstract level, the voting behaviour of decision makers. The focus is on predicting the likely formation of coalitions of decision makers (Newman 1981a, b). It is the formulation of these coalitions which is of interest, not the objectives which such coalitions may seek to achieve. The results of using this approach in accounting have suggested that those affiliated in some ways with large audit firms appear to possess disproportionate powers in standard setting. However, the results of such studies may be very sensitive to the assumptions used to model this behaviour. Moreover, the evidence obtained by looking at specific decisions made by American standard setters does not indicate that any power that exists has been exercised.

Regulation by bureaucracy

The preceding analysis indicates that regulation by governmental agencies such as the SEC in the United States of America could be expected to share many strengths and weaknesses with private sector accounting standard setting bodies. In the United Kingdom, it is at present difficult to believe that the imposition of such a public sector agency is a feasible alternative to the system of self-regulation within what is a fairly complex legislative framework since the Companies Act 1981. The disruption costs and the likely lengthy time scale required to render a 'Securities and Exchange Commission' acceptable to the United Kingdom financial community make such efforts unlikely in the short run.

The demands for a British Securities and Exchange Commission also seem to be cyclical. There is presently little overt demand. The creation of such a body is not particularly high on the agenda of the political parties, if one discounts threats by politicians aimed at obtaining improved results from self-regulation by the accounting profession. If other financial centres find this solution attractive, it is likely that the United Kingdom will have to follow suit. A Securities and Investment Board has recently been set up in the United Kingdom to regulate much of the securities industry. Although it is too early to speculate, it is likely to move into accounting regulation, at least in order to facilitate the discharge of its other functions.

The earlier parts of this chapter sought to compare the strengths and weaknesses of accounting standard setting by the private sector with those of alternative public sector mechanisms for regulating accounting reports. The next main section of this chapter looks at one or two difficulties unique to private sector standard setting.

Specific problems of private sector regulation

The first of these problems is that of showing from where comes the authority of standard setters to lay down 'quasi-laws' affecting a wide range of people.

The authority of standard setters

A clear understanding of the mandate given to private sector standard setters also indicates the likely strength of the enforcement powers which it is claimed they can exercise. As has already been pointed out, the perceived mandate and authority of private sector standard setting bodies differs from country to country, being perhaps strongest for certain activities of the Canadian standard setting body and very nearly non-existent in continental Europe.

As a more detailed example we will discuss the authority of standard setters in the United Kingdom. Here, until recently, any authority given by the British Government to ASC has been implicit. However, a fairly radical reform of the standard setting process was introduced in 1990, following a report sponsored by the accountancy profession (The Dearing Report, 1988). The Companies Act 1989, as part of this process of setting up a more authoritative standard setting body in the United Kingdom, did place a duty on corporate directors to follow accounting standards. This was the first mention of accounting standards in United Kingdom legislation. The other major changes to accounting standard setting in the United Kingdom in 1990 moved the administrative arrangements for this nearer the United States model. The Financial Reporting Council (FRC) is now responsible for raising funds for the Accounting Standards Board and exercises a general policy and supervisory role over the ASB. It has the power to mount cases against individual companies who are not complying with the provisions of the Companies Acts to enforce these provisions by rewriting the accounts. The ASB is now much smaller than its predecessor, the ASC (with some nine rather than over 20 members) and the whole system is much more independent of the accounting profession. The ASB can now issue standards in its own right whereas the ASC had to obtain the agreement of all the sponsoring accounting bodies (of which there are six). The Chairman of the ASB is paid a commercial salary, as are its staff, who will be augmented relative to those employed by ASC. There are also provisions for paying the members of the ASB and some of those with executive responsibility on the FRC. In contrast, the members of the ASC were unpaid.

Both the profession and the Dearing Committee wanted a stronger statutory backing to be given to accounting standards. This was to be accomplished by imposing the general presumption that accounting standards would have the backing of the courts in any legal proceedings, unless departures were necessary to give a true and fair view. The Government refused to give this additional authority on the grounds that it would amount to giving statutory backing to accounting standard setting in the UK and to attenuating the desired self-regulatory character of the standard setting. The full details of all the changes to accounting regulation in the United Kingdom have not yet emerged. For a description of the suggested reforms which led to these and other changes, see the Dearing Report (Dearing, 1988). It is far too early to say whether these changes will increase the authority of United Kingdom standard setters.

No support has yet been forthcoming from the United Kingdom judiciary for accounting standards, though a recent judgement in a lower court does suggest that such support may be forthcoming (see *Lloyd Cheyham & Co.* vs *Little John & Co.*, 1985). Respected legal opinion does suggest that complying with accounting standards yields evidence of the provision of a 'true and fair' view. Opponents to British standard setting endeavours suggest that any lack of detailed Government interference with private sector standards (though such influence has increased since the passing of the 1981 Act) represents indifference to these activities rather than any implied approval. They point also to the Government's willingness to override standard setting efforts, especially in the price change accounting debate, as evidence of a lack of Government backing for private sector standard setting activities in general. However, recent British law does show some signs of codifying proven standards into the law. Current company law although constraining standard setters, perhaps severely in some areas, also does seem to make the profession the repository of the 'true and fair' view, the dominant statutory requirement for accounting reports contained in the law. This legislation suggests that there is a role for the profession in giving guidance on the determination of a 'true and fair' view. A major uncertainty with the law is how the European Court of Justice, which is the ultimate court in the European Community, will respond to accounting cases and how it will seek to balance the many differing European views of accounting, especially of the different meanings of 'true and fair' in the European Community.

More generally, in some countries where statutorily regulated accounts are not the norm, the law does seem to perceive a place for private sector activity to fill in the detail of the legal framework—for example, in laying down generally accepted accounting principles in the United States of America, and by determining what is necessary in order to show a true and fair view in the United Kingdom.

It seems reasonable and efficient that any guidance by private sector standard setters should be given in as an authoritative way as possible. Some authority is given by the business community in a number of countries. Standards, backed by stock exchanges and other influential bodies including the professional accounting organisations, would seem a sensible way of giving this guidance considerable weight. Additional weight is given in those countries—including Australia, New Zealand, the United Kingdom (in some cases) and the United States of America—where the enterprises which do not comply with private sector accounting standards may have their accounts qualified for this reason by auditors. In less serious cases auditors may merely publicly note any non-compliance in their opinion. Whether this type of authority is backed up with sufficient enforcement powers is still an unsettled question, at least in the United Kingdom. Here, such disciplinary powers that are supposed to exist, e.g. the non-listing by the stock exchange and disciplining of accountants by their professional bodies, have not really been invoked, at least publicly. It is sometimes argued that the use of informal enforcement methods by authoritative figures in the business community is sufficient to guarantee compliance. It is very difficult to evaluate this view. Supporters of the endeavours of private sector standard setters often claim to be satisfied with the existing level of compliance, whereas critics are less sanguine. The search by standard setting bodies for ways to enhance their mandates can, therefore, be expected to continue. Some methods of doing this include the use of wide ranging consultation, which encompasses the wide circulation of exposure drafts for comment and the holding of public hearings, and the adoption of many of the aspects of the 'due process' system. Two other major strategies are available to private sector standard setters wishing to enhance their mandates. One of these strategies is to seek a generally accepted conceptual framework for accounting. This process, as illustrated by the FASB's search for such a framework, represents one method of generating accounting theory. This approach will be dealt with in Chapter 12. The remainder of this chapter considers the strengths and weaknesses of consensus seeking as a strategy which may be adopted by standard setters who wish to reinforce their authority.

Consensus seeking

For the reasons given above, private sector agencies, and especially the ASC, and now the ASB, have had to devote their attention to getting voluntary standards accepted by the preparers of accounting reports and by the practising sector of the accounting profession. Self-regulating accounting bodies have, therefore, to attempt to achieve a consensus for each standard of those who have the power to ignore a standard if they wish. This explains the concern of the ASC and other standard setting bodies over increasing their enforcement powers. Sprouse (1983), the then-Vice-Chairman of the American Financial Accounting Standards Board, argues that this body is backed by other bodies with sufficient enforcement power. This has not stopped the FASB from engaging in activities such as seeking a generally accepted conceptual framework (see Chapter 12) and increasing their explicit use of 'due process' procedures. Such activities can be argued to strengthen their authority and, at least, their informal enforcement powers.

Without sufficient enforcement powers, it is difficult to see how a private sector standards body can avoid tempering its suggested standards so that they achieve acceptance by those influential sectors of the community who, by being non-cooperative for any length of time, could put the future of the private sector standard setting body in doubt. Users of accounting reports and many others affected by such reports seem not to have this power and, indeed, tend to go unrepresented in the deliberations of private sector standard setting bodies.

The natural reaction of standard setters in a political environment is to seek to damp down controversy by seeking consensus. This desire to achieve consensus is heightened because strong challenges to standard setting bodies often seem to threaten their survival. The history of standard setting in the United States suggests that the reaction of the accounting profession to challenges to a given type of standard setting mechanism is one of disillusion which leads to reconstituting the standard setting body. British standard setting has recently come near to being completely reorganised. There is little doubt that much of the British financial press and other influential authorities do see major challenges to the British standard setting body as putting its future in doubt.

The problems with seeking to avoid controversy by placing the emphasis in standard setting on acceptability are well known. A consensus may result in standards lacking intellectual rigour. Alternatively, a compromise may require that a number of treatments for a given problem be allowed, not all of which may be desirable. A standard may be fashioned to appeal to those who have the greatest bargaining power. This may make standard setters liable to the criticism that they have acquiesced to the view of one or more influential parties in society (Moonitz, 1974). The standard setting system may, therefore, be seen as unfair to some sections of the community. Alternatively, the search for a consensus may cause the standard setting process to become stagnant or result in a log-jam because of the delays introduced by seeking consensus. The only obvious ways out of these problems are either to attempt to give the standard setting body sufficient authority to be able to overcome the influence of powerful objectors or to encourage the government to become more involved in accounting regulation.

What might be called the theory of coalitions (the theory of games; Luce and Raiffa, 1957) suggests that the rewards in seeking consensus are likely to be fairly small unless the environment is similar to that required for perfect markets.

The theory of games does provide a warning for those who would urge accounting standard setters to seek consensus as a means of getting their reforms accepted. The conditions for such a consensus to work successfully are that the outcome of the consensus operation is first Pareto optimal. Secondly, the outcome must offer all those in the coalition, or consensus group, at least what they could achieve on their own by enforcing the *status quo* or the action which could be obtained solely by their own actions. This condition must also be satisfied for all possible coalitions which can upset the reformer's efforts. Many attempts to obtain consensus do not satisfy these conditions and are thus likely to fail (Kreps, 1990, pp. 355–356).

All the above arguments suggest that consensus seeking by accounting policy makers in the private sector cannot be relied upon to solve their problems, nor is it likely that such efforts will result in the best that can be done for society.

A final weakness of the need for private sector bodies to obtain consensus is that it may encourage too much malleability by standard setters. Critics see flexibility in the face of comments as pandering to powerful preparers, auditors and users.

The progress of some proposed standards does support this view. The history of standard setting concerning research and development accounting and depreciation in the United Kingdom and the Oil and Gas standard in the United States of America are often quoted as examples of overflexibility in the face of criticism. (Contrast the papers by Lafferty and by Slimmings and Watts in Leach and Stamp, 1981.)

Some advantages of consensus seeking

The utility and importance of seeking consensus for accounting issues, even given the above problems, should not be underestimated, at least for private sector standard setting bodies. Bargaining towards a consensus is a fundamental way of proceeding in the face of conflict between individuals. Cushing (1977) has suggested that the generally perceived view in the United States of America that standard setting should remain in the private sector has eased the acceptance of controversial standards. The hope is that the absence of explicit disagreements or conflicts will help repulse any possible governmental intervention. The activities of standard setting bodies suggest that this point has been well taken. The emphasis, for example, in the United States of America and the United Kingdom on 'due process' can be seen in this light, as can the very considerable consultation mechanisms utilised by these bodies. But it is difficult to see that existing standard setting bodies are sufficiently representative in the political sense to purport to be able to generate a political consensus.

Conclusions on accounting regulation

The aim of this chapter was to present critically various views which adopt an economic perspective concerning accounting regulation so that an informed judgement can be reached between the various possible systems of accounting regulation. We adopted a comparative stance when reviewing the likely strengths and weaknesses of accounting regulation by the private sector and by a variety of governmental regulatory mechanisms. The commonality of many of the problems encountered by both types of regulation was emphasised. The contents of this chapter might suggest that at least a minimum of legislative control of accounting has a number of advantages for laying down the framework in which accounting policy makers should work. Most commentators who support such a view would feel that such a legislative role needs to be fleshed out by other bodies. It is unlikely that legislative efforts can deal with all accounting problems in sufficient detail.

All the likely methods for the organising of the necessary subordinate bodies have advantages and disadvantages. One way of proceeding would be to attempt to undertake a cost/benefit analysis of the results likely to be obtained by the alternative methods of organising accounting policy making.

It might be thought from this chapter that the lack of political authority and the difficulties of consensus seeking make private sector standard setting a rather weak instrument for accounting regulation. The contents of this chapter may also lead to predictions of future difficulties for private sector standard setting, though many commentators would regard this as a far too pessimistic view of the future of standard setting.

The next chapter considers the advantages and disadvantages of a generally agreed conceptual framework in aiding regulatory decision making and in helping to improve the authority of the opinions of private sector standard setters.

Chapter summary

The introduction explained why we are dealing with accounting regulation at this stage in the book. It was argued that accounting choices based on accounting theories and theoretical approaches can be expected to have substantial effects on various sectors of society. Each accounting theory therefore should ideally be reviewed in the context of the environment in which the theory might be used. The introduction indicated that these issues are dealt with at a general level in this chapter.

The first major part of this chapter reviewed the various regimes used to regulate external accounting in the practical world. Most of these mechanisms feature both statutory regulation and self-regulation by the profession, though the emphasis between these varies between countries.

The perceived need in most countries to regulate external accounting was suggested to arise because of the perceived societal consequences of the form and contents of accounting reports. Accounting information was said to affect differentially a number of sectors of society. It was suggested that those involved in standard setting were beginning to see that their activities were not just technical but also had a political dimension. The concern in the United States was said to be how to deal with what have been called the economic consequences of standard setting, whilst resisting the pressures to ameliorate such consequences in order to avoid introducing 'politics' into accounting. A second main part of the chapter looked at public sector accounting regulation and compared this with the self-regulation of accounting by the profession.

Some of the advantages of public sector accounting regulation were then presented. These were said to include the fact that accounting choices would be made in the same way as society's other important social choices and by those with a clear mandate, who could lay down clear penalties for non-compliance. A number of tools for dealing with any redistribution effects generated by accounting reforms are available to public sector policy makers but not to private sector accounting policy makers. Public sector authorities may not have to spend so much time and resources on obtaining consensus as do private sector standard setters.

It was then argued that both private and public accounting policy makers may face major problems resulting from the social choice aspects of accounting regulation. The first of these difficulties concerned the problem raised by Arrow that no known social choice mechanism satisfies some simple requirements likely to commend themselves to a liberal society. It was suggested that private sector accounting policy making seems to infringe or ignore most of these criteria. Any of these difficulties experienced by public sector regulators may be ignored by a powerful Government but similar criticisms levelled at private sector policy makers are more difficult to overcome.

A number of technical suggestions for overcoming these problems, especially in an accounting context, were considered and found unlikely to produce general solutions to the difficulties.

The other major problem facing all types of accounting policy regulators and discussed in this chapter was that of ascertaining preferences for various options. It was suggested that mis-statement of preferences is likely where a commodity is not provided by a well functioning market. Methods for discovering preferences in these circumstances are generally thought to require powers to tax and to subsidise and therefore to favour public sector regulation. This second part of the chapter was concluded by considering some problems of accounting regulation by statute.

It was suggested that many of the problems could be overcome by delegating the issuance of accounting regulations to an agency such as the SEC. Such agencies normally have a clear mandate and approach accounting regulation as part of their wider tasks of regulating the securities industry. It was argued that agency regulation may be less costly and more flexible than regulation by the legislature. Disadvantages of this approach were said to include the likelihood of arbitrary action and susceptibility to political and other pressures. A strong agency may be thought to be more likely to be able to resist these pressures than private sector regulators. Charges against accounting regulatory agencies of inefficiencies and the possibility of take-over by those who are supposed to be regulated were then considered. Although these charges are generally levelled against public sector agencies, they would seem equally likely to apply to similar private sector bodies. It was argued that there was a good *prima facie* case for expecting that some elements of the business community would seek to capture regulatory agencies in accounting, whether private or public sector.

The third major part of this chapter considered two problems which seem unique to private sector accounting policy makers. The first is to demonstrate from where accrues the mandate for such policy makers to lay down 'quasi laws' affecting a wide range of people. It was suggested that in the United Kingdom this mandate comes from the power to give guidance in the determination of what is a true and fair view. More generally, the authority for private sector regulators has been argued to come from a need to flesh out whatever framework is laid down by the legislature. It was said that most private sector regulators seek to enhance their mandates by a variety of means including the use of elements of the due process system and widespread consultation. Two major methods of providing standard setters with additional authority are searching for a conceptual framework and seeking to generate consensus concerning accounting standards. The conceptual framework approach is reviewed in the next chapter where it is regarded as an approach for generating accounting theories (see Chapter 12).

The second major problem facing private sector standard setters is that of obtaining consensus for their accounting standards. It was argued that such an approach is natural for those who seek to damp down controversy. The well known problems with this approach were reiterated. Against this, it was suggested that there are clear advantages in consensus seeking.

Finally , some of the conclusions on accounting regulation contained in this chapter were reviewed. Here, it was suggested that the lack of political authority and the difficulties of consensus seeking rendered private sector standard setting a rather weak instrument for accounting regulation, though this may be a far too pessimistic view.

Notes

1. This chapter relies heavily on, and represents a development of, Bromwich (1985, chapters 5 and 6).

2. It is not intended to describe these debates in detail; many of them are well described in the literature. For a British example see Hope and Briggs (1982). An earlier American example is given in Horngren (1973).

3. The outcome of using a majority voting system for pairs of options for this problem depends on the order in which the issues are put to the electorate. Some preferences can therefore never emerge as the winner. In a choice between a private system and a public one with low expenditure, the private system is selected by the rich and the averagely wealthy. In a choice between private and public provision with high expenditure, the latter is preferred by the poor person and the person of average wealth. In the context of the choice between a public system with high and low expenditure, low expenditure wins, preferred by the poor and the rich. The result of such an election with majority voting may be indeterminate because if any one proposal were suggested, the loser could seek to achieve an alternative proposal. This could be done by forming a coalition to seek a further election with the other member of society whom, although voting for the winning option in the original election, would actually prefer another alternative not offered in that original election.

4. Consider a society with three members, of whom one prefers minimum accounting disclosure, one is a moderate disclosurer and one is a full disclosurer. Now consider three levels of depreciation disclosure—a minimum level, a moderate level and a fuller level—to be voted upon in pairs. With majority voting, moderate disclosure, which will be preferred by the middle voter, will get two votes (being those of the moderate and the full disclosurers) relative to minimum disclosure. It will also get two votes relative to full disclosure (the moderate and minimum disclosurers).

5. For example, one system works by attempting to minimise the difference between the sum of the values placed upon a public good by individuals (expressed in money) and its price (if any). This difference is to be funded by lump-sum taxation. The taxation charge for each individual is computed in the following way. The sum of all money votes, except for those of the individual in mind, is obtained and a hypothetical decision taken. The sum is then computed again, now including the valuation in money terms placed on the good by the individual originally left out of the earlier computation. If there is a new outcome, a tax is then levied on this individual equal to the net gains which would have been obtained by the others from what was the preferred option without the additional vote. The gains are

described as net in the sense that they are reckoned for a given choice by summing the gains of those in favour of the existing choice less the gains not achieved by those who favour other options.

Under this type of system, each voter has an incentive to declare true preferences. An individual will not overstate perceived benefits because this would render him or her liable to pay taxes when his or her vote changes the preferences of the community. Understatement does not pay because it may mean forgoing a preferred choice result, for which the costs in terms of taxes will never be greater than the benefits accruing from the individual's desired policy.

Appendix 11.1: Arrow's possibility theorem

This appendix sketches the proof of Arrow' s possibility theorem. The aim should be to obtain the general flavour of the ideas in order to appreciate the importance and strength of Arrow's findings for, at least, private sector standard setting. The presentation is not meant to be rigorous nor does it provide the shortest possible explanation (see Mueller, 1989; Sen, 1970).

Arrow's conclusion

Arrow (1963) shows that no system for making social choices can satisfy five conditions—Pareto optimality, transitivity, irrelevant alternatives, the condition that all options may be chosen as the outcome, and no dictatorship—which it seems reasonable to place on such systems in a liberal society (see pp. 258–9). Arrow proves that no social choice mechanism can satisfy all the five conditions indicated in the chapter. The illustration given here proceeds by showing that, given the satisfaction of any four conditions, the fifth condition must be violated. Here we shall assume that conditions of Pareto optimality, transitivity, irrelevant alternatives, and the condition that all options may be chosen as the outcome, are satisfied. We shall illustrate the proof by showing that, given these four conditions, there must be a dictator if we are to obtain a definite choice from the social choice mechanism being used. The four assumptions we are assuming are satisfied are used implicitly in the proof to allow us to examine the outcome of a given choice without looking directly at society's preferences for this choice.

Decisive groups

For all choices, the largest possible decisive set is the whole of society. If all in society prefer X to Y, then so will society. That is, for pairwise choices,

If $X_i > Y_i$ for all i in I, then $X_s > Y_s$

where the subscript i indexes an individual in a society comprised of I individuals and the subscript s indexes society's preferences. The inequality sign here indicates strict preferences and signifies that option X is shown preferred to option Y.

Here the whole of society is decisive. This is the largest possible decisive set. A smaller set than this may be decisive. For example, there may be a set of people (L) such that if they choose X > Y then so will (or must) society, even if all others in society (R) are indifferent between X and Y choices ($X_r = Y_r$). This can be written formally as:

the set L is decisive when

If $X_l > Y_l$ then $X_s > Y_s$ even though $X_r = Y_r$ for all r in R, where r is not in L.

But such a set may not be the smallest decisive set. This set is that whose pairwise choice wins the day even though all others prefer the alternative outcome. This can be written as:

The set K is the smallest decisive set for a given choice

If $X_k > Y_k$ then $X_s > Y_s$ even though $Y_r > X_r$ where r is not in K.

We now divide the smallest decisive set for our X or Y choice into two smaller non-decisive subsets J and P, where J contains only one individual (j) and P contains all the other members of K.

Z and X choices

Using the above definitions and preference assumptions, we now intend to see whether a societal choice between options Z and X, where Z is a new option, can emerge without breaching Arrow's conditions. We will first make some preliminary assumptions. We will assume that group P prefers Z to X $(Z_p > X_p)$ Z to Y $(Z_p > Y_p)$ and that individual J prefers Z to Y $(Z_j > Y_j)$ and that J prefers X to Z $(X_j > Z_j)$.

In order to give as much information as possible we also consider the choices of that part of society which is not in K, the decisive set above. This we will call group R. We will assume that this group's choices are $Z_r > Y_r$ and $Z_r > X_r$. (The actual assumptions made here make no difference to our conclusions.)

The array of preferences we have for Y and Z and X and Z choices are as follows:

Individual J:	Z > Y	X > Z
Group P:	Z > Y	Z > X
Group R:	Z > Y	Z > X

We will now consider society's choice between Z and Y in order to use the transitivity condition to see what light this casts on society's choice between Z and X. First note that, using the Pareto condition, the preference between Y and Z is that society prefers Z to Y, written as $Z_s > Y_s$.

But this leaves the choice between X and Z indeterminate. This is because $X_s > Y_s$ by the assumption made in the first section above and we have just shown Z is preferred to Y. We have to resolve this indeterminacy between X and Z by breaching one of Arrow's conditions.

If we say that Z_s is preferred to X_s, then the rest of society are dictating to individual J. Similarly, if we say Z_s is preferred to X_s, then individual J becomes a dictator because the only person who prefers X to Z is individual J. This person therefore emerges as a dictator. This illustrates that in this case with four conditions applying the fifth must be breached.

The final step in the analysis is to show that if someone is a dictator for one choice, this individual will be a dictator for all choices.

A dictator for all choices

Let us allow individual J to be a dictator over Z and X choices. Earlier it was assumed that J was not decisive over X and Y choices. We will now show that, given the assumed dictatorship over Z and X choices, J also becomes a dictator over X and Y choices.

To accomplish this, assume that:

$X_j > Z_j$ and $Z_j > Y_j$ and $X_j > Y_j$

(all as above) and

$Z_r > X_r$ and $Y_r > X_r$ and $Z_r > Y_r$

(all as above) where j is not in R

Here we are making a different assumption from that above and assuming that all in group R, now including group P, prefer Y to X. Thus, only individual J prefers X to Y whereas, the rest of society prefer Y to X. The Pareto condition requires that $Z_s > Y_s$ (because all favour this choice). Transitivity therefore implies that $X_s > Y_s$ ($X_s > Z_s$ (by assumption) and $Z_s > Y_s$ implies $X_s > Y_s$). Thus individual J is a dictator over X and Y choices. (This is the case even assuming that the others (group P) in the original decisive set (K) have changed their preferences so that they too now prefer Y to X.)

The only assumptions made concern irrelevant alternatives to the X and Y choices. It can be similarly shown that J is a dictator for all the six combinations of the three options X, Y and Z. Thus with the other conditions set by Arrow in force, a choice can emerge only if dictatorship is allowed. It can be similarly shown that with any of the other four conditions applying, the fifth cannot also apply if a choice for society is to emerge.

12

The conceptual framework approach

Introduction

This chapter concentrates on the Financial Accounting Standards Board's efforts to determine a generally accepted conceptual framework for accounting in the United States of America, all the basic elements of which are now in place. This subject is considered for a number of reasons. First, because the possession of a conceptual framework is another way that was not considered in Chapter 11 for private sector accounting policy makers to enhance their authority in the community. Second, the FASB's conceptual framework project is probably the most comprehensive modern attempt to build a theoretical framework for financial reporting using an economic perspective. Finally, this project represents, perhaps, the major professional attempt so far to utilise some of the elements of the information economics framework of earlier chapters. It thus represents a case study in seeking to make operational some of the more elementary concepts of information economics.

In this chapter the terms 'accounting reports and statements', 'financial statements' and 'financial reports' will all be used interchangeably. In the United States, the term 'financial statements' is usually reserved for the mandatory accounting statements in the accounting package. Financial reports encompass these statements and the other means of communicating information derived from accounting systems. This chapter will concentrate on the accounting information required of profit-seeking enterprises. The FASB has issued statements which deal with non-profit-seeking organisations, but we will not consider these statements.

The objective of the FASB's attempts to determine a conceptual framework for accounting, has been defined as an attempt to discover a structure for thinking about 'better' accounting to be used in clarifying the objectives of financial accounting and guiding in the selection of solutions to accounting problems (Macve, 1981). Statements issued as part of the Conceptual Framework Project thus set forth the objectives and fundamentals of financial reporting. These fundamentals are considered to be the underlying concepts of financial accounting. They are meant to guide in the selection of the items which are deemed to be part of the accounting process, in deciding which items to recognise and measure, and to help in determining the means of summarising and communicating accounting items to the users of accounting reports. Concepts of this type are seen as fundamental because other concepts and accounting treatments flow from them.

Although the FASB see the conceptual framework as mainly helping them in their endeavours as standard setters, they do also see it as a way of achieving common agreement on the objectives of accounting, and the means to be used to obtain these objectives. More specifically, the FASB define the Conceptual Framework as a constitution, a coherent system of interrelated objectives and fundamentals which should lead to the issue of consistent accounting standards and which prescribes the nature, functions and limits of financial accounting statements (FASB, 1978).

The FASB stress that Statements of Financial Accounting Concepts (SFACs) which are the documents in which the FASB's views on the conceptual framework are promulgated, do not establish accounting standards. Rather, statements in this series describe concepts and relations that underlie accounting standards and practices, and are to be used for evaluating existing standards and practices. Such statements, therefore, have less disciplinary authority than accounting standards issued by the FASB. These statements are not subject to the rules of the AICPA (the American Institute of Certified Public Accountants) which require that opinions that financial statements conform with generally accepted accounting principles can only be given if these statements conform to the standards issued by the FASB, unless it can be demonstrated that otherwise the financial statements would be misleading.

The FASB approach, which, as we shall see, places the major weight of their search for a generally accepted conceptual framework on the objectives of accounting, might be thought weaker than an approach which explicitly incorporates the determination of a set of postulates for accounting upon which a theory of accounting is built to allow the derivation of detailed accounting requirements (see Hendriksen, 1982 Chapter 3). In fact, although emphasising the objectives of users, the FASB do use the postulates approach to seeking an accounting theory, although this approach and the postulates themselves generally are left implicit in the conceptual framework. The FASB claim that the objectives they suggest for accounts flow from assumptions about the environment of accounting, the general nature of accounting information, views as to the requirements of the users for information and a consideration of the likely constraints on the accounting process. This loose linking with postulates would seem to rob the conceptual framework process of some of the strength claimed for the postulates approach to accounting theory, where subordinate conclusions gain their authority from their logical derivation for accepted postulates.

The FASB search for objectives in accounting explicitly commences some way down the hierarchy of postulates and principles. This approach might be said to be geared to a lower level of theory than some methodological 'purists' would like (see Hendriksen, 1982, Chapter 3). At the highest level of theory, those who favour adopting a postulates approach see their objective as finding an overall structure for accounting theory from which a variety of more specific hypotheses can be derived (see Mattessich, 1964). Theories concerning specific hypotheses are seen as being at the second level and have been called interpretational or semantic theories. At this level, theory is concerned with the relationship between empirical items and accounting theories and the symbols used in the accounting language being utilised. Many accounting items cannot be easily dealt with, even at this level of theory. Real-world referents for many accounting processes, such as the allocation of depreciation over time, cannot easily be found.

Hendriksen (1982, chapter 3) would relegate the FASB's approach as it is explicitly presented in their Statement of Financial Accounting Concepts No.1 (SFAC No. 1, 1978) to an even lower level of theory which he labels the 'needs of users' approach. This level of theory involves the acceptance of one or more purposes for accounting information and the utilisation of a set of subsidiary hypotheses which seem likely to accomplish this purpose or purposes. Mattessich regards such an approach as being concerned with what he calls 'place holder' assumptions, which allow a theory to be applied in the real world without complete agreement throughout the community on the purpose of the theory.

Some advantages of a conceptual framework for accounting

A paramount aim of the project is to provide a common set of concepts for financial accounting, a widely accepted common terminology and a set of definitions. The potential advantages claimed for the possession of a conceptual framework are substantial (see, for example, Solomons, 1983, 1986). These perceived advantages have been sufficient to persuade the United States financial community to finance the Board's endeavours in this area for a substantial number of years.

As was stated above, the FASB have said that the concepts and relationships that will underlie future financial accounting standards, and those which form the foundations for existing standards, will be evaluated in the light of the conceptual framework. Preparers of financial reports are expected to use the conceptual framework to guide them in their choices of solutions to their accounting problems. Users should gain from the project by increasing their understanding of financial information and of the declared goals which the FASB are seeking to achieve.

The FASB's Conceptual Framework Project is a massive endeavour that has been prosecuted almost from the foundation of the FASB in 1973. The relatively few final documents giving the FASB's formal views on the conceptual framework result from a vast amount of activity. The Conceptual Framework Project has generated a large number and variety of discussion documents, a substantial number of invitations to comment and a large number of responses to such invitations. A number of public hearings and a large number of research projects and task forces have all provided inputs into the project. It has been estimated that as much as 40 per cent of the staff time available to the FASB has been devoted to the project over the FASB's life. This means that several millions of dollars have been spent on the project.

The first major output of this project was three discussion documents in 1976. These first three documents were addressed to the scope and implications of the Conceptual Framework Project, objectives of financial statements (FASB 1976a) and the elements of financial statement and their measurement (FASB, 1976b). This work built on the recommendation of a committee generally referred to as the Trueblood Committee, after its Chairman, Mr Robert M. Trueblood (AICPA, 1973). It was one of two committees set up by the American Institute of Certified Public Accountants which led to the foundation of the FASB. The aim of the Trueblood Committee was to discuss what ought to be the objectives of financial accounting, which it described more fully as general purpose external financial reporting by business enterprises. Much of the Conceptual Framework Project has consisted of refining these original three documents and building on them.

This chapter is not intended to provide a detailed review of the project. Rather, we will concentrate on the strengths and weaknesses of the approach embodied in the search for a conceptual framework as a means of generating accounting theories. The steps which the FASB has gone through in attempting to derive a conceptual framework for accounting, using their term 'financial reporting', will then be presented. These steps will be appraised in a critical way. The following sections will review the promise of this approach for deriving accounting theories.

The possession of a conceptual framework allows many controversial choices concerning accounting standards to be defended as flowing directly from the conceptual framework. Such a framework should, therefore, give a strong defence to accounting policy makers seeking to justify accounting standards. It should also enhance the authority of accounting standards insofar as these can be shown to flow from a logically consistent theoretical framework which has been promulgated only after widespread discussion using many 'due process' procedures, and incorporating any relevant research results. Any authority flowing from such a conceptual framework should be strengthened insofar as this framework can be shown to be generally accepted.

The development of a coherent theoretical foundation for accounting also offers an important, though not complete, defence from what some would call 'political' interference in standard setting. Accounting standards derived from a generally agreed conceptual framework, utilising the technical resources of the accounting profession, should be less liable to political 'manipulation' than standards that cannot be so defended. One of the problems with standard setting in a number of countries is that little attempt is made to present the reasoning underlying standards. A conceptual framework should help here. Standard setters who possess a generally accepted framework would need only to provide additional reasoned arguments for standards which, for some reason, deviate from the conceptual framework, except where they discuss issues not yet considered within the framework.

In addition to the above fairly straightforward advantages for the conceptual framework, a number of more general benefits have been adduced in favour of possessing such a framework. Accounting policy makers must have at least an implicit and partly shared conceptual framework if they are to issue consistent accounting pronouncements over time. A perusal of the outputs of standard setters in the United States of America and United Kingdom might suggest that any such shared framework leans heavily on what might be called conventional accounting. If such a framework exists, it is surely advantageous to users and preparers that this be presented explicitly and set out as clearly and as rigorously as is possible. This should allow users and preparers to predict how accounting policy makers may proceed when faced with new and controversial issues. It should also help accounting policy makers to be as consistent as possible in their judgements.

Insofar as such a conceptual framework is generally accepted, it should reduce controversy in accounting. General agreement concerning fundamentals of accounting should facilitate the writing of generally accepted accounting standards, and reduce the arguments surrounding these standards. It should also allow individual accounting policy makers to distance themselves somewhat from individual standards.

There is little doubt that the genesis of a search for a conceptual framework in the United States of America arose, at least in part, from a desire to protect accounting from the likely intervention of political authorities there (see Zeff, 1972). It also promised to provide a justification for accounting practices in the courts in the face of substantially increasing amounts of litigation, and to provide a protection from criticism by authoritative political bodies and potential competing accounting policy making bodies. One of the major criticisms of the predecessor bodies to the FASB was a lack of any explicit use of accounting principles and accounting research. The conceptual framework project addresses directly the requirement to determine rigorously a framework for accounting and a set of accounting principles. It also allows accounting reform to proceed by demonstrating that existing practices cannot achieve those objectives of accounting which form part of the conceptual framework. The fundamental aim for accounting information adopted by the FASB is to aid in decision making. Accounting standards consistent with this objective are likely to require some degree of change to existing accounting practices. The existence of a conceptual framework should allow accounting reform to be approached as part of a logical and consistent programme of accounting reforms.

Most practitioners in the United States of America are still substantially committed to the Conceptual Framework Project. The perceived slowness of the project, and what its critics regard as its disappointing results, have as yet left this commitment substantially undamaged. A large number of similar, but less substantial, studies at earlier times in America and more recently in other countries—for example, the Corporate Report (ASSC, 1975) in the United Kingdom and the Stamp Report in Canada (CICA, 1980)—have used a similar approach. This suggests that many in the profession believe that a conceptual framework approach (variously defined) is a sensible way to seek to solve problems in accounting. That most of these other studies have had a limited impact on practice is, perhaps, a measure of the challenge facing the FASB's Conceptual Framework Project.

Possible steps in deriving a conceptual framework for accounting

Figure 12.1 indicates the major sequential steps suggested by the FASB as necessary in order to derive a conceptual framework, and to allow that framework to be utilised in accounting policy making. This approach seems a commonsense way of deriving the elements of an accounting system. It owes much to the postulates and principles approach and to earlier efforts in this area; see AICPA (1970, 1973), and the early publications of the FASB (FASB, 1974, 1976a).

The method used is to arrange accounting questions in a hierarchy, the most general issues being considered first. The answers obtained at a higher level are then meant to help yield solutions to lower level questions. Similarly, these lower level solutions are then meant to feed into the determination of accounting standards and to be used by management and auditors to derive accounting practices for specific situations which are consistent with the conceptual framework. The great promise of the approach is that it should culminate in accounting solutions to practical problems which are derived logically from a fully consistent system of accounting thought. As with the postulates and principles approach, subordinate stages in the conceptual framework gain their strength from the general acceptability of the earlier steps in the process.

Figure 12.1 says that the first steps in deriving a conceptual framework for financial reporting (level 1 in the figure) are to determine the basic objective(s) to be pursued, and any subsidiary objectives in the light of the assumed environment in which accounting must work. The completion of this step was reported by the FASB in SFAC

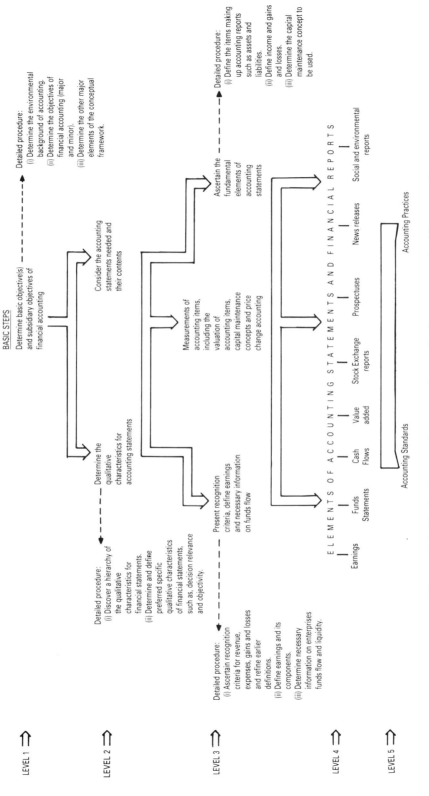

Figure 12.1 The basic steps in generating and using a conceptual framework

LEVEL 1 ⇧

LEVEL 2 ⇧

LEVEL 3 ⇧

LEVEL 4 ⇧

LEVEL 5 ⇧

BASIC STEPS

Determine basic objective(s) and subsidiary objectives of financial accounting

Determine the qualitative characteristics for accounting statements

Consider the accounting statements needed and their contents

Present recognition criteria, define earnings and necessary information on funds flow

Measurements of accounting items, including the valuation of accounting items, capital maintenance concepts and price change accounting

Ascertain the fundamental elements of accounting statements

Detailed procedure:
(i) Determine the environmental background of accounting.
(ii) Determine the objectives of financial accounting (major and minor).
(iii) Determine the other major elements of the conceptual framework.

Detailed procedure:
(i) Discover a hierarchy of the qualitative characteristics for financial statements.
(ii) Determine and define specific preferred qualitative characteristics of financial statements, such as, decision relevance and objectivity.

Detailed procedure:
(i) Ascertain recognition criteria for revenue, expenses, gains and losses and refine earlier definitions.
(ii) Define earnings and its components.
(iii) Determine necessary information on enterprises funds flow and liquidity.

Detailed procedure:
(i) Define the items making up accounting reports such as assets and liabilities.
(ii) Define income and gains and losses.
(iii) Determine the capital maintenance concept to be used.

E L E M E N T S   O F   A C C O U N T I N G   S T A T E M E N T S   A N D   F I N A N C I A L   R E P O R T S

Earnings   Funds Statements   Cash Flows   Value added   Stock Exchange reports   Prospectuses   News releases   Social and environmental reports

Accounting Standards

Accounting Practices

No. 1, *Objectives of Financial Reporting by Business Enterprises* (FASB, 1978).

At the next level (level 2), the FASB considered the necessary qualitative characteristics of accounting statements to achieve the previously determined objectives. The FASB's findings on this issue were reported in SFAC No.2 (FASB, 1980a) which was entitled *Qualitative Characteristics of Accounting Information*.

As the figure suggests, it was planned that the FASB should simultaneously address at this level in the hierarchy both of these characteristics and the type, content and format of the financial statements necessary to achieve FASB's objectives. In fact, their findings on desirable financial statements and their contents were issued later than those concerning qualitative characteristics as part of SFAC No.5 (FASB, 1984), which dealt mainly with recognition issues listed as a level 3 issue in Figure 12.1.

The next step in the process is to determine and define the fundamental items in accounting statements, such as assets, liabilities, costs expenses, revenues and income. These matters were originally dealt with in Concepts Statement No.3 (FASB, 1980b) which has recently been replaced and extended by SFAC No.6 (FASB, 1985). Both statements are entitled *Elements of Financial Statements*. This is a very important stage in the process and is shown as a third-level item on the right of Figure 12.1. This is the first step in the process where the ideas and concepts of earlier stages in the evolution of a conceptual framework really need to be made operational. At this stage, ideas which may have been widely accepted as general principles have to be made operational in the practical accounting environment. A second element at this level of the conceptual framework is to determine recognition criteria for items like revenue and expenses and gains and losses, and to detail income concepts further in a way which is consistent with the favoured criteria. This stage of the process is shown on the left of Figure 12.1 as a level 3 issue. The results of the FASB's work on these issues was reported in Statement No.5, entitled *Recognition and Measurement in Financial Statements of Business Enterprises* (FASB, 1984).

The third item at level 3 in the figure is that of addressing the measurement process in accounting. This involves determining the valuation methods to be used in financial reports and accounting statements (for example, historical cost or current cost) and prescribing the scale of measurement to be used, for example monetary units or units of purchasing power. It also involves selecting either an entity or a proprietary capital maintenance concept. Figure 12.1 indicates that this stage combines measurement issues and recognition matters. Some findings in this area are presented in SFAC No.5 (FASB,1984).

The FASB has thus issued a number of formal statements of its views at all levels of the hierarchy. The work is now seen as mainly completed and the framework as developed is being used to inform of the FASB's endeavours in the area of setting standards and issuing guidance concerning accounting practices.

The above description of the derivation of the conceptual framework is fairly general. The process described reflects what most professional accounting commentators would regard as one variant of the best practice method for seeking a conceptual basis for standard setting.

The next section of this chapter looks at this process in the context of the FASB's actual method of proceeding and considers the results achieved. The aim is not to describe in detail the FASB's findings. Rather, we seek to provide sufficient knowledge of the detailed method of proceeding adopted by FASB, and the results obtained in order to consider whether the use of the conceptual framework approach is likely to be a promising method of arriving at generally accepted accounting theories. Such an evaluation does require a fairly detailed understanding of the output of the project.

Elements of the conceptual framework

The first stage in the process of deriving a conceptual framework is that of determining objectives for financial reporting. Preliminarily to this, it is helpful to decide upon what are to be considered the important items in the environment which influence the characteristics of accounting, i.e. to decide upon a set of environmental postulates for accounting. The postulates of this type chosen by the FASB (though they are not described in this way) represent a fairly bland description of selected aspects of the financial environment in the United States. The chosen postulates emphasise the importance of achieving efficient resource allocation in a sophisticated market-based exchange economy, subject to substantial government intervention, in an environment where investors are separate from managers. An important assumption is that information about enterprises will improve resource allocation and that accounting information has a substantial role to play—in providing information which is useful to those who make decisions about enterprises and about investing in and providing credit to enterprises. This view of the role of accounting is embedded in the environmental postulates entertained. It is not, however, rigorously deduced from these postulates.

The first stage of the Conceptual Framework Project also suggested some general postulates concerning accounting itself (for a comparison, see Moonitz, 1961). These assumptions include that accounting information is generally quantified on the basis of exchange prices, is expressed in monetary units, and is generally capable of verification. This information is seen as normally relating to individual business enterprises and generally relating to past transactions. Again, these are descriptive statements with which few would disagree. However, the implied acceptance of current practice at this stage in the process may make any reforms more difficult to accomplish later in the process (a more detailed discussion was contained in FASB, 1976a, chapters 1–3).

The user orientation

The paramount concern of FASB seems to be to identify the users of accounting reports and determine the possible utilisation of this information. The main steps in this process are:

1 Identify the users or groups of users in mind.
2 For each different type of user identify their decision model(s) and their decision environment(s), including their preferences.
3 For each potential decision, identify the information relevant to the decision in the light of the assumed decision model(s) and consider how far accounting can provide this information.
4 For each accounting system yielding decision-relevant information, consider whether the benefits of providing this information exceed the costs of its provision—the so-called cost/benefit test.

The results achieved at this stage of the process condition much of the results of the remainder of the project.

FASB preferred objectives for accounts, derived implicitly using the above methods, are described in SFAC No.1, (FASB, 1978, p.viii). Three major objectives are identified:

1 Financial reports should provide information that is useful to reasonably informed investors and creditors, and other users who are willing to study information with reasonable diligence, in making rational investment and similar decisions.
2 Financial reporting should aid these users in assessing the amounts, timing and uncertainty of prospective net cash inflows into the enterprise.
3 Finally, financial reporting should provide information about the economic resources of the enterprise, the claims to those resources, and the effects of transactions, events and circumstances which change those resources and claims.

These conclusions concerning objectives are said to flow from what is a rather discursive discussion of possible potential users and the claimed common interest of all the identified potential users in the cash flows generated by enterprises. The above objectives are really those of general purpose financial statements directed towards satisfying a common interest in the ability to generate favourable cash flows. This does not lead the FASB towards favouring cash flow statements. It rather suggests to the FASB that the need is to reform accounting statements so that they yield better guidance in assessing the amounts, timing and uncertainty of favourable net cash flows. The FASB claims that cash flow statements cannot adequately indicate whether or not an enterprise's performance is successful. They therefore assert that accrual accounting should be retained in order better to portray enterprise performance. Many commentators, and perhaps most practitioners, would share this view. It is, however, susceptible to being tested empirically. One of the lynch pins of the whole project might have been substantially strengthened if such empirical studies had been undertaken. It should also be borne in mind that at this stage the FASB were going over ground already well researched by the Trueblood Committee.

Qualitative characteristics

One of the two parallel elements at level 2 of the process is to use the findings in the earlier stage to determine the desirable characteristics for decision-orientated accounting systems and to consider tradeoffs between such characteristics. This element appears as a step in many attempts to derive an accounting theory. Most of these studies have reached generally similar conclusions as to the desirable characteristics of accounting systems, though many have arrived at some different conclusions and often express their conclusions in slightly different words. Stamp (CICA, 1980) presents several different sets of characteristics which have been formulated in a number of different studies (see also Hendriksen, 1982, chapter 3). The Corporate Report's list (ASSC, 1975, para. 3) of the desirable characteristics of accounting information is one of the clearest and is fairly self-explanatory. The list is as follows:

Relevance
Understandability
Reliability
Completeness
Objectivity

Timeliness and
Comparability

All of these characteristics are to be subject to two constraints. One of these is that benefits must exceed costs. The second constraint requires that confidentiality should be preserved. FASB goes further in SFAC No.2 (FASB, 1980a) and attempts to arrange these characteristics or qualities into a hierarchy of qualities which flow from the believed requirements of users but which are derived without using an explicit decision model. This approach seems to have much in common with the information economics approach but in this latter approach the desired information is restricted to signals concerning the likelihood of states of the environment (see Chapter 6) and the decision model used is rigorously defined. This hierarchy takes the shape shown in Figure 12.2.

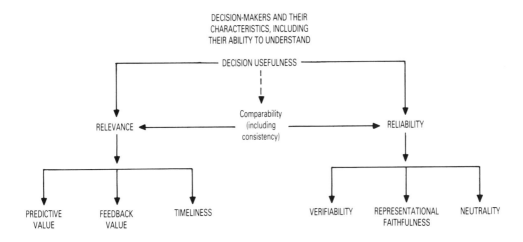

Major constraint: Benefits exceed costs

Items are only to be recognised if they are deemed material

(adapted from SFAC No.2. (1980) p.15)

Figure 12.2 FASB hierarchy of accounting qualities

Most of the characteristics in the figure are self-explanatory. They all flow from the overriding objective of providing accounting information useful for decisions. They therefore suffer from our lack of understanding of the models used for decision making. The hierarchy does, however, reflect a fairly general consensus that these characteristics are likely to be related to decision making. The FASB do not seek to derive these qualities from a specific decision model; rather the qualities flow by deduction from the assumed interest of users in enterprise cash flows.

Relevance and reliability are seen as the two primary qualities that give utility to accounting information. Both contribute to decision usefulness, but accounting policy makers may have to make trade-offs between these two characteristics. Relevant information is defined in a way which owes a substantial debt to modern information economics (see Chapter 6). Information is seen as helping to form or confirm predictions and can change decisions by improving predictions or by altering prior expectations by providing feedback. This is a looser definition than the most popular definition of the nature of information utilised in information economics which restricts the term 'information' to that leading to the revision of probabilities entertained by decision makers which do change decisions (see Chapter 6).

Reliability is the ability of information to correspond with what it purports to portray. Reliability seeks to measure the extent to which users can rely on information to represent what it ostensibly represents.

Figure 12.2 divides relevance into three subordinate qualities, the possession of predictive or feedback value and timeliness. Information can obtain relevance first by possessing predictive value which changes the decision maker's predictions. This is a very important component of the Conceptual Framework Project because it directly relates to the content of the decision models which form the foundation of the conceptual framework. That accounting information should have predictive value is really a central assertion of the Conceptual Framework Project. This is because its dominant aim is to determine useful information for decision making. The future is of the essence of decision making and therefore information about the past activities, to be useful in this process, either must help prediction, i.e. have predictive value, or improve the underlying decision model.

The adoption of a predictive value approach does not mean that the FASB see accounting being reformed so that it provides direct predictions about cash flows. Little of current practice seems to provide direct signals concerning future cash flows. Therefore such an approach might well lead to the abandonment of much of conventional accounting if viewed from this perspective. The predictive value approach rather suggests refining those elements of conventional accounting which are believed to aid in the prediction of items which form part of decision models.

The strengths and weaknesses of a predictive value approach to accounting will be considered in more detail later in this chapter, when we review the promise of the conceptual framework approach for deriving accounting theories.

A second way in which accounting information can obtain decision relevance is for it to have feedback value. This arises where signals provide evidence impacting on existing predictions, by either confirming them or causing changes in existing estimates; only the latter might have value from an information economics perspective (see Chapter 7). The FASB generally expect that items of accounting information will have both predictive and feedback value.

Finally, the decision relevance of otherwise useful information is argued to be reduced by a lack of timeliness. Timeliness is an ancillary aspect of relevance and its lack will damage the relevance of otherwise useful information. Very out-of-date information may be rendered entirely useless either because the information is no longer relevant to the decisions which are now to be made, or because the information may have already become available from other sources.

Problems with this approach to timeliness are that the FASB have not provided a rigorous general definition of this concept and timeliness is not an absolute characteristic, at least when viewed from the perspective of information economics. From this viewpoint, if information can still change decisions it has value and therefore is still timely, irrespective of when it was issued. An earlier receipt of information may have been more timely if it would have led to other decisions which would have yielded greater welfare to the decision maker than the decision made with later access to the information. The FASB points out that increased timeliness may involve some sacrifice of other desirable characteristics of accounting information, such as reliability. We now consider those characteristics, other than relevance, which may aid decision useful-ness. We do this by considering the items shown on the right-hand side of Figure 12.2.

The reliability of an accounting item reflects the degree to which it faithfully represents the item which it purports to portray. From a measurement perspective, we are concerned with the ability of the measure to reflect accurately the underlying quality of concern possessed by the item in mind. An accounting measure which says it measures the historical cost of an item is reliable in so far as it does measure this cost. The FASB seem to have in mind a more sophisticated meaning of representational faithfulness which indicates the validity of a measure being used as a representation of some of the economic characteristics of underlying phenomena. Representational faithfulness seems to be seen as the ability to represent correctly the economic phenomena being measured. This use of the representational faithfulness is problematic because it means that from a measurement perspective we are no longer seeking to measure only empirical characteristics. Restricting measurement to empirical phenomena is a usual criterion necessary before items can be said to be measurable, at least in a rigorous way (see Demski, 1980, pp.11–14). Many accounting phenomena do not exist in the empirical world. The degree to which non-empirical items represent economic phenomena is a value judgement and cannot obviously be represented without reference to the decision maker in mind.

The characteristic of representational faithfulness has to be accompanied by the ability to assure users that the item can be verified by independent measurers. These two properties are shown on the right-hand side of Figure 12.2. Reliable measurers should also not be biased towards any users (that is, in an accounting context, information should be neutral between users). This property is called neutrality in Figure 12.2.

There are a number of interesting and innovative concepts discussed in later stages of the project. We will concentrate on these matters in our briefer review of these later stages.

Elements of financial statements

After dealing with objectives and qualitative characteristics, the FASB proceeded dir-ectly to the third element at the second level in the process. Here, it used the findings in two preceding stages of the project to aid in deriving definitions of the elements of financial statements, such as assets, liabilities, expenses and revenues, at a fairly high level of generality. The declared objective of this study was that such concepts would become operational when combined with other elements in the project, such as recognition criteria.

Definitions of the elements of financial statements were originally given in SFAC No.3, *Elements of Financial Statements*, (FASB, 1980b). This document has been rep-laced by SFAC No.6 (FASB, 1985). (The most important change in this document is that all the elements are redefined in order to apply to not-for-profit organisations as well as business enterprises.) Much of SFAC No.6 seeks to clarify the earlier study and to address criticisms of it.

SFAC No.6 defines ten interrelated elements of financial statements. It also discusses, in some detail, accrual accounting and defines a number of significant concepts used with accrual accounting. We shall not discuss SFAC No.6 in any detail because it generally restates existing practice. The elements of financial statements are defined as the building blocks upon which financial statements are constructed. They are the familiar elements of accounting statements such as assets, liabilities, revenues, expenses, equity and profits. There are fewer surprises here than in earlier parts of the project. The Elements Study does seem to rely heavily upon earlier efforts in these areas (especially Sprouse and Moonitz, 1962, and the Trueblood Report, AICPA 1973). Most of the ten elements are articulated in a very similar way to that used by Sprouse and Moonitz 20 years earlier.

We shall therefore consider only some of the more innovative aspects of the entertained definitions. The FASB go to considerable lengths to indicate that they do not expect any major changes to be caused by the Elements Study in the items which are conventionally categorised as assets or liabilities. These definitions are seen as being helpful in understanding the content of financial statements and in dealing with new accounting issues as they appear. This view must be disappointing to accounting reformers because the definitions in the study do seem to contain the seeds of some radical reforms.

Definitions of elements of financial statements

In the study, assets are defined as possible future economic benefits obtained or controlled by an enterprise as a result of past transactions or events. Liabilities are similarly described as obligations to make probable future sacrifices of economic benefits as a result of past transactions or events affecting the enterprise. Equity is defined, as in existing practice, as the stockholders' interest in the assets of the enterprise. Revenues and expenses are also defined in the usual manner. Gains are taken to refer to increases in owners' equity flowing from the non-operating activities of the enterprise, other than where gains arise from revenues and investments accruing from enterprise owners. Losses are similarly expressed as decreases in ownership interest arising from non-trading activities, except where these result from expenses due to enterprise owners or distributions to them. The final two elements of the study define investments in the enterprise by the owners of a business and distributions to them by the enterprise.

It should be noted that Statement No.6 does not consider whether revenues, expenses, gains and losses, or parts of them, are to be regarded as realised or unrealised. Some topics related to realisation are dealt with in SFAC No.5. SFAC No.6 finally defines comprehensive income as the change in the owners' equity of an enterprise during a period from transactions and from other events and circumstances arising from non-owner sources. Comprehensive income thus incorporates all changes in owners' equity resulting from non-ownership sources.

The essential characteristic of an asset for FASB is consistent with the economic definition of wealth in that it reflects future economic benefits. These benefits are those which the asset should generate for the enterprise in terms of the future net cash inflows it contributes directly or indirectly, either singly or in combination with other assets. The asset must be within the economic control of the enterprise even though it may not be legally owned by the enterprise, for example if leased. Finally, the asset must have been obtained in the past. Basing the definition of an asset on its effect on future cash flows is entirely consistent with the FASB's view that accounting reports should aid decision makers in predicting future cash flows.

The definition of liabilities promulgated by the FASB is symmetrical with this view of assets. It stresses the sacrifice entailed by the requirement to settle a specific obligation, incurred in the past, in the future at a specified or determinable date. Comprehensive income is defined most generally as the amount by which an enterprise is better or worse off at the end of a period than at the beginning. This is an adaptation of what we called the central meaning of income in Chapter 3. Most accounting measurement systems can be accommodated in this definition.

Capital maintenance concepts

Prior to considering the Board's view on recognition criteria, we will consider what they said in Statement No.5 concerning the topic of capital maintenance, which we saw in Chapters 3 and 4 was of fundamental importance to the measurement of economic income. This subject was initially addressed in Statement No.3, which foreshadowed the choice of financial capital maintenance in SFAC No.5. However, few reasons are given in Statement No.5 for opting for financial capital maintenance. These are that it is the concept which is at present in use and that it does not require a specific choice of measurement unit. Physical capital maintenance or the maintenance of operating capacity requires the use of current cost as the attribute which must be used in measurement. This choice is fundamental to accounting, and it is difficult to believe the above reasons are sufficient to justify the FASB's choice, but no further reasons are given.

We now turn to that part of SFAC No.5 which deals for the first time in the Conceptual Framework Project with recognition criteria—a third-level issue. As has been said, it is a fairly crucial issue for the Conceptual Framework Project. In the views of many commentators, this was the first major operational issue dealt with by the FASB. It is, perhaps, the first stage of the project which cannot be proceeded with at only an abstract level.

Recognition criteria

Such criteria are needed to determine when an item should be recorded or incorporated into financial statements. The recognition process must also include changes in already recognised items. The recognition criteria suggested in SFAC No.5 are said to follow from the qualitative characteristics offered in SFAC No.2. These criteria are of two types. Fundamental recognition tests are to be applied to all recognition issues. Other criteria are meant to be helpful in making operational the elements defined in Concepts Statement No.3. The majority of these fundamental criteria restate the Board's earlier findings. To qualify for recognition, an item should:

1 satisfy one of the definitions for being an element of financial statements,
2 give relevant information,
3 yield reliable information, and
4 possess measurability.

The capacity to measure an item is said to flow from its possession of a property that can be measured such as historical cost or current cost, but this measurement must possess sufficient reliability. The test for the possession of sufficient reliability is left undefined here and in Statement No.2. This provides a major problem for users of Concepts Statement 5. The reliability of the information concerning an accounting item may determine the time at which the item can be incorporated into accounting statements. The statement gives no further guidance on this important point, other than to stress that waiting too long in order to improve reliability may involve sacrificing relevance (see Solomons, 1986, chapter 6).

These criteria are subject to the usual cost/benefit test. It is difficult to see how such cost/benefit tests can be applied either by standard setters or by auditors and preparers, other than as value judgements. In the present state of knowledge, it is difficult to assess the benefits to users of accounting information or the costs of its utilisation. Certainly, it is difficult to know how the preparers of accounting reports could have such knowledge. Long experience may help auditors to make such estimates, but these are not central to the auditor's task. There would seem to be a possibility of moral hazard in allowing preparers to make such decisions. The FASB do not intend to make cost/benefit judgements with regard to recognition, other than where they are germane to accounting standards which are being considered for other reasons.

The Board seem to be aware that their tests, as suggested above may be thought to be too imprecise for practical use. They therefore give more detailed advice on using these fundamental criteria for recognition. This guidance is also claimed to be consistent with current practice. The essence of the problem of recognition is that many transactions in a period are uncompleted and their final fruits uncertain. The Board favours sensibly considered conservative reactions as a way of coping with this uncertainty.

These conditions for recognition do little more than summarise, at a fairly high level of generality, the current practice in conventional accounting. It is stated that the essence of recognition is to determine when the uncertainty surrounding an item can be regarded as sufficiently resolved to allow recognition. Ideally, conditions for recognition should be derived from a model of the uncertainty associated with accounting items. Such a model might seek to indicate the perceived likelihood of the states of environment or the events which must occur for realisation to obtain (see Chapters 5 and 6, and Ijiri, 1980; Johnson and Storey, 1982). With such a model, accounting policy makers would still have the difficult task of determining what level of these perceived likelihoods is to be regarded as sufficient to allow recognition in accounting statements. No such model is presented or implicitly entertained in SFAC No.5. The Board seem to be satisfied to reiterate existing accounting conventions with regard to recognition and realisation.

Conventional practice deals with uncertainty by using conservative estimates. The FASB justify this approach by saying that 'in assessing the prospect that as yet uncompleted transactions will be concluded successfully, a degree of scepticism is often warranted . . .. More stringent requirements historically have been imposed for recognizing revenues and gains than for recognizing expenses and losses, and those conservative reactions influence the guidance (in SFAC No.5) for applying the recognition criteria to components of earnings' (FASB, 1984, Concepts Statement No. 5, para 81).

This approach ignores most of the modern understanding of uncertainty. It does not seek to measure the average or expected value of an accounting item, or the possible variability around this value. Reducing the value of accounting items in order to deal with uncertainty makes a number of assumptions, the principal one of which is that any uncertainty will be resolved by the passage of time. This is an empirical matter, but it is easy to think of accounting examples where the passing of time is not of the essence in resolving uncertainty. One illustration would be whether a product which is being considered for development will be a commercial success. The critical event here is whether the market accepts or rejects the product when it is offered for sale.

Many commentators feel that the Conceptual Framework Project has made little progress in this crucial and controversial area. Indeed, many critics of Statement No. 5 argue that the statement is disappointing because, although it uses concepts from the earlier stages of the project, its conclusions amount to recording conventional practice. It is argued that when faced with difficulties the Board does not always follow through its earlier reasoning and seek to provide operational conclusions incorporating this logic. Some critics would say that the Concepts Statements illustrate the propensity of the Board to back away from problems which have direct impact on practical accounting and to seek refuge in confirming current practice.

This completes our review of the formal output of the Conceptual Framework Project of the Financial Accounting Standards Board. The next section briefly summarises the project's progress. It also indicates how far the Board has adhered to fundamental stages of this process. The following major section of this chapter evaluates in a general way the promise of the conceptual framework approach for deriving accounting theories.

Summary of progress on the conceptual framework project

One view of the project's progress since 1974 when one of the first major documents appertaining to the project was issued, to its completion in 1985 with the issue of SFAC No. 6, is that the FASB has moved prudently, and only when consensus is established. It wisely sought to keep all its options open for later stages of the project. In this way, many ideas have been accepted where previous attempts have failed. Some commentators feel, however, that progress has been very slow and that few of the items addressed have been dealt with in an innovative way. With this view, most of the reports in this area published by the FASB are derivative and clearly based on earlier studies. It is somewhat difficult to avoid the view that the FASB have backed off dealing with some of the difficult problems which need to be solved before the Conceptual Framework Project can have any real practical impact. The FASB have not been able to adhere to the sequence of steps they originally regarded as desirable.

This is not to deny the importance of the conceptual framework approach. Some commentators see its concern to satisfy users' needs as representing a revolution in accounting thought.

Indeed, it is important to remember not to be unfair in our criticisms of the conceptual framework. The contribution of this approach cannot be fully evaluated until it has produced a number of operational reforms to accounting which have been tested *in situ*.

Critical evaluation of attempts to ascertain a theoretical framework for accounting

The following criticisms are directed somewhat narrowly towards attempts to seek a theoretical framework for accounting. The emphasis will thus be on the Conceptual Framework Project, which is by far the most ambitious of the recent attempts with this aim. Our critical review will look at a number of the major elements of this project in turn. In Chapter 11 it was suggested that all projects of this type are fatally flawed because there is no objective way of achieving the aim of the FASB standard setters. An accounting framework which serves all, or even a favoured sector of the community (which is FASB's avowed objective), irrespective of their preferences, their beliefs and their endowments, is at present an impossible dream. The earlier parts of this book have attempted to demonstrate that any accounting framework requires value judgements.

These suggested problems with the Conceptual Framework Project are of recent origin and therefore must be considered as tentative. However, they are regarded by many commentators as so fundamental as to require a radical reform of the methodology employed. In evaluating these criticisms it should be borne in mind that many commentators have welcomed the emphasis on identifying the various users of accounts and attempting to construct rational decision models for each class so identified.

The objectives of accounting

It can be argued that the FASB's decision-orientated approach contains the seeds of destruction of the whole process unless handled with great care. In accordance with the FASB's views, most generally accepted decision models involve considering the timing, amounts and uncertainty of potential net cash inflows (see Brealey and Myers, 1988). This supports arguments urging that enterprises should provide forecasts of cash flows and their risk, although the problems which the publication of such forecasts might bring in their wake would still need to be solved. Accounting reports that do not deviate radically from those conventionally issued are not obvious instruments for publishing such forecasts or the elements of such forecasts, even in an imprecise way.

Thus it can be argued that the FASB is at present subscribing to objectives which are probably not well achieved by conventionally prepared accounts. This suggests that much more thorough-going reforms are necessary to achieve these objectives. However, the FASB have shown little wish to overthrow radically what might be called the general principles of conventional accounting. It is difficult to see how these conflicting desires of retaining conservatism when reforming accounting and aiding decision makers can be maintained simultaneously. There is some evidence that this conflict is being reconciled by the FASB in favour of the continuance of the present framework of accounting.

Stewardship issues

It is difficult to escape the view that the emphasis of the Conceptual Framework Project is strongly on accounting information for decision making.

Stewardship objectives do figure in the detailed list of objectives in SFAC No. 1 (FASB, 1978). Feedback information is considered in some detail in SFAC No. 2 (FASB, 1980a). The discussion therein of reliability and its detailed characteristics also indicates the importance attached to stewardship. These latter characteristics are of less importance in a decision-orientated accounting system. This type of information may have different characteristics from stewardship information. Information which is designed to aid stewardship, to allow *ex post* contractual validation and to facilitate the distribution of the enterprise's resources to meet the claims by parties involved with the enterprise have all been strongly argued to require information of as objective a character as possible (see Ijiri, 1967, and Chapter 13).

It is, for example, very difficult to see how monitoring the maintenance of the enterprise asset base can be achieved other than by using objective information. Performance monitoring generally is similarly argued to require an objective foundation, as far as possible. Only the unwise would enter into contracts of which the outcome cannot be validated using objective information. A strong case has been made that information on distributions of resources to parties involved in the enterprise should be as objective as possible in order to reduce debates about the figures on which these distributions are based (Ijiri, 1967).

With this general perspective on *ex post* information, it has been argued that decision-orientated information may not easily serve other purposes. The problem the FASB had in seeking to reconcile the relevance of information to decision making and its reliability when determining recognition criteria (to be discussed later) illustrates this problem. As will be indicated later, the FASB seem to avoid this problem with respect to recognition criteria by opting for current practice with its emphasis on objectivity.

Public choice problems

The public choice literature, which was reviewed in greater detail earlier (see Chapter 11), suggests that the FASB's desire to lay down a 'constitution' for accounting may also cause its endeavours to founder. Many commentators see this as an impossible task. One difficulty associated with seeking a single model of accounting which aids everyone within a sector, or sectors, of the community, is that no generally acceptable method of arriving at such a model exists, given that tastes differ between individuals and that people seek to use published accounting information to solve a variety of problems (Demski, 1973). The selection of such an accounting model, therefore, requires a trade-off between the welfare of members of the community. The present consensus in the literature is that such choices can be generally avoided only with perfect markets in complete equilibrium. As was indicated in Chapter 2, in these situations accounting reports would replicate information conveyed by market prices (Bromwich, 1977). Many accounting statements aid some members of the community and harm others. Decisions concerning the use of accounting systems, therefore, require some type of comparison of the welfare of those who gain and those who are harmed. The FASB have opted to favour those who are making investment and credit decisions, and are capable of using accounting reports in a competent fashion. Other sectors of the community, including those who do not use accounting reports, may be harmed by accounting standards supported by this group. As was indicated in Chapter 11, Arrow (1963) has shown that there exists no method of selecting between rival public choice systems. The methods which might be considered for making such choices, such as majority voting, infringe some seemingly innocuous requirements which might be placed on the choice system (Sen, 1970). Thus, from this perspective, it is unlikely that the FASB can expect that its findings concerning the conceptual framework are likely to be generally accepted.

These findings suggest that standard setting bodies should not be seduced by the blandishments of those who argue that they should seek some universally agreed model for accounting. Such a model may exist, but with the current state of knowledge no method is available for discovering it and for obtaining the community's agreement to its utilisation.

Cushing (1977) (see also Chapter 11) has attempted to blunt the edge of this attack by calling on the literature which questions some of Arrow's assumptions. He argues that some of these assumptions may be reasonable at the level of the individual, but not when society as a whole is concerned. He also advocates a partial approach to accounting standards. The best rule or standard for a given accounting problem is to be sought using cost/benefit analysis, holding constant the accounting principles used in all other areas of controversy.

Choice here may be easier than when the selection of more comprehensive accounting models is required, because simpler options are more readily rendered comparable in terms of the information they convey. Some of the conditions are known which allow the choice of an accounting standard for a given problem to be made without considering the effects of its interaction with other standards on the welfare of those in the community (Bromwich, 1980). These conditions are fairly restrictive but, when applicable, they substantially reduce the problems facing accounting standard setting organisations. Research efforts in the area of social choice may offer further positive aid to standard setters such as the FASB when seeking to deal with these difficult problems.

We will now consider a number of narrower criticisms that have been levelled at the Conceptual Framework Project.

The use of postulates

One criticism of the Conceptual Framework Project is that the axiomatic approach and scientific methods in general, are difficult or impossible to apply in the social sciences. The FASB use of this approach in the Conceptual Framework Project tends to remain implicit, but it is employed nevertheless. That this approach remains implicit suggests that the FASB's ideas concerning the general environment in which accounting works, and of postulates that describe accounting itself, are unlikely to receive general acceptance.

Although the objectives of accounting statements propounded by the FASB do seem logically consistent with the needs of the chosen set of users, their acceptability may be reduced because of the general view in the accounting literature that we do not yet know how accounting figures are utilised in decision making.

Predictive ability

Our review of the qualitative characteristics element of the conceptual framework study indicates the crucial importance given in the study to seeking accounting information which has predictive value. With this approach, the aim is to provide information to decision makers which aids them in predicting the future values of decision variables. This is the way information economics proceeds. This approach was considered in more detail in Chapters 7 and 8. Here our aim is merely to give a sufficient understanding of the predictive value approach to allow us to review critically its role in the Conceptual

Framework Project. As Chapters 7 and 8 indicate, this perspective has been argued to lead to a revolution in the provision of accounting information, and in the testing of views about which accounting information is likely to aid decision makers in making their predictions. This is also the way in which one very well regarded school of the philosophy of science proceeds. Here, theories are judged by their ability to make accurate predictions. The theory which yields the most accurate predictions regarding the issue of concern (ignoring cost considerations) is to be chosen from the available competing theories (see Friedman, 1953; Cohen and Cyert, 1975).

A number of attempts have been made to adopt the predictive value approach in accounting; see, for example, Beaver *et al*, 1968; Carsberg *et al*, 1974. This approach is central to the FASB's Conceptual Framework Project. The method, which is drawn from information economics, is first to assume a decision model which will be utilised by the users of accounting reports. As explained in more detail in Chapter 9, the usual approach in accounting has been to restrict the users in mind to stock market investors and to assume that they use in their decision making variants of the models generally accepted in finance as explaining investment behaviour. Such models emphasise the importance of predictions concerning future cash flows, their timing and risk, though the risk here is not that attaching to an individual security viewed in isolation, but to the change in risk brought about by the addition of an amount of the security to a well diversified portfolio. The role here for accounting information is seen as one of a number of information systems conveying information which will aid in the prediction of the future values of the selected decision variables. Ignoring cost, accounting systems should be selected on the basis of those which aid predictions. One important attribute of this approach is that providing the chosen accounting system is implemented, the results of using the chosen system and the assumed decision model together can be tested in part by observing whether their introduction has any effect on security prices.

We would expect security prices to change on the introduction of accounting systems which yielded information which altered the beliefs of investors concerning the prospects offered by securities. Chapter 9 reviews these studies. It is important to understand that we are seeking to provide accounting information which helps to predict the value of decision variables. We are not trying to provide accounting systems which are best able to predict the future values of accounting items such as accounting profits. Earlier, a number of tests were undertaken that sought to relate to existing accounting information with the predictions it allowed of the values of similar future accounting information (Peasnell, 1974). Nor are we seeking to say that the data provided by accounting systems are themselves predictions. Accounting information as such can only help in forming predictions which have to be made by users (Greenball, 1971).

There are many problems associated with the predictive value approach to accounting information. For example, at present any tests of the predictive value of any accounting system are joint tests of both this hypothesis and of the relevance of the assumed decision model. Although, in finance, there is a fairly general agreement as to the constituents of investor decision models, such models amount to 'as if' hypotheses and may not describe what investors actually do when making decisions. More importantly, the present state of accounting theory is such that we do not know the role, if any, that accounting information plays in investors' decision models. Indeed, we can do little more than sketch the way that, say, accounting income numbers might be used in such models; see, however, Beaver *et al.* (1970). All we can say is that empirical studies have shown that some items of accounting information have a moderate and fairly short-run influence on security prices (see Chapter 9).

There seem to be at least two problems with predictive ability as used in the Conceptual Framework Project. The first is that the FASB have not made explicit the decision model they see investors using, nor have they given any details of this model. They have merely said that investors are assumed to be interested in future cash flows, and their risk and timing. This statement is very general and it is difficult to see how it can be used operationally as it stands. For example, there are many ways of measuring risk. It is not clear which of these the Board has in mind. Indeed, it is not even clear whether the FASB have in mind risk defined with regard to an individual security, or to an optimally diversified security portfolio.

There is a second problem with regard to the FASB's use of the predictive value of accounting information. The FASB have not sought to show how accounting information can obtain predictive value. When the FASB was dealing with the qualitative characteristics of accounting information, a great emphasis was placed upon the relevance of accounting information. The Conceptual Framework Project does not, however, rigorously define relevance nor does it show how relevant accounting information can be utilised in investors' decision models.

Qualitative characteristics

A major criticism has been mounted against the methodology of seeking to deduce desirable characteristics for accounting information as in SFAC No.2, (see Demski, 1973, 1976). These characteristics are meant to be of value in choosing between accounting information systems for all users of accounting reports, or a class of such users, irrespective of their preferences, their decision problems and decision environments. Thus, the FASB are really seeking characteristics for accounting information which are utility- or value-free, i.e. which are of use to all, irrespective of their personal characteristics, at least for their favoured set of users.

Demski (1973) shows that such a test is impossible. Decisions between information systems can be made without reference to preferences and decision problems only in rather restricted circumstances. Information systems can only be ranked in a utility-free way, that is without reference to individual preferences, decision problems and environments, either in ideal markets or where the costless information systems being ranked yield comparable information (Chapter 7). In this case, the information systems being considered can be ranked in terms of the detail they provide (more rigorously, in terms of the fineness of the information they yield) and even here the resulting ranking may apply only to the individual in mind. (For more on this, see Chapter 7.) The problem with this approach arises because information systems are generally not comparable in this way. Any pair of information systems may yield different non-comparable information. For example, published accounting reports for a given enterprise, prepared using conventional accounting principles, are not comparable in terms of the information they provide with accounting reports for the same enterprise, utilising, say, current cost methods. Given only the two sets of accounting reports we cannot convert one of these into the other in any simple way using only the information provided by the two sets of accounting reports.

Where information systems are not comparable in this way, a choice between them can only be made by explicitly considering the various preferences of users. Such a choice thus involves adopting the preferences of one or more favoured users. Demski therefore argues that an exercise such as that undertaken by the FASB in choosing a set of qualitative characteristics cannot be regarded as value-free or neutral between individuals as is suggested by the FASB. Concepts Statement 2 implicitly suggests that each and every individual will gain if the accounting system selected on the basis of the amount of a given characteristic, at least up to some level, provided that the quality is viewed in isolation from other qualities. Demski demonstrates that this assertion can be entertained even for an individual only where the portfolio of accounting systems being considered contains accounting systems which are all comparable in terms of the amount of information they convey.

Demski's requirements for ranking information systems are very stringent. This ranking must be accomplished without reference to individual decision problems or tastes. It must apply to all conceivable decision problems and provide a ranking of all information systems. Vickrey (1982) and others have sought to relax this stringency by suggesting that some characteristics of information systems may be useful even if they do not give an exhaustive ranking of information. Surely, they argue, relevance is a universally desirable characteristic of an accounting system, even if it cannot be utilised generally to rank information systems. If an information system is to be of use, it must be relevant and, thus, the relevance characteristic allows us to screen out those information systems which may be useful from others which are not relevant, even if it does not allow us always to rank them. Moreover, one specific piece of information may be shown to be practically relevant to all decisions. This is what we called the individual's endowment in earlier chapters. Information concerning endowments is necessary to operationalise decision making. Such information is necessary in order for the individual to determine the decision options available. Bromwich and Wells (1983) suggest that information concerning the individual's endowment of tradeable commodities is useful in this sense, even in imperfectly organised markets.

The problem for the general approach of using qualitative characteristics remains. Even if some of the FASB's favoured characteristics can be shown to be necessary properties of information systems, this still would not allow all information systems to be ordered without considering the tastes, decision problems and decision environments faced by individuals in the community. The FASB, in selecting between accounting options, therefore has to make social choice decisions for society.

Trade-offs

SFAC No.2 (FASB, 1980a), on qualitative characteristics, indicates another problem with the conceptual framework approach which is shared by most of the other publications relating to the Conceptual Framework Project, especially Concepts Statement 5, which deals with recognition and measurement. Many of the properties here enunciated as desirable are not absolutely desirable. Often a degree of one property or characteristic can be obtained only by sacrificing to some degree another desirable characteristic. The most obvious example, and that discussed in most detail by the FASB, is the choice between relevance and reliability. In their view the need to ensure the reliability of accounting information may attenuate the pursuit of relevance.

Similarly, in the later Statement dealing with recognition and measurement (FASB, 1984, SFAC No.5), it is said that 'Recognition involves consideration of relevance and comparability, recognition criteria ... are primarily intended to increase reliability.'

Such criteria are seen as 'means of coping with the uncertainty that surrounds business and economic activities'. The response to this uncertainty has been 'to apply conservative procedures in accounting recognition', (FASB, 1984, SFAC No.5, para. 49–50). Here again the need for a trade-off between relevance and reliability is recognised, but is clearly seen as being resolved in favour of reliability. The difficulty is that whilst the trade-off is recognised, no guidance is given as to how this trade-off should be made in operational circumstances. Even what is called 'further guidance for recognition' really states only existing practice without providing any analytical support for these procedures. Nor is it indicated what sort of trade-offs are permissible. It would have been helpful to be told the suggested rates of exchange between relevance and reliability at various levels of these two variables. What is in mind here is some rule that says that for a given problem we have already obtained, say, 90 per cent reliability, we may trade-off, say, 5 per cent of this reliability for an additional, say, 10 per cent of relevance.

Our critical review of the qualitative characteristics stage of the Conceptual Framework Project highlights another more general and major problem. The project seems to adopt either a single person perspective or the assumption of homogeneous tastes across all individuals. The objectives section of the project exemplifies the assumption of homogeneous tastes among the classes of individuals whom the FASB has chosen to aid. In contrast, the FASB's search for qualitative characteristics is approached by considering a single individual's requirements. In this part of the study, the questions asked are what characteristics would be valuable to an individual who subscribes to the FASB's objectives for accounting statements. The FASB's characteristics study does not seek to extend its findings to a multi-person setting. Even if the characteristics presented by the FASB were applicable to all individuals, it is very unlikely that all will have the same preferences for trade-offs between these various characteristics. Thus, in determining such trade-offs, the FASB have to decide which set of users they wish to aid. Earlier chapters indicate some of the difficulties that heterogeneous tastes produce for standard setters and accounting policy makers. Chapter 11 dealt with these problems in more detail.

Elements of accounting statements

The definitions of accounting items such as assets and liabilities that have been derived from the conceptual framework have been argued not to be suitable for solving accounting problems. This is because they do not clearly and completely partition accounting items into separate categories. Armed with these definitions one cannot always clearly place every accounting item into one, and only one, category. Dopuch and Sunder (1980), for example, listed a number of different treatments of a given accounting item which were compatible with the relevant definitions which had then been promulgated by FASB in SFAC No.3.

Many of the then-extant criticisms of the inability of the Elements Study to encompass problematic accounting items, or to deal with them unequivocally, were dealt with in SFAC No.6. Much of this statement seeks to add further details to the FASB's definitions of the elements of accounting statements. It also gives a number of illustrations indicating where accounting items which have been argued to be ambiguous fit into the FASB's definitions for the elements of accounting statements. However, even if Concepts Statement 6 does deal with all the accounting items which so far have been suggested to be problematic, it is unlikely that all similar items raised in the future can be dealt with successfully using the logic given in SFAC No.6. Difficulties are bound to arise as new accounting items emerge.

Dopuch and Sunder (1980) state that they have difficulty in determining the incremental contributions of the FASB endeavours to lay down a framework for accounting over previous efforts. They had equal difficulty in determining the meaning which the FASB attach to the objectives which they seek for accounting. They feel that any attempt to seek those objectives common to all are unlikely to yield a clear set of objectives for accounting. They doubt the appropriateness of what they see as 'the extraordinary emphasis ... on user primacy'. It is argued that this view is a product of looking at the individual information user in isolation and not utilising multi-user perspective when considering accounting information. Some of the difficulties that the existence of a variety of users of accounting might cause have been considered in this chapter and in Chapter 11.

Many of the above sections highlight a final set of problems with the Conceptual Framework Project. The project does seek to discuss the underlying theoretical concepts of accounting. Thus, for example, Concepts Statement 5 underlines the importance of the resolution of uncertainty in dealing with recognition problems. Similarly, the Elements Statement bases its definitions of assets and liabilities on the importance of future cash flows as suggested by modern theory. However, the roles given to these concepts seems to lessen as the project moves towards operational matters. Indeed, our earlier review of the outputs of the Conceptual Framework Project may suggest that as the concerns of the Conceptual Framework Project move nearer to practice, so the outputs of the project tend to converge towards existing practice.

Some commentators are less sceptical concerning the benefits of the Conceptual Framework Project. See Peasnell (1982) for a general review of opinions about the conceptual framework project. Many professional accountants see the adoption of a conceptual framework as the only way forward in standard setting. For example, this was, and indeed still is, the predominant reply when the British standard setting body sought views on how it should proceed after 19 years (ASC, 1979; see also the Dearing Report, 1988). However, the framework in mind seemed to differ substantially from one respondent to another.

Some supporters of the FASB's conceptual framework approach see its objectives as less ambitious than do its critics. Sprouse (1983), who was at the time a Vice-Chairman of the FASB, did not perceive the conceptual framework as a mechanism for making social choice decisions. Rather, he saw it as providing meaningful guidance for resolving issues and ensuring the predictability and consistency of the FASB deliberations. Sprouse sees a major contribution of the Conceptual Framework Project as being to free standard setters from providing only *ad hoc* compromise solutions to the 'hot' issues of the day. By providing a conceptual framework, it is believed that standard setters will be able to enhance the comparability of the information contained in financial statements and thereby increase the 'understanding of such statements and ... confidence in such statements'. In Sprouse's view 'the quest for comparability is a large part of what standard setting is about'.

Others have argued that a private sector standard sitting body has to have a conceptual framework if its views are to have authority and if it is to protect itself from pressure from sectors of the business community (see Macve, 1983; and Solomons, 1983, 1986).

Attacks on a conceptual framework may be less easy to mount than those on individual standards.

Conclusions on the conceptual framework

Many commentators feel that the FASB efforts (and indeed those of others who seek a conceptual framework) have so far failed to provide a useful framework. The statements issued are said to be very general, bland and difficult to utilise in determining a treatment for a given accounting problem. They have often been criticised as supporting a number of different treatments for a given accounting item; they do not seem to stop accounting standards being inconsistent with each other. This is not surprising when it is recalled that many powerful organisations have interests in accounting standards. Dealing directly and clearly with controversial issues may cause major difficulties with these organisations and may bring about the demise of private sector standard setting. A natural tendency to embrace the *status quo* when dealing with practical issues was noted.

The penultimate chapter in this book briefly considers accounting from a stewardship viewpoint. It also briefly reviews the body of accounting theory called positive accounting theory and reviews the empirical evidence so far obtained bearing on this theory. In the final chapter the impact of agency theory on financial reporting is considered, with its concern that accounting for decision making and for control must be considered together.

Chapter summary

It is not intended to summarise in any detail here the discussion of the technical aspects of the FASB's Conceptual Framework Project contained in this already long chapter. This summary will be very selective and will emphasise the strengths and weaknesses of this approach for generating accounting theory. The first two sections of the chapter commenced by introducing some of the advantages claimed for the conceptual framework approach by the FASB including that the conceptual framework acts as a constitution guiding the FASB's endeavours, clarifies the objectives of financial accounting and aids the FASB in selecting solutions to accounting problems.

It was argued that the conceptual framework approach does not really represent a full-blooded application of the postulates and principles approach as it commences some way down the hierarchy of possible steps, commencing at the level of determining the objectives of accounting.

It was suggested that the possession of such a generally accepted framework would provide a defence for controversial standards because they could be shown to flow from a logically consistent framework. This conceptual framework should also provide additional authority for accounting standards and some defence from possible public sector involvement in standard setting. It should also make more explicit the shared theoretical framework used by standard setters, allowing predictions to be made concerning how standard setters might proceed when facing specific accounting problems. The adoption of such a framework should, it was suggested, allow accounting reform to form part of a logical and consistent programme.

It was shown that the detailed objectives of accounting promulgated by the FASB which are to provide information for decision purposes for those making investment, credit and similar decisions are very similar to those of the earlier studies.

Following these introductory sections, we began our review of the Conceptual Framework Project, commencing with a description of the possible steps in the hierarchy to be used in seeking a conceptual framework. The process starts by looking at objectives: those helpful to investors and similar decision makers are then used to inform the FASB of the choice of qualitative characteristics for accounting information at the second level of the hierarchy of items which must be addressed and in determining and defining elements of accounting reports and their measurement at the third level of the hierarchy.

After reviewing the early stages of the process, the remaining part of these two sections concentrated on the innovative aspects of the later publications of the FASB concerning the conceptual framework. The Elements Study was said to provide definitions of assets and liabilities which are clearly consistent with the objectives selected by the FASB and with modern finance theory. Adopting this perspective led to a major innovation in accounting practice in the United State of America—the use of comprehensive or 'all in' income.

Adopting an economic perspective on accounting reports requires the choice of a capital maintenance concept. The Board followed the conventional view and opted for a financial capital maintenance concept. That this important choice was not strongly argued was said to be likely to weaken the Conceptual Framework Project. To conclude these sections, the Board's findings on recognition criteria were presented and discussed. It was suggested that these criteria really amount to restating much of the earlier findings of the project without making these any more suitable for practical use. The further guidance on these issues given by the FASB was said really to represent a statement of conventional practice even though the FASB have a clear view that the recognition of accounting items depends crucially on when the uncertainty about these items is resolved. However, the FASB provide no guidance about this. Some critics would say that the FASB's treatment of recognition criteria illustrates their perceived propensity to take refuge in conventional practice when faced with controversial problems to which they wish to provide a practical solution.

After a brief summary of progress on the Conceptual Framework Project, a critical evaluation of the project was provided in the following main part of the chapter. Here we will only highlight criticisms that have not so far been raised in this chapter summary.

It was argued that there is no objective way of accomplishing the FASB's aims, which may also contain the seeds of their own destruction. This is because it is not clear that accounting statements are the best vehicles for providing information about future cash flows which the FASB see as an essential objective for accounting information. It was argued that accounting standard setting is a public choice problem for which we at present lack a generally accepted system for generating solutions which are acceptable to the community, in that they possess certain simple properties which make them attractive for these purposes. Some attempts to overcome these problems were discussed.

The rigour introduced into the conceptual framework by seeking accounting information with predictive value was welcomed. Two problems with this approach, as it is used by FASB, were considered—that the decision model assumed to be used by investors and others is not made explicit by the FASB, nor is it indicated how accounting information can obtain predictive value. The qualitative characteristics part of the study was also criticised because choices concerning such characteristics cannot, in general, be approached on the assumption that such decisions are neutral between individuals. The presentation of a number of other criticisms and of views supporting the project conclude the chapter.

IV

Accountability, positive accounting theory and agency

13

Accountability, agency and positive accounting theory

Introduction

This chapter considers a number of items which have only been treated briefly so far in this book.

Throughout our study we have generally concentrated on accounting information for decision making, though in a number of chapters we have considered the role of *ex post* information in measuring performance relative to the expected performance in a period, and in defining the prudential distribution of income to security holders (see Chapters 3, 4 and 8). We saw in Chapter 7 on public information that there was a role for *ex post* information in validating the occurrence of contractual conditions. We have also seen that the possible *ex post* information available to the parties entering into the contract will condition the types of contracts that can be written. Contracts can be based rationally on only what is common knowledge to all the parties to the contract, both at its inception and during its span. If the terms of any contract are based on asymmetrical information, any parties with superior knowledge may be able to exploit less informed parties. We are not saying that contractual situations do not involve asymmetrical information but rather that rational contracts should not be based on such information. In Chapter 7, we also indicated that the existence of publicly available *ex post* information about the state of the environment may allow contracts to be formulated which could not otherwise be sustained.

One role of this chapter is to consider some aspects of the use of accounting information *ex post* for the purposes of performance evaluation, for contracting and for monitoring contracts.

In the practical accounting world, the use of accounting for monitoring the results of past periods is of great importance. Accounting information is used in practice for checking whether accountability responsibilities have been satisfactorily discharged, for ensuring that the enterprise is accountable to those with interests in the organisation, for monitoring performance and for ensuring that any prudential responsibilities have been fulfilled. In addition, accounting figures often serve as a basis for distribution of the benefits generated by the enterprise, as the basis for calculating payments due on a contract, for validating contractual performance and as the foundation for tax calculations. Finally, accounting income and changes therein may be a component in determining managerial bonuses.

Accountability information is required to discharge organisational obligations to parties with interests in the enterprise. Such parties may include not only shareholders, creditors and labour, but also the Government and society more generally. Information concerning the fulfilment of prudential requirements indicates whether these have been met by the organisation. These requirements may be imposed by the Government, by accounting or other regulators and by parties who have dealings with the enterprise. Thus, for a number of entities as wide-ranging as banks and charities, the relevant regulators impose a wide variety of capital adequacy conditions which generally involve maintaining minimum asset balances of various types. An example of such a condition would be that liquid funds must represent a specific proportion of the entity's assets, and the requirement that the amount that can be invested in certain types of assets cannot exceed a maximum. Creditors and debt providers may also impose limitations on possible enterprise conduct. For example, many loan agreements require that only certain types of other debt can be issued, subject to conditions aimed at safeguarding the interests of existing debt providers and ensuring that a certain degree of dividend cover is maintained before dividends can be declared. These requirements span a wide variety of types and may be very stringent. Such regulations may therefore substantially influence enterprise conduct. Financial market regulations may also impose restraints expressed using accounting numbers on enterprise conduct. Thus the size of a takeover bid a firm can mount may depend on the amount of its net assets. Where such requirements are imposed, managers may seek to minimise their effects by their choice of accounting policies where this is possible (Watts and Zimmerman, 1986).

This chapter indicates the above subjects are very important and really require a book of their own. Here we shall briefly examine accounting for accountability purposes and its use for bargaining over benefits. We shall also examine the effect of constraints on the enterprise based upon accounting information. In order to continue to employ our decision oriented approach, we shall examine these issues from a decision making perspective.

In this chapter and the next we shall also relax the assumptions generally maintained throughout this text that managers automatically work in the best interests of the security holders. With uncertainty and imperfect information, we would expect managers to seek to maximise their own utility. Managers with superior skills and superior personal information will wish to utilise these advantages in their own best interests. Where managerial effort yields disutility to the manager, other things being equal, the manager will seek to minimise this effort. Such conduct is possible where enterprise owners do not have complete knowledge of managerial conduct. This type of dysfunctional behaviour by managers will be expected by the firm's owners who will seek to reduce it by their own actions.

These problems are not limited to relationships between managers and shareholders but may occur wherever one party employs others to carry out delegated functions. Such a contractual arrangement is described as an agency relationship where one person, usually called the principal, employs one or more other people to undertake tasks on his or her behalf. Agency relations pervade the real world and extend from the relationship between shareholder and manager, senior and junior managers, houseowner or buyer and estate agent (real estate dealer), to interfaces between the Government and local authorities, and regulators and regulatees. They may also be familiar from the law of agency. Agency also includes a myriad of more traditional variants of this relationship where one party offers the other a service — such as client and lawyer, teacher and scholar, and doctor and patient. Agency relationships may also involve settings with multiple agents where, for example, the principal employs a third party to check upon an agent. The employment of an external or internal auditor to validate managerial reports provides an example.

Agency theory seeks to deal with these problems in general. This theory explores, in a general way, the effects on decision making and resource allocation of entertaining various features of the agency model. A narrower approach which employs much of the theory presented in Part II of this book is called the *theory of agent and principal*. Its main concern is to seek reward functions and information systems which allow the principal to motivate the agent in such a way that by maximising the agent's personal utility the agent also maximises for the principal. Both approaches are sometimes labelled agency approaches but the two perspectives differ in that agent and principal models seek to optimise, whereas the term 'agency' used more generally incorporates agency considerations into a wide range of descriptive models. Another distinguishing characteristic of the two approaches is that agent and principal theory explores in much more detail the risk sharing opportunities arising in an agency relationship. Our detailed study of the agent and principal model forms the subject of Chapter 14.

The more general ideas of agency now inform many social science disciplines; agency and principal models are used in economics (see for example Kreps, 1990, chapters 16, 17 and 18), where also a somewhat similar approach called contracting theory focuses especially on settings with incomplete contracts and with transaction costs (see Laffont 1989, chapter 10; Williamson 1975, 1985).

Agent and principal models have been used in the accounting literature mainly in management accounting, but also deal with problems which are important in financial accounting and are of growing importance. For example, this theory yields a strong theoretical foundation for expecting the use of auditors. Similarly, the role of accounting regulators can be better appreciated from this perspective. The current literature applying agent and principal theory to financial accounting issues is still small but it is growing (see Chapter 14).

Plan of the chapter

The first substantive sections of this chapter look at accounting for accountability purposes, including those of stewardship which involve *ex post* information provided to the decision maker after the decision has been executed. Thus, we are altering the focus we have employed in most of this book of considering information provided prior to decision making. *Ex post* information is used to evaluate performance in order to control it, and to motivate the agent to maximise on behalf of the principal. Accountability information motivates the agent because he or she is assumed to know the features of the reporting system which will be used in evaluating performance and to conduct himself or herself accordingly. Additionally, the agent's reward is often linked to such a performance monitoring system. Accountability accounting extends beyond monitoring which reports independently on the state of the environment and on the agent's effort. It includes traditional stewardship accounting which requires the enterprise to demonstrate that it has accounted for its resources in the correct way, has utilised resources only for legitimate purposes and has correctly maintained its assets. Accountability accounting also includes providing information which indicates that the enterprise has followed prudent conduct by, for example, maintaining reasonable cash balances. Finally, this role of accounting provides information which yields the basis for calculating the amount due to parties to the enterprise.

The second section of this chapter looks at some of the general ideas of agency theory. The third and final part of this chapter briefly looks at what is now called 'positive accounting theory', which seeks to incorporate into accounting our understanding of agency and of contracting in markets in order to explain better why enterprise management makes accounting choices in the context of well organised markets. It also tests the hypotheses thus generated utilising the methods explored in Chapter 9. The theory is said to be positive in that it seeks to explain existing accounting phenomena rather than to provide a theory of accounting.

Here markets are assumed to work well. With this view, examples of sub-optimisation which we attributed to market failure in Chapters 10 and 11 are argued rather to represent optimal decisions once transaction costs are taken into account. Our review of positive accounting theory is fairly brief because this is a relatively new area and is subject to some controversy. It is also well explained by its proponents, for example by Watts and Zimmerman (1986). The approach clearly represents a very important and rich research area with probably the fastest growing literature in financial accounting research.

One major difference between our discussion of agency models of both types and accounting for accountability is that the agency models extend the decision making models familiar in this book and expand them to include more explicitly agency considerations, whereas accounting for stewardship and the distribution of enterprise benefits may use information inconsistent with decision making. This is generally the case with accounting figures provided for taxation purposes. Any difference between accounting information for accountability purposes and that required for decision making provides an exemplification of the view that different accounting information may be required for different purposes.

Accounting for accountability

Generally the demand for accountability or stewardship information arises from a wish to know the actions taken by an enterprise and to control them. A reasonably general definition of accountability information is reporting 'on the control and uses of resources by those accountable for their control and use to those to whom they are accountable' (Rosenfield, 1974, p.126). Accountability information covers a wide variety of accounting. The most traditional use of accounting for these purposes is to fulfil stewardship objectives. This involves confirming that corporate resources actually exist, that they have been used for legitimate and legal purposes where utilised during a period, and that assets and resources have been accounted for in a proper way. Auditors play an important role in this area by verifying and validating the enterprise's stewardship reports. Income reporting also fulfils an accountability role because financial reports show the distribution of the enterprise's resources to the various parties involved with the enterprise, and net income indicates the accounting profits available for distribution. More advanced uses of accountability information stem from a wish to ascertain the actions which management have taken during the period.

The accounting literature tends just to assert the need for accountability information and sees this information as distinct from that required for decision making. To a degree this may be the case because many accountability requirements are imposed by law, often in order to solve past difficulties encountered by financial markets which are thought less likely to occur with wider accountability information. Thus, where enterprises have gone bankrupt because of, say, a lack of liquid resources, the law may require clearer reporting of such assets in future. When accountability information is defined as information about past actions for the purpose of controlling future actions, we would normally expect that this information will only be valued if it has some specific benefit to at least some of the parties involved with the enterprise. The existence of this type of information may provide an incentive to management to follow conduct that the security holders regard as optimal. All parties to the enterprise may also wish for accountability information if this leads to better risk sharing between enterprise participants (see Gjesdal, 1981) (risk sharing will be considered in more detail later). Both of these types of information are elements of decision making problems.

Thus, we can say that at least some types of accountability information belongs to the same theoretical framework as does information for decision making. Both theories use the same definition of information as was presented in Part II of this book. However, Gjesdal (1981) shows that the general model for choosing accountability information is different from that utilised for selecting information systems for decision making. With his model, the manager chooses an action and is rewarded by a bonus (an agreed share of the outcome) based on the signals from the information system, the form of which is generally agreed between the manager and a superior at the time of contracting. Using an agent and principal model, Gjesdal shows that this type of information will be useful for stewardship purposes if the actions taken by the manager are reflected in the signal generated by the information system, providing that the manager's bonus varies with the signals. Similarly, accountability systems which generate after-the-event information will have value if the signals from such an information system allow preferred risk sharing.

Gjesdal shows that the criteria for selecting information systems for accountability purposes is different from those for selecting information systems for decision making explained in Chapter 7. In Chapter 7 we said that information systems for decision making could be ranked on the basis of the richness of the decision-relevant information they generate, irrespective of the decision maker's actions, tastes and endowments (see Chapter 7, p 128). Gjesdal shows that this condition is not sufficient for ranking accountability information systems geared to controlling managerial performance. Casually speaking, it can be said that such information systems can be ranked on the basis of their richness in terms of the information they convey about the manager's actions. Thus the practical view that information for accountability purposes may differ from decision making information seems correct, though in some cases both types of information may be generated from the same general framework.

Practical accounting tends to emphasise the need for objectivity in accountability information and therefore stresses the use for these purposes of traditional historical cost information, with its concern to report only events that have actually occurred. Below we review some of the arguments which have been put in favour of using historical accounting for providing accountability information. One of the major proponents of this view has been Ijiri, whose work is reviewed below.

Historical cost and the double entry system

One important strength of the historical cost system (as distinct from accounting statements compiled on this basis) is its intimate connection with double entry bookkeeping which still forms the foundation of even today's very sophisticated financial data processing systems. The double entry system allows vast quantities of data to be handled, classified and aggregated in a flexible way.

Although the double entry system evolved using historical cost, it can be utilised with a variety of other accounting systems. Indeed, most advocates of other accounting systems have felt it incumbent upon them to show that their favoured system of accounting can be put into the double entry framework. Even the present value accounting system (see Chapters 3, 4 and 8) which reports the value of the enterprise's expected cash flows after making due allowance for their timing, can be put in a double entry system. However, the subjectivity of the present value accounting system does weaken its connection with those real-world events that have actually happened. This wish to ground accounting upon actual events has been regarded as a major characteristic of the double entry system, at least for most of its history. The general view is that the double entry system should be based, as far as possible, on prices actually paid or received (Ijiri, 1975, chapter 5). Many accounting systems based on information other than historical cost do not always reflect those actual events which have occurred.

It has been suggested that the figures generated by many non-historical cost accounting systems are not unique. They allow a variety of quantitative representations for some events without any obvious criteria being available for deciding which representation is legitimate. For example, under a current cost accounting system a number of possible measures of replacement costs, which are important elements of these systems, are available, including the cost of replacement with an identical machine, replacement with a machine which renders the same services, replacement with an obvious alternative and replacement with the least-cost new technology. Thus a number of possible ways to represent a given set of events of the past exist under current cost accounting. This is not true of historical cost accounting, at least in an ideal world.

The 'uniqueness' of historical cost accounting

With historical cost accounting, there may exist a unique way of depicting a given set of events. Moreover, ideally historical cost accounting will represent the factual chain of events that really happened, i.e. it will represent actual experience (see Ijiri, 1967, p.66). This quality of the historical cost system is retained in the practical world, but only imperfectly, because accountants find it necessary to allocate items measured at their historical cost to those periods of time which are supposed to benefit from these items. The spreading of the historical cost of an asset over its estimated life, via depreciation, provides a well known example.

Ijiri (1967) argues that this element of uniqueness of the historical cost system actually reduces the problems caused in allocating costs. The uniqueness of the system renders valuation a simpler business than when a number of possible valuations are available. Moreover, unbiased outside observers will have little difficulty in duplicating any allocation used with historical cost systems, providing that the method being used is explained. The valuations used must themselves also be explained before this can be done with other accounting systems (see Ijiri, 1967, pp.58–67). This requirement, to know the measurement or valuation principles used before allocations in accounts can be duplicated by outsiders, is present to a lesser degree with a historical cost system when accepted accounting practice allows options, such as a choice between FIFO and LIFO stock valuation methods and the possibility of the revaluation of assets.

This uniqueness of the historical cost system gives it an advantage relative to other accounting systems which has, perhaps, not been given sufficient prominence in the literature. With this system, users of accounting reports may be more able to see through any accounting tricks and procedures, and more easily discern their quantitative effects. They may, therefore, be able to reconstruct historical cost accounts so that they show the figures free of these tricks and procedures. Chapter 9 briefly reviews some of the empirical evidence for this view. Such adjustments may be easier with the historical cost system than with other accounting systems. Less debate may, therefore, surround the income and position statements (balance sheets) generated by historical cost accounting, at least when these are prepared by unbiased actors.

Hardness of accounting information

Ijiri (1975) has used the uniqueness of historical cost figures to claim that the figures generated by this accounting system are 'harder' than those produced by other valuation methods. Hardness reflects how far the methods used in the construction of accounting figures reduces the ability to disagree with those figures (Ijiri, 1975, pp.35–40). The general correctness of this view follows from our earlier discussion of information for contracting purposes in Chapter 7 (p. 307). This said that contracting could only be based on signals which are available to all contracting parties. More formally and ideally, hard measurement systems are those which generate 'verifiable facts by justifiable rules in a rigid system which allows only a unique set of rules for a given situation' (Ijiri, 1975, p.36). Hardness relates to the amount of disagreement possible about a measure from a given information system. Hardness relates to the degree to which qualified individuals agree on a given measure. Hardness is, thus, a consensus measurement between experts. For any given item, it is likely that its measurement by different individuals will produce a range of values, which can be charted using a frequency-based probability distribution for the item being measured. The degree of objectivity of such a distribution is measured by its dispersion around its mean or average value. Thus, the most objective measurement procedure for a given phenomenon is that which yields the minimum dispersion. However, this assumes that such measurements lack bias.

The bias in a measurement system is determined by the deviation between the mean value given by the measurement procedure and the believed value of the attribute being measured. Since the believed value of an item cannot be ascertained, the amount of bias on a measurement system must depend on expert judgement based on the believed relationship between the characteristics of the measurement system and the item being measured.

Bias arises from two sources. Measurement bias is intrinsic to the measurement system being used. Measurer bias is generated by those characteristics of the measurer which may cause bias, such as lack of skill or a failure of integrity. Seeking objectivity in measurement can be relied on to reduce measurer bias more than bias flowing from the characteristics of the measurement systems being used.

Using these ideas, the reliability of a measurement system is defined as objectivity plus bias, though there are conceptional difficulties in measuring bias because the actual value of the item being measured may not be known (see Ijiri and Jaedicke, 1966). The hardness of information thus indicates the degree of objectivity in its measurement and its lack of bias. Intuitively, these seem sensible requirements for information for accountability purposes. The FASB come to a similar view in the Conceptual Framework Project (see Chapter 12 and FASB, 1980a, SFAC No.2, pp.26–37 especially 33–37). Hardness is argued to be a desirable characteristic for accounting figures which are likely to be used in conflict situations—performance measurement, for example. Such figures reduce any squabbles concerning the figures themselves and therefore allow the true items of debate to emerge. In the practical world this may not be an entirely unmixed blessing because conflict may become less manageable when the true issues of contention are exposed.

Although historical cost accounting has been found wanting as an aid to decision making by many commentators, it may have advantages in some less publicised usages. There are many situations where a figure is required on which the allocation of resources between parties to an agreement can be based. The distinction has also been made between those users' objectives which are legally orientated for which certainty of the accounting figures is a main criterion, and those concerned with economic decisions (Edey, 1970). Taxation, for example, has to be based on some agreed set of figures. One characteristic of information useful for such purposes is that the signals produced should be accepted by all parties. Similarly, for purposes of defining the amount of dividends to be paid to shareholders, it is helpful if the debate is concentrated not upon the accounting figures, but rather upon the reasonableness in the circumstances of the dividend itself. Similarly, in wage negotiations, it is likely to be useful if the bargaining is based on figures accepted by all sides. Bargaining between parties with conflicting interests is difficult enough without additional differences generated by debates about the correctness of the accounting figures.

What is in mind is not that the figures produced are right or wrong but that they constitute an agreed basis for bargaining for contractual purposes. For example, historical cost profit cannot be used to determine the dividend that an enterprise should pay its security holders. Such decisions require a consideration of a number of other variables, including the enterprise's future prospects, its future investment needs, its cash flows and liquidity position. Such deliberations are likely to be easier if all concerned parties are willing to accept accounting profits as a measure of enterprise earnings in their bargaining. It is argued that such an acceptance is more likely for historical cost profits than for any other accounting systems because historical profits contain fewer hypothetical elements than other accounting options.

Ijiri (1967, p.67) explains this well by saying 'Historical valuations play an important part in equity accounting'. Equity accounting is concerned with the distribution of the benefits from the organisation. For accounting to have a useful role in this area, accountants must develop and operate an accounting system in the most objective, consistent and unambiguous manner possible because the data they provide directly affect the way in which conflicting interests are resolved. Such concerns are at present at the centre of accounting research, where one crucial issue is how an agent with superior knowledge, say an enterprise manager, should be rewarded by the enterprise owners, the principals who delegate their decision making power concerning the enterprise to the manager. The aim is to implement a system which will ensure that the agent will work efficiently for the principal even though he or she may have superior knowledge and may use this to favour his or her own interests (see later parts of this chapter, Chapter 14 and Jensen and Meckling, 1976).

Thus, it is argued that whilst historical cost accounting systems do not yield a definite figure for enterprise profit and net worth (value), they give a more precise value than most other accounting systems (Ijiri, 1975, chapter 6). The uniqueness characteristic of historical cost accounting is, therefore, said to be of advantage where performance in some functions is being monitored for performance appraisal and other purposes (see Ijiri 1975, chapter 3). It is argued that individuals will more easily agree to be evaluated on objective rather than subjective information. The needs for monitoring performance are various and include providing feedback for the individual performing a given function for self-appraisal purposes. If one is attempting to accomplish a task, it is necessary to know how well one has done. Other things being equal, a performance measure is likely to be better for feedback purposes, the greater its objectiveness or its factual base. When driving a car that we have managed to crash into an obstacle, it is surely better to have a recording system which signals that this has happened than one which, by careful choice of the measuring device, indicates that we have not actually hit the obstacle.

Similarly, where performance is being monitored for the purposes of rewarding the person in charge of the activity, the use of historical cost accounting may reduce any conflict and help to minimise the incentive for the individual to attempt to enhance performance by manipulating the performance monitoring system itself. This is because, if the performance measure is based on historical costs, the relation between the figures produced and the real-world events, at least for some elements of the performance measure, can be deduced by anyone who understands the system. Ijiri (1975) provides a good review of how well other accounting systems may function as performance measures.

This claimed grounding of historical cost accounting on facts also may aid the traditional stewardship role of accounting reviewed earlier.

More recently, Ijiri (1983) has suggested using the above reasoning that the decision-orientated approach to accounting should be replaced by an approach based upon the concept of fairness. He argues that seeking to aid only decision makers ignores the interests of those who provide information, such as enterprise managers. The argument is that the information to be provided should be based on the agreed accountability relationship between the management and those to whom they are accountable. Such agreements set out what information is expected and also the information over which management may maintain their privacy. The concern for confidentiality arises because publishing certain information may harm management, even though it may aid decision makers external to the firm. Thus, requiring management to publish detailed long-term forecasts may aid external decision makers but harm managers because they may be held accountable for future variations from plans which may be beyond their control. Such a requirement may impose additional risk on the manager.

Here, there is no doubt that information for accountability is seen as being different from the information required for decision making.

The next section gives a general review of some of the characteristics of the agency relationship as a preliminary to our later main section, which provides a presentation of positive accounting theory, and the modelling of the agent and principal relationship in the next chapter.

The general characteristics of agency relationships

The essence of an agency relationship is that one or more people employ one or more other persons as agents. Those who employ others are called principals and those who work for them are called agents. To ease the presentation, we generally assume that we are talking about a setting involving a single agent and a single principal, even though a given setting may actually involve many agents and principals, such as the relationship between shareholders and managers in a firm. The principal is seen as delegating some decision power to the agent. The agent's decision choices are assumed to affect both parties. Such relationships are pervasive in economic and business life and are an element of the more general problem of contracting between entities in the economy.

There are many reasons why these relationships may be entered into by the principal and agent. It is impossible to deal with these in any real detail here. Many of the reasons are similar to those that have been suggested to explain why firms exist, which constitute an enormous literature. For a good brief summary, see Tirole (1988, pp.17–35). These arguments span a wide range of hypotheses including the suggestions that firms are formed to take advantage of economies of scale and scope (see Chandler, 1990, Part 1), to exploit any advantage of asset specificity, to provide an ability to improve on the contracts otherwise available, to allow the avoidance of transaction costs (see Coase, 1937; Williamson, 1975) and to maintain authority relationships including vertical integration (Grossman and Hart, 1983).

Suggested reasons for the existence of agency relationships also have much in common with those used to explain why firms adopt divisional structures of a variety of types, which are the subject of a large literature on divisional performance measurement in managerial accounting (see Kaplan and Atkinson, 1989, chapters 14 and 15).

For our purposes, the reasons an agent is employed may be restricted to three rather general purposes. An agent may be used because of the special skills offered, because the agent may be in possession of private information, and to relax constraints on the principal's time.

The problems with agency relationships arise for a number of reasons. The first is that the parties in the association are assumed, as is usual in economics, to seek to maximise their own best interests subject to the constraints imposed by the agency structure. Differing objectives between the principal and agent arise either because of differences in tastes, especially with regard to risk, or because action by the agent yields disutility to the agent. Generally the principal is seen as being able to choose, at least in part, the structure of the agency relationship. Such choices will seek to guarantee a specific response from the agent, usually by motivating the effort exerted by the agent or more generally by imposing some costs upon the agent. The principal's objective is to structure the agency in a way which ensures that the agent, in maximising his or her best interests subject to the constraints imposed by the principal, will automatically maximise for the principal.

The importance of uncertainty

Such problems would not arise with certainty because here the principal would pay a wage to the agent equal to the marginal value product contributed to the organisation by the agent, where the marginal value product is equal to the agent's output times the incremental revenue obtained on the market for that output. The wage paid will thus be determined by the market, based on what the agent would earn in the next-best alternative employment. Failure to provide the performance implied by the market-determined wages would be immediately apparent to the employer and would result either in an appropriate reduction in wages or the replacement of the agent, if employing less productive agents was not optimal.

It is the existence of uncertainties which gives the agency relationship its interest. The outcome of the agent's delegated functions will depend on the agent's efforts and also the state of the environment that reigns. A low outcome may result because of a poor state of the environment, even where the agent is rendering optimal efforts. Similarily, the occurrence of a favourable state may be used by the agent to disguise shirking. In an agency relationship it is generally impossible for the principal to distinguish between events of this type. The principal is generally assumed to know neither the state of the environment which actually reigns nor the degree of the agent's endeavours. The principal is assumed to know neither of these items because information concerning either one of these elements can be used to ascertain the other. In an agency relationship, the principal typically knows only the outcome produced by employing the agent, and not its two constitutent elements — the state of the environment and the amount of effort expended by the agent.

Information generally, including accounting information, may be helpful here. First, accounting information may serve an accountability role and help in providing information concerning the outcome for the period. Auditors may be useful where the outcome information is issued by the agent, who may be better informed than the principal. Left alone, the agent may provide information which puts his or her actions in the best possible light. Auditing by experts helps to validate and verify such information. Additional information may allow the principal to gain more knowledge concerning either the state of the environment or the agent's endeavours, but at a cost.

Information may play a very strong role in an agency structure because the agent's reward may be based not only on the realised outcome but also on the results signalled by an information system, often an accounting system. Thus, it is typical for managerial remuneration to be based, at least in part, on corporate or divisional accounting profits. As was indicated earlier, such accountability information will work perfectly only if the signals from such an accounting system reflect the endeavours of the agent or if they have relevance to risk sharing.

Effects of uncertainty

The existence of uncertainty has at least three effects on agency models. First, the parties to the relationship may gain from rearranging between themselves the risk they bear where they differ in their attitudes to risk. As the outcomes of the relationships are uncertain, the sharing of these outcomes between principal and agent is an important element of this relationship. Where the shares of the uncertain outcomes do not tally with the attitudes to risk of the parties, rearrangement of risk bearing will improve the welfare of all parties. Such rearrangements should therefore continue until a Pareto efficient allocation (of risk in this case) is attained. Such an equilibrium allocation means that the welfare of one party can not be improved without harming that of another party (see Chapters 2 and 5). The decisions of the parties will be conditioned by the effect of risk without optimal risk sharing. Thus, for example, a risk averse agent forced to bear a risk will seek to protect his or her outcome by seeking to 'insure' against adverse outcomes even though this may not be in the principal's best interest.

The other two results of uncertainty on agency models which we are going to consider in this and the next chapter result from:

1 the actions of the agent not being transparent to the principal — the so-called hidden action problem, and
2 any private information of the agent not being visible to the principal — the so-called hidden information problem (see Arrow, 1985).

With hidden action, the agent can determine to a degree the outcome by his or her actions, and the other party cannot perfectly monitor or enforce an action upon the agent. This is an example of what is called moral hazard. The most obvious example of moral hazard in an agency context is that of the agent's effort. Effort yields rewards to the principal but causes disutility to the agent. Without some monitoring system, the actual effort provided by the agent is unknown to the principal. The lawyer–client relation provides an example of such a relationship. Here the lawyer chooses actions affecting the principal's welfare but because of the superiority of the lawyer's knowledge the principal cannot check whether the lawyer has been diligent. A more relevant example of hidden action to accounting is the relationship between the stockholder (the principal) and management (the agent). Here the stockholder cannot fully observe whether management is working in the security-holder's best interest. The usual solution to moral hazard is the use of incentives which structure activities so that the party who undertakes the action in his or her own best interest will automatically make choices which the other party will prefer (Kreps, 1990, chapter 16).

With hidden information the agent knows something relevant to the transaction which the principal does not know. This is an example of the more general problem of adverse selection where one party to a contracting situation has superior information but the other party cannot check whether this private information has been utilised in his or her best interests. The problem is therefore for the uninformed party to give incentives to the informed party to use the private information at his or her disposal to benefit the uniformed participant (Kreps, 1990, chapter 17).

Insurance provides a very clear example of adverse selection. The population to be insured may consist of individuals with different risk characteristics who are aware of their own characteristics. The insurance company will have to offer the same premium based upon the average characteristics of the population to all individuals if it lacks information about the specific risk characteristics of individuals. This will lead to an inefficient allocation of risk bearing in the community. Quoting the same premium to all will mean that high risk individuals will be undercharged and will therefore buy more insurance than otherwise. Similarly, low risk individuals will purchase a less-than-optimal amount of insurance, given their risk because they are over charged at the going market price for insurance.

A more accounting-orientated example of adverse selection is where firms of auditors offer services of different quality. The adverse selection or the hidden information problem appears in this setting if those employing auditors are not able to distinguish the quality of the services provided by different auditors. To overcome these problems, auditors may resort to advertising or to market signalling, where they seek to signal their quality by their actions. Similarly they may pre-commit themselves publicly to certain actions. Thus an audit firm of high quality may advertise services which only a high quality agent can offer, and pre-commit itself to having its services monitored by an independent third party. Such a firm may also seek to make known the formal qualifications of its members if it is generally believed that such qualifications are correlated with the ability to offer high quality services.

To summarise, in this section we have discussed four types of agency or, more generally, contractual relationships, though other researchers sometimes take a different view of how these models should be categorised. These four types are:

1 moral hazard with hidden action,
2 moral hazard with hidden information,
3 adverse selection, and
4 signalling models.

In understanding agency models, we ought additionally to be clear about the types of information available to the relationship. Here we shall just add to what we have said in previous chapters about information. Information is common knowledge if it is known to all players and if every player knows that all have this common knowledge. Perfect information is defined in the same way as in Chapter 6. Asymmetric information means that the information systems used by the parties in any relationship differ between parties, at least for some time during the relationship. This means that some individual has private information. Thus his or her information system is no worse, at least, than that available to another party and may provide additional information. The agent and principal model provides an example of asymmetric information if only the agent is aware of the chosen act.

Finally, with regard to information, we need to make a rather more technical point, which we shall need later, and distinguish between complete and incomplete information. In Chapters 5 and 6 we implicitly defined complete information as being that information necessary to specify fully the decision problem in mind. However, in some ways this is an unhelpful definition in an agency context, where the agency relationship is ill-defined and therefore difficult to analyse. In order to overcome this problem, it has been suggested that such incomplete relationships can be expressed rather as the possession of complete but imperfect information. This alternative view of incomplete information becomes possible if we allow nature at the beginning of the relationship to choose the rules of the relationship before anything further happens. The resulting model is an example of imperfect information because it is assumed that at least one party does not observe the decision taken by nature.

An example would be a two-person relationship that takes the form of a number of possible different opportunities or decision problems with different pay-offs attached to the same decisions. Assume now that one party knows which actual decision problem will materialise but the other can only assign probabilities to this. Decision models of this type cannot be analysed. However, suppose we add to the decision problem an additional step that involves nature choosing which opportunity will materialise utilising the probabilities of the party who is uncertain about the likely decision problem. With this additional step, the problem is transformed into one of complete but imperfect information as defined above and which can now be analysed (see Rasmusen, 1989, chapters 2 and 6).

Agency costs

The above description of some aspects of the general agency relationship stresses the partial nature of the agency contract, given uncertainty and asymmetric information. As we have seen, the lack of a complete contract allows the participants in an agency relationship scope to pursue their own interests at the expense of other participants. Such activities will include, not only accumulating pecuniary benefits and shirking, but also a wide variety of non-pecuniary benefits, such as luxurious offices, unnecessary 'high tech' equipment and foreign trips. This section is based on the early work of Jensen and Meckling (1976). Realising the possibility of dysfunctional activity, the principal will seek to limit divergencies from his or her interests by incurring costs to provide the agent with incentives to maximise on behalf of the principal and by bearing monitoring costs to limit the activities which do not maximise the principal's interests. Such a monitoring role for accounting is familiar in management accounting. Possible monitoring activities are much more sophisticated than just seeking to measure the behaviour of the agent. These activities include imposing budget and operating restrictions and constraints on the agent, and linking compensation with the outcome of monitoring. Such restrictions are sometimes written into contracts but are often rather more informal, reflecting any authority the principal has over the agent.

A wider view suggested by Jensen and Meckling (1976) considers the firm to be a nexus of contracts embodying the property rights of all the participants in the enterprise. Each set of participants will have contracts that specify how the enterprises' cash flows will be distributed under a variety of contingencies, including bankruptcy. Some of these contracts are embodied in the enterprise's formal legal documents and others will be informal. These property rights are additional to the rights given by those laws which define generally the property rights in enterprise revenue and assets. Debt providers often impose a number of rigorous constraints on the enterprise to which they lend money. Lending agreements thus sometimes require the enterprise to maintain target levels of interest coverage ratios which may be monitored using the financial statements.

Additionally, in some situations the agent may enter into bonding activities which seek to guarantee that the agent will not exploit the principal. This may be sensible conduct but represents costly behaviour on the agent's part. Without such bonding activities, the principal will otherwise seek to adjust in some way the amounts paid to the agent to allow for perceptions of the likely behaviour of the agent. Bonding activities may include items such as accepting contractual limitations on the agent's decision making power and agreeing to have accounts audited by a qualified auditor, i.e. that is to arrange monitoring. Thus, it makes no difference whether the principal or the agent contracts for monitoring and bears the explicit costs of this monitoring, in the first instance.

Both monitoring and bonding activities are costly and are associated to some degree with all contracts written by the enterprise. The costs of these activities are elements of the costs of using the agency relationship. However, these devices are unlikely to be perfect and their utilisation therefore cannot fully ensure that the agent will maximise the principal's utility. The final additional cost of using an agent is the residual loss to the principal arising from the inability to ensure that the agent acts fully in the principal's interest, given existing monitoring and bonding devices. Thus agency costs can be defined in general as:

1 the monitoring costs incurred by the principal,
2 the bonding expenditures undertaken by the agent, and
3 the remaining loss to the principal.

The agency costs in any enterprise will depend on the lack of information about the agent's activities, and on the costs of monitoring and analysing the management's performance, the costs of devising a bonus scheme which rewards the agent for maximising the principal's welfare and the costs of determining and enforcing policy rules. They will also depend on the supply of replacement managers. Competitive pressure in the market for managers will limit the freedom of agents to pursue their own interests (Fama, 1980). Similarly, they will also be limited by the opportunities available to sell the enterprise in the market.

This ability of efficient markets to limit the freedom of action of agents highlights one distinction between the agent and principal model, and agency models more generally. Those who use agency ideas generally tend to assume that markets are important and that they function perfectly (see the review of positive accounting theory in the next section). The agent and principal models tend rather to ignore the effects of markets outside the enterprise, except the labour market. Our detailed review of agent and principal models forms the subject of the next chapter.

The final section this chapter considers positive accounting theory, which seeks to use the general aspects of the agency relationship introduced above to explain the selection of accounting treatments in a perfect market environment. One important aspect of this theory is that the hypotheses generated using the theory are tested against stock market evidence in the way reviewed in Chapter 9.

Positive accounting theory

For the reasons indicated above our survey of this programme of accounting research will be relatively brief. A very clear statement of the general philosophy behind this approach can be found in Jensen (1976). A detailed presentation of the case and current results obtained from this research programme is provided in Watts and Zimmerman (1986). Examples of the research work generated by this theory can be found in the *Journal of Accounting and Economics*.

This theory grew out of a concern that existing accounting theories tended not to reflect fully the existence of markets and the imperfect nature of contractual relationships between parties associated with an enterprise. It also reflected a strong discontent with the rationale for accounting regulation discussed in Chapter 11 of this book. This concern reflected a strong belief, probably garnered from the Chicago school of economics (see Friedman, 1953; Peltzman, 1974; Stigler, 1971) that markets on their own work at least as well as when they are regulated and are less costly to use than regulated markets.

Indeed, the market failure arguments we presented in Chapter 11 are regarded as fallacious by positive accounting theorists (see Watts and Zimmerman, 1986; Leftwich, 1980). Such a statement is representative of the combative style employed by many advocates of positive accounting theory. These views were reviewed in the latter part of Chapter 11. The only common ground between Chapter 11 and the view discussed here is that accounting regulation, and regulation more generally, are political and that differing views concerning the effects of regulation must be subject to empirical testing.

The theoretical foundations of the theory

This view of accounting theory departs from much of the accounting literature in that it does not directly seek accounting theories which aid decision makers in their decisions concerning the enterprise. Rather, the aim is to explain existing accounting phenomena and to predict how these will change in the face of alterations in the variables affecting them. Advocates of the theory thus see themselves as following science and positive economics in seeking theories which are concerned with explaining what *is* rather than reforming it and subjecting such theories to testing by exposure to empirical evidence. Theories which seek to reform are seen as concerned with what *ought to be* and are called normative theories. Normative theories cannot be tested against the empirical evidence as they contain 'ought' statements, though components of the theories can be so tested, as can some of their implications. Debates about scientific method and the history of science are very rigorous and detailed. Thus, elementary or simple distinctions of this type tend to be regarded as unhelpful and misleading. It is not intended to explore this type of debate here. Useful references in an accounting context are Christenson (1983) and Sterling (1990); they support the view of the underlying disciplines that theories cannot be thus categorised in any really meaningful way.

Positive accounting theorists reacted very strongly to the literature of the 1960s and 1970s, which was heavily normative in character. Here the analysis and argument supporting these theories were seen as so compelling, at least by their authors, that no detailed reference to empirical evidence was required for their acceptance. In any case the data for such testing were unavailable at this time. Cited authors of what are called normative theories include Edwards and Bell (1961), who argued strongly for basing accounting statements on current costs, and Chambers (1976), who advocated even more strongly the use of accounting statements based upon net realisable values. Ijiri's (1967, 1975) work discussed earlier in this chapter would be regarded by many as a good exemplar of this type of work. Watts and Zimmerman (1979), leading advocates of positive accounting, have stated that they would prefer to reserve the term 'theory' for principles advanced to explain a set of phenomena. Supporters of positive accounting theory would probably think that this book generally contains far too many normative elements.

Positive accounting theorists believe that other accounting researchers have neglected the need to explain existing accounting practices and variations in them across firms and industries and over time. The domain of the theory is thus the choice of accounting practices and procedures and the objective is to specify testable hypotheses concerning why accounting practices and procedures are selected by organisations. Many commentators have argued that this is a very narrow definition of what can be called accounting phenomena. Much of accounting research would not regarded as such under this criterion.

One very important thrust of positive accounting research is that any theory must be tested against the evidence. This has done much to promote empirical testing in the accounting literature. Again, many debates reign concerning what constitutes an empirical test of a theory but they are beyond the scope of this book. Ideally, theories should be tested not by whether they can be supported by the evidence—everyday experience suggests that such evidence can usually be obtained—but rather, testing should involve seeking continually to refute theory against the evidence. All theories are thus tentative because refuting evidence may become available at any time. Strictly, a useful theory is said to be falsifiable not if that theory can be refuted by existing evidence, but rather if it can be imagined that it could be falsified if certain evidence were available. Positive accounting theorists are willing to tolerate theories that manifest empirical errors, arguing that no theory can predict perfectly and that seeking to reduce prediction errors or what are called anomalies should lead to better explanations. They see as an important empirical result the discovery of general empirical regularities in accounting procedure choices.

The components of the theory

An important assumption of the theory is that a market works well once explicit consideration is given to contracting and other costs of using the market. Thus, the theory fully subscribes to the efficient market hypothesis reviewed in Chapter 9 and also to the validity of the capital asset pricing model. Reigning asset prices quickly impound all public information. Watts and Zimmerman (1986, p. 160) use the material in Chapter 9 to argue that stock and other asset prices reflect rational expectations and therefore insure that participants in the market are price protected. They are price protected in the sense that investors who are not specially informed buy at a price which is fair in that they will obtain a normal return on their investment. Given that the theory subscribes to the efficient market hypothesis, this means that researchers must look at accounting changes which have cash flow consequences, as the market can see through cosmetic accounting changes (see Chapter 9 for a review of the evidence for this).

The other important constituents of the theory are the assumptions presented earlier in this chapter in the section entitled 'The General Characteristics Of Agency Relationships'. In the theory, emphasis is placed upon the assumption that all individuals seek to maximise their personal welfare. Similarly, great weight is given to the possession of asymmetric information. The existence of uncertainty means that some parties associated with the enterprise cannot fully observe the conduct and actions of others in the organisation. However, the market provides prices based on rational expectations of what they are likely to do. Monitoring, auditing and bonding are methods that managers can use to persuade the market that they will constrain activities on their own behalf. As markets are assumed to work, the problem of risk sharing is of less importance than it will be seen to be in the agent and principal models reviewed in the next chapter, because individuals are assumed to use the market to diversify away risk.

Of central importance to positive accounting theory are agency costs. These arise because contracting cannot be complete and therefore contractual relationships allow parties in agency relationships to pursue their own interests to some degree by obtaining pecuniary and non-pecuniary benefits including effort avoidance or shirking. The occurrence of these phenomena is important in explaining the use of accounting in monitoring and auditing. The theory relies fully on Jensen and Meckling's (1976) view of the firm as a nexus of contracts between parties in an agency relationship. Indeed, the theory seems driven by the imperfect character of available contracts and the need to incur agency costs to limit personal utility maximisation by managers. Many of the hypotheses generated by the theory see accounting information being used by managers to maximise their personal interests in a setting where others are using accounting information to safeguard themselves from the dangers of dysfunctional behaviour by managers. The rather different approach used by agent and principal models when looking at the same issues is illustrated in the latter part of the next chapter (pp. 346–53). Here the objective is on determining the optimal use of accounting and auditing to inform the principal and control the agent. These types of agency models tend to ignore the cost of such operations and have not yet been subject to much empirical testing.

Positive accounting theory focuses upon voluntary changes by managers in accounting and models their choices. It also seeks to explain and predict their reactions to mandatory changes in accounting procedures. It can be used to study a large variety of accounting phenomena but so far its actual application has been focused upon a few areas, and even here is regarded by its advocates as a rudimentary theory capable of much further development. Below we will review some of the questions which have been most intensively studied, concentrating on the theory rather than the empirical results. These empirical studies are well reviewed by Watts and Zimmerman (1986) and further and later examples can be found in the *Journal of Accounting and Economics*. The first two areas to be considered are the relationship between owner managers who own all or part of the enterprise and shareholders, and the relationship between debt providers and managers. Finally we will review the understanding the theory currently provides of the effects of the political process on managerial selection of accounting practices.

Contracts between managers and shareholders

Jensen and Meckling (1976) model the contractual relationship between the shareholders in a firm and an owner manager. Consider first the maximising behaviour of a manager who completely owns a firm, obtaining utility from the revenues achieved and non-pecuniary benefits including shirking. These benefits may also include attractive offices, foreign travel and entertaining and they may result in additional cash flows being generated. The value of the firm on a perfect market will be the discounted value of the enterprise cash flows (V_0) for the firm's risk class. These cash flows will reflect any net gains in cash flow terms obtained from the manager's non-pecuniary activities. The manager's consumption of such benefits or perks (job-specific perquisites), because they yield him or her utility, will extend beyond those which are worthwhile in cash flow terms. This is because such benefits yield the manager extra utility. Spending on perks will continue until the marginal utility obtained is equated to the marginal utility of the cash flows foregone to obtain these benefits. Thus the value of the firm on the market with this type of behaviour (V_n) will be less than if the manager had constrained the consumption of perks to those which yield net cash flows to the firm. If the manager were to sell a proportion of these cash flows, say a, on a price-protected market while retaining decision-making power, the maximum receipts obtained would be aV_n. This would be the maximum that could be achieved as with the sale of part of the firm the manager has a clear incentive to extend further the consumption of non-pecuniary benefits. This is because the manager now bears only $(1-a)$ of the cost of perks in terms of the forgone cash flows associated with any extension of the consumption of non-pecuniary benefits. Thus the cost of these benefits is now cheaper and the manager will now consume more non-pecuniary benefits. This will reduce the value of the firm to, say, V'_n. In a fully price-protected market investors will fully anticipate this conduct and will only buy the proportion of the firm they are offered at a price of aV'_n, thereby fully discounting the manager's conduct.

The manager therefore has an incentive to reduce this decline in the value of the firm by accepting the cost of accounting or bonding activities which will assure the market that excessive consumption of benefits will not occur. This is in the manager's best interests providing that the cost of monitoring and bonding activities are less than the required reduction in perks and that the marginal utility obtained from increasing the value of the entity is least equal to that forgone by the reduction in non-pecuniary benefits.

A similar argument applies where investors are not fully informed. Here investors will incur costs to obtain information concerning the consumption of excessive perks by the manager and will deduct this cost from the amount they are willing to pay for a share in enterprise cash flows. It is thus cheaper for the better informed manager to provide this information or to undertake bonding in order to ensure that the discount the market applies to the firm's cash flows is based on accurate information. In this way, the manager will minimise the decline in wealth caused by the consumption of perks.

Thus the demand for accounting is seen to arise from investors' requirements for monitoring information. Watts and Zimmerman (1983) explain the provision of audited statements by firms well before they were required by the law, utilising this type of argument. With this view, managerial compensation packages will be based to a degree on accounting numbers. Managers are therefore postulated to choose those accounting procedures which increase these numbers, subject to any restrictions on accounting choice stipulated in their contracts and the restrictions imposed by the law, accounting standards and any generally accepted accounting principles. One of the hypotheses of this type which has been tested a number of times is called the bonus hypothesis, which postulates that where managers are rewarded by accounting-based bonuses they will seek to choose those accounting procedures which are expected to increase earnings. That this view is supported means it is one of the empirical regularities which positive accounting theorists cite as a contribution to understanding accounting.

Debt contracts

Similar reasoning to the above is argued to apply to the relationship between the firm and debt providers. Accounting numbers seem to figure strongly in debt covenants designed to safeguard the interest of debt providers. Default on these covenants may entail considerable penalties, such as the seizure of collateral or even the winding up of the firm. Dividend and share purchase restrictions are common especially in the United States of America. Dividend restrictions constrain the classes of funds which can be used to pay a dividend to, for example, some proportion of reported accounting earnings plus net stock sales less monetary and stock dividends. The aim of such constraints is to provide management with an incentive not to opt for risky projects which, although having a positive net present value, carry a relatively high chance of default on debt requirements if they go wrong. The acceptance of such projects provides possible wealth transfers away from debt holders where positive variations in cash flows occur if the managers can disguise this risk when funding the project. Similarly, managers will tend to reject projects with positive net present values which reduce the risk of the enterprise cash flows. It has also been argued that management may favour offering a liquidating dividend to debt now, providing that this amount is less than the face value of outstanding debt, rather than accept projects which will guarantee payments to debt which are required later. Debt covenants help to overcome these problems. Other typical restrictions imposed by debt holders are minimum working capital requirements, restrictions of merger activities and purchases of the securities of other companies, in order to stop mergers and investments which may increase the companies' risk and thereby reduce the value of debt. Restrictions on the unauthorised disposition of assets may arise for similar reasons. An obvious further restriction is a prohibition on the issue of later debt on equal or more favourable terms than existing debt.

Accounting-based debt covenants seek to restrict managerial conduct. Management will therefore seek in their permissible accounting choices to select those accounting procedures which reduce the likelihood that the accounting numbers will disclose a breach of a covenant.

Political accounting choices

Here the view is that politicians and regulators, like everyone else, will seek to maximise their personal utility. The political process is seen here to have very similar characteristics to those outlined in Chapter 11 when we discussed the political aspects of accounting regulation, which were seen as possibly altering the wealth of those affected by it. The political process is also seen as leading to wealth transfers, and altering actual and proposed transfers may be very costly to achieve in terms of lobbying and other costs. Such transfers may be more likely to be imposed on enterprises which are politically prominent because of factors such as perceived excess profits and their importance to the economy.

Politically sensitive firms may therefore be expected to select accounting practices which reduce earnings and the value of reported assets. Similarly, we would expected politically regulated firms, such as some public utilities, to opt for accounting methods which reduce earnings both for these reasons and because of the more obvious desire to declare moderate profits.

Such concerns may require trade-offs with some of the motivations which were postulated earlier to affect accounting choices and to favour income-increasing accounting.

The next section looks briefly in a little detail at some of the hypotheses which have been used by positive accounting researchers and gives a flavour of the empirical evidence obtained.

Possible hypotheses: a brief introduction

A number of studies have sought to explain the responses of some of the parties that might be affected by accounting standards to changes in such standards and to proposed new standards. Most of this work has concentrated on the reactions of management to mandated accounting changes and on management's likely attitudes to accounting changes which are in their discretion. As a common approach is used to tackle both of these problems we shall include both types of study in this brief review. The approach used is to take a view as to the objectives management will seek to maximise in reacting to accounting standards and in deciding on discretionary accounting changes. These assumed objectives are then used to predict likely managerial behaviour in a variety of settings.

A large number of factors have been hypothesised to affect management reactions to possible accounting changes. Principal among these are the political sensitivity of the enterprise, the likely effects of such changes on managerial wealth and income, and any effects on the enterprise's ability to conform to the conditions imposed by debt covenants, both of a formal and informal nature. A major contribution of accounting researchers in this area has been to begin to formulate such hypotheses in a way that allows them to be tested using empirical information, though no general theory in this area has yet been produced. This is still a relatively new approach and many methodological problems remain. Some interesting conclusions are beginning to emerge. Management in their lobbying of accounting standard setters do not seem solely concerned with accounting numbers. Their views on accounting changes seem to depend on whether it is in management's interest to have certain elements of the economic reality of the enterprise better portrayed.

Much attention in this empirical research has been focused on the effects of possible accounting changes on enterprise debt convenants. Enterprise leverage does seem correlated with the reaction of management to accounting changes. Closeness to debt constraints has also been found to be statistically significant in explaining managerial attitudes to proposed accounting changes, though these results have not yet been supported in all relevant studies. The political sensitivity of enterprises when enterprise size is used as a surrogate or proxy has been confirmed as seeming to affect managements' accounting choices. The results for most of the other hypotheses discussed above are somewhat disappointing. Most of them have been supported in only a very few studies. For two classic examples of these studies, see Leftwich (1981) and Zmijewski and Hagerman (1981). Leftwich (1981) sought to relate debt variables to unexpected stock market returns. He studied more highly levered firms which faced larger costs in dealing with debt funds. He found that when these enterprises sought to minimise the effects of mandated accounting changes, they experienced more negative unexpected changes in their stock market return than similar but less levered firms. The Zmijewski and Hagerman (1981) study, mentioned earlier, sought to relate voluntary accounting choices by enterprises concerning income-increasing or -decreasing accounting strategies to political costs, bonus plans, leverage and a risk factor. They found that income reduction was favoured in the accounting choices of seemingly monopolistic firms. Highly levered firms with profit sharing management used income-increasing strategies.

That rather weak results have so far been obtained is not very surprising. There have been as yet relatively few studies in these areas. Most of the studies seek to test a number of hypotheses simultaneously, even though there is no general theory of how management may trade off the different items which are hypothesised to affect their accounting choices, nor has much work been done on the relative costs of different possible reactions to accounting changes. More importantly, there is no extant theory which allows predictions concerning the impact of changes in accounting numbers on security values. Major problems in the methodology used also remain to be solved. Even advocates of the approach regard the results obtained so far as nothing more than suggestive. However, findings like those reviewed here do suggest that this approach has considerable promise for increasing our understanding of accounting generally and of accounting standard setting in particular.

Positive accounting: a final word

Above we have tried to explain the case for positive accounting theory in as fair a way as possible. The theory is acknowledged by its adherents to be still fairly unsophisticated and in need of further development. Even its supporters regard its empirical findings as only suggestive. However, they do claim that a contribution to accounting theory has been made by the three general regularities this work has discovered. Managers of firms with accounting profits or income-based bonuses are more likely to choose accounting procedures that enhance profits or income. The second regularity relates to debt and was not discussed explicitly above though it follows fairly obviously from our earlier discussion. This second general finding is that managers are more likely to select procedures which increase current profits or income, the greater the debt/equity ratio of an enterprise. Finally, income-depressing procedures are more likely, the more politically sensitive the enterprise is believed to be by management. More general contributions are a concern to understand the selection of accounting procedures in a clearly specified organisational setting paying due attention to the moderating effects of well functioning markets, and to encourage the use of empirical testing.

The theory is highly controversial and is expressed in strong language which often seems very derogatory of other types of accounting research work. This may explain some of the scathing comments that it has provoked from critics. For example, Solomons (1986, p. 240), a very senior accounting academic, says that this approach when applied to accounting standards provides no room for the consideration of good or bad accounting. The self-interest of managers is all that counts. Solomons is equally deprecating of the evidence provided by positive accounting researchers. Other commentators versed in scientific method, the history of science and philosophy have criticised the underlying view of science and scientific method utilised in positive accounting theory. They have argued that this view does not reflect the permissible methods of selecting theories utilised in science (Christenson, 1983; Sterling, 1990). Especially attacked have been what are seen to be attempts to escape the need to test theories by refutation by labelling counter-evidence as anomalies and then seemingly ignoring them. Other commentators have cast doubt on the validity of the economic reasoning utilised by the advocates of the theory and been dubious of the historical and other evidence adduced in favour of the theory (see Whittington, 1987, and references therein).

Ultimately, the utility of this programme of research depends strongly on the support provided by the empirical evidence. It is as yet too early to judge this and therefore to evaluate how important a contribution this approach makes to accounting.

Chapter 14 looks at the implications for financial accounting theory of that part of general agency theory called principal and agent theory.

Chapter summary

This part of the book began to move to our focus away from information for decision making to accounting for accountability including stewardship and for monitoring, though some aspects of these subjects were taken up throughout the book. This chapter focused on accountability information and introduced the topics of agency and positive accounting theory. The next chapter continues the theme of this one and looks at some of the accounting implications of what are called agent and principal models.

The first substantive part of this chapter looked at accounting for accountability purposes and included the traditional accounting concern of stewardship. Generally, the demand for accountability or stewardship information was said to arise from a wish to know the actions taken by the enterprise and to control them. It was then shown that, at least, some types of accountability information belong to the same theoretical framework as information for decision making. However it was also indicated that certain information for accountability purposes is geared to motivating managers to exert effort by knowing that their conduct will be monitored in a known way. It was shown that the criteria for whether one information system was better for this purpose than another were different from those used for ranking information systems orientated towards decision making. This finding was said to confirm the practical view that different information is required for different purposes.

The next few sections emphasised the need for objectivity in accounting information used for accountability purposes. It was argued that historical cost accounting systems had advantages for this purpose. One argument was that the figures provided by this system had advantages in that they had a uniqueness not possessed by other accounting systems. They were also argued to be more objective (strictly 'harder') than the figures generated by other accounting systems. The view that this accounting system was better able to cope with conflict situations because its use minimised the debate about the meaning of accounting figures was then presented. Finally claims that the decision-orientated approach to accounting should be replaced by an approach based on fairness to the parties in the organisation were presented.

The next major part of the chapter reviewed some of the general characteristics of the agency relationship in order to provide the foundation for our discussion of positive accounting theory later in this chapter and our review of the accounting implications of the agent and principal model in the next chapter. The essence of the agency relationship was said to be the employment of one or more persons by a principal in a situation where the principal does not have full knowledge of employee activities. The overwhelming problem in the agency relationship was said to be that the parties to the relationship may have different objectives and because of uncertainty are free to pursue their personal objectives to a degree. In order to overcome the difficulties that this causes, the agency was indicated to have to incur agency costs, which take the form of monitoring some of the parties in the enterprise, or to require them to bond themselves not to pursue actions that affect other parties adversely.

The final section of the chapter reviewed some of the ideas of positive accounting theory which, in contrast to much of the accounting literature, seeks to explain why managers chose some accounting procedures rather than others. One important aspect of this theory was said to be an insistence on the provision of empirical evidence. The term 'positive' was shown to reflect the desire to explain existing accounting phenomena rather than to reform them. Other distinguishing features of the theory were said to be a belief that markets work and a concern with agency costs. Indeed, it was said that such costs drive positive accounting models. Later sections showed how the foundations of the theory were used to derive seemingly sensible hypotheses describing managerial accounting choices. The empirical evidence in favour of a number of the hypotheses reviewed in this chapter was said to be only suggestive. More general contributions of the theory were said to be to urge the need to investigate accounting choices in clearly specified organisational and market settings and an insistence that hypotheses should be subject to empirical testing. The theory was said still to be developing and to be controversial. The chapter closed by citing some criticisms of the theory.

14

Agent and principal models

Plan of the chapter

This introduction is deliberately kept short because the general elements of this model were introduced in the last chapter. Our discussion of these models will cover a number of subjects. First we shall discuss the general structure of the model and present an initial selection of the usual assumptions used with these models.

We shall assume that the agency comprises one principal and one agent (represented by P or subscript p and A or subscript a respectively). Other more detailed assumptions will be added later. The general form of these models will then be introduced in a non-technical way. Following this, we shall discuss in separate sections the two major elements of the agent and principal model — risk sharing and effort motivation - and then examine the effect of information on agency models. To ease the presentation, we will generally refer to the agent and principal model as the agency model in this chapter. The next section is more technical and introduces the general method of obtaining solutions utilised in the literature. The following section will look briefly at extensions of the agency model. The final section of the chapter considers the uses that have been made of the agency model in financial accounting.

Agency models are based on the theory of games, use advanced mathematical and statistical theory and involve many complex ideas. However, the presentation used here will be as non-technical as possible, given the wish to capture the full analytical richness of this family of models. The aim is to provide an understanding of agency so that its importance to current and future accounting theory can be appreciated. There is now a very large research literature in this area, much of which is very complex. The approach here is generally to introduce the subject in a very informal way and then to provide a somewhat more rigorous presentation. This latter presentation will occasionally deal with quite technical points. This more technical approach is necessary to allow an informed skimming, at least, of the research literature. References in this chapter will not generally be to orginal articles but to survey articles or chapters that are easier to understand. Most of these are very clear and many can be understood without too many technical skills. Note 1 at the end of this chapter provides a selection of references on agency, arranged approximately in terms of their mathematical sophistication.[1]

Initial assumptions and the structure of the model

As agency models are decision theory based, they use the same ideas which served to provide a foundation for decision making under uncertainty presented in Part II of this book, especially in Chapters 5 and 6. We shall therefore use the same basic notation in agency models as was used in those chapters but we shall supplement it to capture the special features of the principal and agent relationship. We shall assume that the agency contract lasts for only one period. The first assumption we shall make is that both parties to the agency relationship seek to maximise on their own behalf.

With agency models, uncertainty external to the enterprise is only about what state of the environment will reign (s_i, where $i = 1, \ldots S$), as it was with decision making under uncertainty. Such uncertainty is captured by the subjective probabilities which individuals assign to each state. Neither party can control the state of the environment, which is realised as a random variable though, as we shall see, effort by the agent may make more favourable states more likely.

The setting is generally fully specified for each party to the agreement, in that all possible states of the environment are known and all the outcomes or payoffs (x_i, $i = 1, \ldots X$) that may arise from the occurrence of a given state in combination with an action by the agent are known, as are all the actions that the agent may take (a_j signifies an action where $j = 1, \ldots A$). The use of A to signify the full set of actions and A to represent an agent should cause no confusion as the intended usage should make the meaning of A clear. Similarly, the different uses of the symbols a and a should cause no difficulty (a used as a subscript indexes the agent; a refers to an action). The preferences of both parties are known. Any hidden or private knowlege possessed by the agent will relate typically either to the action taken or the agent's characteristics, though it could relate to more informed knowledge about possible or actual state realisation.

In contrast to the earlier chapters, all operating decisions are assumed to be taken by the agent. Thus agency adds an uncertainty about what the agent will do to uncertainty about which state will occur. It therefore allows us to model at a very simple level aspects of organisational behaviour.

Both the principal and agent know the payoff from combining any given action with a specific state. The payoff function for all state–action combinations is known, as it was earlier in decision making under uncertainty. What may be unknown to the principal is what action the agent has actually taken. In this case, without additional information, all the principal can observe *ex post* is the outcome for the period, which is a function of the action taken by the agent and the state of the environment which appeared ($x = f(a, s)$).

It will be assumed that the agent and the principal will assign the same prior probabilities to state occurence (except where the agent has private knowledge about state revelation). Similarly, both parties in the agency relationship will be assumed to assign the same signal probabilities to the signals from an information system, even where the output of the system is available to only one person in the agency, though generally the results of any information system will be known to both parties. Where information is truly private, the non-informed individual will know the signals which the information system can provide and their probabilities and all the possible signal-contingent actions available to the informed party. The non-informed party will be ignorant about only the realised signal and therefore of the actual action taken. When we discuss information systems later, we shall find that they now have a second function in addition to state probability revision. They may now additionally give the principal some indication of the effort of the agent.

Preferences for risky outcomes will be measured, as they were earlier, by utility functions which incorporate attitudes to risk, as explained in Chapter 5, with all the assumptions introduced there. Utility functions may differ between the principal and the agent. Typically, the principal is assumed to be risk neutral and the agent risk averse. Technically, it is typically assumed that the agent is strictly risk averse, i.e. the relevant utility function reflects risk aversion everywhere. These assumptions may not be unreasonable where the principal is 'representative' of a fully diversified security holder but the agent will lose his or her job if the enterprise involved does badly. The agent's utility function will measure the utility of the risky rewards the agent achieves, i.e. $E(U_a) = U(F(x))$ where $F(x)$ represents the reward function for the agent — the compensation scheme for the agent where x represents the payoff from the agency relationship. The principal is assumed to obtain the residual outcome after paying the agent. The principal's expected utility (EU_p), can therefore be written as:

$$E(U_p) = U(x - F(x)) \qquad [14.I]$$

It is this function which the principal seeks to maximise.

The agent's utility function may have an additional element where effort is involved. We shall assume that effort is measured by the actions the agent takes with those actions yielding a higher likelihood of more favourable outcomes being assumed to be more effort-intensive. Effort is assumed to yield disutility to the agent. Such disutility can be expressed by a utility function which depends on the action taken. We shall write this negative component of the agent's utility function as $V(a)$. This element of the agents' overall utility function is assumed to reflect increasing effort aversion (that is, it is convex). The assumption is made in the literature that this element of the utility function can be simply added to that element expressing the expected utility the agent obtains from the reward system (technically the agent's utility function is described as additively separable in these two arguments). Thus the agent's expected utility incorporating both elements can be written as:

$$E(U_a) = E(U(F(x))) - V(a) \qquad [14.II]$$

where the disutility associated with effort is assumed to be known with certainty. There is thus no need to apply to this component a utility function which captures risk attitudes.

The agent will seek to maximise this function when working in the agency relationship. The principal's task is therefore to choose a reward system which motivates the agent to take optimum actions from the principal's perspective when the agent maximises the above utility function. Thus, the solutions to agency problems are self-enforcing as the principal seeks a reward function which induces the agent when optimising personally, given the reward function, to optimise also for the principal.

Any agency contract must be based on items observable to and verifiable by both parties, otherwise the contract cannot be enforced by a court or some other superior authority.

Generally the market remains hidden in agency models (however, see Fama, 1980). Basically, the assumption is made that all factors are bought at fixed prices and all outputs are sold at fixed prices. This assumption is usually assumed to apply also to the labour market. This means that we are assuming that there is a perfect market for agency services which determines the agent's reservation utility, the expected utility the agent could obtain in the next-best employment, to be written as U_{ao}.

The general form of the model

The general form of the model comprises a principal (P) who employs an agent (A). As the first sequential action in the model the principal decides upon either (1) or (2):

1 The risk sharing arrangements between the agent (A) and himself or herself, where only risk sharing is of concern. A risk sharing structure will be written as $F(s)$ where s represents the state of the environment and F represents a structure for sharing the outcomes from the agency endeavour.
2 The reward system to be offered to the agent where he or she needs to be motivated to exert effort or to use any private information possessed on the principal's behalf. Effort is shorthand for the disutility associated with the agent's activity, which is typically modelled as being measured by the agent's, action which will be represented by the symbol a in our models. Such a reward function will be represented by $F(x)$ where x is the outcome from the model and, as we would expect from Chapter 5, is function of the state of the environment (s) and the action of the agent (a), that is; $x = f(s,a)$.

In both cases the principal will choose the risk sharing arrangement or fee structure to maximise his or her expected utility, $E(U_p)$. If the principal wishes the agent to enter into the contract, all these schemes will have to offer the agent his or her reservation price expressed in terms of utility, i.e. the expected utility that the agent could obtain in the next-best employment outside the enterprise (U_{ao}). This constraint on viable reward schemes is called by various names — for example the agent's individual rationality or participation constraint, because a rational agent would neither work nor participate in an agency relationship for less than this. Its effect on the risk borne by the agent means that it sometimes has yet another name, the limited liability constraint, so-called because it defines the limit of the agent's risk in uncertain situations. The agent's reward cannot be less than this.

In order to get the agent when acting in his or her own best interests to maximise automatically for the principal also, the reward system offered will have to motivate the agent to follow the principal's wishes. Such a payment scheme is called incentive-compatible, reflecting that it has to offer a pattern of rewards such that in order to achieve the promised benefits the agent has to follow conduct consistent with what the principal wishes to achieve. This need to motivate the agent flows from the lack of direct knowledge by the principal of the agent's activities. The principal is therefore unable to issue direct orders to the agent or to check completely after the event that they have been respected and therefore to reward or penalise the agent appropriately.

Any reward scheme offered by the principal has always to satisfy one restriction. It must yield the agent his or her reservation utility. Where necessary, it has to satisfy a second condition and offer the agent an incentive to follow conduct compatible with the principal's objective. Given our earlier assumption of a perfectly competitive supply of agents, the reward system offered to the agent will always yield an expected utility at least equal to the reserve utility.

The second sequential step in the model is for the agent to choose a personally optimal action prior to the state of the environment being realised in the light of the reward system and the likelihood of expected states of the environment, using any private information system available which maximises his or her utility. The process the agent goes through is fundamentally the same as described in Chapter 5 for a single decision maker under uncertainty where the outcomes from the reward scheme are taken as the possible outcomes, except that the agent will allow for any effort involved in reaching a decision. The reward scheme offered influences the agent *ex ante*. It is the expected rewards rather than the realised reward that motivates the agent.

The third step in the model is for the state of the environment to occur and the outcome for the period to be announced to both parties. Where the principal has access to an additional information system, the signal from this system will typically also appear at this time.

The objective of the agency model is to allow the principal to maximise the residual outcome after paying the agent according to the reward scheme selected by the principal. The reward scheme is structured so that the share of risky outcomes going to the agent, when the agent seeks to maximise given the reward scheme, is such as to motivate the agent to do what is best for the principal when choosing his or her actions purely to maximise personal interests.

Figure 14.1 provides a summary of the most important assumptions and definitions we have discussed so far.

A and P personally maximise

Both are expected utility maximisers

Model is fully specified

Only external uncertainty concerns likelihood of state of environment

A and P know realised payoff

A and P have same prior probability beliefs

Attitudes to risk may differ

A's private knowledge and action may be unknown to P

$U_p = U(x - F(x)) = $ P's utility function

$U_a = U(F(x) - V(a)) = $ A's utility function

Contract based only on items observable to both *A* and P

P selects risk sharing or reward scheme

A Chooses action, given reward scheme

Equilibrium solution self-enforcing

Figure 14.1 Agency: selected assumptions and definitions

The attraction of the model is that it provides a way of analysing the very complex relations within organisations from an economic perspective. Previous models suggested for this purpose lacked rigor and produced rather nebulous results.

These models make a number of reasonable assumptions in modelling the conduct of the parties. The participation constraint states that the agent will only enter into the agreement if promised what could not be obtained elsewhere; otherwise why should the agent participate? That the principal is willing to offer a contract means that the principal is also satisfied that the contract will meet his or her reservation utility.

Following the usual assumptions of the economic models used in this book, both parties will be willing to accept Pareto efficient solutions where available. The above presentation made it clear that the parties do the best they can, given the other's expected actions. The equilibrium solution to the model is thus self-enforcing because both individuals seek to maximise. This equilibrium concept is taken from game theory (see Kreps, 1990, chapters 11 and 12; Rasmusen, 1989, chapter 1).

The connection between game theory and agency is important (Kreps, 1990, pp.603–604) but we need not go down the path of exploring these relationships, other than to look briefly at one of the equilibrium solutions for agency in these terms. For our purposes, we can say that the solution to the agency model is a refinement of what is called a Nash equilibrium (Rasmusen, 1989, p.33; Kreps, 1990, pp.402–407). A Nash equilibrium is one where each party in a conflict situation, an agency relationship in our case, behaves in the obviously sensible way. Informally this means that participants choose their best response to the obviously best actions of the other players. In an agency context, the obviously best strategy for the principal is to assume that the agent will maximise, given the chosen incentive scheme, and to select the optimal scheme for his or her purposes in the light of this assumption. The agent will take a similiar view of the principal's likely conduct and behave in the same way. Such an equilibrium is obtained if no participant has an incentive to deviate from their best strategy, given that the other similarly does not deviate from his or her best strategies. This means that any such equilibrium is self-enforcing. There may be many Nash solutions in a given conflict situation and such solutions may not be Pareto-efficient. Note 2 at the end of this chapter explains informally the actual equilibrium concept used in agency models: it is called a subgame perfect Nash equilibrium.[2] This just allows for the fact that the principal's decision is made before the agent's decision and therefore the decision by the agent must allow for this prior decision.

As was made clear above, agency models deal with two major problems either singly or in combination. These two problems are:

1 risk sharing, and
2 effort inducement.

The next section deals with risk sharing and later sections expand the model to include effort.

Risk sharing

Here the principal selects a risk sharing function $F(s)$ where outcomes depend on the state of the environment and the risk sharing function determines the amount of the outcome which will go to the parties. We will assume here that the agent is hired to take the optimal act for the principal in decision making under uncertainty and that such actions cause the agent no disutility. It is usually assumed that the agent is risk averse and the principal risk neutral. Left alone, the agent will follow his or her personal preferences if paid a bonus based on outcome. The agent will therefore opt for a decision which will reflect personal tastes concerning risk, whereas the principal would prefer that the expected monetary value criterion should be used for the decision. This dysfunctional conduct flows from incorrect risk sharing. In the same way as people with different tastes can both gain from trading, in this setting rearranging risk will be Pareto optimal. Intuitively, it is clear that the optimal solution is for the principal to bear all the risk and the agent to obtain a flat fee. Note that such an arrangement is an extreme version of risk sharing where the principal bears all the risk and the agent none. This procedure means that the principal who does not mind risk insures the agent against all risk which the agent dislikes. With this arrangement the agent will follow orders, because cooperation now costs the agent nothing. This solution is Pareto optimal where the agent is paid a certain fee equal to his or her reservation utility. The agent thus is made no worse off by following this conduct and the principal maximises the amount obtained from the decision. For this reason the risk sharing solution to the agency model is called the first-best solution. This result obtains because the principal has complete knowledge of the agent's actions. Here the agent would either be required to follow the principal's wishes and receive the reservation price or be severely penalised or replaced. We will now state these conclusions more formally using the agency model directly.

Principal's problem

In a risk sharing setting, the principal maximises expected utility (EU_p) by choosing a risk sharing arrangement $F(s)$ with the agent, subject to the constraint that the agent's participation constraint is satisfied, i.e. $U(F(s)) = U_{ao} =$ a constant. More formally:

$$\text{Max} = E(U_p) \tag{14.III}$$
subject to $U(F(s)) = U_{ao}$,

where the second element in the expression is the participation constraint.

The solution to this problem can be found using the Lagrange multipliers familiar from calculus (for an explanation see Copeland and Weston, 1988, appendix D; Kreps, 1990, appendix 1). This approach yields the following solution:

$$L = E(U_p) + \lambda(E(U_a - U_{ao}) \tag{14.IIIa}$$

where λ is the shadow price or opportunity cost of the participation constraint, indicating the increase in the principal's utility if the participation constraint could be relaxed by one unit of the agent's utility. Taking derivatives with respect to the shares of outcome gives:

$$M(U_p)/M(U_a) = \lambda \text{ for all states } (s).$$

This says that the ratio of marginal rates of substitution (the change in preferences with respect to changes in outcomes) is constant over all states. This gives $MU_a =$ $1/\lambda$, again a constant. The solution is thus to pay the agent a constant fee equal to his or her reservation price, just as we worked out above. The amount the agent obtains is constant irrespective of the state of the environment that actually reigns.

The amount of this fee will be that which yields the agent's reservation utility. This is the maximum the agent can expect the principal to pay as the agent offers no additional benefits to the principal relative to all other agents whom the principal could otherwise employ in the perfectly competitive market.

With this compensation agreement, the agent will follow the principal's orders because such conduct leads to a Pareto efficient solution. This course of action by the agent increases the welfare of the principal and causes the agent no harm because we are at present assuming that taking an action is costless for the agent.

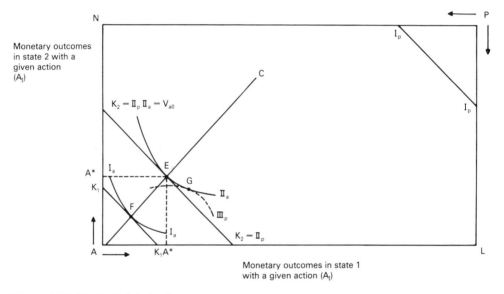

Figure 14.2 Optimal risk sharing

This is shown graphically in Figure 14.2, which is a multi-person variant of Figure 5.2. It shows the total possible outcomes in the two possible states from a specific action, say, A_1. The outcome in the more favourable state, state 1, is shown on the horizontal axis and the outcome in the less favourable state, state 2, is shown on the vertical axis. The horizontal axis is relatively longer because state 1 is assumed to yield greater outcomes than state 2. The agent's share of these outcomes is found by moving away from the left-hand origin. The agent's welfare increases with moves upwards and to the right in the box. The principal's position is shown by reading downwards and to the left from the right-hand corner. The principal's share of the outcomes is shown by reading to the left on the horizontal axis and down the vertical axis. A given point on each axis shows the shares of the two parties according to a given sharing scheme.

Thus, with a scheme which gives the agent a constant amount equal to A* in both states, the principal will obtain the residual amount in whichever state occurs. If state 1 occurs the principal will receive AL minus AA* (as shown on the horizontal axis) and if state 2 appears the receipt will be AN minus AA* (shown on the vertical axis). We wish to use the figure to indicate the optimal sharing arrangement where the principal is risk neutral and the agent risk averse. Recall from Chapter 5 and from the discussion of Figure 5.2 that the agent's preferences for state-contingent outcomes can be illustrated by indifference curves such as I_a and II_a, risk aversion being reflected in their curvature. In a solely risk sharing agency relationship, the highest curve that the agent can expect to obtain is that which yields his or her reservation utility, assumed to be indifference curve II_a in the diagram. The slope of the straight lines such as K_1K_1 and K_2K_2 reflect the identical probability beliefs of the two parties (ϕ_1/ϕ_2). Following the reasoning of Chapter 5, the optimum for the risk averse agent is to obtain his or her certainty line where the ratio of the probabilities is equal to the ratio of preferences between outcomes in the two states as illustrated by points E and F in the figure. The principal's preferences are illustrated by the straight lines such as I_pI_p and II_pII_p. These indifference 'curves' are represented by straight lines because the risk neutral principal values one unit of expected monetary value equally, irrespective of the state in which it occurs.

Optimality requires that the indifference curves of the two parties are tangential. Point E in the figure yields the optimal sharing scheme under our assumptions and shows that the agent achieves his or her certainty line and obtains a fixed fee equal to the reservation utility. The principal obtains the residual outcome.

This straightforward result would disappear if the two parties had different beliefs concerning the probabilities of the outcomes. It was indicated in Chapter 5 that in such a situation a risk averse individual would not seek to obtain the certainty line but would back personal beliefs concerning the likelihood of the states. The simple insurance results obtained here would no longer apply.

If both parties are risk averse, both will bear part of the risk in the optimal risk sharing solution. This is shown in Figure 14.2 where the principal as well as the agent is now risk averse by indifference curves such as III_p. One possible solution is shown where the indifference curve (IIa) representing the agent's reservation utility is tangential to that which reflects the principal's reservation price, taken to be indifference curve III_p. This sharing scheme yields uncertain rewards to both parties. Again our simple solution no longer applies.

This last risk sharing result has been used in management accounting to argue that the conventional view in responsibility accounting that managers should only be held responsible for what they can control is incorrect, as total welfare may be increased if they bear some of the state uncertainty associated with the enterprise if the other parties in the organisation are also risk averse. This may not be a very strong argument where the principals in such an agreement are fully diversified security holders who can be taken to be risk neutral. In practice, a large number of senior managers are rewarded at least in part by bonuses based on corporate or divisional pereformance, some elements of which may be beyond their control. Care has to be taken in designing such systems if they are intended to facilitate risk sharing; otherwise risk averse managers may adopt prudential conduct to avoid risk. In any case, many commentators feel that such schemes are in fact more geared towards stimulating effort than towards risk sharing. We turn to analysing the effect of effort in the agency model in the next section.

Effort inducement

The agent, who will now take effort into account, is effort averse and knows that the principal cannot observe the effort actually deployed. Left alone, the agent will seek to minimise effort. The problem following the introduction of effort into the model is easily illustrated. Assume that the principal adopts the above first-best risk sharing solution in a setting where the agent can improve the quality of the outcomes by exerting effort. Clearly, in an extreme situation where the principal is not able to deduce anything about the effort expended from the realised outcome, the agent will take the fixed fee recommended above and apply no effort. More generally, unless given some incentive the agent will minimise effort. It is this problem that the principal seeks to solve when selecting an incentive scheme. Under any such scheme the rewards offered will be uncertain and require the agent to bear risk. Thus we can solve the motivation problem, but only by deviating from the first-best risk sharing solution. Thus we are dealing with what are called second-best solutions, which involve both risk sharing and effort.

What does effort do?

Agency models are very stylised and no more so than with regard to effort. Above, it was said that effort was not generally defined in any detail but rather expressed costs to the agent of taking action. In the agency literature the effect of effort is assumed to improve the probability of favourable outcomes. This is shown in Figure 14.3, which charts a number of probability distributions showing the probability of each outcome

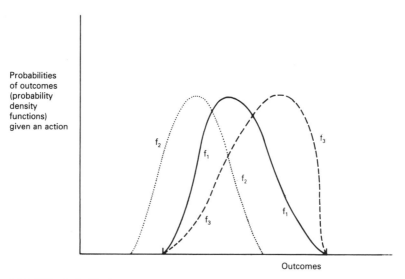

Figure 14.3 Effect of effort

for a given action. Such a probability distribution is called a probability density function (it relates the density of probabilities to outcomes for a given action). It will be written here as $f(x,a)$. A cumulative probability distribution $F(x,a)$ accumulates such densities and therefore, for any outcome, indicates for a given action the accumulated probability of receiving outcomes equal to or less than that outcome; it will sum to 1 over all outcomes. Different probability distributions are associated with different levels of efforts. Assume that the effort associated with probability distribution f_1 in the figure involves low effort and assume that distribution f_3 involves high effort. The effect of effort is thus to shift the distribution to the right and change its shape (by skewing it to the right), thereby increasing the probabilities attached to larger outcomes. Probability distribution f_3 is clearly better than distribution f_1. Technically, the cumulative probability distribution associated with f_3 is said to exhibit stochastic dominance over that associated with the other probability density function.[3] Moving it to the right, as does effort in the figure, increases the return from effort. Thus effort increases outcomes stochastically. This is what effort does in agency theory. With this view, it makes sense for the principal to base any reward scheme on outputs because realised outputs should yield signals as to effort.

The figure is drawn so that both probability distributions we have been considering, f_1 and f_3, have the same extreme values, i.e. they share the same intersections with the horizontal axis or the same supports of the probability distribution. Effort may involve moving supports, as it would if, say, low effort moved distribution f_2, which we shall assume represents the probability density function without effort, so that it becomes identical to distribution f_1. The two distributions are exactly the same except that the latter distribution is moved to the right. Such a movement yields additional information to the principal who, faced with outcomes which only the no-effort distribution could yield, could visit a high penalty on the agent as the principal would know that the agent had shirked. Thus allowing effort to shift supports gives the principal perfect information over some outcomes at least; it converts our problem again into one of risk sharing and amounts to avoiding the agency problem with effort. We shall now present this problem, first in a very informal way.

The principal's problem where effort cannot be observed

The principal's problem now is to maximise personal utility $E(U_p)$, by selecting a reward system for the agent based on outcome, $F(x)$ (where $x = f(s,a)$) subject to:

1 the agent's reserve price (U_{ao});
2 the agent maximising $E(U_a)$,

where $E(U_a) = \{E(U(F(x)) - V(a)\}$, a measures effort and $V(a)$ represents the disutility of effort.

The agent seeks to choose effort so as to maximise the above utility function, given the reward system selected by the principal. This decision can be written using symbols as:

$$\text{Max}_a E(U_a \mid F(x),a) \qquad [14.\text{IVa}]$$

where the vertical line signifies that items to the left, which say maximise expected utility by choosing an act, are conditional on the items to the right, the reward system and the level of effort as measured by the action involved.

This compatibility constraint (14.IVa) can be written in a way which perhaps yields more insight into the agent's decision making process. In order to maximise, the agent will increase effort whilst the incremental reward generated by effort exceeds the additional disutility flowing from the increased effort. Thus, the optimal amount of effort for the agent to expend is obtained at a stationary point where the marginal utility of the fee obtained $M(U_{fee})$ is equal to the marginal disutility flowing from these associated efforts $(-M(U_e)$, where e stands for effort). This approach is standard in economics.

Under certain conditions, the above result is a necessary and sufficient condition for solving the agent's decision problem. It is called the first-order condition because it writes the conditions for solving the agent's decision problem using marginal changes (derivatives of the overall decision problem). Note that, with this approach, s is no longer a decision variable: x now serves to indicate the state of the environment for a given distribution of states via the relation $x = f(a, s.)$ The technical reason for using this condition rather than that in Expression 14.IVa is that strictly the constraint in the form it takes in Expression 14.IVa requires us to select the best action by comparing every pair of possible actions until we arrive at the best action. This is very difficult to do analytically (see Holmstrom, 1979, for a good explanation and references to the literature). Using our reformulated condition, Expression 14.IVa can be written as:

$$M(U_{fee}) = M(U_e) \text{ for the optimal act } (a^*) \text{ for some subset of acts} \qquad [14.IVb]$$

The constraint stated by Expression 14.IVb is an example of an incentive compatibility constraint. If satisfied by the reward structure, it ensures that where the agent maximises given the reward system, the principal will also obtain the maximum utility possible using this reward structure. This should maximise the principal's overall welfare because the reward system used is selected out of all possible reward systems because the principal believes it will induce optimal conduct by the agent.

Providing an incentive to the agent requires that the agent can expect to obtain a higher reward with higher effort. Any such reward will be uncertain because the outcome for the enterprise or agency is uncertain. This means that the solution deviates from the optimal risk sharing solution and requires the agent to bear risk in order to encourage effort. Thus, the solution is regarded as a second-best solution in the literature. The principal will wish to limit this deviation so that rewards are only offered on the expectation of calling forth extra effort.

The solution

In the risk sharing solution, we found that the sharing rule had to take into account the opportunity cost to the principal of satisfying the agent's participation constraint. We have now added a second constraint and therefore we would expect this to figure in the solution to our effort inducing problem. No simple solutions exist to such problems but the general form of the solution is that the ratio of the marginal utilities of the agent and principal weighted by their shares of the outcomes, equals

1 the opportunity cost of the agent's participation constraint as before (λ), *plus*
2 the effect of deviating from optimal risk sharing in order to encourage effort evaluated at the shadow price or opportunity cost of effort (μ), where the effect of extra effort is measured by the change in the outcome distribution due to extra effort over the existing density function distribution. The result of extra effort in terms of increasing the probabilities of more favourable actions is obtained by taking the first derivative of the probability density function $f(x,a)$. This will be written as $f_a(x,a)$

Using the above the general solution, the agency problem can be written as:

$$\{M(U_p)(x-F(x))\}/\{M(U_a)(F(x))\} = \lambda + \mu\{f_a(x,a)/f(x,a)\} \qquad [14.V]$$

where $(x - F(x))$ and $F(x)$ represent the share of outcomes of the principal and agent respectively. With a little manipulation, this expression yields the marginal utility the agent obtains from his or her personal reward as:

$$1/M\{U_a(F(x))\} = \lambda + \mu\{f_a(x,a)/f(x,a)\} \qquad [14.VI]$$

This gives a very straightforward reward function. The agent is paid a fixed sum (measured in utility amounts) plus a reward based on the outcome (x) which is the only thing the principal can observe. Thus, the agent is rewarded depending upon outcome on the assumption that this signals the effort level chosen. Note that if no effort was involved only the first constraint would be binding and there would be no need for the second element of the reward function. We would be back in a pure risk sharing setting.

Below we shall spend a little more time explaining why this works, but the ratio of the probabilities indicates how strongly one can infer effort (a) from observing outcome (x). If a change in action produces a large change in the likelihood of more favourable outcomes, we are safer in paying bonuses on x than where effort makes little difference to the possibilities of more favourable outcomes (see Holmstrom, 1979, pp.74–80). The more we learn about effort from observing output, the higher should be the bonuses based on desirable levels of output.

The meaning of Expression 14.VI is especially clear if we have only two possible effort levels — high effort (a_h) and low effort (a_l). Under these conditions, if we let $f_l(x,a)$ and $f_h(x,a)$ represent the density functions for low and high effort respectively, Expression 14.VI becomes:

$$1/\{M(U_a)(F(x))\} = \lambda + \mu(1 - \{f_l(x,a)/f_h(x,a)\}) \qquad [14.VII]$$

The left-hand element of this expression increases with extra reward ($M(U_a)$ decreases with reward; therefore its reciprocal must increase). The element in curly brackets on the right-hand side decreases with higher effort, i.e. a better outcome is more likely. In this situation therefore the agent's reward should be based on outcome because this signals higher effort. The question remains: under what conditions is it a reasonable assumption that outcomes signal the effort level? The next section considers this matter briefly (see Kreps, 1990, pp. 594–603).

Rewards based on outcomes

The obvious assumption to make is that increased effort yields an increase in uncertain outcome. This can be shown to be insufficient, because in complicated choices the agent takes into account not only the rewards but their probabilities and it is possible that actions which lead to higher rewards in some states may depress the probabilities of rewards in other states. Therefore the agent may opt for a lower effort level which gives a higher probability of reward in those states which are valued more highly, rather than the higher rewards offered in other states by higher effort. To overcome this problem we have to put additional constraints on the ratio of the probability elements contained in curly brackets in Expressions 14.V to 14.VII. Each of these elements are examples of what is called a likelihood ratio. This ratio summarises the relative probabilities of outcomes generated by one action relative to another. Thus in Expression 14.VII, it summarises the relative probabilities of outcomes from high effort relative to those with low effort. What we want is for the probabilities of more favourable outcomes to be greater with high effort than with low effort.

Informally this requires that the appropriate probability distribution for high effort exhibits stochastic dominance over that for low effort. This occurs if a property called in the literature the monotone likelihood property is satisfied. This seems to say what we want, as informally it is satisfied if the ratio of the likelihood of high effort to low effort (as measured by the probability elements of our expressions) rises with observed outcome. If we take two effort levels, low and high (a_l and a_h, where high effort yields the agent greater disutility), and two outcomes, big and small (x_B and x_S), this property is satisfied if the relative likelihood of the better outcome(x_B) with high effort relative to that of the better outcome with lower effort is at least as large as this relative likelihood for the lower outcome (x_s). This condition can be written in symbols as:

$$\phi(x_B \,|\, a_h)/\phi(x_B|\, a_l) \geq \phi(x_S \,|\, a_h)/\phi(x_S \,|\, a_l) \tag{14.VIII}$$

where each element of the two ratios shows the probability of an outcome ($\phi(x)$) conditional on an act having been taken place ($\phi(x|a)$ (see Chapter 6 and Antle and Demski, 1988). Informally, this says that if we observe a high outcome, then the chances are greater that high effort has been expended than is the likelihood that high effort has been utilised when we observe a small outcome. This condition is not quite enough. We also need a condition that stops the agent seeking additional rewards when this is not in the principal's best interests. This requires that we ensure that increases in effort (disutility for the agent) yield diminishing returns in terms of their marginal results on improving the probabilities of more favourable outcomes.

The approach used in the literature

Much of the literature models action choices not as discrete (the choice between high and low effort) but as if any choice were possible from within a range of actions. Actions are treated as if they were continuous. In order to facilitate reading the journals and to allow a comparison between the rather discursive approach in this chapter and the more terse and rigorous treatments in the journals, we shall present the agency model in this form. Technically this requires that we now work with integrals rather than expectations and that density functions are continuous. We use the first-order condition approach outlined above. Recall that the state of the environment is now signalled by the outcome (x) and assume that x is defined for some interval x_0 to x_n The model written in this way is as follows:

$$\underset{F(x),a}{\text{Max}} \int_x U_p \,(x - F(x))(f(x,a))\mathrm{d}x \tag{14.IXa}$$

subject to

$$\int_x U_a(F(x))(f(x,a))\mathrm{d}x - V(a) \geq U_{ao} \tag{14.IXb}$$

and

$$V'(a) = \int_x U_a(F(x))(f_a(x,a))\mathrm{d}x \tag{14.IXc}$$

where $V'(a)$ equals the marginal disutility of effort to the agent. The general solution is unchanged and is

$$1/\{M(U_a)(F(x))\} = \lambda + \mu\{f_a(x,a)/f(x,a)\}$$

The agent's maximisation problem using this notation can be written as:

$$\underset{a}{\text{Max}} \int_x U_a(F(x))(f(x,a))\mathrm{d}x - V(a)$$

which yields the first-order condition

$$\int_x U_a(F(x))(f_a(x,a))\mathrm{d}x - V'(a) = 0$$

Information and communication in agencies

It can be shown that basing $F(x)$, the reward scheme, on even an imperfect information system yielding costless information about the agent's efforts should help the principal in determining the optimal reward system for the agent. This should not surprise us as in Chapter 6 we found that costless information could not harm the decision maker. Here such an information system provides signals about actions and the states of the environment. Therefore, for a fixed action there will be a joint probability distribution formed by its signals and the agent's actions. This should allow the principal to promulgate a reward system that tallies better with his or her interests by making any reward dependent not only on outcomes but also the signals from the information system. Thus access to an information system may allow the principal to reward the agent more correctly because the signals from the information system and the realised outcomes allow the principal to estimate more precisely the agent's effort level and set the reward accordingly. Accounting information may help here if it gives information not otherwise available which helps in deducing the agent's effort. If this were the case, the principal may base any reward also on declared accounting results, perhaps paying a higher bonus when accounting information indicates high effort than when outcomes only are considered.

Holstrom (1979) has developed a solution to the agency problem incorporating a separate information system which may be used by the principal. Let $F(x,z,a)$ be the joint probability distribution of the outcomes and the signals given a specific effort. The associated probability density function is $f(x,z,a)$. Thus we can rewrite Expression 14.VI as:

$$1/\{M(U_a)(F(x))\} = \lambda + \mu\{f_a(x,z,a)/f(x,z,a)\} \tag{14.X}$$

The reward system would be unchanged only if the information system yielded no additional information to the principal. The test for this is very similar to the 'fineness' test for information systems discussed in Chapter 6. This is called the sufficient statistic condition. This says that if outcome (x) is a sufficient statistic for effort (a) relative to an information system yielding signals (z) about effort, the optimal contract need involve only outcomes. A variable (x) is a sufficient statistic for effort in comparison with the information yielded by an information system (identified by its signals z) if the conditional probability of effort given the information yielded by both the outcomes and the information system ($\phi(a|x,z)$ is equal to the conditional probability of effort given outcome information only ($\phi(a \mid x)$)). This can be written as:

$$\phi(a \mid x,z) = \phi(a \mid x) \qquad\qquad [14.\text{XI}]$$

Holmstrom (1979) shows that additional information will have value if Expression 14.XI is not satisfied. Information has value if it is not already available.

This suggests that accounting information may be useful for this purpose. Indeed, accounting information may play an important role in the above models. Managerial bonuses are based on accounting income in many practical incentive schemes. That is, accounting information, with all its faults, is deemed actually to measure outcomes and therefore should ideally yield information about effort. The question therefore arises whether an increase in outcome ascertained using this information system is correlated with effort in the way that was suggested above is necessary if bonuses based upon accounting information are to be successful. As far as is known no results of this type have yet been published though the first part of this chapter presents very strong reasons for exploring these matters. The lack of research findings in this area may reflect the dominance of accounting for decision making. For example, the FASB's Conceptual Project did consider information for stewardship and feedback purposes but it did not explore these matters from an agency perspective (see Chapter 12). This lack of research may also arise because the hypotheses derived using agency models have so far proved very difficult to test. This is due in part to the difficulty of separating the impact of the state variable from that of effort. Another problem in the testing of agency models is that these are generally very simple and the settings reviewed above are not easily found in the practical world. Much work has been done on extending the simple models reviewed above. This work will be reviewed briefly below.

Information value may also help to explain why variables which are not controllable by managers may be used to evaluate senior managers (see Antle and Demski, 1988). Accounting profits, for example, which result from items beyond a manager's control may yield additional indirect information about the manager's efforts not obtained from looking at outcome information. This is because such items may reflect effort levels in some way. For example, although a manufacturing manager may not be responsible for advertising, the success of advertising expenditure may depend on the manager's effort. The utility of an otherwise successful advertising campaign may depend on the effort expended by the manufacturing sector of the enterprise because low effort may mean that the extra orders flowing from advertising cannot be fulfilled. Thus, there is a case for making the production manager's reward dependent on information about advertising because this may yield additional signals about the production manager's efforts.

Finally, we have hardly mentioned the problem of the principal motivating the agent to use and communicate any private information the agent may possess. The logic of agency models with private information in the possession of the agent is generally not dissimilar to the problem of motivating the agent with regard to effort. There is also an important result which shows that ideally it is possible to get the agent to communicate truthfully with the principal (Myerson, 1979). This result shows that, given non-truthful communication, it is possible to provide incentives to the agent to communicate truthfully at no additional cost to the principal. However, this problem is very similiar to the one discussed in Chapter 11 of getting people to reveal their preferences. The practical problems of getting agents to communicate truthfully would seem no less difficult (see Kreps, 1990 chapter 17; Rasmusen, 1989, chapters 7 and 8).

Agency and financial accounting

A strong literature looking at agency and financial accounting is beginning to build up, though it is much less strong than that for managerial accounting (see Baiman, 1990). Generally, this literature looks at the provision of information by enterprise managers after the event, either to the principal or more publicly. This focus seems to produce a much more direct role for accounting information than is provided by the decision making perspective.

This literature generally follows the general approach suggested by Holmstrom (1979) and Gjesdal (1981) (see also Townsend, 1979), which was reviewed briefly in the previous chapter. Another important innovative article was by Butterworth *et al.* (1984). The essence of these models is that the agent has perfect, private information about the state of the environment and the actions taken and therefore about the outcome. This information is not known to the principal, who must rely on the agent to report outcome and other information after the event in some type of accounting report, which is costly to the agency. Thus these models recognise that the manager 'owns' the outcome information. This involves a major departure from the models reviewed so far in this book and even from the agency models discussed above where the principal was assumed to know the outcome and the principal's problem arose because this did not give a perfect indication of effort. Attempts to model financial reporting from an agency perspective go much further and assume that the principal is denied complete knowledge of outcomes, and indeed much else.

Formally, reporting systems transform the actual outcome being reported upon (x) in some way. Thus, rather than directly signalling x, the agent will report $\hat{x}$ using some information system η, the financial reporting system, where $\hat{x}$ is a signal from a financial reporting system and is correlated imperfectly with the realised outcome, x. Such information systems will generally not provide perfect information to the principal.

The contract may also provide for information about the agent's actions. It thus allows the principal to overcome to a degree the lack of outcome and action observability. The choice of reporting system used is very important because it provides the basis for the sharing of outcomes announced by the reporting system between the agent and principal.

Agency contracts must be based on information known to both parties. With this approach therefore the agent and principal write a contract (C) based on reported profit and agree the respective shares of this profit. This contract will be assumed to include the use of auditors to verify such reports. This provides a clear rationale for the use of audit function by providing a signal from a different information system. Here the signals from the auditors' information system will be represented by Y_A and the information system used can be represented by η_A (η_A is an element of symbol H_A where H_A is the set of information systems available). Here the contract will be represented in symbols as $C(\hat{x}, Y_A)$ which represents the principal's share of the outcome where this share is a function of the reported outcome and the signal received from the auditors (Y_A). The agent's share will be the actual outcome less the principal's share, i.e. the agent's share is $x - C(\hat{x}, Y_A)$.

As before, the principal wishes the agent to choose the optimal action from the principal's perspective and seeks to ensure optimal risk sharing in the agency. However, the principal now has to offer an incentive not just for effort but also to motivate the agent to choose the optimal reporting system for the principal.

The principal's first objective is to choose a contract which motivates the agent to choose in his or her self-interest the action level which is also optimal for the principal. The second objective of the principal is to induce the agent similarly to choose the optimal reporting system and signal from that information system, given the agreed auditing system. In addition, the principal is assumed to have some role in designing the reporting system, which will be represented by η_M; signals from this information system will be represented by $\hat{x}$ which represents a message ($\hat{x}$) about the actual outcome x. The most general models assume that the reporting system to be used is mutually agreed by the agent and principal at the time the contract is formulated (Gjesdal, 1981) but others restrict the principal's choice to selecting the general form of the accounting report (Verrecchia, 1986). Additionally, any accounting report made publicly available will have to comply with the relevant company law, to respect the requirements of accounting regulations and to follow any generally accepted accounting principles. Respecting these requirements still leaves the agent with a relatively large degree of freedom as to what to report.

This scenario is much more consistent with practical world views of accounting and does give a basis for explaining some of the institutional characteristics of accounting as observed. However, to better provide a realistic role for accounting, we are making the strong assumption that accounting information provides signals to the principal that are not available from other information. This role for accounting information is assumed. It is not generated from the models used (i.e. it is not endogeneous to the models). However, given this assumption, it can be shown that demands for such information are generated by the models.

As discussed earlier, such information is necessary for decision making and for risk sharing purposes. It is also necessary for the accountability purpose of motivating the agent. It also fulfils a second accountability purpose emphasised by Ijiri (see Chapter 13) of allowing the parties to enforce their rights to their agreed shares in the enterprises' outcomes.

The general model used is represented in Figure 14.4, which divides a single period into a number of sequences. The specification of this model varies between different articles. Thus, much of the literature assumes that the agent alone selects the information system to be used either before or after choosing an act, (see Demski *et al.* 1984; Penno, 1985). The results produced by these models are sensitive to their specifications. We would expect, for example, that where the agent was allowed to choose the information system, the results would differ depending on whether the agent's choice was before or after the selection of action.

The first step in the sequence charted in Figure 14.4 is that the agent enters into a contract $C(\hat{c}, Y_A)$ which determines the shares of the reported outcome ($\hat{x}$).

As part of this contract, the principal and agent agree as to the general reporting system to be used by the manager (η_M) to report an imperfect signal concerning the outcome (x), and an auditing system (η_A) which provides signals (Y_A). The second step in the sequence is that the agent decides what action to take (a) and therefore

Time →

↑	↑	↑	↑	↑	↑	↑
Owner chooses sharing rule $C(\hat{x}, Y_A)$; agent obtains $(x - C(\hat{x}, Y_A))$, determines the feasible reporting system for the manager $(\eta_M \varepsilon H_M)$; agent enters into the contract	Agent takes action (a)	Agent receives private information about state $(1, \ldots S)$	Outcome (x) observed by agent	Agent chooses signal and reports $(\hat{x})$	$(\hat{x})$ audited. Auditors provide signal (Y_A) which may modify $(\hat{x})$	Principal receives Y_A and $\hat{x}$ (as modified); outcome is shared between principal and agent; principal obtains $C(\hat{x}, Y_A)$ and agent receives $(x - C(\hat{x}, Y_A))$

Figure 14.4 Accounting for accountability in agency context

what effort to expend prior to the announcement of state realisation (x) to the agent. The agent then receives private information concerning the state realised and the consequent outcome $x = (x, a)$; such information may be perfect or imperfect. The next step in the process is for the agent to select the details of the information system (η_M) to be used and to generate a signal $\hat{x}$ after receiving private information. In the penultimate step the agent's signal is audited (verified). This procedure yields an auditing signal (Y_A) which may modify the agent's signal. It may occur simultaneously with reporting $\hat{x}$, or later (see Penno, 1985). Finally, the signals are publicly announced and the sharing of the announced outcome between the principal and the agent then occurs according to the terms of the contract.

The principal's problem in models of this type is richer than our earlier agency models which required the selection of only a reward system. Here the principal designs the contract between the two parties to motivate the agent to select the optimal action (a) and the optimal information system, given the auditing requirements stipulated in the contract (if any). This problem is set out informally in Expressions 14.XIIa, b, c, and d.

The principal seeks to maximise personal utility by seeking the optimal personal contract which motivates the agent to choose the optimal effort (a^*) and reporting signal $\hat{x}^*$ (see Expression 14.XIa). This requires that the principal has to maximise his or her personal share of the reported outcome over all possible audit signals, given the actual outcome, and over all outcomes conditional on all acts. The principal does this by maximising subject to three constraints. The first is the familiar participation constraint (Expression 14.XIIb). The other two are an incentive compatability constraint which induces the agent to choose the signals from optimal reporting system $(\hat{x})$ from the principal's perspective (14.XIIc) and the second motivates the agent to choose similarly the best action from this viewpoint (14.XIId).

The first of these two compatibility constraints (Expression 14.XIIc) requires the agent to choose the signal so that it maximises the agent's expected utility $E(U_a)$ conditional on the act chosen and the audit signal (Y_A), less the disutility of the agent's effort $V(a)$. This expected utility is obtained by maximising personal income less the transfer which would otherwise be made to the principal, given the audit signal summed over all audit signals conditional on outcomes (x).

The second constraint (Expression 14.XIId) assumes that the agent selects that act which maximises expected utility less the disutility of effort. Here expected utility is maximised by optimising personal income less the transfer to the principal based on the reported outcome, conditional on the outcome and audit signal summed over all audit signals conditional on outcomes and over all outcomes given all acts. We now write this problem out more formally.

$$\text{Max } E(U_p(a^*x^*)) \qquad\qquad [14.\text{XIIa}]$$

where $E(U_p) = U_p(C(\hat{x}, Y_A)$ conditional on the optimal act and reporting system where the arguments of the utility function are summed over all audit signals (Y_A) weighted by the conditional probabilities of the audit signal given an outcome ($\phi(Y_A \mid (x,a))$) and over all outcomes (x) given an act weighted by the conditional probabilities of the outcome ($\phi(x \mid a)$).

$$E((U_a \mid a, Y) - V(a)) \geqslant V_{oa} \qquad\qquad [14.\text{XIIb}]$$

where the expected utility, $U_a(x - C(\hat{x}, Y_A))$, is conditional on the chosen act and the associated audit signal and the arguments of the expected utility function, $E(U_a)$ are summed over all conditional outcomes and over all conditional signals (as above) weighted by the respective conditional probabilities ($\phi(Y_A) \mid (x,a)$) and $\phi(x \mid a)$

$$\underset{\hat{x}}{\text{Max }} E(U_a, Y_A) - V(a) \qquad\qquad [14.\text{XIIc}]$$

where the expected utility conditional on the audit signal is obtained by maximising personal income less the transfer based on the actual outcome which would be made to its principal ($x - C(\hat{x}, Y_A)$) if the reporting system was not used. Here the arguments of the utility function are summed over all audit signals conditional on outcomes ($\phi(Y \mid x,_a)$)

$$\underset{a}{\text{Max }} E(U_a a, Y_A) - V(a) \qquad\qquad [14.\text{XIId}]$$

where maximum expected utility is obtained by maximising personal income less the actual transfer to the principal ($x - C(x, Y_A)$), conditional on the act and the audit signal. The expected utility is summed over all audit signals conditional on outcomes ($Y_A|x$) and over all outcomes conditional on an act ($x|a$) weighted by the respective conditional probabilities.

This model brings out the importance of auditing as a device for verifying the agent's signal. The possibility of the application of a known auditing technology motivates the agent to report correctly. In these models, it is normally assumed that auditing is costless and perfect and that the detection of any error also provides knowledge of the size of the error. Costly auditing has also been shown to be valuable (see Ng and Stoeckenius, 1979; Verrecchia, 1986). Models of this type have not generally been expanded to allow for the agency characteristics which the presence of the auditor brings to the model, i.e. the auditor requires to be motivated to be efficient in exactly the same way as the manager. Nor has the possibility of collusion between the auditor and the manager been much modelled. For an initial attempt to deal with these problems, see Antle (1982).

Applying the agency approach to financial accounting

The reports provided by managers in the above models are public information; therefore we would expect such information to obtain value in the same situations which we saw in Chapter 7 may generate value for public information. This means that we would expect this type of information to be valuable to the agency if it provides opportunities for improved risk sharing. It seems intuitively reasonable that even imperfect reporting of outcomes by the manager should improve risk sharing, where the principal does not know the actual outcome. Gjesdal (1981) indicates that this is the case providing that the principal's marginal utility obtained from his or her share is correlated with the manager's signals. This means that including the management's information in the agency contract will improve risk sharing possibilities.

Earlier we also showed that public information about productive opportunities may allow a Pareto improvement to be achieved. Similarly, information provided by the agent may yield additional information about the agent's productivity. Gjesdal (1981) again shows this will be the case providing that the signals provided and the agent's actions are correlated. In an agency context, such information is used to motivate the agent. Other work in this area has suggested that information from the agent about the available technology will also be useful to the agency (see Christensen, 1981, 1982).

When reviewing public information we also suggested that this may lead to Pareto improvements where additional information helped to complete the market by allowing trades which otherwise could not be accomplished. Information in an agency model may play a similar role by improving risk sharing possibilities for its agent and managers.

Finally, in Chapter 7 we suggested that public information maybe valuable where it could be provided more cheaply publicly than by each market participant seeking to generate the information privately. Similarly, in an agency context it may be cheaper for the agent to provide the information than for the principal to seek to discover the information privately or to employ a third party to provide it.

There have been a number of other general findings using variants of the approach discussed above. Much of the work using this approach utilises Holmstrom's finding (reviewed above) that *ex post* information will provide a Pareto improvement provided that this information yields information additional to that already possessed. This is a very important result because it suggests that additional, information however imperfect, will be of value.

It has also been shown that increasing the agent's private information available prior to decision may not necessarily lead to a Pareto improvement for the agency (Christenson, 1981, 1982). This is because private information may allow the agent to shirk because it may allow him or her to select a low effort level and say that higher effort has been provided. This would be the case when, using public information, the principal cannot distinguish between the outcomes associated with an unfavourable state but high effort, and a favourable state and low effort. If the agent was given information about these two states, when the favourable state was revealed he or she could opt to provide low effort, knowing that this effort level could not be distinguished from knowledge only of which state was actually realised.

As an illustration consider a two-state and two-effort level problem, where the principal can observe outcomes only. State 1 yields 10,000 monetary units irrespective of whether high or low effort is provided. State 2 yields 10,000 units if low effort is used by the agent and 15,000 units if high effort is provided. This is illustrated in Table 14.1 where e_l stands for low effort and e_h stands for high effort.

Table 14.1 Two-state, two-effort problem

	s_1	s_2
e_l	10 000	10 000
e_h	10 000	15 000

Thus, if the agent receives information that state 2 will reign he or she could opt for low effort knowing the principal cannot detect shirking.

This is not a general conclusion. Two results are possible with private information received prior to the agent making a decision. First, as above, there is a danger that the agent will shirk. Secondly, the reward function chosen, given the knowledge of the private information system and its possible signals, may motivate the agent to maximise effort, given the private information system.

Similar findings apply to public information received prior to agent decision making. Generally following the findings in Chapter 7, we would expect such information to lead to a Pareto improvement but, as in the case of private information, the receipt of such public information may allow the agent to shirk where the agent has additional knowledge relative to the principal.

This literature has produced a wide range of findings. We have already considered Gjesdal's work concerning the comparability of information systems for stewardship. Verrecchia (1986) uses the agency approach described above to consider the situation where the principal is allowed to define partially the set of accounting procedures, thereby restricting the manager's choice. The manager is permitted to select privately between two information systems. One method, which Verrecchia called the financial reporting alternative, reports the true outcome with noise using accounting procedures selected by the agent. The alternative procedure allows the agent to observe the true outcome at a fixed cost to the whole agency. The manager is allowed to select any procedure for determining accounting profits which does not produce larger profits than the greatest profits yielded by the alternatives. The model thus introduces an extra moral hazard into the agency model. It is shown that, under specific assumptions, it is not necessarily in the principal's best interest for the manager to report the maximum profit figure. This is because once a certain profit level is obtained the expected benefit, in terms of further motivating the agent to eliminate noise by paying the costs of obtaining knowledge of the actual outcome, becomes negative.

Penno (1985) introduces one role of auditing which is similar in a way to the general model presented above. Here, however, the agent offers interim reports which are audited later. He shows that there will be gains from this type of communication under certain assumptions. Communication allows the agent to share the risk associated with the audit with the principal (see also Dye, 1983). Penno also considers the effect of the possibility of bankruptcy on the worth of communication. With bankruptcy in certain settings the optimal sharing contract is a constant; that is, the principal gets a fixed sum. There is no advantage to the principal in reporting by the agent or having this report verified. However, it also showed where there is a threat of bankruptcy the principal would gain from a costless auditing function which indicates perfectly that the agent is solvent.

Using a rather different approach, Demski *et al* (1984) show that both the principal and the agent may prefer that the choice of the type of monitoring system be delegated to the manager in order to take advantage of the manager's superior private information which improves the enterprise's contracting and decision making opportunities. The principal can capitalise upon what Demski and colleagues call the manager's 'local expertise' by allowing managers to choose accounting methods and rewarding them accordingly. This model shares with other models reviewed here a wish to reflect the fact that in the practical world it is often managers who decide what to report and in which form, at least within certain limits.

The approach discussed above has been used quite intensively in auditing. For example, Ng (1978) has shown that where managerial remuneration varies proportionally with reported performance the agent would prefer as coarse and positively biased reporting system as possible whereas the principal would prefer as fine and unbiased a system as can be obtained. Auditing may reduce the bias in managerial reports.

More generally, these articles seek to show why there may be a demand for auditing. This is seen to be because auditing may encourage a manager to report truthfully (see, for example, Antle, 1982).

Extensions and criticisms

It is not intended to criticise the agency model here. There are good reviews by Baiman, (1990) and Scapens, (1985). Such criticisms are very wide, ranging from views that people are not motivated in the ways suggested to highly technical debates concerning the mathematics of the models. One obvious problem with the agency model is that its mathematical formulations are very complex, even when they give rise to fairly simple solutions.

Chapter summary

The first substantive section of this chapter introduced the assumptions and structure of the agent and principal model. The agency relationship was said generally to represent a one-period model. The two parties to the relationship are seen as maximising personal expected utilities in a setting where the environment is uncertain in a setting of the same type as we examined in Chapter 6. Generally it was assumed that the principal was risk neutral and the agent strictly risk averse. The components of the model were said generally to be completely specified except that the principal does not know the action taken by the agent or the state of the environment. The payoff from the relationship depends on the state of the environment and the agent's action. The effort associated with such actions were said to cause the agent disutility.

The general form of the model was then described. Here the principal was shown to take the first step in the model by choosing either a risk sharing arrangement or a reward structure for the agency where action by the agent involves effort. Such a reward structure, in order to motivate the agent to maximise for the principal, was shown to require that the agent must be offered a reward system which ensures that the agent automatically maximises for the principal when maximising on his or her own behalf.

The second step in the model was then shown to involve the agent choosing a personal optimal action in the light of the reward system and the likelihood of the state of the environment. The third and final step in the model was for the state of the environment to be realised and the outcome to be announced.

Prior to going on to present the two major variants of the agency model, we then discussed briefly the connection between game theory and agency. The solution to the agency model was indicated to be based on the concept of a Nash equilibrium, which is founded on the idea that parties in the agency relationship choose their obviously best strategy on the supposition that the other party similarly chooses his or her best strategy. Such an equilibrium was said to be self-enforcing if the participants had no incentive to deviate from their personal optimal strategies.

The next two sections looked in sequence at the problems of risk sharing and effort inducement in the agency relationship. With risk sharing, it was shown that the risk neutral principal would optimise by offering the risk averse agent a flat fee equal to the agent's reservation utility. In this way the principal will maximise the residual outcome received and the agent will obtain his or her personal reservation utility, thereby ensuring that the agent will maximise on the principal's behalf as this conduct entails no costs to the agent. This solution was then illustrated graphically.

The section dealing with effort commenced by describing what the agent's efforts achieve. Basically, effort was said to make more likely favourable outcomes. In this setting, the principal's problem is to set a reward structure for the agent which gives the agent his or her reservation utility and provides the agent with an incentive to maximise on behalf of the principal when seeking to maximise personal utility. This incentive is provided by that part of the reward system called the incentive compatibility constraint. The approach used in this chapter to this compatibility constraint utilised what is called the first-order condition, which basically ensures that the agent will seek an outcome where the marginal utility obtained from his or her fee just compensates for the disutility of the marginal effort.

The solution obtained in this way was shown to involve the opportunity cost of the agent's participation constraint plus the effects of deviating from the optimal risk sharing in order to encourage the agent to take effort. This solution was then demonstrated to give rise to a very straightforward reward function which yields the agent a fixed sum plus a reward based on outcome, which is the only thing the principal is assumed to be able to observe.

We then discussed under what conditions observations of output allow the principal to deduce the agent's efforts.

The next main section of the chapter presented the general approach used in the literature in order to allow the findings in this chapter to be reconciled with the more technical journal literature. The chapter then turned to the problem of information and communication in agencies. Here, it was shown that even an imperfect information system can aid the principal in deducing the agent's effort, providing that such information is costless. The conditions for this result were then presented. This basically requires that any information system used should yield additional information about effort over and above that obtained by observing output.

The chapter concluded by considering a number of studies which have used the agent and principal approach to investigate financial accounting. These models were said generally to assume that the principal knows even less than we have assumed so far, and that information is asymmetric in that the agent alone knows the state of the environment and the outcome. The principal has to rely on financial reports provided by the agent in order to learn something of the output of the agency. This was said to introduce a new moral hazard into the agency relationship as the agent now has partial control over the form in which the outcome is reported. To overcome this problem the principal will at the time of contracting seek to restrict the degrees of freedom available to the agent in reporting and insist upon employing auditors. This section therefore provided a strong rationale for the use of auditors. It was also indicated that allowing financial reporting in the model made the principal's problem even more complex as the principal now also has to offer the agent an incentive to report in a way which is optimal for the principal subject to audit signals.

It was said that scenarios produced by these models are much more consistent with practical world views of accounting than those obtained using the decision making perspective entertained throughout much of this book. These models are also consistent with the use of accounting for accountability purposes discussed in Chapter 13. However, we should remember that the utility associated with accounting in these models is assumed and is not generated by the models themselves.

The final section of this chapter appraised the findings obtained by focusing the agent and principal perspective on financial acounting. It was shown that this approach confirmed our earlier findings concerning the value of public information in Chapter 7. Basically, financial reporting by managers was indicated to obtain value for the same reasons as were shown earlier to give public information value. One especially important finding in this area is that which provides an ability to rank accountability information systems (Gjesdal, 1981). Other important findings have been provided by Verrecchia (1986) and Penno (1985).

Notes

1. The following references to agency models are arranged in order of difficulty:

'Introduction' Pratt and Zechauser 'Economics of agency' by K. Arrow in Pratt and Zechauser (1985).
　　Both of these are purely verbal in their presentation.
Kaplan and Atkinson (1989, chapters 16 and 17)
Baiman (1982)
Tirole (1988, chapter 1, especially pp. 34–42 and 51–55)
Kreps (1990, chapters 16 and 17)
Strong and Walker (1987, chapter 8)
Rasmusen (1989, Part II)
(More generally useful in exploring the connection between game theory and agency models; see also Kreps, 1990, part III)
Holmstrong (1979)
Antle and Demski (1988)
(Especially useful for the role of information and communication in agency models).
Baiman (1990)
(Looks in detail at existing and possible future extension of the model).

2. Strictly, the equilibrium concept used in agency models is called a Nash perfect equilibium. As we saw above, the agency model is made up of a number of sequential steps; the equilibrium concept used in agency requires that the strategies chosen provide a Nash equilibrium for the complete process and also for each step in strategies, whether or not these strategies lead to equilibrium. This allows for the fact that it is necessary to model the sequence in which the participants move because different results may follow if a variety of sequences were possible. A full understanding requires a reasonable knowledge of game theory (see Kreps, 1990, part III; and Rasmusen, 1989, Part I).

3. What is called first-order stochastic dominance is displayed by one cumulative probability distribution relative to another if the cumulative probability that an outcome will take a value *less* than, say, x is greater for the second distribution than the first. Thus the probability of receiving less than a certain outcome is greater with distribution f_1, than for f_3. Thus the cumulative probability distribution with respect to high effort rather than low effort will stochastically dominate that distribution for low effort, that is $a_h > a_l \Rightarrow F(x, a_h) < F(x, a)$, where the subscripts h and l index high and low effort respectively and the symbol $\Rightarrow$ stands for 'implies'. The right-hand relationship follows because the low effort distribution accords a higher probability to less valuable outcomes. All decision makers under uncertainty would prefer the dominant distribution over the other. Not all distributions can be compared in this way. Another ranking of distributions is called second-order stochastic dominance, which is satisfied if the area under the cumulative distribution up to some outcome is less than for the other distribution. This is because the latter distribution provides a higher probability of lower outcomes. All risk averse individuals would accept this ranking between pairs of distributions.

4. This optimisation problem can also be solved using the Lagrange multiplier approach where we maximise Expression 14.IXa subject to Expressions 14.IXb and 14.IXc (after some rearrangement). Using this approach we maximise L in the following expression.

(1) $L = \int U_p(x - F(x)) (f(x,a)) \, dx$

(2) $+ \lambda[\int U_a(F(x)) (f(x,a)) \, dx - V(a) - U_{ao}]$

(3) $+ \mu[\int U_a(F(x)) (f(x,a)) \, dx - V'(a)]$ [14.XIII]

Differentiating this whole expression with respect to $F(x)$ yields:

(1) $- U'_p(x - F(x))f(x,a)$

(2) $+ \lambda U'_a(F(x))f(x,a)$

(3) $+ \mu U'_a(F(x))f(x,a)$

where the primes represent first derivatives. Setting this expression to zero yields the classical expression for the optimal reward structure for the agency (see, for example, Holmstrom, 1979):

$$\frac{U'_p(x - F(x))}{U'_a(F(x))} = \lambda + \frac{\mu f_a(x,a)}{f(x,a)}$$ [14.XIV]

The expression generally used in the text follows by rearrangement. Expression 14.IV says that ratio of the principal's and agent's marginal utilities equals a constraint plus a reward term based on the likelihood ratio.

References and further reading

Abdel-Khalik, A.R. *et al.* 1981. *The Economic Effects on Leases of FASB Statement No.13, Accounting for Leases.* Stamford, CT: FASB.

Accounting Standards Steering Committee. 1975. *The Corporate Report.* London: ASSC.

Accounting Standards Committee. 1979. *Consultative Document: Setting Accounting Standards.* London: ASC.

Akerlof, G.A. 1970. 'The Market for Lemons: Quality Uncertainty and the Market Mechanism', *Quarterly Journal of Economics* (August): 488–500.

Alexander, S.S. 1950. 'Income Measurement in a Dynamic Economy', in *Five Monographs on Business Income*, Study Group on Business Income. American Institute of Accountants: 1–97.

Alexander, S.S. 1961. 'Price Movements in Speculative Markets: Trends or Random Walks', *Industrial Management Review* (May): 7–26.

Alexander, S.S. 1977. 'Income Measurement in a Dynamic Economy', revised by Solomons, D. (1950) in Baxter, W.T. and Davidson, S. (eds.), *Studies in Accounting.* The Institute of Chartered Accountants in England and Wales: 35–85.

American Institute of Certified Public Accountants. 1970. *Accounting Principles Board Statement No.4*, 'Basic Concepts and Accounting Principles Underlying Financial Statements of Business Enterprises'. New York: AICPA.

American Institute of Certified Public Accountants. 1973. *Report of the Study Group on the Objectives of Financial Statements.* 'The Trueblood Report'. New York: AICPA.

Amershi, A.H. 1988. 'Blackwell Informativeness and Sufficient Statistics with Applications to Financial Markets and Multiperson Agencies', in Feltham, G.A., Amershi, A.H. and Ziemba, W.T. (eds.), *Economic Analysis of Information and Contracts.* Boston: Kluwer Academic Publishers.

Antle, R. 1982. 'The Auditor As An Economic Agent', *Journal of Accounting Research* (Autumn): 503–527.

Antle, R. and Demski, J.S. 1988. 'The Controllability Principle in Responsibility Accounting', *Accounting Review* (October): 700–719.

Arrow, K.J. 1963. *Social Choice and Individual Values.* New Haven: Yale University Press.

Arrow, K.J. 1964. 'The role of securities in the optimal allocation of risk bearing', *Review of Economic Studies*, Vol. 3: 257–273.

Arrow, K.J. 1974. 'Alternative Approaches to the Theory of Choice in Risk-Taking Situations', in Arrow, K.J. (ed.), *Essays in Risk Bearing.* Amsterdam and New York: North Holland Publishing Co.: 1–43.

Arrow K.J. 1985. 'The Economics of Agency', in Pratt, J.W. and Zeckhauser, R.J. (eds.), *Principals and Agents: The Structure of Business.* Cambridge, MA: Harvard University Press.

Atkinson, A.F. and Stiglitz, J.E. 1980. *Lectures on Public Economics.* New York: McGraw-Hill.

Baiman, S. 1979. 'Discussion of Auditing: Incentives and Truthful Reporting', *Journal of Accounting Research* (Supplement): 25–29.

Baiman, S. 1982. 'Agency Research in Managerial Accounting: A Survey', *Journal of Accounting Literature* (Spring): 154–213.

Baiman, S. 1990. 'Agency Research in Managerial Accounting: A Second Look', *Accounting, Organisations And Society*, Vol.15, No.4: 341–371.

Ball, R.J. and Brown, P. 1968. 'An Empirical Evaluation of Accounting Income Numbers', *Journal of Accounting Research* (Autumn): 159–178.

Barton, A.D. 1974. 'Expectations and Achievements in Income Theory', *Accounting Review* (October): 664–681.

Baxter, W.T. and Davidson, S. (eds.). 1977. *Studies in Accounting*. London: Institute of Chartered Accountants in England and Wales.

Beaver, W.H. 1968. 'The Information Content of Annual Earnings Announcements', *Empirical Research in Accounting: Selected Studies* (Supplement), *Journal of Accounting Research*: 67–92.

Beaver, W.H. 1973. 'What Should be the FASB's Objectives', *Journal of Accountancy* (August): 49–56.

Beaver, W.H. 1974. 'Implications of Security Price Research for Accounting', *Accounting Review* (July): 563–571.

Beaver, W.H. 1981a. *Financial Reporting: An Accounting Revolution*. Englewood Cliffs, NJ: Prentice Hall, 2nd edition 1989.

Beaver W.H. 1981b. 'Market Efficiency', *Accounting Review* (January): 23–37.

Beaver, W.H. 1989. *Financial Reporting: An Accounting Revolution*, 2nd edition. Englewood Cliffs, NJ: Prentice Hall.

Beaver, W.H., Christie, A. and Griffen, P.A. 1980. 'The Information Content of SEC Accounting Series Release No.190', *Journal of Accounting and Economics* (August): 127–157.

Beaver, W.H., Clarke, R. and Wright, W. 1979. 'The Association Between Unsystematic Security Returns and the Magnitude of the Earnings Forecast Error', *Journal of Accounting Research* (Autumn): 316–340.

Beaver, W.H. and Demski, J. 1974. 'The Nature of Financial Accounting Objectives: A Summary and Synthesis', *Journal of Accounting Research* (Supplement): 170–187.

Beaver, W.H. and Demski, J. 1979. 'The Nature of Income Measurement', *Accounting Review* (January): 38–46.

Beaver, W.H. and Dukes, R.E. 1972. 'Interperiod Tax Allocation, Earnings Expectations and the Behaviour of Security Prices', *Accounting Review* (April): 320–332.

Beaver, W.H., Kennelly, J.W. and Ross, W.M. 1968. 'Predictive Ability as a Criterion for the Evaluation of Accounting Data', *Accounting Review* (October): 654–682.

Beaver, W.H., Kettler, P. and Scholes, M. 1970. 'The Association Between Market Determined and Accounting Determined Risk Measures', *Accounting Review* (October): 654–682.

Beaver, W.H. and Landsman, W.R. 1983. 'Incremental Information Content of Statement 33 Disclosures', *Financial Accounting Standards Board*.

Benston, G.J. 1976. *Corporate Financial Disclosure in the UK and USA*. London: D.C. Heath, and Institute of Chartered Accountants in England and Wales.

Benston, G.J. 1983. 'An Analysis of the Role of Accounting Standards for Enhancing Corporate Governance and Social Responsibility', in Bromwich, M. and Hopwood, A.G. (eds.), *Accounting Standards Setting: An International Perspective*. London: Pitman Publishing.

Biddle, G.C. and Lindahl, F.W. 1982. 'Stock Price Reactions to LIFO Adoptions: The Association Between Excess Returns and LIFO Tax Savings', *Journal of Accounting Research* (Autumn): Part 11: 551–588.

Black, F. 1972. 'Capital Market Equilibrium with Restricted Borrowing', *Journal of Business* (July): 444–455.

Bowman, R.G. 1980. 'The Debt Equivalence of Leases: An Empirical Investigation', *Accounting Review* (April): 237–253.

Brealey, R. and Myers, S. 1988. *Principles of Corporate Finance*. New York: McGraw-Hill. (New edition forthcoming.)

Bromwich, M. 1977. 'The Use of Present Value Valuation Models in Published Accounting Reports', *Accounting Review* (July): 587–596.

Bromwich, M. 1980. 'The Possibility of Partial Accounting Standards', *Accounting Review* (April): 288–300.

Bromwich, M. 1985. *The Economics of Accounting Standard Setting*. Englewood Cliffs, NJ: Prentice Hall/ICAEW.

Bromwich, M. and Hopwood, A.G. (eds.). 1983. *Accounting Standards Setting: An International Perspective*. London: Pitman Publishing.

Bromwich, M. and Wells, M.C. 1983. 'The Usefulness of a Measure of Wealth', *Abacus* (December): 119–129.

Butterworth, J.E., Gibbins, M. and King, R.D. 1984. 'The Structure of Accounting Theory: Some Basic Conceptual and Methodological Issues' in Basa, S. and Milburn, J.A. (eds.), *Research to Support Standard Setting in Financial Accounting: A Canadian Perspective*. Proceedings of the 1981 Clarkson Gordon Foundation Research Symposium (Halifax, Nova Scotia) reprinted in Mattessich, R.R. (ed.), *Modern Accounting Research: A Survey and Guide* (Vancouver: General Accountants Research Foundation 1984).

Canadian Institute of Chartered Accountants. 1980. *Corporate Reporting: Its Future Evolution: a research study*. 'The Stamp Report'. Toronto: CICA.

Carsberg, B.V., Hope, A.J.B. and Scapens, R.W. 1974. 'The Objectives of Published Accounting Reports', *Accounting and Business Research* (Summer): 162–173.

Chambers, R.J. 1963. 'Why Bother With Postulates?', *Journal of Accounting Research*, Vol.1, No.1 (Spring): 3–15.

Chambers, R.J. 1966. *Accounting, Evaluation and Economic Behaviour*. Englewood Cliffs, NJ: Prentice Hall.

Chambers, R.J. 1976. 'The Possibility of Normative Accounting Standards', *Accounting Review* (July): 646–652.

Chandler, A.D. Jr. 1990. *Scale and Scope: The Dynamics of Industrial Capitalism*. Cambridge, MA: The Belknap Press of Harvard University Press.

Christensen, J. 1981. 'Communications in Agencies', *Bell Journal of Economics* (Autumn): 661–674.

Christensen, J. 1982. 'The Determination of Performance Standards and Participation', *Journal of Accounting Research* (Autumn): 151–179.

Christenson, C. 1983. 'The Methodology of Positive Accounting', *Accounting Review* (January): 1–22.

Coase, R. 1937. 'The Nature of the Firm', reprinted in Stigler, G. and Boulding, K. (eds.), *Readings in Price Theory*. Homewood, IL. 1952.

Cohen, K.J. and Cyert, R.M. 1975. *Theory of the Firm: Resource Allocation in a Market Economy*. Englewood Cliffs, NJ: Prentice Hall.

Coombs, C.H. *et al*. 1970. *Mathematical Psychology: An Elementary Introduction*. Englewood Cliffs, NJ: Prentice Hall.

Copeland, T.E. and Weston, J.F. 1988. *Financial Theory and Corporate Policy*. Reading, MA: Addison-Wesley.

Cushing, B.E. 1977. 'On the Possibility of Optimal Accounting Principles', *Accounting Review* (April): 308–321.

Davidson, S., Stickney, C.P. and Weil, R.L. 1976. *Inflation Accounts*. New York: McGraw-Hill.

DeAngelo, H. 1981. 'Competition and Unanimity', *American Economic Review* (March): 18–27.

Dearing, R.W. 1988. *The Making of Accounting Standards*. 'The Dearing Report', The Review Committee under the Chairmanship of Sir Ron W. Dearing. The Institute of Chartered Accountants in England and Wales.

Debreu, G. 1959. *Theory of Value*. New Haven: Yale University Press.

DeGroot, M. 1970. *Optimal Statistical Decisions*. New York: McGraw-Hill.

Demski, J.S. 1973. 'The General Impossibility of Normative Accounting Standards', *Accounting Review* (October): 718–723.

Demski, J.S. 1976. 'An Economic Analysis of the Chambers' Normative Standard', *Accounting Review* (July): 653–656.

Demski, J.S. 1980. *Information Analysis*. Reading, MA: Addison-Wesley.

Demski, J.S., Patell, J.M. and Wolfson, M.A. 1984. 'Decentralised Choice of Monitoring Systems', *Accounting Review* (January): 16–34.

Demski, J.S. and Sappington, D.E.M. 1990. 'Fully Revealing Income Measurement', *Accounting Review* (April): 363–383.

Diamond, D.W. 1985. 'Optimal Release of Information By Firms', *Journal of Finance*, Vol.XL, No.4 (September): 1071–1094.

Dimson, E. 1979. 'Risk Measurement When Shares are Subject to Infrequent Trading', *Journal of Financial Economics* (June): 197–226.

Dopuch, N. and Sunder, S. 1980. 'FASB's Statements on Objectives and Elements of Financial Accounting: A Review', *Accounting Review* (January): 1–21.

Dreze, J.H. (ed.). 1974. 'Allocation under uncertainty: equilibrium and optimality'. New York: Macmillan.

Dyckman, T.R. and Morse, D. 1986. *Efficient Capital Markets and Accounting: A Critical Analysis*, 2nd edition. Englewood Cliffs, NJ: Prentice Hall.

Dye, R. 1983. 'Communication and Post-Decision Information', *Journal of Accounting Research* (Autumn): 514–533.

Dye, R.A. 1986. 'Proprietary and Non-proprietary Disclosures', *Journal of Business*, Vol.50, No.2: 331–365.

Edey, H.C. 1970. 'The Nature of Profit', *Accounting and Business Research* (Winter): 50–55.

Edwards, E.O. and Bell, P.W. 1961. *The Theory and Measurement of Income*. Berkeley and Loss Angeles: University of California Press.

Edwards, R.S. 1938. 'The Nature and Measurement of Income', *The Accountant* (July—October), reprinted in Baxter, W.T. and Davidson, S. (eds.). 1977. *Studies in Accounting*. London: Institute of Chartered Accountants in England and Wales.

Edwards, W. and Tversky, A. (eds.). 1967. *Decision Making*. Harmondsworth: Penguin.

Eggington, D.A. 1980. 'Distributable Profits and the Pursuit of Prudence', *Accounting and Business Research* (Winter): 1–44.

Fama, E.F. 1965. 'The Behaviour of Stock Market Prices', *Journal of Business* (January): 34–105.

Fama, E.F. 1970. 'Efficient Capital Markets: A Review of Theory and Empirical Evidence', *Journal of Finance* (May): 383–417.

Fama, E.F. 1976. *Foundations of Finance*. Oxford: Basil Blackwell.

Fama, E.F. 1980. 'Agency Problems And The Theory Of The Firm'. *Journal of Political Economy* (April): 288–307.

Fama, E.F. and Blume, M. 1970. 'Filter Rules and Stock Market Trading Profits', *Journal of Finance* (May): 226–241.

Fama, E.F., Fisher, L., Jensen, M., and Roll, R. 1969. 'The Adjustment of Stock Prices to New Information', *International Economic Review* (February): 1–21.

Fama, E.F., and Miller, M.H. 1972. *Theory of Finance*. New York: Holt, Rinehart and Winston.

Feltham, G.A. 1972. *Information Evaluation*. Studies in Accounting Research, No.3. American Accounting Association.

Feltham, G.A., Amershi, A.H. and Ziemba, W.T. (eds.). 1988. *Economic Analysis of Information and Contracts*. Boston: Kluwer Academic Publishers.

Feltham, G.A. and Christensen, P.O. 1988. 'Firm-specific Information and Efficient Resource Allocation', *Contemporary Accounting Research* (Fall): 133–169.

Financial Accounting Standards Board. 1974. *Discussion Memorandum on the Report of the Study Group on the Objectives of Financial Statements*. Stamford, CT: FASB.

Financial Accounting Standards Board. 1976a. *Tentative Conclusions on the Objectives of Financial Statements of Business Enterprises*. Stamford, CT: FASB.

Financial Accounting Standards Board. 1976b. *Scope and Implications of the Conceptual Framework Project*. Stamford, CT: FASB.

Financial Accounting Standards Board. 1978. *Statement of Financial Accounting Concepts*. 'No.1 Objectives of Financial Reporting by Business Enterprises'. Stamford, CT: FASB.

Financial Accounting Standards Board. 1979. *Statement of Financial Accounting Standards No.33: Financial Reporting and Changing Prices*. Stamford, CT: FASB.

Financial Accounting Standards Board. 1980a. *Statement of Financial Accounting Concepts*. 'No.2 Qualitative Characteristics of Accounting Information' (May). Stamford, CT: FASB.

Financial Accounting Standards Board. 1980b. *Statement of Financial Accounting Concepts*. 'No.3 Elements of Financial Statements'. Stamford, CT: FASB.

Financial Accounting Standards Board. 1984. *Statement of Financial Accounting Concepts*. 'No.5 Recognition and Measurement in Financial Statements of Business Enterprises'. Stamford, CT: FASB.

Financial Accounting Standards Board. 1985. *Statement of Financial Accounting Concepts*. 'No.6 Elements of Financial Statements'. Stamford, CT: FASB.

Fisher, I. 1930a. *Income and Capital*. New York: Macmillan.

Fisher, I. 1930b. 'The Economics of Accountancy', *American Economic Review* (December): 603–618.

Forker, J.J. 1980. 'Capital Maintenance Concepts, Gains from Borrowing and the Measurement of Income', *Accounting and Business Research* (Autumn): 393–402.

Foster, G. 1980. 'Accounting Policy Decisions and Capital Market Research', *Journal of Accounting and Economics* (March): 29–62.

Friedman, M. 1953. 'The Methodology of Positive Economics' in *Essays in Positive Economics*. Chicago: University of Chicago Press. Reprinted by Chicago: Phoenix Books, 1966.

Friend, I. and Blume, M.E. 1975. 'Measurement of Portfolio Performance under Uncertainty', *American Economic Review* (September): 561–575.

Gerboth, D.L. 1973. 'Research, Intuition and Politics in Accounting Inquiry', *Accounting Review* (July).

Gjesdal, F. 1981. 'Accounting for Stewardship', *Journal of Accounting Research* (Spring): 280–331.

Gjesdal, F. 1982. 'Information and Incentives: The Agency Information Problem', *Review of Economic Studies* (July): 373–390.

Gonedes, N. and Dopuch, N. 1974. 'Capital Market Equilibrium, Information Production and Selected Accounting Techniques: Theoretical Framework and Review of Empirical Work', *Journal of Accounting Research Studies on Financial Accounting Objectives* (Supplement): 48–129.

Graham, B., Dodd, E. and Cottle, S. 1962. *Security Analysis*. New York: McGraw-Hill.

Grayson, J.C. 1960. *Decisions Under Uncertainty: Drilling Decisions by Oil and Gas Operations*. (Division of Research.) Boston, MA: Harvard Business School.

Greenball, M.N. 1971. 'The Predictive-ability Criterion: Its Relevance in Evaluating Accounting Data', *Abacus* (July): 1–7.

Grossman, S.J. 1976. 'On the Efficiency of Competitive Stock Markets Where Traders have Diverse Information', *Journal of Finance* (May): 31, 573–585.

Grossman, S.J. 1977. 'The Existence of Future Markets: Noisy Rational Expectations and Information Externalities', *Review of Economic Studies* (October): 431–449.

Grossman, S.J. and Hart, O. 1983. 'An Analysis of the Principal—Agent Problem', *Econometrica* 51: 7–45.

Grossman, S.J. and Stiglitz, J.E. 1976. 'Information and Competitive Price Systems', *American Economic Review*, Vol.66, No.2 (May): 246–253.

Grossman, S.J. and Stiglitz, J.E. 1980. 'On The Impossibility of Informationally Efficient Markets', *American Economic Review* (June): 393–408.

Hagerman, R.C. and Zmijewski, M. 1979. 'Some Economic Determinants of Accounting Policy Choice', *Journal of Accounting and Economics* (August): 141–161.

Hakansson, N.H., Kunkel, G.J. and Ohlson, J.A. 1982. 'Sufficient and Necessary Conditions for Information to Have Social Value in Pure Exchange', *Journal of Finance* (December): 1169–1181.

Hellwig, M.R. 1980. 'On the Aggregation of Information in Competitive Markets', *Journal of Economic Theory*, Vol.22: 477–498.

Hendriksen, E.S. 1982. *Accounting Theory*. Homewood, IL: Richard D. Irwin.

Hicks, J.R. 1946. *Value and Capital*. Oxford: Clarendon Press.

Hicks, J.R. 1979. 'The Concept of Business Income', *Greek Economic Review* (December): Reprinted in Hicks, J.R. 1983. *Classics and Moderns: Collected Essays on Economic Theory*, Vol. III. Oxford: Blackwell.

Hilton, R.W. 1981. 'The Determination of Information Value: Synthesizing Some General Results', *Management Science* (January): 57–64.

Hirshleifer, J. 1970. *Investment, Interest and Capital*. Englewood Cliffs, NJ: Prentice Hall.

Hirshleifer, J. 1971. 'The Private and Social Value of Information and the Reward to Inventive Activity', *American Economic Review* (September): 561–574.

Hirshleifer, J. and Riley, J.G. 1979. 'The Analytics of Uncertainty and Information— An Expository Survey', *Journal of Economic Literature* (December): 1375–1421.

Holmstrom, B. 1979. 'Moral Hazard And Observability', *Bell Journal of Economics* (Spring): 74–91.

Hong, H., Mendelker, G. and Kaplan, R. 1978. 'Pooling *vs* Purchase: The Effects of Accounting for Mergers on Stock Prices', *Accounting Review* (January): 31–47.

Hope, A. and Briggs, J. 1982. 'Accounting Policy Making Some Lessons from the Deferred Taxation Debate', *Accounting and Business Research* (Spring): 83–96.

Horngren, C.T. 1973. 'The Marketing of Accounting Standards', *Journal of Accountancy* (October): 61–66.

Ijiri, Y. 1967. *The Foundations of Accounting Measurement*. Englewood Cliffs, NJ: Prentice Hall.

Ijiri, Y. 1975. 'Theory of Accounting Measurement', *Studies in Accounting Research* No.10, American Accounting Association.

Ijiri, Y. 1980. *Recognition of Contractual Risks and Obligations*, FASB Research Report. Stamford, CT: FASB.

Ijiri, Y. 1983. 'On the Accountability-Based Conceptual Framework', *Journal of Accounting and Public Policy* (Summer): 75–81.

Ijiri, Y. and Jaedicke, R.K. 1966. 'Reliability and Objectivity of Accounting Measurements', *Accounting Review* (July): 474–483.

Inflation Accounting Committee. 1975. *Inflation Accounting: Report of the Inflation Accounting Committee*. London: Her Majesty's Stationery Office.

Jensen, M.C. 1968. 'The Performance of Mutual Funds in the Period 1945–1964', *Journal of Finance* (May): 389–416.

Jenson, M.C. (ed.). 1972. *Studies in the Theory of Capital Markets*. New York: Praeger.

Jenson, M.C. 1976. 'Reflections on the State of Accounting Research and the Regulation of Accounting', *Stanford Lectures in Accounting*. Palo Alto, CA: Stanford University Press.

Jensen, M.C. and Meckling, W.H. 1976. 'Theory of the Firm. Managerial Behaviour, Agency Costs and Ownership Structure', *Journal of Financial Economics* (October): 305–360.

Johnson, L.T. and Storey, K.R. 1982. *Recognition in Financial Statements: Underlying Concepts and Practical Conventions*. FASB Research Report. Stamford, CT: FASB.

Jordon, W.A. 1972. 'Producer Protection from Market Structure and Effects of Governmental Regulation', *Journal of Law and Economics*, Vol.15, No.1 (April): 151–176.

Kaldor, N. 1955. *The Concept of Income in Economic Theory: An Expenditure Tax*. London: Allen and Unwin: 54–78.

Kandel, S. and Stambaugh, R. 1987. 'On the Correlations and Sensitivity of Inferences about Mean-variance Efficiency', *Journal of Financial Economics*, Vol.18, No.1 (March):61–90.

Kaplan, R.S. and Roll, R. 1972. 'Investor Evaluation of Accounting Information: Some Empirical Evidence', *Journal of Business* (April): 225–257.

Kaplan, R.S. and Atkinson, A.A. 1989. *Advanced Management Accounting.* Englewood Cliffs, NJ: Prentice Hall.

Keane, M.S. 1983. *Stock Market Efficiency: Theory, Evidence, Implications.* Deddington, Oxford: Phillip Allan.

Kihlstrom, R. and Mirman, L. 1975. 'Information and Market Equilibrium', *Bell Journal of Economics* (Spring): 357–376.

Kirk, D. 1979. 'Address to the Business Council', reported in *FASB Viewpoints* (9 November).

Kreps, D.M. 1990. *A Course in Microeconomic Theory.* New York: Harvester Wheatsheaf.

Kriple, H. 1979. *The SEC and Corporate Disclosure: Regulation in Search of a Purpose.* San Diego, CA: Harcourt, Brace and Jovanovich.

Krouse, C.G. 1986. *Capital Markets and Prices: Valuing Uncertain Income Streams.* Amsterdam and New York: Elsevier Science Publishers.

Kyburg, H.E., Jr. and Smokler, H.E. (eds.). 1964. *Studies in Subjective Probability.* New York: Wiley.

Lafferty, M. 1981. 'How Good Are The Accounting Standards We Now Have?', in Leach, R. and Stamp, E. (eds.), *British Accounting Standards: The First 10 Years.* Cambridge: Woodhead Faulkner.

Laffont, Jean-Jacques. 1989. *The Economics of Uncertainty and Information.* Cambridge, MA: The MIT Press.

Leach, Sir Ronald. 1981. 'The Birth of British Accounting Standards', in Leach, R. and Stamp, E. (eds.), *British Accounting Standards: The First 10 Years.* Cambridge: Woodhead Faulkner.

Leftwich, R. 1980. 'Market Failure Fallacies and Accounting Information', *Journal of Accounting and Economics* (December): 3–30.

Leftwich, R. 1981. 'Evidence of the Impact of Mandatory Changes in Accounting Principles on Corporate Loan Agreements', *Journal of Accounting and Economics* (March): 3–36.

LeRoy, S. and Porter, R. 1981. 'The Present Value Relation: Test Based on Implied Variance Bounds', *Econometrica* (May): 555–574.

Lev, B. and Ohlson, J.A. 1982. 'Market-Based Empirical Research in Accounting: A Review, Interpretation, and Extension', *Journal of Accounting Research*, Vol.20 (Supplement): 249–332.

Lindahl, E. 1935. *The Concept of Income in Essays in Honour of Gustav Cassel.* London: Allen and Unwin: 399–418.

Lloyd Cheyham & Co. vs *Little John & Co.* 1985. *High Court of Justice.* Queen's Bench Division (30 September).

Lorie, J. and Niederhoffer, V. 1968. 'Predictive and Statistical Properties of Insider Trading', *Journal of Law and Economics* (April): 35–53.

Luce, R.D. and Raiffa, H. 1957. *Games and Decisions.* New York: J. Wiley.

Macve, R.H. 1981. *A Conceptual Framework for Financial Accounting and Reporting: The Possibilities for an Agreed Structure.* London: Institute of Chartered Accountants in England and Wales.

Malinvaud, E. 1972. *Lectures on Micro-economic Theory.* Amsterdam: Elsevier Science Publishers.

Markowitz, H.M. 1952. 'The Utility of Wealth', *Journal of Political Economy*, (Vol.60): 151–158.

Marschak, J. 1974. *Economic Information, Decision and Prediction, Selected Essays: Vol. II.* Dordrecht: D. Reidel.

Marschak, J. and Radner, R. 1972. *Economic Theory of Teams.* New Haven: Yale University Press.

Marshall, J. 1974. 'Private Incentives and Public Information', *American Economic Review* (June): 373–390.

Mattessich, R. 1964. *Accounting and Analytical Methods.* Homewood, IL: Richard D. Irwin.

May, R.G. and Sundem, G.L. 1976. 'Research for Accounting Policy: An Overview', *Accounting Review* (October): 747–763.

Mayers, D. 1972. 'Non-Marketable Assets and Capital Market Equilibrium Under Uncertainty', in Jensen, M.C. (ed.), *Studies in the Theory of Capital Markets*. New York: Praeger.

Mayers, D. and Rice, E. 1979. 'Measuring Portfolio Performance and the Empirical Content of Asset Pricing Models', *Journal of Financial Economics* (March): 3–28.

McGuire, C.B. 1972. 'Comparisons of Information Structures', in McGuire and Radner (1972).

McGuire, C.B. and Radner, R. (eds.). 1972. *Decision and Organisation*. Amsterdam: Elsevier Science Publishers.

Metcalf Report. 1977. *The Accounting Establishment*. United States Senate, Committee on Government Operations. Washington, DC: Government Printing Office.

Meyer, P.E. 1974. 'The APB's Independence and Its Implication for FASB', *Journal of Accounting Research* (Spring): 188–196.

Modigliani, F. and Miller, M.H. 1958. 'The Cost of Capital Corporation Finance and the Theory of Investment', *American Economic Review*, Vol.48 (June): 261–297.

Mood, A.M., Graybill, F.A. and Boes, D.C. 1974. *Introduction to Theory of Statistics*, 3rd edition. New York: McGraw-Hill.

Moonitz, M. 1961. 'The Basic Postulates of Accounting', *Accounting Research Study, No.1*. New York: AICPA.

Moonitz, M. 1974. 'Obtaining Agreement on Standards in the Accounting Profession', *Studies in Accounting Research*, No.8. American Accounting Association.

Mueller, D.C. 1989. *Public Choice II*. Cambridge: Cambridge University Press.

Myerson, R. 1979. 'Incentive Compatibility And The Bargaining Problem'. *Econometrica* (January): 61–73.

Newberry, D.M.G. and Stiglitz, J.E. 1981. *The Theory of Commodity Price Stabilization: A Study in the Economics of Risk*. Oxford: Clarendon Press.

Newman, D.P. 1981a. 'An Investigation of the Distribution of Power in the APB and FASB', *Journal Accounting Research* (Spring): 247–262.

Newman, D.P. 1981b. 'Coalition Formation in the APB and the FASB: Some Evidence on the Size Principle', *Accounting Review* (October): 897–909.

Ng, D.S. 1978. 'An Information Economics Analysis of Financial Reporting and External Auditing', *Accounting Review* (October): 910–920.

Ng, D.S. and Stoeckenius. 1979. 'Auditing: Incentive and Truthful Reporting', *Journal of Accounting Research* (Supplement): 1–24.

Ohlson, J.A. 1987a. *The Theory of Financial Markets and Information*. Amsterdam: Elsevier Science Publishers.

Ohlson, J.A. 1987b. 'On the Nature of Income Measurement: The Basic Results', *Contemporary Accounting Research* (Fall): 1–15.

Ohlson, J.A. 1989. *Accounting Earnings, Book Value and Dividends. The Theory of the Clean Surplus Equation*. Columbia University.

Ohlson, J.A. and Buckman, A.G. 1980. 'Towards a Theory of Financial Accounting', *Journal of Finance* (May): 537–547.

Ohlson, J.A. and Buckman, A.G. 1981. 'Towards a Theory of Financial Accounting: Welfare and Public Information', *Journal of Accounting Research* (Autumn): 399–432.

Parker, R.H., Harcourt, G.C. and Whittington, G. 1986. *Readings in the Concept and Measurement of Income*. Deddington, Oxford: Phillip Allan.

Peasnell, K.V. 1974. 'The Objectives of Published Accounting Reports: A Comment', *Accounting and Business Research* (Winter): 71–77.

Peasnell, K.V. 1982. 'The Function of a Conceptual Framework for Corporate Financial Reporting', *Accounting and Business Research* (Autumn): 243–256.

Peltzman, S. 1974. *Regulation of Pharmaceutical Innovation: The 1962 Amendments*. Washington, DC: American Enterprise Institute for Public Policy.

Peltzman, S. 1976. 'Towards a More General Theory of Regulation', *Journal of Law and Economics* (August): 211–240.

Penno, M. 1985. 'Informational Issues in the Financial Reporting Process', *Journal of Accounting Research* (Spring): 240–255.

Popper, K.R. 1963. *Conjectures and Refutations: The Growth of Scientific Knowledge.* London: Routledge & Kegan Paul.

Posner, R.A. 1974. 'Theories of Economic Regulations', *Bell Journal of Economics and Managerial Science* (Autumn): 335–358.

Pratt, J.W. and Zechauser, R.J. (eds.). 1985. *Principals and Agents: The Structure of Business.* Cambridge, MA: Harvard University Press.

Radner, R. 1968. 'Competitive Equilibrium Under Uncertainty', *Econometrica* (January): 31–58.

Radner, R. 1979. 'Rational Expectations Equilibrium: Generic Existence and the Information Revealed by Prices', *Econometrica* (May): 655–678.

Rasmusen, E. 1989. *Games and Information: An Introduction to Game Theory.* Oxford: Basil Blackwell.

Revsine, L. 1973. *Replacement Cost Accounting.* Englewood Cliffs, NJ: Prentice Hall.

Ricks, W. 1982. 'The Market's Response to the 1974 LIFO Adoptions', *Journal of Accounting Research* (Autumn): Part 1: 367–387.

Ro, B. 1980. 'The Adjustment of Security Prices to the Disclosure of Replacement Cost Accounting Information', *Journal of Accounting and Economics* (August): 159–189.

Roll, R. 1977. 'A Critique of the Asset Pricing Theory's Tests', *Journal of Financial Economics* (May): 129–176.

Roll, R. 1978. 'The Ambiguity When Performance is Measured by the Securities Market Line', *Journal of Finance* (September): 1051–1069.

Roll, R. and Ross, S.A. 1980. 'An Empirical Investigation of the Arbitrage Pricing Theory', *Journal of Finance* (December): 1073–1100.

Ronen, J. 1979. 'The Dual Role of Accounting: A Financial Economic Perspective', in Bicksler, J.L. (ed.), *Handbook of Financial Economics.* Amsterdam and New York: Elsevier Science Publishers.

Rosenfield, P. 1974. In *Objectives of Financial Statements Vol.2 Selected Papers.* New York: AICPA.

Ross, S.A. 1976. 'The Arbitrage Theory of Capital Asset Pricing', *Journal of Economic Theory* (December): 341–360.

Samuelson, P.A. 1966. 'The Pure Theory of Public Expenditure' (1954), in Stiglitz, J. (ed.), *Collected Scientific Papers of Paul A. Samuelson.* Cambridge, MA: MIT Press.

Sandilands, F. 1975. *The Sandilands Report,* see Inflation Accounting Committee 1975.

Savage, L.G. 1954. *The Foundations of Statistics.* New York: J. Wiley.

Scapens, R.W. 1985. *Management Accounting: A Review of Recent Developments.* (New edition forthcoming.) Basingstoke: Macmillan.

Schlaifer, R. 1959. *Probability and Statistics for Business Decisions.* New York: McGraw-Hill.

Schwayder, K. 1967. 'A Critique of Economic Income as an Accounting Concept', *Abacus* (August): 23–35.

Selto, F.M. and Grove, H.D. 1982. 'Voting Power Indices and the Setting of Financial Accounting Standards, Extensions', *Journal of Accounting Research* (Autumn): 676–688.

Sen, A.K. 1970. *Collective Choice and Social Welfare.* San Francisco: Holden-Day.

Sen, A.K. 1977. 'Social Choice Theory: A Re-examination', *Econometrica* (January): 53–89.

Shanken, J. 1985. 'Multivariate Tests of the Zero-beta CAPM', *Journal of Financial Economics,* Vol.14, No.3 (September): 327–348.

Shanken, J. 1987. 'Proxies and Asset Pricing Relations: Living with the Rolls Critique', *Journal of Financial Economics,* Vol.18, No.1 (March): 91–110.

Sharpe, W.F. 1985. *Investments.* Englewood Cliffs, NJ: Prentice Hall International.

Shiller, R. 1981a. 'Do Stock Prices Move Too Much to be Justified by Subsequent Changes in Dividends?', *American Economic Review* (June): 421–436.

Shiller, R. 1981b. 'The Use of Volatility Measures in Assessing Market Efficiency', *Journal of Finance* (May): 291–303.

Simon, H.A. 1959. 'Theories of Decision-Making in Economics and Behavioural Science', *American Economic Review* (June): 253–283.

Slimmings, Sir William. 1981. The Scottish Contribution in Leach, R. and Stamp, E. (eds.), *British Accounting Standards: The First 10 Years*. Cambridge: Woodhead Faulkner.

Smith, C.W. and Warner, J.B. 1979. 'On Financial Contracting: An Analysis of Bond Covenants', *Journal of Financial Economics* (June): 117–161.

Solomons, D. 1961. 'Economic and Accounting Concepts of Income', *Accounting Review XXXVI*, pp. 374–383. Reprinted in Parker, Harcourt and Whittington.

Solomons, D. 1983. 'The Political Implications of Accounting and Accounting Standard Setting', *Accounting and Business Research* (Spring).

Solomons, D. 1986. *Making Accounting Policy: The Quest for Creditability in Financial Reporting*. New York & Oxford: Oxford University Press.

Sprouse, R.T. 1983. 'Standard Setting: The American Experience', in Bromwich, M. and Hopwood, A.G. (eds.), *Accounting Standard Setting: An International Perspective*. London: Pitman Publishing.

Sprouse, R.T. and Moonitz, M. 1962. 'A Tentative Set of Broad Accounting Principles for Business Enterprises', *Accounting Research Study*, No. 3. New York: American Institute of Public Certified Accountants.

Sterling, R.R. 1979. *Towards a Science of Accounting*. Houston, TX: Scholars Book Co.

Sterling, R.R. 1990. 'Positive Accounting Theory: An Assessment', *Abacus* (September): 97–135.

Stigler, G.J. 1971. 'The Theory of Economic Regulation', *Bell Journal of Economics and Management Science* (Spring): 219–255.

Strong, N., and Walker, M. 1987. *Information and Capital Markets*. Oxford: Basil Blackwell.

Sunder, S. 1973. 'Relationship between Accounting Changes and Stock Prices: Problems of Measurement and Some Empirical Evidence', Supplement to *Journal of Accounting Research*, 11: 1–45.

Sunder, S. 1975. 'Stock Price and Risk Related to Accounting Changes in Inventory Valuation', *Accounting Review* (April): 305–315.

Thomas, A.L. 1969. *The Allocation Problem in Financial Accounting Theory*. Accounting Research Study, No.3. American Accounting Association.

Thomas, A.L. 1974. *The Allocation Problem: Part Two*. Accounting Research Study, No.9. American Accounting Association.

Tirole, J. 1988. *The Theory of Industrial Organisation*. Cambridge, MA: MIT Press.

Townsend, R. 1979. 'Optimal Contracts and Competitive Markets with Costly State Verification', *Journal of Economic Theory*, Vol.21, No.2 (October): 265–293.

Trueblood Report. 1973. *Objectives of Financial Statements*. AICPA.

Verrecchia, R.E. 1982. 'The Use of Mathematical Models in Financial Accounting', *Journal of Accounting Research* (Supplement): 1–42.

Verrecchia, R.E. 1986. 'Managerial Discretion in the Choice Among Financial Reporting Alternatives', *Journal of Accounting and Economics*, 8: 175–195.

Vickrey, D.W. 1982. 'Reflections on the Demski—Chambers Debate Concerning the Existence of a Normative Accounting Standard', *Quarterly Review of Economics and Business* (Spring): 130–140, see also Demski (reply), pp. 140–143.

Von Wysocki, K. 1983. 'Research into Processes of Accounting Standard Setting in the Federal Republic of Germany', in Bromwich, M. and Hopwood, A.G. (eds.), *Accounting Standards Setting: An International Perspective*. London: Pitman Publishing.

Watts, R.L. 1982. 'Discussion of The Use of Mathematical Models in Financial Accounting', *Journal of Accounting Research* (Supplement): 48–55.

Watts, R.L. and Zimmerman, J.L. 1978. 'Towards a Positive Theory of the Determination of Accounting Standards', *Accounting Review* (January): 112–134.

Watts, R.L. and Zimmerman, J.L. 1979. 'The Demand for and Supply of Accounting Theories: The Market for Excuses', *Accounting Review* (April): 273–305.

Watts, R.L. and Zimmerman, J.L. 1983. 'Agency Problems, Auditing and the Theory of the Firm: Some Evidence', *Journal of Law and Economics* (October): 613–634.

Watts, R.L. and Zimmerman, J.L. 1986. *Positive Accounting Theory*. Englewood Cliffs, NJ: Prentice Hall.

Watts, T.R. 1981. 'Planning the Next Decade', in Leach, R. and Stamp, E. (eds.), *British Accounting Standards: The First 10 Years*. Cambridge: Woodhead Faulkner.

Whittington, G. 1983. *Inflation Accounting: An Introduction to the Debate*. Cambridge: Cambridge University Press.

Whittington, G. 1987. 'Positive Accounting Theory: A Review Article', *Accounting and Business* (Autumn): 327–336.

Williamson, O. 1975. *Market and Hierarchies: Analysis and Antitrust*. New York: Free Press.

Williamson, O. 1985. *The Economic Institutions of Capitalism*. New York: Free Press.

Zeff, S.A. 1972. *Forging Accounting Principles in Five Countries: A History and Analysis of Trends*. Champaign, IL: Stipes.

Zeff, S.A. 1978. 'The Rise of "Economic Consequences"', *Journal of Accountancy* (December): 56–63.

Zmijewski, M. and Hagerman, R. 1981. 'An Income Strategy Approach to the Positive Theory of Accounting Standard Setting/Choice', *Journal of Accounting and Economics* (August): 129–149.

Author index

Abdel-Khalik, A.R., 217
Accounting Standards Committee (ASC), 301
Accounting Standards Steering Committee
    (ASSC), 282, 286
Alexander, S.S., 46, 62, 68, 173, 213
American Institute of Certified Accountants
    (AICPA), 280, 282, 290
Amershi, A.H., 130
Antle, R., 344, 346, 351, 352, *355*
Arrow, K.J., 106, 258, 275, 295, 318, *355*
Atkinson, A.A., 75, 316
Atkinson, A.F., 28, 241, 247

Baiman, 347, 352, *355*
Ball, R.J., 213, 224, 225
Barton, A.D., 72, 73
Beaver, W.H., 1, 15, 24, 37, 46, 51, 68, 102,
    105, 110, 111, 112, *114*, *116*, 117, 119,
    196, 197, 201, 204, 212, 213, 214, 215,
    216, 220, 223, 224, 225, 239, 243, 297
Bell, P.W., 74, 322
Benston, G.J., 235, 237, 247, 263
Biddle, G.C. 218–19
Black, F., 209
Blume, M.E., 94
Boes, D.C., 137, *142*
Bowman, R.G., 217
Brealey, R., 33, 77, 294
Briggs, J., 274
Bromwich, M., 37, 68, 102, 131, *233*, 239, 252,
    274, 295, 296, 299
Brown, P., 213, 224, 225
Buckman, A.G., 157, 166, 168, 174, 221
Butterworth, J.E., 347

Canadian Institute of Chartered Accountants
    (CICA), 282, 286

Carsberg, B.V., 297
Chambers, R.J., 73, 131,
Chandler, A.D., Jr., 316
Christensen, J., 351,
Christensen, P.O., 177, 193
Christenson, C., 322, 328
Coase, R., 316
Cohen, K.J., 29, 297
Coombes, C.H., 23
Copeland, T.E., 33, 69, 90, 101, *114*, 201, 204,
    209, 337
Cottle, S., 42
Cushing, B.E., 131, 259, 271, 296
Cyert, R.M., 29, 297

Davidson, S., 43
DeAngelo, H., *116*
Dearing Report, 268
Debreu, G., 20, 106
Degroot, M., *142*
Demski, J.S., 15, 23, 24, 37, 68, 102, 105,
    110, 111, 112, *116*, 119, 120, 131, 134,
    142, 146, 149, 151, 196, 197, 203, 239,
    240, 289, 295, 298, 344, 346, 348, 353,
    355
Dimson, E., 209
Dodd, E., 42
Dopuch, N., 300, 301
Dreze, J.H., *114*
Dyckman, T.R., 201, 215
Dye, R., 170, 352

Edey, H.C., 314
Edwards, E.O., 74, 322
Edwards, R.S., 176
Edwards, W., 87
Eggington, D.A., 43

Fama, E.F., 77, 201, 209, 213, 215, 220, 321, 333
Feltham, G.A., 119, 177, 196
Financial Accounting Standards Board (FASB)
  SAFC No. 1 (1978), 140, 279, 284, 294
  SAFC No. 2 (1980a), 140, 284, 287, 291, 292, 294, 298, 314
  SAFC No. 3 (1980b), 284, 289, 291, 300
  SAFC No. 5 (1984), 284, 290, 291, 292, 293, 299, 300, 301
  SAFC No. 6 (1985), 284, 289, 290, 293, 300, 301
  Discussion Memorandum on the Report of the Study Group on the Objectives of Financial Statements (published in 1976), 282
  Scope and Implications of the Conceptual Framework Project (1976b), 280, 282
  Tentative Conclusions on the Objectives of Financial Statements (1976a), 280, 282, 285
Fisher, I., 32
Forker, J.J., 43
Foster, G., 201, 204, 209, 213, 215, 220, 223, 224
Friedman, M., 297, 321
Friend, I., 94

Gerboth, D.L., 255
Gjesdal, F., 311, 347, 348, 350, 351, 355
Graham, B., 42
Graybill, F.A., 137, *142*
Grayson, J.C., 94, 95
Greenball, M.N., 297
Grossman, S.J., 156, 169, 214, 215, 243, 316
Grove, H.D., 266

Hagerman, R., 327
Hakansson, N.H., 167
Hart, O., 316
Hendriksen, E.S., 279, 286
Hicks, J.R., 17, 38, 42, 46, 47, 49, 63, 68, 70, 73, 173
Hilton, R.W., 149, 150, 152, 155
Hirshleifer, J., 18, 30, 46, 69, 81, 83, 90, 97, 99, 101, *114*, 153, 163, 168, 239
Holmstrom, B., 342, 343, 345, 346, 355
Hong, H., 217
Hope, A., 274
Hopwood, A.G., 252
Horngren, C.T., 255, 274

Ijiri, Y., 70, 292, 294, 312, 314, 315, 322
Inflation Accounting Committee, 33, 68

Jaedicke, R.K., 314
Jensen, M.C., 76, 215, 236, 315, 320, 321, 323, 324
Johnson, L.T., 292
Jordan, W.A., 265

Kaldor, N., 38, 46, 49, 50, 63, 176
Kandel, S., 210
Kaplan, R.S., 75, 316, *355*
Keane, M.S., 201, 204, 214
Kihlstrom, S., 215
Kirk, D., 255
Kreps, D.M., 271, 309, 316, 336, 337, 343, 347, *355*
Krouse, C.G., 105, *114*, 181
Kyburg, H.E.Jr., 86

Lafferty, M., 271
Laffont, J-J., 309
Landsman, W.R., 216, 224
Leach, Sir Ronald, 255, 271
Leftwich, R., 246, 321, 327
LeRoy, S. 226
Lev, B., 201, 203, 204, 209, 225
Lindahl, E., 38, 46, 63
Lindahl, F.W., 218–19
Lloyd Cheyham & Co. vs. *Little John & Co.*, 268
Lorie, J. 214
Luce, R.C., 81, 97, 270

Macve, R.H., 278, 301
Malinvaud, E., *114*
Markowitz, H.M., 95
Marschak, J., 119, 120, 122, 126, 129, 130, 133, 151
Marshall, J., 166, 221
Mattessich, R., 279
May, R.G., 255
Mayers, D., 209, 226
McGuire, C.B., 119, 129, *142*
Meckling, W.H., 76, 235, 315, 320, 323, 324
Metcalf Report, 266
Meyers, S., 33, 77, 294
Miller, M.H., 75
Mirman, L., 215
Mood, A.M., 137, *142*
Moonitz, M., 270, 285, 290
Morse, D., 201, 215

Mueller, D.C., 258, 259, 261, 275
Myerson, R., 346

Newberry, D.M.G., 110, *114*
Newman, D.P., 266, 267
Ng, D.S., 350, 352
Niederhoffer, V., 214

Ohlson, J.A., 107, 111, 112, *114*, *116*, 119, 130, 157, 165, 166, 167, 168, 174, 181, 197, 201, 203, 204, 209, 221, 225

Peasnell, K.V., 297, 301
Peltzman, S., 236, 321
Penno, M., 348, 349, 352, 355
Porter, R., 226
Posner, R.A., 265
Pratt, J.W., *355*

Radner, R., 23, 119, 120, 122, 129, 130, 134, *142*, 151, 169
Raiffa, H., 81, 97, 270
Rasmusen, E., 319, 336, 347, *355*
Revsine, L., 43
Rice, E., 226
Ricks, W., 209, 215, 217, 218, 223
Riley, J.G., 46, 83, *114*
Ro, B., 216
Roll, R., 209, 211, 226, *228*
Rosenfield, P., 310
Ross, S.A., 209, 210, 211

Samuelson, P.A., 241
Sappington, D.E.M., 196–7
Savage, L.G., 87
Scapens, R.W., 353
Schlaifer, R., 97
Schwayder, K., 71
Selto, F.M., 266
Sen, A.K., 258, 260, 275, 295
Shanken, J., 210
Sharpe, W.F., 27, 69
Shiller, R., 226

Simon, H.A., 95
Slimmings, Sir William, 255, 271
Smokler, H.E., 86
Solomons, D., 32, 255, 292, 301, 328
Sprouse, R.T., 263, 266, 270, 290, 301
Stambaugh, R., 210
Stamp, E., 271, 286
Sterling, R.R., 23, 322, 328
Stigler, G., 236, 321
Stiglitz, J.E., 28, 110, *114*, 156, 169, 214, 215, 241, 247
Storey, K.R., 292
Strong, N., 107, *114*, 119, 157, 165, 167, 169, *355*
Sundem, G.L., 255
Sunder, S., 218, 300, 301

Thomas, A.L., 44, 69, 73
Tirole, J., 316, *355*
Townsend, R., 347
Tversky, A., 87

Verrecchia, R.E., 168, 348, 350, 352, 356
Vickrey, D.W., 131, 299
Von Wysocki, K., 262

Walker, M., 107, *114*, 119, 157, 165, 167, 169, *355*
Watts, R.L., 168, 201, 219, 235, 236, 246, 308, 309, 321, 322, 323, 324, 325
Watts, T.R., 271
Wells, M.C., 37, 69, 102, 131, 299
Weston, J.F., 33, 69, 90, 101, *114*, 201, 204, 209, 337–9
Whittington, G., 176, 328
Williamson, O., 309, 316

Zechauser, R.J., *355*
Zeff, S.A., 257, 281
Zimmerman, J.L., 201, 219, 235, 236, 246, 308, 309, 321, 322, 323, 324, 325
Zmijewski, M., 327

Subject index

Page numbers in italic refer to items cited in chapter notes

Abnormal performance index (API), 223
Abnormal returns, 213, 214, 222–4
  defined, 223
Accountability, 307, 308
  accounting for, 310–16
    uses of, 310
    general model for, 311
Accounting and information provision, 196–8, 203
Accounting and uncertainty, 102–6
  and multi-periods, 103–6
Accounting information, 122
  a public good, 240–6
    criticisms of, 246–8
  and the market, 235–6, 242
  hardness, 313–15
  impact on security prices, 220–5
    and welfare, 221
  qualitative characteristics of, 286–9, 298–300
  'seeing through', 217–18, 219
Accounting Principles Board (APB), 266
Accounting regulation, 28
  via the legislature, 256–62
    problems, 262–3
Accounting reports, 202
Accounting Standards Board (ASB), 253, 268
Accounting Standards Committee (ASC), 253, 268
Accrual accounting, 286
Adverse selection, 109, 114, 318, 319
  and auditing, 109, 318
Agency, 308
  and financial accounting, 347–53
  and information, 317
  and uncertainty, 316–20
  characteristics, 316
  communications in, 345–6

  costs, 320–1, 323
  defined, 309
  principal's objective, 316
  theory, 9, 10, 76
Agency regulation
  advantages, 263
  disadvantages, 264–7
Agent and principal model, 308 (*see also* Agency)
  and Nash equilibrium, 336
  and risk sharing, 317, 321, 336–9
  assumptions of, 336
  effort motivation in, 321
  first best solution of, 337, 340
  first order condition in, 342
  general form of, 334–6, 344
  scope, 309
  solution with effort, 342–4
  steps in, 335
  theory of, 309
  utility functions for, 333
American Institute of Certified Accountants (AICPA), 279
Arbitrage, 101, 182
Arrow-Debreu securities, 107, 161, 162, 192
Arrow's social choice theorem, 259–60, 275–7
Auditing, 310
  in an agency context, 347–50

Bayes' theorem, 137, *142–3*
Beta factor, 207–8, 218–19
Blackwell's theorem, *142*
Bonding, 320

Capital asset pricing model (CAPM), 107, 202, 204–11, 212, 221, 222, 225, 323
  assumptions, 205

Capital markets and information, 111–12
Capture theory, 265–7
Certainty equivalent wealth, 93
Certainty line, 98
Companies Acts
    1980, 253
    1981, 8, 253, 267, 268
    1985, 8
    1989, 268
Complex securities, 101
Comprehensive income, 290, 303
Conceptual Framework Project (*see also*
        FASB), 9, 117, 131, 140, 265, 278, 279,
        346
    advantages, 280–1
    central assertion, 288
    elements of, 285
    financial reports: objectives in, 286
    single person approach, 300
    steps in deriving, 282–5
Conditional price, 181
Consensus seeking, 270–1
    advantages, 271
    problems, 270–1
Contingent claims
    for commodities, 83
    for consumption, 83
    for income, 83
    over time, 105
Cost/benefit test, 142, 237, 247, 265, 292, 296
Covariance, 207, *228*
Cumulative average of abnormal returns
        (CAR), 223

Dearing Report, 268
Debt contracts, 325–6
Decision making under uncertainty, 81–7
    example, 87–9
    graphical solution, 98–102
    optimality conditions, 100–4
Decision relevance, 131, 140
Decision usefulness (utility), 44, 117–18,
        134
Depreciation (*see* Economic depreciation)
Differential information, 168–70
Disclosure of information, 170
Disutility of effort, 333
'Due Process', 270, 271

Economic consequences, 255, 257
Economic depreciation, 42–3
    criticised, 71–2

Economic income
    aggregation difficulties, 72–3
    as a standard stream, 42–3
    as interest on capital, 41, 42
    criticised, 67–73
    ex ante, 175
        defined, 37–42
        example, 39–41, 183–4
    ex post, 52–4
        example, 65–6
        for total project, *77–8, 199*
        income concept *I*, 58–9, 175, 185–9
        income concept *II*, 59–60, 175
        income concept *I versus* concept *II*, 60–4,
            191–3
        Hicks: concept Number 1, 38–42; concept
            Number 2, 47–9; concept Number 3,
            49–50
        histories, 188, 190
        in imperfect markets, 68
        with risk aversion, 190–1
    In multi-periods, 174
    project based, 68–9
    subjectivity of, 70–1, 73–5
    with certainty, 18–23
    with uncertainty, 46–7, 173, 176–82
        example, 177–82
Economic wealth
    ex ante, 175
    defined, 35–7
        example with uncertainty, 182–4
        with risk aversion, 184–5
    ex post, 54–7
        defined, 54
        with certainty, 18–23
        with risk aversion, 190–1
        with uncertainty, 173, 176–82; example,
            177–82
Economist's income (*see* Economic income)
Efficient market hypothesis, 212, 323
Efficient markets, 202, 204, 213, 214 (*see also*
        Market efficiency)
    and accounting, 215–16
    semi-strong form efficient, 213, 214
    strong form efficient, 214–15
    weak form efficient, 213
Effort, 10,
    inducement, 339–42
Equilibrium conditions for uncertain, multi-
        period problem, 182–3
European Community
    Fourth Directive, 8

Expected monetary value decision rule, 88–9
Expected return, 205
Expected utility, 93–6
  assumptions required, 97
  conditional, 133
  decision rule, 93–4, 120–1
  characteristcs of, 97
  example, 96–7

Feedback value, 288
Financial Accounting Standards Board
      (FASB), 8, 252, 255, 263, 264, 265, 266,
      269, 270, 279
Financial reporting
  defined, 1
Financial Reporting Council (UK), 268
Financial statements
  elements of, 289–93, 300–2
  definitions of, 290–1
Firm specific information, 177
Free riders, 241–4
Futures, 181

Government regulation of accounting, 256–9

Hicksian income concepts (*see* Economic
      income)
Hidden action, 318
Hidden information, 318
Historical cost accounting, 312–16
  uniqueness of, 312–16

Imperfect markets, 108
Incentive compatible reward systems, 334
Income
  central meaning, 38
Income and wealth measurement with risk
      aversion, 84–5
Income measures, 22
  as measures, 23–4
  as present values, 24–6
  for decision making, 33–42
  with uncertainty and multi-periods, 26–8,
      102
Incomplete markets
  and transaction costs, 108
Indifference curves
  under uncertainty, 99
  slope of, 99
Information
  and decision making, 294
    an example, 131–4, 177–82
  asymmetric, 319, 323

complete, 319
defined, 119, 121–2
demand value of, 149–50
expected value of, 146
ex post, 139, 309
incomplete, 319
perfect, 132
private use, for (*see* Private information)
supply value of, 150
value of, 121, 140, 145, 146–52, 151, 203, 213
  and risk, 151–2
  example, 146–9
Information economics, 118, 287, 288
Information(al) perspective, 117, 118, 201,
      215–16, 219–20
  advantages, 118
  defined, 110
Information processing, 202, 204
Information systems, 122, (or information
      functions or structures),
  and outcomes, 123–4
  characteristics of, 19, 122–7
  comparable, 128–31, 298–9, 311
  complete, 119
  decision utility of defined, 123
  fineness of, 128–9
    definition of, 128
    example, 129
  imperfect, 6, 119, 125
    example, 127–30
  measurability of, 125
  multi-period, 103–6
    examples, 104, 186–90, 194–6
  noisy, 6, 119, 125–6
  optimal, costless and perfect, 6, 119
  payoff adequate, 126
  payoff relevant, 126
  value of, 132–4
Informed individuals, 215
Insider trading, 242–3
Insurance, 158

Lagrangean method or multipliers, 30, 337,
      356
Leases, 216–17
LIFO versus FIFO, 217–18
Likelihood ratio, 343, 344, *356*

Market based research, 221–5
  difficulties, 225–7
    and CAPM, 226
    and stock price variability, 226

Market completion, 107
  via assumed beliefs and preferences, 107–8
  with information, 107, 166, 167–8
Market efficiency, 211–15
  defined, 212
Market failure, 239
Market models, 208–11
Markets
  imperfect, 237, 238
  incomplete, 237, 238, 239
Measure theory, *30*
Measurement theory, 16
Mergers, 217
Monitoring, 108, 309, 315
  costs, 316
Monotone likelihood condition, 344
  with high and low effort, 344
Moral hazard, 108–9, 114, 318, 319
Multi-person perspective, 118

Net present value, 17, 33–5
  example, 33–5
Neutral accounting statements
  and map making, 255

Objectivity, 313–14
Options, 107

Pareto
  constrained efficient equilibrium, 107
  efficiency, 146, 158, 159, 161, 162, 163, 165,
    174, 192, 271, 317, 336, 338
    without complete markets, 165
  fully efficient equilibrium, 21, 101–2, 107
    conditions for, 22, *30*, 100–1
  improvement, 156, 258, 351
  in multi-periods, 105–6
Participation constraint, 334
Payoff
  gross, 153
  net, 153
  matrix, 84
    complete, 84; example, 84
Perfectly competitive markets
  defined, *29*
Perfect information
  example, 123
Perfect markets, 16, 64–6
Portfolios
  efficient, 206
  return, 205
  risk: example, 205–6

Positive accounting theory, 10, 267, 310, 321–6
  and empirical regularities, 328
  components of, 323–4
  criticisms, 328
  domain of, 322
  hypotheses, 326–8
  objective of, 322
Postulates approach to accounting theory,
    279–80, 285
Predictive value, 288
  approach, 297
  criticisms, 296–8
Present value, 17
Primitive securities, 101
Principal's problem
  with risk sharing, 337–9
  with unobservable effort, 341
Private Information, 118, 121–2, 214
  defined, 6
  value of, 145
Private sector standard setting (*see* Self-
    regulating profession)
Probabilities
  conditional, *142*
  defined, 86
  frequency based, 86
  joint, *142–3*
  posterior, 137
  revision of, 134–7, *142–3*, 155
    example, 134–7
  subjective, 86–87
    characteristics of, 87
Public choice problems, 295 (*see also* Social
    choice decisions),
Public goods, 7
  and the market, 241
  and the supply of accounting information,
    244–5
  defined, 241
  joint supply characteristics, 241
Public information
  defined, 155–7
  provision of, 157–63
  value of, 145, 155, 163–70,
    example, 164–5, 181–2
  wealth effects of, 156–7

Random walk, 213
Rational expectations, 169
Recognition criteria, 291–3
Regimes (for information provision), 157,
    159–63, 174

Regulation, 236 (*see* Accounting regulation)
Relevance, 287, 299
    defined, 288, 289
Reliability, 287
    defined, 288
    of measurement systems, 313
Revaluation effects, 159
Revelation of preferences, 261–3
Risk
    attitudes, 89–90
        defined, 92–3
    market price of, 208
    neutral, 91, 151
    seeking, 90, 91
Risk aversion, 90, 91, 173
    absolute, 93
    defined, 93
    relative, *115*
Risk premiums, 90, 93
Risk sharing
    in agency models, 10
Risk tolerance, 95–6

Securities and Exchange Commission (SEC),
        251, 263–4, 267
Securities and Investment Board (SIB) 267
Security
    market line, 208
    prices, 100, 157
        and their variability, 226
    risk, 205
    valuation, 202
Self-regulating profession, 242, 252, 253, 259,
        261, 265–6, 267–9, 270, 272
    attacks upon, 265
Signal contingent claims, 161
Signalling, 319
Signals, 134–9
Single person perspective, 118
Social choice decisions, 251
    difficulties, 258–61
Spanning, 106
    example, 106–7
Spot price, 181
'Stamp Report', 282
Standard setting
    authority for, 267–71
    judicial support for, 268
    statutory backing for, 268
State-action matrix, 84
State contingent claims (*see* Contingent
    claims)

State contingent incomes, 102
State preference theory, 82–3
States of environment
    defined, 85
Statements of Financial Accounting Concepts
        (SFAC), 279 (*see also* Conceptual
        Framework Project)
Stewardship, 294–5, 309, 310
Stochastic dominance, 341, 343, *355–6*
Substance over form, 254

Theoretical frameworks for accounting
    critical evaluation, 294–302
Timeliness, 288–9
Time-state contingent claims, 105
Time-state contingent price, 181
    example, 181–2
True and fair view, 253, 268, 269
Trueblood Committee, 280, 286, 290

Unanimity
    of rankings of accounting systems, 15, 111
Uncertainty
    and market imperfections, 106–11
    defined, 81
    event or technological, 83
    market, 83, 109–10
        as a public good, 110
Unsystematic risk, 206
User
    orientation, 285–9
    relevance of information, 118
Utility functions, 90–3
    cardinal defined, 90–1
    characteristics, 92
Utility of a certain sum, 91
Utility of an uncertain sum, 92

Value free
    accounting systems, 4, 15, 17, 68, 69, 103,
        105, 110–11, 239, 250, 298
    choices, 131
Variance, *228*
Voting in standard setting, 266

Wealth measures
    as present values, 24–6
    for decision making, 33–42
    with uncertainty, 26–8, 102–3
Windfall gains and losses, 7, 60–2, 173, 193–6